NINTH CANADIAN EDITION

VOLUME III

Fundamental Accounting Principles

NINTH CANADIAN EDITION

VOLUME III

Fundamental Accounting Principles

Kermit D. Larson
University of Texas—Austin

John J. Wild
University of Wisconsin at Madison

Barbara Chiappetta
Nassau Community College

Morton Nelson
Wilfrid Laurier University

Ray F. Carroll
Dalhousie University

Michael Zin
Professor Emeritus
University of Windsor

McGraw-Hill Ryerson

Toronto Montreal New York Burr Ridge Bangkok Bogotá
Caracas Lisbon London Madrid Mexico City Milan New Delhi
Seoul Singapore Sydney Taipei

McGraw-Hill
Ryerson Limited

A Subsidiary of The ***McGraw-Hill*** *Companies*

FUNDAMENTAL ACCOUNTING PRINCIPLES
Volume III
Ninth Canadian Edition

ISBN: 0-07-560479-5

1 2 3 4 5 6 7 8 9 10 GTC 8 7 6 5 4 3 2 1 0 9

Printed and bound in Canada

Sponsoring Editor: *Jennifer Dewey/Lisa Feil*
Developmental Editor: *Denise McGuinness*
Senior Supervising Editor: *Margaret Henderson*
Production Editor: *Shirley Corriveau*
Production Co-ordinator: *Nicla Dattolico*
Interior Design: *Ellen Pentengell*
Cover Design: *Liz Harasymczuk*
Cover Illustration: *Dave Cutler/SIS©*
Page Make-up: *Valerie Bateman/ArtPlus Limited*
Typeface: *Times Roman*
Printer: *Transcontinental*

Canadian Cataloguing in Publication Data

Main entry under title:

Fundamental accounting principles

9th Canadian ed.
Fourth Canadian ed. written by W.W. Pyle, K.D. Larson and M. Zin.
Includes index.
ISBN 0-07-560477-9 (v.I) ISBN 0-07-560478-7 (v.II) ISBN 0-07-560479-5 (v.III)

1. Accounting. I. Larson, Kermit D.

HF5635.P975 1998 657 C98-932756-6

Contents in Brief

Contents

Preface

Let's Talk

Through extensive market-based surveys, focus groups, and reviews, we discovered several interests and needs in accounting education today. In a nutshell, these desires can be grouped into eight pedagogical areas: (1) motivation, (2) organization, (3) preparation, analysis, and use, (4) ethics, (5) technology, (6) real world, (7) active learning, and (8) flexibility. Our main goal in this edition of *Fundamental Accounting Principles* (F.A.P.) is to address these needs and create the most contemporary, exciting, relevant, and flexible principles book in the market. A quick summary of these areas follows.

Motivation. Motivation drives learning. From the chapter's opening article and its focus on young entrepreneurs to the decision-making prompted by You Make the Call, **F.A.P.** motivates readers. It brings accounting and business to life and demonstrates that this material can make a difference in your life.

Organization. Organization serves the learning process, and **F.A.P.'s** outstanding organization aids that process. From "Chapter Linkages" and learning objectives to chapter outlines and Flashbacks, **F.A.P.** is the leader in lending readers a helping hand in learning about accounting and business.

Preparation, Analysis, and Use. Accounting involves preparing, analyzing, and using information. **F.A.P.** balances each of these important roles in explaining and illustrating topics. From the unique Using the Information section to the creative Hitting the Road projects, **F.A.P.** shows all aspects of accounting.

Ethics. Ethics is fundamental to accounting. **F.A.P.** highlights the roles of ethics and social responsibility in modern businesses. From the Judgment and Ethics decision-making feature to its Ethics Challenge assignments, **F.A.P.** alerts readers to relevant and important ethical concerns.

Technology. Technology continues to change business and accounting, creating new and exciting accounting opportunities. **F.A.P.** is the leader in applying and showing technology in accounting. From the innovative Taking It to the Net projects to its Web-based assignments, **F.A.P.** pushes the accounting frontiers.

Real World. Accounting is important to the information age. From features and assignments that highlight companies like Alliance Communications Corporation, and Atlantis Communications Inc. to the Teamwork in Action and Communication in Practice activities, **F.A.P**. shows accounting in a modern, global context. It also engages both accountants and nonaccountants. From the exciting Did You Know? features to its Business Break, **F.A.P.** shows accounting is relevant to everyone.

Active Learning. Active learning implies active inquiry and interaction. The Teamwork in Action and Communicating in Practice are excellent starting points in developing an active learning environment.

Flexibility. **F.A.P.** is the undisputed leader in offering a strong pedagogical support package. Also, the *MHLA* service is a new, special addition to our support package.

This is just a sneak preview of **F.A.P.'s** new and exciting features. From communication, interpersonal, and critical thinking skills to the development of ethical and global awareness. **F.A.P.** is the leader. We invite you to take a complete look at these and other special features in the remainder of this preface to see why **F.A.P.** is the *first choice* in accounting principles books.

To Instructor

F.A.P. gives Web addresses for current follows-ups to articles, excerpts, and financial statements, and for a real world flavour.

To Student

The chapter's opening article and its *You Make the Call* features drive home the relevance of accounting and business.

Motivation

Motivation is a main goal of **F.A.P.** We know information retention is selective—if it does not apply to the lives of readers, they typically are not motivated to learn. **F.A.P.** explains and illustrates how accounting applies to the reader. Here is a sampling of materials that motivate the reader.

The **Chapter Opening Article** sets the stage and shows how the chapter's contents are relevant to the reader. Articles often focus on young entrepreneurs in business who benefit from preparing, analyzing, and using accounting information. These articles bring the material to life in concrete terms.

Fizzling Inventory

Toronto, ON—By June 1997, 27-year-old Rob Stavos was living his dream. He'd just opened **Liquid Nectar,** a small retail outlet devoted to serving the quirky tastes of young and old alike. But within months, this young entrepreneur's dream had become a nightmare.

Liquid Nectar started out with a bang. Customers raved about its stock of exotic and unique beverage products. Profit margins on successful drinks far outweighed the costs of unsold products. "We were ready to take on the large producers," boasts Rob. Within two months, however, Rob lost control of inventory and margins were being squeezed. What happened? Was Liquid Nectar soon to be another flash-in-the-pan?

You Make the Call features develop critical thinking and decision-making skills by requiring decisions using accounting information. Each chapter contains two to four of these features. They are purposely chosen to reflect different kinds of users. Examples are investors, consultants, programmers, financial planners, engineers, appraisers, and political and community activists. Guidance answers are provided.

Entrepreneur

You are the owner of a small retail store. You are considering allowing customers to purchase merchandise using credit cards. Until now, your store only accepted cash and cheques. What form of analysis do you use to make this decision?

You Make the Call

Company Excerpts call attention to well-known organizations to illustrate accounting topics. These excerpts are often accompanied by text describing the nature of the business and its relevance to readers.

...the Company announced it was proceeding with the construction of a 375,000-tonne smelter at Alma, Quebec. Total cost is estimated at $1,600 [million], most of which will be incurred over the next three years. Approximately $220 [million] is expected to be spent in 1998.

ALCAN

CONSOLIDATED STATEMENTS OF EARNINGS AND RETAINED EARNINGS

ALLIANCE COMMUNICATIONS CORPORATION

For the years ended March 31, 1997, March 31, 1996 and March 31, 1995
(In thousands of Canadian dollars, except per share data)

	1997	1996	1995
REVENUES	$ 282,599	$ 268,945	$ 233,811
DIRECT OPERATING EXPENSES	213,816	209,789	183,685
GROSS PROFIT	68,783	59,156	50,126
OTHER EXPENSES			
Other operating expenses	42,037	40,363	28,643
Amortization	5,160	5,038	5,164
Interest (note 10)	1,296	[illegible]	[illegible]

Financial Statements of familiar companies are used to acquaint readers with the format, content, and use of accounting information. The financial statements for Alliance, and Atlantis are reproduced in an appendix at the end of the book and referenced often.

Organization

Organization is crucial to effective learning. If it is not well-organized or linked with previous knowledge, learning is less effective. **F.A.P.** helps readers organize and link accounting concepts, procedures, and analyses. A **Preview** kicks off each chapter. It introduces the importance and relevance of the materials. It also links these materials to the opening article to further motivate the reader. Here are some additional materials to enhance learning effectiveness.

To Instructor

Use the learning objectives to help structure the course and assignment material to your instructional style.

To Student

Study each of these helpful organizational aids to increase your understanding and learning of accounting and business.

A Look Back

Chapter 1 began our study of accounting by considering its role in the information age. We described accounting for different organizations and identified users and uses of accounting. We saw that ethics and social responsibility are crucial to accounting.

A Look at This Chapter

In this chapter we describe financial statements and the accounting principles guiding their preparation. An important part of this chapter is transaction analysis using the accounting equation. We prepare and analyze financial statements based on transaction analysis.

A Look Forward

Chapter 3 explains the recording of transactions. We introduce the double-entry accounting system and show how T-accounts are helpful in analyzing transactions. Journals and trial balances are also identified and explained.

Chapter linkages launch a chapter and establish bridges between prior, current, and upcoming chapters. Linkages greatly assist readers in effectively learning the materials and help them link concepts across topics.

Learning Objectives

LO 1 Identify and explain the content and reporting aims of financial statements.

LO 2 Describe differences in financial statements across forms of business organization.

LO 3 Explain the roles of preparers, auditors and users of financial statements.

LO 4 Identify those responsible for setting accounting and auditing principles.

LO 5 Identify, explain and apply accounting principles.

LO 6 Analyze business transactions using the accounting equation.

Learning Objectives are shown at the beginning of the chapter to help focus and organize the materials. Each objective is repeated in the chapter at the point it is described and illustrated. Self-contained summaries for learning objectives are provided at the end of the chapter.

Flash back

10. Identify seven internal operating functions in organizations.

11. Why are internal controls important?

A series of **Flashbacks** in the chapter reinforce the immediately preceding materials. Flashbacks allow the reader to momentarily stop and reflect on the topics described. They give immediate feedback on the reader's comprehension before going on to new topics. Answers are provided.

Chapter Outline

- **Communicating with Financial Statements**
  - Previewing Financial Statements
  - Financial Statements and Forms of Organization
- **Transactions and the Accounting Equation**
  - Transaction Analysis—Part I
  - Transaction Analysis—Part II
  - Summary of Transactions

A colour-coded **Chapter Outline** is provided for the chapter. This gives a mental and visual framework to help readers learn the material.

To Instructor

A focus on Using the Information section is a great way to develop analytical thinking.

To Student

Learning accounting principles greatly increases your understanding of articles such as those in *Canadian Business* and other business magazines.

Preparation, Analysis, and Use

Accounting is a service focused on preparing, analyzing, and using information. **F.A.P.** presents a balanced approach to those three crucial aspects of accounting. The preparation aspect of **F.A.P.** is well established and highly regarded. A new progressive emphasis and use continues to put **F.A.P.** in the frontier of practice. Here's a sampling of new or revised textual materials on analysis and use:

The **Accounting Equation** (Assets = Liabilities + Equity) is used as a tool to evaluate a journal entry. The accounting equation is especially useful in learning and understanding the impacts of business transactions and events on financial statements. **F.A.P.** is a pioneer in showing this additional analysis tool.

Aug. 31	Cash	6,300	
	Sales		6,000
	Sales Taxes Payable ($6,000 × 0.05)		300
	To record cash sales and 5% sales tax.		

Assets	= Liabilities	+ Equity
+6,300	+300	+6,000

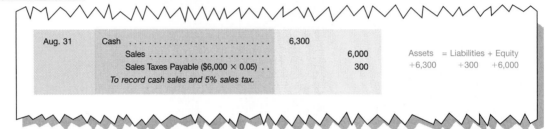

The **Using the Information** section wraps up each chapter and emphasizes critical-thinking and decision-making skills. Each section introduces one or more tools of analysis. It applies these tools to actual companies and interprets the results. The section often focuses on use of ratio analyses to study and compare the performance and financial condition of competitors.

Return on Investment — USING THE INFORMATION

LO 10 Compute and interpret return on investment.

We introduced return on investment in assessing return and risk earlier in the chapter. Return on investment is also useful in evaluating management, analyzing and forecasting profits, and planning future activities. **Dell Computer** has its marketing department compute return on investment for *every* mailing. "We spent 15 months educating people about return on invested capital," says Dell's Chief Financial Offi-

Hitting the Road is a unique addition to the chapter's assignment material. This activity requires readers to work outside the book and often requires application of interpersonal and communication skills. Tasks range from visits to local merchandisers and government offices to conducting phone interviews and Web searches. These activities help readers understand and appreciate the relevance of accounting.

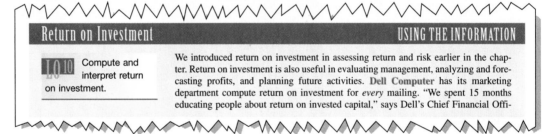

Hitting the Road LO 5

Select a company in your community which you may visit in person or interview on the telephone. Call ahead to the company to arrange a time when you can interview a member of the accounting department who helps in the preparation of the annual financial statements for the company. During the interview inquire about the following aspects of the company's accounting cycle:

Business Break requires the reader to apply the chapter's material to read and interpret a business article. It also aids in developing reading comprehension skills and gives exposure to business happenings.

Business Break LO 11

Read the article, "Car and Strive," in the September 1996 issue of *Canadian Business.*

Required

1. Contrast the profitability of **Magna** in the early 1990s to 1996.
2. What is the amount of revenue for Magna in the 1996 fiscal year?
3. What is the reason for Magna's success?
4. Despite its recent profitability what does the article identify as a possible problem for Magna?

Ethics

Ethics is the most fundamental accounting principle. Without ethics, information and accounting cease to be useful. **F.A.P.** is the leader in bringing ethics into accounting and demonstrating its importance. From the first chapter's article to the ethics codes at the end of the book, **F.A.P.** sets the standard in emphasizing ethical behaviour and its consequences. Here's a sampling of how we sensitize readers to ethical concerns and decision making:

The **Judgment and Ethics** feature requires readers to make accounting and business decisions with ethical consequences. It uses role-playing to show the interaction of judgment and ethics, the need for ethical awareness, and the impact of ethics. Guidance answers are provided.

Judgment and Ethics

Accountant

You are a public accountant consulting with a client. This client's business has grown to the point where its accounting system must be updated to handle both the volume of transactions and management's needs for information. Your client requests your advice in purchasing new software for its accounting system. You have been offered a 10% commission by a software company for each purchase of its system by one of your clients. Do you think your evaluation of software is affected by this commission arrangement? Do you think this commission arrangement is appropriate? Do you tell your client about the commission arrangement before making a recommendation?

A new **Ethics Challenge** is provided in the *Beyond the Numbers* section. It confronts ethical concerns based on material from the chapter. Many of these challenges involve actions where the ethical path is blurred.

Ethics Challenge

LO 2, 3

Randy Meyer is the chief executive officer of a medium-sized company in Regina, Saskatchewan. Several years ago Randy persuaded the board of directors of his company to base a percent of his compensation on the net income the company earns each year. Each December Randy estimates year-end financial figures in anticipation of the bonus he will receive. If the bonus is not as high as he would like he offers several accounting recommendations to his controller for year-end adjustments. One of his favourite recommendations is for the controller to reduce the estimate of doubtful accounts. Randy has used this

Social Responsibility is a major emphasis of progressive organizations. **F.A.P.** is unique in introducing this important topic in Chapter 1. We describe social responsibility and accounting's role in both reporting on and assessing its impact. **F.A.P.** also introduces social audits and reports on social responsibility.

Did You Know?

In Pursuit of Profit

How far can companies go in pursuing profit? Converse proposed to name a new footwear product Run N' Gun. This sparked debate on ethics, social responsibility and profits. Converse said Run N' Gun was a basketball and football term. Critics claimed it invited youth violence and links with the gun culture. To the credit of Converse, it changed the name from Run N' Gun to Run N' Slam prior to its sale to consumers.

To Instructor

The Judgment and Ethics feature raises the role of ethics in accounting and develops critical thinking skills.

To Student

Use these features and book materials to remind us that accounting and business decisions affect peoples' lives.

To Instructor

PowerPoint presentation slides can be customized for your instructional style and are great visual aids to lecture materials.

To Student

Use **F.A.P.**'s Home Page for current updates, hot links to important sites, and much more . . .

Student Software provides several technology-assisted educational activities. These include (1) *Tutorial*—interactive review of topics, and (2) *SPATS*—instructional software to solve problems.

Technology

Technology and innovation can be exciting and fun. **F.A.P.** makes the transition to new technologies easy. It is the leader in demonstrating the relevance of technology and showing readers how to use it. To ensure easy access, all technology offerings are linked to the Larson booksite. The address is **www.mcgrawhill.ca/college/larson**. Here's a sampling of items pushing the technology frontier:

Accounting Web Community

The Financial Accounting Web Community is a place on the Internet designed and built with our adopters in mind. It is a place where instructors can quickly access teaching resources directly related to the text they are using. It is also a place where instructors can share ideas and information with each other.

The Financial Accounting Web Community is the starting point for accessing accounting and business resources on the Web. The book's Web site harnesses technology resources to provide the most up-to-date and powerful Web services available.

Taking It to the Net requires accessing a Web site and obtaining information relevant to the chapter. It aims to make readers comfortable with Web technology, familiar with information available, and aware of the power of Web technology.

Taking It to the Net
LO 1, 7

There is extensive accounting and business information available on the Internet. This includes the **TSE's** on-line address at **http://www.tse.com** and the Depository for Canadian Securities' database referred to as **SEDAR (http://www.sedar.com)** and numerous other Web sites offering access to financial statement information or related data.

Required

Access at least one of the Web sites selected by either you or your instructor and answer the following:

a. Write a brief report describing the types of relevant information available at this Web site.

b. How would you rate the importance of the information available at this Web site for accounting and business?

PowerPoint® Presentations and Supplements augment each chapter with colorful graphics, interesting charts, innovative presentations, and interactive activities. The PowerPoint® materials are flexible and can be customized for any use.

Real World

Showing readers that accounting matters is part of an effective learning package. **F.A.P.** is the leader in real world instructional materials. It offers unique assignments challenging the reader to apply knowledge learned in practical and diverse ways. These challenges include analytical problems, research requirements, comparative analysis, teamwork assignments, and communication exercises. They also allow greater emphasis on conceptual, analytical, communication, and interpersonal skills. Here's a sampling of these materials:

To Instructor and Student

The **glossary** gives complete and accurate definitions of key terms. A key term is set in bold in the chapter, and the glossary references this page number. It also gives synonyms for key terms.

A **summary** describes the chapter in terms of its learning objectives. It assists in assessing one's understanding of key concepts, procedures, and analyses.

Questions give readers quick feedback on their understanding of key chapter topics.

Quick studies are effective checks on concepts, procedures, and analyses. They help build the reader's confidence with the material. Each are keyed to usually one learning objective.

Exercises focus on one or more learning objectives. They are mildly challenging and are an effective way to launch into more challenging problems.

Check Figures serve as an aid to readers.

Questions

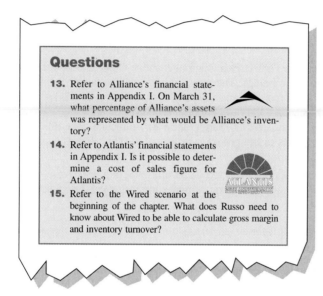

13. Refer to Alliance's financial statements in Appendix I. On March 31, what percentage of Alliance's assets was represented by what would be Alliance's inventory?

14. Refer to Atlantis' financial statements in Appendix I. Is it possible to determine a cost of sales figure for Atlantis?

15. Refer to the Wired scenario at the beginning of the chapter. What does Russo need to know about Wired to be able to calculate gross margin and inventory turnover?

Reporting in Action requires analysis and use of Alliance's annual report information.

Reporting in Action

LO 2, 6, 10

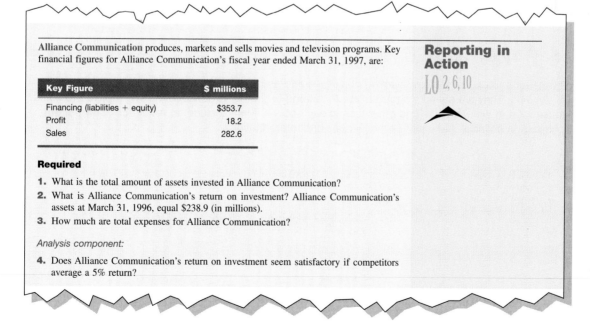

Alliance Communication produces, markets and sells movies and television programs. Key financial figures for Alliance Communication's fiscal year ended March 31, 1997, are:

Key Figure	$ millions
Financing (liabilities + equity)	$353.7
Profit	18.2
Sales	282.6

Required

1. What is the total amount of assets invested in Alliance Communication?

2. What is Alliance Communication's return on investment? Alliance Communication's assets at March 31, 1996, equal $238.9 (in millions).

3. How much are total expenses for Alliance Communication?

Analysis component:

4. Does Alliance Communication's return on investment seem satisfactory if competitors average a 5% return?

Comparative Analysis compares the performance and financial condition of Alliance and Atlantis using the accounting knowledge obtained from the chapter. These activities help develop analytical skills.

Comparative Analysis

LO 2, 6, 10

Both **Alliance Communications** and **Atlantis Communications** produce, market and sell movies and television programs. Key comparative figures ($ millions) for these two organizations follow:

	Alliance	Atlantis
Financing (liabilities + equity)	$353.7	$333.5
Profit	18.2	5.6
Sales	282.6	178.0

Source: Alliance figures are from its annual report for fiscal year-end March 31, 1997. Atlantis figures are from its annual report for fiscal year-end December 31, 1997.

Note: In September 1998 shareholders of Alliance Communications Corp. and Atlantis Communications Inc. approved a merger of the two companies. The new company will be known as Alliance Atlantis Communications Inc. and will "be far more effective around the world and. . . will be positioned for further growth" according to Michael MacMillan, the newly appointed chairman and chief executive officer. Although it will not be possible to compare the Alliance and Atlantis results past 1997, it will be interesting to compare the new company's results to the previous individual entities. Here is an opportunity to see if expected synergies are realized.

Comprehensive and Serial Problems are included in several chapters and focus on multiple learning objectives from multiple chapters. They help integrate and summarize key principles.

Comprehensive Problem

Alpine Company

LO 1

(If the Working Papers that accompany this text are not available, omit this comprehensive problem.)

Assume it is Monday, May 1, the first business day of the month, and you have just been hired as the accountant for Alpine Company, which operates with monthly accounting periods. All of the company's accounting work has been completed through the end of April and its ledgers show April 30 balances. During your first month on the job, you record the following transactions:

May 1 Issued Cheque No. 3410 to S&M Management Co. in payment of the May rent, $3,710. (Use two lines to record the transaction. Charge 80% of the rent to Rent Expense, Selling Space and the balance to Rent Expense, Office Space.)

2 Sold merchandise on credit to Essex Company, Invoice No. 8785, $6,100. (The terms of all credit sales are 2/10, n/30.)

2 Issued a $175 credit memorandum to Nabors, Inc., for defective merchandise sold on April 28 and returned for credit. The total selling price (gross) was $4,725.

Problems often cover multiple learning objectives and usually require preparing, analyzing, and using information. They are paired with **Alternate Problems** for further review of the same topics. Problems are supported with software and other technology options. Many include an **Analytical Component** focusing on financial statement consequences and interpretations.

Problem 7-3A
Income statement comparisons and cost flow assumptions

LO 4, 9

The Denney Company sold 2,500 units of its product at $98 per unit during 19X1. Incurring operating expenses of $14 per unit in selling the units, it began the year with, and made successive purchases of, units of the product as follows:

January 1 beginning inventory . .	740 units costing $58 per unit
Purchases:	
April 2	700 units @ $59 per unit
June 14	600 units @ $61 per unit
August 29	500 units @ $64 per unit
November 18	800 units @ $65 per unit
	3,340 units

Required

Preparation component:

Check Figure Net income (LIFO), $69,020

1. Prepare a comparative income statement for the company, showing in adjacent columns the net incomes earned from the sale of the product, assuming the company uses a periodic inventory system and prices its ending inventory on the basis of (a) FIFO, (b) LIFO, and (c) weighted-average cost.

A **Demonstration Problem** is at the end of the chapter. It illustrates important topics and shows how to apply concepts in preparing, analyzing, and using information. A problem-solving strategy helps guide the reader. Most chapters also have a **Mid-Chapter Demonstration Problem** with solution.

Demonstration Problem

On July 14, 19X1, Truro Company paid $600,000 to acquire a fully equipped factory. The purchase included the following:

Asset	Appraised Value	Estimated Salvage Value	Estimated Useful Life	Amortization Method
Land	$160,000			Not amortized
Land improvements .	80,000	$ -0-	10 years	Straight line
Building	320,000	100,000	10 years	Double-declining balance
Machinery	240,000	20,000	10,000 units	Units of production*
Total	$800,000			

*The machinery is used to produce 700 units in 19X1 and 1,800 units in 19X2.

Required

1. Allocate the total $600,000 cost among the separate assets.

Infographics and Artwork aid in visual learning of key accounting and business topics. Photos, colour, highlighting, and authentic documents all help with visual learning.

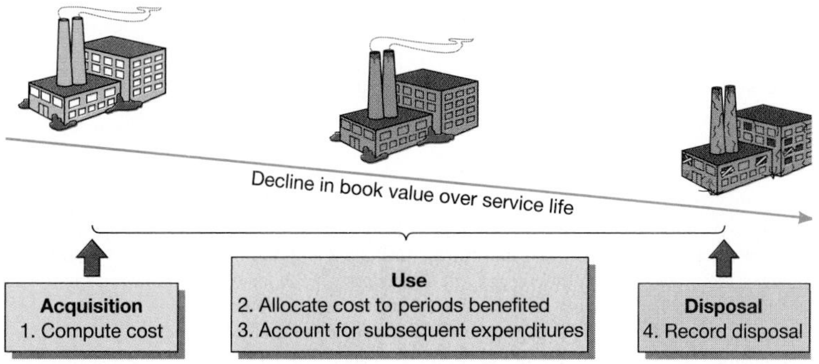

Exhibit 12.2

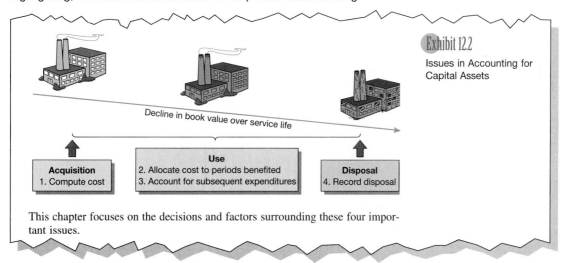

Issues in Accounting for Capital Assets

This chapter focuses on the decisions and factors surrounding these four important issues.

To Instructor

Teamwork in Action and Communicating in Practice are excellent starting points in developing an active learning environment. Both develop communication and interpersonal skills.

To Student

Team-building, collaborative effort skills are usually crucial to career success.

Active Learning

Active learning requires effective assignments. **F.A.P.** is the student-proven and instructor-tested leader in assignment materials. Proven and thoughtful assignments not only facilitate but motivate effective and active learning. many assignments include writing components. Here's a sampling of relevant assignment materials:

Teamwork in Action assignments require preparing, analyzing, and using information in teams. They can be completed in or outside of class. These active learning activities reinforce understanding of key topics and develop interpersonal skills.

Teamwork in Action
LO 5

A team will be called upon to personify the operation of a voucher system. Yet all teams must prepare for the potential to be selected by doing the following:

1. Each team is to identify the documents in a voucher system. The team leader will play the voucher, and each team member is to assume "the role" of one or more documents.
2. To prepare for your individual role you are to:
   a. Find an illustration for the document within the chapter.
   b. Write down your document function, where you originate, and how you flow through the voucher system.
3. Rehearse the role playing of operating the system. You may use text illustrations as props, and for visual effort you may wear a nametag identifying the part you play.

Communicating in Practice exercises aim at applying accounting knowledge to develop written and verbal communication skills.

Communicating in Practice
LO 12

The classroom should be divided into teams. Teams are to select an industry, and each team member is to select a different company in that industry. Each team member is to acquire the annual report of the company selected. Annual reports can be obtained in many ways including accessing this book's Web page or **http://www.sedar.com**. Use the annual report to compute total asset turnover. Communicate with teammates via a meeting, e-mail or telephone to discuss the meaning of this ratio, how different companies compare to each other, and the industry norm. The team must prepare a single memo reporting the ratios for each company and identify the conclusions or consensus of opinion reached during the team's discussion. The memo is to be duplicated and distributed to the instructor and all classmates.

Flexibility

Learning and instructing requires flexibility **F.A.P.** offers flexibility in meeting the unique demands of individual students and teachers. From the conventional classroom to the active learning environment, **F.A.P.'s** new edition and its pedagogical package give more flexibility and options for innovation in learning and instruction. It does this while maintaining the rich content that has made it the market-leading book in accounting principles.

Packaging Options

Unique **packaging options** support **F.A.P.** flexibility. Nobody matches McGraw-Hill Ryerson when it comes to packaging options for accounting principles. Discuss the flexible packaging options with your McGraw-Hill Ryerson sales representative.

To Instructor

F.A.P. supports all instructional and learning styles.

Additional Supporting Materials

Instructor's Resource Manual
Solutions Manual
Test Bank
Solutions Acetates
Teaching Acetates
PowerPoint Slides
Tutorial Software
SPATs
Videos (U.S.)

To Student

F.A.P. provides learning aids.

Additional materials that may be helpful in your accounting course include

Working Papers
Study Guide
GLAS (General Ledger Applications Software)
Essentials of Financial Accounting: A Multimedia Approach

Innovations and Enhancements

In preparing this edition, we asked questions of instructors and students. We asked what topics to add, or change in emphasis. We asked what pedagogical aids would help in teaching and learning. We wanted to know what innovations and enhancements would help them and maintain **F.A.P.** leadership in accounting principles. From these questions came several requests. We listened, and this edition is the result. We have already described major content and pedagogical changes. This section identifies many other chapter-by-chapter innovations and enhancements:

Chapter 1

- New focus on the information age and the relevance of accounting.
- Early introduction to income, revenues, and expenses using Alliance Communications.
- New discussion of return and risk as part of all business decisions.
- New descriptions of business activities: financing, investing, and operating.
- New and unique presentation of ethics and social responsibility.

Chapter 2

- ***FASTForward,*** an athletic service company, introduced as the new focus company for Chapters 2–5.
- New company transactions to add realism and interest.
- Revised discussion and presentation of accounting principles.
- Added analysis of each transaction using the accounting equation.
- New presentation and integration of cash flow statement with other financial statements.
- New description of reporting differences between proprietorships, partnerships, and corporations.

Chapter 3

- Revised presentation of transactions and source documents.
- New exhibits on the accounting equation and double-entry accounting.
- New exhibits and discussion linking transactions to financial statements, including the statement of cash flows.
- Revised discussion and exhibits for recording transactions.
- Expanded discussion of debt ratio with new comparative analysis.

Chapter 4

- New discussion of the accounting period and the motivation for adjusting accounts.
- New framework for preparing and analyzing adjustments.
- Several new exhibits and graphics illustrating adjusting accounts.
- New presentation linking adjustments to financial statements.
- Several new features highlighting current happenings in revenue recognition and the role of technology.
- Revised discussion of profit margin using Loblaw along with comparative analysis.

Chapter 5

- Revised presentation and new exhibits for the closing process.
- Revised presentation and discussion of the statement of cash flow as an integral part of the full set of financial statements.
- New exhibits presenting the accounting cycle.
- New presentation of the classified balance sheet.
- Revised current ratio discussion using Canadian Tire and industry analyses.

Chapter 6

- New discussion comparing a service company and a merchandiser.
- New presentation of the operating cycle of a merchandiser with credit or cash sales.
- New design of source documents including an invoice and debit and credit memoranda.
- Revised presentation of merchandising sales and purchases using the perpetual inventory system.
- Revised discussion on the transfer of ownership for inventory.
- New discussion and presentation of merchandising cost flows across periods.
- New comparison of cash and accrual measures of sales and costs.
- Revised acid-test ratio and gross margin discussion using Mitel and industry analyses.
- New appendix on accounting for merchandise sales and purchases under both the periodic and perpetual inventory systems.

Chapter 7

- Revised presentation of assigning costs to inventory using the perpetual inventory system.
- Revised discussion of inventoriable items and costs.
- New exhibits illustrating statements effects of inventory errors.
- Revised presentation of alternative inventory valuation methods.
- New appendix presentation assigning costs to inventory using the periodic system.
- Expanded merchandise turnover and days' sales in inventory ratio discussion and industry analyses.

Chapter 8

- New section on fundamental system principles.
- Contemporary and streamlined presentation on components of accounting systems.
- Revised discussion of hardware and software for systems.
- Contemporary presentation of Special Journals.
- Revised discussion of technology-based accounting systems.
- Revised layout for Special Journals reflecting current practice.
- New discussion of *enterprise-application software*, including SAP and Oracle.
- New analysis of business segments using a contribution matrix and Bombardier data.

Chapter 9

- New sections on the purpose of internal control and its limitations.
- Revised discussion on the principles of internal control.
- New feature boxes involving current technological developments.
- Revised discussion on control of cash.
- New presentation and exhibits on the voucher system of control.
- New depictions of important source documents.
- New presentation on using banking activities as controls, including the bank reconciliation.
- Revised discussion of days' sales uncollected using comparative analyses of Oshawa Group and George Weston.

Chapter 10

- New organization focuses on receivables first and short-term investments second.
- Revised discussion of credit sales, including use of credit cards.
- New presentation on accounting for accounts receivables.
- New ordering of (simpler) write-off method before (more complex) allowance method.
- New presentation and exhibits for estimating bad debts.
- Revised presentation and exhibits for notes receivable.
- Streamline accounting for investments including unrealized lower of cost and market.
- Revised discussion of accounts receivable turnover using comparative analyses of Imperial Oil and Ocelot Energy.

Chapter 11

- New exhibits including introducing computerized payroll systems.
- Excerpts from Revenue Canada forms.

Chapter 12

- New introduction and motivation on accounting for capital assets.
- New discussion to describe and illustrate amortization.
- Revised presentation and exhibits for disposals of capital assets.
- New discussion on natural resources and intangible assets.
- New discussion on the cash flow impacts of long-term assets.
- Revised total asset turnover illustration using George Weston and Oshawa Group.

Chapter 13

- New introduction on accounting for liabilities.
- Revised presentation of known (determinable) liabilities.
- New exhibits and discussion on promissory notes.
- Revised discussion of accounting for long-term liabilities.
- Transfer of present value discussion of liabilities to Chapter 16.
- Revised presentation of times interest earned with application to Best Buy.

Chapter 14

- New discussion of partnerships, including financial statements, admission/withdrawal, and liquidation.

Chapter 15

- Revised corporation coverage to focus on its characteristics and both common and preferred shares.
- New summary exhibit highlighting differences across alternative forms of organization.

- New exhibits including share certificate.
- Streamlined coverage of share subscriptions.
- Transfer of cash dividends discussions to Chapter 16.
- Revised book value per share discussion with references to Royal Bank.

Chapter 16

- Reorganization into four main sections: dividends; treasury shares; reporting income; and retained earnings.
- New dividends presentation with new exhibits.
- Revised and streamlined discussion on treasury shares.
- Streamlined presentation on reporting income information.
- Revised earnings per share discussion.
- New section on accounting for share options.
- Revised presentation of reporting retained earnings.
- New presentation of dividends yield and price-earnings ratios using Viceroy Homes, Nova Scotia Power, Noranda and CIBC.

Chapter 17

- New introduction to bond (long-term debt) financing.
- Revised bond presentation with new exhibits.
- New layout for effective interest amortization tables.
- Revised presentation of accounting for bond retirements.
- Revised presentation for notes payable.
- New explanation of present value concepts.
- New discussion of present values using interest tables.
- New discussion of collateral agreements for bonds and notes.
- Revised presentation of pledged assets to secured liabilities.

Chapter 18

- Streamlined coverage of investments and international accounting.
- Reorganized into three sections: Classification of investments; long-term investments in securities; and international investments.
- New presentation on the components of return on total assets with real company application.

Chapter 19

- New presentation on the motivation for cash flow reporting.
- New exhibits on the format of the statement of cash flows replacing the statement of changes in financial position.
- Revised discussion on cash from operating activities—both direct and indirect methods.
- New flexible presentation allows coverage of either or both direct or indirect methods.
- New exhibits summarize adjustments for both the direct and indirect methods.
- Revised discussion of cash flows from investing activities.
- Revised discussion of cash flows from financing activities.
- Revised presentation of analysis of cash sources and uses.

Chapter 20

- New discussion on the basics of financial statement analysis.
- New explanation of the building blocks of analysis.
- Revised discussion on analysis tools and standards for comparisons.
- Revised presentation of horizontal and vertical analysis.
- Revised summary exhibit of financial statement analysis ratios.
- New section on analysis reporting.

Chapter 21

- New introduction to managerial accounting.
- New section and exhibit on the purpose of managerial accounting.
- Revised presentation of reporting manufacturing activities.
- New section on cost accounting concepts emphasizing cost identification and classification.
- New discussion of manufacturing management principles.
- New introduction to important managerial topics including prime, conversion, product, and period costs.
- New infographics augment many new and revised topics.
- Transfer of discussion of a manufacturing statement and a general accounting system to Chapter 22.
- New presentation on unit contribution margin with illustrations using a bike manufacturer.

Chapter 22

- New focus on manufacturing and job order cost accounting.
- Revised presentation of manufacturing activities and reporting.

- Revised discussion of the job order cost accounting system.
- Streamlined discussion of underapplied and overapplied overhead.
- New presentation on multiple overhead allocation rates.
- Revised discussion of general accounting system (periodic) in a new appendix.

Chapter 23

- Revised introduction with discussion of motivation for a process manufacturing system.
- New exhibit and discussion comparing job order and process manufacturing systems.
- New exhibit to explain process manufacturing operations.
- Revised discussion of computing and using equivalent units.
- New discussion on the physical flow of units and preparation of a cost reconciliation.
- New presentation on spoilage in process costing and its effects on costs per equivalent unit.

Chapter 24

- New section and exhibits on two-stage allocation.
- New presentation and exhibits for activity-based costing.
- Transfer of activity-based costing upfront to link with Chapter 23.
- Revised discussion of decision-making relevance of cost allocation and performance measurement.
- Revised discussion of department expense allocation.
- New exhibit and presentation of joint costs.
- New presentation of return on assets by investment centres.
- Transfer of discussion of "eliminating an unprofitable department" to Chapter 28.

Chapter 25

- Revised discussion on describing and identifying cost behaviour.
- Revised presentation and comparison of the high-low, scatter diagram, and regression methods.
- Revised presentation on applying cost-volume-profit analysis.
- New presentation of operating leverage and its role in determining income.

Chapter 26

- New presentation of the budget calendar.
- New exhibit showing the master budget sequence.
- Expanded discussion and new exhibits of production and manufacturing budgets.
- Revised discussion motivated by new material on planning objectives.
- New presentation on zero-based budgeting.

Chapter 27

- New discussion and exhibit on the process of budgetary control.
- Revised emphasis on a decision making role for budgets and standard costs.
- New presentation of standard costs and the standard cost card.
- Revised organization of variance analysis.
- New presentation of and visual orientation to variance analysis.
- New separate analysis of variable and fixed overhead variances.
- New presentation on sales variances with illustrations.

Chapter 28

- Revised presentation of capital budgeting.
- New exhibits illustrating capital budgeting and its computations.
- New presentation of the internal rate of return for capital budgeting.
- New section comparing methods of analyzing investments using capital budgeting.
- New section on managerial decision making, information, and relevant costs.
- Revised presentation of short-term managerial decision tools.
- New section on qualitative factors in managerial decisions.
- New presentation of break-even time with illustrations.

Supplements

Instructor's Resource Manual
This manual contains materials for managing an active learning environment and provides new instructional visuals. Each chapter provides a Lecture Outline, a chart linking Learning Objectives to end-of-chapter material, and transparency masters. For instructor's convenience, student copies of these visuals are provided in the *Study Guide*. If students do not acquire the study guide, adopters are permitted to duplicate these visuals for distribution.

Solutions Manual
The manuals contain solutions for all assignment materials. Transparencies in large, boldface type are also available.

Test Bank
The Test Bank contains a wide variety of questions, including true-false, multiple-choice, matching, short essay, quantitative problems, and completion problems of varying levels of difficulty. All Test Bank materials are grouped according to learning objective. A computerized version is also available in Windows.

PowerPoint Slides
This is a package of multimedia lecture enhancement aids that uses PowerPoint® software to illustrate chapter concepts. It includes a viewer so that they can be shown with or without Microsoft PowerPoint® software.

McGraw-Hill Learning Architecture
This Web-based Class Management System distributes product course materials for viewing with any standard Web Browser. This online learning centre is packed with dynamically generated pages of text, graphics, PowerPoint® slides, exercises, and more. Customization possibilities are easily implemented.

PageOut
PageOut is a McGraw-Hill online tool that enables instructors to create and post class-specfic Web pages simply and easily. No knowledge of HTML is required.

Online Learning Centre
A body of online content to augment the text and provide students with interactive quizzing features.

Videos (U.S.)
Lecture Enhancement Video Series. These short, action-oriented videos provide the impetus for lively classroom discussion. There are separate *Financial Accounting and Managerial Accounting* libraries. Available upon adoption.

SPATS (Spreadsheet Applications Template Software).
Excel templates for selected problems and exercises from the text. The templates gradually become more complex, requiring students to build a variety of formulas. What-if questions are added to show the power of spreadsheets and a simple tutorial is included. Instructors may request a free master template for students to use or copy, or students can buy shrinkwrapped versions at a nominal fee.

Tutorial Software
Windows version of multiple-choice, true-false, journal entry review and glossary review questions are randomly assessed by students. Explanations of right and wrong answers are provided and scores are tallied. Instructors may request a free master template for students to use or copy, or students can buy shrinkwrapped versions for a nominal fee.

Solutions Manual to accompany the practice sets.

Student

Working Papers
These new volumes match end-of-chapter assignment material. They include papers that can be used to solve all quick studies, exercises, serial problems, comprehensive problems, and Beyond the Numbers activities. Each chapter contains one set of papers that can be used for either the problems or the alternate problems.

Study Guide
For each chapter and appendix, these guides review the learning objectives and summaries, outline the chapter, and provide a variety of practice problems and solutions. Several chapters also contain visuals to illustrate key chapter concepts.

Additional Software (U.S.)
Essentials of Financial Accounting: A Multimedia Approach
GLAS (General Ledger Applications Software) by Jack E. Terry, ComSource Associates, Inc.

Practice Sets
Student's Name CD Centre, by Harvey C. Freedman of Humber College of Applied Arts and Technology. A manual, single proprietorship practice set covering a one-month accounting cycle. The set includes business papers and can be completed manually and/or using computer data files for use with *Simply Accounting for Windows*. The problem set can be assigned after Chapter 8.

Adders 'N Keyes, Fourth Edition by Brenda Mallouk. *Adders 'N Keyes* is a sole proprietorship practice set that gives students exposure to a real life business setting.

Barns Bluff Equipment, by Barrie Yackness of British Columbia Institute of Technology and Terrie Kroshus. A manual, single proprietorship practice set with business papers that may be assigned after Chapter 9.

Computerized Practice Set
Interactive Financial Accounting Lab by Ralph Smith, Rick Birney and Alison Wiseman.

Acknowledgments

We are thankful for the encouragement, suggestions, and counsel provided by the many instructors, professionals, and students in preparing the 9th Canadian edition. This new edition reflects the pedagogical needs and innovative ideas of both instructors and students of accounting principles. If has been a team effort and we recognize the contributions of many individuals. We especially thank and recognize individuals who provided valuable comments and suggestions to further improve this edition, including:

Reviewers:

John Glendinning	Centennial College
Allen McQueen	Grant MacEwan Community College
Peter Woolley	BCIT
Ann Paterson	Humber College
Bob Holland	Kingstec Community College
David Bopara	Toronto School of Business
Donna Grace	Sheridan College Brampton
Aziz Rajwani	Langara College
Margaret Tough	Seneca College
Neill Nedohin	Red River Community College
Peter Norwood	Langara College
Tony McGowan	Lambton College
Jim Chambers	St. Clair College
Jack Castle	SIAST—Palliser
Cecile Ashman	Algonquin College
Shawn P. Thompson	Algonquin College
Micheal S. Sirtonski	Assiniboine Community College
George Duquette	Canadore College
Denis Woods	Centennial College—Progress Campus
Robin Hemmingsen	Centennial College
Harold J. Keller	College of the Rockies
Joe Pidutti	Durham College
Robert Bryant	Durham College
Ralph Sweet	Durham College
Paul Hurley	Durham College
Bill Rice	Fairview College
Elaine Hales	Georgian College
Don Smith	Georgian College
G. D. McLeod	Humber College—Lakeshore Campus
Gordon Holyer	Malaspina University College
Jeffrey Rudolph	Marianopolis College
Wayne Larson	Northern Alberta Institute of Technology
John Daye	New Brunswick Community College
Brad MacDonald	Nova Scotia Community College—Annapolis Campus
Heather Martin	Nova Scotia Community College—I.W. Akerley Campus
Louise Conners	Nova Scotia Community College—I.W. Akerley Campus
Carol Derksen	Red River Community College
Randy Ross	Ridgetown College, University of Guelph
Greg Fagan	Seneca College
Michael A. Perretta	Sheridan College—Brampton Campus
Don Thibert	Toronto School of Business—Windsor
Pamela Hamm	New Brunswick Community College—Saint John

Problem checkers:

Connie Hahn	Southern Alberta Institute of Technology
Albert Ferris	UPEI
Dirk VanVoorst	Sheridan College—Oakville
Richard Wright	Fanshawe College
Elaine Hales	Georgian College
Maria Belanger	Algonquin College
Karen Matthews	SIAST—Palliser
Neill Nedohin	Red River Community College
Bonnie Martel	Niagara College

Students input plays an important role in the new edition. Over 300 students from the schools below contributed to Student Focus Groups and Student Surveys.

Acadia University
Algonquin College
British Columbia Institute of Technology
Kwantlen College
Northern Alberta Institute of Technology
Nova Scotia Community College
Saskatchewan Institute of Applied Science and Technology (Palliser Campus)
Simon Fraser University
Souther Alberta Institute of Technology

We also want to recognize the contribution of Dennis Wilson of Centennial College who prepared the updates of the payroll liabilities chapter and solutions for this edition and also our final accuracy checker, Elaine Hales of Georgian College. Special thanks also go to Matthew Carroll and Marife Abella for their research assistance.

Morton Nelson *Kermit D. Larson* *Ray Carroll* *Barbara Chiappetta* *Michael Zin* *John J. Wild*

NINTH CANADIAN EDITION

VOLUME III

Fundamental Accounting Principles

21 CHAPTER

Managerial Accounting Concepts and Principles

A Look Back

Chapter 20 described the analysis and interpretation of financial statement information. We applied ratio analyses and other methods to gain a better understanding of company performance and financial condition.

A Look at This Chapter

We begin our study of managerial accounting by explaining its purpose and describing its major characteristics. We also discuss cost concepts and describe how they help managers in gathering and organizing information they need for making decisions. Important management principles are also introduced and discussed.

A Look Forward

Chapters 22 through 28 discuss information that managers need and how they obtain it. We explain the types of decisions managers must make and how managerial accounting helps with these decisions. Chapter 22 looks at how we can measure costs assigned to certain types of processes.

Chapter Outline

Where Do I Start?

Halifax, NS—Sharon West thought she had made it. A graduate of Dalhousie University, she had four years of accounting experience and a new job as manager of special projects at **MacKains**. Yet here she was, asking her supervisor "Where do I start?"

West's new job was to assist managers with accounting analysis. In her first week, she met with managers in marketing, sales, purchasing and manufacturing. Purchasing needed help in setting criteria for selecting suppliers. Manufacturing needed help in planning equipment purchases. Marketing needed help measuring financial effects of promotion strategies. Sales needed help redesigning compensation plans.

West took notes, asked questions, and went back to her new office. She reviewed financial statements, internal monthly reports, and strategic plans. Nowhere did she find the information she needed. Discouraged, she went to the controller. "I'll never forget how helpless I felt," recalls West. "I looked him straight in the eye, swallowed my pride, and said 'I don't know where to start'," West now says with a laugh. "I thought I had it together. But the answers weren't in our accounting records."

West said the controller smiled and told her,"Welcome to management accounting." West says "The answers were in the future, not in past data." West's experience is common. Probably the most important skill of top managers is the ability to go beyond the numbers. Use them, yes. Depend on them, no. West believes one must identify the question and gather relevant data. "But," stresses West, "You then go and learn about operations." These days, West spends much of her time learning operating activities. Little time is spent in her office. And about that question—where do I start? West smiles, "Management accounting is a great beginning, but understanding operations is crucial. And," adds West "don't let anyone tell you this is an office job!"

Learning Objectives

LO 1 Explain the purpose of managerial accounting.

LO 2 Describe the major characteristics of managerial accounting.

LO 3 Explain differences in the balance sheet of manufacturing and merchandising companies.

LO 4 Explain differences in the income statement of manufacturing and merchandising companies.

LO 5 Compute cost of goods sold for a manufacturer.

LO 6 Describe accounting concepts useful in classifying costs.

LO 7 Define product and period costs and explain how they impact financial statements.

LO 8 Explain how a customer orientation in a global economy impacts business operations.

LO 9 Describe current manufacturing management principles.

LO 10 Compute unit contribution margin and describe what it reveals about a company's cost structure.

CHAPTER PREVIEW

Managerial accounting, like financial accounting, provides information to help users make better decisions. Yet there are important differences between managerial and financial accounting. We explain these differences. We also compare accounting and reporting practices used by manufacturing and merchandising companies. Both types of companies earn revenues by selling products.[1] A merchandising company sells products without changing their condition. A manufacturing company buys raw materials and turns them into finished products for sale to customers. We also explain important concepts useful in classifying costs. We conclude the chapter by identifying and describing four management principles. The implications of these principles on management accounting is discussed.

Managerial Accounting

Managerial accounting, also called *management accounting*, is an activity that provides financial and nonfinancial information to managers and other internal decision makers of an organization. This section explains the purpose of managerial accounting and compares it with financial accounting.

Purpose of Managerial Accounting

LO1 Explain the purpose of managerial accounting.

Both managerial accounting and financial accounting share the common purpose of providing useful information to decision makers. They do this by collecting, managing and reporting information in a manner useful to users of accounting data. Both areas of accounting also share the common practice of reporting monetary information.[2] They even report some of the same information. We have already covered areas where the two types of accounting overlap. For example, the financial statements of a company contain information useful for both the managers of a company (insiders) and other persons who are interested in the company (outsiders).

The remainder of this book takes a more careful look at managerial accounting information, how accounting professionals gather it, and how managers use it. The main topic of this chapter and Chapters 22 and 23 is accounting for manufacturing activities. We look at the concepts and procedures used to determine the costs of products a company manufactures and sells. A firm reports these costs on its balance sheet as inventory and on its income statement as cost of goods sold. Later chapters look at budgeting, break-even analysis, activity-based costing, profit planning, cost analysis and other managerial accounting topics.

Information about the cost of products is very important for managers. Managers use information about the cost of producing products for many decisions. This includes predicting the future costs of producing the same or similar items. Predicted costs are used in product pricing, profitability analysis, and even in deciding whether to make or buy a product or component. Much of management accounting is directed at getting useful information about costs to make important planning and control decisions.

Planning is the process of setting goals and making plans to achieve them. Companies formulate long-term strategic plans that usually span a 5- to 10-year horizon and refine them using medium-term and short-term plans. Strategic plans usually set the long-term direction of a firm by developing a road map for the

[1] A service company is another type of company. It earns revenues providing services rather than by selling products. The skills, tools and techniques developed for measuring a manufacturing company's activities apply to service industries.

[2] Modern management accounting practices include the reporting of nonmonetary information in addition to monetary information.

future by thinking about potential opportunities such as new products, new markets and capital investments. The strategic plan can be very "fuzzy" given its long-term orientation. Medium and short-term plans are more operational in nature, thereby translating the strategic plan into actions. These plans are relatively more concrete and consist of objectives and goals that are better defined than in the strategic plan. Short-term plans often cover a one-year period which, when translated into monetary terms, is known as the budget.

Control is the process of monitoring planning decisions and evaluating the organization's activities and employees. Control includes measurement and evaluation of actions, processes and outcomes. The feedback provided by the control function allows managers to revise their plans if necessary. In particular, the measurement of actions and processes allows managers to take timely corrective actions to avoid undesirable outcomes. Exhibit 21.1 portrays these two important management functions.

Managers also use information to plan and control the production process. Information about manufacturing costs helps managers identify problems that require cost management data. In later chapters, we explain more about how managers use cost information in controlling and planning business operations. This includes directing operating activities, improving business operations, and bettering management's decision making.

Exhibit 21.1

Planning and Control

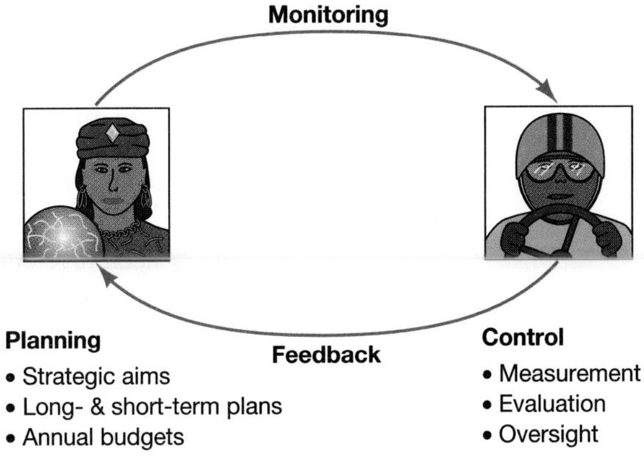

Nature of Managerial Accounting

LO 2 Describe the major characteristics of managerial accounting.

Managerial accounting has its own special characteristics. To understand these characteristics we compare managerial accounting to financial accounting. There are at least seven important differences. These are summarized in Exhibit 21.2.

Exhibit 21.2

Differences between Managerial Accounting and Financial Accounting

	Financial Accounting	Managerial Accounting
1. Users and decision makers	Investors, creditors, and other users external to the organization	Managers, employees, and decision makers internal to the organization
2. Purpose of information	Assist external users in making investment, credit, and other decisions	Assist managers in making planning and control decisions
3. Flexibility of practice	Structured and often controlled by GAAP	Relatively flexible (no GAAP)
4. Timeliness of information	Often available only after an audit is complete	Available quickly without the need to wait for an audit
5. Time dimension	Historical information with minimum predictions	Many projections and estimates; historical information also presented
6. Focus of information	Emphasis on whole organization	Emphasis on projects, processes, and subdivisions of an organization
7. Nature of information	Monetary information	Mostly monetary; some nonmonetary information

Users and Decision Makers

Companies accumulate, process and report financial accounting and managerial accounting information for different groups of decision makers. They provide financial accounting information primarily to external users. These include investors, creditors, regulators and others. External users usually do not have a major role in managing the daily activities of a company. Companies provide managerial accounting information to internal users. These users are responsible for making and implementing decisions about a company's business activities.

Purpose of Information

Investors, creditors and other users of financial accounting information must decide whether to invest in or lend to a company. They also can choose the terms of investment or loan. If they have already invested in a company or loaned to it, they must decide whether to continue owning the company or carrying the loan. Internal decision makers must plan the future of a company. They look to take advantage of opportunities or to overcome obstacles. They also try to control activities and ensure they are being carried out efficiently. Managerial accounting information helps these internal users make both planning and control decisions.

Flexibility of Practice

Because external users make comparisons between companies and because external users need protection against false or misleading information, financial accounting practices are somewhat rigid. This rigid structure is enforced through an extensive set of rules and guidelines called generally accepted accounting principles (GAAP).

Unlike external users, internal users need managerial accounting information for planning and controlling their company's activities rather than for external comparison. Different types of information are required depending on the activity. Because of this it is difficult to standardize managerial accounting systems across companies. Managerial accounting is largely flexible. Also, since managers have access to most company data they require less protection against false or misleading information compared with external users. This reduces the need for a reporting structure.

The design of a company's managerial accounting system largely depends on the nature of the business and the arrangement of the internal operations of the company. Managers of a company can decide for themselves what information they want and how they want it reported. Even within a single company, different managers often can design their own systems to meet their special needs. This flexibility allows managers to modify their systems quickly in response to changes in the environment.

Timeliness of Information

Formal financial statements reporting past transactions and events are not immediately available to outside parties. Independent public accountants often must audit the financial statements a company reports to external users. Because audits can take one to three months to complete, annual financial reports to outsiders usually are not available to users until well after the end of the year.

Managerial accounting information can be forwarded to managers quickly. External auditors need not review it. Estimates and projections are acceptable. Yet, to get information quickly, managers often accept less precision in reports. As an example, an early internal report to management prepared right after the end of the year might say net income for the year is between $4.2 and $4.8 million. An audited income statement might later show net income for the year at $4.55 million. While the internal report is not precise, its information can be more useful because it is available earlier.

Although accounting reports to managers are available without waiting for completion of an audit, internal auditing plays an increasingly important role. Managers are responsible for preventing and detecting fraudulent activities in their companies. Most companies recognize the importance of having strong internal audit functions. In a recent *Report to Shareholders*, the CEO and chief financial officer of **CAE** reported

> Management has established and maintains a system of internal control which is designed to provide reasonable assurance that assets are safeguarded from loss or unauthorized use and that financial information is reliable and accurate. The Corporation also maintains an internal audit department that evaluates and formally reports to management and the Audit Committee on the adequacy and effectiveness of internal controls.

Internal auditors evaluate the flow of information not only inside the company but also outside the company. Internal audits often help avoid situations as depicted in the Judgment and Ethics box.

Production Supervisor

You accept a new job as a production supervisor and invite three of your former classmates for a celebration at a restaurant. When the dinner cheque arrives, David, a self-employed entrepreneur, picks it up saying, "Here, let me pay. I'll deduct it as a business expense on my tax return. It won't cost me as much." Denise, a salesperson for a medium-size company, takes the cheque from David's hand and says, "I'll put this on my company's credit card. It won't cost us anything." Derek, a factory manager for a company, laughs and says, "Neither of you understand. I'll put this on my company's credit card and call it overhead on a cost-plus contract* my company has with the government." Adds Derek, "That way, my company pays for dinner *and* makes a profit on it too." Who should pay the bill?

*A cost-plus contract means the company receives its costs plus a percent of those costs.

Judgment and Ethics

Answer—p. 1016

Time Dimension

To protect external users from false expectations, financial reports deal primarily with both results of past activities and conditions currently existing. While some predictions are necessary, such as service lives and salvage values of capital assets, financial accounting avoids predictions whenever possible. Managerial accounting regularly includes predictions of future conditions and events. As an example, one important managerial accounting report is a budget. A budget predicts sales, expenses and other items. If managerial accounting reports are restricted to the past and present, managers would be less able to plan activities and less effective in managing current activities.

Focus of Information

While companies often organize into divisions and departments, investors do not usually buy shares in one division or department. Neither do creditors lend money to a single division or department of a company. Instead, they own shares in or make loans to the whole company. Since these external users need information about the whole company, financial accounting is focused primarily on a company as a whole. GAAP requires under certain conditions that large companies report information on segments of their operations. The purpose of this requirement is to help external users understand more about the whole company as shown in Exhibit 21.3.

Exhibit 21.3

Focus of External Reports

The focus of managerial accounting is different. Only top-level managers are responsible for managing the whole company. Most managers are responsible for much smaller sets of activities. These middle-level and lower-level managers need managerial accounting reports dealing with specific activities, projects and subdivisions for which they are responsible. For example, division sales managers are

Exhibit 21.4

Focus of Internal Reports

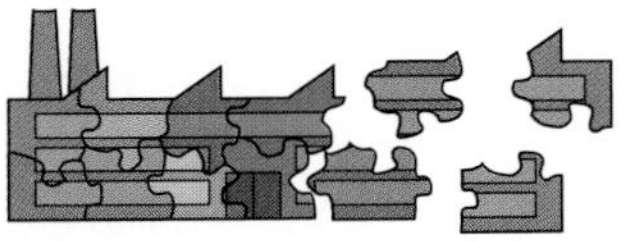

directly responsible only for the results achieved in their divisions. While they often want to see results for all divisions, they usually do not need a company-wide sales report. Division sales managers need information about results achieved in their specific divisions to improve their sales personnel's performance. This information includes the level of success achieved by each salesperson in each division (see Exhibit 21.4).

Nature of Information

Both financial and managerial accounting systems primarily report monetary information. Yet for managerial accounting this is changing. Managerial accounting systems are increasingly reporting nonmonetary information. In the chapter's opening article, we saw Sharon West had to help purchasing, marketing, sales and manufacturing departments with important decisions. While monetary information is an important part of these decisions, nonmonetary information also plays an important role in these decisions. This is especially so in cases where monetary effects are difficult to measure. One common example of important nonmonetary information is the quality and delivery criteria of purchasing decisions.

You Make the Call

Division Manager

You are the manager of a division of a manufacturing company. At a recent executive meeting, you were asked to explore the manufacturing of a component your division has been purchasing from an outside supplier for the past several years. What information do you collect in evaluating these two alternative sources?

Answer—p. 1016

Decision-Making Focus

While we emphasize the differences between financial and managerial accounting, they are not entirely separate. Similar information is useful to both external and internal users. For example, information about costs of manufacturing products is useful to all users in their decisions.

We must also remember that both financial and managerial accounting can affect people's actions. In the chapter's opening article, West's job at MacKains demanded an understanding of accounting. West needed to quantify future costs and revenues associated with projects. But just as important was West's understanding of operations and the people making decisions using cost or revenue data.

Important managerial decisions often are related to each other and people's behaviour. For example, West's design of a sales compensation plan affects the behaviour of the sales force. West also must estimate the dual effects of promotion and sales compensation plans on buying patterns of customers. These estimates impact the equipment purchase decisions for manufacturing. They also can affect the supplier selection criteria established by purchasing. Financial and managerial accounting systems do more than measure, they affect people's behaviour.

Flashback

1. Managerial accounting produces information (a) to meet the needs of internal users, (b) to meet specific needs of a user, (c) often focused on the future, or (d) all of the above.
2. What is the difference between the intended users of financial and managerial accounting information?
3. Do generally accepted accounting principles control the practice of managerial accounting?

Answers—p. 1016

Reporting Manufacturing Activities

Companies with manufacturing activities are different from both merchandising and service companies. The main difference between merchandising and manufacturing companies is that merchandisers buy goods ready for sale while manufacturers produce goods from materials and labour. **Eaton's** is an example of a merchandising company. It buys and sells shoes without physically changing them. **Bata** is a manufacturer of shoes. It purchases materials such as leather, cloth, plastic, rubber, glue and laces. It then uses employees' labour to convert these materials into shoes. **Air Canada** is a service company. It transports people and items.

Much of our focus has been on the business activities of merchandising and service companies. We described these activities and how we account for them. Manufacturing activities are different from both selling merchandise and providing services. This means the financial statements for manufacturing companies have some unique features. This section looks at some of these features and compares them to accounting for a merchandising company.

Balance Sheet of a Manufacturer

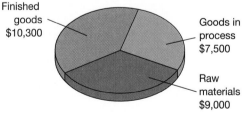

LO 3 Explain differences in the balance sheet of manufacturing and merchandising companies.

Manufacturers carry several different kinds of assets that are unique to them. Manufacturers usually have three inventories instead of a single inventory as carried by merchandising companies. Exhibit 21.5 shows three different inventories in the current asset section of the balance sheet for **Rocky Mountain Bikes**. The three are: raw materials, goods in process, and finished goods.

Raw Materials Inventory

Raw materials inventory refers to the goods a company acquires to use in making products. It uses materials in two ways—directly and indirectly. Most raw materials physically become part of the product and are identified with specific units or batches of product. Raw materials used in this manner are called **direct materials.** For example, the tires, seat and frame of a mountain bike are direct materials. Notice that a mountain bike cannot be produced without these direct materials. The costs of these materials are usually a significant portion of the total cost of producing the bike and therefore must be identified separately.

Other materials used in support of the production process are sometimes not as clearly identified with specific units or batches of product. Examples are a company needing lubricants for machinery and various supplies for cleaning the factory. These materials are called **indirect materials** because they do not become a part of a product and are not clearly identified with specific units or batches of product. Items used as indirect materials often appear on a balance sheet as factory supplies. In other cases, they are included in raw materials.

Inventories of Rocky Mountain Bikes

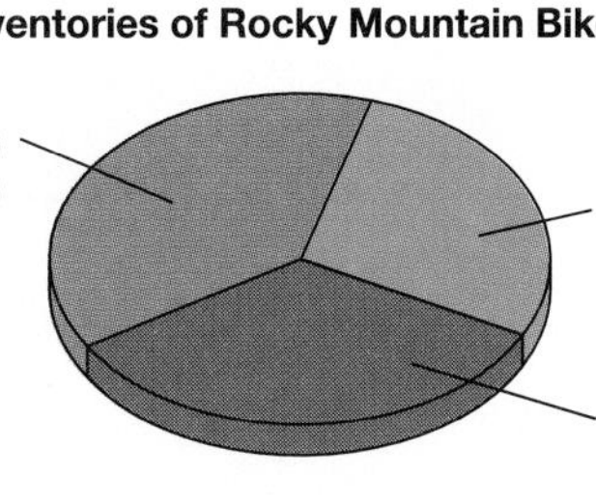

In addition to the indirect materials as defined above, there may be some direct materials that are actually classified as indirect materials. These are so classified because of their low (insignificant) values. Examples include screws and nuts used in assembling mountain bikes, or nails and glue used in manufacturing shoes. Notice that the cost of these materials is likely to be very low compared to the cost of the other direct materials. Using the materiality principle, it does not make much economic sense to individually trace the cost of each of these materials and classify them separately as raw materials. For example, it is not cost-beneficial to maintain an accurate record of the number of nails used in manufacturing one unit of a shoe.

Goods in Process Inventory

Another inventory held by manufacturers is **goods in process inventory,** also called *work in process inventory*. It consists of products in the process of being manufactured but not yet complete. The amount of goods in process inventory depends on the type of production process. If the time required to produce a unit

ROCKY MOUNTAIN BIKES
Balance Sheet
December 31, 1998

Assets			Liabilities and Shareholders' Equity		
Current assets:			Current liabilities:		
Cash		$ 11,000	Accounts payable	14,000	
Accounts receivable	$32,000		Wages payable	540	
Allowance for doubtful accounts	(1,850)	30,150	Interest payable	2,000	
			Income taxes payable	32,600	
Raw materials inventory		9,000	Total current liabilities	49,140	
Goods in process inventory		7,500	Long-term liabilities:		
Finished goods inventory		10,300	Long-term notes payable	50,000	
Supplies		350	Total liabilities		99,140
Prepaid insurance		300	Shareholders' equity:		
Total current assets		68,600	Common shares , no par value	100,000	
Capital assets:			Retained earnings	49,760	
Small tools		1,100	Total shareholders' equity		149,760
Delivery equipment	9,000		Total liabilities and shareholders' equity		$248,900
Accumulated amortization	(4,000)	5,000			
Office equipment	1,700				
Accumulated amortization	(400)	1,300			
Factory machinery	72,000				
Accumulated amortization	(6,500)	65,500			
Factory building	90,000				
Accumulated amortization	(3,300)	86,700			
Land		9,500			
Total tangible capital assets		169,100			
Intangible assets:					
Patents		11,200			
Total assets		$248,900			

Exhibit 21.5

Balance Sheet for a Manufacturer

of product is short, the amount of goods in process inventory is likely small. But, if weeks or months are needed to produce a unit, the amount of goods in process inventory is larger.

Finished Goods Inventory

A third inventory owned by a manufacturer is **finished goods inventory.** Finished goods inventory consists of completed products waiting to be sold. This inventory is similar to merchandise inventory owned by a merchandising company. Both inventories are items ready for sale.

Manufacturers often carry unique plant assets such as *small tools, factory buildings*, and *factory equipment. Patents* are an intangible asset often owned by manufacturers. Companies use these assets to manufacture products. The balance sheet in Exhibit 21.5 shows Rocky Mountain Bikes owns all of these assets. Some manufacturers invest millions or even billions of dollars in production facilities and patents. **Magna's** 1997 balance sheet, for example, shows a net investment in land, buildings, machinery and equipment of $2.1 billion, much of which involves production facilities.

Income Statement of a Manufacturer

LO 4 Explain differences in the income statement of manufacturing and merchandising companies.

The main difference between income statements of manufacturers and merchandisers is the items making up cost of goods sold. Exhibit 21.6 compares the components of cost of goods sold for a manufacturer and a merchandiser. A merchandiser adds beginning merchandise inventory to cost of goods purchased, and then subtracts ending merchandise inventory to get cost of goods sold. A manufacturer adds beginning finished goods inventory to cost of goods manufactured, and then subtracts ending finished goods inventory to get cost of goods sold.

Exhibit 21.6

Cost of Goods Sold Computation

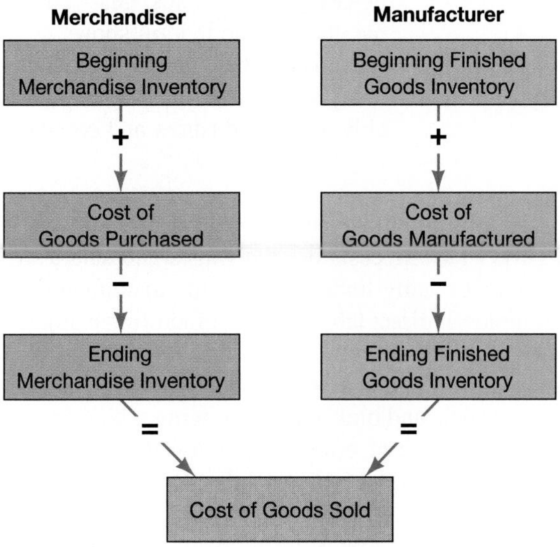

LO 5 Compute cost of goods sold for a manufacturer.

The merchandiser uses the term *merchandise* inventory while the manufacturer uses the term *finished goods* inventory. The manufacturer's inventories of raw materials and goods in process are not included in finished goods because they are not available for sale. The manufacturing company also shows cost of goods *manufactured* instead of cost of goods *purchased.* This difference is because a manufacturer produces its goods instead of purchasing them ready for sale.

We show cost of goods sold sections for a merchandiser (Tele-Mart) and a manufacturer (Rocky Mountain Bikes) in Exhibit 21.7 to highlight these differences. The remaining sections are similar.

Exhibit 21.7

Cost of Goods Sold for a Merchandiser and Manufacturer

Merchandising Company		Manufacturing Company	
Cost of goods sold:		Cost of goods sold:	
Beginning merchandise inventory . .	$ 14,200	Beginning finished goods inventory .	$ 11,200
Total cost of merchandise purchased	234,150	Cost of goods manufactured*	170,500
Goods available for sale	248,350	Goods available for sale.	181,700
Ending merchandise inventory	12,100	Ending finished goods inventory . . .	10,300
Cost of goods sold	$236,250	Cost of goods sold	$171,400

*The cost of goods manufactured amount is reported in the income statement of Exhibit 21.9.

Except for the differences noted, the cost of goods sold computations are the same. But we want to emphasize the numbers used in these computations reflect different activities. The merchandiser's cost of goods purchased is the cost of buying products to be sold. The manufacturer's cost of goods manufactured is the sum of direct materials, direct labour, and overhead costs incurred in producing the products. The details of how to prepare a statement of cost of goods manufactured will be dealt with in Chapter 22. The remainder of this section explains these manufacturing costs, and describes prime and conversion costs.

Direct Materials

Direct materials are tangible components of a finished product. **Direct material costs** are the expenditures for direct materials that are separately and readily traced through the manufacturing process to finished goods. Examples of direct materials in manufacturing a mountain bike include the tires, seat, frame, pedals, brakes, cables, gears and handle bars. The pie chart in the margin shows us that direct materials make up about 45% of manufacturing costs in today's product. But this amount varies considerably across industries and companies.

Manufacturing Cost Components in Today's Products

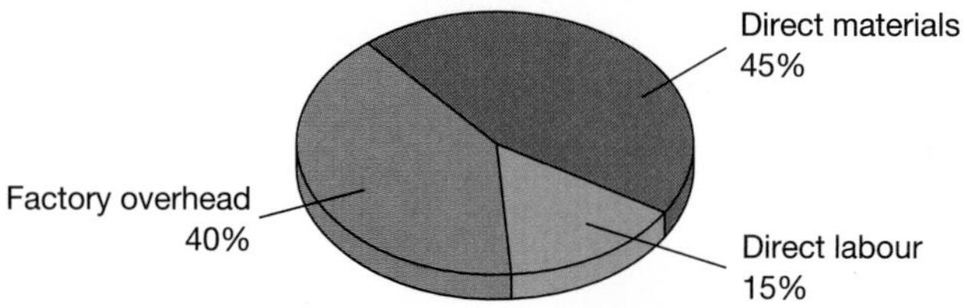

Direct Labour

Direct labour is efforts of employees who physically convert materials to finished product. **Direct labour costs** are the wages and salaries for direct labour that are separately and readily traced through the manufacturing process to finished goods. Examples of direct labour in manufacturing a mountain bike include operators directly involved in converting raw materials into finished products (welding, painting, forming) and assembly line workers who assemble materials such as tires, seats, pedals and brakes to the mountain bike frame. Overtime paid to direct labourers and costs of other workers on the assembly line who assist direct labourers are classified as **indirect labour.**

Factory Overhead

Factory overhead are activities supporting the manufacturing process and are not direct materials or direct labour. **Factory overhead costs** are the expenditures for factory overhead that cannot be separately or readily traced to finished goods. These costs include indirect materials and indirect labour. *Indirect materials* are materials not directly traceable to the product or those that are insignificant. Examples are screws or washers used to assemble the bike, and cleansing agents and lubricants applied to the finished bike. *Indirect labour* is efforts of manufacturing employees who do not work specifically on converting direct materials into finished products and is not clearly linked to specific units or batches of the product.

Factory overhead costs also include maintenance of the mountain bike factory, supervision of its employees, repairing manufacturing equipment, factory utilities (water, gas, electricity), production manager's salary, factory rent, amortization on factory buildings and equipment, factory insurance, property taxes on factory buildings and equipment, and factory accounting and legal services. Factory overhead does *not* include selling and administrative expenses. This is because they are not incurred in manufacturing products. These expenses are called period costs and are recorded as expenses on the income statement when incurred. We describe period costs in detail later in the chapter.

Exhibit 21.8

Prime and Conversion Costs

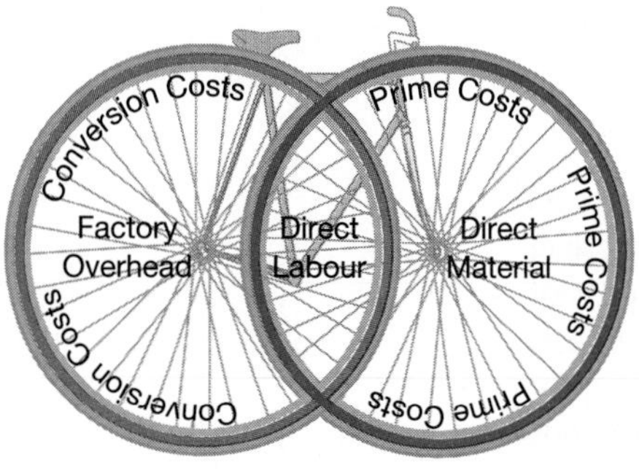

Prime and Conversion Costs

Direct material costs and direct labour costs are also called prime costs. **Prime costs** are expenditures directly associated with the manufacturing of finished goods. Direct labour costs and overhead costs are also called conversion costs. **Conversion costs** are expenditures incurred in the process of converting raw materials to finished goods. Note that direct labour costs often make up both prime costs and conversion costs. Exhibit 21.8 conveys the relation between prime and conversion costs along with their components of direct material, direct labour and factory overhead.

Reporting Performance

Exhibit 21.9 shows the income statement for Rocky Mountain Bikes. Its operating expenses include sales salaries, office salaries, and amortization of delivery and office equipment. Yet operating expenses do not include manufacturing costs such as factory workers' wages and amortization of production equipment and of the factory. These manufacturing costs are not reported as operating expenses. They are part of cost of goods manufactured and included in cost of goods sold. We explain how this is done in the next section under "Classification by Function."

Exhibit 21.9

Income Statement for a Manufacturer

ROCKY MOUNTAIN BIKES
Income Statement
For Year Ended December 31, 1998

Sales			$310,000
Cost of goods sold:			
Finished goods inventory, December 31, 1997		$ 11,200	
Cost of goods manufactured		170,500	
Goods available for sale		181,700	
Finished goods inventory, December 31, 1998		(10,300)	
Cost of goods sold			171,400
Gross profit			138,600
Operating expenses:			
Selling expenses:			
Sales salaries expense	$18,000		
Advertising expense	5,500		
Delivery wages expense	12,000		
Shipping supplies expense	250		
Insurance expense, delivery equipment	300		
Amortization expense, delivery equipment	2,100		
Total selling expenses		38,150	
General and administrative expenses:			
Office salaries expense	15,700		
Miscellaneous expense	200		
Bad debts expense	1,550		
Office supplies expense	100		
Amortization expense, office equipment	200		
Interest expense	4,000		
Total general and administrative expenses		21,750	
Total operating expenses			59,900
Income before income taxes			78,700
Less income taxes expense			(32,600)
Net income			$ 46,100
Net income per common share (20,000 shares)			$ 2.31

Flash back

4. What are the three types of inventory on a balance sheet of a manufacturing company?
5. What is the difference between cost of goods sold in merchandising versus manufacturing companies?

Answers—p. 1017

Mid-Chapter Demonstration Problem

The balance sheet and income statement for a manufacturing company is different than for a merchandising or service company. This problem requires that we understand the important differences between the two.

Required

1. Fill-in the "[BLANKS]" on the balance sheets for both the manufacturing company and merchandising company. Explain why a different presentation is required.

CHIP MAKING SYSTEMS
Balance Sheet
December 31, 1998

Assets	
Current assets:	
Cash	$10,000
[BLANK]	8,000
[BLANK]	5,000
[BLANK]	7,000
Supplies	500
Prepaid insurance	500
Total current assets	$31,000

JOE'S SHOE OUTLET
Balance Sheet
December 31, 1998

Assets	
Current assets:	
Cash	$5,000
[BLANK]	12,000
Supplies	500
Prepaid insurance	500
Total current assets	$18,000

2. Fill-in the "[BLANKS]" on the income statements for the manufacturing company and merchandising company. Explain why a different presentation is required. The manufacturer's cost of good manufactured is the sum of (a) __________, (b) __________, and (c) __________ costs incurred in producing the product.

CHIP MAKING SYSTEMS
Income Statement
For Year Ended December 31, 1998

Sales		$200,000
Cost of goods sold:		
Finished goods inventory, December 31, 1997	$ 10,000	
[BLANK]	120,000	
Goods available for sale	130,000	
Finished goods inventory, December 31, 1998	(40,000)	
Cost of goods sold		90,000
Gross profit		$110,000

JOE'S SHOE OUTLET Income Statement For Year Ended December 31, 1998		
Sales		$190,000
Cost of goods sold:		
Merchandise inventory, December 31, 1997	$12,000	
[BLANK]	108,000	
Cost of goods available for sale	120,000	
Merchandise inventory, December 31, 1998	(40,000)	
Cost of goods sold		80,000
Gross profit		$110,000

Solution to Mid-Chapter Demonstration Problem

1.

CHIP MAKING SYSTEMS December 31, 1998	
Assets	
Current assets:	
Cash	$10,000
[Raw materials inventory]	8,000
[Goods in process inventory]	5,000
[Finished goods inventory]	7,000
Supplies	500
Prepaid insurance	500
Total current assets	$31,000

JOE'S SHOE OUTLET Balance Sheet December 31, 1998	
Assets	
Current assets:	
Cash	$5,000
[Merchandise inventory]	12,000
Supplies	500
Prepaid insurance	500
Total current assets	$18,000

A different presentation of inventory is required for a manufacturing and merchandising company. In a manufacturing company, raw materials are converted to finished goods. In the sequence of making a product the raw materials move into production, labelled goods in process inventory. All raw materials and goods in process inventory at the end of each accounting period are considered current assets. All unsold finished inventory is also considered a current asset at the end of each accounting period. A manufacturing company must control and measure three types of inventory—*raw materials, goods in process*, and *finished goods*. The merchandising company must control and measure one type of inventory, the purchased goods remaining at the end of an accounting period.

2.

CHIP MAKING SYSTEMS Income Statement For Year Ended December 31, 1998		
Sales		$200,000
Cost of goods sold:		
Finished goods inventory, December 31, 1997	$ 10,000	
[Cost of goods manufactured]	120,000	
Goods available for sale	130,000	
Finished goods inventory, December 31, 1998	(40,000)	
Cost of goods sold		90,000
Gross profit		$110,000

JOE'S SHOE OUTLET Income Statement For Year Ended December 31, 1998		
Sales		$190,000
Cost of goods sold:		
Merchandise inventory, December 31, 1997	$ 12,000	
[Cost of Purchases]	108,000	
Cost of goods available for sale	120,000	
Merchandise inventory, December 31, 1998	(40,000)	
Cost of goods sold		80,000
Gross profit		$110,000

Different reporting terms are used for a manufacturing and merchandising company. In particular, the terms "finished goods" and "cost of goods manufactured" are used to reflect the production of goods. Yet the concepts and techniques of reporting cost of goods sold for a manufacturing company and merchandising company are similar. A manufacturer's cost of goods manufactured is the sum of *direct material, direct labour* and *factory overhead* costs incurred in producing the product.

Cost Accounting Concepts

LO 6 Describe accounting concepts useful in classifying costs.

We can classify costs in several different ways. These include assigning costs on the basis of their (1) behaviour, (2) traceability, (3) controllability, (4) relevance, and (5) function. This section explains each of these concepts in classifying costs.

Classification by Behaviour

At the most basic level a cost can be classified as fixed or variable (see Exhibit 21.10). A **fixed cost** does not change with changes in the volume of an activity. Straight-line amortization on a machine is a fixed cost. A **variable cost** changes in proportion to changes in the volume of an activity. Sales commissions based on a percent of units sold is a variable cost. When cost items are combined, total cost can be fixed, variable or mixed. Mixed means it is a combination of fixed and variable costs. Rent of equipment often includes a fixed cost for some minimum amount and a variable cost based on the amount of usage. Classification of costs by behaviour is helpful in cost-volume-profit analyses and short-term decision making. We discuss these in Chapter 25.

Exhibit 21.10

Fixed and Variable Costs

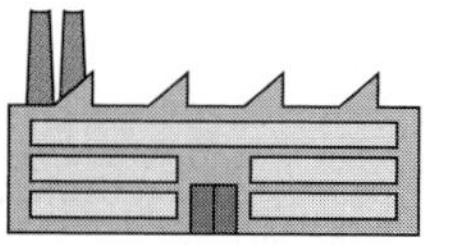

Fixed Cost: The 1998 rent for Rocky Mountain Bikes' factory is $22,000. It does not change with the number of bikes produced.

Variable Cost: The cost of tires is variable with the number of bikes produced. The cost of tires in 1998 is $15 per pair—total of tires is $15,000 if 1,000 bikes are produced or $22,000 if 1,500 bikes are produced.

Classification by Traceability

A cost is often traced to a cost object. A cost object is a product, process, department or customer to which costs are assigned. When a cost is traceable, it is classified as either a *direct* or *indirect cost*. **Direct costs** are those incurred for the benefit of one specific cost object. For example, if we use product as a cost object, material and labour costs are usually directly traceable. **Indirect costs** are incurred for the benefit of more than one cost object. An example of a indirect traceable cost is one benefiting two or more departments such as maintenance which is usually common across more than one department in a firm. As illustrated in Exhibit 21.11, there are several costs in a manufacturing plant that are indirect to a specific department within the plant. Classification of costs by traceability is useful for cost allocation. This is discussed in Chapter 24.

Exhibit 21.11

Direct and Indirect Costs

Direct Costs:
- Salaries of maintenance department employees
- Salary of maintenance department manager
- Equipment purchased by maintenance department
- Materials purchased by maintenance department
- Maintenance department equipment amortization

Indirect Costs:
- Factory accounting
- Factory administration
- Factory rent
- Factory managers' salary
- Factory light and heat

Budget Officer

You are the budget officer of a manufacturer. You are told by your boss to trace as many of the assembly department's direct costs as possible. You are able to trace 90% of the direct costs in an economical manner. To trace the other 10%, you need a sophisticated and costly accounting software package. Do you purchase this package?

Answer—p. 1016

Classification by Controllability

A cost can be defined as **controllable** or **not controllable.** Whether a cost is controllable or not depends on one's responsibilities. This is often referred to as identifying the hierarchical levels in management, or the pecking-order. For example, investments in machinery are controllable by senior-level managers but not low-level managers. Yet many daily operating expenses such as overtime often are controllable by lower-level managers. Classification of costs by controllability is especially useful for evaluating managers.

Exhibit 21.12

Controllability of Costs

Senior Manager Controls costs of investment in land, buildings, and equipment.

Supervisor Controls daily expenses such as supplies, maintenance, and overtime.

Classification by Relevance

A cost can be classified by relevance. This is done by identifying a cost as either a **sunk cost** or an **out-of-pocket cost**. A sunk cost is one already incurred and cannot be avoided or changed. Sunk costs are irrelevant to future decisions. One example is the cost of production equipment previously purchased by a manufacturing company. An out-of-pocket cost requires a future outlay of cash and is relevant for future decision making. Future purchases of production equipment involve out-of-pocket costs.

A discussion of relevant costs must consider **opportunity costs.** An opportunity cost is the potential benefit lost by taking a specific action from two or more alternative choices. One example is a student giving up wages from a job to attend summer school. Consideration of opportunity costs is important when, for example, a computer manufacturer must decide between internally manufacturing a chip versus buying it externally. This is discussed in Chapter 28.

Purchase Manager

You are the purchasing manager of a motorcycle manufacturer. You are evaluating two potential suppliers of seats for your motorcycles. One supplier (A) quotes a price of $75 per seat and assures 100% quality standards and on-time delivery schedules. The second supplier (B) quotes a price of $69 per seat and does not give any written assurances on quality or delivery. You decide to award the contract to the second supplier (B), saving $6 per seat. Are there any opportunity costs of this decision?

Answer—p. 1016

Classification by Function

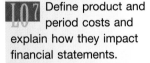

LO 7 Define product and period costs and explain how they impact financial statements.

Another classification of costs for manufacturers is whether a cost is capitalized as inventory or is charged to an expense when incurred. Costs that are capitalized as inventory because they produce benefits that attach to the finished product are called product costs. **Product costs** refer to expenditures necessary and integral to finished products. They can include direct materials, direct labour and overhead costs. Product costs pertain to activities that are carried out to manufacture the product.

Costs that are expensed are called period costs. **Period costs** refer to expenditures identified more with a time period than finished products. They can include selling and general administration expenses. Period costs pertain to activities that are not part of the manufacturing process. A distinction between product and period costs is important. This is because it affects the amount of costs expensed in the income statement and the amount of costs assigned to inventory on the balance sheet.

Our ability to understand and identify product costs and period costs is crucial to using and understanding a company's *manufacturing statement.* Exhibit 21.13 shows the different effects of product and period costs incurred by Rocky Mountain

Exhibit 21.13

Period and Product Costs in Financial Statements

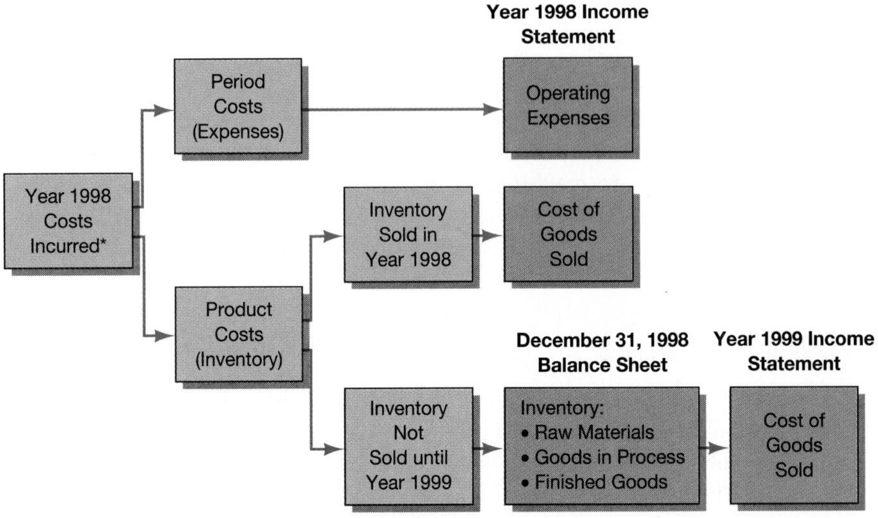

*We exclude from this diagram costs to acquire assets other than inventory, costs to retire debt, and costs of payments to owners.

Bikes, a manufacturer, during 1998. Notice period costs flow directly to its 1998 income statement as expenses. They are not reported as assets.

The product costs for Rocky Mountain Bikes are first assigned to inventory. Final treatment of product costs depends on when inventory is sold or disposed of. Product costs assigned to finished goods in 1998 are reported on Rocky Mountain Bikes' 1998 income statement as part of cost of goods sold. Product costs assigned to unsold inventory are carried forward on Rocky Mountain Bikes' balance sheet at the end of 1998. If this inventory is sold in 1999, product costs assigned to it are reported in the 1999 income statement.

This difference between period and product costs explains why the 1998 income statement of Rocky Mountain Bikes does not report under operating expenses either factory workers' wages or amortization on factory buildings and equipment. Instead, both these costs are combined with the cost of raw materials to compute the product cost of finished goods. A portion of these manufacturing costs are reported in the 1998 income statement as part of cost of goods sold. The other portion is reported on the balance sheet at the end of 1998 as part of the cost of inventory. The portion assigned to inventory could be included in any or all of raw materials, goods in process, or finished goods.

Identifying Cost Classification

It is important we understand that a specific cost item can be classified using any of the five different methods described above. To do this, it is important we understand costs and operations. Using our five classifications, we must be able to identify the: *activity* for behaviour, *cost object* for traceability, *management hierarchical level* for controllability, *opportunity cost* for relevance, and *benefit period* for function. Factory rent, for instance, can be classified as a product cost, is fixed with respect to units produced, indirect with respect to products, and is not controllable by a production supervisor. Potential multiple classifications are shown in Exhibit 21.14 using different cost items incurred in manufacturing mountain bikes. The finished bike is the cost object.

Exhibit 21.14

Potential Multiple Cost Classifications

Cost item	By Behaviour	By Traceability	By Function
Tires	variable	direct	product
Wages of assembly worker	variable	direct	product
Advertising	fixed	indirect	period
Production manager's salary	fixed	indirect	product
Office amortization	fixed	indirect	period

Proper allocation of these costs, and decisions made using cost data, depend on our ability to correctly identify cost classifications.

Cost Concepts for Service Companies

Most of the cost concepts described above are applicable to service organizations. We can consider **Air Canada**, a service firm, as a case example. Air Canada's cost of food for passengers is a variable cost based on the number of passengers. Yet the cost of leasing an aircraft is fixed with respect to the number of passengers. We can also often trace a flight crew's salary to a specific flight whereas wages for ground crew are unlikely directly traceable to a specific flight. Note that classification by function (i.e., product versus period costs) is not relevant to service companies because services are not inventoried. Costs incurred by a service firm are expensed in the reporting period when incurred.

Service Costs
- food
- beverages
- cleaning
- pilots' salaries
- attendants' salaries
- fuel
- travel agents' fees
- ground crew's salaries

Understanding cost concepts is important to managers in service firms. They rely on accurate estimation of costs for many important decisions. An airline manager must often decide between cancelling or rerouting flights. A manager also must be able to estimate costs saved by cancelling a flight versus rerouting. Knowledge of fixed costs is equally important. We explain more about the cost requirements for these and other special accounting decisions in Chapter 27.

Flash back

6. Which type of cost behaviour causes total costs to increase when volume of activity increases?
7. How might traceability of costs improve managerial decisions?

Answers—p. 1017

Manufacturing Management Principles

LO 8 Explain how a customer orientation in a global economy impacts business operations.

Two important factors have encouraged manufacturers to look for more effective and efficient ways to manage their production operations in recent years. First, there is an increased emphasis on *customers* as the most important part of business. This has meant an increasing focus on quality, flexibility and on-time delivery. Second, the expanding *global economy* has fostered greater competition and more opportunities.

The customer focus affects many manufacturing activities. Customers have little tolerance for poor quality. There is very little room for an acceptable defect level. Today's goal is zero defects. Customers also are demanding manufacturers cater to their changing needs. This includes product design, features and even order quantities. This requires manufacturers to adopt more flexible manufacturing practices. There is also increasing importance placed on time. Customers expect their orders to be delivered soon and on time. These changes imply that manufacturers accept the notion of customer orientation. **Customer orientation** means a company's managers and employees are in tune with the changing wants and needs of consumers. They then align their management and manufacturing processes to respond to consumers' wants and needs.

Exhibit 21.15

Manufacturing Management Principles in Action

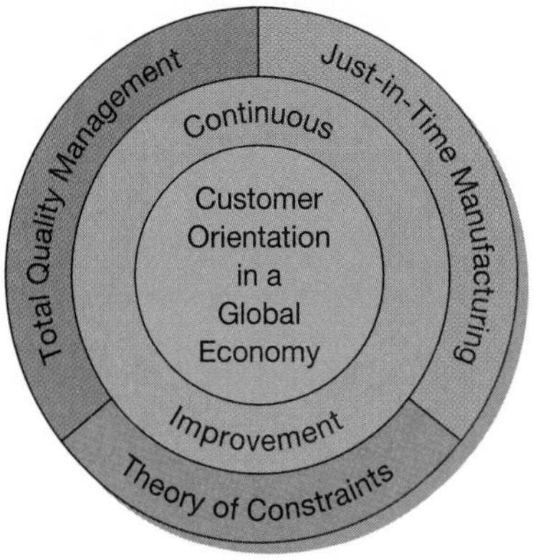

The global economy also produces changes in manufacturing activities. Both global competition and the expansion of competitive boundaries affect today's manufacturers. One notable case of increased global competition is auto manufacturing. The top three Japanese auto manufacturers (**Honda, Nissan** and **Toyota**) once controlled over 40% of the North American auto market. During the 1980s, customers perceived Japanese auto manufacturers provided "value" not obtainable from other manufacturers. They were seen as catering to the quality, flexibility and delivery needs of customers, and as being price competitive.

Many North American and European auto manufacturers faced increased pressure to respond to consumer demands. They have responded constructively with changes in their manufacturing practices. In doing so they have recaptured some of this lost market share. Exhibit 21.15 shows a customer orientation in a global economy as a main focus of manufacturing management principles.

LO 9 Describe current manufacturing management principles.

This focus has led manufacturers to move away from traditional mass production techniques in response to these consumer demands. They are increasingly adopting improved approaches to manufacturing and production management. These approaches include *total quality management (TQM), just-in-time (JIT) manufacturing, theory of constraints (TOC),* and *continuous improvement (CI).* These modern manufacturing management principles apply to the production of both products and services. Customers look for flexibility and quality in services as much as they look for them in products. We describe each of these principles in this section.

Xerox Canada has shown great success by focusing on its customers. Its Customer Satisfaction Measurement System tracks the behaviour and preferences of Xerox equipment owners. This information is used to set benchmarks for quality improvements.

Did You Know?

Airline Quality

For many, airline quality is an oxymoron. Frequent cancellations, late arrivals and lousy food are common complaints. But times are changing. Fueling the quality drive is the stunning turnaround at **Continental Airlines.** Once near the bottom of quality rankings, Continental is now one of the best in on-time performance, baggage handling, and customer satisfaction. **Northwest** recently beefed up its cleaning regimen. It now gives a steam cleaning and deodorizing to lavatories on its DC-10s every 9 days instead of every 14. America West has upgraded food quality, added 60 mechanics to speed repairs, and installed in-flight phones and entertainment systems at every seat. **Delta** says it improved quality by rehiring hundreds of baggage handlers, gate agents, and customer service reps. If we are lucky, air quality will soon include airlines. [Source: *Business Week*, January 21, 1997.]

Total Quality Management

Total quality management, or *TQM* for short, is based on having all managers and employees strive toward higher standards. These higher standards extend to their everyday work and to the products and services offered to customers.

Traditional manufacturers tend to leave the responsibility for quality with an independent group of quality control inspectors. The focus usually is on an inspection of finished products. TQM is different. TQM requires a focus on quality *throughout* the production process. Its strategy is to identify defective work when and where it occurs. This constant focus on quality reminds each employee of the need to eliminate defective work at all stages of production. The expected results are fewer defects in finished products and reduced costs from reworking rejected products.

A company using TQM rewards employees who find defects. With this reward, employees are unlikely to ignore defects in partially completed products arriving at their workstations. We all know pointing out problems can require extra effort, paperwork, and hostile reactions from co-workers. An important part of TQM is changing attitudes of employees to encourage a new commitment to quality. TQM also encourages employees to try new methods to improve quality. With flexibility and rewards, managers committed to TQM try to tap the knowledge and abilities of people closest to the work.

Companies using TQM emphasize the value of reaching higher quality levels. A TQM company sets quality standards and measures quality results at each stage of production. Many companies set maximum rejection rates as targets for each workstation. They encourage employees by rewarding those who reach their targets and by reporting actual rejection rates.

To encourage an emphasis on quality among U.S. companies, Congress established the Malcolm Baldridge National Quality Award in 1987. The award's goals are to enhance competitiveness by promoting quality awareness, recognize quality and business achievements of companies and publicize these companies' successful performance. Entrants must do a painstaking self-analysis using guidelines from the Baldridge Committee. They must also submit to on-site review of operations.

Globe Metallurgical stands out as the only small company to win a Baldridge Award. Using computer-controlled systems and statistical process control, Globe monitors and quantifies every aspect of its manufacturing process. This system advises workers whether processing targets are being met. It also identifies production steps most prone to failure. This system increased worker productivity by 50% in several areas, and customer complaints fell by 91%.

Another winner of a Baldridge is **IBM's** division in Rochester, Minnesota. IBM proudly proclaims[3]:

> IBM Rochester has created a quality policy, a vision, and a set of quality goals that are deployed throughout the site to individual departments. The quality policy is *Rochester Excellence . . . Customer Satisfaction...* This policy is supported by the site vision: *Customer—the final arbiter; Products and services—first with the best; Quality—excellence in education; and People—enabled, empowered, excited and rewarded.*

IBM Rochester's employees also regularly score among the highest in morale across all IBM sites as measured by opinion surveys.

Just-In-Time Manufacturing

A commitment to customers and quality leads to profits only if the company's activities are carried out efficiently. A customer orientation demands efficiency. TQM promotes efficiency because it reduces the cost of reworking or repairing defects. Another means to increase efficiency is to use a just-in-time manufacturing system.

A **Just-In-Time (JIT)** system means a company acquires or produces inventory only when needed. Manufacturing activities are planned so that finished products are produced just as they are needed for delivery to customers. Parts for the finished product are only completed as needed in the manufacturing process. Also, raw materials are acquired only when they are needed. A JIT system tries to stock the minimum amounts of finished goods, goods in process, and raw materials inventories.

A JIT system can be directed to meet the needs of customers. This means companies manufacture products in response to predicted or actual customer wants and needs. As one example, a few years ago, **Toyota** declared all of their automobiles sold in Japan were to be produced only when orders were received from customers. Customers would place orders through dealers and wait only two weeks to take delivery. The advantage to customers is getting exactly what they want after a relatively short wait. The advantage to Toyota and its dealers is the little investment in inventories of automobiles.

An important feature of JIT is the demand-pull system. A *demand-pull* system means products are pulled through the manufacturing process by orders from customers. A *supply-push* system is the old traditional system. This traditional

---

[3] *The Quality Journey Continues...*, IBM, Second Edition, March 1991, © Copyright International Business Machines Corporation (IBM) 1990, 1991. Reprinted with permission.

system pushes products through production by inserting raw materials and applying labour and overhead. It relies on marketing and sales forces to push finished goods to customers after-the-fact. A JIT system does not push but instead is pulled by customer needs. The demand-pull system requires a TQM philosophy and involvement of all employees.

A JIT system can be applied to raw materials and goods in process as well as finished products. To see this, look at the production process for a mountain bike in Exhibit 21.16. This process is split into four parts. Each part is performed in sequence as units move toward completion.

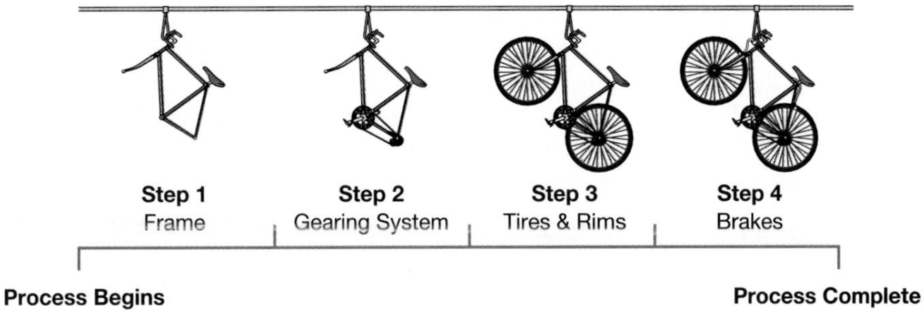

Exhibit 21.16

Production Process—Mountain Bike

A traditional manufacturer allows inventories of mountain bikes to accumulate between workstations. This is to avoid shutting down the production line because of a shortage of any component. The JIT manufacturer aims to get each component to arrive at the production line *just in time* for its use. When successful, the JIT manufacturer needs fewer inventories and is able to use these freed-up assets to reduce debt or invest in other profitable activities.

We must remember not all manufacturing processes can use JIT. To use JIT a company must be able to predict the timing and amount of customer orders. An effective TQM system also must be in place to control the manufacturing process. This is because an unexpected numbers of defects can bring production to a stop. The use of JIT also requires dependable suppliers able to make frequent shipments of small quantities. Good computing and communication equipment are essential. Some JIT companies use systems that send orders directly from their production lines to the supplier's production lines.

The necessary requirements to using a JIT manufacturing system make it more susceptible to disruption than traditional systems. As one example, in 1997 several U.S. plants of **General Motors** were temporarily shut down due to a strike at an assembly plant in Ontario. These U.S. plants supplied components *just in time* to a different Canadian assembly plant.

Theory of Constraints

Another means for improving a company's productive operations is the theory of constraints. The **theory of constraints (TOC)** focuses on identifying factors that constrain or limit a company's operations. Once constraints are identified, managers look for ways to overcome or relax these constraints.

A major emphasis of TOC is to increase **throughput (T)** and reduce investment (I) and operating expenses (OE). Throughput is the added value a company brings to its finished products. We compute throughput as selling price minus costs of direct materials used in production. Investment refers to conversion costs. This includes the cost of property, plant and equipment and inventory for sale. While direct labour is a conversion cost, some companies choose to classify it as an operating expense along with other wages. Operating expenses are the cost of activities required to sell inventory. These include selling and general administration.

While TOC can be applied to the operations of an entire company, including production, sales, engineering, distribution, and administration, it is applied most often in production. Its aim is to synchronize and plan manufacturing operations to minimize processing time. Processing time is the time it takes to produce one item or one order. Shorter processing time helps a company better serve its customers with rapid deliveries.

TOC suggests the key to decreasing processing time is to find the most binding **constraint** (bottleneck), i.e., anything that prevents a company from achieving higher performance in terms of its goals. A constraint can be part of the production process or a resource used in the process. We then manage this constraint to make it nonbinding. A solution may be to add more machinery or labour at the bottleneck of the process to balance the production line. It may also involve redesigning the production process itself.

To illustrate TOC let us return to the production line for mountain bikes (see Exhibit 21.16). This line combines four components to produce finished goods. If the workstation for adding gearing systems (step 2) is the slowest of four workstations, then its output determines the output of the entire line. Workstations pertaining to steps 1, 3 and 4 have idle time while the workstation pertaining to step 2 catches up. One solution is to install more workstations pertaining to step 2 to balance the production flow. While this solution increases throughput because of increased production, it adds inventory costs (more machinery). We should consider ways to increase throughput while minimizing added costs.

Binney & Smith is the manufacturer of Crayola Crayons® with plants in the United States and Lindsay, Ontario. It uses TOC to find and manage manufacturing bottlenecks, to rearrange plant layouts, and to decide the amount of goods-in-process used in its JIT inventory system. Binney & Smith have had great success. Vendors were reviewed and the list of suppliers was shortened. It decreased raw materials inventory by 40%, decreased goods-in-process inventory by 60%, improved on-time shipping performance to 96%, and reduced shipping lead time from 12 to 5 days.

Applying the theory of constraints is a continuous process. After one constraint is identified and relaxed, we search for the next one and so forth. This means as soon as one constraint is relaxed, there is some other constraint that is binding and limiting throughput. We then focus on identifying and relaxing this constraint. In this way, TOC is a regular system aimed at reaching a company's most effective and efficient production process.

Continuous Improvement

Continuous improvement is a management concept where every manager and employee continually looks for ways to improve operations. This extends to customer service, product quality, product features, production process, and employee relations. Continuous improvement rejects the view that an activity is "good enough." New ideas are tried and old ideas are challenged.

There is a relation between continuous improvement and the other manufacturing management principles. There is no place for resisting change with continuous improvement. Instead, managers and employees seek opportunities for growth and increased profitability. In today's global economy, a company is more likely to succeed if its employees are committed to continuous improvement.

Binney & Smith developed and implemented their version of total quality and continuous improvement by using both TOC and JIT principles. They called it High Velocity Manufacturing. It meant encouraging employees to solve problems and accept responsibility for improving the process. They cut the time it takes to change from running one colour of crayon to another. Remarkably, change-over time went from 2 hours to 1/2 hour. They shifted responsibility for quality control from end-of-the-line inspectors to machine operators. Again, defects decreased from 12% to 6%. It worked for Binney & Smith.

Flashback

8. Describe the focus of the theory of constraints.
9. What factors encourage development of new ideas about production management?
10. What is the attitude in a company practising total quality management?

Answers—p. 1017

Implications of Manufacturing Management Principles

Adopting a new manufacturing management principle is challenging. Customer-oriented companies that apply one or more of these principles often end up making several changes to their manufacturing systems. The most common change is a greater use of technology. This usually changes the cost structure in these companies. For example, direct labour often becomes a smaller portion of total cost. It is replaced by machine costs and other overhead. This means total product cost now has a greater proportion of fixed and indirect costs rather than variable and direct costs. A good knowledge of the basic cost concepts discussed earlier in this chapter is essential in understanding the changes to the cost structure when a company's systems and processes are modified.

Did You Know?

Overhead and Proud of It!
Our technology society may not eliminate direct labour, but it can banish us to overhead. We often pride ourselves on our work, a contribution to a product or service. But Roseville Networks Division (RND) of **Hewlett-Packard** now calls us overhead. RND found direct labour to be less than 2% of total manufacturing costs. They then decided to reclassify direct labour from a separate cost item to overhead. Adding insult to injury, this reclassification eliminated about 30 minutes of direct labour per day spent on tracing labour time to products. But at least we're not "immaterial"—yet.
Source: D. Berlant, R. Browning and G. Foster, "How Hewlett-Packard Gets Numbers It Can Trust," *Harvard Business Review*, January–February 1990, pp. 178–183.

A customer orientation necessitates a large amount of information for management decision making. Information on defects, returns, service calls, and on-time delivery is necessary. More accurate cost information is needed to compare different courses of action to satisfy customer needs. This means better methods to track information are required. We discuss many of the changes in managerial accounting resulting from adopting new production management principles.

Unit Contribution Margin

USING THE INFORMATION

LO 10 Compute unit contribution margin and describe what it reveals about a company's cost structure.

We explained in this chapter how managers classify costs by behaviour. This means costs are either fixed or variable with respect to the volume of an activity. In manufacturing companies, volume of activity frequently refers to the number of units produced. We then classify a cost as either fixed or variable depending on whether the cost changes as the number of units produced changes.

Once we separate costs by behaviour, we can then compute the contribution margin of a product. **Contribution margin** is the amount a product's unit selling price exceeds its total unit variable cost. This excess amount contributes to covering fixed costs and generating profits on a per unit basis. Exhibit 21.17 shows the contribution margin formula.

Exhibit 21.17

Contribution Margin

$$\textbf{Contribution margin per product} = \textbf{Sales price per product} - \textbf{Total variable cost per product}$$

Users often use contribution margin in the form of a contribution margin ratio. **Contribution margin ratio** is the *proportion* of a unit's selling price that exceeds total unit variable cost. It can be interpreted as what proportion of each sales dollar remains after deducting total unit variable cost. Exhibit 21.18 shows the formula for the contribution margin ratio, defined as contribution margin divided by sales price.

Exhibit 21.18

Contribution Margin Ratio

$$\textbf{Contribution margin ratio} = \textbf{Contribution margin} \div \textbf{Sales price}$$

We use **Rocky Mountain Bikes'** Tracker8 product to show the usefulness of these measures. The selling price of a Tracker8 mountain bike is $225, and the variable costs of its manufacturing and marketing are $100. The contribution margin per bike is computed as $125 ($225 − $100). This measure is useful to managers in determining the money contributed by each sale of a Tracker8 bike to both (a) fixed costs and (b) profits. Specifically, each sale of a Tracker8 bike yields a $125 contribution margin to cover fixed costs of Rocky Mountain Bikes. Once fixed costs are covered, what is left is profit.

We also compute the contribution margin ratio of the Tracker8 mountain bike as 55.55% ($125 ÷ 225). This information is useful to managers when working with estimates of sales in dollars. Management knows in the case of this product that approximately $0.56 (or 55.55%) of each sales dollar is available as contribution to fixed costs and profits. The contribution margin ratio is also useful in cost-volume-profit (CVP) analysis. CVP analysis is a method we use to assess the volume of activity necessary to achieve different performance levels (including profit, loss, and break-even points). We explain cost-volume-profit analysis in Chapter 25.

You Make the Call

Salesperson

You are a salesperson involved with selling and taking customer orders. You are evaluating orders from two different customers, but you can accept only one of these orders because of your company's limited capacity. The first order is for 100 units of a product with a contribution margin ratio of 60% and a selling price of $1,000. The second order is for 500 units of a product with a contribution margin ratio of 20% and a selling price of $800. The incremental fixed costs are the same for both orders. Which order do you accept?

Answer—p. 1016

Summary

LO1 **Explain the purpose of managerial accounting.** The purpose of managerial accounting is to provide useful information to management and other internal decision makers. It does this by collecting, managing and reporting both financial and nonfinancial information in a manner useful to internal users of accounting data.

LO2 **Describe the major characteristics of managerial accounting.** Major characteristics of managerial accounting include: (1) focus on internal decision makers, (2) emphasis on planning and control, (3) fairly flexible, (4) more timely, (5) reliance on forecasts and estimates, (6) focus on segments and projects, and (7) source of both monetary and nonmonetary information.

LO3 **Explain differences in the balance sheet of manufacturing and merchandising companies.** The main difference is that manufacturers usually carry three inventories instead of a single inventory carried by merchandising companies. These three inventories are: raw materials, goods in process, and finished goods.

LO4 **Explain differences in the income statement of manufacturing and merchandising companies.** The main difference between income statements of manufacturers and merchandisers is the items making up cost of goods sold. A merchandiser adds beginning merchandise inventory to cost of goods purchased, and then subtracts ending merchandise inventory to get cost of goods sold.

LO5 **Compute cost of goods sold for a manufacturer.** A manufacturer adds beginning finished goods inventory to cost of goods manufactured, and then subtracts ending finished goods inventory to get cost of goods sold.

LO6 **Describe accounting concepts useful in classifying costs.** We can classify costs on the basis of their (1) behaviour (fixed vs. variable), (2) traceability (direct vs. indirect), (3) controllability (controllable vs. uncontrollable), (4) relevance (sunk vs. out-of-pocket), and (5) function (product vs. period). It is important to remember that a single cost can be classified in more than one way depending on the purpose for which the cost is being determined. These classifications are useful in understanding cost patterns, analyzing performance, and planning future operations.

LO7 **Define product and period costs and explain how they impact financial statements.** Costs that are capitalized because they are expected to have value in the future are called product costs; whereas costs that are expensed are called period costs. A decision on this classification is important because it affects the amount of costs expensed in the income statement and the amount of costs assigned to inventory on the balance sheet. Product costs are commonly made up of direct materials, direct labour and manufacturing overhead. Period costs include selling and administrative expenses.

LO8 **Explain how a customer orientation in a global economy impacts business operations.** A customer orientation means an increased focus on quality, flexibility and timeliness. An expanding global economy means both greater competition and more business opportunities. Business operations are experiencing an increased alignment between management and manufacturing processes to better respond to and meet consumers' wants and needs.

LO9 **Describe current manufacturing management principles**. Today's business environment emphasizes customer satisfaction. To satisfy the customer, companies increasingly focus on quality, flexibility, timely delivery and cost. Several new manufacturing management principles have emerged to help in this process: total quality management, just-in-time manufacturing, theory of constraints, and continuous improvement.

LO10 **Compute unit contribution margin and describe what it reveals about a company's cost structure.** Contribution margin is a product's sales price less its total variable costs, and the contribution margin ratio is a product's contribution margin divided by its sales price. Contribution margin is the amount received from each sale of the product contributing to fixed costs and profits. Contribution margin ratio tells us what portion of each sales dollar is available as contribution to fixed costs and profits. This information is useful in break-even analysis.

Guidance Answers to **You Make the Call**

Division Manager

You need information from the managerial accounting system to help you decide between making the product in-house versus continuing to buy from outside. You need information pertaining to the costs of making it in-house: raw materials, direct labour and overhead. You also need information about investments in machinery that is required to make the component. Regarding the possibility of continuing to buy from the outside, you need information about the purchase price of components and costs to place the order, along with costs of receiving and storing components. You must also consider nonfinancial factors such as quality of components currently supplied and the quality of in-house production and continued availability.

Budget Officer

It is always desirable if you can trace all costs directly to cost objects. But you need to be able to trace costs in an economically feasible manner. In this case, you are able to trace 90% of costs directly to the assembly department. It may not be economical to spend added money on a new software to trace 10% of costs. This final 10% may be immaterial. You need to make a cost-benefit trade-off. Also, if the software offers benefits beyond tracing the remaining 10% of the assembly department's costs, your decision should take this into account.

Purchase Manager

Opportunity costs relate to the potential quality and delivery benefits given up by not choosing supplier (A) as the preferred supplier. Selecting supplier (B) might involve future costs of poor quality seats (inspection, repairs and returns). Also, because of potential delivery delays, work might be interrupted and increase manufacturing costs. Your company might also incur sales losses if the product quality of supplier (B) is lower. You, as purchase manager, are responsible for these costs and must consider them in making your decision.

Salesperson

The contribution margin for the first order is $600 per unit (60% of $1,000), whereas the contribution margin per unit for the second order is $160 (20% of $800). You are likely tempted to accept the first order based on its high contribution margin per unit. But you must compute total contribution margin based on the number of units sold for each order. Total contribution margin is $60,000 ($600 per unit × 100 units) and $80,000 ($160 per unit × 500 units) for the two orders respectively. The second order provides the largest return in absolute dollars. Another factor you need to consider in your selection is the potential for a long-term relationship with these customers including repeat and increasing sales.

Guidance Answer to **Judgment and Ethics**

Production Supervisor

While someone must pay the bill, it appears that all three of your friends want to pay the bill with someone else's money. David is using money belonging to the tax authorities, Denise is taking money from her company, and Derek is defrauding the government. To prevent such practices, companies have internal audit mechanisms. Also, many companies precisely define the kinds of expenses that can be claimed. Many companies also set up ethical codes of conduct to help guide employees in making decisions.

We must recognize that, depending on the circumstances, some entertainment expenses are justifiable and even encouraged. For example, the tax law allows certain deductions for entertainment that have a business purpose. Corporate policies also sometimes allow and encourage reimbursable spending for social activities, and government contracts sometimes include entertainment as allowable costs. Nevertheless, without further details, payments should be made from their personal accounts.

Guidance Answers to Flashbacks

1. *d.* Managerial accounting information is primarily used by the internal manager, is flexible to meet the needs of individual users and often focuses heavily on the future (e.g., budgets).
2. Financial accounting information is intended for users external to an organization such as investors, creditors, and government authorities. Managerial accounting, on the other hand, focuses on providing information to managers and other decision makers within the organization.
3. No, generally accepted accounting principles (GAAP) do not control the practice of managerial accounting. Unlike external users, internal users need managerial accounting information for planning and controlling their organization's activities rather than for external comparison.

Different types of information may be required depending on the managerial activity. Therefore, it is difficult to standardize managerial accounting systems across companies through the use of GAAP or a similar rigid structure.

4. The three different types of inventory that can be found on the balance sheet of a manufacturing company are raw materials inventory, goods in process inventory and finished goods inventory.
5. The cost of goods sold in merchandising companies includes the purchase price of the merchandise, whereas the cost of goods sold in manufacturing companies includes the three costs of manufacturing, raw materials, direct labour and overhead.
6. Variable costs increase in total when the volume of activity increases.
7. By being able to trace the costs to cost objects (e.g., products, departments), managers have a better understanding of the total costs associated with that cost object. This information is very useful when managers are considering making changes to the cost object (say, dropping the product or expanding the department).
8. The theory of constraints focuses on factors limiting or constraining a company's operations.
9. The factors include: (a) increased demands by customers for higher-quality products, custom-designed products, and faster delivery, (b) increased international competition, and (c) improvements in computers.
10. Under TQM, all managers and employees should strive toward higher standards in their work and in the products and services they offer to customers.

Demonstration Problem

This chapter described several new managerial and cost accounting concepts and terms. It is important we understand these and be able to properly classify terms. This problem assists in this process. Consider the following company, **Chip Making Systems (CMS)**, that manufactures computer chips. CMS incurs various costs in manufacturing both these chips and in the operations of the company. These costs include:

1. Plastic board used to mount the chip, $3.50 each.
2. Assembly worker pay of $15 per hour to attach chips to plastic board.
3. Salary for factory maintenance and repair workers. These workers maintain and repair equipment throughout the factory.
4. Factory foreperson pay of $55,000 per year to supervise employees.
5. Real estate taxes paid on the factory, $14,500.
6. Real estate taxes paid on the company office, $6,000.
7. Amortization costs on machinery used by workers, $30,000.
8. Salary paid to the chief financial officer, $95.000.
9. Advertising costs of $7,800 paid to promote products.
10. Salespersons are paid a commission of $0.50 for each assembled chip sold.
11. Note: Instead of producing and assembling chips, CMS could rent the manufacturing plant to store medical records for six local hospitals.

In the table below classify each of these costs according to the terms labelled across the top of the chart. Refer to the chapter and glossary of terms to help classify these costs. A cost can be classified under more than one category. The plastic board used to mount chips, for instance, is classified as a direct material product cost and as a direct unit cost.

	Period Costs	Product Costs			Unit Cost Classification		Sunk Cost	Opportunity Cost
Cost	Selling and Administrative	Direct Material (prime cost)	Direct Labour (prime and conversion cost)	Factory Overhead (conversion cost)	Direct	Indirect		
1. Plastic board used to mount the chip, $3.50 each		✔			✔			

Solution to Demonstration Problem

	Period Costs	Product Costs			Unit Cost Classification		Sunk Cost	Opportunity Cost
Cost	Selling and Administrative	Direct Material (prime cost)	Direct Labour (prime and conversion cost)	Factory Overhead (conversion cost)	Direct	Indirect		
1.		✔			✔			
2.			✔		✔			
3.				✔		✔		
4.				✔		✔		
5.				✔		✔		
6.	✔							
7.				✔		✔	✔	
8.	✔							
9.	✔							
10.	✔							
11.								✔

Glossary

Constraint Anything that prevents a company from achieving higher performance in terms of its goals. (p. 1012)

Continuous improvement A management concept where every manager and employee continually looks for ways to improve operations. (p. 1012)

Contribution margin A product's sale price less its total variable costs. (p. 1014)

Contribution margin ratio A product's contribution margin divided by its sale price. (p. 1014)

Control Process of monitoring planning decisions and evaluating the organization's activities and employees. (p. 992)

Controllable or not controllable A cost is controllable or not depending on a manager's responsibilities and whether or not they are in position to make decisions on expenditures. (p. 1005)

Conversion costs Expenditures incurred in the process of converting raw materials to finished goods—direct labour costs and factory overhead costs. (p. 1000)

Customer orientation A company's managers and employees are in tune with the changing wants and needs of consumers. (p. 1008)

Direct cost Costs that are incurred for the benefit of one specific cost object. (p. 1005)

Direct labour Efforts of employees who physically convert materials to finished product. (p. 1000)

Direct labour costs Wages and salaries for direct labour that are separately and readily traced through the manufacturing process to finished goods. (p. 1000)

Direct materials Raw materials that physically become part of the product and therefore are clearly identified with specific units or batches of product. (p. 997)

Direct material costs Expenditures for direct materials that are separately and readily traced through the manufacturing process to finished goods. (p. 1000)

Factory overhead Factory activities supporting the manufacturing process and are not direct materials or direct labour. (p. 1000)

Factory overhead costs Expenditures for factory overhead that cannot be separately or readily traced to finished goods. (p. 1000)

Finished goods inventory Products that have completed the manufacturing process and are ready to be sold by the manufacturer. (p. 998)

Fixed cost Does not change with changes in the volume of an activity. (p. 1004)

Goods in process inventory Products that are in the process of being manufactured but that are not yet complete (also called *work in process inventory*). (p. 997)

Indirect cost Costs that are incurred for the benefit of more than one cost object or are immaterial in value. (p. 1005)

Indirect labour Efforts of manufacturing employees who do not work specifically on converting direct materials into finished products and that is not clearly associated with specific units or batches of product. (p. 1000)

Indirect materials Materials that are used in support of the production process but that do not become a part of the product and are not clearly identified with units or batches of product. (p. 997)

Just-in-time (JIT) When a company acquires or produces inventory only when needed. (p. 1010)

Managerial accounting An activity that provides financial and nonfinancial information to managers and other internal decision makers of an organization. (p. 992)

Opportunity costs The potential benefit lost by taking a specific action from two or more alternative choices. (p. 1006)

Out-of-pocket cost Requires a future outlay of cash and is relevant for future decision making. (p. 1005)

Period costs Expenditures identified more with a time period than finished products costs—include selling and general administration expenses. (p. 1006)

Planning Process of setting goals and making plans to achieve them. (p. 992)

Prime costs Expenditures directly associated with the manufacturing of finished goods—direct material costs and direct labour costs. (p. 1000)

Product costs Costs that are capitalized as inventory because they produce benefits that are expected to have value in the future—include direct materials, direct labour and factory overhead costs. (p. 1006)

Raw materials inventory The goods a company acquires to use in making products. (p. 997)

Sunk cost A cost that has already been incurred and cannot be avoided or changed. (p. 1005)

Theory of constraints (TOC) Identifying factors that constrain or limit a company's operations. (p. 1011)

Throughput The added value (selling price minus direct material costs) of finished products processed through the system. (p. 1011)

Total quality management (TQM) A management concept under which all managers and employees at all stages of operations strive toward higher standards and a reduced number of defective units. (p. 1009)

Variable cost Changes in proportion to changes in the volume of an activity. (p. 1004)

Questions

1. Discuss the role of the management accountant in business planning, control and decision making.
2. Distinguish between managerial and financial accounting on the elements of:
   a. users and decision makers
   b. purposes of information
   c. flexibility of practice
   d. time dimension, and
   e. focus of information.
3. Explain the difference between a manufacturing company and merchandising and service companies.
4. Why is managerial accounting required to work with numerous predictions?
5. How does the report content of a manufacturing firm differ from the report content of a merchandising firm?
6. Besides inventories, what other assets often appear on balance sheets of manufacturers but not on balance sheets of merchandisers?

7. Why does a manufacturing firm require three different inventory categories?
8. Distinguish between direct material and indirect material.
9. Explain the difference between direct labour and indirect labour.
10. Distinguish between factory overhead, and selling and administrative overhead.
11. What product cost is listed as both a prime cost and a conversion cost?
12. Assume you complete a tour of NIKE's factory where they make basketball shoes for Canadian university teams. List three direct costs and three indirect costs you are likely to see.
13. Should we evaluate a manager's performance on the basis of controllable or uncontrollable costs? Why?
14. Explain why knowing the cost behaviour is useful in product performance evaluation.
15. Explain why product costs are capitalized but period costs are expensed in the current accounting period.
16. Identify changes a company must make when it adopts a customer orientation.
17. When a company employs "total quality management" throughout its operations the responsibility for quality services and products shifts from __________ to __________. How does this shift relate to what our chapter describes as "continuous improvement"?
18. Explain why a traditional inventory system is labelled a "push" system and a just-in-time inventory system is labelled a "pull" system.
19. When managers use the theory of constraints to streamline a company's production process, what is their plan of action?
20. Describe contribution margin.
21. Explain the contribution margin ratio.
22. Describe the contribution margin ratio in layperson's terms?
23. Why is the contribution margin ratio a useful measure for Bata in deciding on what shoes to manufacture?

Quick Study

QS 21-1
Understand terms
LO1

Managerial and cost accounting:

a. Must follow generally accepted accounting principles.
b. Provide information to aid management in planning and controlling business operations.
c. Are directed at reporting aggregate data on the company as a whole.
d. Information is widely available to all interested parties.

QS 21-2
Understand accounting function
LO2

State whether each of the following most likely describes financial accounting (FA) or managerial accounting (MA):

_____ a. Its practice tends to be flexible.
_____ b. Its users are managers of the corporation.
_____ c. Its primary focus is on the organization as a whole.
_____ d. Its information is available only after the audit is complete.
_____ e. It is directed at external users in making investment, credit and other decisions.

QS 21-3
Determine balance sheet reporting
LO3

Three inventory categories are reported on a manufacturing company's balance sheet: (1) raw materials, (2) goods in process inventory, and (3) finished goods. Identify the order in which these inventory items are normally reported on the balance sheet.

a. (1) (2) (3)
b. (2) (1) (3)
c. (2) (3) (1)
d. (3) (2) (1)

QS 21-4
Calculate cost of goods sold
LO 4

For the month end, Book Time has cost of goods manufactured of $4,000. It also has beginning finished goods inventory of $500 and ending finished goods inventory of $750. The cost of goods sold is:

a. $4,250
b. $4,000
c. $3,750
d. $3,900

QS 21-5
Analyze fixed and variable costs
LO 6

Which one of these statements is true regarding fixed and variable costs?

a. Fixed and variable costs stay the same in total as volume increases.
b. Fixed and variable costs increase as volume increases.
c. Fixed cost stays the same and variable cost increases in total as volume increases.
d. Fixed cost increases and variable cost decreases in total as volume decreases.

QS 21-6
Understand terms
LO 7

Which one of these statements is correct?

a. Sales commission is a product cost and factory rent is a period cost.
b. Factory wages is a product cost and direct materials is a period cost.
c. Factory repair and maintenance is a product cost and sales commission is a period cost.
d. Sales commission is a product cost and amortization on factory equipment is a product cost.

QS 21-7
Evaluate management concepts
LO 8, 9

Match each of the new production management concepts with the phrase that best describes it by filling in the blank with the appropriate letter:

_____ **1.** Customer orientation	**a.** Focuses on factors that limit the operations of a business.
_____ **2.** Total quality management	**b.** Inventory is acquired or produced only as it is needed.
_____ **3.** Just-in-time manufacturing	**c.** Calls for flexible product designs that can be modified to accommodate customer choices.
_____ **4.** Theory of constraints	**d.** Every manager and employee constantly looks for ways to improve company operations.
_____ **5.** Continuous improvements	**e.** Focuses on quality throughout the entire production process.

QS 21-8
Calculate contribution margin ratio
LO 10

Compute the contribution margin ratio from the following data:

Sales	$5,000
Total variable cost	3,000

QS 21-9
Calculate cost of goods sold
LO 5

Calculate cost of goods sold using the following information:

Finished goods inventory, December 31, 19X7	$321,500
Goods in process inventory, December 31, 19X7	74,550
Goods in process inventory, December 31, 19X8	81,200
Cost of goods manufactured, 19X8	972,345
Finished goods inventory, December 31, 19X8	297,200

Exercises

Exercise 21-1
Categorize source of accounting information

LO1

Both managerial accounting and financial accounting provide useful information to decision makers. Indicate in this chart the most likely source of information for each business decision:

Business Decision	Accounting Information Source	
	Managerial	Financial
Estimate product cost for a new line of basketball shoes.		
Plan the budget for next quarter.		
Present financial performance to the board of directors.		
Measure profitability of all store locations.		
Prepare financial reports to GAAP requirements.		
Determine amount of dividends to pay common shareholders		
Determine the location for a new plant.		
Evaluate the purchasing department's performance.		

Exercise 21-2
Define terms

LO1

Complete the following by filling in the blanks:

1. _______ is the process of setting goals and making plans to achieve them.
2. _______ usually covers a period of five to ten years.
3. _______ usually covers a period of one year.
4. _______ is a process of monitoring planning decisions and evaluating an organization's activities and its employees.

Exercise 21-3
Identify characteristics of accounting function

LO2

Complete the chart below comparing financial and managerial accounting. Be specific in your response and *write down* your answer on how both areas of accounting deal with each of the items listed. Experience shows writing out your response increases your likelihood of understanding it.

	Financial Accounting	Managerial Accounting
1. Users and decision makers		
2. Purpose of information		
3. Flexibility of practice		
4. Timeliness of information		
5. Time dimension		
6. Focus of information		
7. Nature of information		

Exercise 21-4
Identify and prepare balance sheets
LO 3

Current assets for two different companies at the end of 1998 are listed below. One is a manufacturer, Roller Blades Co., and the other, Wholesale Distribution Co., a grocery distribution company.

Required

1. Identify which set of numbers relates to the manufacturer and which to the wholesaler.
2. Prepare the current asset section for each company. Discuss why the current asset section is different for these two companies

Account	Company 1	Company 2
Cash	$ 5,000	$ 7,000
Raw materials		60,000
Purchase inventory	40,000	
Goods in process		50,000
Finished goods		30,000
Account receivable	49,000	77,000
Prepaid expenses	2,000	1,000

Exercise 21-5
Identify and prepare income statements
LO 4, 5

Calculate cost of goods sold for each of these two companies for the year ended December 31, 1998:

	The GAP Retail Company	GE Lighting Manufacturing
Beginning inventory:		
Merchandise	$250,000	
Finished goods		$500,000
Cost of Purchases	460,000	
Cost of goods manufactured		886,000
Ending inventory:		
Merchandise	150,000	
Finished goods		144,000

Exercise 21-6
Evaluate and categorize costs
LO 4, 7

The following costs are incurred by **Proctor & Gamble**, a manufacturing company. Classify each cost as either a product or a period cost. If a product cost, identify it as a prime and/or conversion cost. Also state whether each product cost is a direct or indirect cost.

	Product Cost		Period Cost
	Prime Cost	Conversion Cost	
Direct materials used			
Provincial and federal income taxes			
Payroll taxes for production supervisor			
Amortization of patents on factory machine			

Accident insurance on factory workers			
Wages to assembly workers			
Factory utilities			
Small tools used			
Bad debt expense			
Amortization of factory building			
Advertising			
Office supplies used			

Exercise 21-7
Critical thinking about cost concepts
LO 6

Identify each of the five cost accounting concepts discussed in the chapter. Explain the purposes of identifying these separate cost accounting concepts.

Exercise 21-8
Evaluate and categorize costs
LO 6

Listed below are *product costs* for the production of 1,000 soccer balls. Classify each cost as either fixed or variable and as either direct or indirect. What pattern do you see regarding the relation between costs classified by behaviour and costs classified by traceability?

Product Cost	Cost by Behaviour		Cost by Traceability	
	Variable	Fixed	Direct	Indirect
Leather cover for soccer balls				
Lace to hold the leather together				
Assembly works				
Taxes on factory				
Annual flat fee paid to We-Keep-It-Safe Security Company				
Water for cooling machinery				
Machinery amortization				

Exercise 21-9
Link customer orientation theory to practice
LO 8

Customer orientation means a company's managers and employees are responding to changing wants and needs of consumers. You are to stop at a restaurant, hotel or other local business in your area and pick-up a customer response card. On the right-hand side of a blank sheet of paper write down the competitive forces in today's world: time, quality, cost, and flexibility of service. Attach the customer response card to the left side of the sheet. Draw arrows linking questions of the customer response card to the competitive forces. Identify how the response card provides information to management and employees to better meet competitive forces. Be prepared to form small groups to compare and contrast the type of business and customer response cards.

Exercise 21-10
Identify manufacturing management principles
LO 9

The chart below lists recent developments in management accounting systems for several companies (treat each item separately). Match the manufacturing management principle(s) that is likely adopted by each company for the recent development identified. There is overlap in meaning between "customer orientation" and "total quality management" and, therefore, some responses can include more than one answer.

Match	Recent Developments	Manufacturing Management Principle
______	1. Company B starts measuring inventory turnover and discontinues generating elaborate inventory records. Its new focus is to pull inventory through the system.	a. Total quality management (TQM) b. Just-in-time (JIT) c. Theory of constraints (TOC)
______	2. Company A starts reporting measures on customer complaints and product returns from customers.	d. Continuous improvement (CI) e. Customer orientation (CO)
______	3. Company D starts reporting measures such as the percent of defective products and the number of units scrapped.	
______	4. Company F starts a program focusing on its bottlenecks.	

Problems

Problem 21-1
Evaluate management accountant's role
LO 1, 9

The chapter begins with a discussion of the objectives of management and cost accounting. The chapter ends with a discussion on the current business environment. You are to look through the automobile section of your local newspaper. Devote special attention to advertisements of sport utility vehicles and count how many manufactures offer this product today compared to only a few years ago when **Ford** and **General Motors** were the only auto companies offering this product.

Required

What is the responsibility of the management accountant in helping an automobile manufacturing company succeed in our current business environment? (Hint: Think about estimates a management accountant might provide new entrants into this market.)

Problem 21-2
Calculate and evaluate ending inventory
LO 3, 9

Joe Boot Company makes specialty boots for the rodeo circuit. On December 31, 1997, the company had (a) 500 boots in ending inventory valued at $100 per pair and (b) 1,500 heels valued at $5 each in raw materials inventory for boots to be made. During 1998 Joe Boot Company purchased 50,000 heels at $5 each and manufactured 20,000 pairs of boots.

Required

Preparation Component:

1. Determine the value of the heel raw materials inventory at December 31, 1998.

Analysis Component:

2. Write a one-page memo to the plant production manager outlining why a just-in-time inventory management program for heels should be considered. Include in your memo the amount of working capital that can be reduced by December 31, 1998 if the ending heel raw material inventory is cut in half.

Check Figure Ending heel inventory, $57,500

Problem 21-3
Calculate and evaluate inventory values
LO 4,5

Listed below are financial data at December 31, 1998, taken from two different companies.

	Sport World Retail	K2 Ski Manufacturing
Beginning inventory:		
Merchandise	$150,000	
Finished goods		$300,000
Cost of Purchases	250,000	
Cost of goods manufactured		586,000
Ending inventory:		
Merchandise	100,000	
Finished goods		200,000

Required

1. Calculate cost of goods sold at December 31, 1998, for each of the two companies. Include proper title and format in your solution.
2. Write a memo to your supervisor (1) identifying the inventory accounts and (2) describing where each are reported on the balance sheet.

Check Figure K2 Ski's cost of goods sold, $686,000

Problem 21-4
Explain costs
LO 4,7

You must make a presentation to the marketing staff explaining the difference between product and period cost. Your supervisor tells you that the staff would like clarification regarding prime and conversion costs and an explanation of how these terms fit with product and period cost. You are told that many of the staff are unable to identify with these terms in their merchandising activities.

Required

Write a one-page memo in good form (date, to, from, subject, cc, bc—you can refer to a writing text for help in this assignment) to your supervisor outlining your presentation to this group.

Problem 21-5
Evaluate, categorize and compute costs
LO 6,10

Listed below are costs for the production of 1,000 drum sets manufactured by Music Land. They sell for $300 each.

Costs	Cost by Behaviour		Cost by Function	
	Variable	Fixed	Product	Period
Plastic for printers case—$12,000	$12,000		$12,000	
Assembly works—$60,000				
Taxes on factory—$4,500				
Accounting staff's salary—$40,000				

Pay for outsourced roller system (1,000 roller) for a total of $25,000				
Lease cost on sales force office equipment—$7,000				
Top-management salaries—$100,000				
Annual flat fee paid to We-Keep-It-Safe Security Company—$9,000				
Sales commission of $10 for each unit sold				
Machinery amortization—$10,000				

Required

Preparation Component:

1. Classify the costs as fixed or variable, and product or period.
2. Compute:
   a. Contribution margin by filling in the blanks in the table below.
   b. Contribution margin ratio by filling in the blanks in the table below.

MUSIC LAND INC. Contribution Margin Income Statement For the Year Ending December 31, 1998			
Sales ($300 × 1,000)		$[BLANK]	100%
Variable costs			
Plastic for printers case	$[BLANK]		
Assembly works	[BLANK]		
Outsourced roller system	[BLANK]		
Sales commission	[BLANK]	(Check figure for total variable cost) 107,000	36%
Contribution Margin		[BLANK]	Contribution Margin Ratio [BLANK] %
			The contribution margin ratio is calculated: contribution margin, divided by sales.

Analysis Component:

3. What does the contribution margin and contribution margin ratio mean in reference to 2 above?

Check Figure Total variable cost, $107,000

Problem 21-6
Project and estimate costs
LO 1, 6

Refer to "You Make the Call" by the Purchase Manager in this chapter. Assume you are the cost accountant for this company. The purchasing manager asks you about preparing an estimate of the related costs for buying motorcycle seats from supplier (B). She tells you this estimate is needed because unless dollar estimates are attached to nonfinancial factors, such as lost production costs, her supervisor does not give it full attention. The purchase manager also shows you the following information:

- Production is 1,000 motorcycles per year based on 250 production days a year.
- Production time per day is eight hours at a cost of $1,000 per hour to run the production line.
- Lost production time due to poor quality is 1%.
- Satisfied customers purchase, on average, three motorcycles during a lifetime.
- Satisfied customers recommend, on average, the product to five other people.
- Marketing estimates that moving to seat (B) will result in five lost customers per year from repeat business and referrals.
- Average contribution margin per motorcycle is $3,000.

Required

Estimate the costs of buying motorcycle seats from supplier (B). Note that this problem requires you to think creatively and make reasonable estimates and, therefore, there is more than one correct answer. (Hint: Reread the answer to "You Make The Call," and also think about costs of lost production time, repeat business, and other similar factors.)

Check Figure Cost of lost production, $20,000

Problem 21-7
Project and estimate costs
LO 1, 8, 10

The Food King grocery store chain is trying to increase sales to its existing customers by creating a customer orientation in meeting buyer needs and wants. We can see similar strategies by competing grocery stores with the introduction of many new and diverse products in the past five years.

Assume you are hired as a consultant by Food King, a grocery store and market leader, to analyze its operations and suggest improvements. Food King wants to increase its contribution margin by $40,000.

Required

1. Offer three improvements to increase sales to the existing customers of Food King that you have observed in other stores.
2. What level of increase in sales is necessary for Food King to increase total contribution margin by $40,000? (Hint: With each suggestion in 1, you must identify the anticipated sales dollars and contribution margin ratios to meet the $40,000 contribution margin target increase.)

Good in-class group project after students have worked on this alone.

Problem 21-8
Link manufacturing management principles to practice
LO 9

"Lean It Your Way." A trip through a drive-up window of any leading fast food restaurant is useful in understanding manufacturing management principles such as total quality management (TQM), just-in-time (JIT), theory of constraints (TOC), and continuous improvement (CI). Each restaurant can be viewed as a small manufacturing plant. List two fast food restaurants you are familiar with in the first column of the table below (examples include **McDonald's, Taco Bell, Burger King** and **KFC**). Record in the table how each company is putting each of these principles into action, both favourably and unfavourably.

Restaurant	TQM	JIT	TOC	CI

The chapter begins with a discussion of the objectives of management and cost accounting. The chapter ends with a discussion on the current business environment. You are to look through the home electronics section of your local newspaper (the Sunday paper is often best). Devote special attention to the advertisements of TVs and count how many manufactures offer this product.

Alternate Problems

Problem 21-1A
Evaluate management accountant's role
LO 1, 9

Required

What is the responsibility of the management accountant in helping a home electronics manufacturing company succeed in our current business environment? (Hint: Think about estimates a management accountant might provide new entrants into this market.)

Problem 21-2A
Calculate and evaluate ending inventory
LO 3, 9

Candle Skate, Inc. makes specialty skates for the ice skating circuit. On December 31, 1997, the company had (a) 1,500 skates in ending inventory valued at $200 per pair and (b) 2,000 blades valued at $15 each in raw materials inventory for skates to be made. During 1998 Candle Skate, Inc. purchased 45,000 blades at $15 each and manufactured 20,000 pairs of skates.

Required:

Preparation Component:

1. Determine the value of the skate raw materials inventory at December 31, 1998.

Analysis Component:

2. Write a one-page memo to the plant production manager outlining why a just-in-time inventory management program for blades should be considered. Include in your memo the amount of working capital that can be reduced by December 31, 1998, if the ending blade raw material inventory is cut in half.

Problem 21-3A
Calculate and evaluate inventory values
LO 4, 5

Listed below are financial data at December 31, 1998 taken from two different companies.

	Cardinal CD Retail	Van Conversion Inc. Manufacturing
Beginning inventory:		
Merchandise	$50,000	
Finished goods		$200,000
Cost of purchases	350,000	
Cost of goods manufactured		686,000
Ending inventory:		
Merchandise	25,000	
Finished goods		300,000

Required

1. Calculate cost of goods sold at December 31, 1998, for each of the two companies. Include proper title and format in your solution.
2. Write a memo to your supervisor (1) identifying the inventory accounts and (2) describing where each is reported on the balance sheet.

Problem 21-4A
Explain costs
LO 4, 7

You must make a presentation to a client explaining the difference between prime and conversion costs. The client makes and sells bread for 2,000,000 customers per week. The client tells you that the sales staff would like a clarification regarding product and period cost as well. She tells you that many of the staff have had financial accounting training but lack training in managerial accounting topics.

Required

Write a one-page memo in good form (date, to, from, subject, cc, bc—you can refer to a writing text for help in this assignment) to your client outlining your presentation.

Problem 21-5A
Evaluate, categorize and compute costs
LO 6, 10

Listed below are costs for the production of 12,000 CDs manufactured by Music Land Inc. They sell for $15 each.

Costs	Cost by Behaviour		Cost by Function	
	Variable	Fixed	Product	Period
Plastic for CDs—$1,000	$1,000		$1,000	
Assembly works - $20,000				
Rent on factory—$4,500				
Info systems staff's salary—$10,000				
Labels outsourced (12,000) for a total of $2,500				
Lease cost on office equipment—$700				
Top-management salaries—$100,000				
Factory security paid to "We Keep It Safe, Inc." on a yearly contract flat fee basis—$3,000				
Sales commission of $ .5 for each CD sold				
Machinery amortization—$15,000				

Required

Preparation Component:

1. Classify the costs as fixed or variable, and product or period.
2. Compute:
   a. Contribution margin by filling in the blanks in the table below.
   b. Contribution margin ratio by filling in the blanks in the table below.

MUSIC LAND INC. Contribution Margin Income Statement For the Year Ending December 31, 1998			
Sales ($15 × 12,000)		$[BLANK]	100%
Variable costs			
Plastic for CDs	$[BLANK]		
Assembly works	[BLANK]		
Labels outsourced	[BLANK]		
Sales commission	[BLANK]	(Check figure for total variable cost) 29,500	16%
Contribution Margin		[BLANK]	Contribution Margin Ratio [BLANK] %
			The contribution margin ratio is calculated: contribution margin, divided by sales.

Analysis Component:

3. What does the contribution margin and contribution margin ratio mean in reference to 2 above?

Problem 21-6A
Project and estimate costs
LO 1, 6

Refer to "You Make the Call" by the Purchase Manager in this chapter. Assume you are the cost accountant for this company. The purchasing manager asks you about preparing an estimate of the related costs for buying motorcycle seats from supplier (B). She tells you this estimate is needed because unless dollar estimates are attached to nonfinancial factors, such as lost production costs, her supervisor does not give it full attention. The purchase manager also shows you the following information:

- Production is 1,000 motorcycles per year based on 250 production days a year.
- Production time per day is eight hours at a cost of $500 per hour to run the production line.
- Lost production time due to poor quality is 1%.
- Satisfied customers purchase, on average, three motorcycles during a lifetime.
- Satisfied customers recommend, on average, the product to four other people.
- Marketing estimates that moving to seat (B) will result is five lost customers per year from repeat business and referrals.
- Average contribution margin per motorcycle is $2,000.

Required

Estimate the costs of buying motorcycle seats from supplier (B). Note that this problem requires you to think creatively and make reasonable estimates and, therefore, there is more than one correct answer. (Hint: Reread the answer to "You Make the Call," and also think about costs of lost production time, repeat business, and other similar factors.)

Problem 21-7A
Project and estimate costs
LO 1, 8, 10

The Canadian Bagel Store chain is trying to increase sales to its existing customers by creating a customer orientation in meeting buyer needs and wants. We can see similar strategies by competing bagel stores with the introduction of many new and diverse products in the past five years. Assume you are hired as a consultant by Canadian Bagel, a market leader, to analyze its operations and suggest improvements. Canadian Bagel wants to increase its contribution margin by $10,000.

Required

1. Offer three improvements to increase sales to the existing customers of Canadian Bagel that you have observed in other stores.

2. What level of increase in sales is necessary for Canadian Bagel to increase total contribution margin by $10,000? (Hint: With each suggestion in 1, you must identify the anticipated sales dollars and contribution margin ratios to meet the $10,000 contribution margin target increase.)

Good in-class group project after students have worked on this alone.

Problem 21-8A
Link manufacturing management principles to practice
LO 9

"Lean It Your Way." A trip to the photography store can be used to learn "Manufacturing Management Principles" such as total quality management (TQM), just-in-time (JIT), theory of constraints (TOC), and continuous improvement (CI). List two photography stores you are familiar with in the first column of the table below. (Hint: To prepare a response to this question you may want to watch how film is processed and prints prepared within one hour.) Record in the table how each store is putting each of these principles into action, both favourably and unfavourably.

Photography Store	TQM	JIT	TOC	CI

Analytical and Review Problems

A & R Problem 21-1

Amortization of capital assets is normally considered a cost attributable to a specific period of time. For example, the cost of a factory is allocated over the service life of that factory with specific amounts charged to each period. In accounting for manufacturing companies, amortization calculated in a particular period may be carried forward to future period (s). Alternatively, more than the calculated amortization for the current period may be included in the current period's income statement.

Required

Do you agree with the above statements? Using a numerical example, prove or disprove the above statements.

A & R Problem 21-2

In manufacturing accounting, the inclusion of amortization of capital assets as part of the overhead is, in fact, converting a capital (long-term) asset into a current asset.

Required

Does a conversion of capital assets into current assets, via the process of amortization, take place in nonmanufacturing companies, for example merchandising companies? Discuss and support your answer.

BEYOND THE NUMBERS

Reporting in Action

LO 1, 2

Managerial and cost accounting is more than recording, maintaining and reporting financial results. Management accountants must provide managers with both financial and nonfinancial information including estimates, projections and forecasts. Yet looking into the future is not without risk. **Alliance's** managers, including the management accountant, must notify shareholders of this risk.

Required

1. Read Management's Discussion and Analysis contained in Alliance's annual report in Appendix I.
   - **a.** What risks do Alliance's shareholders face as management and employees work to position the company for long-term success?
   - **b.** What is the managerial accountant's role in evaluating risk?
2. Obtain access to Alliance's annual report for a fiscal year ending after March 31, 1997. An annual report can be obtained from various sources including the following Web site: **http://www.sedar.com.** Answer questions 1 *a* and 1 *b* after reading the "To Our Shareholders" section in this recent report. Identify any major changes in this section for the report you collect with the one shown at the end of the book.

Comparative Analysis

LO 6, 9

NIKE and **Reebok** are primarily manufacturing companies.

Required

1. What information on these companies' respective balance sheets would indicate that each is a manufacturing company? Record your clues.
2. What information would you expect to find in the notes to each company's financial statements for evidence that they are manufacturing companies?
3. What impact would a just-in-time inventory management system have on inventory turnover values for these companies?

Ethics Challenge

LO 1, 6, 7

You are the accountant at Music Production, a manufacturer of audio tapes, CDs and record albums. The financial reporting year-end for this company is December 31 and the chief financial officer is concerned about having enough cash to pay the expected corporate tax bill because of poor cash flow management. On November 15 the purchasing department purchased excess inventory of CD raw materials in anticipation of rapid growth of this product beginning in January. To decrease its tax liability the chief financial officer told you to record the purchase of this inventory as a supply and expense it in the current year. This action decreases tax liability by increasing expenses.

Required

1. Where should the purchase of CD raw materials be recorded?
2. How should you respond to this request? (Hint: Check out the Web site listed below under "Taking It to the Net" before answering this question.)

Communicating in Practice

What are the financial rewards of attending college? Write a memo to your classmates about the salary expectations for current graduates in business. Compare and contrast the expected salaries among accounting (use different categories such as public, corporate, tax, audit and so forth), marketing, management, and finance majors. Prepare a graph showing average starting salaries (and salaries for experienced professionals if available). To get this information stop by your school's career services office. Many libraries also have this information. The following Web site can get you started on this project: **http://jobsmart.org/tools/salary/surv-gen.htm**.

Taking It to the Net

Managerial accounting professionals follow a code of ethics. As a member of the Institute of Management Accountants the professional management accountant must comply with the Standards of Ethical Conduct for Management Accountants. Identify the Standards of Ethical Conduct for Management Accountants posted on the following Web site: **http://www.rutgers.edu/Accounting /raw/ima/imaethic.htm**.

Teamwork in Action

LO 3, 4, 5, 6

Your team is to select a manufactured product that each of you is familiar with. The team is responsible for putting together a list of all product components and other costs necessary to manufacture this product. Identify each of these product costs as direct materials, direct labour or factory overhead and provide an explanation for your classification. Also, identify period costs this business is likely to incur. Prepare to report this cost information to your classmates and explain where period and product costs are reported in financial statements. (Note: Each teammate can assume the responsibility of a different part of this assignment.)

Hitting the Road

LO 1, 6

Visit your favourite local fast food restaurant. Observe its business operations. It may be helpful to introduce yourself to the manager and explain that you are doing field research for your class. You might request an opportunity to see business activities that customers do not normally observe. Describe all activities from the time a customer arrives to the time a customer departs. List all costs you can identify from these observations. Classify each of these costs as fixed or variable and provide an explanation for your classification.

Business Break

LO 1, 2, 8, 9

The success and failure of many businesses depends on the profits earned between October 15 and December 24 of any year. Read the article "Why Win98s' Delay is OK" in the September 29, 1997, issue of *Business Week.*

Required

1. Why are businesses—manufacturing, distribution and retail—concerned about the release of Win98 by Microsoft Corporation? Does the management accounting professional need to know about the release of products and customer reactions to any other products except the ones his/her company sells?
2. Assume you make keyboards for Dell Computer. Write a one-page memo to your company's management outlining the possible impact on your product, knowing that Microsoft has delayed the release of its most recent operating system upgrade.

CHAPTER 22

Manufacturing and Job Order Cost Accounting

A Look Back

Chapter 21 introduced us to managerial and cost accounting. We compared it to financial accounting and explained basic cost concepts. We also described several modern manufacturing management principles that are changing the way companies conduct business.

A Look at This Chapter

We begin this chapter by explaining the preparation of a manufacturing statement and describing the accounting systems for manufacturing activities. We also explain how to measure costs in job order production companies, and describe the procedures of a job order costing system.

A Look Forward

Chapter 23 looks at how we measure costs in process production industries. We explain process production in greater detail, describe how to assign costs to processes and also compute the cost per equivalent unit.

Chapter Outline

Hitting the Slopes

Whistler, BC—Roger Worth thought he knew it all. He worked three years with an online service provider as an executive assistant. Yet since starting his new job as a junior manager with Dillon Snowboards, an upstart manufacturer of custom snowboards, he felt as if he was starting over.

It began during Worth's second week at Dillon's. He was given two cost accounting related tasks termed "high-priority" items for use in setting prices of its snowboards. One was to determine the cost of goods manufactured for the most recent six months of activity. The second was to compute the cost of producing an order of 90 "custom snowboards" for a mountain resort. Says Worth, "It was a chance to show off my skills."

Worth devoted much time and energy to both tasks. He obtained a mountain of manufacturing data from the production manager and presented a detailed report to his supervisor. After reading the report his supervisor called Worth into her office. Worth said "She looked me straight in the eye and said, 'This report is useless. There are not even details on work-in-progress in our manufacturing statement. And remember, we're a custom manufacturer'."

Worth returned to his office determined to address the supervisor's challenge. "I read everything I could get on custom manufacturing. And job order manufacturing and costing too," says Worth. "I learned custom manufacturers require special accounting and reports," says Worth. "The supervisor said my new report was first rate," and Worth added, "I'm still learning. But I won't make this same mistake again." Somehow one gets a feeling his supervisor will see to it!

Learning Objectives

LO 1 Explain manufacturing activities and the flow of manufacturing costs.

LO 2 Prepare a manufacturing statement and explain its purpose and links to financial statements.

LO 3 Describe important features of job order manufacturing.

LO 4 Explain job cost sheets and how they are used in job order cost accounting.

LO 5 Describe and record the flow of materials costs in job order cost accounting.

LO 6 Describe and record the flow of labour costs in job order cost accounting.

LO 7 Describe and record the flow of overhead costs in job order cost accounting.

LO 8 Determine adjustments for overapplied and underapplied factory overhead.

LO 9 Apply multiple overhead allocation rates in assigning overhead to products.

CHAPTER PREVIEW

We described managerial concepts and principles, along with differences between merchandising and manufacturing companies, in Chapter 21. In this chapter we spend more time understanding how manufacturing activities are accounted for. We explain how to prepare a manufacturing statement and determine cost of goods manufactured. We also describe two different systems for assigning costs to the movement of goods through the production process. This is often called assigning cost flows to product flows. The *general accounting system*, presented in Appendix 22A, provides information for decision making using a *periodic inventory system*. A *job order costing accounting system* provides information for decision making using a *perpetual inventory system*. A perpetual system provides a continuous record of materials, goods in process, and finished goods on hand. It is also increasingly popular in practice, especially by those companies benefiting from knowing inventory levels. Job order costing is frequently used by manufacturers of custom products or small groups of custom products.

Manufacturing Activities and Information

LO1 Explain manufacturing activities and the flow of manufacturing costs.

Manufacturing activities of a company are described in a special financial report called the manufacturing statement. This report is also called the *schedule of manufacturing activities* or the *schedule of cost of goods manufactured.* The manufacturing statement summarizes the types and amounts of costs incurred in a company's manufacturing process. But for us to understand the manufacturing statement we must first understand the flow of manufacturing costs and activities.

Flow of Manufacturing Activities

Exhibit 22.1 shows the flow of activities for Rocky Mountain Bikes. This exhibit has three important sections: *materials activity, production activity* and *selling activity*. We explain each of these activities in this section.

Exhibit 22.1

Flow of Activities and Costs in Manufacturing

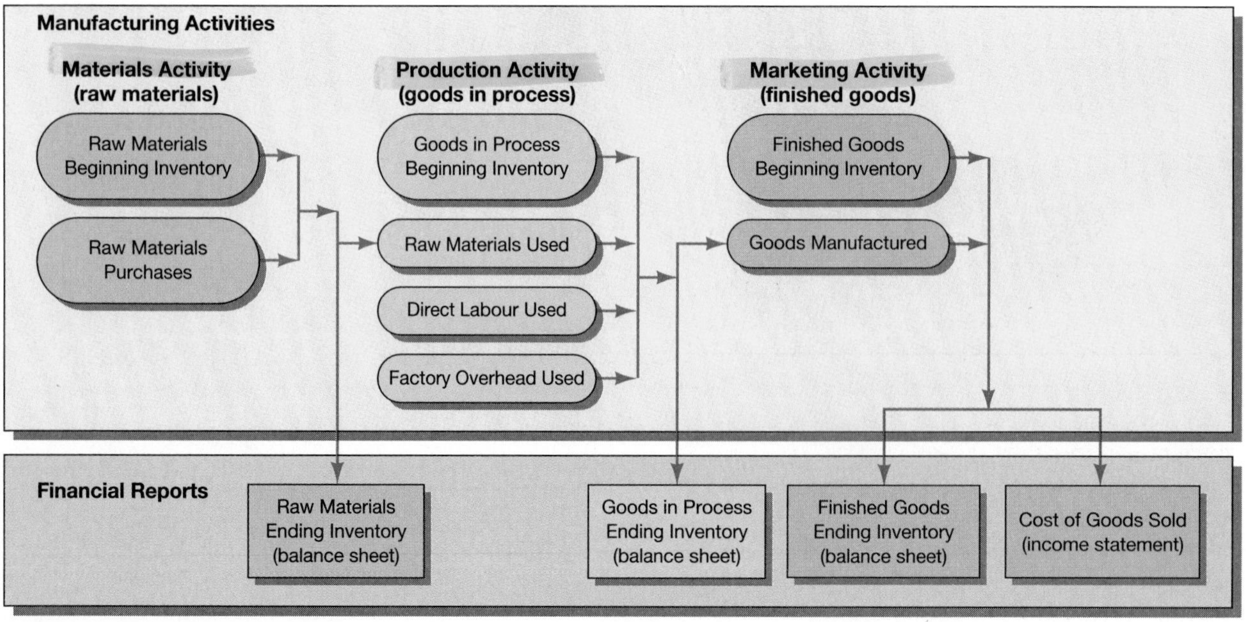

Materials Activity

The left column of Exhibit 22.1 shows the flow of raw materials. **Rocky Mountain Bikes,** like most manufacturers, usually starts a period with a beginning raw materials inventory. This is shown as carried over from 1997 in the exhibit. During 1998, the company acquires additional raw materials. When these purchases are added to beginning inventory, we get the total raw materials available for use in production. These raw materials are then either used in production in 1998 or remain on hand at the end of the period for use in future periods.

Production Activity

The middle column of Exhibit 22.1 describes production activity. Four factors come together in production. They are beginning goods in process inventory, direct materials, direct labour, and overhead. Chapter 21 explained how both direct materials and direct labour are traceable to the manufacturing of a product (mountain bikes in this case). Whereas overhead is not directly traceable to the bikes. Beginning goods in process inventory consists of partly assembled bikes from the previous period, shown as coming from 1997 in Exhibit 22.1.

The production activity results in bikes that are either finished or remain unfinished. The cost of finished bikes makes up the cost of goods manufactured for 1998. Unfinished bikes are identified as ending goods in process inventory at the end of 1998. The cost of unfinished bikes, consisting of direct materials, direct labour and factory overhead, is reported on the 1998 balance sheet. Costs linked with both goods manufactured and goods in process are *product costs.* Period costs are not part of cost of goods manufactured.

Marketing Activity

The company's marketing activity is portrayed in the right column of Exhibit 22.1. Newly completed units are combined with beginning finished goods inventory (from 1997) to make up total finished goods available for sale in 1998. The cost of bikes sold in 1998 is reported on the 1998 income statement as cost of goods sold. The cost of bikes not sold in 1998 is reported on that year's balance sheet as ending finished goods inventory.

Manufacturing Statement

LO 2 Prepare a manufacturing statement and explain its purpose and links to financial statements.

Exhibit 22.2 shows the manufacturing statement for Rocky Mountain Bikes. It reports costs of both materials and production activities as described in Exhibit 22.1. The statement is divided into four parts: *direct material, direct labour, overhead,* and *computation of cost of goods manufactured.* We describe each of these parts in this section.

The manufacturing statement begins by determining the cost of direct materials used. We start by adding the beginning raw materials inventory of $8,000 to this period's purchases of $86,500. This yields $94,500 of total raw materials available for use in 1998. A physical count of inventory shows $9,000 of ending raw materials inventory. We then compute total cost of direct raw materials used during the period as $85,500. This is computed by subtracting the $9,000 ending inventory from the $94,500 total raw materials available for use.

The second part of the manufacturing statement reports direct labour cost. Rocky Mountain Bikes had total direct labour cost of $60,000 in 1998. This amount includes payroll taxes and fringe benefits.

The third part of the manufacturing statement reports on overhead costs incurred. The statement lists each important factory overhead item along with its cost. Total factory overhead cost for the year is $30,000. Some companies report only total factory overhead on the manufacturing statement. But then they report a separate schedule of overhead items listing individual overhead costs. Total manufacturing costs incurred during 1998 is $175,500, computed as $85,500 + $60,000 + $30,000. This is the sum of direct materials used, direct labour incurred, and overhead costs incurred.

The final section of the manufacturing statement computes and reports the *cost of goods manufactured.* First, total manufacturing costs are added to beginning goods in process inventory. This gives the total goods in process inventory of $178,000 for 1998, computed as $175,500 plus $2,500. We then compute cost of goods manufactured of $170,500 for 1998. This is computed by subtracting the cost of ending goods in process inventory of $7,500 from the total goods in process of $178,000. Note that the amount of $7,500 assigned to the ending goods in process inventory consists of direct materials, direct labour and factory overhead. The cost of goods manufactured amount is also called *net cost of goods manufactured* or *cost of goods completed.* Refer to Exhibit 21.9 on page 1001 and see that this item and amount is listed in the cost of goods sold section of Rocky Mountain Bikes' income statement.

Exhibit 22.2

Manufacturing Statement

ROCKY MOUNTAIN BIKES
Manufacturing Statement
For Year Ended December 31, 1998

①	**Direct materials:**		
	Raw materials inventory, December 31, 1997	$ 8,000	
	Raw materials purchases	86,500	
	Raw materials available for use	94,500	
	Raw materials inventory, December 31, 1998	(9,000)	
	Direct materials used		$ 85,500
②	**Direct labour**		60,000
③	**Factory overhead costs:**		
	Indirect labour	9,000	
	Factory supervision	6,000	
	Factory utilities	2,600	
	Repairs, factory equipment	2,500	
	Property taxes, factory building	1,900	
	Factory supplies used	600	
	Factory insurance expired	1,100	
	Small tools written off	200	
	Amortization, factory equipment	3,500	
	Amortization, factory building	1,800	
	Amortization, patents	800	
	Total factory overhead costs		30,000
④	Total manufacturing costs		$175,500
	Add goods in process inventory, December 31, 1997		2,500
	Total cost of goods in process		$178,000
	Deduct goods in process inventory, December 31, 1998		(7,500)
	Cost of goods manufactured		$170,500

Information in the manufacturing statement is used by management in planning and controlling the company's manufacturing activities. To provide timely information for decision making, the statement is often prepared monthly, weekly or even daily. While the manufacturing statement contains information useful to external users, it is not a general-purpose financial statement. Most companies view this information as proprietary and potentially harmful to the company if released to competitors. As a result companies rarely publish the manufacturing statement.

Flashback

1. A manufacturing statement (a) computes cost of goods manufactured for the period, (b) computes cost of goods sold for the period, or (c) reports operating expenses incurred for the period.
2. Does GAAP require companies to report a manufacturing statement?
3. How are both beginning and ending goods in process inventories reported on a manufacturing statement?

Answers—p. 1057

Mid-Chapter Demonstration Problem

The following account balances and other information were taken from the accounting records of Sunny Corporation for the year ended December 31, 1998. Use the information to prepare a schedule of factory overhead costs, a manufacturing statement (show only the total factory overhead cost), and an income statement.

Advertising expense	$ 85,000
Amortization of patents	16,000
Bad debts expense	28,000
Amortization expense, office equipment	37,000
Amortization of factory building	133,000
Amortization of factory equipment	78,000
Direct labour	250,000
Factory insurance expired	62,000
Factory supervision	74,000
Factory supplies used	21,000
Factory utilities	115,000
Finished goods inventory, December 31, 1997	15,000
Finished goods inventory, December 31, 1998	12,500
Goods in process inventory, December 31, 1997	8,000
Goods in process inventory, December 31, 1998	9,000
Income taxes expense	53,400
Indirect labour	26,000
Interest expense	25,000
Miscellaneous expense	55,000
Property taxes on factory equipment	14,000
Raw materials inventory, December 31, 1997	60,000
Raw materials inventory, December 31, 1998	78,000
Raw materials purchases	313,000
Repairs, factory equipment	31,000
Salaries expense	150,000
Sales	1,630,000

Planning the Solution

- Analyze the list of the costs and select those items that are factory overhead.
- Arrange these costs in a schedule of factory overhead costs for 1998.
- Analyze the items remaining on the list and select the ones related to production activity for the year; the selected items should include the materials and goods in process inventories and direct labour.
- Prepare a manufacturing statement for 1998 showing the calculation of the cost of materials used in production, the cost of direct labour, and the total factory overhead cost. When presenting the overhead cost on this statement, show only the total overhead cost from the schedule of overhead costs for 1998. Then show the costs of the beginning and ending goods in process inventory to determine the total cost of goods manufactured. Be certain to include the proper title.
- Combine the remaining revenue and expense items from the list into the income statement for 1998. Combine the cost of goods manufactured from the manufacturing statement with the finished goods inventory amounts to compute the cost of goods sold for 1998.

Solution to Mid-Chapter Demonstration Problem

SUNNY CORPORATION
Schedule of Factory Overhead Costs
For Year Ended December 31, 1998

Amortization of patents	$ 16,000
Amortization of factory building	133,000
Amortization of factory equipment	78,000
Factory insurance expired	62,000
Factory supervision	74,000
Factory supplies used	21,000
Factory utilities	115,000
Indirect labour	26,000
Property taxes on factory equipment	14,000
Repairs, factory equipment	31,000
Total factory overhead	$570,000

SUNNY CORPORATION
Manufacturing Statement
For Year Ended December 31, 1998

Direct materials:		
Raw materials inventory, December 31, 1997	$ 60,000	
Raw materials purchases	313,000	
Raw materials available for use	373,000	
Raw materials inventory, December 31, 1998	(78,000)	
Direct materials used		$ 295,000
Direct labour		250,000
Factory overhead costs		570,000
Total manufacturing costs		1,115,000
Goods in process inventory, December 31, 1997		8,000
Total goods in process		1,123,000
Goods in process inventory, December 31, 1998		(9,000)
Cost of goods manufactured		$1,114,000

Solution to Mid-Chapter Demonstration Problem (continued)

SUNNY CORPORATION
Income Statement
For Year Ended December 31, 1998

Sales		$1,630,000
Cost of goods sold:		
Finished goods inventory, December 31, 1997	$ 15,000	
Cost of goods manufactured	1,114,000	
Goods available for sale	1,129,000	
Finished goods inventory, December 31, 1998	(12,500)	
Cost of goods sold		(1,116,500)
Gross profit		513,500
Operating expenses:		
Advertising expense	85,000	
Bad debts expense	28,000	
Amortization expense, office equipment	37,000	
Interest expense	25,000	
Miscellaneous expense	55,000	
Salaries expense	150,000	
Total operating expenses		(380,000)
Income before income taxes		133,500
Income taxes expense		(53,400)
Net income		$ 80,100

The Inventory System and Accounting for Costs

Reports from the accounting system reflecting manufacturing activities and costs are described above. We now turn to the accounting methods used to compile the information in these reports. We begin with a brief discussion of accounting for manufacturing activities using a general accounting system, but describe it in detail in the appendix to this chapter. We then explain a cost accounting system.

General Accounting System

A **general accounting system** records manufacturing activities using a *periodic* inventory system. A periodic inventory system measures costs of raw materials, goods in process, and finished goods from physical counts of quantities on hand at the end of each period. This information is used to compute amounts of the product used, finished, and sold during a period.

Some companies still use a general accounting system but the frequency of a general accounting system in practice is declining. Competitive forces and customer demands have increased pressure on companies to better manage inventories. This means an increasing number of companies need more timely and precise information on inventories than is provided by a general accounting system.

Cost Accounting System

An ever increasing number of companies use a cost accounting system to generate timely and precise inventory information. A **cost accounting system** records manufacturing activities using a *perpetual* inventory system. A perpetual system continuously updates records for costs of materials, goods in process, and finished goods inventories.

A cost accounting system gives us more timely information about inventories and changes in inventories. This system also give us more timely information about manufacturing costs per unit of product. This is especially helpful for managers in efforts to control costs and determine selling prices. There are two basic types of cost accounting systems: job order cost accounting and process cost accounting. We describe the first type, job order cost accounting, in this chapter. The second type, process cost accounting, is explained in the next chapter.

Job Order Cost Accounting System

This section describes a job order manufacturing and cost accounting system. It is important for us to understand a job order manufacturing system before we can understand manufacturing activities and the accounting for them. We explain the costing system used by job order manufacturers in this section.

Job Order Manufacturing

LO 3 Describe important features of job order manufacturing.

Many companies manufacture products individually designed to meet the needs of each customer. Each unique product is manufactured separately and their production is called job order manufacturing. **Job order manufacturing,** also called *customized production*, is the production of products in response to special orders. In contrast, *process manufacturing,* also called *process production*, is the mass production of products in a sequence of steps (we explain process production and its corresponding cost accounting system in the next chapter).

The production of a unique product is called a **job.** Items that might be produced as jobs include a special machine tool, a building, an airplane and a piece of custom-made jewellery. They are made to meet the unique demands of specific customers. This type of manufacturing system is likely to be very flexible in the number of different products it can produce.

Bombardier's aerospace division is one example of a job order manufacturing system. Its business activities include: (1) design, development and integration of space carriers, (2) design, development, manufacture and support of major airframe components, and (3) joint venture operations in close-air defence systems. Each order is often unique.

When a job involves producing more than one unit of a unique product, it is often called a **job lot.** Products produced as job lots might include benches for a church, imprinted T-shirts for a 10K race or company picnic, and advertising signs for a chain of stores. Although these orders involve more than one unit, the volume of production is typically low (for example 50 benches, 200 T-shirts, or 100 signs).

Another feature of a job order manufacturer is the diversity, often called *heterogeneity*, of the products manufactured. Each customer order is likely different from another in some respect. These variations can be minor or major. T-shirts for a 10K race, for instance, are different than those for a company or family picnic.

Did You Know?

Build to Order Computers

Personal computers are often similar to one another. **Dell Computer** broke this image and adopted a "build to order" strategy. Dell bypasses distributors and sells directly to customers. This means it builds a customized PC for every buyer and sells at below retailer prices. Dell's build-to-order strategy makes it the industry's hottest and fastest growing company. In its first fiscal quarter ended August 3, 1997, profits more than doubled on a 67% increase in sales, and its stock is up 259% this year. Other computer manufacturers, including **Hewlett-Packard** and **Apple**, are trying to copy Dell's strategy. [Source: *Business Week*, September 29, 1997.]

It is important to note that although we have generally described the job order system using manufacturing examples, this system is equally applicable to service firms. Many, if not most, service companies meet their customers' needs by performing a unique service for each customer. Examples of such services include an audit of a client's financial statements, an interior designer's remodelling of an office, a wedding consultant's plan and supervision of a reception, and a lawyer's defence of a client in a lawsuit. Whether the setting is manufacturing or service, job order operations involve meeting the needs of customers by producing or performing unique jobs.

Events in Job Order Manufacturing

The initial event in a normal job order manufacturing operation is the receipt of a customer's order for a unique product. This causes the manufacturer to begin work on the job. A less common case is when management decides to begin work on a job before a contract is signed with a customer. This is referred to as *jobs manufactured on speculation*. Yet in any case, the first step is to predict the cost of completing the job. This depends on the design of the product, prepared by the customer or the manufacturer.

The next step is to negotiate a sales price and decide whether to accept the job. Some jobs are priced on a *cost-plus basis*. This means the customer pays the manufacturer for costs incurred on the job plus a negotiated amount or rate of profit.

The manufacturer must then schedule production of the job to meet the customer's needs and to fit within its own production capacity. This work schedule should take into account workplace facilities including tools, machinery and supplies. Once this schedule is complete the manufacturer can place orders for raw materials. Under JIT, orders for materials call for delivery just in time for use in production. Production occurs as materials and labour are applied to the job.

An overview of job order production activity is given in Exhibit 22.3. This exhibit shows the March 1998 production activity of **Road Warriors.** Road Warriors' manufactures security-equipped cars and trucks. They take any brand vehicle and give it a diversity of security items. These items include special alarms, reinforced exterior, bullet proof glass, and bomb detectors. The company began by catering to high-profile celebrities, but has grown dramatically as it now caters to anyone who wants added security in a vehicle.

Job order manufacturing for Road Warriors requires use of materials, labour and other manufacturing costs. Recall that direct materials are goods used in manufacturing and clearly identified with a particular job. Similarly, direct labour is efforts devoted to a particular job. Overhead costs support production of more than one job. Common manufacturing overhead items are amortization on factory buildings and equipment, factory supplies, supervision, maintenance, cleaning and utilities.

Exhibit 22.3 shows that materials, labour and overhead are added to Job Numbers B15, B16, B17, B18 and B19 during March. Road Warriors completed

Exhibit 22.3

Job Order Manufacturing Activities

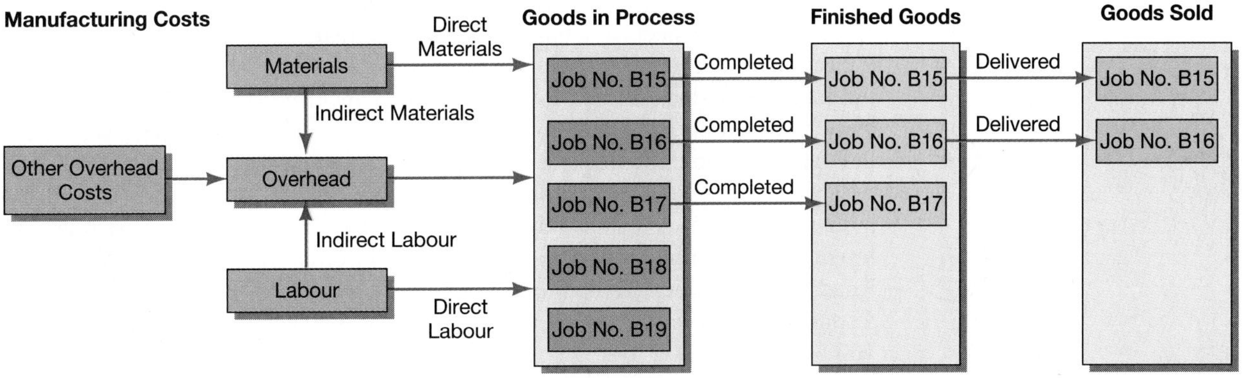

Jobs B5, B6 and B7 in March, and delivered Jobs B5 and B6 to customers. At the end of March, Jobs B8 and B9 remain in goods in process inventory and Job B7 is in finished goods inventory. Labour and materials are divided into their direct and indirect components. Their indirect costs are added to overhead. Total overhead cost is allocated to various jobs.

Flashback

4. Which of these products are likely to involve job order manufacturing? (a) inexpensive watches, (b) racing bikes, or (c) bottled soft drinks.
5. What is the difference between a job and a job lot?

Answers—p. 1057

You Make the Call

Management Consultant

You have recently joined a management consulting company after five years as a cost accountant with a custom manufacturer. One of your tasks is to control and manage costs for the consulting company. At the end of your first month, you find three consulting jobs are complete and two are 60% complete. Both of the unfinished consulting jobs are estimated to cost $10,000 each and earn revenue of $12,000 each. You are unsure about how to recognize goods in process inventory and record costs and revenues. Do you expect to recognize any inventory? If yes, how much? How much revenue is recorded for the first month?

Answer—p. 1057

Job Order Cost Documents

LO 4 Explain job cost sheets and how they are used in job order cost accounting.

Much of the accounting information that managers of job order cost operations use to plan and control production activities is not stored in general ledger accounts. This is because the information often involves very detailed data. Instead it is usually stored in subsidiary records controlled by general ledger accounts. Subsidiary records can store information about raw materials, overhead costs, jobs in process, and finished goods. This section describes the use of these records with job order cost accounting.

A major aim of a **job order cost accounting system** is to determine the cost of producing each job or job lot. In the case of a job lot it also aims to compute the cost per unit. The accounting system must include separate records for each job to accomplish this aim. The system must capture information about costs incurred, and charge these costs to jobs in process.

A **job cost sheet** is a separate record maintained for each job. Exhibit 22.4 shows a job cost sheet for a basic alarm system that Road Warriors produced for a customer. This job cost sheet identifies the customer, the number assigned to the job, the product, and various dates. Costs incurred on the job are immediately recorded on this sheet. When each job is complete, the supervisor enters the date of completion, records any remarks, and signs the sheet.

The job cost sheet in Exhibit 22.4 classifies costs as direct materials, direct labour, or overhead. It shows direct materials are added to Job B15 on four different dates totalling $600. The seven entries for direct labour costs total $1,000. Road Warriors allocated (applied, assigned or charged) overhead costs of $1,600 to this job using an allocation rate of 160% of direct labour cost, computed as 160% × $1,000.

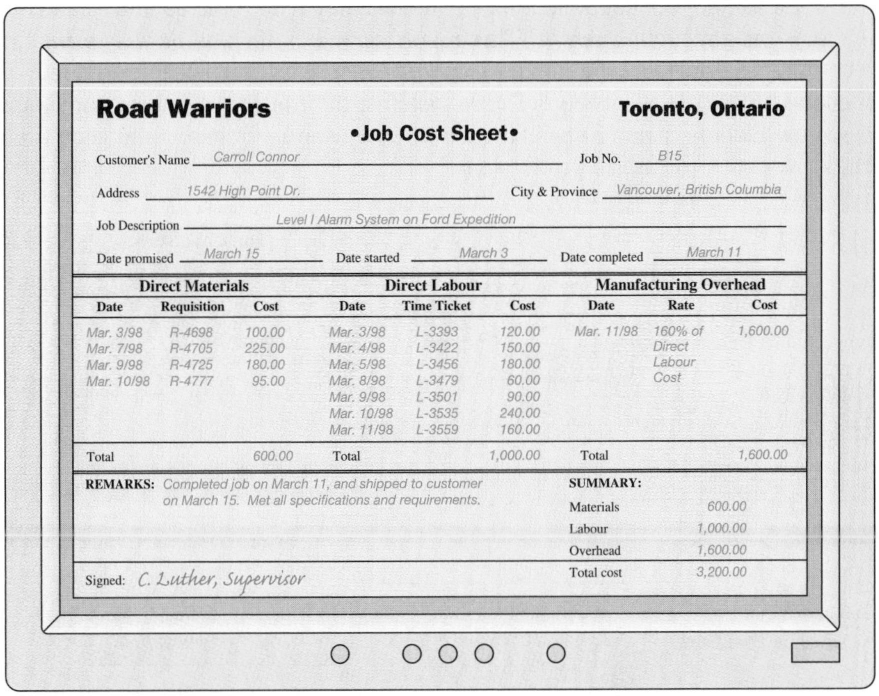

Road Warriors **Toronto, Ontario**

•Job Cost Sheet•

Customer's Name Carroll Connor Job No. B15

Address 1542 High Point Dr. City & Province Vancouver, British Columbia

Job Description Level I Alarm System on Ford Expedition

Date promised March 15 Date started March 3 Date completed March 11

Direct Materials			Direct Labour			Manufacturing Overhead		
Date	Requisition	Cost	Date	Time Ticket	Cost	Date	Rate	Cost
Mar. 3/98	R-4698	100.00	Mar. 3/98	L-3393	120.00	Mar. 11/98	160% of Direct Labour Cost	1,600.00
Mar. 7/98	R-4705	225.00	Mar. 4/98	L-3422	150.00			
Mar. 9/98	R-4725	180.00	Mar. 5/98	L-3456	180.00			
Mar. 10/98	R-4777	95.00	Mar. 8/98	L-3479	60.00			
			Mar. 9/98	L-3501	90.00			
			Mar. 10/98	L-3535	240.00			
			Mar. 11/98	L-3559	160.00			
Total		600.00	Total		1,000.00	Total		1,600.00

REMARKS: Completed job on March 11, and shipped to customer on March 15. Met all specifications and requirements.

SUMMARY:	
Materials	600.00
Labour	1,000.00
Overhead	1,600.00
Total cost	3,200.00

Signed: C. Luther, Supervisor

Exhibit 22.4

Job Cost Sheet

While a job is being manufactured, its accumulated costs are kept in the goods in process inventory. The collection of job cost sheets for all of the jobs in process make up a subsidiary ledger controlled by the Goods in Process Inventory account in the General Ledger. Managers use job cost sheets to monitor costs incurred to date and to predict and control costs to complete each job.

When a job is finished its job cost sheet is completed and moved from the file of jobs in process to the file of finished jobs awaiting delivery to customers. This latter file acts as a subsidiary ledger controlled by the **Finished Goods Inventory** account. When a finished job is delivered to the customer, the job cost sheet is moved to a permanent file supporting the total cost of goods sold. This permanent file contains records from both current and prior periods.

Flash back

6. Which of these statements is correct?
   a. Collection of job cost sheets for unfinished jobs makes up a subsidiary ledger controlled by the Goods in Process account.
   b. Job cost sheets are financial statements provided to investors.
   c. A separate job cost sheet is maintained in the General Ledger for each job in process.
7. What three costs are accumulated on job cost sheets?

Answers—p. 1057

Materials Cost Flows and Documents

LO 5 Describe and record the flow of materials costs in job order cost accounting.

This section and the next two explain the flow of costs and related documents in a job order cost accounting system. We focus on the three cost components: (1) materials, (2) labour, and (3) overhead. Materials cost flows are described in this section, and labour and overhead costs in the following sections.

We begin our analysis of the flow of materials cost data through subsidiary records by looking at Exhibit 22.5. When materials are first received from suppliers, the employees count and inspect them. They record the quantity and cost of items on a receiving report. This report serves as the *source document* for recording materials received in the *materials ledger card* and in the general ledger accounts. In nearly all job order cost systems, the **materials ledger cards** are perpetual records that are updated each time units are purchased and each time units are issued for use in production.

Exhibit 22.5

Job Order Materials Cost Flows Through Subsidiary Records

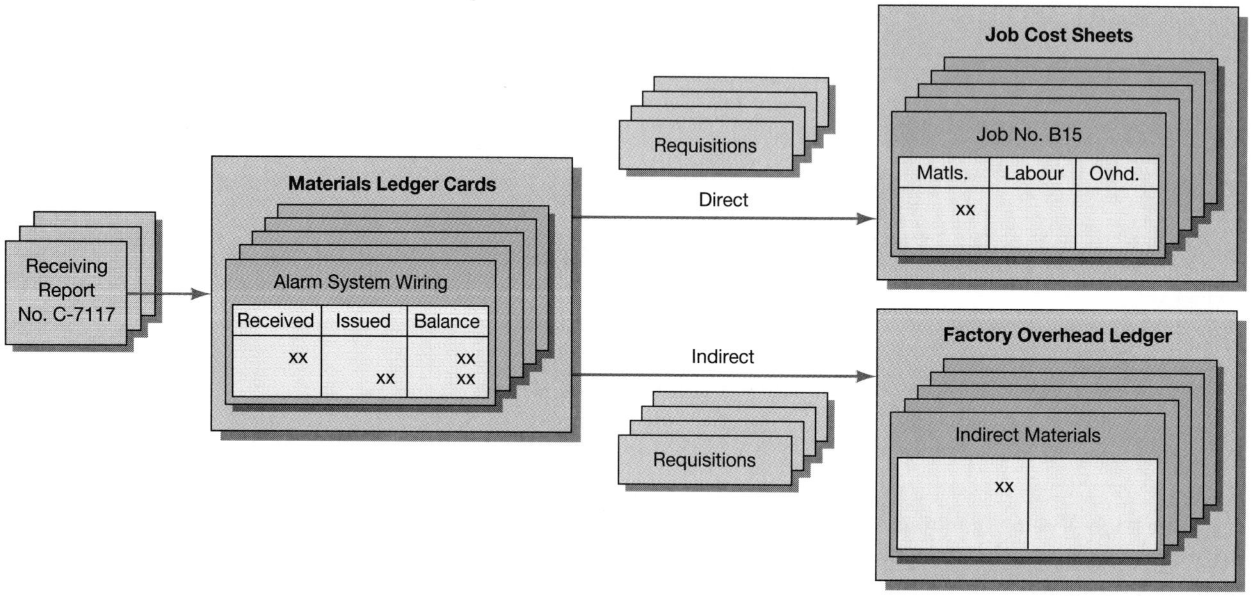

Exhibit 22.5 shows that materials can be requisitioned for use either on a specific job (direct materials) or as overhead (indirect materials). Cost of direct materials flows from the materials ledger card to the job cost sheet. The cost of indirect materials flows from the materials ledger card to the Indirect Materials account in the Factory Overhead Ledger. The Factory Overhead Ledger is a subsidiary ledger controlled by the Factory Overhead account in the General Ledger.

Exhibit 22.6 shows a materials ledger card for material used by Road Warriors. The card identifies the item as alarm system wiring. The card also shows the item's stock number, its location in the storeroom, information about the maximum and minimum quantities that should be on hand, and the reorder quantity. Note the issue of alarm system wiring recorded on March 7, 1998. The job cost sheet in Exhibit 22.4 shows this wiring is used in Job No. B15.

Exhibit 22.6

Materials Ledger Card

Road Warriors

Item *Alarm system wiring* Stock No. *M–347* Location in Storeroom *Bin 137*

Maximum quantity *5 units* Minimum quantity *1 unit* Quantity to reorder *2 units*

	Received				Issued				Balance		
Date	Receiving Report Number	Units	Unit Price	Total Price	Requisition Number	Units	Unit Price	Total Price	Units	Unit Price	Total Price
									1	225.00	225.00
Mar. 4/98	C-7117	2	225.00	450.00					3	225.00	675.00
Mar. 7/98					R–4705	1	225.00	225.00	2	225.00	450.00

When materials are needed in production, a production manager prepares a **materials requisition** and sends it to the materials manager. The requisition shows the job number, the type of material, the quantity needed, and the signature of the manager authorized to make the requisition. Exhibit 22.7 shows the materials requisition for alarm system wiring for Job No. B15. To see how this requisition ties to the flow of costs, compare the information on the requisition with the March 7, 1998, data in Exhibits 22.4 and 22.6.

Exhibit 22.7

Materials Requisition

Road Warriors

MATERIALS REQUISITION NUMBER R-4705

Job No.	B15	Date	March 7/98
Material Stock No.	M-347	Material Description	Alarm system wiring
Quantity Requested	1	Requested By	C. Luther
Quantity Provided	1	Date Provided	March 7/98
Filled By	M. Bateman	Material Received By	C. Luther
Remarks			

Use of alarm system wiring on Job No. B15 yields the following journal entry (locate this item in the job cost sheet shown in Exhibit 22.4):

Mar. 7	Goods in Process Inventory—Job No. B15 .	225	
	Raw Materials Inventory — M-347 . . .		225
	To record use of material on Job No. B15.		

Assets = Liabilities + Equity
+225
−225

This entry is posted to general ledger accounts and to subsidiary records. Posting to subsidiary records includes a debit to a job cost sheet and a credit to a materials ledger card.

An entry to record use of indirect materials is the same as that for direct materials except the debit is to Factory Overhead. In the subsidiary Factory Overhead Ledger, this entry is posted to Indirect Materials.

Labour Cost Flows and Documents

LO 6 Describe and record the flow of labour costs in job order cost accounting.

Exhibit 22.8 shows the flow of labour costs from the Factory Payroll account to subsidiary records of the job cost accounting system. Recall that the costs in subsidiary records give the detailed information needed to manage and control operations.

Factory Labour

The flow of costs in Exhibit 22.8 begins with **clock cards**. These cards are commonly used by employees to record number of hours worked. Clock cards serve as source documents for entries to record labour costs. Clock card data on the number of hours worked is used at the end of each pay period to determine total labour cost. This amount is then debited to the Factory Payroll account. Factory Payroll is a temporary account containing the total payroll cost (both direct and indirect). Payroll cost is later allocated to both specific jobs and overhead.

To assign labour costs to specific jobs and to overhead, we must know how each employee's time is used and how much it costs. Source documents called **time tickets** usually capture this data. Employees fill out time tickets each day to report how much time they spent on each job. An employee who works on several jobs during a day completes a separate time ticket for each job. Tickets are also prepared for time that is charged to overhead as indirect labour. A supervisor signs an employee's time ticket to confirm its accuracy. The hourly rate and total labour cost are computed when the time ticket reaches the accounting area.

Exhibit 22.8

Job Order Labour Cost Flows Through Subsidiary Records

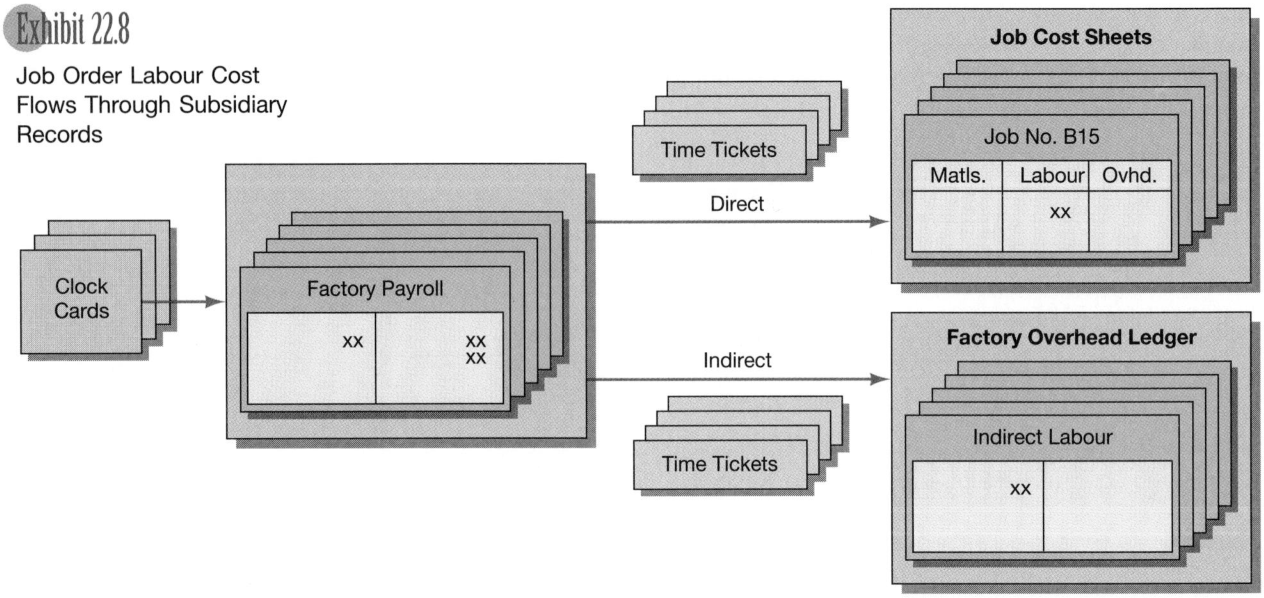

Exhibit 22.9 shows a time ticket reporting the time a Road Warrior employee spent working on Job No. B15. Note the employee's supervisor signed the ticket to confirm its accuracy. The hourly rate and total labour cost are computed after the time ticket is turned in. To see the effect of this time ticket on the job cost sheet, look at Exhibit 22.4 on page 1045 for the entry dated March 8, 1998.

Exhibit 22.9

Labour Time Ticket

Road Warriors

TIME TICKET L–3479

Job No. B15 Date March 8/98

Employee Name T. Zeller Employee Number 3969

TIME AND RATE INFORMATION:

Start Time 9:00 Finish Time 12:00

Elapsed Time 3.0 Hourly Rate $20.00 Total Cost $60.00

Approved By C. Luther

Remarks

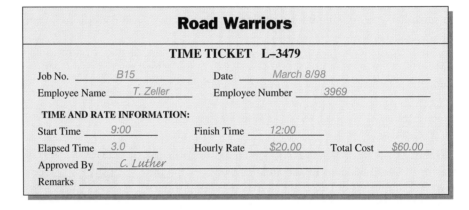

When time tickets report labour used on a specific job, this cost is recorded as direct labour. The following entry records the data from time ticket number L-3479 shown in Exhibit 22.9 (locate this item in the job cost sheet in Exhibit 22.4):

Assets = Liabilities + Equity
+60 +60

Mar. 8	Goods in Process Inventory—Job. No. B15 .	60	
	Factory Payroll		60
	To record direct labour used on Job No. B15.		

The debit in this entry is posted to both the general ledger account and to the appropriate job cost sheet.

An entry to record indirect labour is the same as for direct labour *except* it debits Factory Overhead and credits Factory Payroll. In the subsidiary Factory Overhead Ledger, the debit in this entry is posted to the Indirect Labour account.

Overhead Cost Flows and Documents

LO 7 Describe and record the flow of overhead costs in job order cost accounting.

Factory overhead (or simply overhead) cost flows are shown in Exhibit 22.10. Two of the four sources of overhead costs include indirect materials and indirect labour. These costs are recorded from requisitions for indirect materials and time tickets for indirect labour. The other sources of overhead are (1) vouchers authorizing payments for items such as supplies or utilities and (2) adjusting entries for costs such as amortization.

Because factory overhead usually includes many different costs, a separate account for each overhead cost is often maintained in a subsidiary Factory Overhead Ledger. This ledger is controlled by the Factory Overhead account in the General Ledger. Factory Overhead is a temporary account that accumulates costs until they are allocated (applied, assigned or charged) to specific jobs.

Manufacturing Overhead

Exhibit 22.10

Job Order Overhead Cost Flows Through Subsidiary Records

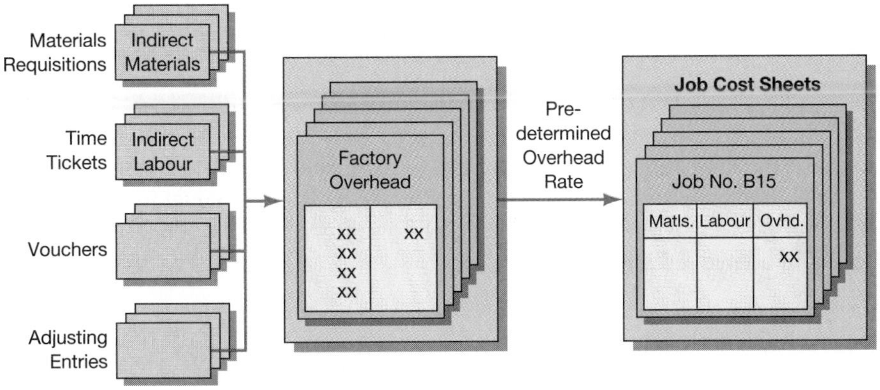

Recall that manufacturing overhead costs are recorded with debits to the Factory Overhead account and credits to other accounts such as Cash, Accounts Payable, and Accumulated Amortization—Equipment. In the subsidiary Factory Overhead Ledger, the debits are posted to their proper accounts such as Amortization on Factory Equipment, Insurance on Factory Equipment, or Amortization of Patents.

Exhibit 22.10 shows overhead costs flow from the Factory Overhead account to job cost sheets. Because manufacturing overhead is made up of costs not directly associated with specific jobs or job lots, we cannot determine the specific dollar amount incurred on a particular job. But we know manufacturing overhead costs are necessary in any manufacturing operation. If the total cost of a job is to include all costs needed to manufacture the job, some amount of manufacturing overhead must be included.

We already know how to allocate overhead to inventories and cost of goods sold by linking overhead to another factor used in production, such as direct labour or machine hours. In Exhibit 22.4, for instance, overhead is expressed as 160% of direct labour. We then allocated overhead by multiplying that percent by the estimated amount of direct labour in both ending inventory and cost of goods sold.

Since perpetual inventory records are used in a job order cost accounting system we cannot wait until the end of the period to allocate overhead to jobs. We must predict overhead in advance and assign it to jobs by using a **predetermined overhead allocation rate,** or simply predetermined overhead rate. This rate requires us to estimate total overhead cost and total direct labour cost (or another factor) before the start of the period. Exhibit 22.11 shows the formula for computing a predetermined overhead allocation rate. These estimates are usually based on annual amounts. We then can use this rate during the period to allocate overhead to jobs.

Exhibit 22.11

Predetermined Overhead Allocation Rate Formula

$$\text{Predetermined overhead allocation rate} = \text{Estimated overhead costs} \div \text{Estimated factor costs}$$

Road Warriors, for instance, allocates overhead by linking it to direct labour. At the start of 1998, management predicted total direct labour cost for 1998 at \$125,000, and predicted total factory overhead costs at \$200,000. Using these estimates, management computed its predetermined overhead allocation rate as 160% of direct labour cost (\$200,000 ÷ \$125,000).

Look back to the job order cost sheet for Job No. B15 in Exhibit 22.4 on page 1045. See that \$1,000 of direct labour is assigned to this job. We then use the predetermined overhead allocation rate of 160% to allocate \$1,600 of overhead to the job. The journal entry to record this allocation is

Mar. 11	Goods in Process Inventory — Job. No. B15	1,600	
	Factory Overhead		1,600
	To assign overhead to Job No. B15.		

Because the allocation rate for overhead is estimated at the start of the period, the total amount assigned to jobs during the period is rarely equal to the amount actually incurred. We explain how this difference is treated at the end of the period in a later section of this chapter.

Judgment and Ethics

Systems Consultant

Your professional services firm is currently working on seven client engagements. Two of these engagements involve significant resources and the clients reimburse your firm for actual costs plus a 10% markup. The other five pay a fixed fee for services. Cost includes labour allocated at \$47 per labour hour. The partner of the firm instructs you to record as many labour hours as possible to the markup engagements by transferring labour hours from others. She says "this will ensure we'll earn an added \$47 markup for each added labour hour recorded." You are the tax manager in charge of these two engagements and your bonus depends on profits generated by the entire seven engagements. What do you do?

Summary of Manufacturing Cost Flows

We showed journal entries for charging Goods in Process inventory and Job No. B15 for the cost of a (1) direct materials requisition, (2) direct labour time ticket, and (3) for manufacturing overhead. While we entered separate entries for each of these costs, they are usually recorded in one entry. Materials requisitions are often collected for a day or a week and recorded with a single entry summarizing these requisitions. The same is done with labour time tickets. When summary entries are made, supporting schedules of the jobs charged and the types of materials used provide the basis for postings to subsidiary records.

To show all the manufacturing cost flows for a period and their related entries, we again look at Road Warriors' activities. Exhibit 22.12 shows costs linked to all of Road Warriors' manufacturing activities for March 1998. Road Warriors did not have any jobs in process at the beginning of March but they did apply materials, labour, and overhead costs to five jobs in March. Specifically, Job Nos. B15 and B16 are completed and delivered to customers in March, Job No. B17 is completed but not delivered, and Job Nos. B18 and B19 are still in process.

Exhibit 22.12 shows purchases of raw materials for $2,750, labour costs incurred for $5,300, and overhead costs of $6,720.

Exhibit 22.12

Job Order Costs of All Manufacturing Activities

ROAD WARRIORS
Job Order Manufacturing Costs
For Month Ended March 31, 1998

Explanation	Materials	Labour	Overhead Incurred	Overhead Assigned	Goods in Process	Finished Goods	Cost of Goods Sold
Job B15	$ 600	$1,000		$1,600			$3,200
Job B16	300	800		1,280			2,380
Job B17	500	1,100		1,760		$3,360	
Job B18	150	700		1,120	$1,970		
Job B19	250	600		960	1,810		
Total job costs	$1,800	$4,200		$6,720	$3,780	$3,360	$5,580
Indirect materials	550		$ 550				
Indirect labour		1,100	1,100				
Other overhead			5,070				
Total costs used in production	$2,350	$5,300	$6,720				
Ending inventory	1,400						
Materials available	$3,750						
Less beginning inv.	(1,000)						
Purchases	$2,750						

Exhibit 22.13 shows the flow of these costs through general ledger accounts and the end-of-month balance in the subsidiary records. The arrow lines are numbered to show the flows of costs for March. Each numbered cost flow reflects several entries made in March.

Exhibit 22.13

Flow of All Job Order Costs and Ending Cost Sheets

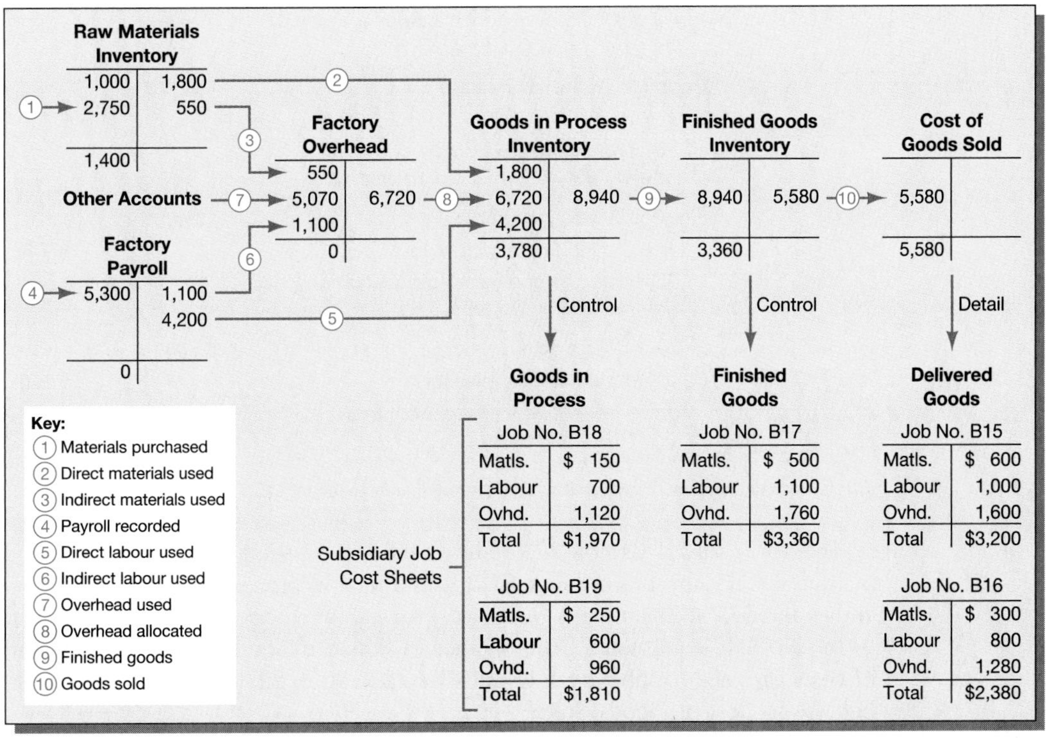

Exhibit 22.14 shows each cost flow with a single entry summarizing the actual individual entries made in March. Each entry is numbered to link with the arrow lines in Exhibit 22.13.

Exhibit 22.14

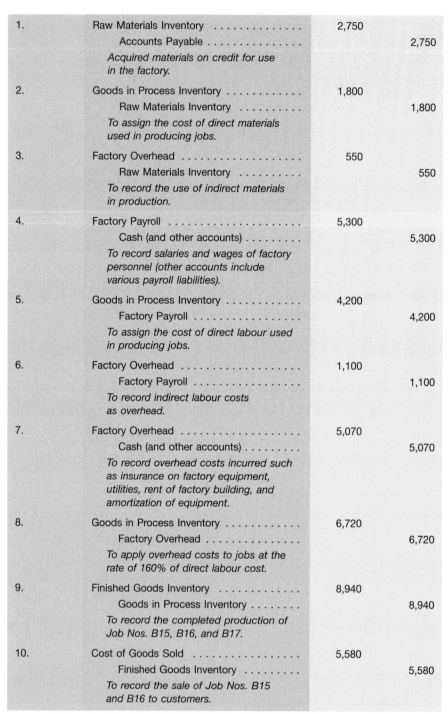

Entries for Job Order Manufacturing Costs

1.	Raw Materials Inventory	2,750	
	Accounts Payable		2,750
	Acquired materials on credit for use in the factory.		
2.	Goods in Process Inventory	1,800	
	Raw Materials Inventory		1,800
	To assign the cost of direct materials used in producing jobs.		
3.	Factory Overhead	550	
	Raw Materials Inventory		550
	To record the use of indirect materials in production.		
4.	Factory Payroll	5,300	
	Cash (and other accounts)		5,300
	To record salaries and wages of factory personnel (other accounts include various payroll liabilities).		
5.	Goods in Process Inventory	4,200	
	Factory Payroll		4,200
	To assign the cost of direct labour used in producing jobs.		
6.	Factory Overhead	1,100	
	Factory Payroll		1,100
	To record indirect labour costs as overhead.		
7.	Factory Overhead	5,070	
	Cash (and other accounts)		5,070
	To record overhead costs incurred such as insurance on factory equipment, utilities, rent of factory building, and amortization of equipment.		
8.	Goods in Process Inventory	6,720	
	Factory Overhead		6,720
	To apply overhead costs to jobs at the rate of 160% of direct labour cost.		
9.	Finished Goods Inventory	8,940	
	Goods in Process Inventory		8,940
	To record the completed production of Job Nos. B15, B16, and B17.		
10.	Cost of Goods Sold	5,580	
	Finished Goods Inventory		5,580
	To record the sale of Job Nos. B15 and B16 to customers.		

Transactions are numbered consistent with the arrow line in Exhibit 22.13.

The lower part of Exhibit 22.13 shows the status of job cost sheets at the end of March. The sum of costs assigned to the jobs in process ($1,970 + $1,810) equals the $3,780 balance in Goods in Process Inventory. Also, costs assigned to Job No. B17 equal the $3,360 balance in Finished Goods Inventory. The sum of costs assigned to Job Nos. B15 and B16 ($3,200 + $2,380) equals the $5,580 balance in Cost of Goods Sold.

Manufacturing Statement in Job Order Costing

A manufacturing statement prepared using a job order cost accounting system is the same as one prepared using a general accounting system. Under both systems, the statement summarizes the total costs of manufacturing activities during the period. The manufacturing statement for Road Warriors is in Exhibit 22.15.

Exhibit 22.15

Manufacturing Statement for Road Warriors

ROAD WARRIORS
Manufacturing Statement
For Month Ended March 31, 1998

Direct materials used	$ 1,800
Direct labour	4,200
Factory overhead	6,720
Total manufacturing costs	$12,720
Add goods in process inventory, February 28, 1998	-0-
Total goods in process during the month	$12,720
Deduct goods in process inventory, March 31, 1998	(3,780)
Cost of goods manufactured	$ 8,940

Did You Know?

Bits and Pieces Accounting
Many job order companies find it easier to maintain job cost records with computers. Yet costs of special software that fulfills all their computing needs can be high. In response, some companies piece together less expensive off-the-shelf software. Emerald Packaging, for instance, expects to save $75,000 by piecing together its own programs rather than buying an entire customized software package. They bought accounting modules and an inventory system off-the-shelf and then developed their own job costing, sales order, pricing and shop-floor programs. [Source: *Business Week*, April 28,1997.]

Flashback

8. In a job order cost accounting system, what account is debited in recording a raw materials requisition? (a) Raw Materials Inventory, (b) Raw Materials Purchases, (c) Goods in Process Inventory if for a specific job, (d) Goods in Process Inventory if they are indirect materials.
9. Which four sources of information lead to recording costs in the Factory Overhead account?
10. Why does a job order cost accounting system use a predetermined overhead application rate?
11. What events result in a debit to Factory Payroll? What events result in a credit?

Answers—p. 1057

Adjusting of Overapplied and Underapplied Overhead

Refer to the debits in the Factory Overhead account in Exhibit 22.13. Note the total cost of factory overhead incurred during March is $6,720, computed as $550 + $5,070 + $1,100. Also note the $6,720 is exactly equal to the amount assigned to production in entry 8. The overhead incurred is equal to the overhead applied in March. But the amount of overhead incurred is rarely equal to the amount of overhead applied. This is because a job order cost accounting system uses a pre-

LO 8 Determine adjustments for overapplied and underapplied factory overhead.

determined overhead rate in applying factory overhead costs to jobs. This rate is determined using estimated amounts before the period begins, and estimates rarely are exactly equal to amounts actually incurred. This section explains what we do when too much or too little overhead is applied to jobs.

Underapplied Overhead

When less overhead is applied than is actually incurred the remaining debit balance in the Factory Overhead account at the end of the period is called **underapplied overhead.** Let us *assume* Road Warriors actually incurred "other overhead costs" of $5,550 instead of the $5,070 shown in Exhibit 22.13. This yields a total overhead cost of $7,200 in March 1998 instead of the $6,720 applied (see Exhibit 22.12). Since the amount of overhead applied was only $6,720, the Factory Overhead account would be left with a $480 debit balance as shown in the ledger account in Exhibit 22.16.

Exhibit 22.16

Underapplied Overhead in the Factory Overhead Ledger Account

Factory Overhead — Acct. No. 540

Date		Explanation	Debit	Credit	Balance	
1998						
Mar.	31	Indirect materials cost	550		550	
	31	Indirect labour cost	1,100		1,650	
	31	Other overhead costs	5,550		7,200	
	31	Overhead costs applied to jobs		6,720	480	(debit)

The $480 debit balance reflects manufacturing costs not charged to jobs. This means the balances in Goods in Process Inventory, Finished Goods Inventory, and Cost of Goods Sold do not include all manufacturing costs incurred. We technically should allocate this underapplied Factory Overhead balance to these accounts. However, the underapplied overhead amount is often immaterial and is entirely allocated (or closed) to the Cost of Goods Sold account.[1] The adjusting entry to record this allocation is made as follows:

Mar. 31	Cost of Goods Sold	480	
	Factory Overhead		480
	To adjust for underapplied overhead cost.		

Overapplied Overhead

When the overhead applied in a period exceeds the overhead incurred the resulting credit balance in the Factory Overhead account is called **overapplied overhead.** We treat overapplied overhead at the end of the period in the same way we treat

[1] When the underapplied overhead is significant, the amount is usually allocated to the Cost of Goods Sold, Finished Goods Inventory and Goods in Process Inventory accounts. The preferred method of allocating underapplied overhead is one consistent with the allocation method used in the period. For Road Warriors this means underapplied overhead is allocated to jobs based on direct labour. Jobs B15 and B16, which are sold, accounted for 42.8% of the total direct labour cost in March 1998. Also, 26.2% of direct labour was consumed by B16 which is in Finished Goods inventory, and the remaining 31% was consumed by jobs B17 and B18 which are in Goods in Process inventory. These percents are multiplied by $480 to compute the amount of underapplied overhead allocated to each account (for example, 42.8% of $480, or $205, is allocated to the Cost of Goods Sold account). An adjusting entry records this allocation:

Mar. 31	Goods in Process Inventory	149	
	Finished Goods Inventory	126	
	Cost of Goods Sold	205	
	Factory Overhead		480
	To adjust the cost of the jobs worked on in March for underapplied overhead cost.		

underapplied overhead. It is ideally allocated to goods in process, finished goods, and cost of goods sold.

When overhead is over- or underapplied, the manufacturing statement must be adjusted by the amount of the over- or underapplied overhead. This adjustment is necessary so that the manufacturing statement reports the actual applied overhead. The adjustment for over- or underapplied overhead is normally reported as the final line item immediately above the total cost of goods manufactured figure in the manufacturing statement (where underapplied overhead is deducted and overapplied overhead is added to cost of goods manufactured). The Demonstration Problem at the end of the chapter illustrates this adjustment and its reporting. (Another common treatment for over- or underapplied overhead is to report it in the factory overhead section of the manufacturing statement.)

Flashback

12. In a job order cost accounting system, why does the Factory Overhead account usually have an overapplied or underapplied balance at the end of a period?

13. The Factory Overhead account has a debit balance at the end of a period. Does this reflect overapplied or underapplied overhead?

Answers—p. 1057

Multiple Overhead Allocation Rates

USING THE INFORMATION

Overhead costs must be allocated to products in some reasonable manner. This chapter described the allocation of overhead using one allocation base. We now explain how managers can use more than one allocation base and how this is useful in management decisions.

The marketing manager, Sam Moore, of the Toronto plant of Rocky Mountain Bikes, requires accurate cost information for pricing purposes. Rocky Mountain Bikes computes current product cost by allocating overhead as a percent of direct labour costs. Moore believes this allocation method distorts the cost of a bike. He prefers a more accurate cost figure so he can make more informed decisions on bike pricing. He also believes that allocation of costs is improved by using multiple overhead rates instead of a single rate.

LO 9 Apply multiple overhead allocation rates in assigning overhead to products.

To determine multiple rates, the total overhead must first be separated, in some meaningful way, into its different components. It is then assigned to products using the allocation bases. The total factory overhead, for instance, at the Toronto plant is $55,000 for the year. This is separated into three components: (1) materials related overhead, $20,000, (2) labour related overhead, $15,000, and (3) machine related overhead, $20,000. The overhead allocation rates are then determined as shown in Exhibit 22.17.

Exhibit 22.17

Computing Multiple Overhead Rates

Overhead Type	Overhead Rate
Materials-related overhead	$20,000 ÷ $100,000 direct materials cost = 20% of direct materials cost
Labour-related overhead	$15,000 ÷ 5,000 direct labour hours = $3 per direct labour hour
Machine-related overhead	$20,000 ÷ 10,000 = $2 per machine hour

To assign overhead to a single job, we must record actual amounts of direct materials cost, direct labour hours, and machine hours consumed by a job. For example, one special order at the Toronto plant recorded the following: direct materials cost, $1,000; direct labour hours, 50 hours at $900; and 200 machine-hours.

If a single overhead allocation rate of 160% of direct labour cost is used to compute overhead, we get total overhead of $1,440 (160% of $900). But when we use the multiple rates computed in Exhibit 22.17, the overhead assigned amounts to $750, computed as (0.20 × $1,000) + ($3 × 50) + ($2 × 200). Note the difference in the overhead amount allocated is $690, a material amount in this case. The new cost figure based on allocation of overhead using multiple overhead rates gave Sam information he needed to reduce the price of mountain bikes. Without this information, the bikes would not have been properly priced and the management of Rocky Mountain Bikes would have been misinformed about the costs of its product.

You Make the Call

Sales Director

You are the manager of a division for your company. Your division's products are facing increasing price competition to the extent that competitors' prices are often lower than your product costs. You learn 53% of total product cost is factory overhead allocated using direct labour hours. You believe product costs from your costing system are distorted and you are wondering if there is a better means to allocate factory overhead. What do you suggest?

Answer—p. 1057

Summary

LO1 Explain manufacturing activities and the flow of manufacturing costs. Manufacturing activities consist of materials, production and marketing activities. The materials activity consists of the purchase and issuance of materials to production. The production activity consists of converting materials into finished goods. At this stage in the process the materials, labour and overhead costs have been incurred and the manufacturing statement is prepared. The marketing activity consists of selling some or all of finished goods available for sale. At this stage in the process the cost of goods sold is determined.

LO2 Prepare a manufacturing statement and explain its purpose and links to financial statements. The manufacturing statement reports the computation of cost of goods manufactured during the period. It begins by showing the period's costs for direct materials, direct labour, and overhead, and then adjusts these numbers for the beginning and ending inventories of goods in process to yield the cost of completed goods.

LO3 Describe important features of job order manufacturing. Certain manufacturers produce unique products for customers and are called job order manufacturers. These unique or special products are manufactured in response to a customer's orders; therefore, such firms are also known as custom manufacturers. The products produced by a job order manufacturer are usually heterogeneous, and typically manufactured in low volumes. The manufacturing systems of job order companies are flexible and are not highly standardized.

LO4 Explain job cost sheets and how they are used in job order cost accounting. In a job order cost accounting system, the costs of producing each job are accumulated on a separate job cost sheet. Costs of direct materials, direct labour, and manufacturing overhead are accumulated separately on the job cost sheet and then added to determine the total cost of a job. Job cost sheets for jobs in process, finished jobs, and jobs that are sold make up subsidiary records that are controlled by general ledger accounts.

LO5 Describe and record the flow of materials costs in job order cost accounting. Costs of materials flow from receiving reports to materials ledger cards and then to either job cost sheets or the Indirect Materials account in the factory overhead ledger.

LO6 Describe and record the flow of labour costs in job order cost accounting. Costs of labour flow from clock cards to the Factory Payroll account and then to either job cost sheets or the Indirect Labour account in the factory overhead ledger.

LO7 Describe and record the flow of overhead costs in job order cost accounting. Manufacturing overhead costs are accumulated in the Factory Overhead account that controls the subsidiary factory overhead ledger. Then, using a predetermined overhead application rate, overhead costs are charged to jobs.

LO8 Determine adjustments for overapplied and underapplied factory overhead. At the end of each period, the Factory Overhead account usually has a residual debit or credit balance. A debit balance reflects underapplied overhead and a credit balance reflects overapplied overhead. If this balance is material, it is allocated to Goods in Process Inventory, Finished Goods Inventory, and Cost of Goods Sold. This allocation uses the same factor, such as direct labour, used to apply overhead during the period. If the balance is not material, it is often transferred to Cost of Goods Sold.

LO 9 **Apply multiple overhead allocation rates in assigning overhead to products.** Total overhead is first separated into its different components—such as materials-related overhead, labour-related overhead, and machine-related overhead. Overhead is then assigned using these different components and their different overhead allocation rates.

Guidance Answers to **You Make the Call**

Management Consultant

Service companies do not recognize goods in process inventory or finished goods inventory. This is an important difference between service and manufacturing companies. As a result, you will not recognize any amount as goods in process inventory at the end of the month. For the two jobs that are 60% complete, you could recognize revenues and costs at 60% of the total expected amount. Therefore, you will recognize revenue of $7,200 (0.60 × $12,000) and costs of $6,000 (0.60 × $10,000).

Sales Director

A faulty cost system can lead to distortions in product costs. The sales director should talk to the controller and ask that individual to study the factory overhead costs in greater detail. Once the different cost elements lumped together in the factory overhead account are known, they can be classified into several groups such as material related, labour related or machine related. Other groups can also be formed (we will discuss more about this in Chapter 24). Once the overhead items are classified into groups, appropriate overhead allocation bases can be established which can be used to compute predetermined overhead allocation rates. These rates can then be used to assign the factory overhead costs to the different products.

Guidance Answer to **Judgment and Ethics**

Systems Consultant

There is an economic incentive to "fudge" the numbers and make some of the assignments "look" more costly. This would also reduce cost on the fixed price assignments. While there is an incentive to act in such a manner, it is clearly unethical. As a professional and as a person, it is your responsibility to engage in ethical behaviour. You must bring to your supervisor's attention the ethical issue involved in the situation. You must first of all refuse to comply with the superior's instructions. If the supervisor forces you into acting in a manner you consider unethical, you should report the matter to a higher authority within the organization.

Guidance Answers to Flashbacks

1. *a*
2. No.
3. Beginning goods in process inventory is added to total manufacturing costs to yield total goods in process. Ending goods in process inventory is subtracted from total goods in process to yield cost of goods manufactured for the period.
4. *b*
5. A job is a special order for a unique product. A job lot consists of a quantity of identical items.
6. *a*
7. The three costs are direct materials, direct labour, and manufacturing overhead.
8. *c*
9. The four sources are materials requisitions, time tickets, vouchers, and adjusting entries.
10. Because a job order cost accounting system uses perpetual inventory records, overhead costs must be assigned to jobs before the end of the period. This requires use of a predetermined overhead application rate.
11. Debits are recorded when wages and salaries of factory employees are paid or accrued. Credits are recorded when direct labour costs are assigned to jobs and when indirect labour costs are transferred to the Factory Overhead account.
12. Overapplied or underapplied overhead exists at the end of a period because application of overhead is based on estimates of overhead and another variable such as direct labour. Those estimates rarely equal the actual amounts incurred.
13. A debit balance reflects underapplied overhead.

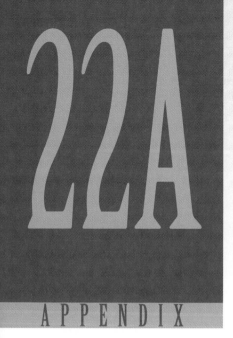

22A General Accounting System for Manufacturing Activities

APPENDIX

Learning Objectives

LO 10 Describe the unique accounts manufacturing companies use in a general accounting system.

LO 11 Describe the flow of manufacturing costs in a general accounting system.

A general accounting system and a cost accounting system are different, yet they have many features in common. They both account for the three elements of manufacturing cost: *direct materials, direct labour, and factory overhead.* They also provide information about the three components of inventory—raw materials, goods in process, and finished goods. The difference is they do not keep records in the same way. The general accounting system uses a *periodic* inventory system in recording raw materials, goods in process, and finished goods. This appendix describes how a general accounting system works. We have previously described in this chapter a cost accounting system (job order costing). A cost accounting system uses the perpetual inventory system.

Accounts Unique to a General Accounting System

LO 12 Prepare entries to record the flow of manufacturing costs in a general accounting system.

LO 13 Explain periodically assigning costs to inventories in a general accounting system.

Many accounts used by manufacturing companies and merchandising companies are the same. Both have accounts for cash, accounts receivable, accounts payable, equity, sales, and selling and administrative expenses. Yet because of the increased complexity of a manufacturing company's operations, its General Ledger usually contains more accounts than a merchandising company's ledger. Accounts used only by manufacturing companies include Factory Equipment, Accumulated Amortization on Factory Equipment, Factory Supplies, and Factory Supplies Used. But there are several accounts that deserve our special attention because of their importance in understanding accounting for manufacturing companies. These accounts are part of the cost flows in manufacturing activities in Exhibit 22.21 and are: Raw Materials Inventory, Raw Materials Purchases, Direct Labour, Factory Overhead, Goods in Process Inventory, Finished Goods Inventory, and Manufacturing Summary. We explain each of these accounts in this section.

Raw Materials Inventory

A company using a general accounting system records the cost of raw materials on hand at the end of a period in its Raw Materials Inventory account. Since periodic inventory is used the amount in this account does not change during an accounting period and remains as its beginning balance. However, at the end of each period the balance in this account is updated in the closing process. A company determines its end-of-period cost of raw materials by a physical count of its materials on hand. It then assigns costs to these materials using an inventory costing method such as FIFO, LIFO, weighted average, or specific identification. We assume a FIFO cost flow in our discussion to avoid unnecessary complexities.

Raw Materials Purchases

A general accounting system records the cost of raw materials purchased during a period by debiting the Raw Materials Purchases account. This account is similar to the Purchases account used for merchandise purchases under a periodic system. Raw Materials Purchases is a temporary account for costs that are later allocated between ending raw materials inventory and the materials used in production for the period. This account starts each period with a zero balance. The balance increases as materials purchases are recorded. It returns to a zero balance when the account is closed at the end of the period. Most companies also use supplementary accounts to record other transactions affecting the cost of purchased materials. These often include accounts for transportation-in, materials purchases returns and allowances, and materials purchases discounts.

Direct Labour

A general accounting system uses a temporary account to record direct labour costs. The Direct Labour account is similar to the Raw Materials Purchases account because it accumulates direct labour costs during the period. The amount in this account in then allocated to other accounts at the end of a period. This means the account begins each period with a zero balance, receives debits throughout the period as direct labour costs are incurred, and is closed at the end of the period. When the Direct Labour account is closed, its accumulated costs are allocated to finished and partially finished goods manufactured during the period. The accounting system also often includes several accounts for different categories of direct labour costs. This information can help managers control direct labour costs. For example, accounts usually distinguish base pay from fringe benefits and payroll taxes. But all these costs are eventually assigned to products.

Factory Overhead

A company's general accounting system often uses many individual overhead accounts to accumulate information about different overhead costs. The manufacturing statement in Exhibit 22.2 illustrates balances from these individual overhead accounts. This information helps management control specific overhead costs such as indirect labour, indirect materials and utilities. However, these individual overhead accounts may sometimes be lumped together in a temporary account to record manufacturing overhead costs, called Factory Overhead.

This Factory Overhead account is like the Direct Labour account because it starts each period with a zero balance. Also during the period, it is debited as overhead costs are incurred. When its accumulated costs are allocated to products in the end-of-period closing process, its account balance is returned to zero. A company often uses many individual overhead accounts to accumulate information about different overhead costs. This information helps management control specific overhead costs such as indirect labour, indirect materials, and utilities.

Goods in Process Inventory

A manufacturer often carries an inventory of partially finished goods in process. These products usually include a portion of their necessary direct materials, direct labour and overhead costs. The cost of these unfinished units is debited to the

Goods in Process Inventory account at the end of the period. The balance of this account remains unchanged during the period when a general accounting system is used. This means that the account is not updated during a period to reflect the completion of products or the start of new units into production. But the year-end closing process updates the account balance to reflect the cost of ending goods in process inventory. The costs recorded in the Goods in Process Inventory account require estimates. Even when products are countable, the process of assigning costs to these units is not precise. Rocky Mountain Bikes, for instance, usually has many partially finished mountain bikes at the end of each period. Determining the cost of these bikes requires estimates. We describe some of the estimation methods later in the chapter.

Finished Goods Inventory

Finished goods are finished products ready for sale. Like the other two inventory accounts, the beginning balance of the Finished Goods Inventory account equals the cost from the prior period's ending balance. When products are finished and sales occur, the account is not updated in a general accounting system. No entries are made to this account until it is updated by the year-end closing process to reflect the cost of finished goods on hand at the end of the period. A physical count of ending finished goods inventory is the primary source of information to update the ending balance in this account.

Manufacturing Summary

A general accounting system also uses a Manufacturing Summary account. This temporary account is similar to the Income Summary account. The Manufacturing Summary account has a zero balance during each period. But during the closing process all manufacturing costs are transferred to this account. The account balance is returned to zero when the costs in this account are allocated among the three ending inventory accounts and cost of goods sold.

Flash back

14. Which of these statements is true about a general accounting system for a manufacturer?

a. Raw materials purchased are debited to Goods in Process Inventory.

b. Goods in Process Inventory account is updated in the end-of-period closing process.

c. FIFO inventory costing method must be used.

15. What is the major difference between a general accounting system and a cost accounting system?

16. Identify an account with a function similar to the Manufacturing Summary account.

Answers—p. 1069

Flow of Manufacturing Cost Information

Detailed manufacturing cost information taken from different accounts in the general accounting system is transferred to the manufacturing statement and then to the income statement. Exhibit 22A.1 shows how cost information for one account, that of overhead, flows from a schedule of factory overhead costs to the manufacturing statement and on to the income statement. Note individual factory overhead costs are listed in a separate schedule. The schedule supports and explains the total factory overhead cost item shown on the manufacturing statement. Since Rocky Mountain Bikes included a detailed list of overhead costs in its manufacturing statement, we show the alternative use of a supporting schedule in this exhibit. The manufacturing statement includes total factory overhead in its computation of cost of goods manufactured. Cost of goods manufactured is then carried to the income statement and shown as part of cost of goods sold.

Exhibit 22A.1

Overhead Cost Flows across Accounting Reports

Rocky Mountain Bikes
Schedule of Overhead Items
For Year Ended December 31, 1998

Indirect labour	$ 9,000
Supervision	6,000
Other overhead items*	15,000
Total overhead	$30,000

*Overhead items are listed in Exhibit 22.2.

Rocky Mountain Bikes
Manufacturing Statement
For Year Ended December 31, 1998

Direct materials	$ 85,500
Direct labour	60,000
Factory overhead	30,000
Total Manuf. costs	$175,500
Beg. goods in process	2,500
Total goods in process	$178,000
End. goods in process	(7,500)
Cost of goods manuf.	$170,500

Rocky Mountain Bikes
Income Statement
For Year Ended December 31, 1998

Sales		$310,000
Cost of goods sold:		
Beg. finished goods	$ 11,200	
Cost of goods manuf.	170,500	
End. finished goods	(10,300)	
Cost of goods sold	$171,400	
Gross profit	$138,600	
Expenses	(59,900)	
Income taxes	(32,600)	
Net income	$ 46,100	

The manufacturing statement and its supporting schedule of overhead items and other accounts are prepared for managers. But financial statements prepared according to GAAP are aimed at external users. Still we see that many management reports are linked to financial statements even though management accounting and financial accounting are aimed at different users.

Journalizing in a General Accounting System

A general accounting system exhibits a flow of manufacturing costs and related entries that explain a company's manufacturing activities. There are five basic cost flows. We list them below by how they are journalized in a general accounting system:

- Recording manufacturing activities
- Closing manufacturing accounts
- Recording ending balances of manufacturing inventories
- Closing the Manufacturing Summary account
- Updating finished goods inventory

These journalizing steps provide information in a form useful for both internal and external decision makers and reports.

Understanding manufacturing and general accounting systems is important to knowing the flow of manufacturing costs and the related entries for manufacturing activities. Our analysis in this appendix uses the information in Exhibit 22A.2 on inventories and events of Rocky Mountain Bikes for 1998.

Exhibit 22A.2

Manufacturing Transactions of Rocky Mountain Bikes in 1998

Beginning inventories:	
Raw materials	$ 8,000
Goods in process	2,500
Finished goods	11,200
Materials and production activity costs for 1998:	
Raw materials purchases	$86,500
Direct labour	60,000
Factory overhead	30,000
Ending inventories:	
Raw materials	$ 9,000
Goods in process	7,500
Finished goods	10,300

The costs of the ending inventories are given. But we describe below how to compute these amounts.

In the upper section of Exhibit 22A.3 we show five boxes on the left reflecting sources of manufacturing costs. They are beginning materials inventory, beginning goods in process inventory, purchases of raw materials, direct labour costs, and factory overhead. In the lower section of this exhibit, we show the beginning balances of the period for the Raw Materials Inventory, Goods in Process Inventory, and Finished Goods Inventory accounts. These amounts of $8,000, $2,500, and $11,200 are carried forward from the end of 1997.

Exhibit 22A.3

Flow of Manufacturing Costs in a General Accounting System

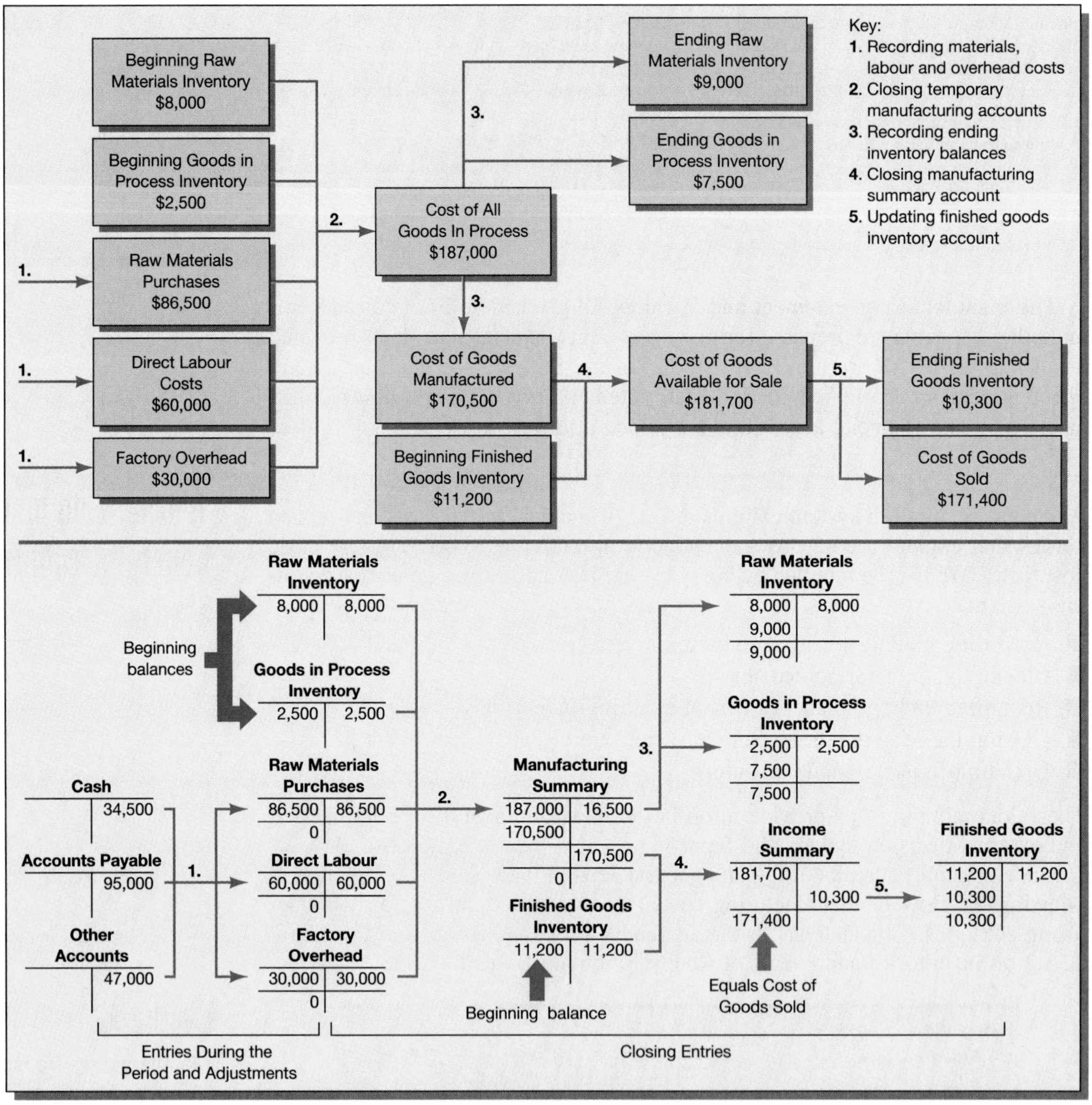

These beginning balances flow into the manufacturing activities of the period. All manufacturing costs eventually end up in one of four places: materials inventory, goods in process inventory, finished goods inventory, or cost of goods sold. Exhibit 22A.3 identifies five major flows and entries for manufacturing costs. These are described in the five remaining sections below corresponding to arrow lines labelled 1 through 5 in this exhibit.

Recording Manufacturing Activities

In the upper section of Exhibit 22A.3, the arrow lines labelled 1 reflect manufacturing events of 1998. These arrows symbolize purchasing raw materials for $86,500 (materials activity), using direct labour at a cost of $60,000 (production activity), and incurring $30,000 of factory overhead costs (production activity).

The lower section of Exhibit 22A.3 shows that Cash, Accounts Payable, and Other Accounts are used with Raw Materials Purchases, Direct Labour, and Factory Overhead to record production costs. The debits and credits linked by arrow lines labelled 1 summarize the journal entries recording the 1998 activities. Arrow lines pointing to Accounts Payable and Raw Material Purchases, for instance, summarize all credit purchases of raw materials for 1998. A typical entry for this company's purchase transactions is:

May 15	Raw Materials Purchases	800	
	Accounts Payable		800
	Purchased raw materials on credit.		

This entry increases the balance of Raw Materials Purchases by the cost of acquired materials. It also increases the balance of Accounts Payable to reflect the liability to pay for this purchase.

Similarly, arrow lines pointing to Direct Labour and Other Accounts reflect all 1998 accruals of direct labour costs. A common entry to record one of those transactions (ignoring withholdings) is:

Aug. 21	Direct Labour	2,550	
	Wages Payable		2,550
	To accrue direct labour payroll.		

This entry increases the balance of the temporary Direct Labour account and increases Wages Payable (Other Accounts in the exhibit) by the amount accrued. To simplify this exhibit, it uses an "Other Accounts" T-account to reflect all accounts other than Cash and Accounts Payable that are credited in 1998 while recording manufacturing costs.

The arrow line pointing to Factory Overhead reflects all overhead costs incurred in 1998. This exhibit uses only one Factory Overhead account instead of the many detailed overhead accounts that many companies use. A common item in factory overhead is amortization on the factory building. The following adjusting entry is one example of this cost:

Dec. 31	Factory Overhead	1,800	
	Accumulated Amortization, Building . .		1,800
	To record amortization on the factory building.		

The lower section of Exhibit 22A.3 shows the arrow line labelled 1 that reflects all entries made in 1998 including adjusting entries. The cost flow arrow lines labelled 2, 3, 4 and 5 all reflect closing entries.

Closing Temporary Manufacturing Accounts

The upper section of Exhibit 22A.3 shows arrow line 2 indicating the five sources of manufacturing costs total $187,000 for 1998. This total is made up of:

Beginning inventories:	
Raw materials	$ 8,000
Goods in process	2,500
Materials and Production activity costs:	
Raw materials purchases	86,500
Direct labour	60,000
Factory overhead	30,000
Total costs to be accounted for in 1998	$187,000*

* Note the amount of $187,000 is different from the $175,500 listed as total manufacturing costs in the middle box of Exhibit 22.2 (the manufacturing statement). Total manufacturing cost of $175,500 is derived after deducting from $187,000 both the ending raw materials inventory of $9,000 and the $2,500 beginning goods in process inventory. Total manufacturing costs in Exhibit 22.2 is the sum of raw materials used, direct labour incurred and factory overhead incurred. Exhibit 22A.3 shows the flow of manufacturing activities and how beginning inventories and the costs incurred in 1998 are accounted for as finished goods and ending inventories.

The lower section of Exhibit 22A.3 shows that entry 2 transfers the balances of these five sources to the temporary Manufacturing Summary account at the end of 1998. This closing entry is:

Dec. 31	Manufacturing Summary	187,000	
	Raw Materials Inventory		8,000
	Goods in Process Inventory		2,500
	Raw Materials Purchases		86,500
	Direct Labour		60,000
	Factory Overhead		30,000
	To close the 1998 production accounts to Manufacturing Summary.		

When several factory overhead accounts are used, the above closing entry includes a credit to each of them. If a separate account is used for each overhead cost listed in the manufacturing statement in Exhibit 22.2 on page 1038, then the closing entry is replaced by:

Dec. 31	Manufacturing Summary	187,000	
	Raw Materials Inventory		8,000
	Goods in Process Inventory		2,500
	Raw Materials Purchases		86,500
	Direct Labour		60,000
	Indirect Labour		9,000
	Factory Supervision		6,000
	Factory Utilities		2,600
	Repairs, Factory Equipment		2,500
	Property Taxes on Factory Building		1,900
	Factory Supplies Used		600
	Factory Insurance Expired		1,100
	Small Tools Written Off		200
	Amortization of Factory Equipment		3,500
	Amortization of Factory Building		1,800
	Amortization of Patents		800
	To close the 1998 production accounts to Manufacturing Summary.		

Recording Ending Balances of Inventory Accounts

Arrow lines labelled 3 in Exhibit 22A.3 indicate $9,000 of the $187,000 total cost for 1998 is allocated to ending inventory of raw materials and another $7,500 is allocated to ending goods in process inventory. The remaining $170,500 is assigned to the cost of units completed in the period.

In the lower section of this exhibit, arrow line 3 reflects the entry to record the cost of ending raw materials and goods in process inventories. This entry is:

Dec. 31	Raw Materials Inventory	9,000	
	Goods in Process Inventory	7,500	
	Manufacturing Summary		16,500
	To update the raw materials and goods in process inventories.		

The $170,500 cost of completed units temporarily remains as the balance of Manufacturing Summary. Look at Exhibit 22.2 on page 1038 to find this amount as the last line of the Manufacturing Statement. We also see it in the Cost of Goods Sold section of the income statement in Exhibit 21.9 on page 1001.

Closing Manufacturing Summary Account

Arrow line labelled 4 in Exhibit 22A.3 reflects the cost of goods available for sale. The lower section of this exhibit shows arrow line 4 transferring both the Manufacturing Summary balance and the beginning Finished Goods Inventory to Income Summary.

The entire closing entry is not reflected in Exhibit 22A.3 because of its focus on manufacturing cost flows. But we show the closing entry below that closes all 1998 expense accounts for Rocky Mountain Bikes. Balances of expense accounts are taken from the 1998 income statement in Exhibit 21.9.

Dec. 31	Income Summary	274,200	
	Manufacturing Summary		170,500
	Finished Goods Inventory		11,200
	Sales Salaries Expense		18,000
	Advertising Expense		5,500
	Delivery Wages Expense		12,000
	Shipping Supplies Expense		250
	Insurance Expense, Delivery Equipment		300
	Amortization Expense, Delivery Equipment		2,100
	Office Salaries Expense		15,700
	Miscellaneous Expense		200
	Bad Debts Expense		1,550
	Office Supplies Expense		100
	Amortization Expense, Office Equipment		200
	Interest Expense		4,000
	Income Taxes Expense		32,600
	To close the Manufacturing Summary and expense accounts, and to clear the Finished Goods Inventory account.		

Updating Finished Goods Inventory Account

The upper section of Exhibit 22A.3 shows arrow line 5 reflecting the allocation of cost of goods available for sale to the ending inventory of finished goods and the cost of goods sold. The lower section of this exhibit shows arrow line 5 reflecting the allocation entry. This completes the process of accounting for Rocky Mountain Bikes' manufacturing costs in 1998. The final entry leaves $171,400 cost of goods sold in the Income Summary account. While the exhibit does not show the Sales account, the complete closing entry includes a debit to Sales as follows:

Dec. 31	Finished Goods Inventory	10,300	
	Sales	310,000	
	Income Summary		320,300
	To close the Sales account and update the Finished Goods Inventory account.		

After this entry is posted the Income Summary account has a credit balance of $46,100. This equals net income for 1998. The entry to close the Income Summary account and update the Retained Earnings account is:

Dec. 31	Income Summary	46,100	
	Retained Earnings		46,100
	To close Income Summary and update Retained Earnings.		

Observe this last closing entry is the same whether the company is engaged in merchandising, manufacturing or service activities.

Flashback

17. In recording closing entries for a manufacturing company using a general accounting system, the beginning balance of Finished Goods Inventory is:

a. Debited to Finished Goods Inventory and credited to Income Summary.

b. Debited to Finished Goods Inventory and credited to Manufacturing Summary.

c. Credited to Finished Goods Inventory and debited to Income Summary.

18. What accounts are summarized in the Manufacturing Summary account?

19. What accounts are summarized in the Income Summary account?

Answers—p. 1069

Inventory Valuation in a General Accounting System

A general accounting system measures ending inventories of raw materials, goods in process, and finished goods using physical counts of units on hand. Assigning costs to raw materials inventory is the same as assigning costs to the merchandise inventory of a retailer. Items in both of these companies' inventories are often in the same condition as when they were purchased. But determining the value of costs of goods in process and finished goods inventories is more complex. Companies simply cannot measure costs of goods in process and finished goods by the amounts paid to suppliers. This is because these inventories have been partially or entirely converted from raw materials into finished products. The manufacturing costs of these inventories must be estimated by considering the relevant amounts of each of the three product costs: direct materials, direct labour and factory overhead. This section describes the estimation of these costs.

Estimating Direct Material and Direct Labour Costs in Ending Inventories

Measuring the direct materials and direct labour costs in both goods in process and finished goods inventories is often difficult for manufacturing processes. A production manager who understands the manufacturing process must often estimate these costs. This manager must first estimate the quantity of direct materials in each goods in process inventory. Costs are then assigned based on a cost flow assumption such as FIFO. The estimated direct material costs for products in goods in process inventory are totalled to measure the direct material cost of the entire inventory. This same process is used to compute the cost of direct materials in finished goods inventory.

The method for estimating direct labour cost of goods in process is similar to that used for direct materials. A production manager usually estimates the hours of direct labour applied to the units in goods in process inventory. Then, based on the cost per hour of labour, this manager computes total direct labour cost of these units. The manager makes similar estimates of direct labour cost for finished goods inventory.

Estimating Factory Overhead Cost in Ending Inventories

Since factory overhead is not clearly linked with specific units or batches of product, estimating the overhead cost assigned to the ending inventories is challenging. The usual method of assigning overhead is to relate factory overhead to a factor common to most manufacturing activities. A company, for instance, can express total factory overhead cost as a percent of *total machine hours used in production*. The company then assigns overhead cost to units of product by multiplying that percent by the number of machine hours used to produce each product. An alternative is to express total factory overhead cost as a percent of *direct labour cost*. In this case the company assigns overhead cost to units of product by multiplying that percent by the direct labour cost assigned to each product.

We use Rocky Mountain Bikes to see how this method is carried out. This company's total overhead costs for 1998 are $30,000 and its total direct labour costs are $60,000. This means $1 of factory overhead cost is incurred for each $2 of direct labour cost. Exhibit 22A.4 shows how overhead costs are computed as a percent of direct labour cost.

$$\textbf{Overhead Rate} = \frac{\textbf{Factory overhead}}{\textbf{Direct labour}} = \frac{\$30{,}000}{\$60{,}000} = 50\%$$

Exhibit 22A.4

Overhead Rate in a General Accounting System

Rocky Mountain Bikes then applies this percent to management's estimates of direct labour cost per product to determine the factory overhead cost per product. Exhibit 22A.5 shows how we assign all three types of cost to products in the different ending inventories.

Exhibit 22A.5

Estimating Cost of Inventories—General Accounting System

	Goods in Process			Finished Goods		
	Cost per Unit	Units of Products	Total Cost	Cost per Unit	Units of Product	Total Cost
Direct materials (estimated)	$3.75	1,000	$3,750	$11.00	515	$ 5,665
Direct labour (estimated)	2.50	1,000	2,500	6.00	515	3,090
Factory overhead (50% of direct labour)	1.25	1,000	1,250	3.00	515	1,545
Total cost			$7,500			$10,300

This exhibit shows management estimates direct materials costs at $3.75 per unit for goods in process and $11 per finished unit. Estimates of direct labour cost are $2.50 per unit for goods in process and $6.00 per finished unit. Factory overhead cost is then assigned at the rate of 50% of direct labour cost. A physical count of each ending inventory shows there are 1,000 partially finished bikes in process and 515 bikes in finished goods inventory. Each per unit cost is then multiplied by the number of bikes in each inventory to get the total cost assigned to both inventories. Note the $7,500 cost of ending goods in process and the $10,300 cost of ending finished goods inventory are the amounts reported in Exhibit 22A.1.

Companies often link factory overhead to direct labour when assigning overhead to inventories. But alternative methods are used. Factory overhead is also linked to machine hours used in manufacturing. When products are manufactured by machine, total overhead cost can be divided by total machine hours used to get overhead cost per machine hour. Companies then assign overhead to units based on the number of machine hours it takes to produce a unit.

Other factors such as the quantity of direct materials used in production are also used as a basis for assigning overhead to inventories. While these methods yield estimates, they are based on an often reasonable assumption that overhead incurred in producing a product is proportional to the amount of the factor selected (such as direct labour) in producing the product.

Flash back

20. Why are assignments of direct material and direct labour costs to goods in process and finished goods inventories often based on estimates by managers familiar with the production process?

21. CompTech uses an overhead rate of 60% of direct labour cost to assign overhead cost to its cost of products in goods in process inventory. CompTech's manufacturing statement reports total overhead cost of $156,000. How much direct labour did CompTech report?

Answers—p. 1069

Summary of Appendix 22A

LO 10 Describe the unique accounts manufacturing companies use in a general accounting system. Unique accounts used by manufacturers with general accounting systems include Raw Materials Inventory, Raw Materials Purchases, Direct Labour, Factory Overhead, Goods in Process Inventory, Finished Goods Inventory, and Manufacturing Summary. Additional accounts may provide more detailed information for management use in planning and controlling operations.

LO 11 Describe the flow of manufacturing costs in a general accounting system. During each period, manufacturers use separate accounts to record their raw materials purchases, direct labour costs, and factory overhead costs. After end-of-period adjustments are recorded in the closing process, all manufacturing costs are transferred to the Manufacturing Summary account. Next, the Manufacturing Summary balance is allocated to cost of goods manufactured (Income Summary) and to the ending inventories of raw materials and goods in process. At the same time, the beginning finished goods inventory balance is transferred to Income Summary. Another closing entry records the ending finished goods inventory.

LO 12 Prepare entries to record the flow of manufacturing costs in a general accounting system. A general accounting system exhibits five basic cost flows: recording manufacturing activities; closing manufacturing accounts; recording ending balances of manufacturing inventories; closing the Manufacturing Summary account; and updating finished goods inventory. Each of these are journalized.

LO 13 Explain periodically assigning costs to inventories in a general accounting system. When determining costs of ending inventories, a manufacturer allocates raw materials and direct labour costs to goods in process and finished goods using estimates from production managers. Factory overhead cost is linked with another factor used in production such as direct labour or machine hours. The manufacturer then allocates overhead costs to ending work in process and finished goods inventories based on estimated quantity of direct labour or machine hours used to produce the units in the inventories.

Guidance Answers to Flashbacks

14. *b*

15. A cost accounting system will contain many more accounts because of Raw Materials and Goods in Process inventories.

16. Income summary

17. *c*

18. Accounts that enter into the computation of goods manufactured are summarized in the Manufacturing Summary account. They include the beginning and ending balances of the Raw Materials Inventory and Goods in Process Inventory accounts, and the preclosing balances of the Raw Materials Purchases, Direct labour, and Factory Overhead accounts.

19. Accounts that enter into the computation of the year's net income are summarized in the Income Summary account. They include the beginning and ending balances of the Finished Goods Inventory account, the balance of the Manufacturing Summary account, and the balances of all revenue and expense accounts.

20. Direct material and direct labour costs for both goods in process and finished goods inventories often must be estimated because quantities of direct materials and direct labour used in these inventories are not known certainly.

21. $260,000 ($156,000 ÷ 0.6)

Demonstration Problem

The following information describes the job order manufacturing activities of Peak Manufacturing Company for May:

Raw materials purchases	$16,000
Factory payroll cost	15,400
Overhead costs incurred:	
Indirect materials	5,000
Indirect labour	3,500
Other factory overhead	9,500

The predetermined overhead rate is 150% of the direct labour cost. These costs are allocated to the three jobs worked on during May as follows:

	Job 401	Job 402	Job 403
Balances on April 30:			
Direct materials	$3,600		
Direct labour	1,700		
Applied overhead	2,550		
Costs during May:			
Direct materials	3,550	$3,500	$1,400
Direct labour	5,100	6,000	800
Applied overhead	?	?	?
Status on May 31	Finished (sold)	Finished (unsold)	In process

Required

1. Determine the total cost of:
   a. April 30 inventory of jobs in process.
   b. Materials used during May.
   c. Labour used during May.
   d. Factory overhead incurred and applied during May and the amount of any over- or underapplied overhead on May 31.
   e. Each job as of May 31, the May 31 inventories of goods in process and finished goods, and the goods sold during May.
2. Prepare summarized journal entries for the month to record
   a. Materials purchases (on credit), the factory payroll (paid with cash), indirect materials, indirect labour, and the other factory overhead (paid with cash).
   b. Assignment of direct materials, direct labour, and overhead costs to the Goods in Process Inventory account. (Use separate debit entries for each job.)
   c. Transfer of each completed job to the Finished Goods Inventory account.
   d. Cost of goods sold.
   e. Removal of any underapplied or overapplied overhead from the Factory Overhead account. (Assume the amount is not material.)
3. Prepare a manufacturing statement for May.

Planning the Solution

- Determine the cost of the April 30 in-process inventory by adding up the materials, labour, and applied overhead costs for Job 401.
- Compute the cost of materials used and labour by adding up the amounts assigned to jobs and to overhead.
- Compute the total overhead incurred by adding the amounts of the three components; compute the amount of applied overhead by multiplying the total direct labour cost by the predetermined overhead rate; compute the underapplied or overapplied amount as the difference between the actual cost and the applied cost.
- Determine the total cost charged to each job by adding any costs incurred in April to the materials, labour, and overhead applied during May.
- Group the costs of the jobs according to their status as completed.
- Record the direct materials costs assigned to the three jobs using a separate Goods in Process Inventory account for each job; do the same thing for the direct labour and the applied overhead.
- Transfer the costs of Jobs 401 and 402 from Goods in Process Inventory to Finished Goods Inventory.
- Record the costs of Job 401 as the cost of goods sold.
- Record the transfer of the underapplied overhead from the Factory Overhead account to the Cost of Goods Sold account.
- On the manufacturing statement, remember to include the beginning and ending in-process inventories, and to deduct the underapplied overhead.

Solution to Demonstration Problem

1. Total cost of:
   a. April 30 inventory of jobs in process (Job 401):

Direct materials	$3,600
Direct labour	1,700
Applied overhead	2,550
Total	$7,850

   b. Materials used during May:

Direct materials:		
Job 401	$ 3,550	
Job 402	3,500	
Job 403	1,400	
Total direct materials	8,450	
Indirect materials	5,000	
Total materials	$13,450	

c. Labour used during May:

Direct labour:	
Job 401	$ 5,100
Job 402	6,000
Job 403	800
Total direct labour	11,900
Indirect labour	3,500
Total labour	$15,400

d. Factory overhead incurred during May:

Indirect materials	$ 5,000
Indirect labour	3,500
Other factory overhead	9,500
Total actual overhead	18,000
Overhead applied (150% × $11,900)	17,850
Underapplied overhead	$ 150

e. Total cost of each job:

	401	402	403
From April:			
Direct materials	$ 3,600		
Direct labour	1,700		
*Applied overhead	2,550		
From May:			
Direct materials	3,550	$ 3,500	$1,400
Direct labour	5,100	6,000	800
*Applied overhead	7,650	9,000	1,200
Total costs	$24,150	$18,500	$3,400

**Equals 150% of the direct labour cost.*

Total cost of the May 31 inventory of goods in process (Job 403) = $3,400

Total cost of the May 31 inventory of finished goods (Job 402) = $18,500

Total cost of goods sold during May (Job 401) = $24,150

2. Journal entries:

a.

Raw Materials Inventory	16,000	
Accounts Payable		16,000
To record materials purchases.		
Factory Payroll	15,400	
Cash		15,400
To record factory payroll.		
Factory Overhead	5,000	
Raw Materials Inventory		5,000
To record indirect materials.		
Factory Overhead	3,500	
Factory Payroll		3,500
To record indirect labour.		
Factory Overhead	9,500	
Cash		9,500
To record other factory overhead.		

b. Assignment of costs to goods in process:

Goods in Process Inventory (Job 401)	3,550	
Goods in Process Inventory (Job 402)	3,500	
Goods in Process Inventory (Job 403)	1,400	
Raw Materials Inventory		8,450
To assign direct materials to jobs.		
Goods in Process Inventory (Job 401)	5,100	
Goods in Process Inventory (Job 402)	6,000	
Goods in Process Inventory (Job 403)	800	
Factory Payroll		11,900
To assign direct labour to jobs.		
Goods in Process Inventory (Job 401)	7,650	
Goods in Process Inventory (Job 402)	9,000	
Goods in Process Inventory (Job 403)	1,200	
Factory Overhead		17,850
To apply overhead to jobs.		

c.

Finished Goods Inventory	42,650	
Goods in Process Inventory (Job 401)		24,150
Goods in Process Inventory (Job 402)		18,500
To record completion of jobs.		

d.

Cost of Goods Sold	24,150	
Finished Goods Inventory		24,150
To record sale of Job 401.		

e.

Cost of Goods Sold	150	
Factory Overhead		150
To assign underapplied overhead.		

3.

PEAK MANUFACTURING COMPANY
Manufacturing Statement
For Month Ended May 31

Direct materials used		$ 8,450
Direct labour used		11,900
Factory overhead:		
Indirect materials	$5,000	
Indirect labour	3,500	
Other factory overhead	9,500	18,000
Total manufacturing costs		$38,350
Add goods in process, April 30		7,850
Total goods in process during the month		46,200
Deduct goods in process, May 31		(3,400)
Deduct underapplied overhead		(150)
Cost of goods manufactured		$42,650

Glossary

Clock card A source document that an employee uses to record the number of hours at work and that is used to determine the total labour cost for each pay period. (p. 1047)

Cost accounting system An accounting for manufacturing activities based on the *perpetual* inventory system. (p. 1041)

Finished goods inventory Products that have completed the manufacturing process and are ready to be sold by the manufacturer. (p. 1045)

General accounting system An accounting for manufacturing activities based on the *periodic* inventory system. (p. 1041)

Job The production of a unique product or service. (p. 1042)

Job cost sheet A separate record maintained for each job. (p. 1044)

Job lot Producing more than one unit of a unique product. (p. 1042)

Job order cost accounting system A cost accounting system that is designed to determine the cost of producing each job or job lot. (p. 1044)

Job order manufacturing The production of products in response to special orders, also called *customized production.* (p. 1042)

Materials ledger card A perpetual record that is updated each time units are both purchased and issued for use in production (p. 1046)

Materials requisition A source document that production managers use to request materials for manufacturing and that is used to assign materials costs to specific jobs or to overhead. (p. 1046)

Overapplied overhead The amount by which the overhead applied to jobs during a period with the predetermined overhead application rate exceeds the overhead incurred during the period. (p. 1055)

Predetermined overhead application rate The rate established prior to the beginning of a period that relates estimated overhead to another variable such as estimated direct labour, and that is used to assign overhead cost to jobs. (p. 1049)

Time ticket A source document that an employee uses to report how much time was spent working on a job or on overhead activities and that is used to determine the amount of direct labour to charge to the job or to determine the amount of indirect labour to charge to factory overhead. (p. 1047)

Underapplied overhead The amount by which overhead incurred during a period exceeds the overhead applied to jobs with the predetermined overhead application rate. (p. 1054)

A superscript letter A indicates material based on Appendix 22A.

Questions

1. Manufacturing activities of a company are described in a special financial report called the ______. This statement summarizes the types and amounts of costs incurred in a company's manufacturing ________.
2. What are the three categories of manufacturing cost?
3. List several examples of factory overhead costs.
4. What is the difference between factory overhead and selling and administrative overhead?
5. List the components of a manufacturing statement for a manufacturer of running shoes and provide specific examples of each.
6. Does the date of a manufacturing statement match the balance sheet or income statement and why?
7. Describe the relationships among the income statement, the manufacturing statement, and a detailed schedule of factory overhead costs.
8. If NIKE were to set up a manufacturing operation in Toronto what inventories would you expect the company to hold?
9. Why must a manufacturer estimate the amount of factory overhead assigned to individual jobs or job lots?
10. The text used a percent of labour cost to assign factory overhead to individual jobs. Identify another approach that a company may use to assign factory overhead costs.
11. What types of information are recorded on a job cost sheet? How are job cost sheets used by management and employees?
12. In a job order cost accounting system, what records serve as a subsidiary ledger for Goods in Process Inventory? For Finished Goods Inventory?
13. What journal entry is recorded when a materials manager receives a materials requisition and then issues materials for use in the factory?
14. What role does the materials requisition slip play to safeguard the company's assets?
15. What is the difference between a "clock card" and a "time ticket"?

16. What events cause debits to be recorded in the Factory Overhead account? What events cause credits to be recorded in the account?
17. What accounts are used to eliminate overapplied or underapplied overhead from the Factory Overhead account, assuming the amount is not material?
18. NIKE just finished production on a batch of 300 football shoes, specially coloured green and gold, for a NFL team. How should they account for this, as 300 individual jobs or a job lot? Why?
19. Why must a company prepare a predetermined factory overhead rate?
20. How would a hospital apply job order costing?
21.[A] Identify the seven accounts used in general accounting systems for manufacturers that are not used by merchandising or service companies.
22.[A] If a general accounting system is used, at what point in the accounting cycle are the costs of raw materials purchases, direct labour, and factory overhead allocated to the cost of goods sold and to the ending raw materials, goods in process, and finished goods inventories?
23.[A] In the general accounting system model, all manufacturing accounts are closed to the ________ summary account.
24.[A] How does the process of determining the ending goods in process in a job order cost accounting system differ from the process used in a general accounting system?

Quick Study

QS 22-1
Identify manufacturing flow
LO 1

Identify the order of manufacturing activities—which is performed first, second and third (circle).

a. Production activity 1, 2, 3
b. Selling activity 1, 2, 3
c. Materials activity 1, 2, 3

QS 22-2
Determine Cost of Goods Manufactured
LO 1

Max-it Company's manufacturing statement includes the following information. Determine the cost of goods manufactured.

Direct materials used	$189,760
Direct labour	65,100
Total factory overhead costs	24,720
Goods in process, December 31, 1997	299,400
Goods in process, December 31, 1998	234,210

QS 22-3
Determine factory overhead rates
LO 4

Secor Company incurred the following manufacturing costs for the period:

Direct labour	$468,000
Direct materials	354,500
Factory overhead	117,000

Compute overhead cost as a percentage of (a) direct labour and (b) direct materials.

QS 22-4
Review job and job lot differences
LO 2

Determine which products from the following list would most likely be manufactured as a job and which as a job lot:

1. Hats imprinted with a company logo.
2. A hand-crafted table.
3. A custom-designed home.
4. A 30-metre motor yacht.
5. Little League trophies.
6. Wedding dresses for a chain of department stores.

QS 22-5
Determine job cost
LO 3

The following information was found on materials requisitions and time tickets for Job 9-1005, which was completed by Beaufort Boats for Redfish Rentals. The requisitions are identified by code numbers starting with the letter Q and the time tickets start with W:

Date	Document	Amount
July 1/X4	Q-4698	$1,250
July 1/X4	W-3393	600
July 5/X4	Q-4725	1,000
July 5/X4	W-3479	450
July 10/X4	W-3559	300

At the beginning of the year, management estimated that the overhead cost would equal 140% of the direct labour cost for each job. Determine the total cost on the job cost sheet for Job 9-1005.

QS 22-6
Prepare material journal entries
LO 2

During one month, a company that uses a job order cost accounting system purchased raw materials for $50,000 cash. It then used $12,000 of the raw materials indirectly as factory supplies and used $32,000 as direct materials. Prepare entries to record these transactions.

QS 22-7
Prepare labour journal entries
LO 3

During one month, a company that uses a job order cost accounting system had a monthly factory payroll of $120,000, paid in cash. Of this amount, $30,000 was classified as indirect labour and the remainder as direct. Prepare entries to record these transactions.

QS 22-8
Prepare factory overhead entries
LO 4

During the current month, a company that uses a job order cost accounting system had a monthly factory payroll of $120,000, paid in cash. Of this amount, $30,000 was classified as indirect labour and the remainder as direct for the production of 100 water skis. Factory overhead is applied at 150% of direct labour payroll. Prepare the entry to record manufacturing overhead to this job lot.

QS 22-9
Prepare over/underapplied overhead entry
LO 5

Relay Company allocates overhead at a rate of 150% of direct labour cost. Actual overhead for the period was $950,000 and direct labour was $600,000. Prepare the closing entry of over- or underapplied overhead to cost of goods sold.

QS 22-10A
Identify general accounting system terms
LO 4

Complete the following sentences about accounts unique to a manufacturing company:

a. The temporary account that has a zero balance until the closing process starts and is similar to Income Summary is the ______________________________ account.

b. The temporary accounts in which manufacturing costs are recorded throughout the period are ________________, ________________, and ________________.

QS 22-11A
Prepare general accounting system closing entries
LO 5, 6

The Intermat Company manufactures products and accounts for its activities using a general accounting system. The following account balances are taken from the company's ledger at the end of the year before closing:

Raw Materials Inventory	$ 20,000
Goods in Process Inventory	16,000
Raw Materials Purchases	84,000
Direct Labour	110,000
Factory Overhead	220,000

Physical counts at the end of the year show:

Raw Materials Inventory	$ 18,000
Goods in Process Inventory	17,600

Prepare the closing entries that should be made to the Manufacturing Summary account, except for the entry to the Income Summary account.

QS 22-12^A
Prepare general accounting system closing entries
LO 5, 6

These additional account balances are taken from the ledger of the Intermat Company described in QS 22-11^A.

Finished Goods Inventory	$ 30,000
Sales	800,000
Selling Expenses	120,000
General and Administrative Expenses	87,000
Income Taxes Expense	73,440

A physical count at the end of the year shows:

Finished Goods Inventory	$37,000

Prepare the closing entries that should be made to the Income Summary account. Assume that the balance of the Manufacturing Summary account is $414,400 (debit) after the entries in QS 22-11^A are posted.

Exercises

Exercise 22-1
Computing cost of goods manufactured and cost of goods sold
LO 2

The following information is taken from the accounting records of Bean Company and Baby Company.

	Bean Company	Baby Company
Beginning finished goods inventory	$10,000	$15,800
Beginning goods in process inventory	12,400	22,000
Beginning raw materials inventory	6,400	8,240
Lease on factory equipment	24,000	35,000
Direct labour	15,000	16,000
Ending finished goods inventory	12,300	21,800
Ending goods in process inventory	15,400	19,000
Ending raw materials inventory	4,600	3,400
Factory utilities	8,000	6,400
Factory supplies used	5,600	2,800
General and administrative expenses	24,000	40,000
Indirect labour	1,300	1,920
Repairs, factory equipment	3,320	5,100
Raw materials purchases	27,000	32,600
Sales salaries	30,000	28,000

Compute the cost of goods manufactured and the cost of goods sold for each company.

Exercise 22-2
Identifying components of financial statements
LO 1, 2

For each of the following account balances for a manufacturing company, indicate by a ✓ in the appropriate column whether it will appear on the balance sheet, the income statement, the manufacturing statement, or a detailed schedule of factory overhead costs. Assume that the income statement shows the calculation of cost of goods sold and the manufacturing statement shows only the total amount of factory overhead. Note that an account balance may appear on more than one report.

Account	Balance Sheet	Income Statement	Manufacturing Statement	Overhead Schedule
Accounts receivable				
Computer supplies for office				
Beginning finished goods inventory				
Beginning goods in process inventory				
Beginning raw materials inventory				
Cash				
Amortization of factory building				
Amortization of factory equipment				
Amortization expense, office building				
Amortization expense, office equipment				
Direct labour				
Ending finished goods inventory				
Ending goods in process inventory				
Ending raw materials inventory				
Factory maintenance employee				
Computer supplies for factory				
Income taxes				
Insurance on factory building				
Rent on office building				
Office supplies used				
Property taxes on factory building				
Raw materials purchases				
Sales				

Exercise 22-3
Preparing a manufacturing statement
LO 2

Given the selected account balances of Packer Corp. shown below, prepare its manufacturing statement in proper form on December 31, 1998. Include the individual overhead account balances in this statement.

Sales	$1,000,000
Raw materials inventory, December 31, 1997	25,000
Goods in process inventory, December 31, 1997	45,525
Finished goods inventory, December 31, 1997	57,375
Raw materials purchases	120,825
Direct labour	136,650
Factory computer supplies used	13,800

Indirect labour	33,600
Repairs, factory equipment	6,000
Rent on factory building	49,500
Advertising expenses	86,400
General and administrative expenses	100,950

The ending inventories are:

Raw materials inventory, December 31, 1998	$ 35,625
Goods in process inventory, December 31, 1998	31,650
Finished goods inventory, December 31, 1998	53,475

Exercise 22-4
Preparing a manufacturing company's income statement
LO 2

Use the information provided in Exercise 22-3 to prepare an income statement for Packer Corporation. Assume that the cost of goods manufactured is $363,625.

Exercise 22-5
Understanding the manufacturing process
LO 1, 2

The following partially completed flowchart shows how cost flows through a business as the product is manufactured. Some of the boxes in the flowchart show cost amounts while other boxes contain question marks. Compute the cost that should appear in each box containing a question mark.

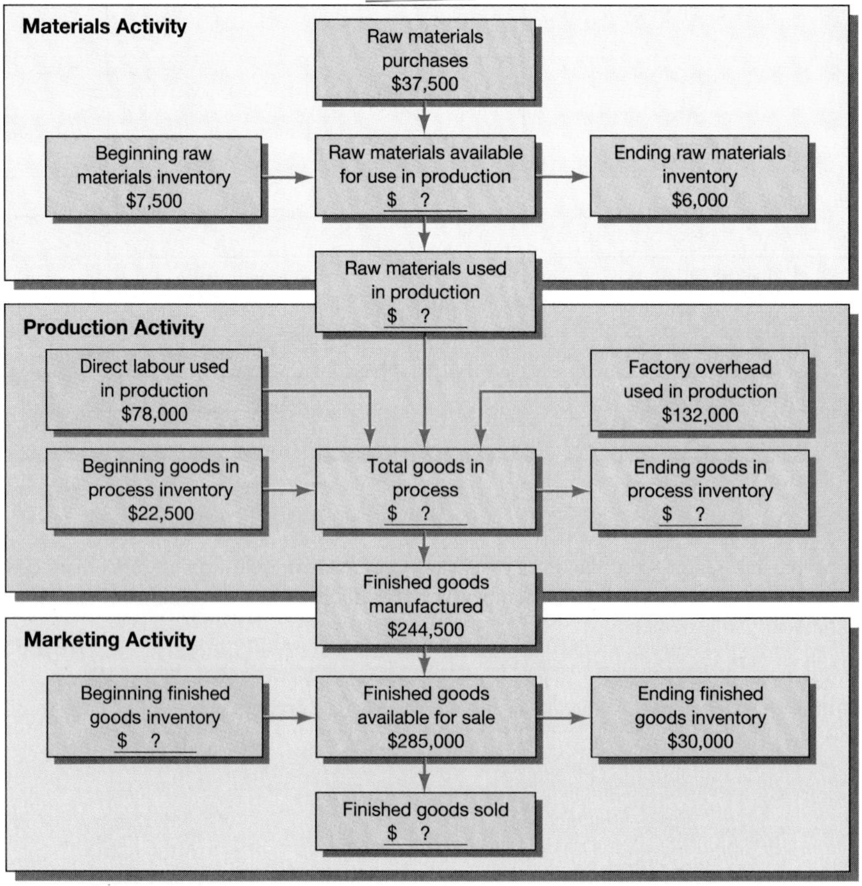

Exercise 22-6
Documents used in job order cost accounting systems
LO 3, 4, 5, 6, 7

The following left column includes the names of several documents used in job order cost accounting systems. The right column presents short descriptions of the purposes of the documents. In the blank space beside each of the numbers in the right column, write the letter of the document that serves the described purpose.

a. Factory Payroll account	_____ **1.** Communicates to the storeroom that materials are needed to complete a job.
b. Materials ledger card	_____ **2.** Shows only the total amount of time that an employee works each day.
c. Time ticket	_____ **3.** Shows the amount approved for payment of an overhead cost.
d. Voucher	_____ **4.** Shows the amount of time an employee worked on a specific job.
e. Materials requisition	_____ **5.** Temporarily accumulates the cost of incurred overhead until the cost is assigned to specific jobs.
f. Factory Overhead account	_____ **6.** Temporarily accumulates labour costs incurred until they are assigned to specific jobs or to overhead.
g. Clock card	_____ **7.** Perpetual inventory record of raw materials received, used, and on hand.

Exercise 22-7
Analysis of cost flows
LO 3, 6, 7, 8

As of the end of June, the job cost sheets at Skateboards for You, Inc. showed that the following total costs had been accumulated on three jobs:

	Job 102	Job 103	Job 104
Direct materials	$15,000	$33,000	$27,000
Direct labour	8,000	14,200	21,000
Overhead	4,000	7,100	10,500

Job 102 had been started in production during May and the following costs had already been assigned to it in that month: direct materials of $6,000, direct labour of $1,800, and overhead of $900. Jobs 103 and 104 were started during June. Overhead cost was applied with a predetermined application rate based on direct labour cost. Jobs 102 and 103 were finished during June, and it is expected that Job 104 will be finished in July. No raw materials were used indirectly during June. Using this information, answer the following questions:

a. What was the cost of the raw materials during June for the three jobs?
b. How much direct labour cost was incurred during June?
c. What predetermined overhead application rate was used during June?
d. How much cost was transferred to finished goods during June?

Exercise 22-8
Computing overhead application rate; assigning costs to jobs
LO 7

In December 1998, Dana Company's management established the 1999 overhead application rate based on direct labour cost. The information used in setting the rate included the cost accountant's estimates that the company would incur $756,000 of overhead costs and $540,000 of direct labour cost during 1999. During March of 1999, Dana began and completed Job No. 13-56.

Required

a. Compute the overhead application rate for 1999.
b. Use the information on the following job cost sheet to determine the total cost of the job.

JOB COST SHEET

Customer's Name Keiser Co. **Job No.** 13-56

Job Description 5 Two-Page Color Monitors—21 inch

	Direct Materials		Direct Labour		Overhead Costs Applied	
Date	**Requisition No.**	**Amount**	**Time-Ticket No.**	**Amount**	**Rate**	**Amount**
Mar. 8	4-129	5,000	T-306	640		
11	4-142	7,050	T-432	1,280		
18	4-167	3,550	T-456	1,280		
Total						

Exercise 22-9
Analysis of costs assigned to goods in process
LO 7

Angus Company uses a job order cost accounting system that charges overhead to jobs on the basis of direct material cost. At the end of last year, the company's Goods in Process Inventory account showed the following:

Goods in Process Inventory					Acct. No. 121
Date		**Explanation**	**Debit**	**Credit**	**Balance**
1998					
Dec.	31	Direct materials cost	1,500,000		1,500,000
	31	Direct labour cost	240,000		1,740,000
	31	Overhead costs	450,000		2,190,000
	31	To finished goods		2,100,000	90,000

Required

1. Determine the overhead application rate (based on direct material cost) used.
2. Only one job was in the goods in process inventory at the end of December, 1998. Its direct materials cost was $30,000. How much direct labour cost must have been assigned to it? How much overhead cost must have been assigned to it?

Exercise 22-10
Understanding cost flows in a job order cost accounting system
LO 1, 4, 7

The Auto Security Company produces special order security products and uses a job order cost accounting system. The system provided the following information:

	April 30	May 31
Inventories:		
Raw materials	$40,000	$ 50,000
Goods in process	9,600	19,500
Finished goods	60,000	33,200
Information about May:		
Raw materials purchases (paid with cash)		$ 189,000
Factory payroll (paid with cash)		400,000
Factory overhead:		
Indirect materials		12,000
Indirect labour		75,000
Other overhead costs		100,500
Sales (received in cash)		1,200,000
Predetermined overhead application rate based on direct labour cost		65%

Compute the following amounts for the month of May:

a. Cost of direct materials used.
b. Cost of direct labour used.
c. Cost of goods manufactured.
d. Cost of goods sold.
e. Gross profit.

Exercise 22-11
Recording journal entries for a job order cost accounting system
LO 5, 6, 7

Using the information provided in Exercise 22-10, prepare general journal entries to record the following events for May:

a. Raw materials purchases.
b. Direct materials usage.
c. Indirect materials usage.
d. Factory payroll costs.
e. Direct labour usage.
f. Indirect labour usage.
g. Factory overhead other than indirect materials and indirect labour (record the credit in Other Accounts).
h. Application of overhead to goods in process.
i. Transfer of finished jobs to the finished goods inventory.
j. Sale and delivery of finished goods to customers.

Exercise 22-12
Eliminating end-of-period balance in Factory Overhead
LO 7, 8

In December 1998, Entertainment Inc. established its predetermined overhead application rate for movies produced during 1999 by using the following predictions:

Overhead costs	$1,800,000
Direct labour costs (e.g. set construction crew)	450,000

At the end of 1999, the company's records showed that actual overhead costs for the year had been $1,770,000. The actual direct labour cost had been assigned to jobs as follows:

Movies completed and released	$400,000
Movies still in production	45,000
Total actual direct labour cost	$445,000

Required

1. Compute the predetermined overhead application rate for 1999.
2. Set up a T-account for overhead and enter the overhead costs incurred and the amounts applied to movies during the year with the predetermined rate.
3. Determine whether overhead was overapplied or underapplied during the year.
4. Prepare the general journal entry to close any over- or underapplied overhead to cost of goods sold.

Exercise 22-13
Eliminating end-of-period balance in Factory Overhead
LO 7, 8

In December 1998, Setter Company established its predetermined overhead application rate for jobs produced during 1999 by using the following predictions:

Overhead costs	$600,000
Direct labour costs	500,000

At the end of 1999, the company's records showed that actual overhead costs for the year had been $680,000. The actual direct labour cost had been assigned to jobs as follows:

Jobs completed and sold	$420,000
Jobs still in the finished goods inventory . . .	84,000
Jobs in the goods in process inventory	56,000
Total actual direct labour cost	$560,000

Required

1. Compute the predetermined overhead application rate for 19X2.
2. Set up a T-account for Factory Overhead and enter the overhead costs incurred and the amounts applied to jobs during the year with the predetermined rate.
3. Determine whether overhead was overapplied or underapplied during the year.
4. Prepare the general journal entry to allocate any over- or underapplied overhead to cost of goods sold.
5. Prepare the general journal entry to allocate any over- or underapplied overhead assuming the amount is material.

Exercise 22-14A
Identifying facts about manufacturing accounts
LO 10

The following chart lists seven accounts in general accounting systems used by manufacturers. Fill in the requested facts for each account. The first row is completed for you.

Account	Balance at Beginning of Year	Entries to Account Prior to Closing	Closing Entries Made to Account	Closed at End of Year?	Financial Statements on Which Balance is Reported
Raw Materials Inventory	Cost of raw materials on hand at end of prior year	None	Credited for beginning balance. Debited for ending balance	No	Manufacturing Statement
Balance Sheet					
Raw Materials Purchases					
Direct Labour					
Factory Overhead					
Goods in Process Inventory					
Finished Goods Inventory					
Manufacturing Summary					

Exercise 22-15A
Closing entries for a manufacturing company
LO 10, 11

Use the information provided in Exercise 22-3 and prepare closing entries for Packer Corporation.

Exercise 22-16A
Closing entries for a manufacturing company
LO 11, 12, 13

The following account balances are taken from the Helix Co.'s accounting records after adjustments as of December 31, 1998. Also presented are the results of physical counts and valuations of the ending inventories.

Sales	$422,400
Raw materials purchases	67,200
Direct labour	99,120
Factory overhead	81,600
Selling expenses	45,840
General and administrative expenses	41,760
Income taxes expense	47,520
Beginning inventories:	
Raw materials inventory	12,480
Goods in process inventory	17,040
Finished goods inventory	10,320
Ending inventories:	
Raw materials	19,440
Goods in process	25,200
Finished goods	15,840

Prepare closing entries for the company.

Exercise 22-17A
Overhead rate calculation and analysis
LO 11, 13

Cardinal Company uses the proportional relationship between factory overhead and direct labour costs to assign factory overhead to its inventories of goods in process and finished goods. The company incurred the following costs during 1998:

Direct materials used	$ 637,500
Direct labour costs	2,500,000
Factory overhead costs	1,000,000

a. Determine the company's overhead rate for 1998.

b. Under the assumption that the company's $57,000 ending goods in process inventory had $18,000 of direct labour costs, determine the inventory's direct material costs.

c. Under the assumption that the company's $337,485 ending finished goods inventory had $137,485 of direct material costs, determine the inventory's direct labour cost and its factory overhead costs.

Exercise 22-18A
Allocating costs to ending inventories
LO 11, 13

Monarch Company's ending goods in process inventory consisted of 4,500 units of partially completed product and its finished goods inventory consisted of 11,700 units of product. The factory manager determined that the goods in process inventory included direct materials cost of $10 per unit and direct labour cost of $7 per unit. Finished goods were estimated to have $12 of direct materials cost per unit and $9 of direct labour cost per unit. During the period, the company incurred these costs:

Direct materials	$460,000
Direct labour	277,000
Factory overhead	332,400

The company allocates factory overhead to goods in process and finished goods inventories by relating overhead to direct labour cost.

a. Compute the overhead rate.

b. Compute the total cost of the two ending inventories.

c. Because this was Monarch's first year, there were no beginning inventories. Compute the cost of goods sold for the year.

Exercise 22-19A
Allocating costs to goods in process; preparing manufacturing statement
LO 1, 13

Hudson Company's General Ledger included the following items related to its manufacturing activities for 1998. The accounts have been adjusted, but have not yet been closed.

Raw materials inventory	$ 94,600
Goods in process inventory	99,360
Raw materials purchases	311,400
Direct labour	450,000
Indirect labour	194,200
Factory utilities	109,440
Repairs, factory equipment	30,060
Rent on factory building	84,600
Property taxes on factory building	19,260
Factory insurance expired	16,020
Factory supplies used	34,920
Amortization of factory equipment	82,800
Amortization of patents	13,680

In addition, the ending inventory of raw materials is known to be $91,080. The ending inventory of goods in process is not known, but it is known that the company makes a single product and 4,500 units of goods were in process on December 31, 1998. Each unit of the product contained an estimated $18.00 of direct materials and had $7.50 of direct labour cost assigned to it.

Required

Preparation component:

1. Compute the overhead rate based on the relationship between total factory overhead cost and total direct labour cost. Then, determine the cost of the ending goods in process inventory.
2. Prepare a manufacturing statement for 1998. Be certain to include a title on this statement.
3. Prepare entries to close the manufacturing accounts to Manufacturing Summary and to close the Manufacturing Summary account.

Check Figure Overhead rate, 130.0%

Analysis component:

4. Compute the overhead rate based on the relationship between total factory overhead and total direct materials used. Then, without providing additional calculations, explain how Hudson's manufacturing statement would be affected if this rate were used instead of one based on direct labour cost.

Problems

Problem 22-1
Preparing manufacturing and income statements
LO 2

The following alphabetical list of items was taken from the adjusted trial balance and other records of Floral Company before the 1999 year-end closing entries were recorded:

Advertising expense	$ 16,200
Amortization expense, office equipment	6,750
Amortization expense, selling equipment	8,100
Amortization of factory equipment	28,350
Direct labour	523,800
Factory supervision	97,200
Factory supplies used	4,850
Factory utilities	27,000
Income taxes expense	109,350
Indirect labour	47,250

Inventories:	
Raw materials, January 1	132,300
Raw materials, December 31	136,350
Goods in process, January 1	10,700
Goods in process, December 31	11,250
Finished goods, January 1	141,750
Finished goods, December 31	113,400
Miscellaneous production costs	6,750
Office salaries expense	56,700
Raw materials purchases	695,250
Rent expense, office space	18,900
Rent expense, selling space	21,600
Rent on factory building	74,800
Maintenance, factory equipment	24,300
Sales	3,431,350
Sales discounts	45,900
Sales salaries expense	236,250
Transportation-in on raw materials	20,250

Required

Preparation component:

1. Prepare a manufacturing statement and an income statement for the company. The income statement should present separate categories for (a) selling expenses and (b) general and administrative expenses.

Check Figure: Cost of goods manufactured, $1,545,200

Analysis component:

2. Review what you learned about merchandise turnover (Chapter 7) and compute the turnover rates for Floral's raw materials and finished goods inventories. Then, discuss some possible reasons for the differences between the turnover rates for the two inventories.

Problem 22-2
Recording manufacturing costs and preparing financial reports
LO 1, 2, 4, 5, 6, 7

The following information refers to the job order manufacturing activities of Lawn Company for April: The March 31 inventory of raw materials was $150,000. Raw materials purchases during April were $400,000. Factory payroll cost during April was $220,000. Overhead costs incurred during April were:

Indirect materials	$30,000
Indirect labour	14,000
Factory rent	20,000
Factory utilities	12,000
Factory equipment amortization	30,000

The predetermined overhead rate was 50% of the direct labour cost. Costs allocated to the three jobs worked on during April were:

	Job 306	Job 307	Job 308
Balances on March 31:			
Direct materials	$14,000	$18,000	
Direct labour	18,000	16,000	
Applied overhead	9,000	8,000	
Costs during April:			
Direct materials	100,000	170,000	$80,000
Direct labour	30,000	56,000	120,000
Applied overhead	?	?	?
Status on April 30	Finished (sold)	Finished (unsold)	In process

Job 306 was sold for $380,000 cash during April.

Required

Preparation component:

1. Determine the total of each manufacturing cost incurred for April (direct labour, direct materials, allocated overhead), and the total cost assigned to each of the three jobs (including the balances from March 31).
2. Present journal entries for the month to record:
   a. The materials purchases (on credit), the factory payroll (paid with cash), and the actual overhead costs, including indirect materials and indirect labour. (The factory rent and utilities were paid with cash.)
   b. The assignment of direct materials, direct labour, and applied overhead costs to the Goods in Process Inventory.
   c. The transfer of Jobs 306 and 307 to the Finished Goods Inventory.
   d. The cost of goods sold for Job 306.
   e. The revenue from the sale of Job 306.
   f. The assignment of any underapplied or overapplied overhead to the Cost of Goods Sold account. (The amount is not material.)
3. Prepare a manufacturing statement for April (use a single line presentation for direct materials and show the details of overhead cost). Also, present a calculation of gross profit for April and show how the inventories would be presented on the April 30 balance sheet.

Check Figure: Cost of goods manufactured, $485,000

Analysis component:

4. When the over- or underapplied overhead adjustment is made, you are closing Factory Overhead to Cost of Goods Sold. Discuss how this adjustment impacts business decision making regarding individual jobs or batches.

Problem 22-3
Source documents, journal entries and financial statements
LO 2, 5, 6, 7, 8

The following trial balance of the Scobey Company was generated by the computer system on the morning of December 31, 1998. Warren Kemp, the company's accountant, knows that something is wrong with the trial balance because it does not show any balance for goods in process inventory and it still shows balances in the Factory Payroll and Factory Overhead accounts:

Cash	$ 48,000	
Accounts receivable	42,000	
Raw materials inventory	26,000	
Goods in process inventory	-0-	
Finished goods	9,000	
Prepaid rent	3,000	
Accounts payable		$ 10,500
Notes payable		13,500
Common shares		30,000
Retained earnings		87,000
Sales		180,000
Cost of goods sold	105,000	
Factory payroll	16,000	
Factory overhead	27,000	
Miscellaneous expenses	45,000	
Total	$321,000	$321,000

After a few moments of searching a cluttered in-box, Kemp found six source documents that needed to be processed to bring the accounting records up to date:

Materials requisition 21-3010:	$4,600	direct materials to Job 402
Materials requisition 21-3011:	7,600	direct materials to Job 404
Materials requisition 21-3012:	2,100	indirect materials
Labour time ticket 6052:	5,000	direct labour to Job 402
Labour time ticket 6053:	8,000	direct labour to Job 404
Labour time ticket 6054:	3,000	indirect labour

Jobs 402 and 404 are the only units in process at the end of the year. The predetermined overhead application rate is 200% of direct labour cost.

Required

Preparation component:

1. Use the information on the six source documents to prepare journal entries to assign the following costs:
   a. Direct material costs to goods in process inventory.
   b. Direct labour costs to goods in process inventory.
   c. Overhead costs to goods in process inventory.
   d. Indirect material costs to the overhead account.
   e. Indirect labour costs to the overhead account.
2. Determine the new balance of the Factory Overhead account after making the entries in requirement 1. Determine whether there is any under- or overapplied overhead for the year. If so, prepare the appropriate adjusting entry to close the overhead account, assuming that the amount is not material.
3. Prepare a revised trial balance.
4. Prepare an income statement for 1998 and a balance sheet as of December 31, 1998.

Check Figure: Net income, $23,900

Analysis component:

5. Assume that the $2,100 on materials requisition 21-3012 should have been direct materials charged to Job 404. Without providing specific calculations, describe what impact this error would have on Scobey's 1998 income statement and balance sheet.

Problem 22-4
Source documents and journal entries in job order cost accounting

LO 7, 8

The predetermined overhead application rate for 1998 was 200% of direct labour for Skidoo Watercraft Inc. The company's activities related to manufacturing during May 1998 were:

a. Purchased raw materials on account, $125,000.
b. Paid factory wages with cash, $84,000.
c. Paid $11,000 cash to computer consultant to reprogram factory equipment.
d. Materials requisitions for the month show that the following materials were used on jobs directly and indirectly:

Job 136	$30,000
Job 137	20,000
Job 138	12,000
Job 139	14,000
Job 140	4,000
Total direct materials ...	$80,000
Indirect materials	12,000
Total materials used	$92,000

e. Labour time tickets for the month show the following labour was used on jobs directly and indirectly:

Job 136	$ 8,000
Job 137	7,000
Job 138	25,000
Job 139	26,000
Job 140	2,000
Total direct labour	$68,000
Indirect labour	16,000
Total	$84,000

f. Overhead was applied to Jobs 136, 138, and 139.

g. Jobs 136, 138, and 139 were transferred to finished goods.

h. Jobs 136 and 138 were sold on account for a total price of $340,000.

i. Overhead costs incurred during the month were as follows. (Credit Prepaid Insurance for the expired factory insurance.)

Amortization of factory building	$37,000
Amortization of factory equipment	21,000
Expired factory insurance	7,000
Accrued property taxes payable	31,000

j. At the end of the month, overhead is applied to the goods in process (Jobs 137 and 140) using the predetermined rate of 200% of direct labour cost.

Required

1. Prepare general journal entries to record the events and transactions *a* through *j*.

2. Set up T-accounts for each of the following general ledger accounts, each of which started the month with a zero balance. Then, post the journal entries to these T-accounts and determine the balance of each account.

Raw Materials Inventory	Factory Payroll
Goods in Process Inventory	Factory Overhead
Finished Goods Inventory	Cost of Goods Sold

3. Prepare a job cost sheet for each job worked on during the month. Use the following simplified form of the job cost sheet:

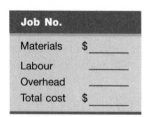

Job No.	
Materials	$______
Labour	______
Overhead	______
Total cost	$______

Check Figure: Finished goods inventory, $92,000

4. Prepare a schedule showing the total cost of each job in process and proving that the sum of the costs equals the Goods in Process Inventory account balance. Prepare similar schedules for the finished goods inventory and the cost of goods sold.

Problem 22-5
Allocating overhead using predetermined overhead application rate
LO 4, 7, 8

In December 1998, Cantu Company's accountant estimated the next year's direct labour as the cost of 50 persons, working an average of 2,000 hours each at an average wage rate of $15 per hour. The accountant also estimated the following manufacturing overhead costs for 1999:

Indirect labour	$159,600
Factory supervision	120,000
Rent on factory building	70,000
Factory utilities	44,000
Factory insurance expired	34,000
Amortization of factory equipment	240,000
Repairs, factory equipment	30,000
Factory supplies used	34,400
Miscellaneous production costs	18,000
Total	$750,000

At the end of 1999, the cost records showed the company had incurred $725,000 of overhead costs. It had completed and sold five jobs with the following direct labour costs:

221	$354,000
222	330,000
223	175,000
224	420,000
225	184,000

In addition, Job 226 was in process at the end of the year and had been charged $10,000 for direct labour. The company's predetermined overhead application rate is based on direct labour cost.

Required

1. Determine:
   a. The predetermined overhead application rate for 1999.
   b. The total overhead cost applied to each of the six jobs during 1999.
   c. The over- or underapplied overhead at year-end.
2. Assuming that the amount of over- or underapplied overhead is not material, prepare the appropriate journal entry to close the Factory Overhead account at the end of 1999.

Check Figure: Factory overhead, $11,500 debit.

Problem 22-6
Recording manufacturing transactions; subsidiary records
LO 5, 6, 7, 8

If the working papers that accompany this text are not available, do not attempt to solve this problem.

The Kaplan Company manufactures special variations of its product, a technopress, in response to special orders from its customers. On May 1, the company had no inventories of goods in process or finished goods but held the following raw materials:

Material M	120 units @	$200	=	$24,000
Material R	80 units @	160	=	12,800
Paint	44 units @	72	=	3,168
Total				$39,968

On May 4, the company began working on two technopresses: Job 102 for Grobe Company and Job 103 for Reynco Company.

Required

Follow the instructions given in this list of activities and then complete the statements provided in the working papers:

Check Figure: Balance in Factory Overhead, $1,536 credit, overapplied

a. Purchased raw materials on credit and recorded the following information from the receiving reports and invoices:

Receiving Report No. 426, Material M, 150 units at $200 each.
Receiving Report No. 427, Material R, 70 units at $160 each.

(*Instructions: Record the purchases with a single general journal entry and post it to the appropriate general ledger T-accounts, using the transaction letter to identify the entries. Also, enter the receiving report information on the materials ledger cards.*)

b. Requisitioned the following raw materials for production:

Requisition No. 35, for Job 102, 80 units of Material M.
Requisition No 36, for Job 102, 60 units of Material R.
Requisition No. 37, for Job 103, 40 units of Material M.
Requisition No. 38, for Job 103, 30 units of Material R.
Requisition No. 39, for 12 units of paint.

(*Instructions: Enter the amounts for the direct materials requisitions only on the materials ledger cards and the job cost sheets. Enter the indirect material amount on the raw materials ledger card and record a debit to the Indirect Materials account in the subsidiary Factory Overhead Ledger. Do not record a general journal entry at this time.*)

c. Employees turned in the following time tickets for work in May:

Time tickets Nos. 1 to 10 for direct labour on Job 102, $40,000.
Time tickets Nos. 11 to 30 for direct labour on Job 103, $32,000.
Time tickets Nos. 31 to 36 for equipment repairs, $12,000.

(*Instructions: Record the direct labour reported on the time tickets only on the job cost sheets and debit the indirect labour to the Indirect Labour account in the subsidiary Factory Overhead Ledger. Do not record a general journal entry at this time.*)

d. Paid cash for the following items during the month:

Factory payroll, $84,000.
Miscellaneous overhead items, $36,000.

(*Instructions: Record the payments with general journal entries and then post them to the general ledger accounts. Also record a debit in the Miscellaneous Overhead account in the subsidiary Factory Overhead Ledger.*)

e. Finished Job 102 and transferred it to the warehouse. The company assigns overhead to each job with a predetermined overhead application rate equal to 70% of direct labour cost. (*Instructions: Enter the allocated overhead on the cost sheet for Job 102, fill in the cost summary section of the cost sheet, and then mark the cost sheet as "Finished." Next, prepare a journal entry to record the job's completion and transfer to finished goods, and then post it to the general ledger accounts.*)

f. Delivered Job 102 and accepted the customer's promise to pay $290,000 within 30 days. (*Instructions: Prepare general journal entries to record the sale of Job 102 and the cost of goods sold. Post them to the general ledger accounts.*)

g. Applied overhead to Job 103, based on the job's direct labour to date. (*Instructions: Enter the overhead on the job cost sheet but do not make a general journal entry at this time.*)

h. Recorded the total direct and indirect materials costs as reported on all the requisitions for the month. (*Instructions: Prepare a general journal entry to record these costs, and post it to the general ledger accounts.*)

i. Recorded the total direct and indirect labour costs as reported on all the time tickets for the month. (*Instructions: Prepare a general journal entry to record these costs, and post it to the general ledger accounts.*)

j. Recorded the total overhead costs applied to jobs.
(Instructions: Prepare a general journal entry to record the application of these costs, and post it to the general ledger accounts.)

k. Determine the balances in the raw materials inventory, goods in process inventory, and factory overhead accounts.

l. Determine if the balance of the factory overhead account is over- or underapplied.

Problem 22-7A
Adjusting and closing entries, allocating overhead costs
LO 3, 4, 10–13

Following is the unadjusted trial balance of the Titus Company as of December 31, 1999:

Cash	$ 62,500	
Accounts receivable	230,000	
Raw materials inventory	220,000	
Goods in process inventory	100,000	
Finished goods inventory	225,000	
Factory equipment	500,000	
Accumulated amortization, factory equipment		$ 112,500
Accounts payable		162,500
Wages payable		
Income taxes payable		
Common shares		397,000
Retained earnings		418,000
Sales		1,562,500
Raw materials purchases	625,000	
Direct labour	232,500	
Indirect labour	87,500	
Factory utilities	67,500	
Repairs, factory equipment	15,000	
Amortization of factory equipment		
Selling expenses	162,500	
General and administrative expenses	125,000	
Income taxes expense		
Total	$2,652,500	$2,652,500

The following adjusting entries need to be made:

a. Amortization on the factory equipment for the year is $75,000.
b. Accrued direct labour wages are $17,500.
c. Accrued indirect labour wages are $5,000.
d. Accrued income taxes are estimated to be $80,000.

The raw materials ending inventory was $210,000. These facts were known about the other ending inventories:

	Materials Cost per Unit	Labour Cost per Unit	Units
Goods in process	$25.00	$10.00	2,500
Finished goods	40.00	22.50	6,000

Required

1. Present the prescribed adjusting entries.
2. Determine the total adjusted overhead cost, the total adjusted direct labour cost, and the overhead cost to direct labour cost ratio.
3. Determine the cost of the ending inventories of goods in process and finished goods.
4. Present the closing entries.

Check Figure Ending finished goods inventory, $510,000

Alternate Problems

Problem 22-1A
Preparing manufacturing and income statements

LO 2

The following alphabetical list of items was taken from the adjusted trial balance and other 1999 records of Vacation Home Building, Inc. before the year-end closing entries were recorded:

Advertising expense	$ 16,200
Amortization expense, office equipment	6,750
Amortization expense, selling equipment	8,100
Amortization of factory equipment	28,350
Direct labour	450,000
Factory supervision	97,200
Factory supplies used	4,850
Factory utilities	30,000
Income taxes expense	109,350
Indirect labour	47,250
Inventories:	
Raw materials, January 1	132,300
Raw materials, December 31	136,350
Goods in process, January 1	10,000
Goods in process, December 31	11,250
Finished goods, January 1	141,750
Finished goods, December 31	113,400
Miscellaneous production costs	6,750
Office salaries expense	56,700
Raw materials purchases	695,250
Rent expense, office space	18,900
Rent expense, selling space	21,600
Rent on factory building	74,800
Maintenance, factory equipment	24,300
Sales	4,000,000
Sales discounts	45,900
Sales salaries expense	236,250
Transportation-in on raw materials	20,250

Required

Preparation component:

Check Figure Cost of goods manufactured, $1,473,700

1. Prepare a manufacturing statement and an income statement for the company. The income statement should present separate categories for (a) selling expenses and (b) general and administrative expenses.

Analysis component:

2. Review what you learned about merchandise turnover (Chapter 7) and compute the turnover rates for Vacation's raw materials and finished goods inventories. Then, discuss some possible reasons for the differences between the turnover rates for the two inventories.

Problem 22-2A
Recording manufacturing costs and preparing financial reports

LO 1, 4, 5, 6, 7

The following information refers to the job order manufacturing activities of Cowan Company for April:

The March 31 inventory of raw materials was $16,000. Raw materials purchases during April were $60,000. Factory payroll cost during April was $68,000. Overhead costs incurred during the month of April were:

Indirect materials	$ 6,000
Indirect labour	4,000
Factory rent	24,000
Factory utilities	22,000
Factory equipment amortization	25,000

The predetermined overhead rate was 130% of the direct labour cost. Costs allocated to the three jobs worked on during April were:

	Job 114	Job 115	Job 116
Balances at March 31:			
Direct materials	$4,000	$6,000	
Direct labour	2,000	2,200	
Applied overhead	2,600	2,860	
Costs during April:			
Direct materials	10,000	30,000	$16,000
Direct labour	16,000	28,000	22,000
Applied overhead	?	?	?
Status at April 30	Finished (sold)	Finished (unsold)	In process

Job 114 was sold for $100,000 cash during April.

Required

Preparation component:

1. Determine the total of each manufacturing cost incurred for April (direct labour, direct materials, allocated overhead), and the total cost assigned to each of the three jobs (including the balances from March 31).
2. Present journal entries for the month to record:
   a. The materials purchases (on credit), the factory payroll (paid with cash), and the actual overhead costs, including indirect materials and indirect labour. (The factory rent and utilities were paid with cash.)
   b. The assignment of direct materials, direct labour, and applied overhead costs to the Goods in Process Inventory.
   c. The transfer of Jobs 114 and 115 to the Finished Goods Inventory.
   d. The cost of Job 114 in the Cost of Goods Sold account.
   e. The revenue from the sale of Job 114.
   f. The assignment of any underapplied or overapplied overhead to the Cost of Goods Sold account. (The amount is not material.)
3. Prepare a manufacturing statement for April (use a single-line presentation for direct materials and show the details of overhead cost). Also, present a calculation of gross profit for April and show how the inventories would be presented on the April 30 balance sheet.

Analysis component:

4. When the over- or underapplied overhead adjustment is made, you are closing Factory Overhead to Cost of Goods Sold. Discuss how this adjustment impacts business decision making regarding individual jobs or batches.

Problem 22-3A
Source documents, journal entries and preparing financial statements
LO 2, 5, 6, 7, 8

Following is the trial balance of the Velcro Company as generated by the computer system on the morning of December 31, 1998. Bruce Moore, the company's accountant, knows that something is wrong with the trial balance because it does not show any balance for the goods in process inventory and it still shows balances in the Factory Payroll and Factory Overhead accounts:

Cash	$ 40,000	
Accounts receivable	80,000	
Raw materials inventory	24,000	
Goods in process inventory	-0-	
Finished goods	50,000	
Prepaid rent	4,000	
Accounts payable		$ 16,000
Notes payable		30,000
Common shares		60,000
Retained earnings		33,800
Sales		250,000
Cost of goods sold	140,000	
Factory payroll	20,000	
Factory overhead	9,800	
Miscellaneous expenses	22,000	
Total	$389,800	$389,800

After a few moments of searching a cluttered in-box, Moore finds six source documents that need to be processed to bring the accounting records up to date:

Materials requisition 94-231:	$ 5,000	direct materials to Job 603
Materials requisition 94-232:	8,000	direct materials to Job 604
Materials requisition 94-233:	1,500	indirect materials
Labour time ticket 765:	6,000	direct labour to Job 603
Labour time ticket 766:	12,000	direct labour to Job 604
Labour time ticket 777:	2,000	indirect labour

Jobs 603 and 604 are the only units in process at the end of the year. The predetermined overhead application rate is 80% of direct labour cost.

Required

Preparation component:

1. Use the information on the six source documents to prepare journal entries to assign the following costs:
   a. Direct materials costs to goods in process inventory.
   b. Direct labour costs to goods in process inventory.
   c. Overhead costs to goods in process inventory.
   d. Indirect materials costs to the overhead account.
   e. Indirect labour costs to the overhead account.
2. Determine the new balance of the Factory Overhead account after making the entries in requirement 1. Determine whether there is under- or overapplied overhead for the year. If so, prepare the appropriate adjusting entry to close the overhead account, assuming that the amount is not material.
3. Prepare a revised trial balance.
4. Prepare an income statement for 1998 and a balance sheet as of December 31, 1998.

Analysis component:

5. Assume that the $1,500 indirect materials on materials requisition 94-233 should have been direct materials charged to Job 604. Without providing specific calculations, describe what impact this error would have on Velcro's 1998 income statement and balance sheet.

Problem 22-4A
Source documents and journal entries in job order cost accounting
LO 7, 8

Back Pack Company's predetermined overhead application rate during a recent month was 90% of direct labour. The company's activities related to manufacturing during the month were:

a. Purchased raw materials on account, $57,000.
b. Paid factory wages with cash, $99,750.
c. Paid miscellaneous factory overhead costs with cash, $11,250.
d. Materials requisitions for the month show that the following materials were used on jobs and indirectly:

Job 487	$13,500
Job 488	9,000
Job 489	12,000
Job 490	10,500
Job 491	1,500
Total direct materials	$46,500
Indirect materials	3,750
Total materials used	$50,250

e. Labour time tickets for the month show the following labour was used on jobs and indirectly:

Job 487	$16,500
Job 488	19,500
Job 489	25,500
Job 490	18,000
Job 491	7,500
Total direct labour	$87,000
Indirect labour	12,750
Total	$99,750

f. Jobs 487, 489 and 490 were completed and overhead was allocated to them with the predetermined overhead application rate of 90% of direct labour cost.
g. Jobs 487, 489 and 490 were transferred to finished goods.
h. Jobs 487 and 489 were sold on account for a total price of $225,000.
i. Overhead costs incurred during the month were as follows. (Credit Prepaid Insurance for the expired factory insurance.)

Amortization of factory building	$24,750
Amortization of factory equipment	18,750
Expired factory insurance	2,250
Accrued property taxes payable	5,250

j. At the end of the month, overhead is applied to the goods in process (Jobs 488 and 491) using the predetermined rate of 90% of direct labour cost.

Required

1. Prepare general journal entries to record the events and transactions *a* through *j*.
2. Set up T-accounts for each of the following general ledger accounts, each of which started the month with a zero balance. Then, post the journal entries to these T-accounts and determine the balance of each account:

Raw Materials Inventory	Factory Payroll
Goods in Process Inventory	Factory Overhead
Finished Goods Inventory	Cost of Goods Sold

3. Prepare a job cost sheet for each job worked on during the month. Use the following simplified form of the job cost sheet:

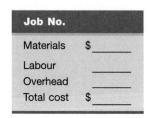

Job No.	
Materials	$______
Labour	______
Overhead	______
Total cost	$______

4. Prepare a schedule showing the total cost of each job in process and proving that the sum of the costs equals the Goods in Process Inventory account balance. Prepare similar schedules for the finished goods inventory and the cost of goods sold.

Problem 22-5A
Allocating overhead using predetermined overhead application rate
LO 4, 7, 8

In December 1998, Watson Company's accountant estimated the next years direct labour as the cost of 40 persons, working an average of 1,500 hours each at an average wage rate of $50 per hour. The accountant also estimated the following manufacturing overhead costs for 1999:

Indirect labour	$540,000
Factory supervision	450,000
Rent on factory building	360,000
Factory computer system	200,000
Factory insurance expired	60,000
Amortization of factory equipment	300,000
Repairs, factory equipment	180,000
Factory supplies used	110,000
Miscellaneous production costs	200,000
Total	2,400,000

At the end of 1999, the cost records showed the company had incurred $2,200,000 of actual overhead costs. It had completed and sold five jobs with the following direct labour costs:

625	$300,000
626	225,000
627	975,000
628	240,000
629	375,000

In addition, Job 630 was in process at the end of the year and had been charged $75,000 for direct labour. The company's predetermined overhead application rate is based on direct labour cost.

Required

1. Determine:
   a. The predetermined overhead application rate for 1999.
   b. The total overhead cost applied to each of the six jobs during 1999.
   c. The over- or underapplied overhead at year-end.

2. Assuming that the amount of over- or underapplied overhead is not material, prepare the appropriate journal entry to close the Factory Overhead account at the end of 1999.

Problem 22-6A
Recording manufacturing transactions; subsidiary records
LO 5, 6, 7

If the working papers that accompany this text are not available, do not attempt to solve this problem.

The Natkin Company manufactures special variations of its product (called a megatron) in response to orders from its customers. On March 1, the company had no inventories of goods in process or finished goods but held the following raw materials:

Material M	150 units @	$ 40 =		$6,000
Material R	50 units @	160 =		8,000
Paint	20 units @	20 =		400
Total				$14,400

On March 3, the company began working on two megatrons: Job 450 for Ancira Company and Job 451 for Montero, Inc.

Required

Follow the instructions given in the list of activities below and then complete the statements provided in the working papers.

a. Purchased raw materials on credit and recorded the following information from the receiving reports and invoices:

Receiving Report No. 20, Material M, 150 units at $40 each.
Receiving Report No. 21, Material R, 200 units at $160 each.

(*Instructions: Record the purchases with a single general journal entry and post it to the appropriate general ledger T-accounts, using the transaction letter to identify the entries. Also, enter the receiving report information on the materials ledger cards.*)

b. Requisitioned the following raw materials for production:

Requisition No. 223, for Job 450, 60 units of Material M.
Requisition No 224, for Job 450, 100 units of Material R.
Requisition No. 225, for Job 451, 30 units of Material M.
Requisition No. 226, for Job 451, 75 units of Material R.
Requisition No. 227, for 10 units of paint.

(*Instructions: Enter the amounts for the direct materials requisitions only on the materials ledger cards and the job cost sheets. Enter the indirect material amount on the raw materials ledger card and record a debit to the Indirect Materials account in the subsidiary Factory Overhead Ledger. Do not record a general journal entry at this time.*)

c. Employees turned in the following time tickets for work in March:

Time tickets Nos. 1 to 10 for direct labour on Job 450, $24,000.
Time tickets Nos. 11 to 20 for direct labour on Job 451, $20,000.
Time tickets Nos. 21 to 24 for equipment repairs, $4,000.

(*Instructions: Record the direct labour reported on the time tickets only on the job cost sheets and debit the indirect labour to the Indirect Labour account in the subsidiary Factory Overhead Ledger. Do not record a general journal entry at this time.*)

d. The company paid cash for the following items during the month:

Factory payroll, $48,000.
Miscellaneous overhead items, $47,000.

(Instructions: Record the payments with general journal entries and then post them to the general ledger accounts. Also record a debit in the Miscellaneous Overhead account in the subsidiary Factory Overhead Ledger.)

e. Finished Job 450 and transferred it to the warehouse. The company assigns overhead to each job with a predetermined overhead application rate equal to 120% of direct labour cost.

(Instructions: Enter the allocated overhead on the cost sheet for Job 450, fill in the cost summary section of the cost sheet, and then mark the cost sheet as "Finished." Next, prepare a journal entry to record the job's completion and transfer to finished goods, and then post it to the general ledger accounts.)

f. Delivered Job 450 and accepted the customers' promise to pay $130,000 within 30 days.

(Instructions: Prepare general journal entries to record the sale of Job 450 and the cost of goods sold. Post them to the general ledger accounts.)

g. At the end of the month, used the predetermined rate to assign overhead cost to Job 451, based on the direct labour cost used on the job up to that date.

(Instructions: Enter the overhead on the job cost sheet but do not make a general journal entry at this time.)

h. Recorded the total direct and indirect materials costs as reported on all the requisitions for the month.

(Instructions: Prepare a general journal entry to record these costs, and post it to the general ledger accounts.)

i. Recorded the total direct and indirect labour costs as reported on all the time tickets for the month.

(Instructions: Prepare a general journal entry to record these costs, and post it to the general ledger accounts.)

j. Recorded the total overhead costs applied to jobs.

(Instructions: Prepare a general journal entry to record the application of these costs, and post it to the general ledger accounts.)

k. Determine the balances in the raw materials inventory, goods in process inventory, and factory overhead accounts.

l. Determine if the balance of the factory overhead account is over- or underapplied.

Problem 22-7A[A]
Adjusting and closing entries, allocating overhead costs
LO 3, 4, 10–13

The unadjusted trial balance of the Titus Company as of December 31, 1999 is shown at the top of page 1099.

The following adjusting entries need to be made:

a. Amortization on the factory equipment for the year is $75,000.

b. Accrued direct labour wages are $17,500.

c. Accrued indirect labour wages are $5,000.

d. Accrued income taxes are estimated to be $70,000.

The raw materials ending inventory was $210,000. These facts were known about the other ending inventories:

	Materials Cost per Unit	Labour Cost per Unit	Units
Goods in process	$25.00	$10.00	2,500
Finished goods	30.00	32.50	6,000

Cash	$ 162,500	
Accounts receivable	250,000	
Raw materials inventory	300,000	
Goods in process inventory	100,000	
Finished goods inventory	225,000	
Factory equipment	500,000	
Accumulated amortization, factory equipment		$ 112,500
Accounts payable		162,500
Wages payable		
Income taxes payable		
Common shares		397,000
Retained earnings		618,000
Sales		1,562,500
Raw materials purchases	625,000	
Direct labour	232,500	
Indirect labour	87,500	
Factory utilities	67,500	
Repairs, factory equipment	15,000	
Amortization of factory equipment		
Selling expenses	162,500	
General and administrative expenses	125,000	
Income taxes expense		
Total	$2,852,500	$2,852,500

Required

1. Present the prescribed adjusting entries.
2. Determine the total adjusted overhead cost, the total adjusted direct labour cost, and the overhead cost to direct labour cost ratio.
3. Determine the cost of the ending inventories of goods in process and finished goods.
4. Present the closing entries.

Check Figure Ending finished goods inventory, $570,000

Analytical and Review Problems

A & R 22-1

Klapstein Watch Company has recently automated its production line. "This automation is great," said Jack Duffy, the company production superintendent. "It has enabled us to reduce our throughput time by about 35 %. We have been able to rid ourselves of many costs that do not add value to our product.

"I agree," said Ray Klapstein, the company president. "Let's keep in mind that manufacturing time consists of process time, inspection time, move time, and wait time, and it is only process time that adds value to our product."

"I guess that is why the other costs are called nonvalue-added activities?" mumbled Adam Upp, a trainee in the accounting department. Adam is a little overwhelmed at how the new technology seems to be affecting accounting. Adam is unclear on how total costs flow through the system with a just-in-time system in comparison with the traditional job order system. "I would like to know more about how JIT actually saves costs and how it might affect the accounting system."

Required

Explain to Adam how JIT can save costs and speculate as to how the accounting might differ from traditional job order accounting.

A & R 22-2

The president of Vernon Company has hired you as the new accountant. He has asked you to prepare the financial statements for the year ended December 31, 1998, based on the adjusted trial balance that follows:

VERNON COMPANY
Adjusted Trial Balance
December 31, 1998

Cash	$ 50,000	
Accounts receivable	58,440	
Raw materials inventory	4,200	
Goods in process inventory	28,500	
Finished goods inventory	47,600	
Store equipment	73,780	
Accumulated amortization, store equipment		$ 27,080
Accounts payable		25,200
Long-term notes payable		69,600
Common shares		71,600
Retained earnings		63,940
Sales		193,000
Sales returns and allowances	2,500	
Cost of goods sold	138,000	
Factory payroll	5,000	
Factory overhead	2,500	
Miscellaneous expenses	39,900	
	$450,420	$450,420

The president has informed you that this trial balance was prepared by the previous accountant and is supposedly ready to be used in preparing the statements. He has also told you that Vernon uses a job order cost accounting system and assigns factory overhead using a predetermined overhead rate that relates overhead to direct labour.

After taking a brief look at the adjusted trial balance, you suspect that some items of information for the period were not processed, or were processed incorrectly, and that you need some time to research the problem. Explain the basis of your suspicions to the president and describe the nature of the entries that will probably be required to correct the adjusted trial balance.

BEYOND THE NUMBERS

Reporting in Action

Magna Corporation continues to grow and expand its auto parts business. According to Magna's annual report, much of this growth comes from international sales.

Required

1. Predict the type of costs that will increase as a percent of sales with expansion in international sales.

2. Explain why you think the types of costs identified for part 1 will increase for Magna. (Hint: Think about why a cost increase is anticipated in the product and/or period cost category as international sales increase. You can begin to develop answers by evaluating the gross margin percent for the years reported in their annual reports.)

Comparative Analysis

The management of both **Budd Canada** and **Magna International** want to know the importance of a "just in time" inventory system for their operating cash flows. The following information is provided from their balance sheets:

	Budd Canada		Magna	
	Sept. 1997	Sept. 1996	July 1997	July 1996
Finished goods	4,078,077	4,614,900	99,300,000	81,500,000
Work-in-process.	22,068,252	21,953,267	97,300,000	125,900,000
Raw materials	3,125,960	2,743,326	189,800,000	149,500,000
Tooling			282,900,000	169,200,000
Total	29,272,289	29,311,493	669,300,000	526,100,000

Required

1. Identify the impact on operating cash flows (increase or decrease) for changes in inventory levels (increasing or decreasing) for each year reported.
2. What impact would a JIT inventory system have on both Budd's and Magna's level of raw materials on hand and their operating cash flows? Link your answer to your response to part 1.
3. Would the move to a JIT system be a one time or recurring impact on operating cash flow?

Ethics Challenge

An accounting professional needs at least two skill sets. The first and most obvious is to be technically competent. Knowing how to capture, manage and report information are valuable and necessary skills. Being able to anticipate management's and employees' bias is the second skill. Knowing how a person is compensated, for instance, helps an accounting professional anticipate information biases from that person.

Required

Draw on these two skills and write a memo to the chief financial officer regarding the practice of allocating overhead in your company. Information about your company and situation follows:

Background

Your company sells portable housing to general contractors and the Nova Scotia Government. Jobs sold to general contractors are won on a bid basis. A contractor will ask for three bids from different manufactures, for example, eight portable housing units for an upcoming road construction project. The combination of low bid and high quality usually wins the job. Jobs sold to the Nova Scotia Government are bid on a cost-plus basis. That is, the selling price is determined by adding all costs to a job and then adding on a profit based on cost at a specified percent, such as 10%. The Nova Scotia Government buys products from you because the production facility is in an economically deprived section of Nova Scotia. As the accounting professional, you have observed some very unusual dollar values allocated between general contractor jobs and Nova Scotia Government jobs. The amount of factory overhead allocated to Nova Scotia Government jobs is higher than that allocated to general contract jobs. You are trying to understand the problem in allocating costs and why it exists.

Communicating in Practice

You are preparing for a second interview with a growth manufacturing company. The company is impressed with your credentials and experience, but has indicated they have a number of other qualified applicants. You anticipate this second interview will necessitate that you exhibit how you can offer something special over other candidates. You learn the company currently uses a general accounting system and is not satisfied with the lack of timeliness of its information. The company manufactures holiday decoration and display items. They produce different items at different times of the year for stock as well as products that are custom designed to meet special orders for commercial window displays. To show an understanding of the business and your ability to improve the operation, you plan to recommend they consider using a cost accounting system.

Required

In preparation for the interview you are required to prepare notes outlining:

1. The cost accounting system recommendation and why it is suitable for this business;
2. How your recommendation improves the available information compared to the system currently used;
3. A general description of the documents this system requires; and
4. How the documents are used to facilitate the operation of the system.

Taking It to the Net

Many manufacturing companies use "Job Order Costing" computer software to help measure the cost of individual jobs or batches. As the consultant for a newly established boat manufacturer, you need to find a good job order costing software package.

Required

Visit the Web site **http://www.classic.on.ca/** or search the Web to find a Canadian site that promotes job order costing.. Prepare a memo to the chief operating officer of the company reporting relevant information about job order costing software and any recommendation.

Teamwork in Action

The following alphabetical list of items is taken from the adjusted trial balance and other records of Make-it-Better Company before the year-end closing entries are recorded:

Advertising expense	$ 15,300
Amortization expense, office equipment	7,000
Amortization expense, selling equipment	8,000
Amortization of factory equipment	26,000
Direct labour	520,600
Factory supervision	98,000
Factory supplies used	12,600
Factory utilities	29,000
Indirect labour	48,000
Inventories:	
Raw materials, January 1	142,000
Raw materials, December 31	134,500
Goods in process, January 1	12,700
Goods in process, December 31	11,250
Finished goods, January 1	131,000
Finished goods, December 31	103,200
Miscellaneous production costs	6,800
Office salaries expense	60,700
Raw materials purchases	698,000
Rent expense, office space	16,900
Rent expense, selling space	20,600
Rent on factory building	63,800
Repairs, factory equipment	22,300
Sales	2,620,000
Sales discounts	46,000
Sales salaries expense	229,000

Required

1. *Each* member of the team is to assume the responsibility for computing *one* of the amounts listed below. You are not to duplicate your teammates work. Get necessary amounts from a teammate. Each member is to explain their computation to the team in preparation for reporting to the class.
   a. Materials used
   b. Factory overhead
   c. Total manufacturing costs of period
   d. Total cost of goods in process during period
   e. Cost of goods manufactured
2. Check your cost of goods manufactured with the instructor. If correct, proceed to part 3.
3. *Each* member of the team is to assume the responsibility for computing *one* of the amounts listed below. You are not to duplicate your teammates work. Get necessary amounts from a teammate. Each member is to explain their computation to the team in preparation for reporting to the class.
   a. Net Sales
   b. Cost of goods sold
   c. Gross profit
   d. Total operating expenses
   e. Net income or loss before taxes

Hitting the Road

Job order costing is frequently used by builders. For example, one residential building contractor keeps a record of direct cost and applies overhead to single-family homes in a housing development project.

Required

1. In teams of two or three you are to prepare a job order cost sheet for a condo, duplex and single-family home under construction in a real estate development project. List four materials, labour and other direct costs. Write down how the team thinks overhead should be applied to a condo, duplex and single-family home.
2. Contact a builder and compare your job order cost sheet to the job cost sheet of this builder. If possible, speak to the accountant for that company.

Business Break

Managing raw materials entering the production process is a challenging and crucial task for a company. Read the article "Porsche Is Back—And Then Some" in the September 15, 1997 issue of *Business Week* and discuss how Wendelin Wiedeking used supply management at Porsche.

Required

1. In groups of three discuss how Wiedeking saved Porsche.
2. Discuss what Wiedeking accomplished in comparison to what you observe in a successful grocery store.

23 CHAPTER

Process Cost Accounting

A Look Back

Chapter 21 introduced managerial accounting, described cost concepts, and discussed modern manufacturing management principles. Chapter 22 introduced the manufacturing statement and how we account for cost flows. We also explained job order costing—an important cost accounting system.

A Look at This Chapter

This chapter focuses on how we measure and account for costs in process production businesses. We explain process production, describe how to assign costs to processes, and compute cost per equivalent unit for a process.

A Look Forward

Chapter 24 describes managerial accounting reports useful in directing a company's activities. We explain how to allocate factory overhead costs to different products and describe the activity-based costing method of overhead allocation.

Chapter Outline

Tea Time

Niagara Falls, ON—Christine Butler, fresh out of college with a business degree, recently joined **Tasty Tea**, a processor and distributor of tea. Tasty Tea offers 15 different blends of tea to gourmet shops in one 500-gram bag. After finishing a two-week training period, all new employees such as Butler must write a detailed report on Tasty Tea's production process in making tea. "The company's expectations for us are high, and the competition is fierce," say Butler. The report must identify the flow of information on product costs for Tasty Tea and estimate total costs.

Butler's report identified three major processes: drying tea leaves, blending the different teas, and packaging the product. She explains the drying and packaging processes are highly automated and computer controlled. But, the blending process is more labour intensive. When Butler looked over her finished report, she was satisfied it covered all important processes and flows with one exception. "I just couldn't figure out how to come up with the cost of a kilogram of tea," says Butler. "It's a simple concept, but implementing it was tough." Butler knew this cost estimate was crucial for setting selling prices and planning operations.

Butler recalled from her training course that companies with continuous processing, such as Tasty Tea, must use a different costing system as compared to custom manufacturers. She eventually pursued colleagues and additional readings for help with process costing. "It took me about 40 hours of work to get my estimate," says Butler, "and I'm still not entirely sure of it." Using both process cost accounting methods and process cost summaries, she finally got her estimate. Adds Butler, "And I thought school was tough!"

Learning Objectives

LO 1 Explain process operations and how they differ from job order operations.

LO 2 Compare process cost accounting and job order cost accounting systems.

LO 3 Record the flow of direct materials costs in a process cost accounting system.

LO 4 Record the flow of direct labour costs in a process cost accounting system.

LO 5 Record the flow of factory overhead costs in a process cost accounting system.

LO 6 Define equivalent units and explain their use in process cost accounting.

LO 7 Compute equivalent units produced in a period.

LO 8 Explain the four steps in accounting for production activity in a period.

LO 9 Define a process cost summary and describe its purposes.

LO 10 Prepare a process cost summary.

LO 11 Record the transfer of goods between departments.

LO 12 Record the transfer of completed goods to Finished Goods Inventory and Cost of Goods Sold.

LO 13 Analyze cost per equivalent unit with and without spoiled units of production.

CHAPTER PREVIEW

The type of product or service a company offers determines its cost accounting system. We focused on job order costing in Chapter 22. Companies use job order costing to account for manufacturing when each product or job consists of one unit (or a group of units) that is uniquely designed to meet the requirements of a particular customer. Each unit, or group of units, is a distinct product or job requiring unique applications of material, labour and overhead. We also explained that not all products are manufactured in this way. Many products carry standard designs where one unit of product is no different than any other unit. This type of system often produces large numbers of products on a continuous basis, period after period. All units pass through similar manufacturing steps or processes. In this chapter we describe how to use a process cost accounting system to account for these types of products. We explain how manufacturing costs are accumulated for each process and then assigned to units passing through processes. This knowledge helps in understanding the cost of each process and in finding ways to reduce this cost and improve processes.

Process Manufacturing Operations

LO1 Explain process operations and how they differ from job order operations.

There are many manufacturers engaged in continuous processing of similar, often called *homogenous*, products. **Process manufacturing,** also called *process production*, is the mass production of products in a sequence of steps. This means products pass through a series of sequential processes.

Petroleum refining is a common example of a process production system. Crude oil passes through a series of steps before it is processed into three grades of petroleum. The assembly line at the Ford plant in Oakville, Ontario, resembles a process production system. An important characteristic of a process production system is its high level of standardization. This is necessary if the system is to produce large volumes of products. Other examples of products manufactured in a process manufacturing system are carpeting, hand tools, personal computers, furniture, skis, television sets, compact disks, building supplies (lumber, doors, paint, etc.), greeting cards, calculators, and small pleasure boats. **Michelin**, for instance, uses a process manufacturing system and a process cost accounting system for a portion of its operations. Process operations also extend to services. Examples include mail sorting at **Canada Post** and order processing in large mail-order firms. The common feature in these service organizations is that operations are performed in a sequential manner using a series of standardized processes.

Each of these examples of products and services involve operations having a series of processesor steps. Each process involves a different set of activities. A manufacturing operation, for instance, that processes chemicals, may include the four steps as shown in Exhibit 23.1

Exhibit 23.1

Processing of Chemicals

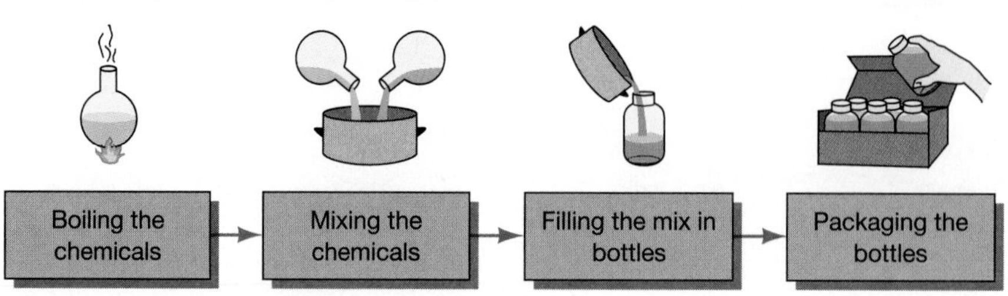

Comparing Job Order and Process Production

LO 2 Compare process cost accounting and job order cost accounting systems.

Important features of both job order and process production systems are shown in Exhibit 23.2. It is important to note that while we often describe job order and process operations with manufacturing examples, they also apply to service companies. In a job order costing system the measurement focus is on the individual job or batch. In a process costing system the measurement focus is on the process itself and the standardized units produced.

Exhibit 23.2

Features of Job Order and Process Production Systems

Job Order Manufacturing Systems	Process Production Systems
• Custom orders	• Repetitive production
• Heterogeneous products	• Homogenous products
• Low production volume	• High production volume
• High product flexibility	• Low product flexibility
• Low to medium standardization	• High standardization

Did You Know?

Mix and Match

A recent survey of 155 manufacturing companies showed 41 (26.5%) are organized as predominantly job order systems and 13 (8.4%) as predominantly process production systems. In addition, of these 54 companies using either job order or process production, 30 (55.6%) of these said they are adopting or using just-in-time manufacturing principles. [Source: Lindsay, M. and S. Kalagnanam, *The Adoption of Just-In-Time Production Systems in Canada and Their Association with Management Control Practices*, Hamilton, Ontario: The Society of Management Accountants of Canada, 1993.]

Organization of Process Manufacturing Operations

In a process manufacturing operation, each process is identified as a separate *production department, workstation*, or *work centre*, and a manager is usually responsible for one or more processes. With the exception of the first department or process, each receives the output from the prior department as a partially processed product. Depending on the nature of the process, direct labour, manufacturing

Exhibit 23.3

Manufacturing Operation with Parallel and Sequential Processes

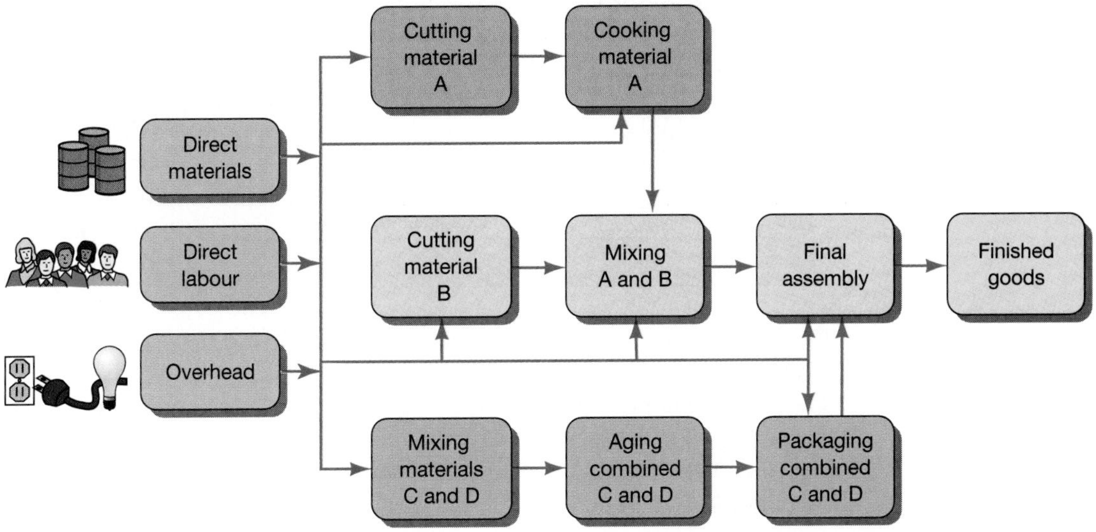

overhead, and, perhaps, additional direct materials are combined to move the product further toward completion. Only the last department in the series produces finished goods ready for sale to customers.

Most process manufacturing operations are more complex than the one shown in Exhibit 23.1. For example, Exhibit 23.3 shows an operation in which components of a final product are manufactured in three parallel processes and then combined at different stages of production. In addition to the parallel processes, many manufacturing operations involve hundreds of different components and related production processes.

GenX Company—An Illustration

We look at **GenX Company** to provide a basis for illustrating process manufacturing. GenX produces Profen, an over-the-counter pain reliever for athletes. GenX sells Profen to wholesale distributors who in turn sell it to retailers. Profen is produced in two steps. Step one uses a grinding process to pulverize blocks of its active ingredient, Profelene. Step two mixes the resulting powder with flavourings and preservatives, and molds it into Profen tablets. This process also packages the Profen tablets.

Exhibit 23.4 shows a summary floor plan of the GenX factory, which has five rooms:

- *Storeroom*, where materials are received and then distributed in response to requisitions.
- *Production support office*, used by administrative and maintenance employees who support manufacturing operations.
- Employees' *locker rooms*, where workers change from street clothes into uniforms before working in the factory.
- *Production floor*, divided into two areas for use by the grinding and mixing departments.
- *Warehouse*, where finished products are stored before being shipped to wholesalers.

Exhibit 23.4

Floor Plan of GenX's Factory

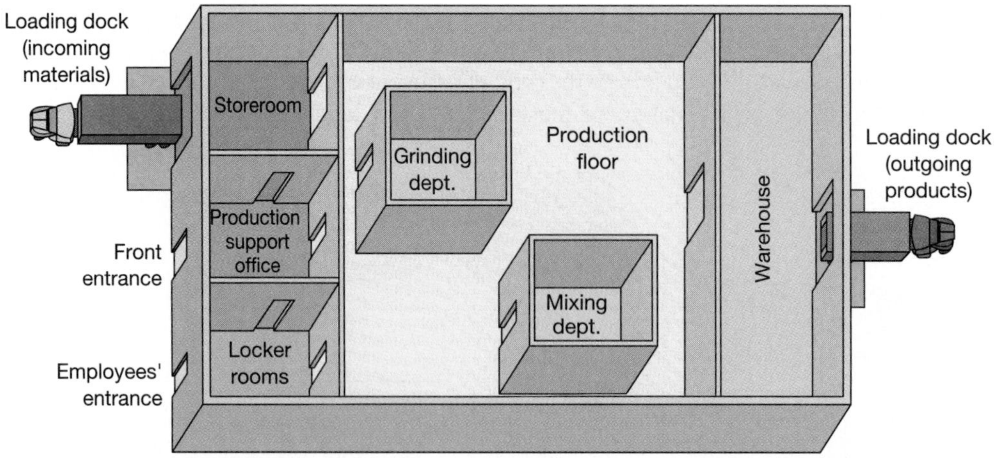

Even though GenX's manufacturing process is fairly simple, its factory can support five or more managers as shown in Exhibit 23.5.

The first step in process manufacturing is the decision to produce a product. Management must determine the types and quantities of materials and labour needed and then schedule the work for departments. Based on these plans, production begins.

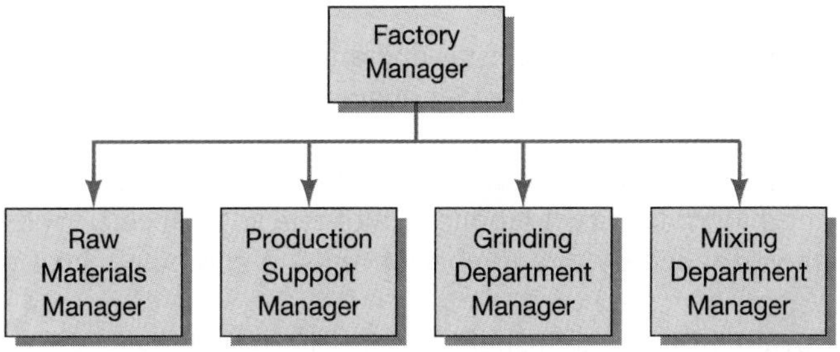

Exhibit 23.5

Partial Organization Chart of GenX's Factory

The flowchart at the top of Exhibit 23.6 shows the production steps for GenX. The table at the bottom of the exhibit summarizes GenX's manufacturing inventories at the beginning of April 1998, the manufacturing costs GenX incurred during April, and the application of these costs to the grinding and mixing departments. In the following sections, we explain how GenX uses a process cost accounting system to account for these costs.

Exhibit 23.6

Process Manufacturing Operations—GenX

A. Process Manufacturing Operations

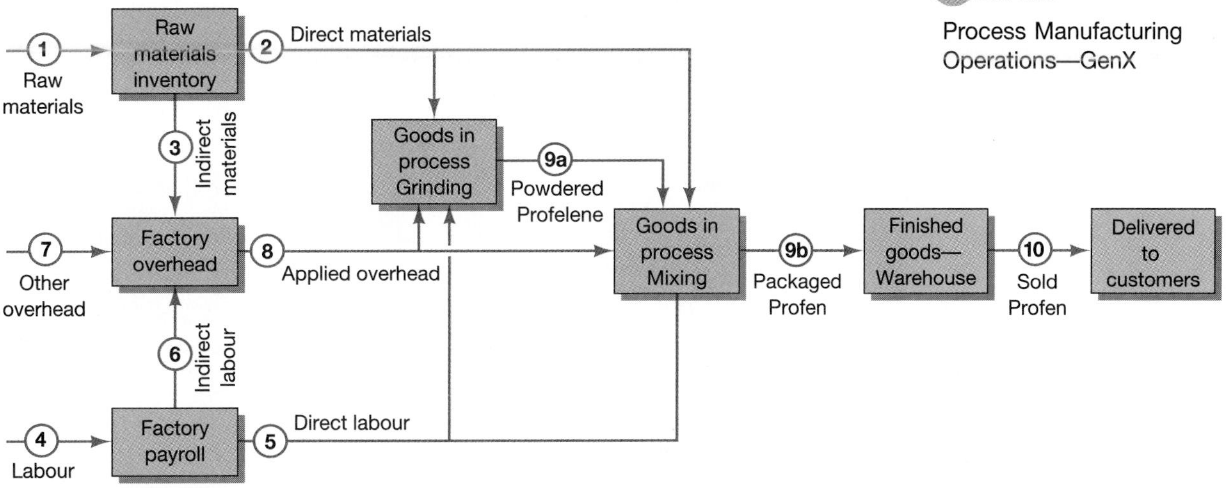

B. Manufacturing Costs During April 1998

	Raw Materials	Factory Payroll	Factory Overhead	Grinding Department	Mixing Department
Beginning balance	$4,000			$4,250	$3,520
Purchases and costs incurred	14,135	$14,020	$880		
Application of costs:					
Direct materials	(11,940)			9,900	2,040
Indirect materials	(1,195)		1,195		
Direct labour		(10,800)		5,700	5,100
Indirect labour		(3,220)	3,220		
Overhead applied			(5,295)	4,275	1,020

Flash back

1. A process manufacturing operation (a) is another name for a job order operation, (b) does not use the concepts of direct materials or direct labour, (c) assigns responsibility for each process to a manager.
2. Under what conditions is a process cost accounting system more suitable for measuring manufacturing costs than a job order cost accounting system?

Answers—p. 1132

Process Cost Accounting

Process and job order manufacturing operations are similar in that they both combine materials, labour, and other manufacturing overhead items in the process of producing products. Yet they differ in the way they are organized and managed. In job order operations, the job order cost accounting system assigns direct materials, direct labour, and overhead to specific jobs. The total job cost is then divided by the number of units to compute a cost per unit for that job.

By comparison, in a process manufacturing operation, the **process cost accounting system** assigns direct materials, direct labour, and overhead to specific manufacturing processes. The total costs associated with each process are then divided by the number of units passing through that process to determine the cost per equivalent unit (defined later in the chapter) for that process. The cost per equivalent unit for each process is summed for all processes to determine the total cost per unit of a product. We explain how to compute unit costs later in the chapter.

The focus of job order operations is on specific jobs while the focus of process operations is on the series of processes used to complete the production of the product. This difference is highlighted in Exhibit 23.7.

Exhibit 23.7

Job Order and Process Cost Accounting

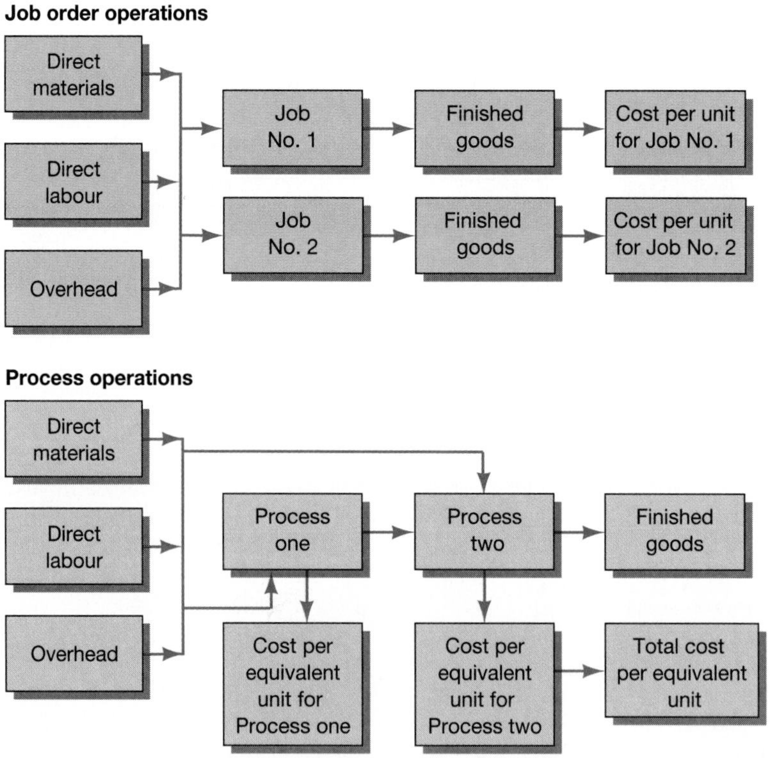

Direct and Indirect Costs in Process Cost Accounting

In Chapter 21, we explained that direct material and direct labour costs can be directly linked with specific units or batches of product. Other manufacturing costs that cannot be clearly associated with specific units or batches of product are defined as manufacturing overhead. Chapter 22 explained how the concepts of direct and indirect materials and labour are used in job order cost accounting. This means materials and labour used on jobs are charged to the jobs as direct costs. Materials and labour that contribute to manufacturing but that are not clearly associated with specific jobs are indirect costs and are allocated to jobs as manufacturing overhead.

Process cost accounting systems also use the concepts of direct and indirect manufacturing costs. Materials and labour that are clearly associated with specific manufacturing processes are assigned to those processes as direct costs. Materials and labour that are not clearly associated with a specific process are indirect costs and are assigned to overhead. Some costs classified as manufacturing overhead in a job order system may be classified as direct costs in process cost accounting. For example, amortization of a machine used entirely by one process is a direct cost of that process. The next three subsections explain the accounting for materials, labour and overhead costs in a process cost accounting system.

Did You Know?

Factory Smarts
Robots, computers, and online information are all common in today's factory. This means more is expected of today's factory workers. The ranks of manufacturers putting a majority of their workers through training programs are triple what they were a decade ago. Also, the percent of the roughly 20 million factory workers with a college education has jumped to 25% vs. 17% in 1985. And 19% have college degrees today, up from 16% a decade ago. [Source: *Business Week*, September 30, 1996.]

Accounting for Materials Costs

LO 3 Record the flow of direct materials costs in a process cost accounting system.

In Exhibit 23.6, arrow 1 reflects the arrival of materials at GenX's factory. These materials include Profelene, flavourings, preservatives, packaging supplies, and supplies for the production support office. GenX uses a perpetual inventory system and makes all purchases on credit. The entry to summarize the receipts of raw materials during April is:[1]

1.	Raw Materials Inventory	14,135	
	Accounts Payable		14,135
	Acquired materials on credit for use in the factory.		

The accounting department makes entries to record receipt of materials when it receives copies of receiving reports from the storeroom.

Arrow 2 in Exhibit 23.6 reflects the flow of direct materials to the grinding and mixing departments, where they are used in producing Profen. Most direct materials are physically combined into the finished product. But, in process cost accounting, direct materials include supplies used in a specific process because they can be clearly associated with that process.

As in a job order system, the manager of a process usually obtains material for use in the process by submitting a materials requisition to the raw materials storeroom manager. Yet, in some situations, materials move continuously from the raw materials inventory to a manufacturing process. **Coca-Cola Bottling**, for instance, uses a manufacturing process in which inventory moves through the system continuously. In these cases, a **materials consumption report** summarizes the materials used by a department during a reporting period and replaces materials requisitions.

[1] We omit the transaction date in the journal entries for brevity since each of the entries designated 1–10 are dated April 30.

The following entry records the use of direct materials by GenX's two production departments during April:

2.	Goods in Process Inventory—Grinding	9,900	
	Goods in Process Inventory—Mixing	2,040	
	Raw Materials Inventory		11,940
	To assign costs of direct materials used in the grinding and mixing departments.		

Two goods in process inventory accounts allow the costs incurred by each process to be separately accumulated. This entry does not increase or decrease the company's assets because it merely transfers costs from one asset account to two other asset accounts.

In Exhibit 23.6, arrow 3 shows the flow of indirect materials from the storeroom to factory overhead. These materials are not clearly associated with either the grinding or the mixing departments. They are used in support of production.

The following entry records the cost of indirect materials used by GenX during April:

3.	Factory Overhead	1,195	
	Raw Materials Inventory		1,195
	To record indirect materials used in April.		

After the entries for materials are posted, the Raw Materials Inventory account appears as shown in Exhibit 23.8.

Exhibit 23.8

Raw Materials Inventory Ledger Account

Date		Explanation	Debit	Credit	Balance
		Raw Materials Inventory			**Acct. No. 132**
1998					
Mar.	31	Beginning balance			4,000
Apr.	30	Materials purchases	14,135		18,135
	30	Direct materials usage		11,940	6,195
	30	Indirect materials usage		1,195	5,000

The April 30 balance sheet reports the balance of this account as a current asset.

Accounting for Labour Costs

Exhibit 23.6 shows the factory payroll cost for GenX reflected in arrow 4. Total labour cost of $14,020 is paid with cash and is recorded in the Factory Payroll account with this entry:

4.	Factory Payroll	14,020	
	Cash		14,020
	To record factory wages for April.		

LO 4 Record the flow of direct labour costs in a process cost accounting system.

This entry is triggered by time reports sent to the company's accountant from the two production departments and the production support office. For simplicity, we do not identify withholdings and additional payroll taxes for the employees.

In a process operation, the direct labour of a production department includes all labour used exclusively by that department, even if it is not applied to the product itself. If a production department, for instance, has a full-time manager and a full-time maintenance worker, their salaries are direct labour costs, not factory overhead.

Arrow 5 in Exhibit 23.6 shows GenX's use of direct labour in the grinding and mixing departments. The following entry transfers April's direct labour costs from the Factory Payroll account to the two goods in process accounts:

5.	Goods in Process Inventory—Grinding	5,700	
	Goods in Process Inventory—Mixing	5,100	
	Factory Payroll		10,800
	To assign costs of direct labour used in the grinding and mixing departments.		

Arrow 6 in Exhibit 23.6 reflects the indirect labour of GenX. These employees provide the clerical, maintenance, and other services that help the grinding and mixing departments produce Profen more efficiently. For example, they order materials, deliver them to the factory floor, repair equipment, operate and program computers used in production, keep payroll and other production accounting records, clean up, and move the finished goods to the warehouse. The following entry charges these indirect labour costs to factory overhead:

6.	Factory Overhead	3,220	
	Factory Payroll		3,220
	To record indirect labour as overhead.		

After these entries for labour are posted, the Factory Payroll account looks as shown in 23.9.

Exhibit 23.9

Factory Payroll Ledger Account

Factory Payroll					Acct. No. 530
Date		**Explanation**	**Debit**	**Credit**	**Balance**
1998					
Mar.	31	Beginning balance			-0-
Apr.	30	Total payroll for April	14,020		14,020
	30	Direct labour costs		10,800	3,220
	30	Indirect labour costs		3,220	-0-

This account is now closed and ready to receive entries for May.

Accounting for Factory Overhead

LO 5 Record the flow of factory overhead costs in a process cost accounting system.

Overhead costs other than indirect materials and indirect labour are reflected by arrow 7 in Exhibit 23.6. These overhead items include the costs of insuring manufacturing assets, renting the factory building, using factory utilities, and depreciating the equipment not directly related with a specific process. The following entry records these costs for the month of April:

7.	Factory Overhead	880	
	Prepaid Insurance		80
	Accrued Utilities Payable		200
	Cash		250
	Accumulated Amortization, Factory Equipment		350
	To record manufacturing overhead items incurred during April.		

After this entry is posted, the Factory Overhead account balance is $5,295. Total overhead cost for April includes indirect materials of $1,195, indirect labour of $3,220, and $880 of other overhead items.

Arrow 8 in Exhibit 23.6 reflects the application of factory overhead to the production departments. Recall from Chapters 21 and 22 that factory overhead is applied to products or jobs by relating overhead cost to another variable such as direct labour hours or machine hours used in production. Process cost systems also use predetermined application rates

In many situations, a single allocation basis such as direct labour hours fails to provide useful allocations. As a result, management may use different rates for different production departments. Based on an analysis of each department's operations, GenX applies overhead as shown in Exhibit 23.10.

Exhibit 23.10

Application of Factory Overhead

A. Predetermined Overhead Application Rates

Grinding department	75% of its direct labour cost
Mixing department	20% of its direct labour cost

B. Overhead Applied in April

Production Department	Direct Labour Cost	Predetermined Rate	Overhead Applied
Grinding	$5,700	75%	$4,275
Mixing	5,100	20	1,020
Total			$5,295

Judgment and Ethics

Budget Officer

You are working on identifying the direct and indirect costs of a new processing department containing several automated machines. The manager of this department instructs you to classify a majority of the costs as indirect to take advantage of the direct labour based overhead allocation method and be charged with a lower amount of overhead (owing to the small direct labour component within the department). You know this penalizes other departments who will then be hit with higher allocations. This means the performance ratings of managers in these other departments will suffer. What action(s) do you take?

Answer—p. 1132

GenX records these overhead applications with the following entry:

8.	Goods in Process Inventory—Grinding	4,275	
	Goods in Process Inventory—Mixing	1,020	
	Factory Overhead		5,295
	Allocated factory overhead costs to the grinding department at 75% of direct labour cost and to the mixing department at 20% of direct labour cost.		

After posting this entry, the Factory Overhead account looks as shown in Exhibit 23.11.

For GenX, the amount of overhead applied equals the actual overhead incurred during April. In most cases, using a predetermined overhead application rate nearly always leaves an overapplied or underapplied balance in the Factory Overhead account. At the end of the period, this overapplied or underapplied bal-

Factory Overhead				Acct. No. 540	
Date		**Explanation**	**Debit**	**Credit**	**Balance**
1998					
Mar.	31	Beginning balance			0
Apr.	30	Indirect materials	1,195		1,195
	30	Indirect labour costs	3,220		4,415
	30	Other overhead costs	880		5,295
	30	Applied to production depts.		5,295	0

Exhibit 23.11

Factory Overhead Ledger Account

ance should be either closed to the Cost of Goods Sold account or allocated among the cost of goods sold and the goods in process and finished goods inventories. Procedures for making this allocation are the same as that described in Chapter 22 for job order cost accounting systems.

Flash back

3. When Department X sends partially completed units to Department Y, the entry that records the transfer includes:
   a. A debit to Goods in Process Inventory—Department X.
   b. A debit to Goods in Process Inventory—Department Y.
   c. A credit to Goods in Process Inventory—Department Y.
4. What are the three categories of costs incurred by both job order and process manufacturing operations?
5. How many Goods in Process Inventory accounts are needed in a process cost accounting system?

Answers—p. 1132

Full Service Accounting

Many service companies use process departments to perform specific tasks for consumers. Hospitals, for instance, have radiology and physical therapy facilities with special equipment and trained employees. When patients need services, they are processed through proper departments and receive prescribed care. In a different setting, **MT&T** uses a system similar to process cost accounting to accumulate costs for services such as directory assistance. Service companies need cost accounting information as much as manufacturers. Managers use information about the cost of providing services to plan future operations, to control costs, and to determine charges to customers. All the basic techniques of process cost accounting are applied equally well to service operations.

Did You Know?

Computing and Using Equivalent Units of Production

In the previous sections, we explained how manufacturing costs for a period are accumulated in separate Goods in Process accounts for each manufacturing process. But we have not explained the flows labelled 9a, 9b, and 10 in Exhibit 23.6. These arrows reflect the transfer of products from the grinding department to the mixing department, from the mixing department to finished goods inventory, and from finished goods inventory to cost of goods sold. To determine the costs recorded for these flows, we must first determine the cost per unit of product and then apply this result to the number of units transferred.

Accounting for Goods in Process Inventories

If a manufacturing process has no beginning and ending goods in process inventory, the unit cost computation is simple. The unit cost of goods transferred out of a process when there is no beginning and ending goods in process inventory is:

$$\frac{\textbf{Total cost assigned to the process (direct materials, direct labour and factory overhead)}}{\textbf{Total number of units started and finished during the period}}$$

However, if a process has a beginning or ending inventory of partially processed units, the cost assigned to the process is allocated to all units worked on during the period. The denominator must be a measure of the entire production activity of the process during the period. This measure is called **equivalent units of production**, sometimes abbreviated *EUP*. Equivalent units of production measures the activity of a process as the number of units that would be completed if all efforts during a period had been applied to units that were started and finished. This measure of production activity is used in computing the cost per equivalent unit and also to assign the costs to finished goods and goods in process inventory (this is explained later in the chapter).

For example, assume GenX adds (or introduces) 100 units of material into the grinding process. Suppose at the end of the day the production supervisor determines 100 units are 60% processed. The equivalent units of production for that day is computed as 60 (100 × 60%). This means if we had introduced 60 units into the process, we would have completely processed these 60 units.

Equivalent Units for Materials May Not Be the Same for Direct Labour and Overhead

LO 6 Define equivalent units and explain their use in process cost accounting.

In many manufacturing processes, the equivalent units of production for materials is not the same as it is for labour and overhead. To see this, consider the manufacturing process shown in Exhibit 23.12:

Exhibit 23.12

Process Manufacturing System

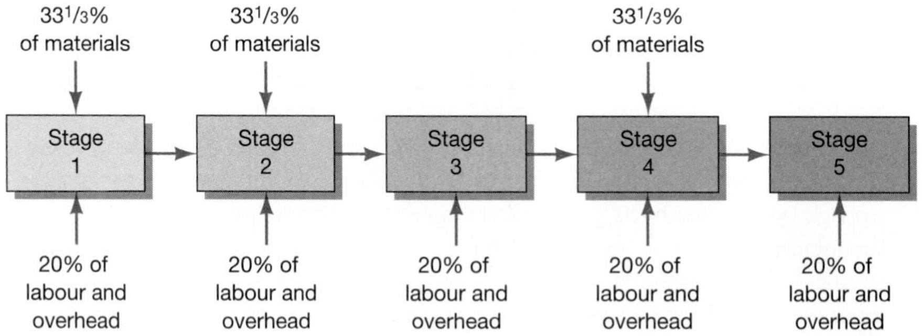

This exhibit shows a single production process consisting of five stages. One-third of the direct material cost is added at each of three stages: Stage 1, Stage 2, and Stage 4. One-fifth of the direct labour cost is added at each of the five stages. Because overhead is applied as a percentage of direct labour, one-fifth of the overhead also is added at each of the five stages.

When units finish Stage 1, they are one-third complete with respect to materials but only one-fifth complete with respect to labour and overhead. If they finish Stage 2, they are two-thirds complete with respect to materials, but only two-fifths complete with respect to labour and overhead. If they finish Stage 3, they remain two-thirds complete with respect to materials, but three-fifths complete with respect to labour and overhead. When they finish Stage 4, they are

100% complete with respect to materials but only four-fifths complete with respect to labour and overhead.

If 300 units of product are started and processed through Stage 1 during a month, at month-end they are one-third complete *with respect to materials.* Expressed in terms of equivalent finished units, the processing of these 300 units is equivalent to finishing 100 units. This is computed as 300 units × 33 1/3%, or 100 units. But note that only one-fifth of direct labour and overhead are included in the 300 units at the end of Stage 1. The equivalent units of production *with respect to direct labour and overhead* equals 300 units × 20%, or 60 units.

May I Help You?

Customer-interaction software is one of the hottest areas in customer-service processes. Whether the business is insurance, long-distance phone service, or selling high-tech gear, companies are finding this software can turn their customer-service process into an asset. What does it do? For starters, its cuts time spent on 800-service calls because a customer only describes a problem once, it yields a database of customer questions and complaints that gives insights into needed improvements, it can recognize incoming phone numbers and immediately direct them to the proper personnel along with data on previous dealings. [Source: *Business Week*, April 29, 1996.]

Did You Know?

Accounting for GenX's Grinding Department

Exhibit 23.13 shows the information needed to compute equivalent units of production for GenX's grinding department for the month of April, 1998:

Exhibit 23.13

GenX Grinding Department Production Data—April 1998

Beginning inventory:	
Units of product	30,000
Percentage of completion — direct materials	100%
Percentage of completion — direct labour	33⅓%
Units started during April	90,000
Units transferred from grinding to mixing	100,000
Ending inventory:	
Units of product	20,000
Percentage of completion — direct materials	100%
Percentage of completion — direct labour	25%

LO 7 Compute the equivalent units produced in a period.

LO 8 Explain the four steps in accounting for production activity in a period.

In computing equivalent units, we assume each of GenX's production departments process units on a first-in, first-out basis.[2] Accounting for the month's activity involves four steps: *physical flow, equivalent units, cost per equivalent unit* and *cost reconciliation.* Each of these steps is described in this section.

Physical Flow of Units

Physical flow is a reconciliation of (a) physical units started with and (b) physical units completed. This is shown in Exhibit 23.14.

[2] We assume a FIFO flow for all related computations in this chapter. Weighted average and LIFO also can be used. But they are less useful for measuring how effectively costs are controlled during a period.

Exhibit 23.14

GenX Grinding Department Physical Flow—April 1998

Units to account for:		Units accounted for as:	
Beginning inventory	30,000 units	Units transferred from grinding to mixing	100,000 units
Units started during April	90,000 units	Ending inventory:	20,000 units
Total number of units	120,000 units	Total number of units	120,000 units

The 100,000 units transferred from grinding to mixing during April include the 30,000 units from the beginning goods in process inventory (or simply beginning inventory). The remaining 70,000 units transferred out are started during April. Note a total of 90,000 units are started during April. Because 70,000 of these 90,000 units are completed, 20,000 units remain unfinished at the end of the month.

Computing Equivalent Units of Production

Our next step is to compute equivalent units of production in the grinding department for direct materials, direct labour, and factory overhead for April.

Equivalent Units—Direct Materials

Direct materials (the Profelene blocks) are added at the beginning of the process. A unit of product is 100% complete with respect to materials as soon as it is started. This means beginning goods in process inventory for April received all its materials in March and is not assigned any additional materials. The 70,000 units started and completed in April and the 20,000 units in ending goods in process inventory (or simply ending inventory) on April 30 received all their materials in April. With respect to materials, the grinding department's equivalent units of production are computed in Exhibit 23.15.

Exhibit 23.15

GenX Grinding Department Direct Materials Equivalent Units of Production—April 1998

	Units of Product		Percent Added This Period		Equivalent Units
Beginning goods in process . . .	30,000	×	0%	=	-0-
Goods started and completed .	70,000	×	100	=	70,000
Ending goods in process	20,000	×	100	=	20,000
Total units	120,000				90,000

Equivalent Units—Direct Labour and Factory Overhead

Direct labour and factory overhead (i.e., conversion costs) are assigned uniformly throughout the process.[3] Recall that beginning inventory of 30,000 units are partially completed in March. In April, additional labour and overhead is assigned to these units to complete them. This means these units were 33 1/3% complete during March, and the remaining 66 2/3% is assigned in April. The 70,000 units started and completed in April are assigned 100% of labour and overhead. The 20,000 units in ending inventory are assigned only 25% of labour at the end of April. Exhibit 23.16 summarizes these computations.

[3] Note factory overhead is applied using direct labour as an allocation base. This means the equivalent units are the same for both labour and overhead.

Exhibit 23.16

GenX Grinding Department Direct Labour and Factory Overhead Equivalent Units of Production—April 1998

	Units of Product		Percent Added This Period		Equivalent Units
Beginning goods in process . . .	30,000	×	$66\frac{2}{3}\%$	=	20,000
Goods started and completed .	70,000	×	100	=	70,000
Ending goods in process	20,000	×	25	=	5,000
Total units	120,000				95,000

A summary of April 1998 equivalent units of production for the grinding process is shown in Exhibit 23.17.

Exhibit 23.17

GenX Grinding Department Equivalent Units of Production—April 1998

Activities during April 1998	Direct Materials	Direct Labour	Factory Overhead
Units from beginning inventory processed in current period	-0-	20,000	20,000
Units started and completed in current period . . .	70,000	70,000	70,000
Units in ending inventory at end of current period . .	20,000	5,000	5,000
Equivalent units of production for period	90,000	95,000	95,000

Cost per Equivalent Unit

We next compute the *cost per equivalent unit* for direct materials, direct labour and factory overhead. Recall from Exhibit 23.6 that GenX's grinding department incurred \$9,900 in direct materials and \$5,700 in direct labour for April. Also, factory overhead of \$4,275 is applied to the grinding process. These costs are assigned to the partially completed units from beginning inventory, the units started and completed during the current period, and to units in ending inventory at the end of the period. The use of direct labour in April is shown in Exhibit 23.18.

These costs and the equivalent units computed above are used in determining the cost per equivalent unit for each cost element for April. These equivalent unit costs are shown in Exhibit 23.19.

Exhibit 23.18

GenX Grinding Department Use of Direct Labour—April 1998

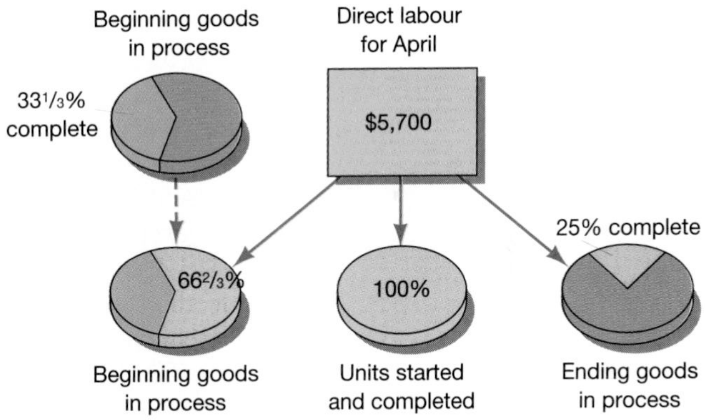

Exhibit 23.19

GenX Grinding Department Cost Per Equivalent Unit—April 1998

Activities during April 1998	Direct Materials	Direct Labour	Factory Overhead
Costs assigned to grinding in current period	\$9,900	\$5,700	\$4,275
Equivalent units of production in current period . .	90,000	95,000	95,000
Cost per equivalent unit for period	\$0.11	\$0.06	\$0.045

Total cost per equivalent unit for the grinding process amounts to \$0.215, computed as \$0.11 + \$0.06 + \$0.045.

Cost Reconciliation

The final step in this process is to reconcile costs associated with the process for the month by assigning them to units transferred from grinding to mixing and to those units in ending inventory. Exhibit 23.20 summarizes this cost reconciliation.

Exhibit 23.20

GenX Grinding Department Cost Reconciliation—April 1998

Costs to Account for:		Amount
From beginning inventory		4,250
Assigned in April 1998 (direct materials, direct labour and factory overhead)		19,875
Total costs to account for		**$24,125**
Costs Accounted for as:		
Beginning inventory completed in April 1998:		
Costs from previous period		$4,250
Costs assigned during current period:		
Direct materials (0 units × $0.11)	-0-	
Direct labour (20,000 units × $0.06)	1,200	
Factory overhead (20,000 units × $0.045)	900	$ 2,100
Total costs to process beginning inventory in current period		6,350
Cost of units started and completed in April 1998 (70,000 × $0.215)		15,050
Units in ending inventory:		
Direct material (20,000 × $0.11)	2,200	
Direct labour (5,000 × $0.06)	300	
Factory overhead (5,000 × $0.045)	225	
Total costs of units in ending inventory		2,725
Total costs accounted for		$24,125

Note the following points from Exhibit 23.20. First, total costs to be accounted for must equal the costs accounted for (minor differences can exist due to rounding). Second, costs of units transferred out from grinding to mixing include costs associated with the beginning inventory processed in the current period ($6,350) and costs of units started and completed in the current period ($15,050). This amounts to $21,400 for 100,000 units transferred out, or $0.214 per unit. Ending inventory is valued at $2,725, and is transferred to the next period.

Total cost per equivalent unit for April is computed as $0.215. But the cost per unit for the units transferred out is $0.214. The difference of $0.001 is because the total cost per equivalent unit is slightly different for March—recall that $4,250 of the $21,400 is carried forward from March. As explained in footnote 1, the FIFO method considers only current period's costs and activity in computing the cost per equivalent unit for the period.

Flashback

6. Equivalent units are:
   a. A measure of a production department's productivity in using direct materials, direct labour, or overhead.
   b. Units of a product produced by a foreign competitor that are similar to units produced by a domestic company.
   c. Generic units of a product similar to brand-name units of a product.
7. Interpret the meaning of a department's equivalent units of production with respect to direct labour.
8. A department began an accounting period with 8,000 units that were one-fourth complete, started and completed 50,000 units, and ended with 6,000 units that were one-third complete. How many equivalent units did it produce during the period?

Answers—p. 1132

Process Cost Summary—Grinding Department

LO 9 Define a process cost summary and describe its purposes.

A primary managerial accounting report for a process cost accounting system is the **process cost summary.** A separate process cost summary is prepared for each process or production department. Three purposes of the report are to (a) help managers control their departments, (b) help factory managers evaluate department managers' performance, and (c) provide cost information for financial statements. A process cost summary achieves these purposes by describing the costs charged to the department, the equivalent units of production achieved by the department, and the costs assigned to the output.

LO 10 Prepare a process cost summary.

A summary report is prepared by combining exhibits 23.14, 23.17, 23.19 and 23.20. An alternative format of the process cost summary is shown in Exhibit 23.21. Note the summary shown in Exhibit 23.21 on the following page is divided into three sections. Section 1 summarizes total costs charged to the department, including direct materials, direct labour, and overhead costs incurred, plus the cost of the beginning goods in process inventory.

Section 2 describes the equivalent units of production produced by the department. Equivalent units for materials and equivalent units for direct labour and overhead are in separate columns. Section 2 also shows direct materials, direct labour, and overhead costs per equivalent unit.

Section 3 allocates total costs among products worked on in the period. Costs of finishing beginning inventory units are computed and added to the cost carried forward from March to get total processing cost of $6,350 for beginning inventory units. Next, costs of processing 70,000 units from start to finish are computed and added to get their total processing cost of $15,050. The $6,350 and $15,050 are added to give us $21,400 total cost of goods transferred out of the department.

The bottom portion of section 3 computes the $2,725 cost of partially processing the ending inventory units. All the assigned costs are added to show the total $24,125 cost charged to the department in section 1 is now assigned to the units in section 3.

Flashback

9. A process cost summary for a department has three sections. What information is presented in each of them?

Answers—p. 1132

You Make the Call

General Manager

You are the general manager of a new company manufacturing two distinctly different types of tiny electronic components. Both components are produced in very large quantities using the same process consisting of four departments. You are preparing for a meeting with your management accountant to discuss whether to report the cost per equivalent unit for both products together or separately for each product. What do you advise?

Answer—p. 1132

Transferring Goods between Departments

Arrow 9a in Exhibit 23.6 reflects the transfer of units (powdered Profelene) from the grinding department to the mixing department. The $21,400 cost of this transfer, as computed in Section 3 of the process cost summary of Exhibit 23.21, is recorded with the entry at the top of page 1123:

Exhibit 23.21

GenX Grinding Department Process Cost Summary

GENX COMPANY
Process Cost Summary for Grinding Department
For Month Ended April 30, 1998

①	**Costs Charged to Department**	
	Direct materials requisitioned	$ 9,900
	Direct labour charged	5,700
	Overhead allocated (at predetermined rate)	4,275
	Total processing costs for the period	19,875
	Goods in process at the beginning of the period	4,250
	Total costs to be accounted for	**$24,125**

			Equivalent Units	
②	**Equivalent Unit Processing Costs:**	**Units of Product**	**Direct Materials**	**Labour and Overhead**
	Units processed:			
	Beginning goods in process	30,000	-0-	20,000
	Units started and completed	70,000	70,000	70,000
	Ending goods in process	20,000	20,000	5,000
	Total	120,000	90,000	95,000
	Total direct materials cost for the period			$9,900
	Direct materials cost per equivalent unit ($9,900/90,000 units)			$0.110
	Total direct labour cost for the period			$5,700
	Direct labour cost per equivalent unit ($5,700/95,000 units)			$0.060
	Total overhead cost for the period			$4,275
	Overhead cost per equivalent unit ($4,275/95,000 units)			$0.045

③	**Assignment of Costs to Output of Department:**	**Equivalent Units**	**Cost per Unit**	**Total Cost**
	Goods in process, March 31, 1998, and completed in the period			
	Costs from prior month			$ 4,250
	Direct materials added (none)			-0-
	Direct labour added	20,000	$0.060	1,200
	Overhead applied	20,000	0.045	900
	Total costs to process			6,350
	Goods started and completed in the period			
	Direct materials added	70,000	0.110	7,700
	Direct labour added	70,000	0.060	4,200
	Overhead applied	70,000	0.045	3,150
	Total costs to process			15,050
	Total costs transferred to mixing department (unit cost = $21,400/100,000 units = $0.214)			21,400
	Goods in process, April 30, 1998:			
	Direct materials added	20,000	0.110	2,200
	Direct labour added	5,000	0.060	300
	Overhead applied	5,000	0.045	225
	Total costs to process			2,725
	Total costs accounted for			**$24,125**

9a	Goods in Process Inventory—Mixing	21,400	
	Goods in Process Inventory—Grinding .		21,400
	To record the transfer of partially completed goods from the grinding department to the mixing department.		

After this entry is posted, the Goods in Process Inventory account for the grinding department is as shown in Exhibit 23.22.

Exhibit 23.22

Goods in Process Inventory (Grinding) Ledger Account

Goods in Process Inventory — Grinding					Acct. No. 133	
Date		**Explanation**	**Debit**	**Credit**	**Balance**
1998					
Mar.	31	Beginning balance			4,250
Apr.	30	Direct materials	9,900		14,150
	30	Direct labour costs	5,700		19,850
	30	Applied overhead	4,275		24,125
	30	Transfer to mixing department		21,400	2,725

Note the $2,725 ending balance equals the cost assigned to these partially completed units in Section 3 of the process cost summary in Exhibit 23.21.

LO 11 Record the transfer of goods between departments.

Flash back

10. What effect does the transfer of a partially completed product from one production department to another have on the total assets of the company?

Answers—p. 1132

Accounting for GenX's Mixing Department

The mixing department begins working on Profelene when it is received from the grinding department. It adds direct materials in the form of flavouring, preservatives and packaging supplies. Direct labour and overhead are added at the same rate as direct materials.

Equivalent Units of Production—Mixing Department

In the grinding department, the equivalent units of production for direct labour and overhead are not the same as for direct materials. But the mixing department requires only one computation of equivalent units of production. This is because direct materials, direct labour, and overhead are used at the same rate. Exhibit 23.23 provides the data needed to compute equivalent units of production in the mixing department.

Exhibit 23.23

GenX Mixing Department Production Data—April 1998

Beginning inventory (March 31):		
Units of product	16,000	
Percentage of completion—Direct materials, direct labour, and overhead		25%
Units received from grinding department	100,000	
Units transferred to finished goods	101,000	
Ending inventory (April 30):		
Units of product	15,000	
Percentage of completion—Direct materials, direct labour, and overhead		33 1/3%

A total of 101,000 units are transferred to finished goods in April. Based on a first-in, first-out assumption, 16,000 of these units came from beginning goods in process inventory and 85,000 are started and completed in April. Because 100,000 units are received from the grinding department in April and 85,000 of these units are completed, the ending goods in process inventory is 15,000 units. Exhibit 23.24 computes the mixing department's equivalent units of production for direct materials, direct labour and overhead for April.

Exhibit 23.24

GenX Mixing Department Equivalent Units of Production

	Units of Product		Percent Added This Period		Equivalent Units
Beginning goods in process . . .	16,000	×	75%	=	12,000
Goods started and completed .	85,000	×	100	=	85,000
Ending goods in process	15,000	×	$33^1/_3$	=	5,000
Total units	116,000				102,000

Process Cost Summary—Mixing Department

Exhibit 23.25 shows the process cost summary for the mixing department. The costs charged to the department in section 1 include $21,400 transferred in from the grinding department. Section 2 shows the equivalent units of production for the direct materials, direct labour, and overhead added by the mixing department. Section 2 also computes the costs per equivalent unit added during the mixing process. Section 3 shows how costs charged to the department are assigned to the output of the department. The $29,470 cost of the units transferred to finished goods is computed as the combined cost of the beginning units in process and the started and completed units in the period.

Because all Profelene received from the grinding department enters production at the beginning of the mixing process, the beginning goods in process inventory is 100% complete with respect to Profelene. None of the Profelene transferred in during April is used to finish the beginning inventory units. The $21,400 cost transferred in during April relates to the 100,000 units that the mixing department started to process in April. In section 3 of Exhibit 23.25, $18,190 of the $21,400 is assigned to the 85,000 units started and finished in April (85,000 × $0.214). The remaining $3,210 is assigned to the 15,000 units in ending inventory (15,000 × $0.214).

Flash back

11. A ski manufacturer's total processing costs are $262,500 for its waxing department in the month of December. To complete beginning goods in process, this department added 20,000 equivalent units of materials, labour, and overhead. This department also started and completed 70,000 units during the month and had 15,000 equivalent units remaining in process at month-end. Costs transferred in from the sanding department for December total $300,000, of which 25% relates to units the waxing department didn't finish at month-end. For the waxing department's process cost summary, what is reported as the total costs to process goods started and completed?

Answers—p. 1132

Exhibit 23.25

GenX Mixing Department Process Cost Summary

GENX COMPANY
Process Cost Summary for Grinding Department
For Month Ended April 30, 1998

①

Costs Charged to Department	
Direct materials requisitioned	$ 2,040
Direct labour charged	5,100
Overhead allocated (at predetermined rate)	1,020
Total processing costs for the period	$ 8,160
Goods in process at the beginning of the period	3,520
Costs transferred in from the grinding department (100,000 units at $0.214 each)	21,400
Total costs to be accounted for	**$33,080**

②

Equivalent Unit Processing Costs:	**Units of Product**	**Equivalent Units of Production**
Units processed:		
Beginning goods in process	16,000	12,000
Units started and completed	85,000	85,000
Ending goods in process	15,000	5,000
Total	116,000	102,000
Total direct materials cost for the period		$ 2,040
Direct materials cost per equivalent unit ($2,040/102,000 units)		$ 0.020
Total direct labour cost for the period		$ 5,100
Direct labour cost per equivalent unit ($5,100/102,000 units)		$ 0.050
Total overhead cost for the period		$ 1,020
Overhead cost per equivalent unit ($1,020/102,000 units)		$ 0.010

③

Assignment of Costs to Output of Department:	**Equivalent Units**	**Cost per Unit**	**Total Cost**
Goods in process, March 31, 1998, and completed during April:			
Costs from prior period			$3,520
Direct materials added	12,000	$0.020	240
Direct labour added	12,000	$0.050	600
Overhead applied	12,000	$0.010	120
Total costs to process			$4,480
Goods started and completed in the period:			
Costs transferred in (85,000 x $0.214)			$18,190
Direct materials added	85,000	$0.020	1,700
Direct labour added	85,000	$0.050	4,250
Overhead applied	85,000	$0.010	850
Total costs to process			$24,990
Total costs transferred to finished goods (unit cost = $29,470/101,000 units = $0.2918)			$29,470
Goods in process, April 30, 1998:			
Costs transferred in (15,000 x $0.214)			$3,210
Direct materials added	5,000	$0.020	100
Direct labour added	5,000	$0.050	250
Overhead applied	5,000	$0.010	50
Total costs to process			$3,610
Total costs accounted for			**$33,080**

Mid-Chapter Demonstration Problem

A production department in a process manufacturing system of Golden Company completed 500,000 units of product and transferred them to finished goods during a recent month. Of these units, 150,000 were in process at the beginning of the week. The other 350,000 units were started and completed during the week. At the end of the period, 60,000 units were in process.

Required

Compute the department's equivalent units of production with respect to direct materials under each of the following unrelated assumptions:

a. All direct materials are added to the products when processing begins.

b. The direct materials are added to the products evenly throughout the process. The beginning goods in process inventory was 30% complete and the ending goods in process inventory was 60% complete.

c. One-quarter of the direct materials are added to the products when the process begins and the other three-quarters is added when the process is 75% complete as to direct labour. The beginning goods in process inventory was 40% complete as to direct labour and the ending goods in process inventory was 80% complete as to direct labour.

Solution to Mid-Chapter Demonstration Problem

a. Ending inventory is 100% complete with respect to materials.

	Units of Products	Percent Added	Equivalent Units
Beginning goods in process	150,000	0%	-0-
Goods started and completed	350,000	100	350,000
Ending goods in process	60,000	100	60,000
Total units	560,000		410,000

b. Beginning inventory is 30% complete with respect to materials, so 70% must be added in the current week. Ending inventory is 60% complete with respect to materials.

	Units of Products	Percent Added	Equivalent Units
Beginning goods in process	150,000	70%	105,000
Goods started and completed	350,000	100	350,000
Ending goods in process	60,000	60	36,000
Total units	560,000		491,000

c. Beginning inventory is 25% complete with respect to materials, so the additional 75% must be added in the current week. Ending inventory is 100% complete with respect to materials because direct labour has passed the 75% level.

	Units of Products	Percent Added	Equivalent Units
Beginning goods in process	150,000	75%	112,500
Goods started and completed	350,000	100	350,000
Ending goods in process	60,000	100	60,000
Total units	560,000		522,500

Transferring Costs To Finished Goods Inventory and Cost of Goods Sold

Arrow 9b in Exhibit 23.6 reflects the transfer of finished products from the mixing department to Finished Goods Inventory. The process cost summary for the mixing department shows 101,000 units of packaged Profen are assigned a cost of $29,470. The following entry records the transfer:

9b	Finished Goods Inventory	29,470	
	Goods in Process Inventory—Mixing . .		29,470
	To record transfer of completed units of Profen out of production.		

After this entry is posted, the mixing department's Goods in Process Inventory account appears as shown in Exhibit 23.26.

Exhibit 23.26

Goods in Process Inventory (Mixing) Ledger Account

Goods in Process Inventory — Mixing					Acct. No. 134
Date		Explanation	Debit	Credit	Balance
1998					
Mar.	31	Beginning balance			3,520
Apr.	30	Direct materials	2,040		5,560
	30	Direct labour costs	5,100		10,660
	30	Applied overhead	1,020		11,680
	30	Transfer from grinding dept.	21,400		33,080
	30	Transfer to warehouse		29,470	3,610

The ending balance equals the cost assigned to the partially completed units in section 3 of Exhibit 23.25.

LO 12 Record the transfer of completed goods to Finished Goods Inventory and Cost of Goods Sold.

GenX sells 106,000 units of Profen in April. The beginning inventory of finished goods consists of 23,000 units with a cost of $6,440. The remaining 83,000 units sold are the 101,000 completed in April. Ending finished goods inventory amounts to 18,000 units. Section 3 of Exhibit 23.25 showed total manufacturing cost per unit finished in April is $0.2918 ($29,470/101,000). We compute cost of goods sold for April in Exhibit 23.27.

Exhibit 23.27

GenX Cost of Goods Sold—April 1998[a]

23,000 units from the beginning inventory	$ 6,440
83,000 units manufactured during April (83,000 × $0.2918)	24,219
Total cost of goods sold	$30,659

[a] Computations assume a FIFO inventory system.

The following entry records the cost of goods sold for April:

10.	Cost of Goods Sold	30,659	
	Finished Goods Inventory		30,659
	To record cost of goods sold during April.		

After this entry is posted, the Finished Goods Inventory account appears as shown in Exhibit 23.28.

Exhibit 23.28

Finished Goods Inventory Ledger Account

Finished Goods Inventory					Acct. No. 135
Date		Explanation	Debit	Credit	Balance
1998					
Mar.	31	Beginning balance			6,440
Apr.	30	Transfer from mixing department	29,470		35,910
	30	Cost of goods sold		30,659	5,251

Summary of GenX's Manufacturing Cost Flows

Exhibit 23.29 shows manufacturing cost flows of GenX for April. Each of these cost flows and their entries to record them are explained in the prior sections. The flow of costs through accounts reflects the flow of manufacturing activities and products in its factory.

Exhibit 23.29

Cost Flows through GenX—April 1998

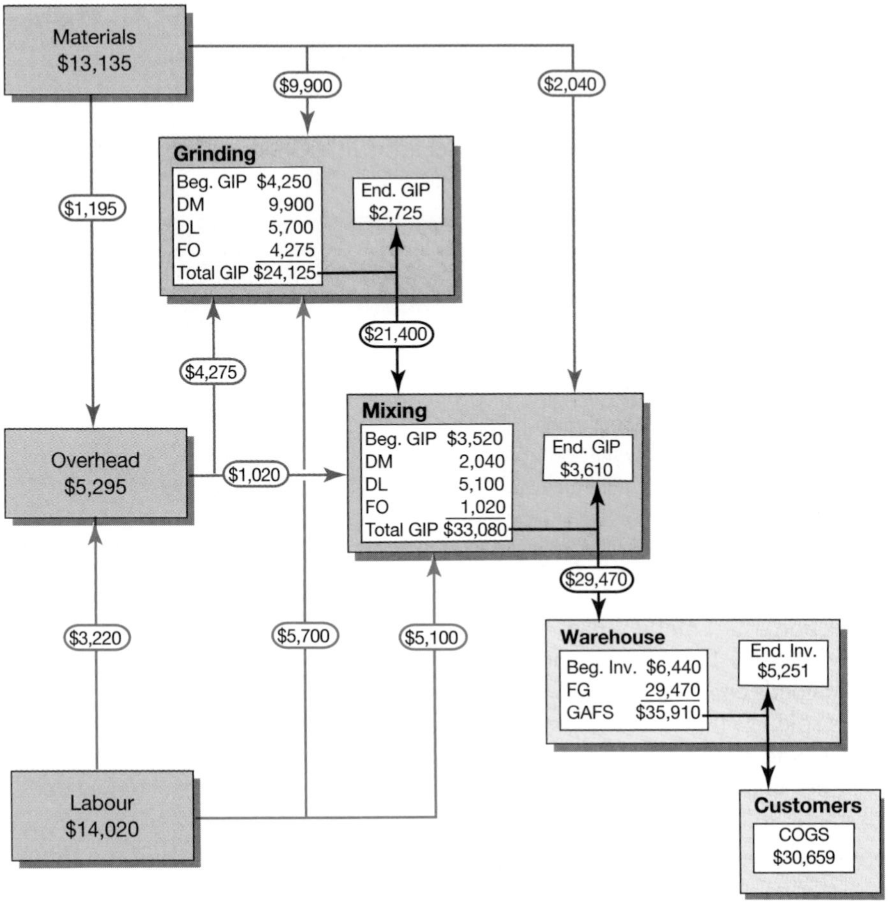

*Abbreviations: GIP (goods in process); DM (direct materials); DL (direct labour); FO (factory overhead); FG (finished goods); GAFS (goods available for sale); COGS (cost of goods sold).

Modern Manufacturing Management Principles and Process Manufacturing Operations

We described several modern manufacturing management principles in Chapter 21. Adopting these concepts brings about changes in some process manufacturing operations. Management concerns with throughput and just-in-time manufacturing, for instance, cause boundary lines between departments to become less distinct. In some cases, higher quality and better efficiency are obtained by reorganizing production processes. Instead of producing the different types of Bata shoes in a series of departments, a separate work centre for each shoe can be established in one department. When this rearrangement occurs, the process cost accounting system is changed to account for costs of each work centre.

When a company adopts just-in-time (JIT) manufacturing methods, the inventories described in the chapter can virtually disappear. For example, if raw materials are not ordered or received until needed, a Raw Materials Inventory account may be unnecessary. Instead, materials cost is immediately debited to the Goods in Process Inventory account. Similarly, a Finished Goods Inventory account may not be needed. Instead, cost of finished goods can be debited to the Cost of Goods Sold account instead of the Finished Goods Inventory account.

Best of Both Worlds

Customer orientation demands *both* flexibility and standardization to better serve customers. While flexibility allows companies to supply products or services to each customer's unique specifications such as in a job order setting, standardization helps achieve efficiencies and lower costs to customers such as in a process production operation. **Ford** and **Toyota** attempt to combine flexibility and standardization with breaks in their assembly lines processes. This is done by using equipment to speed up the changeovers of jigs, tools and fixtures for machines on the line. These companies get the best of both worlds and are better able to satisfy customers. [Source: P. F. Drucker, "The Emerging Theory of Manufacturing," *Harvard Business Review*, May–June 1990, pp. 94–102.]

Did You Know?

When a company uses the theory of constraints to increase throughput, the cost accounting system helps managers locate bottlenecks. A bottleneck, for instance, can be seen by the presence of large upstream or downstream inventories. Based on analysis of inventories, managers can pinpoint the bottleneck and manage it to improve efficiency.

Gadgets at Work

A unique order-processing system makes it possible for Polycan Industries to deliver bumpers about 80 kilometres to **Ford's** Oakville, Ontario, facility just-in-time for assembly, four hours after they are ordered. The just-in-time system developed by Polycon engineers is based on Sectim, a real-time information and control system from **Aspen Technology Inc**. The real-time capabilities of the system make it possible to provide management with up-to-the-minute information on plantwide operations. [Source: M. Ngo and P. Szucs, *Canadian Plastics*, August 1996, pp. 12–15.]

Did You Know?

Flashback

12. A company successfully uses just-in-time manufacturing and essentially eliminates its goods in process inventories. How does this affect its computations of equivalent units of production?

Answers—p. 1132

Spoiled Units of Production

USING THE INFORMATION

LO 13 Analyze cost per equivalent unit with and without spoiled units of production.

We have described how to compute product cost in process manufacturing companies. But our discussion assumes either there are no *spoiled* units of production or they are not considered in computing cost per unit. Managers, of course, prefer no spoiled units but recognize the likely existence of some spoiled units. By not explicitly considering spoiled units in computing the equivalent units of production (and therefore the cost per equivalent unit), the good units are forced to *absorb* the cost of errors resulting from spoilage. This can impact decision making based on cost per equivalent unit.

Managers find it useful to know the actual cost per equivalent unit *without* the good units absorbing the cost of the spoiled ones. This involves adding the spoiled units while computing the equivalent units of production for a period. Let's assume a simple production process where 900 good units and 100 spoiled units are produced in 1999. If there are no goods in process inventories, the equivalent units of production can be computed as 900 or 1,000 units, depending on whether we count spoiled units. The greater the percent of spoiled units, the larger the impact on computing and using the equivalent units of production figure.

To illustrate, suppose this same company has production costs in 1999 equal to $18,000. The cost per equivalent unit of production can be determined in two ways as shown in Exhibit 23.30.

Exhibit 23.30

Computing Costs per Equivalent Unit with and without Spoilage

For Calendar Year 1999	Spoilage Ignored	Spoilage Considered
Production cost incurred	$18,000	$18,000
Equivalent units of production	900 units	1,000 units
Cost per equivalent unit	$20 per unit	$18 per unit

Note the marked difference in the cost per equivalent unit in this case. Managers are often tempted to use the higher cost when pricing products. The thinking behind this approach is that using the higher cost allows them to determine a price to "cover" all expenses. The downside of using the information in this way is that companies can price themselves out of a market with too high of a price and never notice the high cost of spoiled goods.

You Make the Call

Process Manager

You are the manager of a crucial process in your company's manufacturing cycle. During the recent quarter, your process generated an unusually high percent of scrap (spoilage). Yet, the monthly process cost report does not show the cost of this scrap. You want to submit a proposal to top management to obtain resources for implementing process improvement measures and need information on the cost of scrap to include in your proposal. What do you do?

Answer—p. 1132

Summary

LO1 Explain process operations and how they differ from job order operations. Process operations produce large quantities of identical products or services by passing them through a series of processes or steps in production. Like job order operations, they combine direct materials, direct labour, and overhead in the manufacturing operation. Unlike job order operations that assign the responsibility for each job to a manager, process operations assign the responsibility for each process to a manager. The primary focus is on the series of processes used to complete the production of products.

LO2 Compare process cost accounting and job order cost accounting systems. Process and job order manufacturing operations are similar in that they both combine materials, labour, and other manufacturing overhead items in the process of producing products. Yet they differ in the way they are organized and managed. In job order operations, the job order cost accounting system assigns direct materials, direct labour, and overhead to specific jobs. The total job cost is then divided by the number of units to compute a cost per unit for that job. By comparison, in a process manufacturing operation, the process cost accounting system assigns direct materials, direct labour, and overhead to specific manufacturing processes. The total costs associated with each process are then divided by the number of units passing through that process to determine the cost per equivalent unit for that process. The costs per equivalent unit for each process are added to determine the total cost per unit of a product.

LO 3 **Record the flow of direct materials costs in a process cost accounting system.** The materials purchased are debited to a Raw Materials Inventory account. As direct materials are issued to processes, they are separately accumulated to the Goods in Process Inventory account for that process.

LO 4 **Record the flow of direct labour costs in a process cost accounting system.** The direct labour costs are first debited to the Factory Payroll account. The total amount in Factory payroll is then assigned to the Goods in Process Inventory account pertaining to each process.

LO 5 **Record the flow of factory overhead costs in a process cost accounting system.** The cost of factory overhead items are first accumulated in the Factory Overhead account and then allocated, using a predetermined overhead rate, to the different processes. The allocated amount is debited to the Goods in Process Inventory account pertaining to each process.

LO 6 **Define equivalent units and explain their use in process cost accounting.** Equivalent units of production measure the activity of a process as the number of units that would be completed if all efforts during a period had been applied to units that were started and finished. This measure of production activity is used in computing the cost per equivalent unit and also to assign the costs to finished goods and goods in process inventory.

LO 7 **Compute equivalent units produced in a period.** To compute equivalent units, determine the number of units that would have been finished if all of the direct materials (or direct labour or overhead) had been used to manufacture units that were started and completed during the period. The costs incurred by a process are divided by its equivalent units of production to determine cost per unit.

LO 8 **Explain the four steps in accounting for production activity in a period.** The four steps involved in accounting for production activity in a period are (1) recording the physical flow of units, (2) computing the equivalent units of production, (3) computing the cost per equivalent unit of production, and (4) cost reconciliation. The last step involves assigning the costs to finished goods and goods in process inventory for the period. These four steps are helpful in preparing the process cost summary report.

LO 9 **Define a process cost summary and describe its purposes.** A process cost summary is a managerial accounting report that summarizes the activity of a production process or department during a period. Three purposes of the report are to (a) help managers control their departments, (b) help factory managers evaluate department managers' performance, and (c) provide cost information for financial statements. A process cost summary achieves these purposes by describing the costs charged to the department, the equivalent units of production achieved by the department, and the costs assigned to the output.

LO 10 **Prepare a process cost summary.** A process cost summary can be prepared by including the physical flow of units, equivalent units of production, costs per equivalent unit, and cost reconciliation in one summary report. The report shows the units and costs to account for during the period and how these were accounted for during the period. In terms of units, the report includes the beginning goods in process inventory and the units started during the month. These are accounted for in terms of goods completed and transferred out and ending goods in process inventory at the end of the period. With respect to the costs, the report includes the direct materials, direct labour, and factory overhead costs assigned to the process during the period, and how these costs were assigned to goods completed and transferred out and goods in process inventory at the end of the period.

LO 11 **Record the transfer of goods between departments.** As units of product are transferred from one manufacturing process to the next, the accumulated cost of those units is transferred from one goods in process account to the next. Once the goods are completed in the preceding process, they are transferred out to the next process in the sequence. The costs associated with the goods completed in the preceding process are then debited to the goods in process inventory of the next process. With this transaction, the costs of the preceding process are accumulated in the next process.

LO 12 **Record the transfer of completed goods to Finished Goods Inventory and Cost of Goods Sold.** As units complete the last manufacturing process and are eventually sold, their accumulated cost is transferred to Finished Goods Inventory and finally to Cost of Goods Sold.

LO 13 **Analyze cost per equivalent unit with and without spoiled units of production.** Failure to consider spoiled units in computing the equivalent units of production, and the cost per equivalent unit, means good units are forced to absorb the cost of spoiled units. This can negatively impact decision making based on cost per equivalent unit. Decision makers should examine costs both with and without spoiled units.

Guidance Answers to **You Make the Call**

General Manager

As per the information, both components are produced using the same process. This means that the conversion activity is likely to be very similar to both products. Therefore, the conversion cost per equivalent unit can be computed for both products combined. However, it is likely that the materials consumed by each component may be different. If they are different, then the materials cost per equivalent unit must be computed and also reported separately for each component.

Process Manager

In such a situation, it is important for you to meet with the cost/management accountant and explain the situation to him or her. Assuming you can collect the information on scrap, you must compute the total equivalent units produced including scrap and recompute the cost per equivalent unit. The new cost per equivalent unit will be lower than what was previously computed. You can then multiply the new cost per equivalent unit by the number of scrap units to determine the cost of scrap. This scrap cost information can be shown to top management to inform them about the financial implications of scrap.

Guidance Answer to **Judgment and Ethics**

Budget Officer

By instructing you to classify a majority of the costs as indirect, the manager is passing on some of his department's costs to a common overhead pool which will be partially absorbed by each department within the company. Moreover, the overhead costs are allocated on the basis of direct labour and the new department has a relatively low direct labour component. Therefore, the new department will be assigned less overhead whereas portions of it will be assigned to other departments. You recognize the unethical behaviour of the department manager; it is your duty to bring this to the attention of the department manager first. If this individual refuses to listen, you must then inform someone in a position of authority.

Guidance Answers to Flash backs

1. *c*

2. When a company produces large quantities of identical products, a process cost accounting system is more suitable.

3. *b*

4. The costs are direct materials, direct labour, and manufacturing overhead.

5. One Goods in Process Inventory account is needed for each production department.

6. *a*

7. Equivalent units with respect to direct labour is the number of units that would have been produced if all of the labour had been used on units that were started and finished during the period.

8.

	Units of Product		Percent Added		Equivalent Units
Beginning inventory . .	8,000	×	75%	=	6,000
Units started and finished	50,000	×	100	=	50,000
Ending inventory	6,000	×	33⅓	=	2,000
Equivalent units					58,000

9. The first section shows the costs charged to the department. The second section describes the equivalent units produced by the department. The third section shows how the total costs are assigned to units worked on during the period.

10. The transfer decreases one Goods in Process Inventory account and increases another. Therefore, the transfer has no effect on total assets.

11. Equivalent unit processing cost:

$$\frac{\$262{,}500}{20{,}000 + 70{,}000 + 15{,}000} = \$2.50$$

Goods started and completed:

Costs transferred in	$225,000
Total costs added (70,000 × $2.50)	175,000
Total costs to process	$400,000

12. If goods-in-process inventories are eliminated, equivalent units of production is the number of units started and completed during the period.

Demonstration Problem

The Canadiana Company produces a product by passing it through a molding process and then through an assembly process. Information related to manufacturing activities during July follows:

Raw materials:	
Beginning inventory	$100,000
Raw materials purchased on credit	300,000
Direct materials used in molding	(190,000)
Direct materials used in assembling	(88,600)
Indirect materials used	(51,400)
Ending inventory	$ 70,000
Factory payroll:	
Direct labour used in molding	$ 42,000
Direct labour used in assembling	55,375
Indirect labour used	50,625
Total payroll cost (paid with cash)	$148,000
Factory overhead incurred:	
Indirect materials used	$ 51,400
Indirect labour used	50,625
Other overhead costs	71,725
Total factory overhead incurred	$173,750
Factory overhead applied:	
Molding (150% of direct labour)	$ 63,000
Assembling (200% of direct labour)	110,750
Total factory overhead applied	$173,750

Molding department:	
Beginning goods in process inventory (units)	5,000
Percentage completed—materials	100%
Percentage completed—labour and overhead	60%
Units started and completed	17,000
Ending goods in process inventory (units)	8,000
Percentage completed—materials	100%
Percentage completed—labour and overhead	25%
Costs:	
Beginning in process inventory	$ 53,000
Direct materials added	190,000
Direct labour added	42,000
Overhead applied (150% of direct labour)	63,000
Total costs	$348,000
Assembling department:	
Beginning goods in process inventory	$154,800
Ending goods in process inventory	108,325
Finished goods inventory:	
Beginning inventory	$ 96,400
Cost transferred in from assembling	578,400
Cost of goods sold	(506,100)
Ending inventory	$168,700

Required

1. Compute the equivalent units of production for the molding department for July, and determine the costs per equivalent unit for direct materials, direct labour, and overhead.
2. Compute the cost of the units transferred from molding to assembling during the month and the cost of the ending goods in process inventory for the molding department.
3. Prepare summary journal entries to record the events of July.

Planning the Solution

- Compute the molding department's equivalent units of production and cost per unit with respect to direct materials.
- Compute the molding department's equivalent units of production with respect to direct labour and overhead and determine the cost per unit for each.
- Compute the total cost of the goods transferred to the assembly department by using the equivalent units and unit costs to determine (a) the cost of the beginning in-process inventory, (b) the materials, labour, and overhead costs added to the beginning in-process inventory, and (c) the materials, labour, and overhead costs added to the units that were started and completed in the month.
- Use the information to record entries for (a) raw materials purchases, (b) direct materials usage, (c) indirect materials usage, (d) factory payroll costs, (e) direct labour usage, (f) indirect labour usage, (g) other overhead costs (credit Other Accounts), (h) application of overhead to the two departments, (i) transferring partially completed goods from molding to assembling, (j) transferring finished goods out of assembling, and (k) the cost of goods sold.

Solution to Demonstration Problem

1. Equivalent units of production—direct materials:

	Units of Product		Percent Added		Equivalent Units
Beginning goods in process . . .	5,000	×	0%	=	-0-
Goods started and completed . .	17,000	×	100	=	17,000
Ending goods in process	8,000	×	100	=	8,000
Total units	30,000				**25,000**

Materials cost per equivalent unit = \$190,000/25,000 = \$7.60 per unit

Equivalent units of production—direct labour and overhead:

	Units of Product		Percent Added		Equivalent Units
Beginning goods in process . . .	5,000	×	40%	=	2,000
Goods started and completed . .	17,000	×	100	=	17,000
Ending goods in process	8,000	×	25	=	2,000
Total units	30,000				**21,000**

Labour cost per equivalent unit = \$42,000/21,000 = \$2 per unit

Overhead cost per equivalent unit = \$63,000/21,000 = \$3 per unit

2. Cost of units transferred from molding to assembling during the month:

	Equivalent Units	Cost per Unit	Total Cost
Beginning goods in process:			
Costs from prior month			\$ 53,000
Direct materials added	-0-	\$7.60	-0-
Direct labour added	2,000	2.00	4,000
Overhead applied	2,000	3.00	6,000
Total cost to process			\$ 63,000
Units started and completed:			
Direct materials added	17,000	\$7.60	\$129,200
Direct labour added	17,000	2.00	34,000
Overhead applied	17,000	3.00	51,000
Total cost to process			\$214,200
Cost of transferred units			**\$277,200**

3. Summary general journal entries for July:

Raw materials purchases:

Raw Materials Inventory	300,000	
Accounts Payable		300,000

Direct materials usage:

Goods in Process Inventory—Molding	190,000	
Goods in Process Inventory—Assembling . .	88,600	
Raw Materials Inventory		278,600

Indirect materials usage:

Factory Overhead	51,400	
Raw Materials Inventory		51,400

Factory payroll costs:

Factory Payroll	148,000	
Cash		148,000

Direct labour usage:

Goods in Process Inventory—Molding	42,000	
Goods in Process Inventory—Assembling	55,375	
Factory Payroll		97,375

Indirect labour usage:

Factory Overhead	50,625	
Factory Payroll		50,625

Other overhead costs:

Factory Overhead	71,725	
Other Accounts		71,725

Application of overhead:

Goods in Process Inventory—Molding	63,000	
Goods in Process Inventory—Assembling	110,750	
Factory Overhead		173,750

Transferring partially completed goods from molding to assembling:

Goods in Process Inventory—Assembling	277,200	
Goods in Process Inventory—Molding		277,200

Transferring finished goods:

Finished Goods Inventory	578,400	
Goods in Process Inventory—Assembling		578,400

Cost of goods sold:

Cost of Goods Sold	506,100	
Finished Goods Inventory		506,100

Glossary

Equivalent units of production The number of units that would be completed if all effort during a period had been applied to units that were started and finished. (p. 1116)

Materials consumption report A document that summarizes the materials used by a department during a reporting period and replaces materials requisitions. (p. 1111)

Process cost accounting system A system of assigning direct materials, direct labour, and overhead to specific manufacturing processes. The total costs associated with each process are then divided by the number of units passing through that process to determine the cost per equivalent unit. (p. 1110)

Process cost summary A primary managerial accounting report for a process cost accounting system. The report describes the costs charged to a department, the equivalent units of production by the department, and how the costs were assigned to the output. (p. 1121)

Process manufacturing The mass production of products in a sequence of steps; this means products pass through a series of sequential processes; also called process production. (p. 1106)

Questions

1. Can services be delivered by process operations? Give an example.
2. You have studied two types of cost accounting systems up to this point in your accounting course. What is the determinant for a business in selecting the type of cost accounting system? Give two examples of each.
3. Identify the control document for material flows when a material requisition slip is not used.
4. The primary focus in a job order costing system is the job or batch. Identify the two primary focuses in process costing.
5. Are the journal entries to match cost flows to product flows in process costing primarily the same or much different from those in job order costing? Explain.
6. Explain in your own words equivalent units of production (EUP). Why is it necessary to use EUP in process costing?
7. Why is it possible for direct labour in a process manufacturing operation to include the labour of employees who do not work specifically on products?
8. A manufacturing company produces a single product by processing it first through a mixing department and next through a cutting department. What accounts do direct labour costs flow through in this company's process cost system?
9. After all labour costs for a period are allocated, what balance should remain in the Factory Payroll account?
10. Is it possible to have underapplied or overapplied overhead costs in a process cost accounting system?
11. Explain why equivalent units of production for direct labour and overhead may be the same and why they may differ from equivalent units for direct materials.
12. List the four steps in accounting for production activity in a period.
13. What purposes are served by a process cost summary?
14. You are the production manager of a shoe manufacturing operation in Kitchener, Ontario. Your company has taken on a special order to produce the shoes for *all* the employees of **Canadian Tire** stores across the country. Draw the production process assuming three production departments: cutting, Canadian Tire design set to the material, and assembly. Your picture should begin with the delivery of raw materials and finish with the shipment of goods.

Quick Study

QS 23-1
Match product to cost system
LO 1

For each of the following, indicate whether it is most likely to be produced in a process operation or a job-order operation:

a. Door hinges.
b. Wall clocks.
c. Custom cut flower arrangements.
d. Bolts and nuts.
e. House paint.
f. Folding chairs.
g. Custom tailored suits
h. Sport shirts
i. Concrete swimming pools
j. Pianos.

QS 23-2
Match cost flows to product flows
LO 3, 4, 5

Texton Company manufactures a product requiring two processes: cutting and sewing. During August, partially completed units with a cost of $297,500 were transferred from cutting to sewing. The sewing department requisitioned $58,200 of direct materials and incurred direct labour of $96,000. Overhead is applied to the sewing department at 100% of direct labour. Units with a cost of $102,400 were completed and transferred to finished goods. Prepare the journal entries to record the August activities of the sewing department.

QS 23-3
Compute EUP
LO 6, 7

The following information pertains to units processed in the binding department of Lowe Printing Company during March:

	Units of Product	Percent of Labour Added
Goods in process	150,000	25%
Goods started and completed	340,000	100
Ending goods in process	120,000	40

Compute the total equivalent units of production with respect to labour for March.

QS 23-4
Compute EUP cost
LO 7, 10

The following information for a company's assembly department describes its manufacturing operations for one month:

Costs charged to the department:	
Goods in process at the beginning of the month	$ 10,000
Total processing costs for the month	208,000
(Direct Material = $52,000 Labour and Factory Overhead = $156,000)	
Cost transferred from prior department (26,000 units)	104,000
Total costs to be accounted for	$322,000
Equivalent units produced during month for direct materials, direct labour and factory overhead:	
Beginning in process inventory	4,000
Units started and completed	24,000
Ending in process inventory	2,000
Total units	30,000

The units transferred to the assembly department were immediately placed in production, with the result that none of their $104,000 cost was added to the beginning in process inventory. Their cost was divided between the units started and completed and the units in the ending goods in process inventory. What is the equivalent unit cost for transferred in, direct material, and direct labour and factory overhead? What is the total cost per unit of a finished product?

QS 23-5
Compute EUP cost
LO 10

The cost of beginning inventory plus the costs added during the period should equal the cost of _______ plus the cost of _______ .

Exercises

Exercise 23-1
Terms used in process cost accounting systems
LO 1–13

Match each of the following items with the appropriate description of its purpose:

a. Materials consumption report
b. Process cost summary
c. Equivalent units of production
d. Goods in process inventory—Department A
e. Raw materials inventory account
f. Materials requisition
g. Finished goods inventory account
h. Factory overhead account

_____ **1.** Holds costs of finished products until sold to customers.
_____ **2.** Holds costs for indirect materials, indirect labour, and other similar costs until assigned to production departments.
_____ **3.** Describes the direct materials used in a production department.
_____ **4.** Notifies the materials manager that materials should be sent to a production department.
_____ **5.** Holds costs of materials until they are used in production departments or as factory overhead.
_____ **6.** Holds costs of direct materials, direct labour, and applied overhead until products are transferred from Department A.
_____ **7.** A periodic report that describes the activity and output of a production department.
_____ **8.** Partially completed units standardized to completed units

Exercise 23–2
Journal entries in a process cost accounting system
LO 3, 4, 5

The Model Toy Company manufactures products with two processes: sanding and painting. Prepare entries to record the following activities for January:

a. Purchased raw materials on credit at a cost of $40,000.

b. Used direct materials with costs of $19,000 in the sanding department and $5,000 in the painting department.

c. Used indirect materials with a cost of $20,500.

d. Incurred total labour cost of $75,000, all of which was paid in cash.

e. Used direct labour with costs of $30,000 in the sanding department and $24,000 in the painting department.

f. Used indirect labour with a cost of $11,000.

g. Incurred other overhead costs of $24,000 (credit Cash).

h. Applied overhead at the rates of 125% of direct labour in the sanding department and 75% of direct labour in the painting department.

i. Transferred partially completed products with a cost of $79,900 from the sanding department to the painting department.

j. Transferred completed products with a cost of $145,000 from the painting department to the finished goods inventory.

k. Sold products on credit for $300,000. Their accumulated cost was $150,000.

Exercise 23–3
Interpreting journal entries in a process cost accounting system
LO 3, 4, 5

The following journal entries were recorded in the "Clothing For Your Pet, Inc." process cost accounting system. The company produces pet clothing by passing them through a cutting department and an assembly department. Overhead is applied to production departments based on the direct labour cost during the period. Provide a brief explanation of the event recorded by each entry.

a.	Raw Materials Inventory	26,000	
	Accounts Payable		26,000
b.	Goods in Process Inventory—Cutting	12,000	
	Goods in Process Inventory—Assembly	9,000	
	Raw Materials Inventory		21,000
c.	Goods in Process Inventory—Cutting	8,000	
	Goods in Process Inventory—Assembly	5,000	
	Factory Payroll		13,000
d.	Factory Payroll	16,000	
	Cash		16,000
e.	Factory Overhead	5,000	
	Other Accounts		5,000
f.	Factory Overhead	5,000	
	Raw Materials Inventory		5,000
g.	Factory Overhead	3,000	
	Factory Payroll		3,000
h.	Goods in Process Inventory—Cutting	6,000	
	Goods in Process Inventory—Assembly	7,000	
	Factory Overhead		13,000
i.	Goods in Process Inventory—Assembly	30,000	
	Goods in Process Inventory—Cutting		30,000
j.	Finished Goods Inventory	44,000	
	Goods in Process Inventory—Assembly		44,000
k.	Cost of Goods Sold	50,000	
	Finished Goods Inventory		50,000
	Accounts Receivable	125,000	
	Sales		125,000

Exercise 23-4
Recording cost flows in a process cost system—service business
LO 3, 4, 5

The Nixon Company specializes in shredding government documents in a two-step process. The system begins by processing documents through the shredding department and then through the bagging department. The following information describes the manufacturing operations for April:

	Shredding Department	Bagging Department
Direct materials used	$ 40,000	$460,000
Direct labour used	45,000	75,000
Predetermined overhead application rate (based on direct labour)	120%	200%
Goods transferred from shredding to bagging	$(145,000)	
Goods transferred from bagging to finished goods		(403,000)

In addition, service revenue for the month totalled $900,000 on credit and cost of goods sold was $300,000.

Required

Prepare summary general journal entries to record the April activities.

Exercise 23-5
Computing equivalent units
LO 6, 7

During a recent month, a production department in a process manufacturing system completed a number of units of product and transferred them to finished goods. Of these units, 50,000 were in process in the department at the beginning of the month and 220,000 were started and completed during the month. The beginning inventory units were 60% complete with respect to materials and 40% complete with respect to labour when the month began. At the end of the month, 66,000 additional units were in process in the department and were 80% complete with respect to materials and 30% complete with respect to labour.

Required

Compute (a) the number of physical units transferred to finished goods and (b) the number of equivalent units with respect to materials and with respect to labour produced in the department during the month.

Exercise 23-6
Assigning costs to inventories in a process cost system
LO 7, 8, 10

The production department described in Exercise 23-5 had $700,000 of direct materials and $500,000 of direct labour cost charged to it during the month. Compute the direct materials cost and the direct labour cost per equivalent unit in the department and allocate the costs among the units in the goods in process inventories and the units started and completed during the month.

Exercise 23-7
Computing equivalent units
LO 6, 7, 10

A production department in a process manufacturing system completed 250,000 units of product and transferred them to finished goods during a recent week. Of these units, 75,000 were in process at the beginning of the week. The other 175,000 units were started and completed during the week. At the end of the period, 50,000 units were in process.

Required

Compute the department's equivalent units of production with respect to direct materials under each of the following unrelated assumptions:

a. All direct materials are added to the products when processing begins.

b. The direct materials are added to the products evenly throughout the process. The beginning goods in process inventory was 50% complete and the ending goods in process inventory was 70% complete.

c. One-half the direct materials are added to the products when the process begins and the other half is added when the process is 75% complete as to direct labour. The beginning goods in process inventory was 40% complete as to direct labour and the ending goods in process inventory was 60% complete as to direct labour.

Exercise 23-8
Completing a flowchart for a process system
LO 3, 4, 5, 11

The following flowchart shows the production activity of the punching and bending departments of the Laker Company for August. Use the amounts shown on the flowchart to compute the missing numbers identified by question marks.

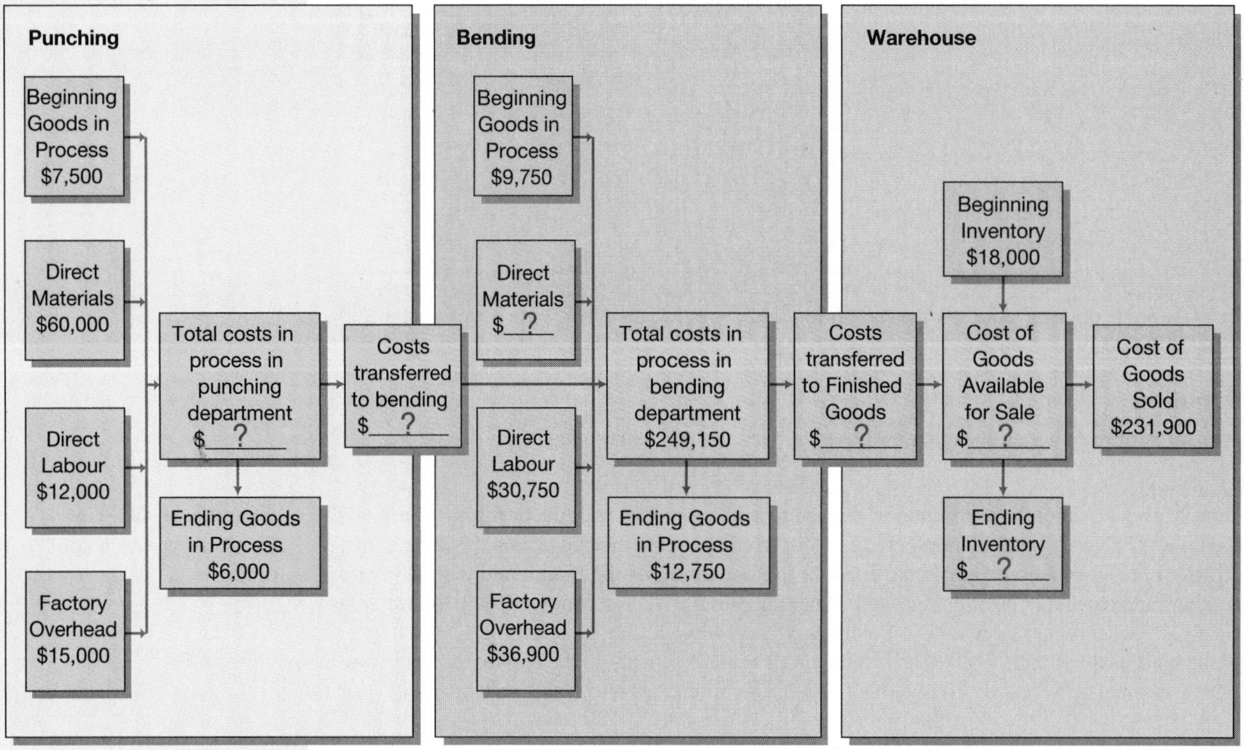

Exercise 23-9
Completing a process cost summary
LO 7

The following partially completed process cost summary describes the July activities of the slicing department of the Serranos Company. The output of the slicing department is sent to the canning department, which sends the finished goods to the warehouse for shipping. A partially completed process cost summary for the slicing department follows:

Costs Charged to the Department	
Direct materials requisitioned	$224,000
Direct labour charged	39,000
Overhead allocated (at 200% predetermined rate)	78,000
Total processing costs for the month	341,000
Goods in process at the beginning of the month	59,000
Total costs to be accounted for	$400,000

		Equivalent Units	
Equivalent Unit Processing Costs	**Units of Product**	**Direct Materials**	**Labour and Overhead**
Beginning goods in process	1,600	1,600	1,200
Units started and completed	20,000	20,000	20,000
Ending goods in process	2,400	2,400	1,800
Total	24,000	24,000	23,000

Prepare the process cost summary for the slicing department by completing the Equivalent Unit Processing Costs section and the Assignment of Costs to the Output of the Department section.

Problems

Problem 23-1
Measuring production costs and preparing journal entries

LO 3, 4, 5, 11, 12

The NHLL Logo Company manufactures blankets by passing the products through a weaving department and a sewing department. This information is known about its inventories for May:

	Beginning Inventory	Ending Inventory
Raw materials	$ 120,000	$ 185,000
Goods in process—Weaving	300,000	330,000
Goods in process—Sewing	570,000	700,000
Finished goods	1,266,000	1,206,000

The following information describes the company's activities during May:

Raw materials purchases (on credit)	$ 500,000
Factory payroll cost (paid with cash)	3,060,000
Other overhead cost (credit Other Accounts)	156,000
Materials used:	
Direct—Weaving	240,000
Direct—Sewing	75,000
Indirect	120,000
Labour used:	
Direct—Weaving	1,200,000
Direct—Sewing	360,000
Indirect	1,500,000
Overhead rates as a percentage of direct labour:	
Weaving	80%
Sewing	150%
Sales (on credit)	$4,000,000

Required

1. Compute (a) the cost of products transferred from weaving to sewing, (b) the cost of products transferred from sewing to finished goods, and (c) the cost of goods sold.
2. Prepare summary general journal entries to record the activities during May.

Check Figure Cost of goods sold, $3,275,000

Problem 23-2
Computing costs per equivalent unit and allocating costs to products

LO 7

The PeaPood Carver Company passes its product through several departments, the last of which is the carving department. Direct labour is added evenly throughout the process in this department. One-fourth of direct materials are added at the beginning of the process and the remaining three-fourths is added when the process is 50% complete with respect to direct labour. During November, 575,000 units of product were transferred to finished goods from the carving department. Of these units, 100,000 units were 40% complete with respect to labour at the beginning of the period and 475,000 were started and completed during the period. At the end of November, the goods in process inventory consisted of 300,000 units that were 25% complete with respect to labour.

The carving department's direct labour cost for November was $1,220,000 and direct materials cost was $1,875,000.

Required

Preparation component:

1. Determine the carving department's equivalent units of production with respect to direct labour and with respect to direct materials.
2. Compute the direct labour cost and the direct materials cost per equivalent unit.
3. Compute the amount of direct labour cost and the amount of the direct materials cost assigned to the beginning goods in process inventory, to the units started and completed, and to the ending goods in process inventory.

Check Figure Direct labour cost per equivalent unit, $2.00

Analysis component:

4. PeaPood sells and ships all units to customers as soon as they are completed. Assume that an error was made in determining the percentage of completion for the units in ending inventory. Instead of being 25% complete with respect to labour, they were actually 60% complete. Write a brief essay describing how this error would affect PeaPood's November financial statements.

Problem 23–3
Journal entries in a process cost accounting system and using equivalent units
LO 3, 4, 5, 6

The Walden Company produces large quantities of a product that goes through two processes—spinning and cutting. These facts are known about the factory's activities for March:

Raw materials:	
Beginning inventory	$ 32,000
Raw materials purchased (on credit)	221,120
Direct materials used in spinning	(160,000)
Direct materials used in cutting	(37,120)
Indirect materials used	(40,560)
Ending inventory	$ 15,440
Factory payroll:	
Direct labour used in spinning	$ 68,000
Direct labour used in cutting	55,680
Indirect labour used	36,320
Total payroll cost (paid with cash)	$160,000
Factory overhead incurred:	
Indirect materials used	$ 40,560
Indirect labour used	36,320
Other overhead costs	91,640
Total factory overhead incurred	$168,520
Factory overhead applied:	
Spinning (125% of direct labour)	$ 85,000
Cutting (150% of direct labour)	83,520
Total factory overhead applied	$168,520

The following facts are known about the inventory in the spinning department:

Units:	
Beginning in process inventory	4,000
Started and completed	12,000
Ending in process inventory	8,000
Percentage completed:	
Beginning in process inventory	
Materials	100%
Labour and overhead	25%
Ending in process inventory	
Materials	100%
Labour and overhead	25%
Costs:	
Beginning in process inventory	$ 41,000
Direct materials added	160,000
Direct labour added	68,000
Overhead applied (125% of direct labour)	85,000
Total costs	$354,000
Transferred out to cutting department	(272,000)
Ending in process inventory	$ 82,000

These facts are known about the goods in process inventories for the cutting department:

Beginning in process inventory	$174,000
Ending in process inventory	177,120

These facts are known about the finished goods:

Beginning inventory	$148,400
Cost transferred in from cutting	445,200
Cost of goods sold	(530,000)
Ending inventory	$ 63,600

During the month, 10,000 units of finished goods were sold for cash at the price of $120 each.

Required

Preparation component:

1. Prepare entries to record the activities of March.
2. Compute the equivalent units of production for the spinning department for March, and compute the costs per equivalent unit for direct materials, direct labour, and overhead.
3. Compute the cost of the ending goods in process inventory for the spinning department.

Check Figure Cost per equivalent unit: materials, $8.00; labour, $4.00; overhead, $5.00

Analysis component:

4. Walden provides incentives to managers of the processing departments by paying monthly bonuses based on their success in controlling costs per equivalent unit of production. Assume that the spinning department underestimated the percentage of completion for the units in ending inventory, with the result that the equivalent units of production in ending inventory for March were understated. What impact would this error have on the bonuses paid to the manager of the spinning department and the manager of the cutting department? What impact, if any, would this error have on April bonuses?

Problem 23-4
Preparing a process cost summary
LO 7, 10

Praxair Company produces its product by passing it through a single processing department. Direct materials, direct labour, and overhead are added to the product evenly throughout the process. The company uses month-long reporting periods for its process cost accounting system.

The Goods in Process Inventory account appears as follows after posting entries for direct materials, direct labour, and overhead costs during October:

Goods in Process Inventory					Acct. No. 133
Date		Explanation	Debit	Credit	Balance
Oct.	1	Beginning balance			40,800
	31	Direct materials	100,200		141,000
	31	Direct labour costs	400,500		541,500
	31	Applied overhead	123,000		664,500

During October, the company finished and transferred 150,000 units of the product to finished goods. Of these units, 30,000 were in process at the beginning of the month and 120,000 were started and completed during the month. The beginning goods in process inventory was 30% complete. At the end of the month, the goods in process inventory consisted of 20,000 units that were 80% complete.

Required

1. Compute the number of equivalent units of production for October.
2. Prepare the department's process cost summary for October.
3. Prepare an entry to transfer the cost of the completed units to finished goods inventory.

Check Figure Total cost transferred to finished goods, $600,711

Problem 23-5
Preparing a process cost summary
LO 7, 10, 11, 13

Manchaca Company manufactures a single product in one department. All direct materials are added at the beginning of the manufacturing process. Direct labour and overhead are added evenly throughout the process. The company uses month-long reporting periods for its process cost accounting system.

During May, the company completed and transferred 22,200 units of product to the finished goods inventory. The beginning goods in process inventory consisted of 3,000 units that were 100% complete with respect to direct materials and 40% complete with respect to direct labour and overhead. The other 19,200 completed units were started during the month. In addition, 2,400 units were in process at the end of the month. They were 100% complete with respect to direct materials and 80% complete with respect to direct labour and overhead.

After posting the entries to record direct materials, direct labour, and overhead during May, the company's Goods in Process Inventory account appears as follows:

Goods in Process Inventory					Acct. No. 133
Date		Explanation	Debit	Credit	Balance
May	1	Beginning balance			181,320
	31	Direct materials	496,800		678,120
	31	Direct labour costs	1,185,600		1,863,720
	31	Applied overhead	948,480		2,812,200

Required

1. Compute the department's equivalent units of production for May.
2. Compute the cost per equivalent unit.
3. Prepare the department's process cost summary for May.
4. Prepare the entry to transfer the cost of the completed units to finished goods inventory.

Check Figure Total cost transferred to finished goods, $2,578,230

Analysis component:

5. Throughout the course you have been exposed to the fact that accountants rely upon estimates.
   a. Identify the two major estimates that influence the cost per equivalent unit.
   b. In what direction do you anticipate a bias from the operations management team for each estimate, given you know their compensation is based on maintaining low inventory values? Explain.
6. The approach to measuring spoilage can impact the equivalent unit cost. In the above problem, without computation, would the cost per equivalent unit increase or decrease if management only counted the good units of production? (Assume the current problem includes spoiled units.) Explain why management would want to know the cost of spoiled units.

Alternate Problems

Problem 23-1A
Measuring production costs and preparing journal entries
LO 3, 4, 5, 11, 12

The Tots Toys Company manufactures dolls by passing the products through a molding department and an assembly department. This information is known about its inventories for June:

	Beginning Inventory	Ending Inventory
Raw materials	$36,000	$55,000
Goods in process—molding	12,000	21,000
Goods in process—assembly	66,000	54,000
Finished goods	78,000	99,000

The following information describes the company's activities during June:

Raw materials purchases (on credit)	$ 100,000
Factory payroll cost (paid with cash)	200,000
Other overhead cost (credit Other Accounts)	50,000
Materials used:	
Direct—molding	$6,000
Direct—assembly	54,000
Indirect	21,000
Labour used:	
Direct—molding	$ 100,000
Direct—assembly	75,000
Indirect	25,000
Overhead rates as % of direct labour:	
Molding	80%
Assembly	75%
Sales (on credit)	$500,000

Required

1. Compute (a) the cost of products transferred from molding to assembly, (b) the cost of products transferred from assembly to finished goods, and (c) the cost of goods sold.
2. Prepare entries to record the activities during June.

Problem 23-2A
Computing costs per equivalent unit and allocating costs to products

LO 7

The Penbrook Company passes its product through several departments, the last of which is the bagging department. Direct materials are added evenly throughout the process. One-half of the direct labour is added at the beginning of the process and the other half is added when the process is 50% complete with respect to materials. During September, 80,000 units of product were transferred to finished goods from the bagging department. Of these units, 18,000 units were 60% complete at the beginning of the period and 62,000 were started and completed during the period. At the end of September, the goods in process inventory consisted of 8,000 units that were 25% complete with respect to materials. The bagging department's direct materials cost for September was $712,000 and direct labour cost was $1,980,000.

Required

Preparation component:

1. Determine the bagging department's equivalent units of production with respect to direct labour and with respect to direct materials.
2. Compute the direct labour cost and the direct materials cost per equivalent unit.
3. Compute the amount of direct labour cost and the amount of the direct materials cost assigned to the beginning goods in process inventory, to the units started and completed, and to the ending goods in process inventory.

Check Figure Direct labour cost per equivalent unit, $30.00

Analysis component:

4. Penbrook sells and ships all units to customers as soon as they are completed. Assume that an error was made in determining the percentage of completion for the units in ending inventory. Instead of being 25% complete with respect to materials, they were actually 75% complete. Write a brief essay describing how this error would affect Penbrook's September financial statements.

Problem 23-3A
Journal entries in a process cost accounting system and using equivalent units
LO 3, 4, 5, 7

The Trimble Company produces large quantities of a product that goes through two processes—tooling and machining. These facts are known about the factory activities for May:

Raw materials:	
Beginning inventory	$ 84,000
Raw materials purchased (on credit)	500,000
Direct materials used in tooling	(248,200)
Direct materials used in machining	(178,200)
Indirect materials used	(101,600)
Ending inventory	$ 56,000
Factory payroll:	
Direct labour used in tooling	$318,000
Direct labour used in machining	35,640
Indirect labour used	46,360
Total payroll cost (paid with cash)	$400,000
Factory overhead incurred:	
Indirect materials used	$101,600
Indirect labour used	46,360
Other overhead costs	50,520
Total factory overhead incurred	$198,480
Factory overhead applied:	
Tooling (40% of direct labour)	$127,200
Machining (200% of direct labour)	71,280
Total factory overhead applied	$198,480

The following facts are known about the inventory in the tooling department:

Units:	
Beginning in process inventory	40,000
Started and completed	120,000
Ending in process inventory	20,000
Percentage completed:	
Beginning in process inventory	
Materials	80%
Labour and overhead	40%
Ending in process inventory	
Materials	90%
Labour and overhead	75%
Costs:	
Beginning in process inventory	$ 99,200
Direct materials added	248,200
Direct labour added	318,000
Overhead applied (40% of direct labour)	127,200
Total costs	$792,600
Transferred out to machining department	(720,000)
Ending in process inventory	$ 72,600

These facts are known about the goods in process inventories for the machining department:

Beginning in process inventory	$249,000
Ending in process inventory	229,320

These facts are known about the finished goods:

Beginning inventory	$ 36,600
Cost transferred in from machining	1,024,800
Cost of goods sold	(1,000,400)
Ending inventory	$ 61,000

During the month, 80,000 units of finished goods were sold for cash at the price of $20 each.

Required

Preparation component:

1. Prepare entries to record the activities of May.
2. Compute the tooling department's equivalent units of production for May, and compute the costs per equivalent unit for direct materials, direct labour, and overhead, assuming all product costs are added evenly throughout the process.
3. Compute the cost of the ending goods in process inventory for the tooling department.

Analysis component:

4. Trimble provides incentives to managers of the processing departments by paying monthly bonuses based on their success in controlling costs per equivalent unit of production. Assume that the tooling department overestimated the percentage of completion for the units in ending inventory, with the result that the equivalent units of production in ending inventory for May was overstated. What impact would this error have on the bonuses paid to the manager of the tooling department and the manager of the machining department? What impact, if any would this error have on June bonuses?

Problem 23-4A
Preparing a process cost summary
LO 7, 10

Osorio Company produces its product by passing it through a single processing department. Direct materials, direct labour, and overhead are added to the product evenly throughout the process. The company uses month-long reporting periods for its process cost accounting system.

The Goods in Process Inventory account appears as follows after posting entries for direct materials, direct labour, and overhead costs:

Goods in Process Inventory					Acct. No. 133
Date		Explanation	Debit	Credit	Balance
Nov.	1	Beginning balance			70,000
	30	Direct materials	115,000		185,000
	30	Direct labour costs	425,000		610,000
	30	Applied overhead	600,000		1,210,000

During November, the company finished and transferred 100,000 units of the product to finished goods. Of these units, 7,500 were in process at the beginning of the month, and 92,500 were started and completed during the month. The beginning goods in process inventory was 80% complete. At the end of the month, the goods in process inventory consisted of 12,000 units that were 25% completed.

Required

1. Compute the number of equivalent units of production for November.
2. Prepare the department's process cost summary for November.
3. Prepare an entry to transfer the cost of the completed units to Finished Goods Inventory.

Problem 23-5A
Preparing a process cost summary
LO 7, 10, 11, 13

Jiffy Manufacturing Company manufactures a single product in one department. Direct labour and overhead are added evenly throughout the process. Direct materials are added as needed. The company uses month-long reporting periods for its process cost accounting system.

During January, the company completed and transferred 220,000 units of product to the finished goods inventory. The beginning in process inventory consisted of 20,000 units that were 75% complete with respect to direct materials and 60% complete with respect to direct labour and overhead. The other 200,000 completed units were started during the month. In addition, 40,000 units were in process at the end of the month. They were 50% complete with respect to direct materials and 30% complete with respect to direct labour and overhead.

The company has only one Goods in Process Inventory account. At the end of the month, the account appeared as follows after entries for direct materials, direct labour, and overhead had been posted:

Goods in Process Inventory					Acct. No. 133
Date		Explanation	Debit	Credit	Balance
Jan.	1	Beginning balance			41,100
	31	Direct materials	112,500		153,600
	31	Direct labour costs	176,000		329,600
	31	Applied overhead	440,000		769,600

Required

1. Compute the equivalent units of production for direct materials and for direct labour and factory overhead.
2. Compute the cost per equivalent unit for direct materials, direct labour and factory overhead.
3. Prepare the department's process cost summary for January.
4. Prepare an entry to transfer the cost of the completed units to finished goods inventory.

Analysis component:

5. Throughout the course you have been exposed to the fact that accountants rely upon estimates.
   a. Identify the two major estimates that influence the cost per equivalent unit.
   b. In what direction would you anticipate a bias from the operations management team for each estimate, given you know their compensation is based on maintaining low inventory values? Explain.
6. The approach to measuring spoilage can impact the equivalent unit cost. In the above problem, without computation, what would be the cost per equivalent unit if management only counted the good units of production? (Assume the current problem includes spoiled units.) Explain why management would want to know the cost of spoiled units.

Comprehensive Problem

Corked Bat Company

This Comprehensive Problems acts as a review of Chapters 3, 6, 7, 21, and 23.

The Corked Bat Company produces baseball bats for yet-to-be homerun hitters. The bats go through two processes, one cuts the wood into bats and drills a hole for the cork, labelled Department One, and the other fills the hole with cork and stamps the company's logo on the bat, labelled Department Two. All of Department One's output is transferred to Department Two. In addition to the goods in process inventories in Departments One and Two, the Corked Bat Company maintains inventories of raw materials and finished goods. The Corked Bat Company uses raw materials as direct materials in Departments One and Two and as indirect materials. Its factory payroll costs include direct labour for each department and indirect labour. All materials in each department are added at the beginning and direct labour and factory overhead are applied uniformly.

Required

In this problem, you are to maintain certain records and produce various measures of the inventories to reflect the events of July. Round all computations of unit costs to the nearest penny and all other dollar amounts to the nearest whole dollar. To begin, set up the following general ledger accounts and enter their June 30 balances:

Acct. 132	Raw Materials Inventory	$ 50,000
Acct. 133	Goods in Process Inventory—Department One	130,000
Acct. 134	Goods in Process Inventory—Department Two	50,000
Acct. 135	Finished Goods Inventory	200,000
Acct. 413	Sales	-0-
Acct. 502	Cost of Goods Sold	-0-
Acct. 530	Factory Payroll	-0-
Acct. 540	Factory Overhead	-0-

1. Prepare entries to record the following events that occurred in July
   a. Purchased raw materials for $250,000 cash (use a perpetual inventory system).
   b. Used raw materials as follows:

Department One	$60,000
Department Two	45,000
Indirect materials	20,000

   c. Incurred factory payroll cost of $454,500 paid with cash (ignore income and other taxes).
   d. Assigned factory payroll costs as follows:

Department One	$270,000
Department Two	134,500
Indirect labour	50,000

   e. Incurred additional factory overhead costs of $160,000, paid in cash.
   f. Allocated factory overhead to Departments One and Two at 50% of the direct labour costs.
2. Information about the units of product on hand or worked on during July follows:

	Department One	Department Two
Bats in beginning inventory	500	1,000
Percent completed with respect to:		
Materials	100%	100%
Labour and overhead	20%	75%
Bats started and finished in July	2,000	1,800
Percent completed with respect to:		
Materials	100%	100%
Labour and overhead	100%	100%
Bats in ending inventory	1,000	1,600
Percent completed with respect to:		
Materials	100%	100%
Labour and overhead	30%	40%

Use this information and the facts from part 1 to make the following computations:
   a. Equivalent units of production in Department One and the per unit costs for labour, materials, and overhead.
   b. Equivalent units of production in Department Two and the per unit costs for labour, materials, and overhead.
3. Using the results from part 2 and previously given information, make the following computations, and prepare general journal entries to record:
   g. Total cost of units transferred from Department One to Department Two during July.
   h. Total cost of units transferred from Department Two to finished goods during July.
   i. Sale of finished goods that cost $531,400 for $1,250,000 cash.
4. Post the journal entries from parts 1 and 3 to the ledger accounts that you set up at the beginning of the problem.
5. Compute the amount of gross profit from the sales in July.

Analytical and Review Problems

A & R 23-1

For Ying company, which uses a process cost system, you are given the following selected information for the month of August 1998.

	Physical Units %	Complete
Beginning work in process	3,000	50%
Units started	12,000	
Units in ending work in process	5,000	30%

The total cost of the beginning work in process was $18,500, of which $3,500 represented direct labour costs. Overhead is applied on the basis of direct labour costs.

During August, the company added $34,700 of direct materials, $25,250 of direct labour, and $30,300 of overhead to work in process.

All direct materials are added at the beginning of the process, and the conversion costs are incurred uniformly throughout the process.

Required

1. What is the overhead rate?
2. Show the direct materials, the direct labour, and the overhead components of the beginning work in process.
3. What is the number of equivalent units used to establish the weighted average cost for direct materials, direct labour, and overhead?
4. What is the number of equivalent units used to establish the cost for direct materials, direct labour, and overhead?
5. What is the cost of ending work in process inventory for direct materials, direct labour, and overhead? Show each component separately.

(CGA-Adapted)

A & R 23-2

Vancouver Canners Ltd. has recently modernized its canning process by installing updated, more efficient machines. The process has become much less labour intensive.

Required

Indicate what changes you would expect to see in the company's process costing system as a result of the modernization.

A & R 23-3

The Dessau Company produces a product by sending it through two processes, one of which takes place in Department One and the other in Department Two. All the Department One's output is transferred to Department Two. In addition to the goods in process inventories in Departments One and Two, Dessau maintains inventories of raw materials and finished goods. Dessau uses raw materials as direct materials in Departments One and Two and as indirect materials. Its factory payroll costs include direct labour for each department and indirect labour.

Required

In the problem, you are to maintain certain records and produce various measures of the inventories to reflect the events of July. Round all calculations of unit costs to the nearest penny and all other dollar amounts to the nearest whole dollar. To begin, set up the following general ledger accounts and enter their June 30 balances:

Acct. 132	Raw Materials Inventory	$ 64,000
Acct. 133	Goods in Process Inventory—Department One	128,440
Acct. 134	Goods in Process Inventory—Department Two	50,000
Acct. 135	Finished Goods Inventory	220,000
Acct. 413	Sales	-0-
Acct. 502	Cost of Goods Sold	-0-
Acct. 530	Factory Payroll	-0-
Acct. 540	Factory Overhead	-0-

1. Prepare entries to record the following events that occurred in July:

a. Purchased raw materials for $200,000 cash (use a perpetual inventory system).

b. Used raw materials as follows:

Department One	$72,000
Department Two	89,600
Indirect materials	42,000

c. Incurred factory payroll cost of $360,000, paid with cash (ignore income and other taxes).

d. Assigned factory payroll costs as follows:

Department One	$200,000
Department Two	100,000
Indirect materials	60,000

e. Incurred additional factory overhead costs of $48,000, paid in cash.

f. Allocated factory overhead to Department One and Two as percentage of the direct labour costs. (To make this entry, you must first compute the overhead allocation rate using direct labour and overhead costs incurred during July.)

2. Information about the units of product on hand or worked on during July follows:

	Department One	Department Two
Units in beginning inventory	500	1,000
Percent completed with respect to:		
Materials	50%	40%
Labour and overhead	40%	62%
Units started and finished in July	2,000	1,800
Percent completed with respect to:		
Materials	100%	100%
Labour and overhead	100%	100%
Units in ending inventory	1,000	1,600
Percent completed with respect to:		
Materials	15%	25%
Labour and overhead	20%	20%

Use this information and the facts from part 1 to make the following calculations:

i) Equivalent units of production in Department One and the per unit costs for labour materials, and overhead.

ii) Equivalent units of production in Department Two and the per units costs for labour, materials, and overhead.

3. Using the results from requirements 2 and previously given information, make the following calculations, and prepare general journal entries to record:

g. Total cost of units transferred from Department One to Department Two during July.

h. Total cost of units transferred from Department Two to finished goods during July.

i. Sale of finished goods that cost $531,400 for $1,250,000 cash.

4. Post the journal entries from parts 1 and 3 to the ledger accounts that you set up at the beginning of the problem.

5. Compute the amount of gross profit from the sales in July.

BEYOND THE NUMBERS

Reporting in Action

Consider the costs and benefits for external reporting of making certain the ending work-in-process percent complete values are precise. Also consider whether reasonable estimates are acceptable. Global Shoes reported raw materials inventory as follows:

	1998	1997	1996
Net income	$800,000,000	$795,822,000	$553,190,000
Raw material	60,275,000	55,275,000	16,399,000

Now assume that the raw material value for 1997 is overstated by 10% and for 1996 is understated by 15% due to estimation errors.

Required

a. By how much is ending inventory (i) overstated for 1997 and (ii) understated for 1996, before and after tax? Assume a 40% tax each year. Round calculations to the nearest thousands.

b. By how much (in percent) does net income increase and decrease for 1997 and 1996 respectively? (Hint: Work out a simple example to see how an error in ending inventory impacts net income.)

c. Are the amounts in (b) material or immaterial? Explain in reference to costs and benefits.

Take a look at the 1998 work-in-process inventory value and assume a 10% understatement and a 40% tax rate. Does your answer change from the above?

Comparative Analysis

Leading competitive process manufacturers such as Nike and Reebok usually work to maintain a high-quality and low-cost operation. One ratio routinely watched is the cost of goods sold divided by total expenses. Assume for this problem that total expenses equal cost of goods sold plus selling and administrative expenses. If this ratio declines, for instance, it could mean the company is spending too much on operations and not enough on production. If this ratio increases beyond a specified target, it could mean the company is spending too much on manufacturing or not enough on selling and administration. (Note: Financial ratio analysis is an interactive process focusing on several ratios. The following questions focus our attention on only one issue and therefore the analysis is limited.)

	Nike		Reebok	
	1997	1996	1997	1996
Cost of goods sold	$5,502,993	$3,906,746	$2,144,442	$2,114,084
Total expenses	$7,806,697	$5,495,358	$3,210,214	$3,113,815

Required

a. For both Nike and Reebok, compute the percent of cost of goods sold to total expenses for each year available.

b. Comment on the similarities or differences you identify from your computations.

Ethics Challenge

Many accounting professionals are skilled in financial analysis. But most are not skilled in the highly technical world of manufacturing, especially the process manufacturing environment (for example, a bottling plant or chemical manufacturer). Yet to provide professional accounting services you must understand the industry, product, and processes associated with your business. This is your ethical responsibility.

Required

Write a one-page action plan, in a memo format, on how you would go about becoming educated regarding a key business process of a company that hired you to provide it with professional financial advice. One example might be the packaging process for "double-stuffed" Oreo Cookies. The memo should specify an industry, product, and one selected process. Second, the memo should minimally draw on one professional journal in the industry and one professional industry organization.

Communicating in Practice

LO 1, 2

You hire a new assistant production manager. His prior experience is with a company that produced goods to order. Your firm engages in continuous production of homogeneous products that go through various manufacturing processes. Your new assistant sends you an e-mail questioning some cost classifications on an internal report. He questions why the cost of some materials that do not actually become part of the finished product, and some labour costs that are not directly associated with producing the product are classified as direct costs. Respond to his question via memo or e-mail.

Taking It to the Net

You've learned teamwork is essential for business success. The same is true for business and accounting software. Software products must work together to be value added in providing information in support of decision making. Check out the following Web location [**www.uec-usx.com/spts.htm**] and answer the following questions:

Required

1. Identify three systems that must work together to support the business information needs of a steel manufacturer.
2. Identify the role each system plays in coordinating the system applications and/or the respective type of information each system manages.

Teamwork in Action

LO 1, 3, 4, 5

The purpose of this team activity is to ensure each member of the team understands processing manufacturing operations and the related accounting entries. Turn to Exhibit 23.6 and find the activities identified with numbers 1–10. Pick a member of the team to start. This team member is to describe activity number 1 in this exhibit, then verbalize the related journal entry and describe how the amount(s) in the entry are computed. The other members of the team are to voice agreement or disagreement—discussion is to continue until all express understanding. Rotate to the next numbered activity and next team member until all activities and entries are discussed. If at any point a team member is stumped, the team member may "pass" and volunteer to get back in the rotation at whatever point he/she can contribute to the team's discussion. Teams should call the instructor if assistance is needed.

Hitting the Road

In the study of process costing you learned that the process is measured first and then a unit measure is taken in the form of equivalent units—direct material, direct labour, overhead and all three combined. Also, you learned the same thinking applies to service industry processes.

Required

Take a trip to your local **Canada Post** centre. Look into the back room and you will see several processes ongoing. Select one process, such as sorting, and *list the costs associated with this process*. Your list should include material, labour and overhead (be specific). Classify each cost as fixed or variable. At the bottom of your list, outline how overhead should be assigned to your identified process. The following format is suggested:

Cost description	Direct Material	Direct Labour	Process Overhead	Variable cost	Fixed cost
Workforce sorting		X		X	
Overhead allocation suggestions:					

Business Break

Does a change in company strategy result in changes to the process costing system? Read the article "Microprocessors Are for Wimps" in the December 15, 1997, issue of *Business Week* and answer the following questions in a one-page memo to your instructor.

1. Identify the shift in **Motorola's** market focus regarding microprocessor production.
2. What changes can you suggest to Motorola regarding the process costing system to better support the new market focus?

24 CHAPTER

Cost Allocation and Performance Measurement

A Look Back

Chapter 21 introduced managerial accounting and cost concepts, and discussed new manufacturing management principles. Chapter 22 extended these cost concepts and introduced the manufacturing statement and job order costing. Chapter 23 described process cost accounting.

A Look at This Chapter

This chapter describes cost allocation and activity-based costing. It identifies managerial reports useful in directing a company's activities. It also describes allocating common costs among departments, responsibility accounting, and measuring departmental performance.

A Look Forward

Chapter 25 looks at cost behaviour and describes how this is useful to managers in performing cost-volume-profit analyses.

Chapter Outline

Chasing Costs and Finding Gold

Montreal, PQ—Karla Sellers, a department manager for **AeroTech**—a commercial aerospace manufacturer—was confronted with several strategic initiatives launched by top management. These initiatives were directed at improving AeroTech's competitive position. Its management pursues continuous improvement, but it aims to strategically identify specific areas for improvement. Says Sellers, "My department was the guinea pig, and I was leery to put it politely."

To identify opportunities for improvement, Seller's supervisors examined cost data based on an analysis of processes and activities. This required designing an accounting system so that cost information tracked the flow of underlying resources in the processes at AeroTech. Management considered this necessary if they were to confidently use data in targeting and measuring AeroTech's continuous quality improvement.

Sellers' department—the Small Aircraft Division—was the target of the Process and Activity Analysis project. Its aim was to implement an activity-based cost system to meet management's information demands. Sellers and her team identified four main goals of their activity-based cost system:

1. Increase cost visibility, specifically when processes crossed organizational boundaries.
2. Identify major cost drivers for analysis and prediction of cost behaviour.
3. Improve tracing of overhead costs.
4. Identify activities adding value to the product and those that do not.

"I felt uneasy about the whole project," says Sellers. "I had never participated in such a major overhaul of an information system." Before beginning, Sellers says she needed to get a better understanding of how costs are traced to processes, how they are accumulated, and how costs per unit were computed for each process.

"It all eventually came together," says Sellers. She admits her team's lack of knowledge in activity-based costing slowed its progress. "In the end, we cut costs by nearly 17%, which drove price reductions," says Sellers. "Our competitors did not react and we gained 9% in market share." Sellers reward? She's now Vice-President of Strategic Operations with a hefty salary to boot!

Learning Objectives

LO 1 Assign factory overhead costs using two-stage cost allocation.

LO 2 Assign factory overhead costs using activity-based costing.

LO 3 Explain departmentalization and the role of departmental accounting.

LO 4 Distinguish between direct and indirect expenses.

LO 5 Identify bases for allocating indirect expenses to departments.

LO 6 Prepare departmental income statements.

LO 7 Prepare departmental contribution reports.

LO 8 Explain controllable costs and responsibility accounting.

LO 9 Describe allocation of joint costs across products.

LO 10 Analyze investment centres using return on total assets.

CHAPTER PREVIEW

The three prior chapters focused on measuring the costs of products manufactured, including reporting and analyzing the results in financial statements. This chapter discusses further the issue of cost allocation. It describes how we allocate manufacturing costs shared by more than one product across these products, and how we allocate indirect costs of shared items such as utilities, advertising and rent. The chapter next describes activity-based costing and its tracing of the costs of individual activities. This knowledge helps us better understand how resources are consumed as illustrated in the opening article. The chapter also shifts our focus to managerial accounting reports useful in directing a company's activities. It explains how and why management divides companies into departments.

Additional Methods of Overhead Cost Allocation

Chapter 22 explained how we allocated factory overhead cost to jobs using a predetermined overhead allocation rate based on direct labour cost. When a single overhead allocation rate is used on a plant-wide basis, all overhead is lumped together and a predetermined overhead allocation rate is computed and used to assign overhead to jobs. This section considers additional cost allocation issues.

Two-Stage Cost Allocation

LO1 Assign factory overhead costs using two-stage cost allocation.

This section considers a case where multiple overhead allocation rates are used to assign overhead. This case is illustrated in Chapter 22 on page 1049. We apply a two-stage cost allocation procedure in this situation to assign all pertinent direct and indirect costs to the products.

In the first stage, costs are assigned to cost centres or operating departments. An operating department carries out the main function(s) of an organization. These cost centres are usually production departments such as machining and assembly. We explain this stage in a later section of this chapter. Costs assigned to a cost centre consist of those directly incurred by the centre and those allocated to it from one or more service departments within the company. A service department, for instance, supports activities of many centres. The second stage computes a predetermined overhead allocation rate for each cost centre. This rate is used to assign overhead to jobs.

Illustration of Two-Stage Cost Allocation

The case in Exhibit 24.1 helps us understand the two-stage procedure. Consider the manufacturer, **Custom Autos**. It consists of five manufacturing related departments: janitorial, maintenance, factory accounting, machining and assembly. The expenses incurred by each department are considered a product cost. The three service departments—janitorial, maintenance and factory accounting— expect to incur $10,000, $15,000 and $8,000 (total $33,000) of expenses respectively for the first quarter of 1998. These amounts consist of expenses directly traceable to the three departments and include items such as salaries and other expenses not shared with another department.

The resources of these service departments are consumed by two cost centres (machining and assembly) as shown in the exhibit for each service department; for example, 60:40 in the case of janitorial. In the first step, the service department costs are assigned to the two cost centres based on the use of services by the cost centres. This means 60% or $6,000 of the janitorial costs are assigned to the machining cost centre and 40% or $4,000 to the assembly cost centre.

For costs assigned from the service departments, those costs directly incurred by the cost centre ($10,000 in the case of machining) are added to determine total costs assigned to each cost centre. This means a total of $25,000 and $36,000 are assigned to machining and assembly respectively.

In the second stage, predetermined overhead rates for each cost centre are computed. In the case of machining, this rate is computed using machine hours as the allocation base. In the case of assembly, the rate is computed using labour hours as the allocation base. The predetermined overhead rates are computed as $2.50 per machine hour for machining and $1.80 per labour hour for assembly.

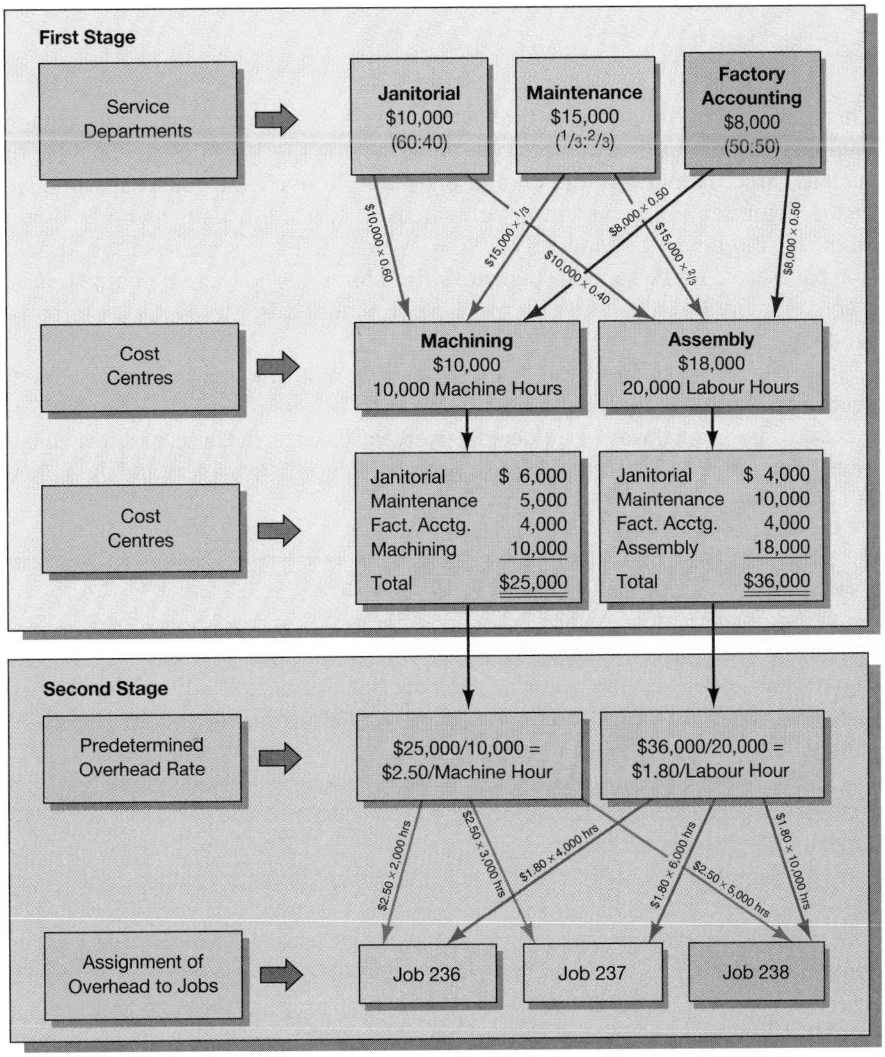

Exhibit 24.1

Two-Stage Cost Allocation

The predetermined overhead rates are then used to assign overhead to jobs. In particular, three jobs were started and finished in the first quarter of 1998. These jobs consumed resources as follows: Job 236—2,000 machine hours in machining and 4,000 labour hours in assembly; Job 237—3,000 machine hours and 6,000 labour hours; Job 238—5,000 machine hours and 10,000 labour hours. The overhead assigned to these three jobs is shown in Exhibit 24.2. Total overhead assigned to each job is $12,200, $18,300 and $30,500. This adds to $61,000, which is the total amount of overhead we started with.

Exhibit 24.2

Assignment of Overhead to Jobs

Overhead Assignment	Job 236	Job 237	Job 238
Machining:			
$2.50 × 2,000	$ 5,000		
$2.50 × 3,000		$ 7,500	
$2.50 × 5,000			$12,500
Assembly:			
$1.80 × 4,000	$ 7,200		
$1.80 × 6,000		10,800	
$1.80 × 10,000			18,000
Total overhead assigned .	$12,200	$18,300	$30,500

Activity-Based Costing

This chapter and the previous three chapters show that overhead costs are too complex to be simply explained as the result of the variation in one factor such as direct labour.[1] While computing multiple overhead rates as explained in the prior section is an improvement over allocation using simply direct labour, it too doesn't adequately assign overhead. This is because the allocation bases used in the second stage are still volume-based (e.g., machine hours) whereas many overhead cost items are not actually driven by the volume of production.

Inappropriate allocations can distort unit costs. When the number of jobs, products or departments increases, the possibility of improperly assigning costs increases. Traditional ways of allocating overhead costs on the basis of direct labour often distort unit costs. This can cause poor decisions by managers and the failure of companies.

Did You Know?

Overhead Kills

Futura Computer Company faced two opportunities. First, bankruptcy of a competitor offered it an opportunity to pick up half a million units of incremental sales of its seemingly best product on top of existing sales of three million units. Second, it had an opportunity to outsource two million units of a money-losing product to a Korean firm that submitted an attractive bid. The senior vice president of production recommended manufacturing the less profitable product in Korea and retooling its own domestic plant to produce the extra units of the better product. This strategy aimed to convert the company's current $11 million loss to a $17.5 million profit. But profits never materialized, and losses ballooned to $20 million! What went wrong? It turns out the "best" product was a loser, while the "worst" product was a consistent moneymaker. The root of the problem was allocation of overhead items like amortization on the basis of direct labour cost. This meant a product using, say, 20% of total labour was assigned 20% of amortization. But where labour was being used, machinery wasn't. Labour-heavy products should have been assigned less amortization. Poor cost allocation brought this company to its knees. [Source: "Overhead Can Kill You," *Forbes*, October 2, 1997.]

[1] Because technological advances increase the extent of automated manufacturing, direct labour costs have declined as a percent of total production cost. In some companies, direct labour cost is such a small part of total cost that it is treated as overhead.

In practice, indirect costs are the result of many different factors. **Activity-based costing** attempts to deal with this complexity by better allocating costs to the users of overhead activities. The idea of using activities to allocate costs is not new. But companies are increasingly attracted by the potential benefits of activity-based costing. In a survey conducted by MANAGEMENT ACCOUNTING®, most respondents felt activity-based costing is definitely worth the investment.[2]

Exhibit 24.3 shows the *two-step activity-based factory overhead cost allocation.* Note the first step includes identifying activities involved in the manufacturing process and forming activity cost "pools" by combining activities into sets. The second step involves computing predetermined overhead cost allocation rates for each cost pool and assigning costs to jobs.

Exhibit 24.3

Activity-Based Cost Allocation

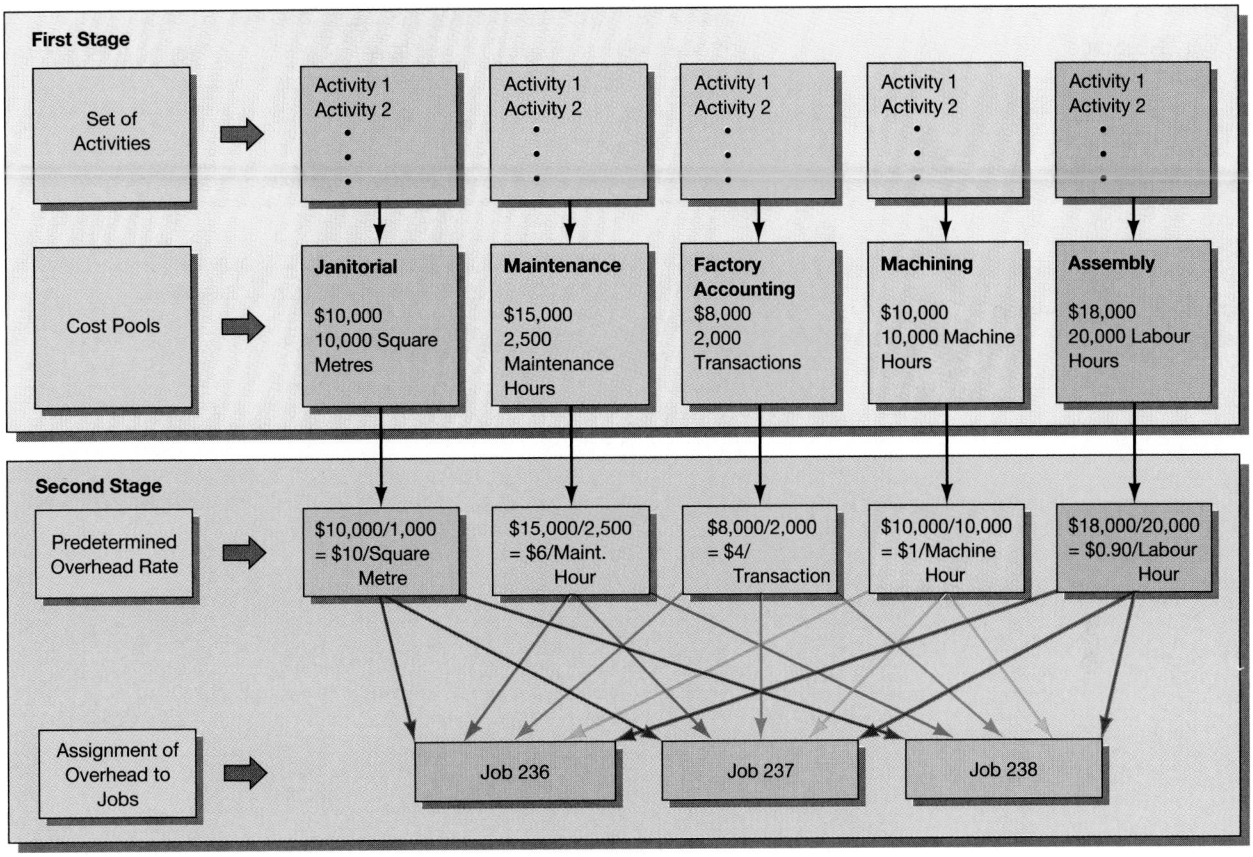

We start at the top of Exhibit 24.3. Costs of separate activities of overhead items or *resources* are collected in separate temporary accounts. The cost of each activity is driven by what is called a cost driver. A **cost driver** causes the cost of an activity to go up or down. The cost driver for a purchase order processing activity, for instance, is the number of purchase orders processed.

Activities are then pooled in a logical manner into **activity cost pools.** An activity cost pool is a temporary account accumulating costs a company incurs to support an identified set of activities. Costs accumulated in an activity cost pool include variable and fixed costs of the activity. Variable costs pertain to resources acquired as needed (e.g., materials) whereas fixed costs pertain to resources acquired in advance (e.g., equipment).

---

[2] S. Jayson, "ABC Is Worth the Investment," *Management Accounting*, April 1994, p. 27. Another relevant article is "Does Your Company Need a New Cost System?" by Robin Cooper, *Harvard Business Review,* Spring 1987.

LO 2 Assign factory overhead costs using activity-based costing.

In practice, an activity cost pool account is handled like a manufacturing overhead account. After all activity costs are accumulated in an activity cost pool account, users of the activity, called *cost objects*, are assigned a portion of the total activity cost. This is done using a cost driver or allocation base.

Illustration of Activity-Based Costing

To illustrate, let's return to the three jobs of Custom Autos. Assume resources are consumed by Jobs 236, 237, and 238 as shown in Exhibit 24.4. We then assign overhead to these three jobs using activity-based costing as shown in Exhibit 24.5.

Exhibit 24.4

Activity Resource Consumption

Resource Use	Job 236	Job 237	Job 238
Square metres of space .	500	300	200
Maintenance hours	1,250	750	500
Number of transactions .	500	700	800
Machine hours	2,000	3,000	5,000
Direct labour hours	4,000	6,000	10,000

Exhibit 24.5

Activity-Based Overhead Assignment

Overhead Assignment	Job 236	Job 237	Job 238
Janitorial			
$10.00 × 500	$ 5,000		
$10.00 × 300		$ 3,000	
$10.00 × 200			$ 2,000
Maintenance			
$6.00 × 1,250	7,500		
$6.00 × 750		4,500	
$6.00 × 500			3,000
Factory Accounting			
$4.00 × 500	2,000		
$4.00 × 700		2,800	
$4.00 × 800			3,200
Machining			
$1.00 × 2,000	2,000		
$1.00 × 3,000		3,000	
$1.00 × 5,000			5,000
Assembly			
$0.90 × 4,000	3,600		
$0.90 × 6,000		5,400	
$0.90 × 10,000			9,000
Total overhead assigned .	$20,100	$18,700	$22,200

Note from Exhibits 24.2 and 24.5 the overhead amounts assigned to the three jobs vary markedly depending on whether two-stage cost allocation or activity-based costing is applied. Overhead assigned to Job 236 goes up from $12,200 using two-stage cost allocation to $20,100 under activity-based approach. Yet overhead assigned to Job 238 declines from $30,500 to $22,200. This difference in amounts assigned results from more accurately tracing overhead resource use to each job. This is because activity-based costing uses allocation bases reflecting actual cost drivers.

Broad Application

Activity-based costing is used in many industries. ABC has been used by banks such as the **Bank of Nova Scotia**, automotive manufacturers such as **Volkswagon Canada** and in many other organizations such as universities, health care providers and computer manufacturers. The only requirements are the existence of overhead costs and the need to determine the activities that cause overhead costs. Results of using ABC include more accurate costing that enables management to make better resource allocation decisions leading to improved profitability.

Did You Know?

Comparing Two-Stage and Activity-Based Cost Allocation

Differences between traditional allocation methods and activity-based costing are mainly due to how many cost drivers are used and how many allocations are made. Traditional cost systems commonly accumulate overhead in one overhead account or a small number of overhead accounts. Companies often assign these overhead costs to jobs or products using a single allocation base such as direct labour. Service department costs may be allocated to cost centres or production departments separately (see Exhibit 24.1).

Under activity-based costing, the costs of activity resources (sometimes including service departments) are assigned to activities using the resources. These activities are then accumulated into activity cost pools. A company selects a cost driver (allocation base) for each activity pool. It uses this cost driver to assign the accumulated activity costs to cost objects (such as jobs or products) benefitting from the activity.

It is common for an activity-based costing system to involve 6 to 12 (or more) times as many allocations as a traditional cost system. As one example, a Montreal-based manufacturer currently uses nearly 20 different activity cost drivers to assign overhead costs to its products.

An activity-based cost system was recently set up at **Perkin-Elmer,** a maker of analytical instruments. John Bennett, the controller, says at first they tried to analyze too many cost drivers. Then, they set up cross-functional teams able to identify the important cost drivers in each area. Examples of indirect cost pools (i.e., activity cost pools for indirect costs) and their cost drivers are listed in Exhibit 24.6. We use these cost drivers to assign activity costs to cost objects and, then, to products produced.

Exhibit 24.6

Costs and Cost Drivers in Activity-Based Costing

Cost	Cost Driver
Materials purchasing	Number of purchase orders
Materials handling	Number of materials requisitions
Personnel processing	Number of employees hired or laid off
Equipment amortization	Number of products produced or hours of use
Quality inspection	Number of units inspected
Indirect labour in setting up equipment	Number of setups required
Engineering costs for product modifications	Number of modifications (engineering change orders)

You Make the Call

Director of Operations

You are the director of operations for a promotional company. Two department managers approach you with a complaint. Both feel they are unduly assigned high overhead costs. Overhead is currently assigned on the basis of labour hours for artwork designers. These managers argue overhead does not only depend on the designers' hours and that many overhead items are unrelated to these hours. How do you respond?

Answer—p. 1182

Activity-based costing is especially effective when many different kinds of products are manufactured in the same department or departments. Some products produced in a department might be simple, while others are more complex. More complex products likely require more help from service departments such as engineering, maintenance, and materials handling. If the same amount of direct labour is applied to the complex and simple products, a traditional overhead allocation system assigns the same overhead cost to them. But with activity-based costing, the complex products are assigned a greater portion of overhead because they consume more company resources.

This difference in overhead assigned can affect product pricing, make-or-buy, and other important decisions. Also, production managers can focus on managing activities that drive overhead cost instead of reducing allocated overhead by reducing direct labour cost. But managers cannot focus solely on activities. The contribution of an activity to the entire production process must be kept in mind.

Activity-based costing also causes managers to pay closer attention to all activities. If overhead costs are accumulated in one account, attention is less likely to be directed at controlling any individual cost item. Activity-based costing requires managers to look at each item. This encourages them to manage each cost to increase the benefit from each dollar spent. It also encourages managers to cooperate because it shows how their efforts are interrelated. This results in *activity-based management.*

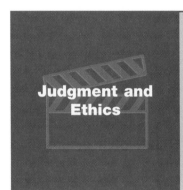

Judgment and Ethics

Accounting Officer

You are an accounting officer working for a company producing expensive women's footwear, the production of which involves many complicated and specialized activities. The company's general manager recently learned about activity-based costing (ABC) and thinks it might be appropriate to use. But your current supervisor does not want to disturb the existing cost accounting system and instructs you to prepare a report stating "the implementation of ABC is a complicated process involving too many steps and may not be worth the effort." You actually believe ABC will help the company in identifying sources of costs and controlling them. What action do you take?

Flashback

1. What is a cost driver?
2. When activity-based costing is used rather than traditional allocation methods:
   a. Managers must identify cost drivers for various components of overhead cost.
   b. Individual cost items in service departments are allocated to products manufactured or sold in production or selling departments.
   c. Managers can direct their attention to the activities that drive overhead cost.
   d. All of the above.

Answers—p. 1183

Mid-Chapter Demonstration Problem

Leonard Company produces two products: Zig and Zag. Overhead is estimated at $600,000 and the company expects to use 1,000 labour hours to produce Zig and 3,000 hours to produce Zag. Overhead is caused by purchase orders costing $120,000, inspections costing $270,000, and materials handling costing $210,000. The company estimates the following activity information:

	Zig	Zag	Total
Number of purchase orders	1,000	500	1,500
Number of inspections	1,000	500	1,500
Number of times material is handled	1,500	500	2,000

Required

a. Compute the amount of overhead assigned to each product using direct labour hours as the base.

b. Compute the amount of overhead assigned to each product using ABC.

c. What insight is provided by ABC?

Planning the Solution

- Determine the total overhead costs and divide this amount by the total estimated labour hours.
- Allocate the overhead to each product by multiplying the overhead rate by the number of labour hours used by each product.
- Establish a separate overhead rate for each activity that causes the overhead cost. To assign overhead to each product multiply each separate rate by the quantity of the activity consumed by each product.

Solution to Mid-Chapter Demonstration Problem

a.

Overhead rate based on direct labour hours $= \frac{\$600,000}{4,000 \text{ DLH}} = \$150$ per hour

Overhead assigned to Zig: $150 × 1,000	=	$150,000
Overhead assigned to Zag: $150 × 3,000	=	$450,000
Total		$600,000

b.

Purchase order overhead = $120,000 ÷ 1,500 = $80 per purchase order

Inspection rate = $270,000 ÷ 1,500 = $180 per inspection

Materials handling rate = $210,000 ÷ 2,000 = $105 per handling

Allocation Using ABC

						Zig	Zag
Purchase order overhead							
Zig	1,000	×	$ 80	=		$ 80,000	
Zag	500	×	$ 80	=			$40,000
Inspection overhead							
Zig	1,000	×	$180	=		180,000	
Zag	500	×	$180	=			90,000
Materials handling							
Zig	1,500	×	$105	=		157,500	
Zag	500	×	$105	=			52,500
Total						$417,500	$182,500

c. Using labour hours as the overhead base assigned too little overhead to Zig and too much overhead costs to Zag. ABC gives a more accurate assignment of overhead to the products. Since Zig uses more of the activities that cause overhead it should be assigned more of the overhead costs. A more accurate determination of overhead costs will help management make better decisions regarding the employment of resources and lead to better product pricing decisions.

Departmental Accounting

LO3 Explain departmentalization and the role of departmental accounting.

Managerial accounting information about subunits of a company is useful for managers. When companies are too large to be managed effectively as a single unit, they are divided into subunits or departments. Our discussion of process cost accounting in Chapter 22 showed how manufacturing systems are subdivided into departments for better management.

Managerial accounting for departments has two main goals. The first is to provide information that managers use to evaluate the profitability or cost effectiveness of each department's activities. This goal is met by **departmental accounting.** The second goal is to assign costs and expenses to managers who are responsible for controlling those costs and expenses. This information is used to control those costs and to evaluate the performance of managers. This goal is met by responsibility accounting. Departmental and responsibility accounting systems are related and share much information. We discuss departmental accounting in this and the next section. Responsibility accounting is described later in the chapter.

Motivation for Departmentalization

Many companies are sufficiently large and complex, requiring division into subunits or departments. When a company is departmentalized, each department is often placed under the direction of a manager. As a company grows, management often divides departments into new departments. This is so that responsibilities for the activities of a department do not overwhelm a manager's ability to oversee and control them effectively. A company also creates departments to take advantage of the skills of individual managers.

Basis of Departmentalization

The two basic categories of departments are *production* and *service*. For a manufacturer, production departments engage directly in manufacturing. Departments are often organized to put each manufacturing process under the direction of one manager. This is defined by activities it carries out or products it manufactures.

For a merchandiser, production departments make sales directly to customers. Merchandisers often organize each department around the product it sells. For instance, each *selling department* often has the task of selling one or more lines of merchandise.

Service departments help both production and selling departments by providing support. Examples are advertising, purchasing, payroll, human resource management, and top management. Service departments do not directly manufacture products or produce revenues through sales. Their support is important for the success of other departments and the company.

Information for Departmental Evaluation

When a company is divided into departments, managers need to know how well each department is performing. The accounting system must supply information about the resources used and outputs achieved by each department. This requires a system to measure and accumulate revenue and expense information for each department wherever possible. Because of its potential usefulness to competitors, this information is not distributed publicly. Information about departments is prepared for internal managers to help control operations, appraise performance, allocate resources, and strategic actions. If a department is highly profitable, management may decide to expand its operations. Or, if a department is showing poorly, information about revenues and expenses may suggest useful changes.

More companies are emphasizing customer satisfaction as a main responsibility of each operating department. This has led to changes in the measures reported in responsibility accounting systems. Increasingly, financial measurements are being supplemented with quality and customer satisfaction indexes. **Motorola**, for instance, uses two key measures: the number of defective parts per million parts produced and the percent of orders delivered on time to customers.

Financial information used to evaluate a department depends on whether it is a profit centre or a cost centre. A **profit centre** incurs costs and generates revenues. Selling departments are often evaluated as profit centres. A **cost centre** incurs costs or expenses without directly generating revenues. Manufacturing departments of a manufacturer and the service departments such as accounting, advertising, and purchasing are all cost centres.

More Than Profit!
A recent survey shows many companies use nonfinancial performance measures as part of the information package reported to management. Approximately 63% of respondents indicated they use nonfinancial measures, and 87% indicated these measures should be used even more. Nonfinancial measures being used most often are: cycle time, defect rate, on-time deliveries, inventory turns, customer satisfaction, and safety. About one-quarter of respondents indicated they are implementing an activity-based management project as part of their performance measurement system. [Source: Cost Management Group, "Companies Continue to Adjust Their Performance Measurement Systems," *Cost Management Update*, April 1997, page 1].

Did You Know?

Evaluating the performance of managers depends on whether they are responsible for profit centres or cost centres. Managers of profit centres are judged on their ability to generate revenues in excess of the department's expenses. It is assumed they influence both revenue generation and cost incurrence. Managers of cost centres are judged on their ability to control costs by keeping them within a satisfactory range under an assumption they only influence costs.

Departmental Reporting and Analysis

Companies use various means to obtain information about their departments. The needed information depends on the focus and philosophy of management. **Air Canada's** statement of corporate objectives, for instance, indicates its reason for existence is to satisfy customer needs. The challenge in this case is to set up management responsibility accounting systems to provide relevant feedback for evaluating performance in terms of a company's objectives. The means of obtaining information about departments depend on the extent a company uses computer and information technology.

Computerized Departmental Systems

Sophisticated cash registers allow managers of a merchandising company access to information about each department's sales, sales returns, and other crucial data. In a networked system, registers transfer this information directly to computers for reporting and analysis purposes. Registers are capable of doing much more than accumulating sales information. They can print detailed information on sales tickets given to customers, total the ticket, and initiate entries to record credit sales in a customer's account. If information about sold goods is recorded at the register by a scanner or a keyboard, the system can produce detailed departmental summaries of items sold and those remaining in inventory.

Separate Accounts by Department

Sophisticated systems allow companies to compute total sales and sales returns for each department on a regular basis. More clerical effort is needed for less sophisticated systems. In these systems, totals are often accumulated by one of two ways: (a) separate Sales and Sales Returns accounts in its general ledger for each department, (b) supplementary spreadsheet analysis of departmental sales and sales returns. Information systems can also accumulate information about purchases and purchases returns by departments.

If a company uses special journals and has separate Sales, Sales Returns, Purchases, and Purchases Returns accounts for each selling department, then its special journals often have separate columns for routine transactions by departments. Exhibit 24.7 shows a sales journal used to record information by selling departments. The amounts debited to customers' accounts are entered in the Accounts Receivable Debit column and posted to these accounts daily. Less frequently, perhaps monthly, this column's total is posted to the Accounts Receivable controlling account. Amounts sold to a customer for each department are entered in the last three columns. Totals of these three columns are posted to the ledger accounts at least monthly.

Exhibit 24.7

Departmentalized Sales Journal

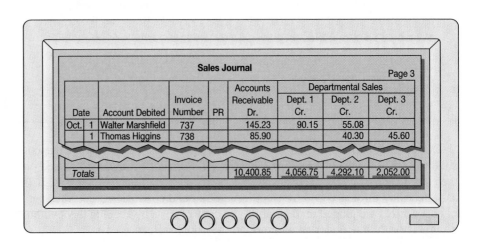

Sales Journal Page 3

Date		Account Debited	Invoice Number	PR	Accounts Receivable Dr.	Departmental Sales Dept. 1 Cr.	Dept. 2 Cr.	Dept. 3 Cr.
Oct.	1	Walter Marshfield	737		145.23	90.15	55.08	
	1	Thomas Higgins	738		85.90		40.30	45.60
Totals					10,400.85	4,056.75	4,292.10	2,052.00

Departmental Spreadsheet Analysis

If separate accounts are not maintained in the general ledger by department, a company can create departmental information by using a supplemental spreadsheet analysis. In this case, a company records sales, sales returns, purchases, and purchases returns as if the company is not departmentalized. Then, it identifies each department's transactions and enters these amounts on a spreadsheet.

For example, after recording sales in its usual manner, a company can compute daily total sales by department and enter these totals on a sales spreadsheet. Exhibit 24.8 shows such a spreadsheet. At the end of a period, column totals of the spreadsheet show sales by department. The combined total of all columns equal the balance of the Sales account.

Exhibit 24.8

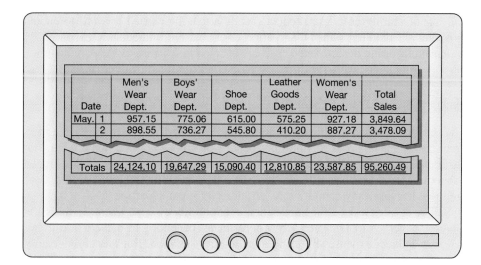

Departmental Sales Spreadsheet

Date		Men's Wear Dept.	Boys' Wear Dept.	Shoe Dept.	Leather Goods Dept.	Women's Wear Dept.	Total Sales
May.	1	957.15	775.06	615.00	575.25	927.18	3,849.64
	2	898.55	736.27	545.80	410.20	887.27	3,478.09
Totals		24,124.10	19,647.29	15,090.40	12,810.85	23,587.85	95,260.49

When a merchandiser uses a spreadsheet analysis of department sales, it often uses separate spreadsheets to accumulate sales, sales returns, purchases, and purchases returns by department. If each department counts its inventory, it can also compute its gross profit. Accumulating information and computing gross profit by department is not difficult. Yet some companies do not measure profits by department because of difficulties in allocating expenses across departments. We consider these difficulties in the next section.

Flash back

3. What is the difference between departmental accounting systems and responsibility accounting systems?
4. Service departments (a) manufacture products, (b) make sales directly to customers, (c) produce revenues, (d) assist production departments.
5. Explain the difference between a cost centre and a profit centre, and give an example of each.
6. A company that develops departmental information by using supplemental sales analysis spreadsheets would probably:
   a. Have a sophisticated computerized cash register system.
   b. Use separate spreadsheets to accumulate sales, sales returns, purchases, and purchases returns.
   c. Provide separate Sales accounts for each department in its general ledger.

Answers—p. 1183

Departmental Expense Allocation

When a company computes departmental profits, it confronts some accounting challenges. These challenges involve allocating the company's expenses across its selling departments.

LO 4 Distinguish between direct and indirect expenses.

Direct Expenses Require No Allocation

Direct expenses are readily traced to a department because they are incurred for the sole benefit of that department. They require no allocation across departments. For example, the salary of an employee who works in only one department is a direct expense of that one department.

The concept of direct expense is similar to the concept of direct cost introduced in Chapter 21. We used the term *direct cost* in the context of a manufacturer where all manufacturing costs are product costs that can be carried forward to ending inventory if required rather than period costs that are immediately expensed. In *non*manufacturing departments, costs are charged to expense as they are incurred. In these situations, the term direct expense is used instead of direct cost.

Indirect Expenses Require Allocation

A company's expenses include indirect expenses. **Indirect expenses** (like indirect costs) are incurred for the joint benefit of more than one department. For example, if two or more departments share a single building, they both enjoy the benefits of the expenses of renting, heating, and lighting. These expenses are indirect because they cannot be readily traced to one department.

There is often a need for information about profits by department. In this case, indirect expenses are allocated across departments benefiting from them. Ideally we allocate indirect expenses by using a cause-effect relation. But identifying cause-effect relations is not always possible. In these situations, each indirect expense is allocated on a basis approximating the relative benefit received by each department. Measuring the benefit each department receives from an indirect expense is difficult or sometimes impossible. Even when a reasonable allocation basis is chosen, considerable doubt often exists regarding the amount charged to each department.

Illustration of Indirect Expense Allocation

To illustrate how an indirect expense can be allocated, we look at a jewellery store that purchases janitorial services from an outside company. Management allocates this cost across the store's three departments according to the floor space each occupies. Costs of janitorial services for a recent month are $300. Exhibit 24.9 shows the square metres of floor space occupied by each department. This store then computes the percent of the total square metres taken up by each department, and then allocates the $300 cost across them using these percents.

Exhibit 24.9

Indirect Expense Allocation

Department	Square Metres	Percent of Total	Allocated Cost
Jewellery	400	25.0%	$ 75
Watch repair	240	15.0	45
China and silver	960	60.0	180
Total	1,600	100.0%	$300

This exhibit shows the jewellery department occupies 25% of the floor space in the store. The allocation assumes 25% of janitorial services are applied to cleaning its space. This results in 25% of the total $300 cost being assigned to the jewellery department. When the allocation process is complete, these and other allocated costs are deducted from gross profits for each department to determine the net income for each.

We can apply the concepts of direct and indirect costs or expenses in a variety of cases. We can readily link direct costs or expenses with a *cost object*. Here, the relevant cost object is a department. Other cost objects may be relevant for other decisions. For general accounting and job order cost systems in manufacturing operations (Chapter 22) the cost object is a job or a group of products. For process cost systems (Chapter 23) the cost object is a process.

One consideration in allocating costs is to motivate managers and employees toward desired behaviour. This means a cost incurred in one department might be allocated to another department because the latter department caused the cost and can control it. For example, the controller of **AeroTech** captures the costs of reworking, delivering, and reinstalling defective aerospace components in separate accounts. She then removes these costs from manufacturing accounts and allocates them to individual salespersons who serviced the customers receiving defective components. This reassigns costs from manufacturing to those who best control them.

Identifying Indirect Expenses and Allocation Bases

LO5 Identify bases for allocating indirect expenses to departments.

This section describes how to allocate the usual indirect expenses across departments and identifies the bases used. There is no standard rule about what basis is best. This is because expense allocation involves several factors and the relative importance of these factors varies across cases. Judgment is required, and people do not always agree. In our discussion, note the parallels between activity-based costing and the allocation procedures described here.

Wages and Salaries

Employees' wages and salaries can be part of either direct or indirect expenses. If their time is spent entirely in one department, their wages are a direct expense of that department. But, if employees work in more than one department, their wages are an indirect expense and must be allocated across the departments benefited. An employee's contribution to a department usually depends on the hours worked in that department. A reasonable basis for allocating employees' wages and salaries is the *relative amount of time spent in each department*.

A supervisory employee often manages more than one department. Time spent in each department is often a useful basis for allocating a supervisor's salary. It is sometimes not practical to record a supervisor's time spent in each department. In this case, a company can allocate supervisory salaries to departments on the basis of the number of employees in each department. This basis is reasonable if a supervisor's main task is managing people. Another basis of allocation is on sales across departments. This basis is reasonable if a supervisor's job reflects on departments' sales.

Rent, Amortization, and Related Building Expenses

Rent expense for a building is reasonably allocated to departments on the basis of floor space occupied by each department. Yet some floor space is often more valuable than other space because of location. If so, the allocation method charges departments with more valuable space a higher expense per square metre. Ground-floor retail space, for instance, is often more valuable than basement or upper-floor space because all customers pass departments near the entrance while fewer go beyond the first floor. When there are no precise measures of floor space values, it is helpful to base allocation on data such as customer traffic and real estate assessments. When a company owns a building, then its expenses for amortization, taxes, insurance, and other building-related expenses are allocated like rent expense.

Advertising

Effective advertising of a department's products increases customer traffic and sales. These customers also often buy unadvertised products during their visit. This means advertising of products for some departments often help sales of all departments, and many stores treat advertising as an indirect expense. Advertising is often allocated on the basis of each department's proportion of total sales. For example, a department with 10% of a store's total sales is assigned 10% of advertising expense. Another method is to analyze each advertisement to compute the newspaper space or TV/radio time devoted to the products of a department. A department is then charged with the actual costs of advertisements. Management must consider whether this more detailed and costly method justifies the effort.

Equipment and Machinery Amortization

Amortization on equipment and machinery used only in one department is a direct expense of that department. Amortization on equipment and machinery used by more than one department is an indirect expense to be allocated across all of them. Accounting for each department's equipment amortization expense requires a company to keep records showing which departments use specific assets. Relative number of hours equipment and machinery are used by departments is a reasonable basis for allocating amortization.

Utilities

Utilities expenses such as heating and lighting are usually allocated on the basis of floor space occupied by departments. This practice assumes the amounts for heat and lighting, and the extent of their use, are uniform across departments. When this is not the case, a more involved allocation may be necessary. There is often a trade-off between the usefulness of more precise information and the effort in getting it.

Services

To generate products and sales, production departments require services by departments such as personnel, payroll, advertising, and purchasing. Because these service departments do not produce revenues, they are evaluated as cost centres. A departmental accounting system can accumulate and report costs incurred directly by each service department for this purpose. It then allocates a service department's indirect costs to other departments benefiting from them.

When a production department's effectiveness is assessed, we consider the cost of any benefits it receives from service departments. This means after the costs of service departments are compiled, they are allocated to production and selling departments. This is done using traditional two-stage cost allocation (see Exhibit 24.1). The costs of service departments are shared indirect expenses of production departments. If management wants to evaluate selling departments as profit centres using net income instead of gross profit, service department costs are also allocated to them. Exhibit 24.10 shows some commonly used bases for allocating service department costs to production and selling departments.

Exhibit 24.10

Allocation Bases for Services

Service Departments	Common Allocation Bases
Office	Number of employees or sales in each department
Personnel	Number of employees in each department
Payroll	Number of employees in each department
Advertising ...	Sales or amounts of advertising charged directly to each department
Purchasing ...	Dollar amounts of purchases or number of purchase orders processed
Cleaning	Square metres of floor space occupied
Maintenance ..	Square metres of floor space occupied

Preparing Departmental Income Statements

Each profit centre is assigned its full expenses to yield a complete income statement. These costs include direct expenses and indirect expenses shared with other departments. It is often useful to compile the full amount of expenses incurred in service departments and then assign them to production departments or cost centres. This is the first stage of the two-stage cost allocation procedure described at the beginning of this chapter (see Exhibit 24.1).

LO 6 Prepare departmental income statements.

To illustrate, let's look at Exhibit 24.11 **Acer Hardware** has five departments. Two of them (office and purchasing) are service departments and the other three (hardware, housewares, and appliances) are selling departments. There are three steps in allocating costs to its selling departments.

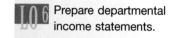

Step One

Step one accumulates direct expenses for each service and selling department as shown in Exhibit 24.11.

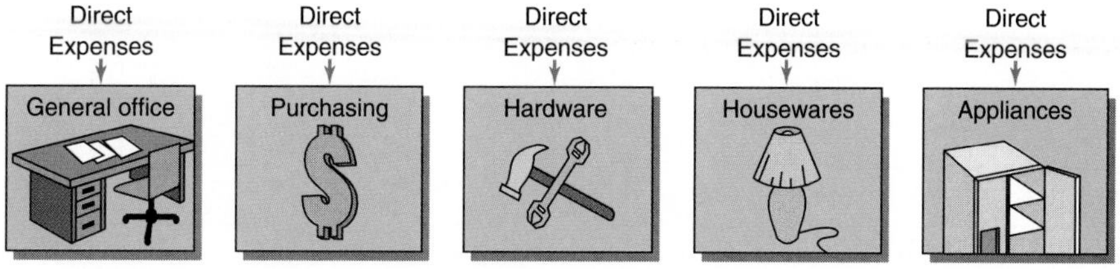

Exhibit 24.11

Step 1: Direct Expense Accumulation

Direct expenses include salaries and other expenses each department incurs but does not share with any other department. This information is accumulated in departmental expense accounts.

Step Two

Step two allocates indirect expenses across all departments using the allocation base identified for each expense. This step is shown in Exhibit 24.12.

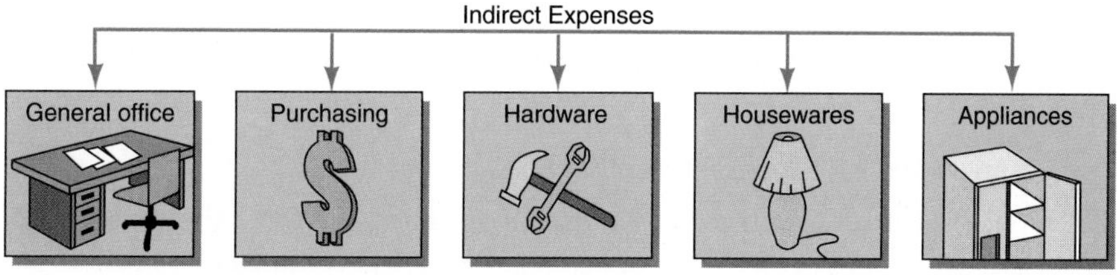

Exhibit 24.12

Step 2: Indirect Expense Allocation

Indirect expenses include items discussed in the prior section such as wages, amortization, rent, and advertising. Indirect expenses are recorded in expense accounts, and allocation is done using a *departmental expense allocation spreadsheet.* We describe this spreadsheet below.

Step Three

Step three allocates expenses of the two service departments (office and purchasing) to the three selling departments. Exhibit 24.13 reflects the process of step three.

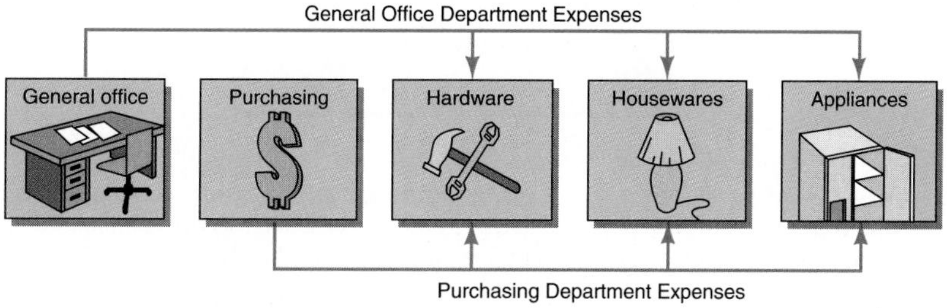

Exhibit 24.13

Step 3: Service Department Expense Allocation

Exhibit 24.14

Departmental Expense Allocation Spreadsheet

Service department expenses are allocated using one of the bases described in the prior section. Computations for both steps two and three are made on a *departmental expense allocation spreadsheet* as shown in Exhibit 24.14.[3]

ACER HARDWARE
Departmental Expense Allocations
For Year Ended December 31, 1998

			Allocation of Expenses to Departments				
	Allocation Base	Expense Account Balance	General Office Dept.	Purchasing Dept.	Hardware Dept.	House-wares Dept.	Appliances Dept.
Direct expenses:							
Salaries expense	Payroll records	$51,900	$13,300	$8,200	$15,600	$7,000	$7,800
Amortization on equipment	Amortization records	1,500	500	300	400	100	200
Supplies expense	Requisitions	900	200	100	300	200	100
Indirect expenses:							
Rent expense	Amount and value of space	12,000	600	600	4,860	3,240	2,700
Utilities expense	Floor space	2,400	300	300	810	540	450
Advertising expense	Sales	1,000			500	300	200
Insurance expense	Value of insured assets	2,500	400	200	900	600	400
Total department expenses		$72,200	$15,300	$9,700	$23,370	$11,980	$11,850
Service department expenses:							
General office department	Sales		$15,300		7,650	4,590	3,060
Purchasing department	Purchase orders			$9,700	3,880	2,630	3,190
Total expenses allocated to operating departments		$72,200			$34,900	$19,200	$18,100

The upper part of column one in Exhibit 24.14 lists both direct and indirect expenses. The lower part of column one lists service departments. The allocation bases are identified in the second column, and total expense amounts are in the third.

Using a Departmental Expense Allocation Spreadsheet

This spreadsheet reflects the three steps above. First, the three direct expenses of salaries, equipment amortization, and supplies are accumulated in each of the five departments. Second, the four indirect expenses of rent, utilities, advertising, and insurance are allocated to all departments using the allocation bases identified. To illustrate, let's look at allocation of rent. Exhibit 24.15 lists the five departments' square metres of space occupied.

Exhibit 24.15

Departments' Square Metres

General office	500
Purchasing	500
Hardware	1,350
Housewares	900
Appliances	750
Total	4,000

[3] In some cases, we might allocate costs of a service department to other service departments because they also use its services. For example, costs of a payroll office benefit all service and production departments and some of its costs can be assigned to all departments. Nearly all examples and assignment materials in this book allocate service cost only to production departments for simplicity.

The two service departments occupy 25% of the total space (1,000 sq. metres/4,000 sq. metres). But they are located near the back of the building and the space is of lower value than space near the front occupied by selling departments. Management estimates space near the back accounts for $1,200 of total rent expense of $12,000. Exhibit 24.16 shows how we allocate the $1,200 rent expense between these two service departments in proportion to their square metres.

Exhibit 24.16

Allocating Indirect (Rent) Expense to Service Departments

Department	Square Metres	Percent of Total	Allocated Cost
General office	500	50.0%	$ 600
Purchasing	500	50.0	600
Total	1,000	100.0%	$1,200

We then allocate the remaining $10,800 of rent expense to the three selling departments as shown in Exhibit 24.17.

Exhibit 24.17

Allocating Indirect (Rent) Expense to Selling Departments

Department	Square Metres	Percent of Total	Allocated Cost
Hardware	1,350	45.0%	$ 4,860
Housewares	900	30.0	3,240
Appliance	750	25.0	2,700
Total	3,000	100.0%	$10,800

We also apply step two in allocating the $2,400 of utilities expense to all departments based on the square metres occupied as shown in Exhibit 24.18.

Exhibit 24.18

Allocating Indirect (Utilities) Expense to All Departments

Department	Square Metres	Percent of Total	Allocated Cost
General office	500	12.50%	$ 300
Purchasing	500	12.50	300
Hardware	1,350	33.75	810
Housewares	900	22.50	540
Appliances	750	18.75	450
Total	4,000	100.00%	$2,400

Note the rows in Exhibit 24.14 for rent and utilities expenses show the amounts from these exhibits. The allocation of the two other indirect expenses of advertising and insurance are similarly computed. But note that since advertising expense is allocated on the basis of sales, and since service departments do not have sales, it is allocated to only the three selling departments.

The third step allocates total expenses of the two service departments to the three selling departments. The allocations use the identified allocation bases as shown in the lower part of Exhibit 24.14.

When the spreadsheet is complete, the amounts in the departmental columns are used to prepare departmental income statements as reported in Exhibit 24.19.

Exhibit 24.19

Departmental Income Statements

ACER HARDWARE Departmental Income Statements For Year Ended December 31, 1998	Hardware Department	Housewares Department	Appliances Department	Combined
Sales	$119,500	$71,700	$47,800	$239,000
Cost of goods sold	73,800	43,800	30,200	147,800
Gross profit on sales	$ 45,700	$27,900	$17,600	$ 91,200
Operating expenses:				
Salaries expense	$ 15,600	$ 7,000	$ 7,800	$ 30,400
Amortization expense, equipment	400	100	200	700
Supplies expense	300	200	100	600
Rent expense	4,860	3,240	2,700	10,800
Utilities expense	810	540	450	1,800
Advertising expense	500	300	200	1,000
Insurance expense	900	600	400	1,900
Share of general office expenses	7,650	4,590	3,060	15,300
Share of purchasing expenses	3,880	2,630	3,190	9,700
Total operating expenses	$ 34,900	$19,200	$18,100	$ 72,200
Net income (loss)	$ 10,800	$ 8,700	$ (500)	$ 19,000
Analysis:				
Gross profit as percent of sales	38.2%	38.9%	36.8%	38.2%

Flash back

7. If a company has two sales departments (shoes and hats) and two service departments (payroll and advertising), which of the following statements is correct?
   a. Wages incurred in the payroll department are direct expenses of the shoe department.
   b. Wages incurred in the payroll department are indirect expenses of the sales departments.
   c. Advertising department expenses are allocated to the other three departments.
8. Which of the following bases can be used to allocate salaries of supervisors across production departments?
   a. Hours spent in each department.
   b. Number of employees in each department.
   c. Sales achieved in each department.
   d. Any of the above, depending on which is most relevant.
9. What are the three steps in allocating expenses to profit centres?

Answers—p. 1183

Departmental Contributions to Overhead

Departmental income statements like those in Exhibit 24.19 are not always best for evaluating each department's performance. This is especially the case when indirect expenses are a large portion of total expenses. This results from weaknesses in assumptions and decisions in allocating indirect expenses. We overcome this limitation of departmental income statements by evaluating departmental performance with **departmental contributions to overhead.** A departmental contribution to overhead is a report of the amount of revenues less *direct* expenses.[4]

LO 7 Prepare departmental contribution reports.

Exhibit 24.20 shows a departmental contribution report for ACER Hardware. Using the information in Exhibits 24.19 and 24.20, we can perform a more complete evaluation of the profitability of the three selling departments. For instance, let's compare the performance of the appliance department as described in these two exhibits. Exhibit 24.19 shows a net loss of $500 resulting from the department's operations, whereas Exhibit 24.20 shows a positive contribution to overhead of

Exhibit 24.20

Departmental Contributions to Overhead

ACER HARDWARE
Income Statement Showing Departmental Contributions to Overhead
For Year Ended December 31, 1998

	Hardware Department	Housewares Department	Appliances Department	Combined
Sales	$119,500	$71,700	$47,800	$239,000
Cost of goods sold	73,800	43,800	30,200	147,800
Gross profit on sales	$ 45,700	$27,900	$17,600	$ 91,200
Direct expenses:				
Salaries expense	$ 15,600	$ 7,000	$ 7,800	$ 30,400
Amortization expense, equipment	400	100	200	700
Supplies expense	300	200	100	600
Total direct expenses	$ 16,300	$ 7,300	$ 8,100	$ 31,700
Departmental contributions to overhead	$ 29,400	$20,600	$ 9,500	$ 59,500
Indirect expenses:				
Rent expense				$ 10,800
Utilities expense				1,800
Advertising expense				1,000
Insurance expense				1,900
General office department expense				15,300
Purchasing department expense				9,700
Total indirect expenses				$ 40,500
Net income				$ 19,000
Contribution percents	24.6%	28.7%	19.9%	24.9%

Flash back

10. On an income statement showing departmental and combined contributions to overhead (a) indirect expenses are subtracted from each department's revenues, (b) only direct costs and expenses are subtracted from each department's revenues, (c) net income is shown for each department.

Answers—p. 1183

[4] A department's contribution is said to be "to overhead" because of the traditional practice of considering all indirect expenses as overhead. This meant the excess of a department's revenues over direct expenses was a contribution to paying total overhead.

$9,500, which is 19.9% of sales. While the contribution of the appliance department is not as large as the other selling departments, a $9,500 contribution to overhead is better than a $500 loss. This tells us that the Appliances Department is not a money loser; on the contrary, it is contributing $9,500 towards defraying the indirect expenses of $40,500.

Controllable Costs and Responsibility Accounting

Departmental accounting reports are often used to evaluate a department's performance. But are these reports useful in assessing how well a department *manager* performs? The answer is neither departmental income nor its contribution to overhead may be useful because many expenses are outside the control of a manager. Instead, we evaluate a manager's performance using *responsibility accounting reports* describing a department's activities in terms of **controllable costs.**[5] Chapter 21 explained that a cost is controllable if a manager has the power to determine or at least strongly affect the amounts incurred. **Uncontrollable costs** are not within the manager's control or influence.

Distinguishing Controllable and Direct Costs

LO 8 Explain controllable costs and responsibility accounting.

Controllable costs are not always the same as direct costs. Direct costs are readily traced to a department, but their amounts may or may not be under the control of the department manager. For example, department managers often have little or no control over amortization expense because they cannot affect the amount of equipment assigned to their departments. Department managers also usually have no control over their salaries. But department managers can control or influence items such as the cost of goods sold and supplies used in the department. When controllable costs are used to judge managers' performances, managers must use data describing their departments' outputs and controllable costs and expenses. A manager's performance is often judged by comparing current period's results with planned levels and those of prior periods.

Identifying Controllable Costs

Controllable and uncontrollable costs are identified with a particular manager and a definite time period. Without defining these two reference points, we do not know whether a cost is controllable or uncontrollable. For example, the cost of property insurance is usually not controllable at the department manager's level, but it is controllable by the executive responsible for obtaining the company's insurance coverage. Likewise, this executive may not have any control over costs resulting from insurance policies already in force. But, when a policy expires, this executive is free to renegotiate a replacement policy and now controls these costs. This means all costs are controllable at some level of management if the time period is sufficiently long, and we must use judgment in identifying controllable costs.

Responsibility Accounting

The concept of controllable costs provides the basis for a responsibility accounting system. A **responsibility accounting system** assigns managers the responsibility for costs and expenses under their control. Prior to each reporting period,

[5] The terms *cost* and *expense* are often used interchangeably. But they are not the same. A cost is the monetary value of acquiring some resource that may have present and future benefit. An expense is an expired cost, i.e., as the benefit of a resource expires, a portion of the cost is written off as an expense.

a company prepares plans that identify costs and expenses under the control of each manager. These plans are called **responsibility accounting budgets.** To ensure cooperation of managers and the reasonableness of budgets, the managers are involved in preparing their budgets.

A responsibility accounting system prepares performance reports. A **performance report** accumulates costs and expenses for managers about costs for which they are responsible. These reports show actual costs and expenses alongside budgeted amounts. Managers use performance reports to focus attention on differences between actual costs and budgeted amounts. This information often results in corrective or strategic actions. Upper management uses performance reports to evaluate the effectiveness of lower-level managers in controlling costs and keeping them within budgeted amounts. Chapter 25 further explains the nature and use of performance reports.

A responsibility accounting system must reflect that control over costs and expenses belongs to several levels of management. Let's consider the organization chart in Exhibit 24.21. The lines in this chart connecting the managerial positions reflect channels of authority. This means while the three department managers are responsible for the controllable costs and expenses incurred in their departments, these same costs are subject to the overall control of the Western plant manager. Similarly, the Western plant's costs are subject to the control of the vice president of production, the president, and ultimately the board of directors.

Exhibit 24.21

Organizational Responsibility

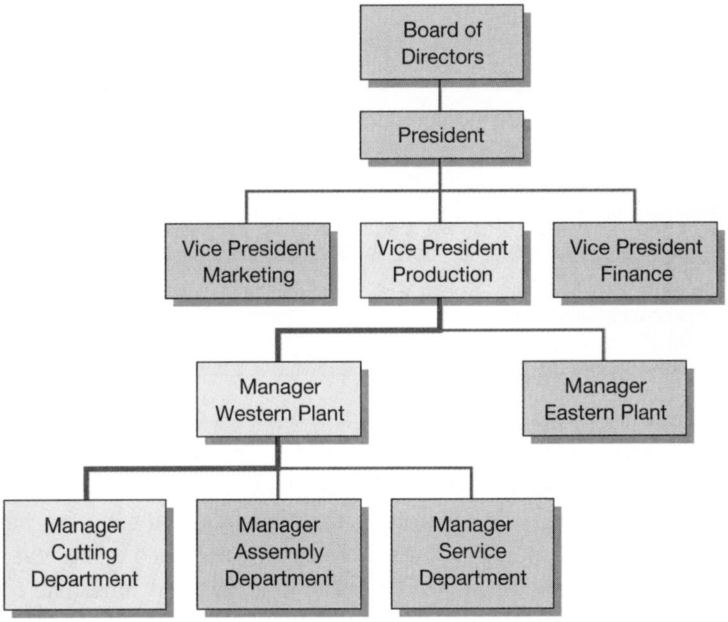

At lower levels, managers have limited responsibility and relatively little control over costs. Performance reports for this management level cover only the few controllable costs. Responsibility and control broaden at higher levels. Reports to higher-level managers therefore span a wider range of costs. But reports to higher-level managers often do not contain the details reported to their subordinates. These details are summarized for two reasons: (1) lower-level managers are often responsible for these detailed costs and (2) detailed reports can obscure important points. Detailed reports to higher-level managers can detract attention from the broader, more important issues facing a company.

Exhibit 24.22 shows summarized performance reports for the three management levels identified in Exhibit 24.21. Note in Exhibit 24.22 that costs under the control of the cutting department manager are totalled and included among controllable costs of the Western plant manager. Also, costs under the control of the plant manager are totalled and included among controllable costs of the vice president for production. In this way a responsibility accounting system provides relevant information for each management level.

Exhibit 24.22

Responsibility Accounting Performance Reports

Vice President, Production	For July		
Controllable Costs	**Budgeted Amount**	**Actual Amount**	**Over (Under) Budget**
Salaries, Plant managers	$ 80,000	$ 80,000	$ -0-
Quality control costs	21,000	22,400	1,400
Office costs	29,500	28,800	(700)
Western plant	276,700	279,500	2,800
Eastern plant	390,000	380,600	(9,400)
Total	$797,200	$791,300	$(5,900)

Manager, Western Plant	For July		
Controllable Costs	**Budgeted Amount**	**Actual Amount**	**Over (Under) Budget**
Salaries, Department managers	$ 75,000	$ 78,000	$3,000
Amortization	10,600	10,600	-0-
Insurance	6,800	6,300	(500)
Cutting department	**79,600**	**79,900**	**300**
Assembly department	61,500	60,200	(1,300)
Service department 1	24,300	24,700	400
Service department 2	18,900	19,800	900
Total	$276,700	$279,500	$2,800

Manager, Cutting Department	For July		
Controllable Costs	**Budgeted Amount**	**Actual Amount**	**Over (Under) Budget**
Raw materials	$26,500	$25,900	$ (600)
Direct labour	32,000	33,500	1,500
Indirect labour	7,200	7,000	(200)
Supplies	4,000	3,900	(100)
Other controllable costs	9,900	9,600	(300)
Total	**$79,600**	**$79,900**	**$ 300**

We must recognize that technology means our ability to produce vast amounts of information exceeds our ability to use information. Good managers select relevant data for planning and controlling the areas under their responsibility. A good responsibility accounting system reflects this need and makes every effort to get relevant information to the right person at the right time. The right person is the one who controls the cost, and the right time is before a cost gets out of control.

Let's return to the case of **AeroTech** in the opening article for an example. Its controller changed the basis for computing commissions paid to salespersons this past year. Sales revenues previously were the sole basis for computing commissions. But the new system reduced these sales revenues by the raw materials, direct labour, delivery, and reinstallation costs of reworking aerospace components. The new system combines the concepts of cost allocation, controllable costs and responsibility accounting to motivate salespersons to control reworking costs. Because salespersons are now rewarded on sales net of the cost of controllable errors, their behaviour changed. They verified specifications before submitting component orders. This led to reduced costs and an income increase of more than 20%.

Flashback

11. Are departmental net income and contribution to overhead useful when assessing the performance of a department manager? Explain why.

12. Performance reports used to evaluate managers should (a) include data about controllable expenses, (b) compare actual results with planned levels, (c) both a and b.

Answers—p. 1183

Joint Costs

LO 9 Describe allocation of joint costs across products.

Most manufacturing processes involve joint costs. A **joint cost** is a single cost incurred in producing or purchasing two or more essentially different products. A joint cost is related to an indirect expense in the sense it is shared across more than one cost object. For example, a petroleum refining company incurs a joint cost when it buys crude oil that it separates into different grades of gasoline, lubricating oil, kerosene, paraffin, ethylene, and other products as shown in Exhibit 24.23. Likewise, a sawmill incurs joint costs when it buys a log and cuts it into boards classified as Clear, Select, No. 1 Common, No. 2 Common, No. 3 Common, and other types of lumber and by-products.

Exhibit 24.23

Joint Products from Petroleum Refining

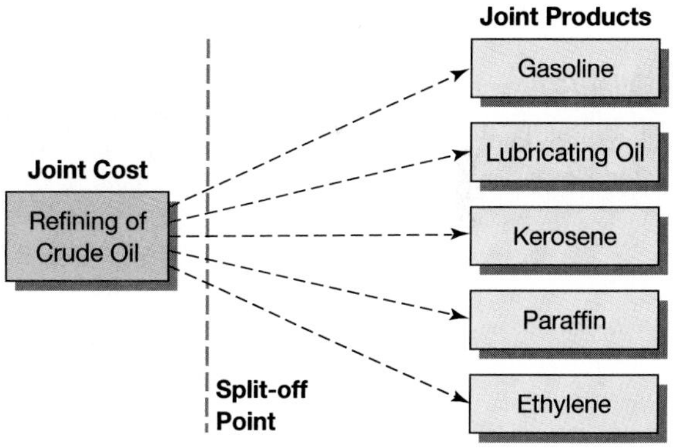

When a joint cost is incurred, a question arises as to whether its amount should be allocated to different products produced from it. When management wishes to estimate the total cost of a product, joint costs are included in the computation. But when management needs information to help decide whether to sell a product at a certain point in the production process or process further, joint costs are ignored. For example, many managerial decisions such as whether to continue buying logs and cutting lumber, are based on unallocated cost information.

When GAAP financial statements are prepared, joint cost is assigned to products. We then face a problem of deciding how to allocate joint cost across products resulting from the cost. For example, if some products are sold and others remain in inventory, allocating joint cost allows us to assign costs to both cost of goods sold and ending inventory.

A joint cost is sometimes allocated on a physical basis, such as the ratio of kilograms, cubic metres, or litres of each joint product to the total kilograms, cubic metres, or litres of all joint products flowing from the cost. But this method is not usually applied because the resulting cost allocations do not reflect the relative market values generated from the joint cost. For example, in Exhibit 24.24, the portion of log producing Structural grade lumber is worth more than the portion used to produce No. 3 Common lumber. A simple physical basis for allocating joint cost would not reflect the extra value flowing into some products or the inferior value flowing into others. Also, a physical basis can cause the sale of some joint products to appear more profitable than others when they are not.

Illustrating Physical Allocation of Joint Cost

To illustrate a physical measure of allocating a joint cost, let's consider a sawmill that bought logs for $30,000. When cut, these logs produce 30,000 cubic metres of lumber in the grades and amounts shown in Exhibit 24.24. Note the logs produce 6,000 cubic metres of No. 3 Common lumber, which is 20% of the total. With physical allocation, the No. 3 Common lumber is assigned 20% of the $30,000 cost of the logs, or $6,000 ($30,000 × 20%). Because this low-grade lumber sells for $4,000, this allocation gives a $2,000 loss from its production and sale.

Exhibit 24.24

Allocating Joint Costs on a Physical Basis

Grade of Lumber	Board Metres Produced	Percent of Total	Allocated Cost	Selling Price	Gross Profit
Structural	3,000	10.0%	$3,000	$12,000	$9,000
No. 1 Common ...	9,000	30.0	9,000	18,000	9,000
No. 2 Common ...	12,000	40.0	12,000	16,000	4,000
No. 3 Common ...	6,000	20.0	6,000	4,000	(2,000)
Total	30,000	100.0%	$30,000	$50,000	$20,000

Illustrating Value-Based Allocation of Joint Cost

A better approach allocates joint cost in proportion to the sales value of the output produced by the process at the point of separation. Exhibit 24.25 reflects this approach to allocation. Here, the percents of the total cost allocated to each grade are determined by the ratio of each grade's sales value to the total sales value of $50,000. (Note: Sales value is the unit selling price multiplied by the number of units produced.) The Structural grade lumber receives 24% of the total cost ($12,000/$50,000) instead of the 10% portion based on a physical measure. The No. 3 Common lumber receives only 8% of the total cost, or $2,400, which is much less than the $6,000 assigned to it with the physical basis.

An outcome of value-based allocation is that *every* grade produces exactly the same 40% gross profit on its sales value. This 40% rate equals the gross profit rate from selling all the lumber made from the $30,000 logs for a combined price of $50,000.

Exhibit 24.25

Allocating Joint Costs on a Value Basis

Grade of Lumber	Sales Value	Percent of Total	Allocated Cost	Gross Profit
Structural	$12,000	24.0%	$ 7,200	$ 4,800
No. 1 Common	18,000	36.0	10,800	7,200
No. 2 Common	16,000	32.0	9,600	6,400
No. 3 Common	4,000	8.0	2,400	1,600
Total	$50,000	100.0%	$30,000	$20,000

Flash back

13. A company produces three products: B1, B2 and B3. The joint cost incurred for the current month for these products is $180,000. The following data relate to this month's production:

Product	Units Produced	Unit Sales Price
B1	96,000	$3.00
B2	64,000	6.00
B3	32,000	9.00

The amount of joint cost allocated to B3 is: (a) $30,000, (b) $54,000, (c) $90,000.

Answers—p. 1183

Return on Total Assets by Investment Centres

USING THE INFORMATION

LO 10 Analyze investment centres using return on total assets.

We described how to evaluate a department as a profit centre or as a cost centre. Large companies are often broken into several divisions that are evaluated as investment centres. An **investment centre** incurs investments and generates profits. The investment centre manager is responsible for its revenues and expenses along with the cost of the investment.

The measure often used to evaluate an investment centre manager is the centre's return on total assets; also called return on investment. This measure is computed as net income divided by average total assets (see Chapter 1). Net income is for the centre, and average total assets reflects the centre's investment level. If a centre with an average investment of $1 million yields a net income of $210,000, its return on total assets is 21%.

A centre's return on total assets provides top management with an assessment of how well a centre manager has utilized the centre's productive assets to generate returns for the company. Top managers can also compare performance across divisions using this same measure. Many companies establish a centre's target return on total assets and reward managers depending on whether the targets are met. Centre managers often rely upon return on total assets to decide whether they want to reinvest resources in new centre opportunities.

Centre Manager

You are the centre manager of a growing investment centre. Your centre's return on total assets has averaged 19%. You are considering two new potential investing opportunities for your centre. The first requires a $250,000 investment and is expected to yield annual net income of $50,000. The second requires a $1 million investment with an expected annual net income of $175,000. Do you pursue either opportunity?

Answer—p. 1182

Summary

LO 1 **Assign factory overhead costs using two-stage cost allocation.** In the traditional two-stage cost allocation procedure, costs are first assigned to cost centres which are typically production departments such as machining and assembly. Then, in the second stage, a predetermined overhead allocation rate is computed for each cost centre which is used to assign overhead to jobs.

LO 2 **Assign factory overhead costs using activity-based costing.** In activity-based costing, the costs of separate activities of overhead items or *resources* are first collected in separate temporary accounts. Then, the activities are pooled together in some logical manner into activity cost pools. After all activity costs have been accumulated in an activity cost pool account, consumers of the activity, termed *cost objects*, are assigned a portion of the total activity cost using an appropriate cost driver or allocation base.

LO 3 **Explain departmentalization and the role of departmental accounting.** Companies are divided into departments whenever they become too large to be effectively managed as a single unit. Production departments either manufacture products in a factory or sell products in a store. Service departments support the activities of these production departments. Departmental accounting systems provide information for evaluating departments' performances and responsibility accounting systems provide information for evaluating the performance of department managers. Departments are evaluated as cost centres if they incur costs but do not generate revenues. Departments are evaluated as profit centres if they generate revenues.

LO 4 **Distinguish between direct and indirect expenses.** Direct expenses are easily traced to a specific department because they are incurred for the sole benefit of one department. Indirect expenses, on the other hand, benefit more than one department. If departmental net incomes are measured, indirect expenses are allocated to the departments on some reasonable basis. The allocation basis selected for an indirect expense is a matter of judgment but should reflect the relative benefit the departments receive from the expense.

LO5 Identify bases for allocating indirect expenses to departments. There is no standard rule about what allocation base is best to allocate indirect expenses to departments. Ideally we allocate indirect expenses by using a cause-effect relation. But identifying cause-effect relations is not always possible. In these situations, each indirect expense is allocated on a basis approximating the relative benefit received by each department.

LO6 Prepare departmental income statements. Each profit centre (department) is assigned its full expenses to yield a complete income statement. These costs include direct expenses and indirect expenses shared with other departments. The departmental income statement begins by listing the revenues and the cost of goods sold of the department to determine the gross profit. The operating expenses (direct and indirect expenses allocated to the departments) are then deducted from the gross profit to compute the department's net income. It is often useful to compile the full amount of expenses incurred in service departments and then assign them to operating departments (or cost centres).

LO7 Prepare departmental contribution reports. The departmental contribution report is somewhat similar to the departmental income statement in terms of computing the gross profit for each department. Then, the direct operating expenses for each department are deducted from the gross profit to determine the contribution generated by each department. The indirect operating expenses are not allocated to individual departments but are deducted in total from the total contribution generated by the company as a whole.

LO8 Explain controllable costs and responsibility accounting. A controllable cost must be identified with a specific level of management and a specific time period. The total expenses of operating a department often include items that are not controllable by the department manager. To be useful, performance reports produced by a responsibility accounting system for evaluating departmental managers should include only the expenses (and revenues) controllable by the managers.

LO9 Describe allocation of joint costs across products. A joint cost is a single cost incurred in producing or purchasing two or more different products. When income statements are prepared, joint costs should be allocated to the resulting joint products based on the relative market value of the joint products at the point of separation.

LO10 Analyze investment centres using return on total assets. The measure often used to evaluate an investment centre manager is the centre's return on total assets, also called return on investment. This measure is computed as net income divided by average total assets. Net income is for the centre, and average total assets reflects the centre's investment level.

Guidance Answers to **You Make the Call**

Director of Operations

First and foremost, you should collect details of the overhead items and review them to see if direct labour does indeed drive these costs. If it does not, then the department managers are correct in pointing out that the overhead was unduly assigned to their departments. Given that the current overhead allocation base is direct labour, you may not be able to reverse the situation. However, the situation provides an opportunity to consider other overhead allocation bases including the use of activity-based costing.

Centre Manager

One must first realize that the investment's are not comparable on the basis of absolute dollars of income. For instance, the second investment provides a higher income in absolute dollars but requires a greater investment. Rather, one needs to compute the return on total assets for each alternative: (1) $50,000 ÷ $250,000 = 20%, and (2) $175,000 ÷ $1 million = 17.5%. Alternative 1 has the higher return and is preferred over alternative 2. But do you pursue one, both or neither? Given that alternative 1's return is higher than the centre's usual return of 19%, it should be pursued assuming its risks are acceptable. Also, since alternative 1 requires a small investment, the corporate office is likely more agreeable to pursuing it. But alternative 2's return is lower than the usual 19% and is not likely to be acceptable.

Guidance Answer to **Judgment and Ethics**

Accounting Officer

You should not write a report as requested by your current supervisor because you may be misrepresenting the situation. It is your responsibility, as an accountant, to ascertain all the facts regarding activity-based costing (the implementation procedure to be followed, advantages and disadvantages of ABC, costs involved, etc.). You should then approach your supervisor with all the facts and suggest that you would like to modify the report to request a pilot implementation of the system before proceeding with a full-fledged implementation. The pilot test will allow you to further assess the suitability of ABC in your company. You should realize that your supervisor may refuse to accept your suggestion, at which time you may wish to speak to some other person of authority.

Guidance Answers to Flashbacks

1. A cost driver is a factor that affects the amount of a component of overhead cost. In activity-based costing, cost drivers are the allocation bases used to assign overhead costs to products and processes.
2. *d*
3. Departmental accounting systems provide information used to evaluate the performance of *departments*. Responsibility accounting systems provide information used to evaluate the performance of *department managers*.
4. *d*
5. A cost centre incurs costs without directly generating revenues, like a manufacturing or service department. A profit centre incurs costs but also generates revenues, like a selling department.
6. *b*
7. *b*
8. *d*
9. (1) Assign the direct expenses to each department. (2) Allocate indirect expenses to all departments. (3) Allocate the service department expenses to the production departments.
10. *b*
11. No, because many of the expenses that enter into these calculations are beyond the control of the manager, and managers should not be evaluated using costs they do not control.
12. *c*
13. *b*

Demonstration Problem

Use the following information to prepare departmental income statements for Hacker's Haven, a computer store. The store has five departments. Three of them are selling departments (hardware, software, and repairs), and two are service departments (general office and purchasing).

Some accounting information about the five departments' activities for 19X1 follows:

	General Office	Purchasing	Hardware	Software	Repairs
Sales	—	—	$960,000	$600,000	$840,000
Cost of goods sold	—	—	500,000	300,000	200,000
Direct expenses:					
Payroll	$60,000	$45,000	80,000	25,000	325,000
Amortization	6,000	7,200	33,000	4,200	9,600
Supplies	15,000	10,000	10,000	2,000	25,000

In addition, several indirect expenses are incurred in the departments. In preparing an income statement, these indirect expenses are allocated among the five departments. Then, the expenses of the two service departments are allocated to the three production departments. The total amounts and the allocation bases for each expense are as follows:

Type of Indirect Expense	Total Cost	Allocation Basis
Rent	$150,000	Square metres occupied
Utilities	50,000	Square metres occupied
Advertising	125,000	Dollars of sales
Insurance	30,000	Value of assets insured
Service departments:		
General office	?	Number of employees
Purchasing	?	Dollars of cost of goods sold

The following information is needed for the allocations:

Department	Square Metres	Sales	Insured Assets	Employees	Cost of Goods Sold
General office	500		$ 60,000		
Purchasing	500		72,000		
Hardware	4,000	$ 960,000	330,000	5	$ 500,000
Software	3,000	600,000	42,000	5	300,000
Repairs	2,000	840,000	96,000	10	200,000
Total	10,000	$2,400,000	$600,000	20	$1,000,000

Required

1. Complete a departmental expense allocation work sheet for Hacker's Haven.

2. Prepare a departmental income statement reporting net income for each selling department and for all selling departments combined.

Planning the Solution

- Set up and complete four schedules to allocate the indirect expenses for rent, utilities, advertising, and insurance.
- Allocate the departments' indirect expenses with a six-column work sheet like the one in Exhibit 24.14. Enter the given amounts of the direct expenses for each department. Then enter the allocated amounts of the indirect expenses that were just computed.
- Complete two schedules for allocating the general office and purchasing department costs to the three selling departments. Enter these amounts on the work sheet and determine the total expenses allocated to the three selling departments.
- Prepare a four-column departmental income statement like the one in Exhibit 24.19. Show sales, cost of goods sold, the gross profit from sales, the individual direct and indirect expenses, and the net income for each of the three selling departments and for the entire company.

Solution to Demonstration Problem

Allocations of indirect expenses among the five departments:

Rent	Square Metres	Percent of Total	Allocated
General office	500	5.0%	$ 7,500
Purchasing	500	5.0	7,500
Hardware	4,000	40.0	60,000
Software	3,000	30.0	45,000
Repairs	2,000	20.0	30,000
Total	10,000	100.0%	$150,000

Utilities	Square Metres	Percent of Total	Allocated Cost
General office	500	5.0%	$ 2,500
Purchasing	500	5.0	2,500
Hardware	4,000	40.0	20,000
Software	3,000	30.0	15,000
Repairs	2,000	20.0	10,000
Total	10,000	100.0%	$50,000

Advertising	Sales Dollars	Percent of Total	Allocated
Hardware	$ 960,000	40.0%	$ 50,000
Software	600,000	25.0	31,250
Repairs	840,000	35.0	43,750
Total	$2,400,000	100.0%	$125,000

Insurance	Assets Insured	Percent of Total	Allocated
General office	$ 60,000	10.0%	$ 3,000
Purchasing	72,000	12.0	3,600
Hardware	330,000	55.0	16,500
Software	42,000	7.0	2,100
Repairs	96,000	16.0	4,800
Total	$600,000	100.0%	$30,000

Departmental Expense Allocation Spreadsheet for Year Ended December 31, 19X1

Expense	Allocation Bases	Expense Account Balance	General Office	Purchasing	Hardware Dept.	Software Dept.	Repairs Dept.
Direct expenses:							
Payroll		$ 535,000	$60,000	$45,000	$ 80,000	$ 25,000	$325,000
Amortization		60,000	6,000	7,200	33,000	4,200	9,600
Supplies		62,000	15,000	10,000	10,000	2,000	25,000
Indirect expenses:							
Rent	Square metre	150,000	7,500	7,500	60,000	45,000	30,000
Utilities	Square metre	50,000	2,500	2,500	20,000	15,000	10,000
Advertising	Sales	125,000	—	—	50,000	31,250	43,750
Insurance	Assets	30,000	3,000	3,600	16,500	2,100	4,800
Total		$1,012,000	$94,000	$75,800	$269,500	$124,550	$448,150
Service dept. expenses:							
General office	Employees		$94,000		23,500	23,500	47,000
Purchasing	Goods sold			$75,800	37,900	22,740	15,160
Total expenses allocated to selling departments		$1,012,000			$330,900	$170,790	$510,310

Allocations of service department expenses among the three selling departments:

General Office:	Employees	Percent of Total	Allocated Cost
Hardware	5	25.0%	$23,500
Software	5	25.0	23,500
Repairs	10	50.0	47,000
Total	20	100.0%	$94,000

Purchasing:	Cost of Goods Sold	Percent of Total	Allocated Cost
Hardware	$ 500,000	50.0%	$37,900
Software	300,000	30.0	22,740
Repairs	200,000	20.0	15,160
Total	$1,000,000	100.0%	$75,800

HACKER'S HAVEN COMPUTER STORE
Departmental Income Statement
For Year Ended December 31, 19X1

	Hardware	Software	Repairs	Combined
Sales	$960,000	$600,000	$840,000	$2,400,000
Cost of goods sold	500,000	300,000	200,000	1,000,000
Gross profit	460,000	300,000	640,000	1,400,000
Expenses:				
Payroll	80,000	25,000	325,000	430,000
Amortization	33,000	4,200	9,600	46,800
Supplies	10,000	2,000	25,000	37,000
Rent	60,000	45,000	30,000	135,000
Utilities	20,000	15,000	10,000	45,000
Advertising	50,000	31,250	43,750	125,000
Insurance	16,500	2,100	4,800	23,400
General office	23,500	23,500	47,000	94,000
Purchasing	37,900	22,740	15,160	75,800
Total expenses	330,900	170,790	510,310	1,012,000
Net income	$129,100	$129,210	$129,690	$ 388,000

Glossary

Activity-based costing A two-stage allocation system where the first stage includes identifying the activities involved in the manufacturing process and forming cost pools by combining activities into sets and the second stage involves computing the predetermined overhead cost allocation rates for each cost pool and assigning the costs to jobs. (p. 1159)

Activity cost pool A temporary account that accumulates the costs a company incurs to support an identified activity. (p. 1159)

Controllable costs Costs with amounts that the manager has the power to determine or at least strongly influence. (p. 1176)

Cost centre A department or unit that incurs costs, alone, such as the accounting department. (p. 1165)

Cost driver A driver that causes the cost of an activity to go up or down. (p. 1159)

Departmental accounting system An accounting system that provides information that management can use to evaluate the profitability or cost effectiveness of a department's activities. (p. 1164)

Departmental contribution to overhead The amount by which a department's revenues exceed its direct costs and expenses. (p. 1175)

Direct expenses Expenses that are easily traced to a specific department because they are incurred for the sole benefit of that department. (p. 1168)

Indirect expenses Expenses incurred for the joint benefit of more than one department. (p. 1168)

Investment centre A centre in which a manager is responsible for revenues, costs and investments. (p. 1181)

Joint cost A single cost incurred in producing or purchasing two or more essentially different products. (p. 1179)

Performance report A responsibility accounting report that compares actual costs and expenses for a department with the budgeted amounts. (p. 1177)

Profit centre A unit of a business that incurs costs and also generates revenues. (p. 1165)

Responsibility accounting budget A plan that specifies the expected costs and expenses under the control of a manager. (p. 1177)

Responsibility accounting system An accounting system that provides information that management can use to evaluate the performance of a department's manager. (p. 1176)

Uncontrollable costs Costs that the manager does not have the power to determine or at least strongly influence. (p. 1176)

Questions

1. Why are businesses divided into departments?
2. Identify the two stages in a "two-stage" allocation system by completing the following: In the first stage, costs are assigned to ______ centres which are typically production departments such as machining and assembly. Then, in the second stage, a predetermined overhead allocation rate is computed for each cost centre which is used to assign overhead to ______.
3. What is the difference between production departments and service departments?
4. What is activity-based costing?
5. Identify five typical cost pools for activity-based costing.
6. In activity-based costing costs in a cost pool are allocated to ______.
7. Why would a business use activity-based costing?
8. What are the two primary goals for managerial accounting for departments?
9. Is it possible to evaluate the profitability of a cost centre? Why?
10. How is a departmental sales analysis spreadsheet used in determining sales by departments?
11. What is the difference between direct and indirect expenses?
12. Suggest a reasonable basis for allocating each of the following indirect expenses to departments: (a) salary of a supervisor who manages several departments, (b) rent, (c) heat, (d) electricity used for lighting, (e) janitorial services, (f) advertising, (g) expired insurance on equipment, and (h) amortization on equipment.
13. How is a department's contribution to overhead measured?
14. What are controllable costs?
15. Controllable and uncontrollable costs must be identified with a particular ______ and a definite ______ period.
16. Why should managers be closely involved in preparing their responsibility accounting budgets?
17. In responsibility accounting, who is the right person to be given timely reports and statistics for a specific cost?
18. What is a joint cost? How are joint costs usually allocated among the products produced from them?
19. Give two examples of joint costs. Explain with examples.
20. NIKE receives telephone orders for merchandise sold in different types of stores, i.e. sporting goods super stores and specialty running shoe stores. Why would it be useful to (a) collect information for each particular store category and (b) treat each category as a profit centre?
21. Reebok delivers orders to many different locations in North and South America. List three controllable and three uncontrollable costs for Reebok's delivery department.

Quick Study

QS 24-1

Activity-based costing

LO 2

The following is taken from Foster's internal financial reports of a factory with two production departments:

	Direct Labour	Hours of Machine Use
Department 1	$ 9,400	1,200
Department 2	6,600	2,000
Totals	$16,000	3,200
Factory overhead:		
Rent and utilities		$ 6,100
Indirect labour		2,700
General office expense		1,700
Equipment amortization		1,500
Supplies		900
Total overhead		$12,900

Compute the total amount of overhead cost that would be allocated to Department 1 for Foster if activity-based costing is used. Assume the cost driver for indirect labour and supplies is direct labour and the cost driver for the remaining overhead items is hours of machine use.

QS 24-2
Allocation and measurement terms
LO 3-8

In each of the blanks next to the following terms, place the identifying letter of the description that best matches each term.

_____ **1.** Cost centre
_____ **2.** Investment centre
_____ **3.** Departmental accounting system
_____ **4.** Production department
_____ **5.** Profit centre
_____ **6.** Responsibility accounting system
_____ **7.** Service department

a. Provides information used to evaluate the performance of a department.
b. Provides information used to evaluate the performance of a department manager.
c. Does not directly manufacture products, but contributes to the profitability of the entire company.
d. Engages directly in manufacturing or in making sales directly to customers.
e. Incurs costs without directly generating revenues.
f. Incurs costs but also generates revenues.
g. Manager is responsible for revenues, costs and investments

QS 24-3
Basis for allocation
LO 5

For each of the following types of indirect and service department expenses, name one possible allocation basis that could be used to distribute it to the departments indicated:

a. Computer services for the factory production schedule:
____

b. Electric utility expense to all departments:
____

c. Maintenance department expenses to the production departments:
____

d. General office department expenses to the production departments:
____

QS 24-4
Departmental contributions to overhead
LO 7

Using the following information, compute each department's contribution to overhead (both in dollars and as a percent). Which department contributes the highest dollar amount to total overhead? Which department's contribution percent is the highest?

	Dept. A	Dept. B	Dept. C
Sales	$53,000	$170,000	$84,000
Cost of goods sold	34,185	103,700	49,560
Gross profit	18,815	66,300	34,440
Total direct expenses	6,360	37,060	8,736
Contribution to overhead	$	$	$
Contribution percent	%	%	%

QS 24-5
Joint cost allocation
LO 9

A 1,002 square metre commercial building was purchased for $325,000. An additional $50,000 was spent to split the space into two separate rental units and to get it ready to rent. Unit A, which has the desirable location on the corner and contains 334 square metres, will be rented out for $10.00 per square metre. Unit B contains 668 square metres and will be rented out for $7.50 per square metre. How much of the joint cost should be assigned to Unit B?

QS 24-6
Investment centre
LO 10

Compute return on assets for each of the three **NIKE** shoe divisions below (each division is an investment centre).

Division	Net Income	Assets	Return on Assets
Basketball	$4,000,000	$20,000,000	
Soccer	$1,500,000	$15,000,000	
Cross-trainer	$ 750,000	$10,000,000	

Exercises

Exercise 24-1
Allocating rent expense to departments
LO 1, 5

The National Auto Component, Inc. pays $128,000 rent every year for its two-story building. The space in the building is occupied by five departments as follows:

Paint department	1,390 square metres of first-floor space
Engine department	3,410 square metres of first-floor space
Window department	2,040 square metres of second-floor space
Electrical department	960 square metres of second-floor space
Auto accessory department	1,800 square metres of second-floor space

The company allocates 65% of the total rent expense to the first floor and 35% to the second floor. It then allocates the rent expense for each floor to the departments on that floor on the basis of the space occupied. Determine the rent to be allocated to each department. (Round all percents to the nearest one-tenth and all dollar amounts to the nearest whole dollar.)

Exercise 24-2
Departmental expense allocations
LO 1, 5

Pembroke Corporation has four departments: materials, personnel, manufacturing, and packaging. In a recent month, the four departments incurred three shared indirect costs. The amounts of these expenses and the bases used to allocate them are:

Expense	Cost	Allocation Base
Supervision	$ 75,000	Number of employees
Utilities	60,000	Square metres occupied
Insurance	16,500	Value of assets in use
Total expense	$151,500	

These quantities are to be used in allocating the costs for the month:

Department	Employees	Square Metres	Assets Value
Materials	18	3,000	$ 6,000
Personnel	6	500	1,200
Manufacturing	66	5,000	37,800
Packaging	30	1,500	15,000
Total	120	10,000	$60,000

Using this information, prepare allocations of each of the three indirect expenses among the four departments. Then, prepare a table that shows the total expenses assigned to the four departments.

Exercise 24-3
Activity-based costing

LO 2

The Glass Company manufactures two types of glass shelving, rounded edge and squared edge, on the same production line. Last month, the company experienced the following costs and results:

	Rounded Edge	Squared Edge	Total
Direct materials	$ 9,500	$21,600	$ 31,100
Direct labour	6,100	11,900	18,000
Overhead (300% of labour)	18,300	35,700	54,000
Total cost	$33,900	$69,200	$103,100
Quantity produced	10,500	14,100	
Average cost per unit	$ 3.23	$ 4.91	

Several of the managers have approached the cost accounting department for help in understanding activity-based costing. Their specific request is that ABC be applied to the production results to see whether the average cost per unit is significantly changed. This additional information is extracted from the production records for the month:

- The overhead cost for supervision was $2,160. The cost driver for supervision is direct labour cost.
- The overhead cost for machinery amortization was $28,840. The cost driver for this cost is hours of use. The machinery was used 300 hours for rounded edge shelves and 700 hours for squared edge shelves.
- The overhead cost for preparing the line to manufacture products was $23,000. The cost driver for this cost is number of setup times. The line was set up 31 times to produce different kinds of rounded edge and 94 times to produce different kinds of squared edge shelves.

Required

Use this information to:

a. Assign the overhead cost to the products using activity-based costing.

b. Determine the average cost per unit of the two products using direct materials, direct labour, and overhead allocated under ABC.

c. Compare and explain the average per unit cost under ABC to the average cost per unit found in the data section of this problem.

Exercise 24-4
Allocating service department expenses to production departments

LO 6

The following partially completed lower section of a departmental allocation spreadsheet is being prepared for Early Bird Bookstore. At this stage it shows only the amounts of direct and indirect expenses that have been allocated to the five departments:

Expense	Allocation Bases	Expense Account Balance	Advertising Office	Purchasing Dept.	Book Dept.	Magazine Dept.	Newspaper Dept.
Total		$654,000	$22,000	$30,000	$425,000	$86,000	$91,000
Service dept. expenses:							
Advertising	Sales		?		?	?	?
Purchasing	Purchase orders			?	?	?	?
Total expenses allocated to selling departments		?			?	?	?

Complete the spreadsheet by allocating the two service departments' expenses to the three selling departments. These amounts were known about the allocation bases for the three selling departments:

	Sales	Purchase Orders
Books	$448,000	424
Magazines	144,000	312
Newspapers	208,000	264
Total	$800,000	1,000

Exercise 24-5
Allocating indirect payroll expense to departments
LO 5, 6

Eliza Short works in both the jewellery department and the hosiery department of Fine's Department Store. Short assists customers in both departments and also straightens and stocks the merchandise in both departments as needed. The store allocates Short's annual wages of $30,000 between the two departments based on a sample of the time worked in the two departments. The sample was obtained from a diary that Short kept of hours worked in a randomly chosen two-week period. The diary showed that the following hours were spent in these activities:

Selling in the jewellery department	64
Straightening and rearranging merchandise in the jewellery department	6
Selling in the hosiery department	14
Straightening and stocking merchandise in the hosiery department	12
Idle time spent waiting for a customer to enter one of the selling departments	4

Required

Prepare calculations to allocate Short's wages between the departments. Round all percents to the nearest tenth of a percent and all dollar amounts to the nearest whole dollar.

Exercise 24-6
Departmental expense allocation spreadsheet
LO 5, 6

The ProCycle Shop has two service departments (advertising and administrative), and two sales departments (motorcycles and clothing). During 1998, the departments had the following direct expenses:

Advertising department	$ 10,560
Administrative department	12,740
Motorcycle department	101,600
Clothing department	11,900

The departments occupy the following square metres of floor space:

Advertising department	340
Administrative department	360
Motorcycle department	1,980
Clothing department	1,320

The advertising department developed and distributed 100 ad pieces during the year. Of these, 76 promoted motorcycles and 24 promoted clothing. The store sold $300,000 of merchandise during the year. Of this amount, $225,000 was from the motorcycle department while the remainder was from the clothing department.

Required

Prepare an expense allocation sheet for the ProCycle Shop that assigns the direct expenses to all four departments and the year's $64,000 of utilities expense to the four departments on the basis of floor space occupied. In addition, allocate the advertising department expenses on the basis of the number of ads placed and the administrative department expenses based on the amount of sales. Provide supplemental schedules showing how you computed the expense allocations. (Round all percents to the nearest one-tenth and all dollar amounts to the nearest whole dollar.)

Exercise 24-7
Evaluating managerial performance
LO 8

Cathy Shore manages the auto stereo department of a large auto dealership. This is the 1998 income statement for her department:

Revenues:		
Sales of parts	$ 72,000	
Sales of services	105,000	$177,000
Costs and expenses:		
Building amortization	9,300	
Cost of parts sold	30,000	
Income taxes allocated to department	8,700	
Interest on long-term debt	7,500	
Manager's salary	12,000	
Payroll taxes	8,100	
Supplies	15,900	
Utilities	14,400	
Wages (hourly)	6,000	
Total costs and expenses		111,900
Department net income		$ 65,100

Analyze the items on the income statement to identify those that clearly should be included on a performance report used to evaluate Cathy's performance. List them and explain why you have chosen them. Then, list and explain the items that should clearly be excluded. Finally, list the items that are not clearly included or excluded and explain why they fall in that category.

Exercise 24-8
Assigning joint real estate costs
LO 9

Capital Properties just completed developing a subdivision that includes 400 home sites. The 300 lots in the Canyon section are below a ridge and do not have views of the neighbouring canyons and hills, while the 100 lots in the Hilltop section offer unobstructed views. The Canyon lots are expected to sell for $50,000 each, while the Hilltop lots are expected to sell for $90,000 each. The developer acquired the land for $2,500,000 and spent another $2,500,000 on street and utilities improvements. Assign the joint land and improvement costs to the lots and determine the average cost per lot. (Round all percents to the nearest one-tenth and all dollar amounts to the nearest whole dollar.)

Exercise 24-9
Assigning joint product costs
LO 9

Tasty Seafood Company purchases lobsters and processes them into tails and flakes. It then sells the lobster tails for $42 per kilogram and sells the flakes for $28 per kilogram. On average, 100 kilograms of lobster can be processed into 52 kilograms of tails and 22 kilograms of flakes, with 26 kilograms of waste.

Assume that 1,200 kilograms of lobster are purchased for $9 per kilogram. The lobsters are then processed with an additional labour cost of $1,800. No materials or labour costs are assigned to the waste. If 548 kilograms of tails are sold and 162 kilograms of flakes are sold, what is the allocated cost of the sold items and the cost of the remaining inventory?

Exercise 24-10
Investment centre
LO 10

You have been asked to prepare a return on investment analysis by the regional manager of Dog Café. This growing chain is trying to decide which outlet to open among two alternatives. The first location requires a $600,000 investment in an area primarily populated by Saint Bernards and is expected to yield annual net income of $175,000 (Saint Bernard's love burgers). The second location requires a $200,000 investment in an area primarily populated by French poodles and is expected to yield annual net income of $78,000 (French poodles love small, but expensive burgers).

Required

1. Compute the return on investment for each dog burger alternative.
2. Write up your recommendation to the regional manager. Be prepared to explain your reasoning in class. (Hint: Think of market conditions.)

Problems

Problem 24-1
Allocation of building occupancy costs
LO 1, 6

Toy Time, Inc., has several departments that occupy both floors of a two-story building. The departmental accounting system has a single account in the ledger called Building Occupancy Cost. These types and amounts of costs were recorded in this account for last year:

Amortization, building	$18,000
Interest, building mortgage	27,000
Taxes, building and land	8,000
Gas expense	2,500
Lighting expense	3,000
Maintenance expense	5,500
Total	$64,000

The building has 1,250 square metres on each floor. For simplicity, the bookkeeper merely divided the $64,000 occupancy cost by 2,500 square metres to find an average cost of $25.60 per square metre. Then, each department was charged with a building occupancy cost equal to this rate times the number of square metres that it occupies.

Joan French manages a first-floor department that occupies 330 square metres and Leo Perry manages a second-floor department that occupies 600 square metres of floor space. In discussing the departmental reports, they have questioned whether using the same rate per square metre for all departments makes sense because the first-floor space has a greater value. Looking further into the issue, the two managers checked a recent real estate study of average rental costs for similar space. The amounts do not include costs for heating, lighting, and cleaning. They found that ground-floor space is worth $90 per square metre while second-floor space is worth only $60.

Required

Use the preceding information to:

1. Allocate the occupancy cost to the two departments by the bookkeeper's method.
2. Allocate the occupancy cost to the two departments in proportion to the relative market values of the space, except for the heating, lighting, and cleaning costs, which should be allocated on an equal basis per square metre occupied. Round costs per square metre to the nearest cent.

Check Figure Part 2. Total occupancy cost to French, $10,012.20.

Analysis Component:

3. If you were a manager of a second floor department, which method would you prefer, and why?

Problem 24-2
Activity-based costing
LO 2

Surgery Centre, Inc. is a growing outpatient surgery centre that has enjoyed excess profits from many years. However, now Medicare is beginning to cut reimbursement by as much as 50%. As a result the centre is trying to get a better understanding of its cost of resources. You have been hired to prepare an activity-based cost analysis with the following data. The key question is what does it cost to offer on average a general surgery compared to an orthopedic surgery?

The cost centres and respective drivers are:

Activity Centre	Cost	Driver	Quantity
Professional salaries	$1,500,000	Professional hours	10,000
Service patients/supplies	25,000	Number of patients	500
Building cost	150,000	Square metres*	1,500

The professional services:

Service	Pro. Hours	Square Metres*	No. of Patients
General surgery	2,500	500	400
Orthopedic	7,500	1,000	100

* Orthopedic surgeries require more space for patients, supplies, and special equipment.

Required

Check Figure Average cost of general surgery, $1,113

1. Compute the cost per driver.
2. Compute the average cost for a general and an orthopedic surgery.

Analysis component:

3. Without computation, would the average cost of a general surgery be more or less if activity centre cost were allocated on number of surgeries alone. Why?

Problem 24-3
Departmental income statement
LO 6

Looking-At-You, Inc., began operating in January 1998 with two selling departments and one office department. The 1998 departmental net incomes are:

LOOKING-AT-YOU, INC.
Departmental Income Statement
For Year Ended December 31, 1998

	Clocks	Mirrors	Combined
Sales	$122,500	$52,500	$175,000
Cost of goods sold	60,000	32,000	92,000
Gross profit from sales	62,500	20,500	83,000
Direct expenses:			
Sales salaries	20,000	7,000	27,000
Advertising	1,200	500	1,700
Store supplies used	900	400	1,300
Amortization of equipment	1,500	300	1,800
Total direct expenses	23,600	8,200	31,800
Allocated expenses:			
Rent expense	7,020	3,780	10,800
Utilities expense	2,600	1,400	4,000
Share of office department expenses	10,500	4,500	15,000
Total allocated expenses	20,120	9,680	29,800
Total expenses	43,720	17,880	61,600
Net income	$ 18,780	$ 2,620	$ 21,400

Starting in January 1999, Looking-At-You plans to open a third department that will sell paintings. Management predicts that the new department will produce $35,000 in sales with a 55% gross profit margin and that it will require the following direct expenses: sales salaries, $8,000; advertising, $800; store supplies, $500; and equipment amortization, $200.

Since opening, the store has rented space in a building. It will be possible to fit the new department into the same overall space by taking some square metres from the other two departments. When the new painting department is opened, it will fill one-fifth of the space presently used by the clock department and one-sixth of the space used by the mirror department. Management does not predict any increase in utilities costs, which are allocated among the departments in proportion to occupied space.

The company allocates its office department expenses among the selling departments in proportion to their sales. It expects the painting department to increase office department expenses by $7,000.

Because the painting department will bring new customers into the store, management expects sales in the clock and mirror departments to increase by 7%. Those departments' gross profit percents are not expected to change. No changes are expected in their direct expenses, except for store supplies used, which will increase in proportion to sales.

Required

Prepare a departmental income statement that shows the company's predicted results of operations for 1999 with three selling departments. (Round all percents to the nearest one-tenth and all dollar amounts to the nearest whole dollar.)

Check Figure Forecasted combined net income, $29,815

Problem 24-4
Responsibility accounting performance reports

LO 8,7

Vi Symanski, the manager of Royal Manufacturing Company's Victoria plant, is responsible for all costs of the plant's operation other than her own salary. The plant has two production departments and one service department. The camper and trailer departments manufacture different products and have their own managers. The office department provides services equally to the two production departments. Symanski manages the office department. A budget is prepared for each production department and the office department. The responsibility accounting system must assemble the information to present budgeted and actual costs in performance reports for each of the production department managers and the plant manager.

Each performance report includes only those costs that the particular manager can control. The production department managers control the costs of raw materials, wages, supplies used, and equipment amortization. The plant manager is responsible for the department managers' salaries, utilities, building rent, office salaries other than her own, other office costs, plus all the costs controlled by the two production department managers.

The annual departmental budgets and cost accumulations for the two production departments were as follows:

	Budget			Actual		
	Campers	Trailers	Combined	Campers	Trailers	Combined
Raw materials	$160,000	$250,000	$ 410,000	$159,400	$246,500	$ 405,900
Wages	99,000	191,000	290,000	102,300	193,700	296,000
Department manager salary	40,000	44,000	84,000	41,000	47,000	88,000
Supplies used	34,000	83,000	117,000	31,900	84,600	116,500
Equipment amortization	58,000	110,000	168,000	58,000	110,000	168,000
Utilities	2,800	4,200	7,000	2,700	3,800	6,500
Building rent	5,000	8,000	13,000	4,800	7,200	12,000
Office department costs	54,000	54,000	108,000	52,000	52,000	104,000
Total	$452,800	$744,200	$1,197,000	$452,100	$744,800	$1,196,900

Office department budget and actual costs consisted of the following:

	Budget	Actual
Plant manager salary	$ 56,000	$ 57,100
Other office salaries	30,000	27,700
Other office costs	22,000	19,200
Total	$108,000	$104,000

Required

Prepare responsibility accounting performance reports that list the costs controlled by the following managers:

1. Manager of the camper department.
2. Manager of the trailer department.
3. Manager of the Victoria plant.

Check Figure Part 3. Victoria plant controllable costs, $1,200 under budget

In each report, include the budgeted and actual costs and show the amount that each actual cost is over or under the budgeted amount.

Analysis component:

4. Who did a better job of managing cost, the plant manager or the production department managers? Why?

Problem 24-5
Allocating joint costs
LO 9

Jack Tandy's orchards produced a good crop of peaches in 1998. After preparing the following income statement, Tandy concluded that he should have given the No. 3 peaches to charity and saved a lot of money and trouble.

JACK TANDY ORCHARDS
Income from Peaches
For Year Ended December 31, 1998

	No. 1	No. 2	No. 3	Combined
Sales (by grade):				
No. 1: 120,000 kg @ $3.75 . . .	$450,000			
No. 2: 120,000 kg @ $2.50 . . .		$300,000		
No. 3: 300,000 kg @ $0.50 . . .			$ 150,000	
Total sales				$900,000
Costs:				
Tree pruning and care @ $0.50/kg	60,000	60,000	150,000	270,000
Picking, sorting, and grading @ $0.30/kg	36,000	36,000	90,000	162,000
Delivery @ $0.075/kg	9,000	9,000	22,500	40,500
Total costs	105,000	105,000	262,500	472,500
Net income (loss)	$345,000	$195,000	$(112,500)	$427,500

In preparing the statement, Tandy allocated the joint costs among the grades as an equal amount per kilogram. Records about the delivery cost show that $30,000 of the $40,500 was the cost of crating the No. 1 and No. 2 peaches and hauling them to the buyer. The remaining $10,500 of delivery cost was the cost of crating the No. 3 peaches and hauling them to the cannery where they were used to make preserves.

Required

Preparation component:

1. Prepare allocation schedules showing how the costs would be allocated on the basis of the relative sales values of the three grades. Separate the delivery cost into the amounts directly identifiable to the grades. (Round all percents to the nearest one-tenth and all dollar amounts to the nearest whole dollar.)
2. Using your answers to requirement 1, prepare an income statement that shows the results of producing and delivering the peaches.

Check Figure Part 2. Net income from No. 1 peaches, $216,000

Analysis component:

3. Do you think the delivery cost is a true joint cost? Explain your answer.

Alternate Problems

Problem 24-1A
Allocation of building occupancy costs

LO 1, 6

DuPree's has several departments that occupy all three floors of a two-story building with a basement. The store has rented this building under a long-term lease negotiated when rental rates were much lower. The departmental accounting system has a single account in the ledger called Building Occupancy Cost. These types and amounts of costs were recorded in this account for last year:

Building rent	$300,000
Lighting expense	24,000
Cleaning expense	16,000
Total	$340,000

The building has 750 square metres on each floor but only 500 square metres in the basement. For simplicity, the bookkeeper merely divided the $340,000 occupancy cost by 2,000 square metres to find an average cost of $170 per square metre. Then, each department was charged with a building occupancy cost equal to this rate times the number of square metres that it occupies.

Manny Malone manages a department that occupies 200 square metres of floor space in the basement. In discussing the departmental reports with other managers, Malone has questioned whether using the same rate per square metre for all departments makes sense considering the fact that different floors have different values. Looking further into the issue, Malone checked a recent real estate study of average rental costs for similar space. The amounts do not include costs for lighting and cleaning. The report shows that ground-floor space is worth $400 per square metre while second-floor space is worth $200 and basement space is worth only $100.

Required

Use the preceding information to:

1. Allocate the occupancy cost to Malone's department by the bookkeeper's method.
2. Allocate the occupancy cost to Malone's department in proportion to the relative market value of the space, except for the lighting and cleaning costs, which should be allocated on an equal basis per square metre occupied.

Analysis Component:

3. If you were a manager of a second-floor department, which method would you prefer, and why?

Problem 24-2A
Activity-based Costing

LO 2

Bill's Landscaping Centre, Inc. is a growing landscaping business that has enjoyed excess profits from many years. However, now competition is beginning to cut service revenue by as much as 30%. As a result the centre is trying to get a better understanding of its cost of resources. You have been hired to prepare an activity-based cost analysis with the following data. The key question is what does it cost to offer on average general landscaping services compared to a custom-designed with water flow landscaping services?

The cost centres and respective drivers are:

Activity Centre	Cost	Driver	Quantity
Professional salaries	$500,000	Professional hours	10,000
Customer supplies	125,000	Number of customers	500
Building cost	150,000	Square metres*	150

The professional services:

Service	Pro. Hours	Square Metre*	No. of Customers
General services	2,500	50	400
Water services	7,500	100	100

* Landscaping services including water flow require more space for equipment, supplies, and planning.

Required

1. Compute the cost per driver.
2. Compute the average cost for a general and a water flow landscaping service.

Analysis component:

3. Without computation, would the average cost of a general landscaping service be more or less if activity centre costs were allocated on number of customers alone? Why?

Problem 24-3A
Departmental income statement

LO 6

Crane Entertainment, Ltd., began operating in January 1998 with two selling departments and one office department. The 1998 departmental net incomes are shown below:

CRANE ENTERTAINMENT, LTD.
Departmental Income Statement
For Year Ended December 31, 1998

	Movies	Video Games	Combined
Sales	$540,000	$180,000	$720,000
Cost of goods sold	378,000	138,600	516,600
Gross profit from sales	162,000	41,400	203,400
Direct expenses:			
Sales salaries	35,000	14,000	49,000
Advertising	10,500	5,500	16,000
Store supplies used	3,300	700	4,000
Amortization of equipment	4,200	2,800	7,000
Total direct expenses	53,000	23,000	76,000
Allocated expenses:			
Rent expense	29,520	6,480	36,000
Utilities expense	4,100	900	5,000
Share of office department expenses	39,000	14,000	53,000
Total allocated expenses	72,620	21,380	94,000
Total expenses	125,620	44,380	170,000
Net income	$ 36,380	$ (2,980)	$ 33,400

Starting in January 1999, Crane plans to open a third department that will sell compact discs. Management predicts that the new department will produce $250,000 in sales with a 35% gross profit margin and that it will require the following direct expenses: sales salaries, $18,000; advertising, $10,000; store supplies, $1,500; and equipment amortization, $1,000.

Since opening, the store has rented space in a building. It will be possible to fit the new department into the same overall space by taking some square metreage from the other two departments. When the new compact disc department is opened, it will fill one-fourth of the space presently used by the movie department and one-third of the space used by the video game department. Management does not predict any increase in utilities costs, which are allocated among the departments in proportion to occupied space.

The company allocates its office department expenses among the selling departments in proportion to their sales. It expects the compact disc department to increase office department expenses by $8,000.

Because the compact disc department will bring new customers into the store, management expects sales in the movie and video game departments to increase by 10%. Those departments' gross profit percents are not expected to change. No changes are expected in their direct expenses, except for store supplies used, which will increase in proportion to sales.

Required

Prepare a departmental income statement that shows the company's predicted results of operations for 1999 with three selling departments. (Round all percents to the nearest one-tenth and all dollar amounts to the nearest whole dollar.)

Problem 24-4A
Responsibility accounting performance reports
LO 8,7

Margaret Penny, the manager of a manufacturing company's Montreal plant, is responsible for all costs of the plant's operation other than her own salary. The plant has two production departments and one service department. The refrigerator and dishwasher departments manufacture different products and have their own managers. The office department provides services equally to the two production departments. Penny manages the office department. A monthly budget is prepared for each production department and the office department. After the end of each month, the responsibility accounting system must assemble the information to present budgeted and actual costs in performance reports for each of the production department managers and the plant manager.

Each performance report includes only those costs that the particular manager can control. The production department managers control the costs of raw materials, wages, supplies used, and equipment amortization. The plant manager is responsible for the department managers' salaries, utilities, building rent, office salaries other than her own, other office costs, plus all the costs controlled by the two production department managers.

The April departmental budgets and cost accumulations for the two production departments were as follows:

	Budget			Actual		
	Refriger-ators	Dish-washers	Combined	Refiger-ators	Dish-washers	Combined
Raw materials	$400,000	$200,000	$ 600,000	$375,000	$200,000	$ 575,000
Wages	172,000	80,000	252,000	174,700	76,800	251,500
Dept. mgr. salary	55,000	49,000	104,000	55,000	46,500	101,500
Supplies used	15,000	9,000	24,000	14,000	10,000	24,000
Equipment amortization	53,000	37,000	90,000	53,000	37,000	90,000
Utilities	30,000	18,000	48,000	34,500	20,700	55,200
Building rent	63,000	17,000	80,000	61,000	15,000	76,000
Office dept. costs	71,000	71,000	142,000	75,000	75,000	150,000
Total	$859,000	$481,000	$1,340,000	$842,200	$481,000	$1,323,200

Office department budget and actual costs for April consisted of the following:

	Budget	Actual
Plant manager salary	$ 81,000	$ 85,000
Other office salaries	40,000	35,200
Other office costs	21,000	29,800
Total	$142,000	$150,000

Required

Prepare responsibility accounting performance reports that list the costs controlled by the following managers:

1. Manager of the refrigerator department.
2. Manager of the dishwasher department.
3. Manager of the Montreal plant.

In each report, include the budgeted and actual costs for the month, and show the amount that each actual cost is over or under the budgeted amount.

Check Figure Part 3. Montreal plant controllable costs, $20,800 under budget

Analysis Component:

4. Who did a better job of managing cost, the plant manager or the production department managers? Why?

Problem 24-5A
Allocating joint costs
LO 9

Kathy and Ken Vine own a tomato farm. After preparing the following income statement, Kathy remarked to Ken that they should have fed the No. 3 tomatoes to the pigs and saved a lot of money and trouble.

KATHY AND KEN VINE
Income from Tomatoes
For Year Ended December 31, 19X1

	No. 1	No. 2	No. 3	Combined
Sales (by grade):				
No. 1: 200,000 kg @ $3.00 . . .	$600,000			
No. 2: 150,000 kg @ $2.00 . . .		$300,000		
No. 3: 50,000 kg @ $0.60			$ 30,000	
Total sales				$930,000
Costs:				
Land preparation, seed, planting, and cultivating @ $1.00/kg	200,000	150,000	50,000	400,000
Harvesting, sorting, and grading @ $0.04/kg	8,000	6,000	2,000	16,000
Delivery @ $0.02/kg	4,000	3,000	1,000	8,000
Total costs	212,000	159,000	53,000	424,000
Net income (loss)	$388,000	$141,000	$(23,000)	$506,000

In preparing the statement, Kathy and Ken allocated the joint costs among the grades as an equal amount per kilogram. Records about the delivery cost show that $7,000 of the $8,000 was the cost of crating the No. 1 and No. 2 tomatoes and hauling them to the buyer. The remaining $1,000 of delivery cost was the cost of crating the No. 3 tomatoes and hauling them to the cannery where they were stewed and canned.

Required

Preparation component:

1. Prepare allocation schedules showing how the costs would be allocated on the basis of the relative sales values of the three grades. Separate the delivery cost into the amounts directly identifiable to the grades. Then, allocate any shared delivery cost on the basis of the relative sales values of the grades. (Round all percents to the nearest one-tenth and all dollar amounts to the nearest whole dollar.)

2. Using your answers to requirement 1, prepare an income statement that shows the results of producing and delivering the tomatoes.

Analysis component:

3. Do you think the delivery cost is a true joint cost? Explain your answer.

Analytical and Review Problems

A & R 24-1

Many accountants and analysts hold that whatever method is used for common costs or joint costs allocation is arbitrary and an exercise in futility. Allocation obscures rather than illuminates the essential data on which evaluation and decision must be made. Consequently, allocation of costs should only be made where it is absolutely necessary; for example, amount of cost to be matched with the current period (cost of goods sold) and the amount of cost to be carried to future period(s) as inventory. Allocation for evaluation of performance should, however, not be made because such allocations are at best meaningless and at worst misleading and obscure the facts of a situation.

Required

Do you agree with the view expressed? Discuss your answer.

A & R 24-2

It has been stated that in eliminating a profit centre, you eliminate all of the revenue but not all the costs.

Required

Do you agree? Support your answer with an illustration.

A & R 24-3

To allocate or not to allocate; that is the question.

Required

Make a case for allocation and a case against allocation of common and/or joint costs.

BEYOND THE NUMBERS

Reporting in Action

LO 8

A careful review of **Alliance's** financial statements offers clues as to where growth in sales revenue is coming from. In particular, examine Results of Operations.

Required

1. Compute the growth in sales percent, using 1995 as a base for 1996 and 1996 as the base for 1997. Do this for each of the five business segments listed.
2. What area is growing the fastest for Alliance?
3. How can Alliance's managers use this information?
4. Compute the growth in sales by segments for the most recent reporting period. Compare these results to those computed above. What growth patterns, if any, do you observe?

Comparative Analysis

LO 6

Alliance and **Atlantis** compete in the production and distribution of television programs and broadcasting.

Required

1. Design a three-stage "Responsibility Accounting Performance Report," assuming you have available internal information for both companies. Exhibit 24.22 can be used as an example. The goal of this assignment is to design a reporting framework for the companies; numbers are not required. Limit your reporting framework to sales activity only. Prepare to share your answers in a class discussion regarding responsibility accounting.
2. Explain why it is important to have identical "responsibility accounting performance reports," when comparing performance within a company and across different companies. Be specific in your response.

Ethics Challenge

LO 6

Remember receiving your grade report? How did you feel? This is how managers feel when they are handed their individual performance reports in a responsibility accounting system. Individuals are hired, fired, and promoted based on information in a performance report. The preparer of these reports has at least two key responsibilities. First, be certain the values reported reflect actual performance. Second, report information in a clear and concise manner. Graphing information is a popular means for presenting this information. Complete the following requirements and discuss which method best communicates the performance of Randy Ltd.

Required

1. Assume that net incomes for 1997, 1996 and 1995 are $1,295,222, $899,090, and $649,864 respectively.
   a. Prepare a textual (traditional) one-page report listing total operating income by year.
   b. Prepare a bar chart report showing total operating income by year.
2. Which report carries the strongest message? Explain.

Communicating in Practice

LO 9

Canadian Tire is a national home improvement chain with stores located all over the country. The manager of each store receives a salary as well as a bonus equal to a percent of the store's net profit for the reporting period. Assume that the following net income calculation appeared on the Antigonish store manager's performance report for a recent three-month period:

Sales	$2,500,000
Cost of goods sold	(800,000)
Wages expense	(500,000)
Utilities expense	(200,000)
Home office expense	(75,000)
Net income	$ 925,000
Manager's bonus (5%)	$ 46,250

In previous periods, the bonus percent had been 5% but the performance report had not included any charges for the home office expense. The home office expense is now assigned to every store as a percent of its sales.

Required

Assume you are the national office manager. Write a short memorandum that includes three reasons why "home office expense" is included in the new performance report to store managers. (Remember, the store manager's salary is reduced by 5% of $75,000.)

Taking It to the Net

LO 10

This chapter introduced spreadsheet files used to prepare financial reports. You can download from various sources tutorials showing how spreadsheets can be used in many different business applications. Check out this Web page: **www.lacher.com**.

Required

1. Open up the table of contents (TOC) on the bottom of this Web page. Select "Business Solutions Tutorials," and read through the tutorials. Identify three tutorials for review.
2. Describe in a memo how the three tutorials are used to aid business decision making.

Teamwork in Action

LO 4

Activity-based costing is increasingly popular as a useful tool in (1) measuring the cost of resources consumed and (2) assigning cost to individual products. Yet, this accounting tool has been available to decision makers for more than 30 years.

Required

Break into teams and prepare a list of at least three reasons why activity-based costing has gained in popularity in recent years. Be prepared to present your answers is a class discussion. (Hint: What changes exist in products and services over the past 30 years?)

Hitting the Road

LO 6

Visit a local movie theatre and check out the concession area and its theatres. The manager of a theatre often focuses on questions such as:

- How much money do we make on concessions?
- What types of movies generate the greatest sales?
- What types of movies generate the greatest profits?

Required

As the new accounting manager for a 16-screen movie theatre, you are required to:

1. Set up a responsibility accounting reporting framework for the movie theatre. In particular, how would you segment the different departments of a movie theatre for responsibility reporting?
2. Recommend how to allocate to the different segments heat, rent, insurance and maintenance costs to help answer the question above.

Business Break

LO 8

Assume you are the manager of the truck division of a large **Ford** dealership in Calgary, Alberta. The owner of the dealership asks you to read "AUTO—Prognosis 1998" in the January 12, 1998, issue of *Business Week*, pp. 102–103 and make changes to the budget prepared in late 1997.

Required

Below are the controllable costs supplied by the owner in preparing your 1998 budget. Identify whether you plan to increase, decrease or make no change in modifying this budget given the auto industry prognosis described in *Business Week*. Explain briefly. Be prepared to compare your answers in a class discussion.

Description	Amount	I=increase, D=decrease NC=no change
Sales	$10,000,000	
Commissions	500,000	
Advertising	2,500,000	
Training	750,000	
Heat/lights	1,000,000	
Maintenance	500,000	
Projected profits	$ 4,750,000	

25

CHAPTER

Cost-Volume-Profit Analysis

A Look Back

Chapter 24 focused on cost allocation and activity-based costing. We identified several managerial reports useful in directing a company's activities.

A Look at This Chapter

This chapter shows how information on both cost and sales behaviour is useful to managers in performing cost-volume-profit analyses.

A Look Forward

Chapter 26 describes the budgeting process and its importance. It also explains the master budget.

Chapter Outline

High and Dry

Victoria, BC—Cara McKey is the marketing manager for **Maxum,** a leading manufacturer of sealant for water sports equipment and gear. This past year, McKey helped close one of the company's biggest deals ever. But the big deal came close to being the big bust.

Maxum had been working with **Sport Marine** over the past two years supplying goods and services to its water sports division. "Then," says McKey, "they asked about a long-term contract that would nearly double yearly sales. I was ecstatic." McKey quickly put things in motion. But, McKey next got a call from Maxum's controller. He wanted to go over the proposed contract with her.

"I knew he was a numbers person," says McKey, "so I hit him hard." She pointed out the new contract would not impact any current business, and that the new business would require no added advertising or servicing costs. "Then, to top it off," adds McKey, "I proposed we offer a contract price 10% to 12% lower than normal, still insisting we would cover current inventory costs and maintain our 15% gross profit margin."

Then it was the controller's turn. McKey says he showed her that current inventory product cost was an average of current manufacturing costs at today's sales level. He pointed out that such a major shift in sales leads to many changes in cost behaviour. "The next thing I knew," adds McKey, "he and I were running cost-volume-profit analyses on the contract." In the end, Maxum got the contract, but not at the price cut McKey originally thought. Maxum did slice about 3% off the price and still maintained its 15% margin. "If it wasn't for the controller, I'd be looking at about a 5% gross margin today, and," adds McKey, "a different job."

Learning Objectives

LO 1 Describe different types of cost behaviour in relation to production and sales volume.

LO 2 Determine cost estimates using three different methods.

LO 3 Compare the scatter diagram, high-low, and least-squares regression methods of estimating costs.

LO 4 Compute a break-even point for a single product company.

LO 5 Graph the costs and revenues for a single product company.

LO 6 Identify assumptions in cost-volume-profit analysis and explain how they impact the analysis.

LO 7 Describe several applications of cost-volume-profit analysis.

LO 8 Compute the break-even point for a multiproduct company.

LO 9 Analyze changes in sales using the degree of operating leverage.

CHAPTER PREVIEW

This chapter explains different kinds of costs and shows how they are affected by changes in the operating volume of a business. We analyze the costs and revenues of a company to understand how different operating strategies affect its profit or loss. Managers use this kind of analysis to forecast what will happen if changes are made in costs, sales volume, selling prices, or product mix. They then use these forecasts to select the best strategy for the future such as whether to price a special order below the usual selling price as seen with Maxum in the opening article.

Cost-Volume-Profit Analysis and Cost Behaviour

Planning a company's future activities and events is a crucial phase in successful management. One of the first steps in planning is predicting the volume of activity, the costs to be incurred, revenues to be received, and income (or profit) to be earned. An important tool to help managers carry out this step is **cost-volume-profit (CVP) analysis.**

CVP helps managers predict how income is affected by changes in costs and sales levels. In its basic form, CVP involves computing the sales level at which a company neither earns an income nor incurs a loss. This is called the break-even point. For this reason, this basic form of cost-volume-profit analysis is often called *break-even analysis*. But managers use many other applications of this analysis to answer questions such as:

- What sales volume is needed to earn a target income?
- What is the change in income if unit selling prices are reduced and sales volume is increased?
- How much will income increase if we install a new machine to reduce labour costs?
- What is the income earned if we change the sales mix of our products?

The phrase *cost-volume-profit analysis* is better than break-even analysis as a description of this tool when it is used to address questions like these.

Did You Know?

Breaking Even
Compaq Computer got its start when Rod Canion, Jim Harris, and Bill Murto, all prior senior managers at **Texas Instruments,** had a good plan and a solid product. They raised start-up capital of $20 million using cost-volume-profit forecasts showing break-even volumes attainable within the first year after product development. Compaq's first year sales totalled more than $100 million. [Source: R. Venkatesan, "Bootstrap Finance: The Art of Startup," *Harvard Business Review*, November–December 1992.]

Conventional cost-volume-profit analysis requires management to classify all costs as either *fixed* or *variable* with respect to production or sales volume. We introduced different cost behaviours in Chapter 21. The remainder of this section extends our discussion of cost behaviours.

LO1 Describe different types of cost behaviour in relation to production and sales volume.

Fixed Costs

The amount of a **fixed cost** incurred each period remains unchanged even when production volume varies from period to period within a specified relevant range. For example, $5,000 monthly rent paid for a factory building remains the same whether the factory operates with a single eight-hour shift or around the clock with three shifts. Also, rent cost is the same each month at any level of output from zero on up to the full production capacity of the plant (2,000 units per month).

While *total* fixed cost remains constant as the level of production changes, the fixed cost *per unit* of product decreases as volume increases. For instance, if 20 units are produced when monthly rent is \$5,000, the average factory building rent cost per unit is \$250 computed as \$5,000 ÷ 20 units. When production increases to 100 units per month, the average cost per unit decreases to \$50 (\$5,000 ÷ 100 units). The average cost decreases to \$10 per unit if production increases to 500 units per month. Other common examples of fixed costs include amortization, property taxes, office salaries, and many service department costs.

When production volume and costs are graphed, units of product are usually plotted on the *horizontal axis* and dollars of cost are plotted on the *vertical axis*. Fixed costs are represented as a horizontal line because the total amount remains constant at all levels of production. The graph in Exhibit 25.1 shows this fixed cost behaviour. Fixed costs remain at \$32,000 at all production levels up to the factory's monthly capacity of 2,000 units of output. The relevant range for fixed costs in Exhibit 25.1 is 0 to 2,000 units. If the relevant range changes (i.e., production capacity increases or decreases), it is likely the amount of fixed costs will change.

Exhibit 25.1

Relations of Fixed and Variable Costs to Volume

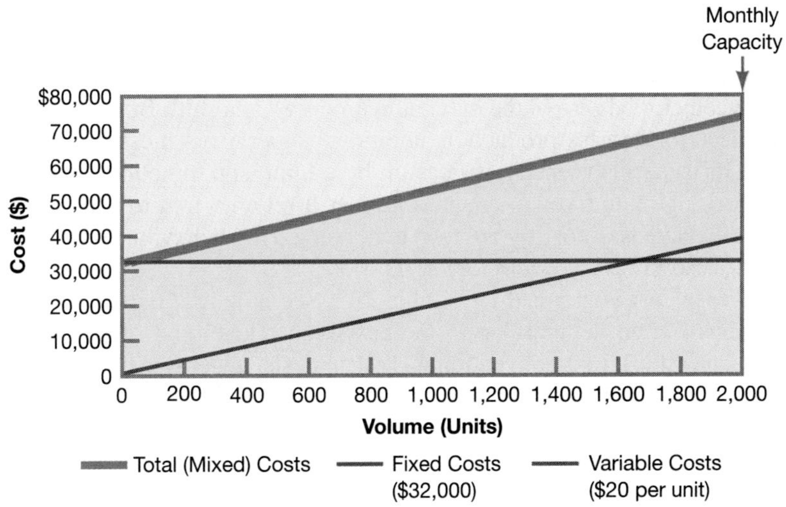

Variable Costs

The total amount of a **variable cost** changes in proportion to changes in volume. The direct material cost of a product is one example of a variable cost. If one unit of product requires material costing \$20, total material costs are \$200 when 10 units of product are manufactured, \$400 for 20 units, \$600 for 30 units, and so on. The variable cost *per unit* produced remains constant while the *total* amount of variable cost changes with the level of production. Other variable costs include direct labour (if workers are paid for completed units), some overhead costs, selling commissions, and shipping costs.

When variable costs are plotted on a graph of cost and volume, it appears as a straight line starting at the zero cost level. This line is upward (positive) sloping. The line rises as production volume increases. The variable cost line using \$20 per unit is graphed in Exhibit 25.1.

Mixed Costs

Mixed costs reflect both fixed and variable costs. Compensation for sales representatives often includes a fixed monthly salary and a variable commission based on sales. The total cost line in Exhibit 25.1 is a mixed cost. Like a fixed cost, it is greater than zero even when volume is at zero. But unlike a fixed cost, it increases steadily in proportion to increase in volume. The mixed cost line in Exhibit 25.1 starts on the vertical axis at the $32,000 fixed cost point. This means at the zero level of output, total cost equals only the fixed costs. Total cost increases as the activity level increases. The amount of the increase equals the variable cost per unit for each additional unit produced and is the highest when production volume is 2,000 units (the end point of our graph).

The simplest way to include mixed costs in a CVP analysis is to separate them into fixed and variable components. The fixed component is added to other fixed costs for the planning period, and the variable component is added to other variable costs.

Recall the opening article involving Maxum. In analyzing the potential sales order, the controller's first course of action was to separate all manufacturing and selling costs into variable and fixed categories. The controller concluded only raw materials and sales commissions were variable costs. Direct labour was added in eight-hour shifts and was called a step-wise cost (see below). All other manufacturing costs were categorized as fixed costs.

Step-Wise Costs

Step-wise costs reflect a step pattern. Salaries of production supervisors often behave in a step-wise manner. Their salaries are fixed for a certain production volume, whether it be zero or the maximum produced in a shift. But when another shift is added to increase production, additional supervisors must be hired. The total cost for supervisory salaries goes up by a lump-sum amount. Total supervisory salaries remain fixed at this new, higher level until a third shift is added. A third shift increases cost by another lump sum. This behaviour reflects step-wise costs, also known as *stair-step costs.*

A step-wise cost is graphed in Exhibit 25.2. See how it is flat within narrow ranges (steps). Then it jumps up to the next higher level and stays there over another range (step). In a conventional CVP analysis, a step-wise cost is treated as either a fixed cost or a variable cost. This treatment involves judgment on the part of the manager and mostly depends on the width of the range.

To illustrate, suppose after the production of every 25 snowboards, the operator adds a special oil to the finishing machine. The cost of this oil reflects a step-wise pattern. As another example, suppose after the production of every 1,000 units, a maintenance person must replace the snowboard cutting tool. Again, this is a step-wise cost. But note the range of 25 snowboards is much narrower than the range of 1,000 snowboards. This means some managers might treat the cost of the oil as a variable cost and the cost of the cutting tool as a fixed cost.

Exhibit 25.2

Step-Wise and Curvilinear Costs

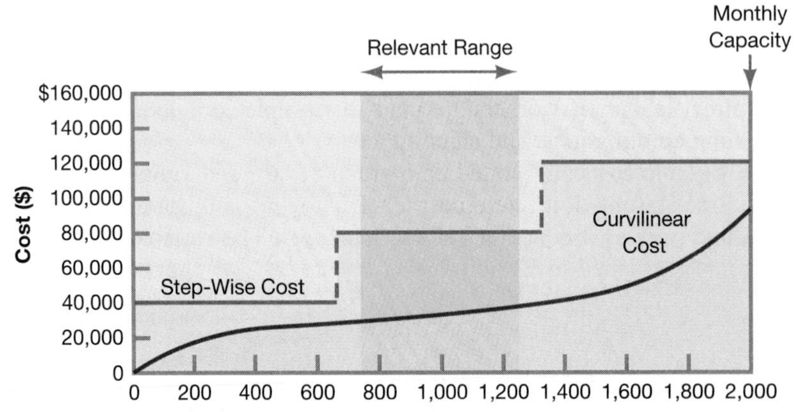

Curvilinear Costs

A variable cost, as explained above, is a *linear* cost. This means it increases at a constant rate as production volume increases. **Curvilinear costs,** also called *non-linear*, increase as volume increases but not at a constant rate like variable costs. When graphed, curvilinear costs appear as a curved line. Exhibit 25.2 shows a curvilinear cost beginning at zero when production is zero and then increasing at different rates. Its highest rate is when sales volume reaches the maximum for the month.

An example of a curvilinear cost is total direct labour cost when workers are paid by the hour. At low levels of production, adding more workers allows each of them to specialize by doing the same task over and over again instead of doing several different tasks. The work crew becomes more efficient and able to produce additional units for lower costs. But a point is eventually reached where adding more workers begins to create inefficiencies. For instance, a large crew may demand more time and effort in communicating or coordinating their efforts. While adding workers increases output, the labour cost per unit increases and the total labour cost goes up with a steeper slope. This pattern is seen in Exhibit 25.2 where the curvilinear cost curve starts at zero, rises, flattens out, and then increases at a faster rate as output nears the maximum for the month.

Flashback

1. Which of the following statements is typically true?
   a. Variable cost per unit increases as volume increases.
   b. Fixed cost per unit decreases as volume increases.
   c. A curvilinear cost includes both fixed and variable elements.
2. Describe the behaviour of a fixed cost.
3. If a raw material cost per unit remains constant (fixed), why is it called a variable cost?

Answers—p. 1226

Identifying and Measuring Cost Behaviour

LO 2 Determine cost estimates using three different methods.

Identifying cost behaviour requires careful analysis and judgment. We first want to analyze and identify individual costs that can be classified as either fixed or variable. When it is difficult to classify a cost as either fixed or variable, an analysis of past cost behaviour is useful. Three methods are usually used in analyzing past costs: scatter diagrams, high-low, and least-squares regression. Each method is discussed below using the sales and cost data from calendar year 1999 for a start-up company. The data are shown in Exhibit 25.3. Sales volume in dollars is used as the activity base in estimating cost behaviour.

Exhibit 25.3 Data for Estimating Cost Behaviour

Month	Sales Volume ($)	Total Cost ($)
January	17,500	20,500
February	27,500	21,500
March	25,000	25,000
April	35,000	21,500
May	47,500	25,500
June	22,500	18,500
July	30,000	23,500
August	52,500	28,500
September	37,500	26,000
October	57,500	26,000
November	62,500	31,000
December	67,500	29,000

Scatter Diagrams

Scatter diagrams display data about past costs in graphical form as in Exhibit 25.4. In preparing a scatter diagram, sales volume in dollars or units is plotted on the horizontal axis and cost is plotted on the vertical axis. Each individual point on the diagram reflects the cost and volume levels for a prior period. In Exhibit 25.4, twelve prior months' figures are graphed. Each point reflects total costs incurred and sales volume for one of those months. For instance, note the point labelled March. March sales were $25,000 and its total costs were also $25,000.

Exhibit 25.4

Scatter Diagram

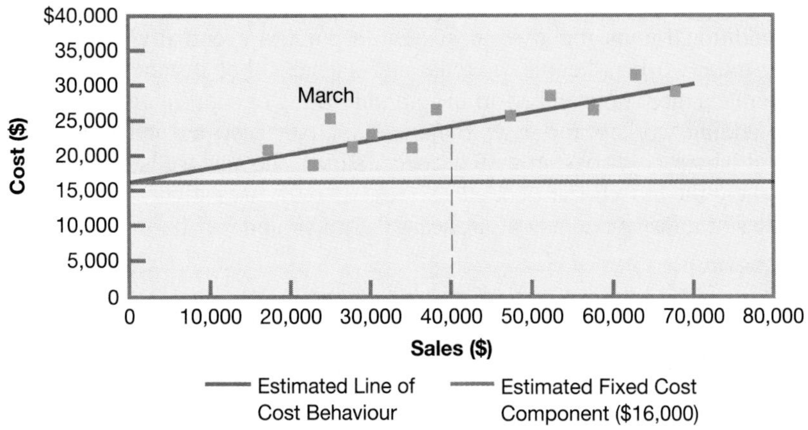

The **estimated line of cost behaviour** is drawn on a scatter diagram to reflect the past relation between cost and sales volume. This line best "fits" visually the points in a scatter diagram. This demands judgment. The line drawn in Exhibit 25.4 intersects the vertical axis at approximately $16,000. This amount reflects its fixed cost estimate. To compute variable cost per unit, or the slope, involves several steps. First, we select any two points on the horizontal axis (sales), say 0 and $40,000. Second we draw a vertical line from the $40,000 point to intersect the estimated line of cost behaviour. The point on the vertical axis (cost) corresponding to the intersection point on the estimated line is roughly $24,000. Similarly, the cost corresponding to zero sales is $16,000 (the fixed cost point). Third we compute the slope of the line, or variable cost, as the "change in cost" divided by the "change in sales" as shown in Exhibit 25.5.

Variable cost is $0.20 per sales dollar. The cost equation to predict costs at different sales levels for our illustration is: $16,000 plus $0.20 per sales dollar.

Exhibit 25.5

Formula for Slope of Line

$$\frac{\textbf{Change in cost}}{\textbf{Change in sales}} = \frac{\$24{,}000 - \$16{,}000}{\$40{,}000 - \$\,0} = \frac{\$8{,}000}{\$40{,}000} = \$0.20 \text{ per sales dollar}$$

High-low Method

High-low method is another means to estimate the cost equation. To apply this method, we connect the two points in the diagram representing the highest and lowest sales volume. In our case, the lowest sales volume is $17,500 and the highest is $67,500, and the costs corresponding to these sales volumes are $20,500 and $29,000 (see data in Exhibit 25.3). The estimated line of cost behaviour for the high-low method is drawn by connecting the two points on the scatter diagram corresponding to the lowest and highest sales volumes as follows:

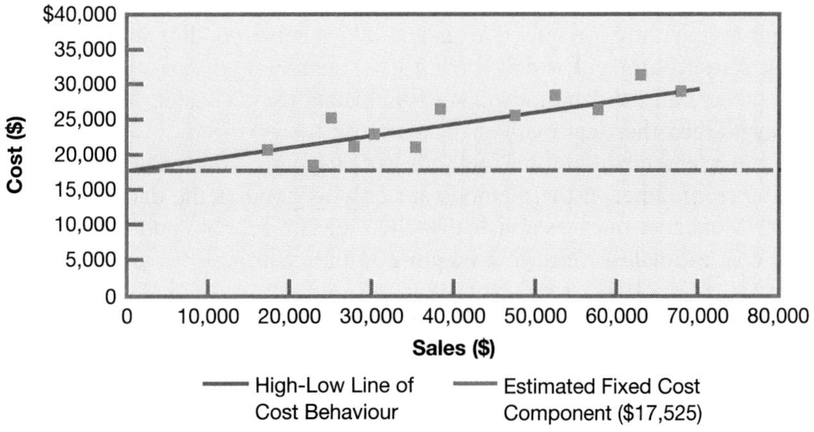

If we extend this line to the vertical axis, it intersects it at a cost of $17,525. This amount is the fixed cost. The variable cost per unit is determined using the data presented in Exhibit 25.3 corresponding to the two sales volumes, and is $0.17 per sales dollar as shown in Exhibit 25.6.

$$\frac{\textbf{Change in cost}}{\textbf{Change in sales}} = \frac{\$29{,}000 - \$20{,}500}{\$67{,}500 - \$\ 17{,}500} = \frac{\$\ 8{,}500}{\$50{,}000} = \$0.17 \text{ per sales dollar}$$

Exhibit 25.6

Formula for Variable Cost per Unit for High-Low Method

The cost equation to estimate costs at different sales levels is: $17,525 plus $0.17 per sales dollar. This cost equation is slightly different from that determined using the scatter diagram method. A deficiency of the high-low method is that it ignores all sales points except the highest and lowest. The outcome is less precise because it uses the most extreme points rather than the more usual conditions likely to occur in future periods.

Least-Squares Regression

Least-squares regression is a statistical method of identifying cost behaviour. The details of this method are covered in advanced cost accounting courses. The computations, however, are easily made on most spreadsheet programs and calculators. The cost equation for the data presented in Exhibit 25.3 works out to: $16,947 plus $0.19 per sales dollar. This means fixed cost is estimated as $16,947 and variable cost as $0.19 per sales dollar. Both costs are reflected in the graph below:

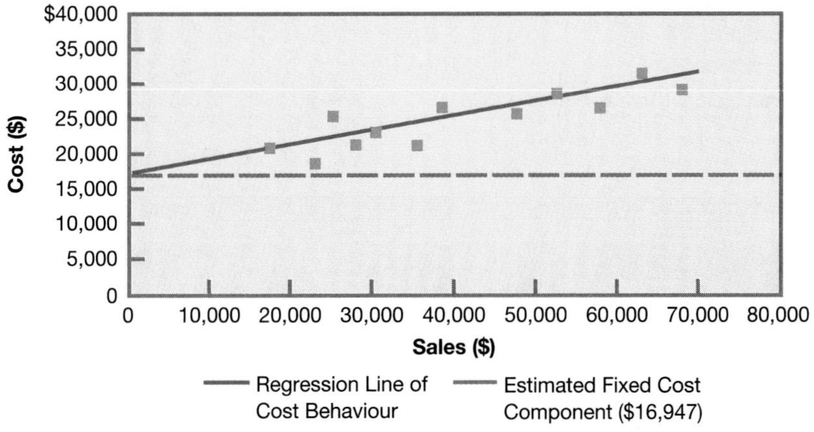

The three methods result in slightly different estimates of fixed and variable costs as shown in Exhibit 25.7. Estimates from the scatter diagram are based on

LO3 Compare the scatter diagram, high-low and least-squares regression methods of estimating costs.

a "visual fit" of the cost line and are subject to interpretation. Estimates from the high-low method use only two sets of values corresponding to the lowest and highest sales volumes. Estimates from least-squares regression use a statistical technique and all the data points available. Many users consider least-squares as superior to the other two methods.

We must remember all three methods use *past data*. This means cost estimates resulting from either of the methods are only as good as the data used for estimation. Managers must establish that the data are reliable and can be used to derive cost estimates useful in predicting future costs.

Exhibit 25.7

Comparison of Cost Estimation Methods

Estimation Method	Fixed Cost	Variable Cost
Scatter Diagram	$16,000	$0.20 per sales dollar
High-Low	$17,525	$0.17 per sales dollar
Least-Squares Regression . .	$16,947	$0.19 per sales dollar

Flash back

4. Which of the following is likely to yield the more precise estimated line of cost behaviour? (a) high-low method, (b) least-squares method, or (c) scatter diagram.
5. What is the primary weakness of the high-low method?
6. Using conventional CVP, a mixed cost should be (a) disregarded, (b) treated as a fixed cost, or (c) separated into fixed and variable components.

Answers—p. 1226

Mid-Chapter Demonstration Problem

Total factory overhead costs for Landry Company has been fluctuating considerably from year to year in relation to increases and decreases in the number of direct labour hours worked in the factory.

The factory overhead costs above consist of indirect materials, rent, and maintenance. The company has analyzed these costs at the 50,000-hour level of activity and has determined that at this activity level these costs exist in the following proportions:

Indirect materials (V)	$25,000
Rent (F)	80,000
Maintenance (M)	35,000
Total factory overhead costs	$140,000

V = variable; F = fixed; M= mixed.

Total factory overhead costs at high and low levels of activity for recent years are:

	Level of Activity	
	Low	High
Direct labour hours	50,000	80,000
Total factory overhead costs	$140,000	$170,000

To have data available for planning, the company wants to break down the maintenance cost into its variable and fixed cost elements.

Required

1. Determine how much of the $170,000 factory overhead cost at the high level of activity above consists of maintenance cost.
2. By means of this high-low method of cost analysis, determine the cost formula for maintenance.
3. Express the company's maintenance costs in the linear equation form $Y = a + bX$.
4. What *total* factory overhead costs would you expect the company to incur at an operating level of 75,000 direct labour hours? Show computations.

Planning the Solution

- Find the periods of the highest and lowest activity. In this problem these activity points are given.
- Next, determine maintenance costs by first deducting the costs of all other overhead items from the total overhead costs.
- Determine the change in cost and the change in activity and the high and low points.
- Compute the variable maintenance cost per unit by dividing the change in maintenance costs by the change in activity.
- Compute the fixed maintenance cost by deducting the variable maintenance cost from the total maintenance costs at either the high or low activity level.
- Combine the variable and fixed components of maintenance costs and express this relationship as a formula.
- Using the formula found, determine maintenance costs at the 75,000-hour level of activity and add the other component overhead costs to arrive at total overhead costs.

Solution to Mid-Chapter Demonstration Problem

1. Maintenance cost at the low and high levels of direct labour hour activity can be isolated as follows:

	Level of Activity	
	50,000 DLH	80,000 DLH
Total factory overhead cost	$140,000	$170,000
Deduct:		
Indirect materials @ $.50 per DLH*	(25,000)	(40,000)
Rent	(80,000)	(80,000)
Maintenance cost	$ 35,000	$ 50,000

*$25,000 ÷ 50,000 DLH = $0.50 per DLH

2. High-low analysis of maintenance cost:

	Direct Labour Hours	Maintenance Cost
High level of activity	80,000	$50,000
Low level of activity	50,000	35,000
Change observed	30,000	$15,000

Variable cost element:

$$\frac{\text{Change in cost}}{\text{Change in activity}} = \frac{\$15{,}000}{30{,}000 \text{ DLH}} = \$0.50 \text{ per DLH}$$

Solution to Mid-Chapter Demonstration Problem (continued)

Fixed cost element:

Total cost at the high level of activity	$50,000
Less variable cost element ($0.50 × 80,000 DLH)	40,000
Fixed cost element	$10,000

Therefore, the cost formula for maintenance is: $10,000 per year plus $.50 per direct labour hour.

3. Y = $10,000 + $.50X.

4. Total factory overhead cost at 75,000 direct labour hours would be:

Maintenance:		
Variable cost element (75,000 DLH × $.50)	$37,500	
Fixed cost element	10,000	$ 47,500
Indirect materials (75,000 DLH × $.50)		37,500
Rent		80,000
Total factory overhead cost		$165,000

Break-Even Analysis

Break-even analysis is a special case of cost-volume-profit analysis. This section describes break-even analysis including computation of the break-even point and preparing a CVP (or break-even) chart.

Computing Break-Even Point

LO 4 Compute a break-even point for a single product company.

The **break-even point** is the sales level at which a company neither earns a profit nor incurs a loss. The break-even point can be expressed either in units of product or in dollars of sales.

To illustrate, Rydell sells footballs for $100 per unit and incurs $70 of variable costs per unit sold. Fixed costs are $24,000 per month and the monthly capacity is 1,800 units of product. Rydell breaks even for the month when it sells 800 footballs, with a sales volume of $80,000. We compute this break-even point using the formula in Exhibit 25.8.[1]

---

[1] The mathematics of this formula are shown here:

Define:	S = sales in units	R = revenue per unit
	F = fixed costs per month	V = variable cost per unit
	$S \times R$ = dollar sales	$S \times V$ = total variable cost

Then: Contribution margin per unit = $R - V$

At break-even: Sales = Fixed Costs + Variable Costs

$(S \times R) = F + (S \times V)$

$S \times R) - (S \times V) = F$

$S \times (R - V) = F$

$S = F/(R - V)$

$S = F/\text{Contribution margin per unit}$

Also: Contribution margin ratio = $(R - V)/R$

At break-even: $S = F/(R - V)$

$S \times R = (F \times R)/(R - V)$

$S \times R = F \times [R/(R - V)]$

$S \times R = F/[(R - V)/R]$

$S \times R = F/\text{Contribution margin ratio}$

$$\textbf{Break-even point in units} = \frac{\textbf{Fixed costs}}{\textbf{Contribution margin per unit}}$$

Exhibit 25.8

Formula for Computing Break-Even Sales (in units)

As explained in Chapter 21, the **contribution margin per unit** is the difference between the selling price and the variable cost per unit. It is computed using the formula shown in Exhibit 21.17. For Rydell Company, the contribution margin per unit is $30 ($100 − $70). This means break-even sales volume is $24,000 ÷ $30 = 800 units. At a price of $100 per unit, sales of 800 units generate revenues of $80,000 (break-even sales dollars). The break-even sales volume of $80,000 can also be computed without computing sales units. This involves using the formula shown in Exhibit 25.9.

$$\textbf{Break-even point in dollars} = \frac{\textbf{Fixed costs}}{\textbf{Contribution margin ratio}}$$

Exhibit 25.9

Formula for Computing Break-Even Sales (in dollars)

As explained in Chapter 21, **contribution margin ratio** is the *proportion* of a unit's selling price that exceeds total unit variable cost. It is computed as the unit contribution margin divided by the unit selling price (see Exhibit 21.18). For Rydell the contribution margin ratio is 30% ($30 ÷ $100). Break-even sales dollars is computed as $24,000 ÷ 0.30 = $80,000.

To verify that Rydell's break-even point equals $80,000 and 800 units, prepare a simple income statement similar to the one in Exhibit 25.10. It shows the $80,000 revenue from sales of 800 units exactly equals the sum of fixed and variable costs.

Exhibit 25.10

Income Statement for Break-Even Sales

RYDELL COMPANY
Forecasted Income Statement

Sales (800 units @ $100 each) .		$80,000
Costs:		
Fixed costs	$24,000	
Variable costs (800 units @ $70 each)	56,000	80,000
Net income		$ -0-

Preparing a Cost-Volume-Profit Chart

LO5 Graph the costs and revenues for a single product company.

Exhibit 25.11 is a graph of the cost-volume-profit relations for Rydell Company for a month. This graph is called a **CVP chart,** also called a *break-even graph* or *break-even chart.* The horizontal axis is the number of units sold and the vertical axis is dollars of sales and costs. We assume straight lines depict both costs and revenues on the graph. To prepare a CVP chart, we complete the following steps: [2]

1. Plot fixed costs on the vertical axis (i.e., $24,000). Draw a horizontal line at this level to show fixed costs remain unchanged regardless of sales volume. Exhibit 25.11 includes this line, although the fixed cost line is not essential to the analysis.
2. Draw a line reflecting total costs (variable costs plus fixed costs). For any sales level, this line shows the sum of both fixed and variable costs for that level. This line starts at the fixed costs on the vertical axis because total costs equal fixed costs at the zero sales level. The slope of the total cost

[2] These instructions are provided to guide you through a manual drafting process. The graph can also be drawn with computer assistance, including spreadsheet programs that can convert numeric data to graphs.

line equals the variable cost per unit ($70). To draw the line, compute the total costs for any sales level, and connect this point with the vertical axis intercept ($24,000). Do not draw this line beyond the productive capacity for the planning period (1,800 units for Rydell).

3. Draw a sales line starting at the origin (zero units and zero dollars of sales). The slope of this line equals the selling price per unit ($100). To draw the line, compute the total revenues for any sales level, and connect this point with the origin. Do not extend this line beyond the productive capacity for the planning period. The total revenue is at its highest level at maximum capacity. It is likely the relevant range is near the middle of the graph.

Exhibit 25.11

Cost-Volume-Profit Chart

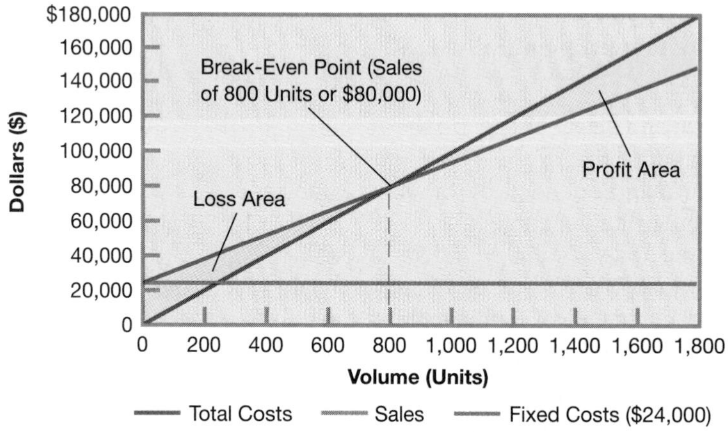

The total cost line and the sales line intersect at 800 units of product in Exhibit 25.11. This intersection is the break-even point. It is the point where total sales revenue of $80,000 equals the sum of both fixed and variable costs ($80,000).

On either side of the break-even point, the vertical distance between the sales line and the total cost line at any specific sales volume measures the profit or loss expected at that volume. At volume levels to the left of the break-even point, this vertical distance is the amount of the loss because the total cost line is above the total sales line. At volume levels to the right of the break-even point, the vertical distance represents the amount of profit because the total sales line is above the total cost line.

Assumptions of Cost-Volume-Profit Analysis

Cost-volume-profit analysis assumes relations can be expressed as straight lines similar to those in Exhibit 25.1. This assumption allows users of CVP to classify all costs as either fixed or variable. CVP analysis also treats revenues as variable, with all units of a product being sold at the same unit price. These assumptions allow users to answer several important questions. But the usefulness of these answers depends on the validity of at least three assumptions:

LO6 Identify assumptions in cost-volume-profit analysis and explain how they impact the analysis.

1. Selling price per unit is constant.
2. Variable cost of output is constant.
3. Fixed costs are constant.

While these assumptions are not always realistic, they don't necessarily limit the usefulness of CVP as a first step in forecasting the effects of an operating plan. This section discusses these and other assumptions of CVP.

Production Output Versus Sales Volume

We normally define variable costs and fixed costs in terms of the level of *output produced.* But CVP usually describes the planning period's level of activity in terms of *sales volume* rather than production output. Sales volume can be described as either the number of units sold or the dollars of sales.

To simplify analysis, users often assume the level of production will be the same as the level of sales. This means we do not have to be concerned with costs flowing into inventory instead of being sold or with costs flowing into cost of goods sold from the prior period's inventory. This assumption is justified because CVP provides only a tentative plan not based on inventory management.

Manager of Operations

You are the manager of operations for a *new* manufacturing plant set up to produce a variety of gift articles. One of your immediate and important tasks is to coordinate with the accountant to identify the behaviour of manufacturing costs to develop a production cost budget. You know three methods can be used to identify cost behaviour from past data. But past data is not available as this is a new plant. What do you do?

You Make the Call

Answer—p. 1225

Working with Assumptions

The behaviour of individual costs and revenues often is not perfectly consistent with CVP assumptions. If the expected cost and revenue behaviour is different from the assumptions, the results of a CVP analysis may be limited. Still, there are several reasons why we can perform useful analyses using these assumptions.

Summing Costs Can Offset Deviations

Deviations from assumptions with individual costs are often minor when these costs are summed. For instance, while the individual variable cost items may not be perfectly variable, when we sum all variable costs their individual deviations can offset each other. This means the assumption of variable cost behaviour may be proper for total variable costs even when it is not for individual variable cost items. Similarly, an assumption that total fixed costs are constant may be proper even when individual fixed cost items are not exactly constant.

Relevant Range of Operations

Revenues, variable costs, and fixed costs are reasonably reflected in straight lines on a graph when the assumptions are applied only over a **relevant range of operations.** The relevant range of operations is the normal operating range for a business. Assumptions about fixed and variable costs are valid within this range. Except for unusually difficult or prosperous times, management typically plans for operations within a range of volume neither close to zero nor maximum capacity. The relevant range for planning excludes extremely high and low operating levels that are unlikely to occur. Assuming a specific cost is fixed or variable is more likely valid when operations are within the relevant range. As shown in Exhibit 25.2, a curvilinear cost can be treated as perfectly variable if the relevant range covers volumes where it has a near constant slope.

A relevant range may not be applicable to all cost items. For example, production supervisory salaries will increase as more production shifts are added. If production in each shift is 1,000 units, the initial relevant range for supervisory salaries is 0 to 1,000 and increases in steps of 1,000. But factory rent increases only when a company rents more space. Rental cost remains the same up to a production level of 3,000 units from the three shifts. The initial relevant range for this cost item is 0 to 3,000 units of production and increases in steps of 3,000. A company cannot keep track of all these different relevant ranges. Management must plan according to the normal relevant range of activity. If the normal range of activity changes, some costs may need reclassification.

Estimates from Cost-Volume-Profit Analysis

CVP analysis yields approximate answers to questions about costs, volumes, and profits. These answers do not have to be precise because the analysis makes rough estimates about the future. As long as managers understand that CVP analysis gives estimates, then it can be a useful tool for starting the planning process.

Recall the opening article and the decision by the controller at Maxum to use CVP. While Maxum's variable costs per unit appeared to be stable, the proposed volume was well beyond the current relevant range of its production capacity. Maxum was already near capacity during peak months and the current location could not be expanded. After including the new fixed costs necessary to expand capacity, Maxum set a rough price to recover all relevant costs and contribute 15% to overhead and operating income.

CVP analysis is only a starting point. Other qualitative factors must be considered. The large capital outlay for a second manufacturing facility would increase Maxum's fixed costs. These fixed costs would leverage the company and make it vulnerable in a business downturn. This is because fixed costs do not decline if volume does. Also, the proposal would mean about 50% of Maxum's business is with one buyer. Maxum could end up being a *captive supplier for Sport Marine*. This would make it vulnerable to pressure for future price concessions.

Flash back

7. Fixed cost divided by the contribution margin ratio yields the:
   a. Break-even point in dollars.
   b. Contribution margin per unit.
   c. Break-even point in units.
8. A company sells a product for $90 per unit with variable costs of $54 per unit. What is the contribution margin ratio?
9. Refer to question 8. If fixed costs for the period are $90,000, what is the break-even point in dollars?
10. What are the three basic assumptions used in CVP?

Answers—p. 1226

Applying Cost-Volume-Profit Analysis

LO 7 Describe several applications of cost-volume-profit analysis.

Managers consider a variety of strategies in planning business operations. These strategies often affect costs and revenues for the company. Cost-volume-profit analysis is useful in helping managers evaluate the likely effects of these strategies. This explains several applications of cost-volume-profit analysis.

Computing Income from Expected Sales

An important question managers need an answer to is, "What is the amount of income from expected sales?" To answer this, we look at four factors in the CVP analysis. These factors are shown in Exhibit 25.12.

Exhibit 25.12

Relations in CVP Analysis

Income (pre-tax) = Sales − [Fixed costs + Variable costs]

or

Income (pre-tax) = Sales − Fixed costs − Variable costs

We use these relations to compute income from predicted sales and cost levels.

To illustrate, let's assume the management of Rydell expects to sell 1,500 product units. What is the amount of income if this monthly sales level is achieved? At this level, revenues are $150,000, computed as 1,500 units × $100. Rydell's fixed costs are $24,000 per month. Its variable costs per unit are $70 per unit, and total variable costs for 1,500 units of product are $105,000 (1,500 units × $70). Using the relations from Exhibit 25.12, and substituting these amounts, we compute Rydell's income as shown in Exhibit 25.13.

Exhibit 25.13

Computing Income From Expected Sales

$$\text{Income} = [1{,}500 \text{ units} \times \$100] - \$24{,}000 - [1{,}500 \text{ units} \times \$70] = \$21{,}000$$

The $21,000 income does not include the effects of income taxes. Recall that corporations must pay income taxes. If management wants to find the amount of after-tax income from selling 1,500 units, they must apply the proper tax rate to the $21,000. If the tax rate is 25%, the income tax is $5,250 and net income is $15,750. Management would then determine whether this net income is an adequate return on the assets invested. Management should also look at whether sales and income can be increased by raising or lowering prices. CVP is a good tool for addressing these kinds of "what if" questions.

Computing Sales for a Target Income

"How many units must I sell to earn $50,000?"

Many companies' annual plans are based on certain income targets. Rydell's income target for 2000 is to increase 1999 income by 10%. When 1999 income is known, Rydell easily computes its target income for 2000. CVP analysis helps us in determining the sales level needed to achieve the target income. Computing this sales level is important because planning for the year is then based on this level. We use the formula shown in Exhibit 25.14 to compute sales for a target income.[3]

Exhibit 25.14

Formula for Computing Sales (Dollars) for a Target Income

$$\textbf{Dollar sales} = \frac{\textbf{Fixed costs + Target income + Income taxes}}{\textbf{Contribution margin ratio}}$$

To illustrate, we return to Rydel, which has monthly fixed costs of $24,000 and a 30% contribution margin ratio. Let's assume it sets a target monthly income of $18,000 after income taxes at the rate of 25%. This means the before-tax income is targeted at $24,000 [$18,000/(1–.25)] since the tax is $6,000. Using the formula in Exhibit 25.14 we find $160,000 of sales are needed to produce an $18,000 net income. We show this computation in Exhibit 25.15.

---

[3] The mathematics of this formula are shown here:

Define:	S = sales in units	R = revenue per unit
	F = fixed costs per month	V = variable cost per unit
	N = target net income	T = income taxes
	$S \times R$ = dollar sales	$S \times V$ = total variable cost

We know: Contribution margin ratio $= (R - V)/R$

Then:

$(S \times R) - F - (S \times V) - T = N$

$(S \times R) - (S \times V) = F + N + T$

$S \times (R - V) = F + N + T$

$S = (F + N + T)/(R - V)$

$S \times R = [(F + N + T) \times R]/(R - V)$

$S \times R = (F + N + T) \times [R/(R - V)]$

$S \times R = (F + N + T)/[(R - V)/R]$

$S \times R = (F + N + T)/\text{Contribution margin ratio}$

Exhibit 25.15

Computing Sales for a Target Income

$$\text{Dollar sales at target income} = \frac{\$24{,}000 + \$18{,}000 + \$6{,}000}{30\%}$$
$$= \$160{,}000$$

We can alternatively use the formula in Exhibit 25.14 to compute *unit sales* instead of dollar sales. To do this we need only substitute the *contribution margin* in place of the contribution margin ratio as the denominator. This gives us the number of units needed to be sold to reach the target income level. Exhibit 25.16 illustrates this application to Rydell Company.

Exhibit 25.16

Formula for Computing Sales (Units) for a Target Income

$$\textbf{Unit sales} = \frac{\textbf{Fixed costs + Net income + Income taxes}}{\textbf{Contribution margin}}$$
$$= \frac{\$24{,}000 + \$18{,}000 + \$6{,}000}{\$30}$$
$$= 1{,}600 \text{ units}$$

The two computations in Exhibits 25.15 and 25.16 are equivalent because sales of 1,600 units at \$100 per unit equal \$160,000 of sales.

Judgment and Ethics

Management Trainee

You are part of a management trainee group debating a proposed product launch. A crucial factor is the range of income levels from different sales projections. Sales projections are very subjective given the product has not been produced before. One team member suggests they pick numbers producing income because any estimate is "as good as any other." Another crucial factor is fixed and variable cost predictions that are being estimated from a scatter diagram of 20 months' production on a comparable product. But cost predictions are not supportive of the investment. A team member asks whether less favourable data points can be dropped from the analysis to see if the cost picture is improved. Your role is to do a cost-volume-profit analysis to reflect these suggestions. What do you do?

Answer—p. 1226

Computing the Margin of Safety

All businesses desire to sell more than the break-even number of units and thereby earn profits. The excess of expected sales over sales at the break-even point is a company's margin of safety. The **margin of safety** is the amount sales can drop before the company incurs a loss. It can be expressed in units, in dollars, or even as a percent of the predicted level of sales. To illustrate, if Rydell's expected sales are \$100,000, the margin of safety is \$20,000 above break-even sales of \$80,000. As a percent, the margin of safety is 20% of expected sales as shown in Exhibit 25.17.

Exhibit 25.17

Formula for Computing Margin of Safety Percent

$$\textbf{Margin of safety percent} = \frac{\textbf{Expected sales} - \textbf{Break-even sales}}{\textbf{Expected sales}}$$
$$= \frac{\$100{,}000 - \$80{,}000}{\$100{,}000} = 20\%$$

Management needs to assess whether this margin of safety is adequate in light of various factors. These factors include sales variability, competition, consumer tastes, and economic conditions.

Paging Out of Business!
Just a few years ago, the paging industry buzzed with promise. As the rage to page swept the nation, beeper operators saw subscriber rolls triple. But recently, messages beeped to paging executives are coming from concerned shareholders. Determined to outdo competitors, operators spent freely to expand their networks, and many relied on low-margin paging to grab market share. Price competition led to paging companies giving business to resellers—companies that lease services at a discount and then resell it to subscribers. Resellers allow companies to acquire customers without costs of billing and customer service—but many companies are charging resellers less than $3 a month, compared with the $9 they charge consumers. **Paging Network,** the biggest carrier, charged some resellers under $1, less than a third of what is needed to break even. Its CEO now admits the low-price strategy was flawed, and claims "We don't want to be in that [price-cutting] business." [Source: "Scary Signals on Pagers," *Business Week*, December 29, 1997.]

Did You Know?

Sensitivity Analysis

It is often useful for us to know the effects of changing some estimates used in CVP analysis. This is because they are *estimates* and not actual values. For instance, we may want to know what happens if we reduce a product's selling price to increase sales. Or, we may want to know what happens to income if we install a new machine that increases fixed costs but reduces variable costs. If we can describe how these changes affect a company's fixed costs, variable costs, selling price, and volume, we can use CVP to predict income.

"Will automation lower break-even sales?"
MANAGER

To illustrate, let's assume Rydell Company is looking into buying a new machine that would increase monthly fixed costs from $24,000 to $30,000, but decrease variable costs from $70 per unit to $60 per unit. The product's selling price will remain unchanged at $100. This results in increases in both the unit contribution margin and the contribution margin ratio. The new contribution margin per unit is $40 ($100 − $60) and the new contribution margin ratio is 40% of selling price ($40/$100). The manager wants to know what the break-even point is if the machine is bought.

If Rydell buys the machine, its new break-even point in dollars is $75,000. This is computed as shown in Exhibit 25.18.

Exhibit 25.18

Formula for Computing Break-Even When Changes Occur

$$\textbf{New break-even point in dollars} = \frac{\textbf{New fixed costs}}{\textbf{New contribution margin ratio}} = \frac{\$30{,}000}{40\%} = \$75{,}000$$

The new fixed costs and the new contribution margin ratio can also be used to address other issues including computation of (a) expected income for a given sales level, and (b) the sales level needed to earn a target income. Sensitivity analysis can also be used to generate different sets of revenue and cost estimates that are optimistic, pessimistic, and most likely. Different CVP estimates provide management with various scenarios to analyze and input into their business planning strategy.

Flash back

11. A company has fixed costs of $50,000 and a 25% contribution margin ratio. How many dollars of sales are necessary for the company to achieve a net income of $120,000 if the tax rate is 20%? (a) $800,000, (b) $680,000, or (c) $600,000.

12. If the contribution margin ratio decreases from 50 to 25%, what can be said about unit sales needed to achieve a target income level?

13. What is a company's margin of safety?

Answers—p. 1226

Computing Multiproduct Break-Even Point

LO 8 Compute the break-even point for a multiproduct company.

To this point we have looked only at cases where the company produces a single product. This was to keep the basic CVP analysis simple. But many companies produce multiple products. We can modify the basic CVP analysis for use when a company produces and sells several products.

An important assumption in a multiproduct setting is the sales mix of different products is *known* and *constant* in the planning period. **Sales mix** is the ratio of the sales volumes for various products. For instance, if a company normally sells 10,000 footballs, 5,000 baseballs, and 4,000 basketballs, then its sales mix is said to be 10:5:4 for footballs, baseballs, and basketballs.

To apply multiproduct CVP analysis, we need to estimate the break-even point by using a composite unit. A *composite unit* is defined as a specific number of units of each product in proportion to their expected sales mix. Multiproduct CVP analysis treats this composite unit like a single product.

To illustrate, let's look at **Hair-Today,** a stylist salon, that offers three cuts: Basic, Ultra, and Budget in the ratio of 4 units of Basic to 2 units of Ultra to 1 unit of Budget (expressed as 4:2:1). Management wants to estimate its break-even point for the next year. Unit selling prices for the three cuts are:

Basic	$10
Ultra	16
Budget	8

Using this sales mix, the selling price of a composite unit of the three products is computed as:

4 units of Basic @ $10 per unit	$40
2 units of Ultra @ $16 per unit	32
1 unit of Budget @ $8 per unit	8
Selling price of a composite unit	$80

The company's fixed costs are $96,000 per year and the variable costs of the three products are:

Basic	$6.50
Ultra	9.00
Budget	4.00

This means the variable costs of a composite unit of the products are:

4 units of Basic @ $6.50 per unit	$26
2 units of Ultra @ $9.00 per unit	18
1 unit of Budget @ $4.00 per unit ...	4
Variable costs of a composite unit ...	$48

After we compute the variable costs and selling price of a composite unit of the company's products we can compute Hair-Today's contribution margin for a composite unit. This is computed as $32 by subtracting the variable costs of a composite unit from its selling price ($80 − $48).

We can use the $32 contribution margin to determine Hair-Today's break-even point in composite units. The break-even point is 3,000 composite units as shown in Exhibit 25.19.

Exhibit 25.19

Formula for Break-Even Point in Composite Units

$$\text{Break-even point in composite units} = \frac{\text{Fixed costs}}{\text{Contribution margin per composite unit}}$$

$$= \frac{\$96{,}000}{\$32} = 3{,}000 \text{ composite units}$$

This computation implies Hair-Today breaks even when it sells 3,000 composite units of its products. To determine how many units of each product must be sold to break even, we multiply the number of units of each product in the composite unit by 3,000:

Basic: 4 × 3,000	12,000 units
Ultra: 2 × 3,000	6,000 units
Budget: 1 × 3,000	3,000 units

The schedule in Exhibit 25.20 verifies these results by showing Hair-Today's revenues and costs at the break-even point.

Exhibit 25.20

Multiproduct Break-Even Income Statement

HAIR-TODAY
Forecasted Product Income Statement at Break-Even Point

	Basic	Ultra	Budget	Combined
Sales:				
Basic (12,000 @ $10)	$120,000			
Ultra (6,000 @ $16)		$96,000		
Budget (3,000 @ $8)			$24,000	
Total revenues				$240,000
Variable costs:				
Basic (12,000 @ $6.50)	78,000			
Ultra (6,000 @ $9.00)		54,000		
Budget (3,000 @ $4.00)			12,000	
Total variable costs				144,000
Contribution margin	$42,000	$42,000	$12,000	$ 96,000
Fixed costs				96,000
Net income				$ -0-

A CVP analysis using composite units can be used to answer a variety of planning questions. Once a product mix is set, all answers are based on the assumption it remains constant at all sales levels, just like other factors in the analysis. But we can vary the sales mix to see what happens under alternative strategies.

Marketing Manager
You are the marketing manager of a medium-sized communications firm, responsible for marketing cellular phones and accessories. A CVP analysis report that you have just received indicates that with the current sales mix and price levels, the product line will just break even. You want to earn at least 10% more income than you earned in 1997. What alternatives do you have for achieving the desired income level?

Answer—p. 1225

Flash back

14. The sales mix of a company's two products, X and Y, is 2:1. Unit price and variable cost data are:

	X	Y
Unit sales price	$5	$4
Unit variable cost	2	2

What is the contribution margin per composite unit? (a) $5, (b) $10, or (c) $8.

15. What additional assumption about sales mix must be made in doing a conventional CVP analysis in a company that produces and sells more than one product?

Answers—p. 1226

Operating Leverage

USING THE INFORMATION

LO 9 Analyze changes in sales levels using the degree of operating leverage.

CVP analysis is especially useful when management begins the planning process and needs to predict the outcomes of alternative strategies. These strategies can involve selling prices, fixed costs, variable costs, sales volume, and product mix. Managers are interested in looking at the effects of changes in some of these factors.

One goal of all managers is to get maximum benefits from its fixed costs (resources). Managers would like to use 100% of the production capacity so that fixed costs are spread over a greater number of units. This decreases fixed cost per unit and increases income.

The extent, or relative size, of fixed costs in a firm's total cost structure is known as **operating leverage.** Companies with a large proportion of fixed costs in their cost structure are said to have high operating leverage (e.g., highly automated companies) A useful tool in assessing the effect of changing sales on profits is the **degree of operating leverage (DOL).** The DOL is computed by taking a ratio of total contribution margin to pre-tax income.

To illustrate, let's return to Rydell Company. At a sales level of 1,600 units, the total contribution margin for Rydell is $48,000 (1,600 × $30) and income, after subtracting fixed costs of $24,000, is $24,000. This means the degree of operating leverage is 2.0, computed as $48,000 ÷ $24,000. We can use this ratio to measure the effect of changes in sales to changes in income. For instance, suppose Rydell expects sales to increase by 10%. If this is within the relevant range of operations, we can expect this 10% increase in sales to result in a 20% increase in income (2.0 × 10%). Similar analysis can be done for expected decreases in sales.

Summary

LO1 Describe different types of cost behaviour in relation to production and sales volume. A cost's behaviour is described in terms of how its amount changes in relation to production and sales volume changes in a relevant range. As volume increases, total fixed costs remain unchanged. Total variable costs change in direct proportion to volume changes. Mixed costs display the effects of fixed and variable components. Stepwise costs remain constant over a small volume range, increase by a lump-sum, then remain constant over another volume range, and so on. Curvilinear costs change in a nonlinear relationship to volume changes.

LO2 Determine cost estimates using three different methods. The three different methods used to estimate costs are the scatter graph method, the high-low method and the least-squares regression method. All three methods use past data to estimate costs.

LO3 Compare the scatter diagram, high-low and least-squares regression methods of estimating costs. Estimates from the scatter diagram are based on a "visual fit" of the cost line and are subject to interpretation, whereas estimates from the high-low method are based only on two sets of values corresponding to the lowest and highest sales volumes. The least-squares regression method, on the other hand, follows a statistical technique and uses all the data points. Therefore, the regression method is considered as superior to the other two methods.

LO4 Compute a break-even point for a single product company. A company's break-even point for a period is the sales volume at which total revenues equal the total costs. To compute a break-even point in terms of units, divide total fixed costs by the contribution margin per unit. To compute a break-even point in terms of sales dollars, divide total fixed costs by the contribution margin ratio.

LO5 Graph the costs and revenues for a single product company. The costs and revenues for a company can be graphically illustrated. This type of presentation is called a CVP chart. In this chart, the horizontal axis represents the number of units sold and the vertical axis represents dollars of sales and costs. In accordance with the simplifying assumptions used in basic analyses, straight lines depict the costs and revenues on the graph.

LO6 Identify assumptions in cost-volume-profit analysis and explain how they impact the analysis. Conventional cost-volume-profit analysis is based on assumptions that the selling price of the single product remains constant and that variable and fixed costs behave consistently with those classifications. These assumptions are not likely to hold at volume levels outside the relevant range of operations of the business. If the assumptions do not lead to valid predictions of future costs, the CVP is less helpful.

LO7 Describe several applications of cost-volume-profit analysis. Cost-volume-profit analysis can be used to develop initial predictions of what would happen under alternative strategies concerning sales volume, selling prices, variable costs, or fixed costs. Applications include "what-if" analysis, computing sales for a targeted income, and break-even analysis.

LO8 Compute the break-even point for a multiproduct company. CVP can be applied to a multiproduct company by expressing the predicted sales volume in terms of composite units of product. A composite unit consists of a specific number of units.

LO9 Analyze changes in sales using the degree of operating leverage. The extent or relative use of fixed costs in a firm's cost structure to which a firm can utilize fixed resources is known as operating leverage. One tool useful in assessing the effect of changes in sales on profits is the degree of operating leverage or DOL, which is the ratio of the contribution margin to the profit. This ratio can be used to determine the expected percentage change in profits for a given percentage change in sales.

Guidance Answers to **You Make the Call**

Manager of Operations

Without the availability of past data, none of the three methods described in the chapter can be used to identify cost behaviour. In this situation, the manager must investigate if he can get access to such data from similar manufacturing systems, such as from other plants within the company. If not, it will usually be difficult to obtain such information from other companies due to the sensitive nature of the data. The manager must then develop a list of the different production inputs and establish input-output relationships for each input. This understanding will provide preliminary guidance to the manager to identify cost behaviour. After several months actual cost data are available for analysis.

Marketing Manager

You must first compute the level of sales required to achieve the desired net income using the existing assumptions. Then you must conduct sensitivity analysis by varying the price, sales mix and cost estimates. Results from the sensitivity analysis will provide you with information which you can use to assess the possibility of reaching the target sales levels based on the price and sales mix estimates. You may then have to pursue aggressive marketing strategies to push the high margin products or you may have to cut prices to increase sales and profits or some other strategy may emerge.

Guidance Answers to **Judgment and Ethics**

Management Trainee

Your dilemma is whether to go along with the suggestion to "manage" the numbers to make the project look like it will achieve sufficient profits to allow it to be approved. Because not telling the truth is in and of itself unethical, you should not succumb to this suggestion. Many people will likely be affected negatively if you "manage" the predicted numbers and the project eventually is unprofitable. Moreover, if it does fail, it is likely an investigation would reveal that the data in the proposal had been "fixed" to make it look good. Professional accounting bodies generally include provisions that apply to this situation in their ethical codes of conduct.

Perhaps the best way to deal with the dilemma and comply with one's professional responsibilities is to prepare several analyses showing results under different assumptions, and then let senior management decide whether to go ahead in light of the information about the uncertainties of success. A point to remember is that it seldom makes sense for groups within an organization to attempt to deceive each other. Major decisions often affect many people in addition to those who make them, and their effects can linger for a long time.

You might also recall the Institute of Management Accountants' Standards of Ethical Conduct include several provisions that apply to this situation.

Guidance Answers to Flashbacks

1. *b*
2. A fixed cost remains unchanged in total amount regardless of production levels within a relevant range.
3. The cost of raw materials is a variable cost because the total cost changes in proportion to volume changes.
4. *b*
5. The high-low method ignores all of the cost/volume data points except the high and low extremes.
6. *c*
7. *a*
8. ($90 – $54)/$90 = 40%
9. $90,000/40% = $225,000
10. The three basic assumptions are: (1) that the actual selling price per unit remains constant for all units sold during the planning period; (2) that for costs classified as variable, the actual costs per unit of output will remain constant; and (3) that for costs classified as fixed, the total amount will remain constant over the volumes projected for the planning period.
11. *a* Before-tax income = $120,000/(1 − .20) = $150,000

$$\frac{\$50,000 + \$120,000 + (\$150,000 \times 20\%)}{25\%} = \$800,000$$

12. If the contribution margin ratio decreases by 50%, unit sales would have to double.
13. The margin of safety is the excess of the predicted sales level over its break-even sales level.
14. *c* Selling price of a composite unit:

2 units of X @ $5 per unit	$10
1 unit of Y @ $4 per unit	4
Selling price of a composite unit	$14

Variable costs of a composite unit:

2 units of X @ $2 per unit	$4
1 unit of Y @ $2 per unit	2
Variable costs of a composite unit	$6

Contribution margin per composite unit is $8

15. It must be assumed that the sales mix remains unchanged at all sales levels in the relevant range.

Demonstration Problem

Scissors Manufacturing Co. produces and sells a special type of scissors for cutting heavy cloth material. The fixed costs of operating the business have averaged about $150,000 per month, and the variable costs for a pair of scissors have been about $5 per unit. All the manufactured scissors can be sold at $8 per unit and the fixed costs provide a production capacity of up to 100,000 units per month.

Required

1. Use formulas to compute the following:
   a. Contribution margin per pair of scissors.
   b. Break-even point in terms of the number of scissors produced and sold.

c. Amount of profit at 30,000 scissors sold per month (ignore income taxes).
d. Amount of profit at 85,000 scissors sold per month (ignore income taxes).
e. Quantity of scissors to be produced and sold to provide $45,000 of after-tax profits, assuming an income tax rate of 25%.

2. Draw a CVP chart for the company, showing a volume of scissors of output on the horizontal axis. Identify the break-even point and the amount of pre-tax profit when the level of scissors production is 75,000. (Omit the fixed cost line.)
3. Use formulas to compute the following:
   a. Contribution margin ratio.
   b. Break-even point in terms of sales dollars.
   c. Amount of profit at $250,000 of sales per month (ignore income taxes).
   d. Amount of profit at $600,000 of sales per month (ignore income taxes).
   e. Dollars of sales needed to provide $45,000 of after-tax profits, assuming an income tax rate of 25%.

Planning the Solution

- Find the formulas in the chapter for the required items concerning volumes expressed in units and solve them using the original data given in the problem.
- Draw a CVP chart that reflects the facts given in the problem. The horizontal axis should plot the volume in units up to 100,000, and the vertical axis should plot the total dollars up to $800,000. Plot the total cost line as upward-sloping, starting at the fixed cost level ($150,000) on the vertical axis and increasing until it reaches $650,000 at the maximum volume of 100,000 units. Verify that the break-even point (where the two lines cross) equals the amount you computed in Part 1.
- Find the formulas in the chapter for the required items concerning volumes expressed in units and solve them using the original data given in the problem.

Solution to Demonstration Problem

1. a. Contribution margin per scissors = Selling price per unit − Variable cost per unit
   = $8 − $5 = $3

   b. Break-even point in scissors = $\dfrac{\text{Fixed costs}}{\text{Contribution margin per scissors}} = \dfrac{\$150{,}000}{\$3}$ = 50,000 scissors

   c. Profit at 30,000 scissors sold = (Units × Contribution margin per unit) − Fixed costs
   = (30,000 × $3) − $150,000 = −$60,000 (a loss)

   d. Profit at 85,000 scissors sold = (Units × Contribution margin per unit) – Fixed costs
   = (85,000 × $3) − $150,000 = $105,000 profit

   e. Pre-tax profit = $45,000 / 75% = $60,000
   Income taxes = $60,000 × 25% = $15,000

   Units needed for $45,000 profit = $\dfrac{\text{Fixed costs + Net income + Income taxes}}{\text{Contribution margin per scissors}}$

   = $\dfrac{\$150{,}000 + \$45{,}000 + \$15{,}000}{\$3}$ = 70,000 scissors

2. CVP chart:

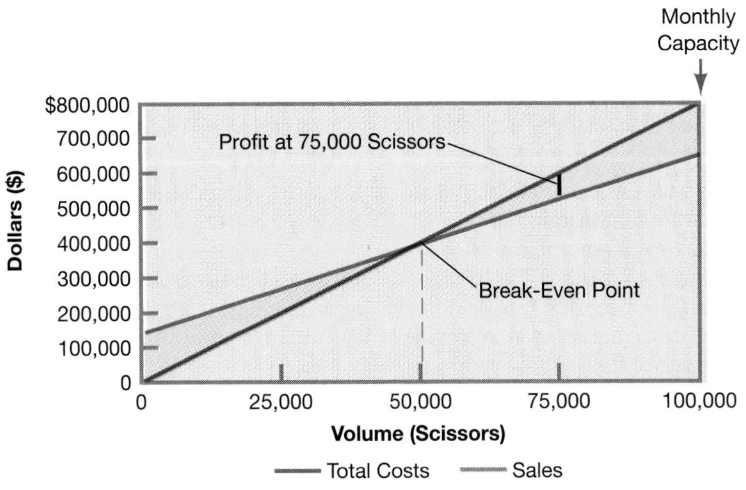

3. a. Contribution margin ratio $= \dfrac{\text{Contribution margin per unit}}{\text{Selling price per unit}} = \dfrac{\$3}{\$8} = \underline{\underline{.375}}, \text{ or } \underline{\underline{37.5\%}}$

b. Break-even point in dollars $= \dfrac{\text{Fixed costs}}{\text{Contribution margin ratio}} = \dfrac{\$150{,}000}{37.5\%} = \underline{\underline{\$400{,}000}}$

c. Profit at sales of $250,000 = (Sales × Contribution margin ratio) − Fixed costs
= ($250,000 × 37.5%) − $150,000 = $\underline{\underline{-\$56{,}250 \text{ (a loss)}}}$

d. Profit at sales of $600,000 = (Sales × Contribution margin ratio) – Fixed costs
= ($600,000 × 37.5%) − $150,000 = $\underline{\underline{\$75{,}000 \text{ profit}}}$

e. Dollars of sales to have $45,000 profits $= \dfrac{\text{Fixed costs + Net income + Income taxes}}{\text{Contribution margin ratio}}$

$$= \frac{\$150{,}000 + \$45{,}000 + \$15{,}000}{37.5\%} = \underline{\underline{\$560{,}000}}$$

Glossary

Break-even point The unique sales level at which a company neither earns a profit nor incurs a loss. (p. 1214)

Contribution margin per unit The amount that the sale of one unit contributes toward recovering fixed costs and profit. (p. 1215)

Contribution margin ratio The contribution margin per unit expressed as a percentage of the product's selling price. (p. 1215)

Cost-volume-profit analysis The first step in the planning phase is predicting the volume of activity, the costs to be incurred, revenues to be received, and profits to be earned. (p. 1206)

Curvilinear cost A cost that changes with volume but not at a constant rate like pure variable costs. (p. 1209)

CVP chart A graphic representation of the cost-volume-profit relationships. (p. 1215)

Degree of operating leverage (DOL) The ratio of contribution margin divided by pre-tax income; used in assessing the effect on income of changes in sales. (p. 1224)

Estimated line of cost behaviour A line on a scatter diagram drawn to identify the past relationship between cost and sales volume. (p. 1210)

Fixed cost A cost that remains unchanged in total amount even when production volume varies from period to period. (p. 1206)

High-low method A simple way to draw an estimated line of cost behaviour by connecting the highest and lowest costs on a scatter diagram with a straight line. (p. 1210)

Least-squares regression A statistical method for deriving an estimated line of cost behaviour that is more precise than the high-low method. (p. 1211)

Margin of safety The excess of expected sales over the sales at the break-even point. (p. 1220)

Mixed cost A cost that acts like a combination of a fixed and a variable cost. (p. 1206)

Operating leverage The extent, or relative size, of fixed costs in the total costs structure. (p. 1224)

Relevant range of operations A business's normal operating range; excludes extremely high and low volumes that are not likely to be encountered. (p. 1217)

Sales mix The ratio of the volumes of the various products sold by a company. (p. 1222)

Scatter diagram A graph used to display data about past cost behaviours and volumes for each period as points on the diagram. (p. 1210)

Step-wise cost A cost that remains fixed over limited ranges of volumes but increases by a lump sum when volume increases beyond maximum amounts. (p. 1208)

Variable cost A cost that changes in proportion to changes in production volume. (p. 1206)

Question

1. Why is cost-volume-profit analysis used?
2. What is a variable cost? Identify two variable costs.
3. When volume increases, do variable costs per unit increase, decrease, or stay the same within the relevant range of activity? Why?
4. When volume increases, do fixed costs per unit increase, decrease, or stay the same within the relevant range of activity? Why?
5. How do step-wise costs and curvilinear costs differ?
6. In performing a conventional CVP analysis for a manufacturing company, what simplifying assumption is usually made about the volume of production and the volume of sales?
7. What two factors tend to justify classifying all costs as either fixed or variable even though individual costs might not behave perfectly consistently with these classifications?
8. How does assuming a relevant range affect cost-volume-profit analysis?
9. List three ways to identify cost behaviour.
10. How can a scatter diagram be used in identifying the behaviour of a company's costs?
11. In CVP analysis, what is the estimated profit at the break-even point?
12. Assume that a straight line on a CVP chart intersects the vertical axis at the level of fixed costs and has a positive slope, such that it rises with each additional unit of volume by the amount of the variable costs per unit. What would this line represent?
13. Why are fixed costs depicted as a horizontal line on a CVP chart?
14. Two similar companies each have sales of $20,000 and total costs of $15,000 for a month. Company A's total costs include $10,000 of variable costs and $5,000 of fixed costs. If Company B's total costs include $4,000 of variable costs and $11,000 of fixed costs, which company will enjoy a greater profit if sales double?
15. _______ __ _______ measures the expected sales in excess of the sales at the break-even point.
16. Consider the process of manufacturing hats for sale during the Olympic games. Identify some of the variable and fixed product costs associated with that process. [Hint: Your costs are limited to product costs.]
17. Reebok is thinking of expanding production of its most popular walking shoe by 65%. Will variable and fixed costs stay within the relevant range? Why or why not?

Quick Study

QS 25-1

Identify cost behaviour

LO1

Following are four series of costs measured at various volume levels. Examine each series and identify which is fixed, variable, step-wise and curvilinear.

Volume (Units)	Series 1	Series 2	Series 3	Series 4
0	$ -0-	$450	$ 800	$100
100	800	450	800	105
200	1,600	450	800	120
300	2,400	450	1,600	145
400	3,200	450	1,600	190
500	4,000	450	2,400	250
600	4,800	450	2,400	320

QS 25-2
Identify cost behaviour
LO 1

For each of the following, determine whether it would best be described as a fixed, variable, or mixed cost:

a. Maintenance of factory machinery.
b. Packaging expense.
c. Wages of an assembly-line worker paid on the basis of acceptable units produced.
d. Factory supervisor's salary.
e. Taxes on factory building.
f. Rubber used in manufacture of athletic shoes.

QS 25-3
Identify cost behaviour
LO 1 2

The following scatter diagram reflects past maintenance hours and corresponding maintenance costs:

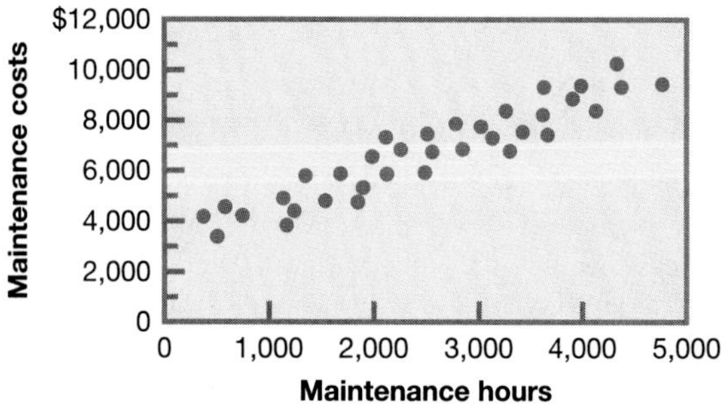

Draw an estimated line of cost behaviour and determine the fixed and variable components of maintenance costs.

QS 25-4
Recognize CVP assumptions
LO 6

Which of the following is one of the assumptions that underlie cost-volume-profit analysis?

a. The actual selling price per unit must change in proportion to the number of units sold during the planning period.
b. Assumptions regarding cost behaviour are constant within the relevant range.
c. For costs classified as variable, the actual costs per unit of output must change constantly.
d. For costs classified as fixed, the actual costs per unit of output must remain constant.

QS 25-5
Find contribution margin and BE in units
LO 4

The Flip Phone Company sells a product for $100 per unit. Fixed costs for the period total $180,000 and variable costs are $40 per unit. Determine (a) the contribution margin per unit and (b) the break-even point in units.

QS 25-6
Find contribution margin ratio and BE in dollars
LO 4

Refer to QS 25-5. Determine the (a) contribution margin ratio and (b) the break-even point in dollars.

QS 25-7
CVP analysis and taxes
LO 7

Refer to QS 25-5. Assume that Flip Phone is subject to a combined federal and provincial income tax rate of 30%. Compute the units of product that must be sold to earn after-tax income of $140,000.

QS 25-8
Multiproduct break-even
LO 8

Beeper Company manufactures and sells two products, green and gold beepers, in the ratio of 5:3. Fixed costs are $85,000 and the contribution margin per composite unit is $170. What is the number of green and gold beepers that will be sold at the break-even point?

QS 25-9
Evaluate operating leverage
LO 9

Consider the following information about Company A and Company B. A high proportion of Company A's total costs are variable with respect to units sold whereas a high proportion of Company B's costs are fixed with respect to units sold. Which company is likely to have a higher degree of operating leverage? Why?

Exercises

Exercise 25-1
Identifying categories of cost behaviour
LO 1

The left column presents the names of several categories of costs. The right column presents short definitions of those costs. In the blank space beside each of the numbers in the right column, write the letter of the cost described by the definition.

a. Total cost	_____ **1.**	This cost remains constant over a limited range of volume that is less than the total productive capacity; when it reaches the end of its limited range, it increases by a lump sum and remains at that level until another limited range is exceeded.
b. Mixed cost	_____ **2.**	This cost has a component that remains the same over all volume levels and another component that increases in direct proportion to increases in volume.
c. Variable cost	_____ **3.**	This cost increases when volume increases, but the increase is not constant for each unit produced.
d. Curvilinear cost	_____ **4.**	This cost remains the same over all volume levels within the productive capacity for the planning period.
e. Step-wise cost	_____ **5.**	This cost increases in direct proportion to increases in volume because its amount is constant for each unit produced.
f. Fixed cost	_____ **6.**	This cost is the combined amount of all the other costs.

Exercise 25-2
Recognizing cost behaviour patterns
LO 1

Following are five series of costs measured at various volume levels. Examine each series and identify which is fixed, variable, mixed, step-wise and curvilinear:

Volume (Units)	Series A	Series B	Series C	Series D	Series E
0	$ -0-	$2,200	$ -0-	$1,000	$3,000
400	3,200	2,700	6,000	1,000	3,000
800	6,400	3,200	6,600	2,000	3,000
1,200	9,600	3,700	7,200	2,000	3,000
1,600	12,800	4,200	8,200	3,000	3,000
2,000	16,000	4,700	9,600	3,000	3,000
2,400	19,200	5,200	13,500	4,000	3,000

Exercise 25-3
Recognizing cost behaviour graphs
LO 1

The following five graphs represent various cost behaviours.

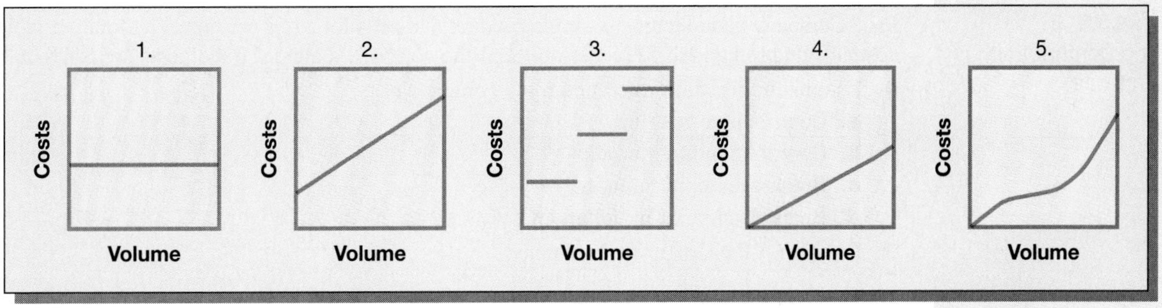

Required

a. Identify the type of cost behaviour that each graph represents —mixed, step-wise, fixed, variable and curvilinear.

b. For each of the following items, identify the graph that best illustrates the cost behaviour described:

(1) Material handling workers are required for every 300 direct factory workers.

(2) Real estate taxes on factory.

(3) Electricity charge in total that includes the standard monthly charge plus a charge for each kilowatt hour.

(4) Commissions to salespersons.

(5) An addition of hourly paid workers that provides substantial gains in efficiency as a few workers are added, but gradually smaller gains in efficiency as more workers are added

---

Exercise 25-4
Scatter diagram and cost behaviour—six data points
LO 2

A sail company's accounting system provides the following information about its monthly sales and the amount of a specific cost in those months. Each unit sells for $500.

Month	Sales	Cost
1	$15,000	$10,100
2	11,500	7,500
3	10,500	7,000
4	7,500	5,500
5	9,000	6,000
6	12,500	9,500

Use this data to prepare a scatter diagram. Then, draw an estimated line of cost behaviour and determine whether the cost appears to be variable, fixed, or mixed.

Exercise 25-5
Scatter diagram and cost behaviour—15 data points
LO 2

Use the following information about monthly sales volume and the amount of a specific cost to prepare a scatter diagram. Then, draw a cost line that reflects the behaviour displayed by this cost. Finally, determine whether the cost is variable, step-wise, fixed, mixed or curvilinear.

Period	Sales	Cost	Period	Sales	Cost
1	$380	$295	9	290	$195
2	400	280	10	160	120
3	100	115	11	120	115
4	200	200	12	360	275
5	240	195	13	140	130
6	310	275	14	222	205
7	340	295	15	190	130
8	270	215			

Exercise 25-6
Computing contribution margin and rate
LO 4, 5

Pace Company manufactures a single product that sells for $168 per unit. The total variable costs of the product are $126 per unit and the company's annual fixed costs are $630,000.

1. Use this information to compute the company's:

a. Contribution margin.

b. Contribution margin ratio.

c. Break-even point in units.

d. Break-even point in dollars of sales.

2. Draw a CVP chart for the company.

Exercise 25-7
Computing additional sales necessary to break even
LO 7

Prepare an income statement for Pace Company's operations (from Exercise 25-6) showing sales, variable costs, and fixed costs at the break-even point. If Pace's fixed costs were to increase by $135,000, what amount of sales (in dollars) would be needed to break even?

Exercise 25-8
Computing sales required to obtain desired income
LO 7

The management of Pace Company (in Exercise 25-6) wants to earn an annual after-tax income of $840,000. Because of special tax incentives, the company is subject to a combined federal and provincial income tax rate of 20%. Compute:

a. The units of product that must be sold to earn the target after-tax net income.
b. The dollars of sales that must be reached to earn the target after-tax net income.

Exercise 25-9
Estimating the income result from increased volume
LO 7

The sales manager of Pace Company (in Exercise 25-6) predicts that the annual sales of the company's product will soon reach 40,000 units even though the price will increase to $200 per unit. According to the production manager, the variable costs are expected to increase to $140 per unit but fixed costs will remain at $630,000. The company's tax adviser expects that the combined federal and provincial income tax rate will still be 20%. What amounts of before-tax and after-tax income can the company expect to earn from selling units at this expected level with these expected costs?

Exercise 25-10
Computing unit and dollar sales using contribution margin
LO 7

In predicting the events of the upcoming quarter, the management of the Grant Company thinks that it will incur a total of $500,000 of variable costs and $800,000 of fixed costs while earning a pre-tax income of $100,000. The management predicts that the contribution margin per unit will be $60. Using this information, determine (a) the total expected dollar sales for the quarter and (b) the number of units expected to be sold in the quarter.

Exercise 25-11
Computing total variable and fixed costs
LO 5

Snap Company expects to sell 100,000 units of its product next year, which should produce total revenues of $12 million. Management predicts that the pre-tax net income for the year will be $3,000,000 and that the contribution margin per unit will be $40.

Required

a. Using this information, compute (i) the total expected variable costs and (ii) the total expected fixed costs for next year.
b. Prepare a CVP chart from this information.

Exercise 25-12
Computing sales and variable costs using contribution margin ratio
LO 7

The management of the Waterloo Company predicts that it will incur fixed costs of $250,000 next year and that the pre-tax income will be $350,000. The expected contribution margin ratio is 60%. Use this information to compute the amounts of (a) total dollar sales and (b) total variable costs.

Exercise 25-13
CVP analysis using composite units
LO 8

The Home Company sells windows and doors in the ratio of 8:2 (8 windows for every 2 doors). The selling price of each window is $100 and the selling price of each door is $450. The variable cost of a window is $60 and the variable cost of a door is $300. Next year's fixed costs are expected to be $750,000. Use this information to determine:

a. The selling price of a composite unit of these products.
b. The variable costs per composite unit.
c. The break-even point in composite units.
d. The number of units of each product that will be sold at the break-even point.

Exercise 25-14
Calculate and evaluate operating leverage
LO 9

Compute the operating leverage for each company. Identify which one benefits more from a 20% increase in sales and explain why.

Company A: A heavy machinery manufacturer with current sales of $1,000,000 and a 65% contribution margin. Fixed costs equal $500,000.

Company B: A consulting firm with current service revenues of $1,000,000 and a 25% contribution margin. Fixed costs equal $100,000.

Problems

Problem 25-1
Scatter diagram and estimating cost behaviour
LO 2

Bricks Co.'s monthly sales and cost data for its operating activities of the past year are shown below. The management of the company wants to use these data to predict future fixed and variable costs.

Period	Sales	Total Cost
1	$160,000	$ 80,000
2	80,000	50,000
3	140,000	110,000
4	100,000	50,000
5	150,000	115,000
6	100,000	60,000
7	170,000	110,000
8	140,000	80,000
9	10,000	40,000
10	80,000	70,000
11	50,000	50,000
12	55,000	40,000

Required

1. Prepare a scatter diagram with sales volume (in $) plotted on the horizontal axis and total cost plotted on the vertical axis for Bricks Co.
2. Estimate the line of cost behaviour by a visual inspection and draw it on the scatter diagram. (Assume a linear relation, which means that you should draw a straight cost line on the graph.)
3. Using the estimated line of cost behaviour and the assumption that the future will be like the past, predict an amount of monthly fixed costs for Brick Co. Also, predict future variable costs per sales dollar.
4. Use the estimated line of cost behaviour to predict future total costs when the sales volume is (a) $100,000 and (b) $150,000.

Check Figure Approximate slope of cost line, $0.50 per sales dollar

Problem 25-2
Completing CVP analyses, including a chart
LO 4, 5

Long Company manufactures and markets a number of rope products. Management is considering the future of Product XT508CV, a special rope for hang gliding, which has not been as profitable as planned. Because this product is manufactured and marketed independently from the other products, its total costs can be precisely measured. The plan for the next year calls for a selling price of $150 per 100 metres. The fixed costs for the year are expected to be $200,000, up to the maximum capacity of 600,000 metres. The forecasted variable costs are $100 per 100 metres.

Required

1. Predict the break-even point for Product XT508CV in terms of (a) units and (b) dollars of sales.
2. Prepare a CVP chart for Product XT508CV. Use 550,000 metres as the maximum number of metres sold on the graph and $900,000 as the maximum number of sales dollars.
3. Prepare an income statement showing sales, fixed costs, and variable costs for Product XT508CV at the break-even point.

Problem 25-3
Income statements to confirm projections
LO 7

In 1998, Little Company sold 20,000 units of its only product and incurred a $50,000 loss (ignoring income taxes), as follows:

LITTLE COMPANY Income Statement For Year Ended December 31, 1998	
Sales	$750,000
Variable costs	600,000
Contribution margin	$150,000
Fixed costs	200,000
Net loss	$ (50,000)

During a planning session for 1999 activities, the production manager has pointed out that variable costs can be reduced 50% by installing a machine that automates several operations presently being done by hand. To obtain these savings, the company must increase its annual fixed costs by $150,000. The maximum capacity of the system would be 40,000 units per year.

Required

1. Compute 1998 break-even point in terms of dollars.
2. Compute the dollar break-even point for 1999 under the assumption that the new machine is installed.
3. Prepare a forecasted income statement for 1999 that shows the expected results with the new machine installed. Assume that there will be no change in the selling price and no change in the number of units sold. The combined federal and provincial income tax rate is 30%.
4. Compute the sales level required to earn $140,000 of after-tax income in 1999 with the new machine installed and with no change in the selling price.
5. Prepare a forecasted income statement that shows the results at this sales level.

Check Figure Requirement 4: Unit sales, 24,445 units

Problem 25-4
Break-even analysis comparing different cost structures
LO 7

Beach Company produces and sells two products, T and O. These products are manufactured in separate factories and marketed through completely different channels. Thus, they do not have any shared costs. Last year, Beach sold 50,000 units of each product. The following income statements describe the financial results:

	Product T	Product O
Sales	$800,000	$800,000
Variable costs	560,000	100,000
Contribution margin	$240,000	$700,000
Fixed costs	100,000	560,000
Income before taxes	$140,000	$140,000
Income taxes (32% rate)	44,800	44,800
Net income	$ 95,200	$ 95,200

Required

Preparation component:

1. Compute the break-even point in dollars for each product.
2. Assume that the company expects the sales of each product to decline to 33,000 units in the upcoming year, even though the price will remain unchanged. Prepare a forecasted income statement that shows the expected profits from the two products. Follow the format of the preceding statement and assume that any loss before taxes results in a tax savings.

Check Figure After-tax income, Product O, $228,480

3. Assume that the company expects the sales of each product to increase to 64,000 units in the upcoming year, even though the price will remain unchanged. Prepare a forecasted income statement that shows the expected profits from the two products. Follow the format of the preceding statement.

Analysis component:

4. If sales were to greatly decrease, which of these products would experience the greater loss? Why?
5. Describe some factors that might have created the different cost structures for these two products.

Problem 25-5
Analyzing the effects of price and volume changes on profits
LO 7

This year, Clark Company sold 35,000 units of product at $16 per unit. Manufacturing and selling the product required $120,000 of fixed manufacturing costs and $180,000 of fixed selling and administrative expenses. This year's variable costs and expenses per unit were:

Material	$4.00
Direct labour (paid on the basis of completed units)	3.00
Variable manufacturing overhead costs	0.40
Variable selling and administrative expenses	0.20

Next year the company will use new raw material that is easier to work with and cheaper than the old material. A switch to the new material will reduce material costs by 60% and direct labour costs by 40%. The new material will not affect the product's quality or marketability. The next set of decisions concerns the marketing strategy to be used. Because the factory's output is creeping up to its annual capacity of 40,000 units, some consideration is being given to increasing the selling price to reduce the number of units sold. At this point, two strategies are being considered. Under Plan 1, the company will keep the price at the current level and sell the same volume as last year. This plan increases profits because of the materials change. Under Plan 2, the product's price will be increased by 25%, but unit sales volume will fall only 10%. Under both Plan 1 and Plan 2, all of the fixed costs and variable costs (per unit) will be exactly the same.

Required

1. Compute the break-even point in dollars for Plan 1 and Plan 2.
2. Prepare side-by-side condensed forecasted income statements showing the anticipated results of Plan 1 and Plan 2. The statements should show sales, total fixed costs, total variable costs and expenses, income before taxes, income taxes (30% rate), and net income.

Check Figure Net income under Plan 2, $142,800

Problem 25-6
Break-even analysis with composite units
LO 8

Peabody Company manufactures and sells three products, Red, White, and Blue. Their individual selling prices are:

Red	$ 55.00 per unit
White	$ 85.00 per unit
Blue	$110.00 per unit

The variable costs of manufacturing and selling the products have been:

Red	$ 40.00 per unit
White	$ 60.00 per unit
Blue	$ 80.00 per unit

Their sales mix is reflected in a ratio of 5:4:2. The annual fixed costs shared by all three products are $150,000. One particular item of raw materials is used in manufacturing all three products. Management has learned that a new material is just as good and cheaper. The new material would reduce the variable costs as follows: Red by $10, White by $20, and Blue by $10. But, the new material requires new equipment, which will increase annual fixed costs by $20,000. (In preparing your answers always round up to the nearest whole composite unit.)

Required

1. Assuming that the company continues to use the old material, determine the company's break-even point in dollars and units of each product that would be sold at the break-even point.
2. Assuming that the company decides to use the new material, determine the company's new break-even point in dollars and units of each product that would be sold at the break-even point.

Check Figure New plan break-even point, 442 composite units

Analysis:

1. What insight does this problem offer to management in planning for the long-term success of a business?

Alternate Problems

Problem 25-1A
Scatter diagram and estimating cost behaviour

LO 2

Inland Co.'s monthly sales and cost data for its operating activities of the past year are shown below. The management of the company wants to use these data to predict future fixed and variable costs.

Period	Sales	Total Cost
1	$390	$194
2	250	174
3	210	146
4	310	178
5	190	162
6	430	220
7	290	186
8	370	210
9	270	170
10	170	130
11	350	190
12	230	158

Required

1. Prepare a scatter diagram with sales volume (in $) plotted on the horizontal axis and total cost plotted on the vertical axis for Inland Co.
2. Estimate the line of cost behaviour by a visual inspection and draw it on the scatter diagram. (Assume a linear relation, which means that you should draw a straight cost line on the graph.)
3. Using the estimated line of cost behaviour and the assumption that the future will be like the past, predict an amount of monthly fixed costs for Inland Co. Also, predict future variable costs per sales dollar.
4. Use the estimated line of cost behaviour to predict future total costs when the sales volume is (a) $150 and (b) $250.

Problem 25-2A
Completing CVP analyses, including a chart

LO 4, 5

Saskatoon Company manufactures and markets a number of products. Management is considering the future of one product, electronic keyboards, which has not been as profitable as planned. Because this product is manufactured and marketed independently from the other products, its total costs can be precisely measured. The plan for the next year calls for a selling price of $225 per unit. The fixed costs for the year are expected to be $30,000, up to the maximum capacity of 700 units. The forecasted variable costs are $150 per unit.

Required

1. Predict the break-even point for keyboards in terms of (a) units and (b) dollars of sales.
2. Prepare a CVP chart for keyboards. Use 700 as the maximum number of units on the graph and $180,000 as the maximum number of dollars.
3. Prepare an income statement showing sales, fixed costs, and variable costs for keyboards at the break-even point.

Problem 25-3A
CVP chart and income statements to confirm projections
LO 7

In 1998, the Capital Company sold 50,000 units of its only product, and incurred a $200,000 loss (ignoring income taxes), as follows:

CAPITAL COMPANY Income Statement For Year Ended December 31, 1998	
Sales	800,000
Variable costs	900,000
Contribution margin	$ (100,000)
Fixed costs	100,000
Net loss	$ (200,000)

During a planning session for 1999's activities, the production manager has pointed out that variable costs can be reduced 72.22% by installing a machine that automates several operations presently being done by hand. To obtain these savings, the company must increase its annual fixed costs by $200,000. The maximum capacity of the system would be 80,000 units per year.

Required

1. Compute 1998 break-even point in terms of dollars.
2. Compute the dollar break-even point for 1999 under the assumption that the new machine is installed. (Round the change in variable cost to a whole number.)
3. Prepare a forecasted income statement for 1999 that shows the expected results with the new machine installed. Assume that there will be no change in the selling price and no change in the number of units sold. The combined federal and provincial income tax rate is 40%.
4. Compute the sales level required to earn $300,000 of after-tax income in 1999 with the new machine installed and with no change in the selling price.
5. Prepare a forecasted income statement that shows the results at this sales level.

Check Figure Requirement 4: Unit sales, 72,728 units

Problem 25-4A
Break-even analysis comparing different cost structures
LO 7

Model Company produces and sells two products, BB and TT. These products are manufactured in separate factories and marketed through completely different channels. Thus, they do not have any shared costs. Last year, Model sold 120,000 units of each product. The following income statements describe the financial results:

	Product BB	Product TT
Sales	$3,000,000	$3,000,000
Variable costs	1,800,000	600,000
Contribution margin	1,200,000	2,400,000
Fixed costs	600,000	1,800,000
Income before taxes	600,000	600,000
Income taxes (35% rate)	210,000	210,000
Net income	$ 390,000	$ 390,000

Required

Preparation component:

1. Compute the break-even point in dollars for each product.
2. Assume that the company expects the sales of each product to decline to 104,000 units in the upcoming year, even though the price will remain unchanged. Prepare a forecasted income statement that shows the expected profits from the two products. Follow the format of the preceding statement.
3. Assume that the company expects the sales of each product to increase to 190,000 units in the upcoming year, even though the price will remain unchanged. Prepare a forecasted income statement that shows the expected profits from the two products. Follow the format of the preceding statement.

Analysis component:

4. If sales were to greatly increase, which of these products would experience the greater increase in profit? Why?
5. Describe some factors that might have created the different cost structures for these two products.

Problem 25-5A
Analyzing the effects of price and volume changes on profits
LO7

Last year, White Company earned a disappointing 4.2% after-tax return on sales from marketing 100,000 packages of its only product, orange watch bands. The company buys orange watch bands in bulk and repackages them in bags for resale at the price of $25 per bag. White incurred these costs last year:

Cost of bulk product for 100,000 packages	$1,000,000
Packaging materials and other variable packaging costs	100,000
Fixed costs	1,250,000
Income tax rate	30%

The marketing manager has reported that this year's results will be the same as last year's unless some changes are made. The manager has suggested that the company can increase the number of bags sold by 80% if it reduces the selling price by 20% and upgrades the packaging. The change would increase variable packaging costs by 25%, but increased sales would allow the company to take advantage of a 20% quantity discount on the product's bulk purchase price. Neither the packaging nor the volume change would affect fixed costs, which provide an annual capacity of 200,000 units.

Required

1. Compute the dollar break-even points for selling orange watch bands (a) under the existing price strategy and (b) under the new strategy that alters the selling price and the variable costs.
2. Prepare side-by-side condensed forecasted income statements showing the anticipated results of (a) continuing the existing strategy and (b) changing to the new strategy. Determine whether the after-tax return on sales will be changed by the new strategy.

Check Figure Net income under Plan 2, $479,500

Problem 25-6A
Break-even analysis with composite units
LO8

Unity Company manufactures and sells three products, Product 1, Product 2, and Product 3. Their individual selling prices are:

Product 1	$40.00 per unit
Product 2	$30.00 per unit
Product 3	$14.00 per unit

The variable costs of manufacturing and selling the products have been:

Product 1 . .	$30.00 per unit
Product 2 . .	$20.00 per unit
Product 3 . .	$ 8.00 per unit

Their sales mix is reflected in a ratio of 6:3:5. The annual fixed costs shared by all three products are $200,000. One particular item of raw materials is used in manufacturing products 1 and 2. Management has learned that a new material is just as good and cheaper. The new material would reduce the variable costs as follows: Product 1 by $10.00, Product 2 by $5.00. But, the new material requires new equipment, which will increase annual fixed costs by $50,000.

Required

1. Assuming that the company continues to use the old material, determine the company's break-even point in dollars and the units of each product that would be sold at the break-even point.
2. Assuming that the company decides to use the new material, determine the company's new break-even point in dollars and the units of each product that would be sold at the break-even point.

Check Figure New plan break-even point, 1,282 composite units

Analysis:

What insight does this problem offer to management in planning for the long-term success of a business?

Analytical and Review Problems

A & R 25-1

Utilizing the following diagram of cost/volume relationship, demonstrate your understanding of (a) the relevant range and (b) cost behaviour. (Hint: Identify the relevant ranges by lettering the appropriate points on the diagram.)

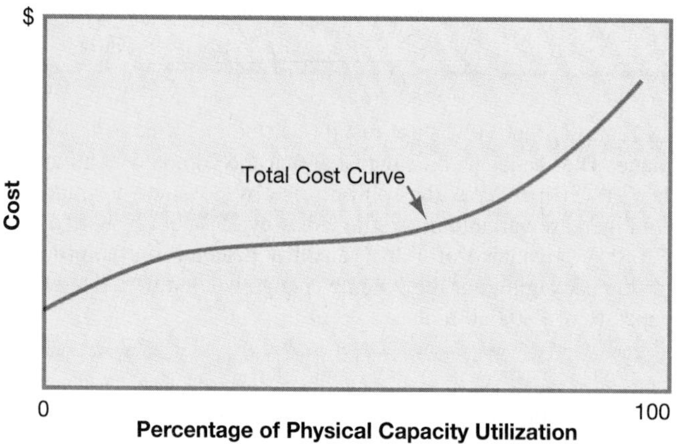

A & R 25-2

Fixed and variable costs are also viewed a capacity and activity costs.

Required

Discuss the basis for the alternate view of fixed and variable costs.

A & R 25-3

For companies using full costing (fixed and variable costs are included in the overhead rate in estimating the cost of goods manufactured) reported net income tends to correlate with the level of production. On the other hand, for companies using variable costing (only variable costs are included in the overhead rate in determining costs of goods manufactured) net income tends to correlate with the level of sales.

Required

Do you agree with the above statements? Set up a numerical example to support or disprove the above statements.

BEYOND THE NUMBERS

Reporting in Action

LO 1

NIKE has expanded its product lines from running shoes to a full-line of athletic shoes to athletic apparel and more over the past decade. Assume you are assigned to head up NIKE's new product, snowboards, to be sold through its sporting goods distribution channels across Canada. You are given permission to use all existing resources in getting the product to market, such as NIKE's purchasing department, legal department, building and equipment, and so forth.

Required

1. What costs are your most immediate concerns and why?
2. Identify the direct costs of snowboards and where these costs are primarily reflected in financial reports.
3. Assume you are successful in selling snowboards. The contribution margin is 60% and you anticipate sales of $5 million in 1998. Discuss why gross margin on the income statement will not reflect in total your success. (Hint: What is the difference between gross margin and contribution margin?)

Comparative Analysis

LO 4, 5

Both NIKE and Reebok make basketball shoes that are widely sold in Canada and throughout the world, yet one company is often more profitable than the other in sales of these shoes. We want to understand how this is possible. Each company makes decisions about purchasing assets to produce basketball shoes, similar to the decisions described in the chapter. In particular, fixed asset and variable cost decisions determine the break-even point and profitability of the company.

Required

1. Using the data below, compute the monthly cost per pair of basketball shoes for Nike and Reebok. (Assume sales equals production volume.)

	NIKE	Reebok
Estimated pair sales	10,000@ $60 ea.	10,000@ $60 ea.
Material/unit	$10/unit	$10/unit
Direct labour/unit	$30/unit	$34/unit
Factory rent/month	$30,000	$10,000
Factory equipment (amortization)	$50,000	$60,000

2. Compare and explain why one company is more profitable than the other.
3. If sales sharply decline, which company will be more profitable (computations are unnecessary)?

Ethics Challenge

The labour time we pay for an auto mechanic to repair a car is not usually based on actual hours worked. Instead, the amount paid to a mechanic is based on an industry average amount of time estimated to complete a repair job. The repair shop bills the customer for the industry average amount of time at the repair centre's billable cost per hour. This means a customer can pay, for example, $120 for two hours of work on a car, when the actual hours worked may be only one hour. Many experienced mechanics can complete repair jobs well under the industry average. The average data is compiled by engineering studies and surveys completed by participates in the auto repair business. Most reputable auto repair centres use the industry average in billing customers.

Assume you are asked to complete the survey for a repair centre. The survey calls for objective input and many questions require detailed cost behaviour analysis. The mechanics and business owner know you have the survey and are encouraging you to complete the survey in a way that increases the average billable cost per hour for repair work.

Required

Write a report to the mechanics and business owner describing the direct labour data analysis you will undertake in completing this report.

Communicating in Practice

LO 6

The chapter explained the important assumptions underlying CVP analysis. There are still further assumptions that impact CVP analysis. (CVP analysis is a tool that can be used to forecast future revenues and costs).

Required

Assume you are a college student actively engaged in job searching. You should prepare a short report identifying three assumptions relating to your expected salary and three assumptions relating to your expected costs for your first year out of college. (Hint: While you have various expectations, many uncertainties exist in your first year out of college.) Be prepared to present and discuss your assumptions in class.

Taking It to the Net

Creativity is a skill all persons must build and maintain. This is evidenced in this chapter by how CVP analysis is used to project revenue and costs into the future. Locate the following Web site: **[http://www.ozemail.com.au/~caveman/Creative/Bsics/Index.html]**. Click on and read: *"What can I do to increase my creativity?"*

Required

Identify and explain activities that can help build and maintain your creativity.

Teamwork in Action

LO 6

The owner of a local movie theatre presents to your class and describes the follow strategy: Ticket sales on weekends and evenings are strong. But attendance during the days, Monday–Thursday, is poor. She proposes to offer to the local grade schools a contract having educational material shown at her movie theatre for a set charge per student. The owner asks your help to prepare a CVP analysis listing the cost and revenue projections for her plan. She must tell the school's administration the charge per child. At a minimum, she needs to set the charge per child to break even.

Required

Break into teams and prepare a list of questions that must be answered by the school's administration and the owner of the movie theatre for you to complete a reliable CVP analysis.

Hitting the Road

LO 8

Multiproduct break-even point analysis is often viewed differently when actually applied in practice. You are to visit a local fast food restaurant and count the number of items on the menu. You often find as many as 75 items on a menu. To apply multiproduct break-even point analysis to a restaurant, similar menu items must be fit into groups. A reasonable approach may be to classify menu items into five categories—for example, one group can be soft drinks with an estimate of average selling price and variable cost used to calculate an average contribution margin. (Hint: The contribution margin on soft drinks is about 90%.).

Required:

1. Prepare a one-year multiproduct break-even point analysis for the restaurant visited. You must begin by establishing groups. Next, estimate the volume and contribution margin for each category. These estimates are necessary to estimate the contribution margin of all categories. Use the following value in your computations: fixed cost in total is $1,000,000 per year. (Hint: You must develop your own estimates on volume and contribution margin for each group to obtain the break-even value point and sales value.)
2. Report on the volume of sales necessary to break even at this fast food restaurant.

Business Break
LO7

We normally applaud deflation in the prices we pay for products and services. But is this good news for the business world? Read "The Zero Inflation Economy" in the January 19, 1998, issue of *Business Week,* pp. 28–31, and answer the following questions to see the impact deflation has on a business in making decisions about cost behaviour and CVP analysis.

Required

1. Define price stability.
2. List advantages of price stability in predicting revenue and cost behaviour within the relevant range.
3. Explain why the metal industry discussed in this article is negatively impacted by deflation.
4. What impact does deflation have on companies in the metal industry when preparing a CVP analysis?

26 CHAPTER

Master Budgets and Planning

A Look Back

Chapter 25 looked at cost behaviour and described its usefulness for managers in performing cost-volume-profit analysis.

A Look at This Chapter

This chapter explains the importance of budgeting and describes the master budget. It also discusses the value of the master budget to the planning of future company activities.

A Look Forward

Chapter 27 focuses on flexible budgets, standard costs, and variance reporting.

Chapter Outline

- **Importance of Budgeting**
  - Budgeting Promotes Analysis and a Focus on the Future
  - Budgeting Provides a Basis for Evaluating Performance
  - Budgeting Motivates Employees
  - Budgeting Coordinates Business Activities
  - Budgeting Communicates Plans and Instructions
- **Budget Administration**
  - Budget Committee
  - Budget Period
- **The Master Budget**
- **Preparing the Master Budget**
  - Preparing Operating Budgets
  - Preparing the General and Administrative Expense Budget
  - Preparing the Capital Expenditures Budget
  - Preparing Financial Budgets
  - Preparing the Cash Budget
- **Using the Information—Zero-Based Budgeting**

Easy Rider

Edmonton, AB—**BIKER** is one of the hottest, new manufacturers of coil springs. Its target customers are domestic and international manufacturers of sports bikes, both bicycles and motorcycles. BIKER has developed and patented a unique spring design that substantially cushions the jolts of on- and off-road biking. The growth in mountain bikes has further fuelled its double-digit sales growth over the past five years.

Candy Bergman, with brother Michael, launched the company from her parents' garage only eight short years ago. "Dad loved off-road biking, and really got us hooked," says Bergman, now 29. "But the ride was horrible, and we started tinkering with the springs. Dad was an auto mechanic and got us on the right track."

But BIKER came close to folding. "We didn't run a profit until our fourth year," complains Bergman. "Both Michael and I had other jobs, and the money demands were almost too much." It was not until BIKER's fourth year that they turned a profit. Bergman points to several problems, but one was budgeting. "We give our customers a better ride, at less cost," says Bergman. "But this demands careful budgeting and planning. And we didn't do either well."

But Bergman learned fast. "We now run budgets for everything," says Bergman. "Estimates of the demand for sports bikes, and our sales in particular, enable us to forecast sales and prepare budgets for the next three years. We know things change, but at least we know what happens when they change." While Bergman is far from a numbers person, she knows the importance of income and cash flow. She points to the sales budget as the starting point. "I don't pay employees, customers do. If we don't serve customers, none of us gets paid," adds Bergman. "What's the use of other budgets or plans if there are no sales? The sales budget is key." For now, BIKER's ride looks smooth.

Learning Objectives

LO 1 Describe the importance and benefits of budgeting.

LO 2 Explain the process of budget administration.

LO 3 Describe a master budget and the process of preparing it.

LO 4 Prepare each component of a master budget and link them to the budgeting process.

LO 5 Link both operating and capital expenditure budgets to budgeted financial statements.

LO 6 Analyze expense planning using zero-based budgeting.

CHAPTER PREVIEW

After management applies cost-volume-profit analysis in devising a strategy for the upcoming period, it then looks to turn this strategy into specific plans. These plans are usually compiled in a master budget. The budgeting process serves several purposes, including motivation and communication. The budget coordinates a company's activities toward common goals. It also serves as a standard for evaluating actual results and performance. In this chapter, we explain how to prepare a master budget and use it as a formal plan in the future activities of a company. This kind of planning was crucial to the success of **BIKER.** One's ability to prepare this kind of formal plan is of enormous help in starting and operating a company. It gives us a glimpse into the future and attempts to translate plans into actions as described by Candy Bergman in the opening article.

Importance of Budgeting

LO1 Describe the importance and benefits of budgeting.

Management often must carefully plan a company's activities for weeks, months, and even years ahead to successfully achieve its goals. Managers then monitor and control activities so that they conform to the plan. In many situations, particularly in a continuous improvement environment, management will also update the plan to reflect new information. This revised plan then serves as the basis for controlling current company activities.

Budgeting is the process of planning future business actions and expressing them as formal plans. The **budget** is a formal statement of a company's future plans expressed in quantitative terms. Because the economic or financial aspects of the business are the primary relevant factors involved in management decisions, budgets are usually expressed in monetary terms.

All managers should be involved in planning. Managers who plan carefully and formalize plans in a budgeting process can increase the likelihood of company success.

Budgeting Promotes Analysis and a Focus on the Future

When management plans the future with the care and attention to detail needed for preparing a budget, it requires thorough analysis. A good budgeting process requires careful attention to detail and thorough analysis of business operations. The budgeting process facilitates good decision making.

The relevant focus of a budgetary analysis is the future. It directs management's attention to future events and the opportunities available to the company. A focus on the future is important because the pressures of daily operating problems often divert management's attention and take precedence over planning. A good budgeting system counteracts this tendency by formalizing the planning process and demanding relevant input. Budgeting makes planning an explicit management responsibility.

Budgeting Provides a Basis for Evaluating Performance

The control function requires management to evaluate business operations against some norm. Evaluation involves comparing actual results against one of two usual alternatives: (1) past performance or (2) expected performance. An evaluation assists management in taking corrective actions if necessary.

Evaluation using expected, or budgeted, performance as a benchmark is potentially superior to past performance in deciding whether actual results trigger a need for corrective actions. This is because past performance is often inferior as a standard for evaluation as it fails to take into account several changes that may affect current activities. Changes in economic conditions, shifts in competitive advantages within the industry, new product developments, increased or decreased advertising, and other factors all reduce the usefulness of comparisons with past results. In the computing industry, for instance, increasing competition and decreasing prices often reduce the usefulness of performance comparisons across different years.

Budgeted performance levels are computed after careful analysis and research. The budgeting process requires management to anticipate and adjust for changes in company, industry, and economic conditions.

Budgeting Motivates Employees

Because budgeting provides standards for evaluating performance, it can affect the attitudes of employees who are evaluated. The budgeting process can have a positive effect on employees' attitudes, but it can also trigger negative feelings if care is not taken. Budgeted levels of performance, for instance, must be realistic to avoid discouraging employees. Also, personnel who will be evaluated should be consulted and involved in preparing the budget to increase their commitment to meeting it. The practice of involving employees in the budgeting process is known as participatory budgeting. Evaluations of performance also must allow the affected employees to explain the reasons for apparent performance deficiencies. Managerial accounting reports do not tell the whole story.

Three important guidelines in the budgeting process are:

1. Employees affected by a budget should be consulted during the budget preparation period.
2. Goals reflected in a budget should be attainable.
3. Evaluations of performance should be made carefully with opportunities to explain any failures.

Budgeting can be a positive motivating force when these guidelines are followed. Budgeted performance levels can provide goals for employees to attain or even exceed as they carry out their responsibilities.

Budgeting Coordinates Business Activities

An important management objective in larger companies is that activities of all departments contribute to meeting a company's overall goals. This requires careful coordination. Budgeting provides a way to achieve this coordination. We describe later in this chapter how a company's budget, or operating plan, is based upon its objectives. This operating plan starts with the sales budget, which drives all other budgets including production, materials, labour, and overhead. The budgeting process coordinates the activities of these various departments to meet the company's overall goals.

Budgeting Communicates Plans and Instructions

A manager can help explain business plans directly to employees. This can occur through conversations and other informal communication. But conversations can create uncertainty and confusion if not supported by clear documentation of the plans. A written budget that informs employees throughout the organization about management's plans is preferred. This budget can communicate both management's broad plans for the organization as well as specific action plans that employees should take to meet the budget's objectives.

Judgment and Ethics

Budgeting Staffer

You are working in the budget office of a company. You learn that earnings for the current quarter are going to be far below the budgeted amount announced in the press. You also learn one of the company's top officers, who is also aware of the impending news of the earnings shortfall, has decided to take an upper management position with a competitor in the same industry but in a different part of the country. Before his departure is announced to the public, he decides to sell all shares of the company that you and he are working for. His leaving will hurt your company's ability to improve earnings. Does this action bother you? Is there anything you would do?

Answer—p. 1268

Budget Administration

Budgeting is an important and detailed activity that must be properly administered. This section explains the details of budget administration.

Budget Committee

LO 2 Explain the process of budget administration.

The task of preparing a budget should not be the sole responsibility of any one department. Similarly, the budget should not be simply handed down as top management's final word. Instead, budget figures and budget estimates usually are more useful if developed through a bottom up process. This includes, for instance, involving the sales department in preparing sales estimates. Likewise, the production department should have initial responsibility for preparing its own expense budget. Without active employee involvement in preparing budget figures, there is a risk these employees will feel as if the numbers fail to reflect their special problems and needs.

Although budgets usually should be developed by this bottom up process, the budgeting system also requires central guidance to keep matters in balance. In some companies this guidance comes from the chief executive officer alone. In other companies a budget committee composed of department heads and other executives is formed to ensure that budgeted amounts are realistic before giving final approval. If a department submits initial budget figures not reflecting efficient performance, the budget committee should return them with explanatory comments on how to improve them. Then, the originating department must either adjust its proposals or explain why they are acceptable. Communication between the originating department and the budget committee should continue as needed to ensure that both parties accept the budget as reasonable, attainable, and desirable.

The budget committee is responsible for settling disputes that may occur between different units within an organization. Sometimes fear and distrust leads to internal conflict as business segments compete for limited budgeted resources. An awareness of potential turf battles among segment managers is an important step in preventing any dysfunctional behaviour that might otherwise occur.

The concept of continuous improvement applies to budgeting as well as production. **Amoco** recently streamlined its monthly budget reporting package from a one-inch-thick stack of monthly control reports to a tidy, two-page flash report on monthly earnings and key production statistics. The key to this efficiency gain was the integration of new budgeting and cost allocation processes with Amoco's strategic planning process. Amoco's controller explained the new role of the finance department with respect to the budgetary control process as follows:[1]

[1] Stephen Barr, "Grinding It Out," *CFO Magazine*, January 1995.

> There's less of an attitude that finance's job is to control. People really have come to see that our job is to help attain business objectives.

Budget Period

We explained in Chapter 21 how companies prepare long-term strategic plans spanning 5 to 10 years. These are then "fine tuned" in preparing medium-term and short-term plans. Strategic plans usually set the long-term direction of a company. They provide a road map for the future about potential opportunities such as new products, markets and investments. The strategic plan can be "rough" given its long-term focus. Medium- and short-term plans are more operational, and translate strategic plans into actions. These action plans are fairly concrete and consist of defined objectives and goals.

The short-term plans are usually called budgets and cover a one-year period. For convenience, the budget period usually coincides with the accounting period.

Exhibit 26.1

Comparing Actual Performance with Budgeted Performance

ECCENTRIC MUSIC
Income Statement with Variations from Budget
For Month Ended April 30, 1999

	Actual	Budget	Variance
Sales	$63,500	$60,000	$+3,500
Less:			
Sales returns and allowances	1,800	1,700	+100
Sales discounts	1,200	1,150	+50
Net sales	60,500	57,150	+3,350
Cost of goods sold:			
Merchandise inventory, April 1, 1999	42,000	44,000	−2,000
Purchases, net	39,100	38,000	+1,100
Transportation-in	1,250	1,200	+50
Goods available for sale	82,350	83,200	−850
Merchandise inventory, April 30, 1999	41,000	44,100	−3,100
Cost of goods sold	41,350	39,100	+2,250
Gross profit	$19,150	$18,050	$+1,100
Operating expenses:			
Selling expenses:			
Sales salaries	6,250	6,000	+250
Advertising	900	800	+100
Store supplies	550	500	+50
Amortization, store equipment	1,600	1,600	
Total selling expenses	9,300	8,900	+400
General and administrative expenses:			
Office salaries	2,000	2,000	
Office supplies used	165	150	+15
Rent	1,100	1,100	
Insurance	200	200	
Amortization, office equipment	100	100	
Total general and administrative expenses	3,565	3,550	+15
Total operating expenses	12,865	12,450	+415
Income from operations	$ 6,285	$ 5,600	$ +685

Most companies, therefore, prepare at least an annual budget. An annual budget reflects the objectives for the next year. To provide more specific guidance, the annual budget usually is separated into quarterly or monthly budgets. These short-term budgets allow management to quickly evaluate performance and take corrective action. Managers can compare actual results to budgeted amounts in a report such as that illustrated in Exhibit 26.1. This report shows actual results, budgeted results, and any differences. A difference is called a *variance*, which we discuss in detail in Chapter 27. Management examines variances to identify areas for improvement.

Many companies apply **continuous budgeting** by preparing **rolling budgets.** As each monthly or quarterly budget period goes by, these companies revise their entire set of budgets for the months or quarters remaining, and add new monthly or quarterly budgets to replace the ones that have lapsed. This means at any point in time, monthly or quarterly budgets are available for the next 12 months or four quarters.

Exhibit 26.2 shows five rolling budgets starting in December 1998. The first one covers the next four quarters through December 1999. Then, in March 1999, the company prepares another rolling budget for the next four quarters through March 2000. This same process is repeated every three months. As a result, management is continuously planning ahead. Note that a quarter's budget is drawn up four times using the most recent information available. For example, Exhibit 26.2 shows the budget for the fourth quarter of 1999 is prepared in December 1998, and revised in March, June, and September of 1999. But when continuous budgeting is not used, the fourth-quarter budget is nine months old and, perhaps, out of date when applied.

Exhibit 26.2

Rolling Budgets

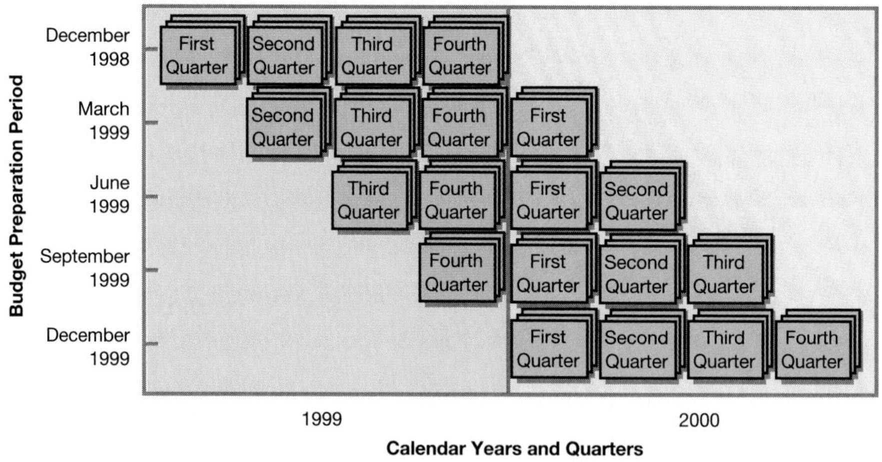

Did You Know?

Budget Calendar

Penn Fuel Gas (PFG), a public utility, initiated its first annual and long-range and operating budget process in early 1995. Three stakeholder groups influenced the creation of its budgeting system: bankers, board of directors, and management. All three were interested in cash flow projections and future earnings potential. PFG's budgeting process begins six months before the budget is due to the board of directors. The utility's budget calendar, provides information on the activities of the budget group during this period. [Source: R.N. West, and A.M. Snyder, "How to Set Up a Budgeting and Planning System," *Management Accounting*, January 1997, pp. 20–26].

Flash back

1. What are the major benefits of budgeting?
2. What is the chief responsibility of the budget committee?
3. What is the usual time period covered by a budget?
4. What are rolling budgets?

Answers—p. 1268

The Master Budget

LO 3 Describe a master budget and the process of preparing it.

A **master budget** is a formal, comprehensive plan for the future of a company. To include definite plans for all activities, a master budget contains several individual budgets. These individual budgets are linked with each other to form a coordinated plan for the company. The master budget typically includes individual budgets for sales, purchases, production, various expenses, capital expenditures, and cash. Managers often express the expected financial results of these planned activities with both a budgeted income statement for the budget period and a budgeted balance sheet at the end of the budget period.

The usual number and types of budgets included in a master budget depend on the size and complexity of the company. A master budget should include, at a minimum, the budgets listed in Exhibit 26.3.

Exhibit 26.3

Components of the Master Budget

1. **Operating budgets.**
   a. *Sales budget.*
   b. For merchandisers: *Merchandise purchases budget* (specifying units to be purchased).
      For manufacturers:
         (i) *Production budget* (specifying units to be produced).
         (ii) *Manufacturing budget* (specifying planned manufacturing costs).
   c. *Selling expense budget.*
   d. *General and administrative expense budget.*
2. **Capital expenditures budget (specifying budgeted expenditures for plant and equipment).**
3. **Financial budgets.**
   a. *Cash budget* (specifying budgeted cash receipts and disbursements).
   b. *Budgeted income statement.*
   c. *Budgeted balance sheet.*

In addition to these individual budgets, managers often include supporting calculations and schedules along with the master budget.

Management cannot prepare certain budgets until other budgets are complete. For example, the merchandise purchases budget cannot be prepared until the sales budget is because the number of units to be purchased depends on how many units are expected to be sold. As a result, we must prepare budgets within the master budget in a sequence. A typical sequence is that followed by **HON Company**, a furniture manufacturer, in its quarterly budgeting process.[2] Its quarterly budget consists of five steps as shown in Exhibit 26.4 and is completed over a six-week period.

At any stage in this budgeting process, undesirable outcomes might be revealed. This means that changes must be made to prior budgets and the previous steps repeated. For instance, an early version of the cash budget might

[2] R. Drtina, S. Hoeger and J. Schaub, "Continuous Budgeting at the HON Company," *Management Accounting*, January 1996, pp. 20–24.

Exhibit 26.4

Master Budget Sequence

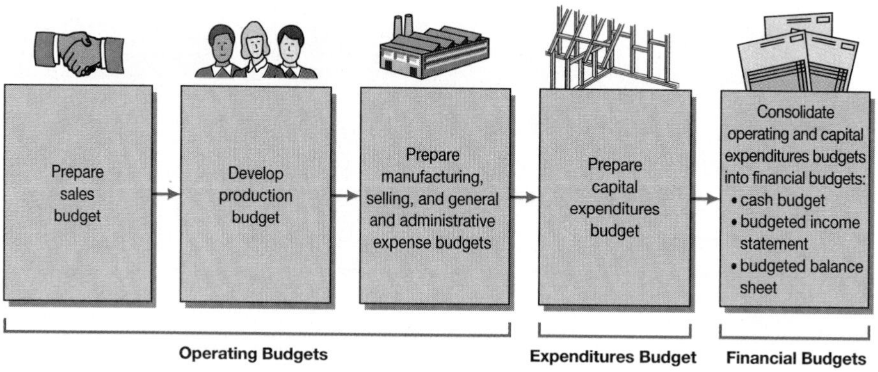

show an insufficient amount of cash unless cash outlays are reduced. This might yield a reduction in planned equipment purchases. Or, a preliminary budgeted balance sheet may reveal too much debt from an ambitious expenditures budget. These findings often result in revised plans.

Did You Know?

Budgeting and Acquisition

Budgeting is a crucial part of management's analysis at Koch Industries for potential acquisitions. Analysis begins by projecting annual sales volume, prices, and total revenues. They then estimate cost of sales for each revenue item along with selling, general, and administrative expenses. These are combined to form projected net income of the potential acquisition for the next several years. They also predict expenditures and other costs. By comparing the budgeted cost of a potential acquisition with its expected future income, they decide the price to offer for the potential acquisition.

Flash back

5. What is a master budget?
6. A master budget:
   a. Always includes a manufacturing budget specifying the number of units to be produced.
   b. Is prepared with a process starting with the operating budgets and continues with the capital expenditures budget, the cash budget, and the budgeted financial statements.
   c. Is prepared with a process ending with the budgeted income statement.
7. What are the three primary categories of budgets in the master budget?

Answers—p. 1268

Preparing the Master Budget

LO 4 Prepare each component of a master budget and link them to the budgeting process.

This section explains how the master budget for Hockey Den (HD), a retailer of children's hockey sticks, is prepared. The company's master budget includes operating, capital expenditure, and cash budgets for each month in a quarter. It also includes a budgeted income statement for each quarter and a budgeted balance sheet as of the last day of each quarter. On the following pages, HD's budgets are shown for October, November, and December 1999. Exhibit 26.5 presents the beginning balance sheet for this budgeting period.

Exhibit 26.5

Balance Sheet Prior to Future Budgeted Periods

HOCKEY DEN Balance Sheet September 30, 1999		
Assets		
Cash		$ 20,000
Accounts receivable		42,000
Inventory (9,000 units @ $6)		54,000
Equipment*	$200,000	
Less accumulated amortization	(36,000)	164,000
Total assets		$280,000
Liabilities and Shareholders' Equity		
Liabilities:		
Accounts payable	$ 58,200	
Income taxes payable (due October 31, 1999)	20,000	
Note payable to bank	10,000	$ 88,200
Shareholders' equity:		
Common shares	150,000	
Retained earnings	41,800	191,800
Total liabilities and shareholders' equity		$280,000

*Equipment is amortized on a straight-line basis over 10 years where salvage value is $20,000.

Preparing Operating Budgets

This section explains the preparation of operating budgets for Hockey Den. Operating budgets consist of the sales budget, merchandise purchases budget, selling expense budget, and general and administrative expense budget. The preparation of a production budget and related manufacturing budgets are also described, although Hockey Den does not prepare these budgets because it is a merchandiser.

Preparing the Sales Budget

The first step in preparing the master budget is planning the **sales budget.** This budget shows the planned sales units and the revenue derived from these sales. The sales budget is the starting point in the budgeting process because plans for most departments are linked to sales. The sales budget should emerge from a careful analysis of forecasted economic and market conditions, plant capacity, proposed selling expenses (such as advertising), and predictions of unit sales. Because people normally feel a greater commitment to goals they have had a hand in setting, the sales personnel of a company are usually asked to develop predictions of sales for each territory and department. Another advantage of using this participatory budgeting approach is it draws on knowledge and experience of people involved in the activity.

In September 1999, **Hockey Den** sold 7,000 hockey sticks at $10 per unit. After considering sales predictions and market conditions, Hockey Den's sales budget is prepared for the next quarter plus one extra month, see Exhibit 26.6. The sales budget includes January 2000 because the purchasing department relies on estimated January sales in deciding on December 1999 purchases.

The sales budget in Exhibit 26.6 includes forecasts of both unit sales and unit prices. While some companies prepare a sales budget expressed only in total sales dollars, most sales budgets are more detailed. This is because they must show units and unit prices for many different products, regions, departments, and sales representatives.

Exhibit 26.6

Sales Budget Showing Planned Unit Sales and Dollar Sales

HOCKEY DEN Monthly Sales Budget October 1999–January 2000	Budgeted Unit Sales	Budgeted Unit Price	Budgeted Total Sales
September 1999 (actual)	7,000	$10	$ 70,000
October 1999	10,000	$10	$100,000
November 1999	8,000	10	80,000
December 1999	14,000	10	140,000
Total for the quarter	32,000	$10	$320,000
January 2000	9,000	$10	$ 90,000

This chapter's opening article described budgets and planning at **BIKER**. In prior years, BIKER had classified its sales budget by the type of coil (steel versus titanium). This past year it expanded the classifications by type of bike. It used the planning process to identify industries other than sports bikes that can benefit from the high tensile strength and lightweight properties of titanium coil springs. It identified and successfully marketed a new coil spring to NASCAR racing vehicles. Both strength and weight are crucial in this sport, and important enough to justify the added expense of titanium coil springs. By using the budgeting and planning process, BIKER successfully increased its sales. Projections for the next two years have titanium coil spring sales increasing 30% to 50%. The majority of this growth is from NASCAR parts.

You Make the Call

Sales Manager

You are a sales manager for a designer clothes manufacturer. Business is highly seasonal and you find that fashions and designs are continuously changing. How do you prepare annual sales budgets?

Answer—p. 1267

Preparing the Merchandise Purchases Budget

Various methods are used to help managers make inventory purchasing decisions. These methods all recognize that the number of units added to inventory depends on budgeted sales volume. Whether a company manufactures or purchases the product it sells, budgeted future sales volume is the primary factor in most inventory management decisions.

Just-in-Time Inventory Systems

Managers of *just-in-time* (JIT) inventory systems use sales budgets for covering short periods (often as few as one or two days) to order just enough merchandise or materials to satisfy the immediate sales demand. As a result, the level of inventory on hand is held to a minimum (or zero in an ideal situation). A just-in-time system minimizes the costs of maintaining inventory. But just-in-time systems are practical only if customers are content to order in advance or if managers can accurately determine short-term sales demand. Also, suppliers must be able and willing to ship small quantities regularly and promptly.

Safety Stock Inventory Systems

Market conditions and manufacturing processes for many products do not allow a just-in-time system to be used. Instead, many companies keep enough inventory on hand to reduce the risk of running short. This practice requires enough purchases to satisfy the budgeted sales amounts and to maintain an additional quantity of inventory as a **safety stock.** The safety stock provides protection against lost sales caused by unfulfilled demands from customers or delays in shipments from suppliers.

Merchandise Purchases Budget

Companies usually express a **merchandise purchases budget** in both units and dollars. Exhibit 26.7 shows the general layout for computing a purchases budget.

Exhibit 26.7

Layout for a Merchandise Purchases Budget

	Units
Budgeted ending inventory	720
Add budgeted sales	1,000
Required units of available merchandise	1,720
Deduct beginning inventory	(900)
Inventory to be purchased	820

We can express this layout in equation form as shown in Exhibit 26.8.

Exhibit 26.8

Formula for a Merchandise Purchases Budget

Inventory to be purchased = Budgeted ending inventory + Budgeted sales for the period − Budgeted beginning inventory

If this formula is expressed in units and only one product is involved, we can compute the number of dollars of inventory to be purchased for our budget by multiplying the units to be purchased by the cost per unit.

After Hockey Den assessed the cost of keeping inventory along with the risk of a temporary inventory shortage, it decided the number of units in its inventory at the end of each month should equal 90% of next month's predicted sales. For example, inventory at the end of October should equal 90% of budgeted November sales, and the November ending inventory should equal 90% of budgeted December sales, and so on.

Hockey Den's suppliers expect the September 1999 per unit cost of $6 to remain unchanged through January 2000. This information along with knowing 9,000 units are on hand at September 30 (see Exhibit 26.5), allows the company to prepare the merchandise purchases budget shown in Exhibit 26.9.

Exhibit 26.9

Merchandise Purchases Budget

HOCKEY DEN
Merchandise Purchases Budget
October, November, and December 1999

	October	November	December
Next month's budgeted sales (units)	8,000	14,000	9,000
Ratio of inventory to future sales	× 90%	× 90%	× 90%
Budgeted ending inventory (units)	7,200	12,600	8,100
Add budgeted sales for the month (units)	10,000	8,000	14,000
Required units of available merchandise	17,200	20,600	22,100
Deduct beginning inventory (units)	(9,000)	(7,200)	(12,600)
Number of units to be purchased	8,200	13,400	9,500
Budgeted cost per unit	$ 6	$ 6	$ 6
Budgeted cost of merchandise purchases	$49,200	$80,400	$57,000

The first three lines of Hockey Den's merchandise purchases budget determine the required ending inventories. Budgeted unit sales are then added to the desired ending inventory to give us the required units of available merchandise. We then subtract beginning inventory to determine the budgeted number of units to be purchased. The last line is the budgeted cost of the purchases, computed by multiplying the units to be purchased by the predicted cost per unit.

We already indicated that some budgeting systems describe only the total dollars of budgeted sales. Likewise, a system can express a merchandise purchases budget only in terms of the total cost of merchandise to be purchased, omitting the number of units to be purchased. This method assumes a constant relation between sales and cost of goods sold. Hockey Den, for instance, might assume the expected cost of goods sold to be 60% of sales, computed from the budgeted unit cost of $6 and the budgeted sales price of $10. Here its cost of goods sold can be budgeted in dollars on the basis of budgeted sales without requiring information on the number of units involved. But it is still necessary to consider the effects of beginning and ending inventories in determining the amounts to be purchased.

Preparing the Production and Manufacturing Budgets

Because Hockey Den does not manufacture its product, its budget for acquiring goods to be sold is a *merchandise purchases budget*, as explained in the prior section. But a manufacturer must prepare a **production budget** instead of a merchandise purchases budget. A production budget shows the number of units to be produced each month. Production budgets are similar to merchandise purchases budgets except the number of units to be purchased each month (as shown in Exhibit 26.9) is replaced by the number of units to be manufactured each month. A production budget does not show costs because it is *always expressed in units of product*. Exhibit 26.10 shows the production budget for **H-Puck**, a manufacturer of hockey pucks.

Exhibit 26.10

Production Budget

H-PUCK
Production Budget
October, November, and December 1999

	October	November	December
Next month's budgeted sales (units)	8,000	14,000	9,000
Ratio of inventory to future sales	× 90%	× 90%	× 90%
Budgeted ending inventory (units)	7,200	12,600	8,100
Add budgeted sales for the month (units) . . .	10,000	8,000	14,000
Required units of available production	17,200	20,600	22,100
Deduct beginning inventory (units)	(9,000)	(7,200)	(12,600)
Number of units to be produced	8,200	13,400	9,500

A **manufacturing budget** shows the budgeted costs for raw materials, direct labour, and manufacturing overhead. It is based on the budgeted production volume from the production budget. The manufacturing budget for most companies consists of three individual budgets: direct materials budget, direct labour budget, and overhead budget. Exhibits 26.11–26.13 show these three manufacturing budgets for H-Puck. These budgets show the total cost of goods to be manufactured in the budget period.

The *direct materials budget* starts with computing the budgeted materials needed to satisfy each month's production requirement. We must also add the desired ending inventory requirements. The desired ending inventory of direct materials as shown in Exhibit 26.11 is 50% of next month's budgeted material requirements of vulcanized rubber. For instance, in the month of October 1999, an ending inventory of 3,350 lbs. of material is desired (50% of 6,700 lbs.). The desired ending inventory for December 1999 is 2,250 lbs., computed from the direct material requirement of 4,500 lbs. for a production level of 9,000 units in January 2000.

Exhibit 26.11

Direct Materials Budget

H-PUCK
Direct Materials Budget
October, November, and December 1999

	October	November	December
Budgeted production (units)	8,200	13,400	9,500
Material requirements per unit (lbs.)	× 0.5	× 0.5	× 0.5
Materials needed for production (lbs.)	4,100	6,700	4,750
Add desired ending inventory (lbs.)	3,350	2,375	2,250
Total materials requirements (lbs.)	7,450	9,075	7,000
Deduct beginning inventory (lbs.)	(2,050)	(3,350)	(2,375)
Pounds of materials to be purchased	5,400	5,725	4,625
Material price per pound	$ 6	$ 6	$ 6
Total cost of direct materials purchases	$32,400	$34,350	$27,750

The total material requirements are computed by adding the desired ending inventory figures to that month's budgeted production material requirements. For October 1999, the total material requirement is 7,450 lbs., computed from 3,350 + 4,100. From the total material requirement we then subtract the pounds of materials available in beginning inventory. For October 1999, the materials available from September 1999 are computed as 50% of October's material requirements to satisfy production, or 2,050 lbs. (50% of 4,100). This means the direct materials to be purchased in October 1999 are budgeted at 5,400 lbs., computed from 7,450 – 2,050 (see Exhibit 26.11).

The *direct labour budget* for H-Puck is shown in Exhibit 26.12. About 15 minutes of labour time is required to produce one unit for H-Puck. Labour is paid at the rate of $12 per hour. Budgeted labour hours is computed by multiplying the budgeted production level for each month by one-quarter (or 0.25) of an hour. Direct labour cost is then computed by multiplying budgeted labour hours by the labour rate of $12 per hour.

Exhibit 26.12

Direct Labour Budget

H-PUCK
Direct Labour Budget
October, November, and December 1999

	October	November	December
Budgeted production (units)	8,200	13,400	9,500
Labour requirements per unit (hours)	× 0.25	× 0.25	× 0.25
Total labour hours needed	2,050	3,350	2,375
Labour rate (per hour)	$ 12	$ 12	$ 12
Labour dollars	$24,600	$40,200	$28,500

The *manufacturing overhead budget* for H-Puck is shown in Exhibit 26.13. The variable portion of overhead is assigned at the rate of $2.50 per unit of production for H-Puck. The fixed portion stays constant at $15,000 per month for H-Puck. The condensed manufacturing overhead budget is shown here. Most overhead budgets are more detailed, listing each overhead cost item.

Exhibit 26.13
Manufacturing Overhead Budget

H-PUCK Manufacturing Overhead Budget October, November, and December 1999	October	November	December
Budgeted production (units)	8,200	13,400	9,500
Variable manufacturing overhead rate	× $2.50	× $2.50	× $2.50
Budgeted variable overhead	$20,500	$33,500	$23,750
Budgeted fixed overhead	$15,000	$15,000	$15,000
Budgeted total overhead	$35,500	$48,500	$38,750

Did You Know?

Activity/Process-Based Budgeting

Paul Sharman, president of **Focused Management Information**, says companies that use activity-based costing and analysis of processes should consider activity/process-based budgeting. He says activity-based costing information is useful for strategic goal setting, and process analysis is useful for process goal setting. This is followed by activity analysis and the preparation of budgets for each major process. Sharman claims activity/process-based budgeting "offers a most powerful device [available] to ... organizations in driving change and human behaviour." [Source: Sharman, P., "Activity/Process Budgets: A Tool for Change Management," *CMA Magazine*, March 1996, pp. 21-24.]

Mid-Chapter Demonstration Problem

A sales budget for the first six months of 1999 is given below for Clarke Manufacturing Ltd.

Month	Budgeted Sales (units)
January	7,000
February	10,000
March	16,000
April	9,000
May	7,000
June	7,500

The finished goods inventory on hand at the end of each month are engineered to equal 30% of the budgeted sales for the subsequent month. Each unit of product requires six metres of material A at $5 per metre. In an effort to minimize cost, Clarke Company's policy is to carry inventory not in excess of 10% of the next month's production needs. Assume goods in process are not material in amount. On January 1, there were 2,000 units of product on hand.

Required

Prepare a budget showing the quantity of material A to be purchased for each month in the first quarter.

Planning the Solution

- First prepare a materials purchases budget. Start with the budgeted sales for January and add the desired ending inventory. The desired ending inventory is determined by multiplying February budgeted sales by 30%. Deduct the number of units in the beginning inventory (2,000) to arrive at the units to be produced.
- Repeat this same sequence for February, March, and April.
- Prepare a purchases budget by taking the units to be produced in January and multiplying this number by six metres to arrive at the total production needs for the month. Add the desired ending inventory in metres needed to arrive at the required metres to be purchased in January. Repeat this sequence for February and March.
- Add the rows together to arrive at the figures for the quarter.

Solution to Mid-Chapter Demonstration Problem

Production Budget

	January	February	March	April	May
Budgeted Sales	7,000	10,000	16,000	9,000	7,000
Add: Desired ending inventory	3,000	4,800	2,700	2,100	
Total needs	10,000	14,800	18,700	11,100	
Less: Beginning inventory	2,000	3,000	4,800	2,700	
Units to be produced	8,000	11,800	13,900	8,400	

Purchases Budget

	January	February	March	Quarter
Units to be produced	8,000	11,800	13,900	33,700
Material A needed per unit (m)	6	6	6	6
Production needs in metres	48,000	70,800	83,400	202,200
Add: Desired ending inventory	7,080	8,340	5,040*	5,040
Total metres needed	55,080	79,140	88,440	207,240
Less: Beginning inventory	4,800	7,080	8,340	4,800
Required metres to be purchased	50,280	72,060	80,100	202,440
Material price per metre ($5)	5	5	5	5
Total cost of material purchased	$251,400	$360,300	$400,500	$1,012,200

*(8,400 × 6 = 50,400 × .10)

Preparing the Selling Expense Budget

The **selling expense budget** is a plan listing the types and amounts of selling expenses expected during the budget period. Its initial responsibility usually rests with the vice president of marketing or an equivalent sales manager. The selling expense budget is normally created to provide sufficient selling expenses to meet sales goals reflected in the sales budget. Predictions of selling expenses are based on both the sales budget and on the experience of previous periods. After some or all of the master budget is prepared, management may decide that projected sales volume is inadequate. If so, subsequent adjustments in the sales budget may require corresponding adjustments in the selling expense budget.

Hockey Den's selling expense budget is shown in Exhibit 26.14. Hockey Den's selling expenses consist of commissions paid to sales personnel and a $2,000 monthly salary paid to the sales manager. Sales commissions equal 10% of total sales and are paid in the month sales occur. Sales commissions are variable with respect to sales volume whereas the sales manager's salary is fixed. No advertising expenses are budgeted for this particular quarter.

Exhibit 26.14

Selling Expense Budget

HOCKEY DEN Selling Expense Budget October, November, and December 1999	October	November	December	Total
Budgeted sales	$100,000	$80,000	$140,000	$320,000
Sales commission percentage	× 10%	× 10%	× 10%	× 10%
Sales commissions	10,000	8,000	14,000	32,000
Salary for sales manager . . .	2,000	2,000	2,000	6,000
Total selling expenses	$ 12,000	$10,000	$ 16,000	$ 38,000

Preparing the General and Administrative Expense Budget

The **general and administrative expense budget** is a plan showing the predicted operating expenses not included in the selling expenses budget. The general and administrative expenses may consist of items that are variable or fixed with respect to sales volume. The office manager, or the person responsible for general administration, usually has the responsibility for preparing the initial general and administrative expense budget.

While interest expense and income tax expense are often classified as general and administrative expenses in published income statements, they normally cannot be planned for at this stage of the budgeting process. The prediction of interest expense follows the preparation of the cash budget and the decisions regarding debt. The predicted income tax expense depends on the budgeted amount of pretax income. Also, both interest and income taxes are usually beyond the control of the office manager. As a result, they should not be used in evaluating that person's performance in comparison to the budget.

Exhibit 26.15 shows the general and administrative expense budget for Hockey Den. General and administrative expenses include salaries of $54,000 per year, or $4,500 per month. Salaries are paid each month when they are earned. Using the information in Exhibit 26.5, the amortization on equipment is $18,000 per year [($200,000 – $20,000)/10 years], or $1,500 per month ($18,000/12 months).

Exhibit 26.15

General and Administrative Expense Budget

HOCKEY DEN General and Administrative Expense Budget October, November, and December 1999	October	November	December	Total
Administrative salaries	$4,500	$4,500	$4,500	$13,500
Amortization of equipment . .	1,500	1,500	1,500	4,500
Total general and administrative expenses . .	$6,000	$6,000	$6,000	$18,000

Flash back

8. In preparing monthly budgets for the third quarter, a company budgeted 120 unit sales for July and 140 unit sales for August. The June 30 finished goods inventory consists of 50 units and management wants each month's ending inventory to be 60% of next month's sales. How many units of product should the production budget for the third quarter specify for July production? (a) 84, (b) 120, (c) 154, or (d) 204.
9. What is the difference between operating budgets for merchandising and manufacturing companies?
10. How does a just-in-time inventory system differ from a safety stock system?

Answers—p. 1268

Preparing the Capital Expenditures Budget

The **capital expenditures budget** lists dollar amounts to be received from disposing of equipment and to be spent on purchasing additional equipment if the proposed production program is carried out. It is usually prepared after the operating budgets. Because production capacity is limited by the company's plant and equipment, this budget is usually affected by long-range plans for the business instead of short-term sales budgets for the next year or quarter. But still the process of preparing a sales or manufacturing budget can reveal that the company needs more capacity and additional equipment is necessary.

Capital budgeting is the process of evaluating and planning for capital (plant and equipment) expenditures. Planning for capital expenditures is an important task of management because these expenditures often involve long-run commitments of large amounts. Also, capital expenditures often have a major effect on predicted cash flows and the company's need for debt or equity financing. This means the capital expenditures budget is often linked with management's evaluation of the company's ability to take on more debt. We discuss capital budgeting in detail in Chapter 28.

In the case of Hockey Den, it does not anticipate any disposals of equipment through December 1999. But it does plan to acquire additional equipment for $25,000 cash near the end of December 1999. Since this is the only budgeted capital expenditure from October 1999 through January 2000, no separate budget is shown. The cash budget in Exhibit 26.16 (see page 1262) reflects this $25,000 planned expenditure.

Preparing Financial Budgets

After preparing the operating and capital expenditures budgets, a company uses information from these budgets to prepare three financial budgets: cash budget, budgeted income statement, and budgeted balance sheet. It is important to note that information from the production and manufacturing budgets (Exhibits 26.10 through 26.13) is not used in preparing financial budgets for Hockey Den. Again, this is because Hockey Den is a merchandiser.

LO 5 Link both operating and capital expenditure budgets to budgeted financial statements.

Preparing the Cash Budget

After developing budgets for sales, merchandise purchases, expenses, and capital expenditures, the next step is preparing the cash budget. The **cash budget** shows expected cash inflows and outflows during the budget period. It is especially helpful in maintaining a cash balance necessary to meet a company's obligations. By preparing a cash budget, management can prearrange loans to cover any anticipated cash shortages before they are needed. A cash budget also helps management avoid a cash balance that is too large. Too much cash is undesirable because it earns a relatively low rate of return.

Managing Cash

Harley's net cash flows from investing activities were negative and averaged $150 million per year from 1994–1996. This was due mainly to increases in capital expenditures. Harley said it "is pursuing a long-term manufacturing strategy to increase its motorcycle production capacity." During this time period, Harley's cash balance fell by more than 50%. [Source: *1996 Annual Report*, Harley-Davidson.]

Did You Know?

Similarly, Candy Bergman of BIKER was very interested in cash flow projections. BIKER attained its success with the titanium coil springs because of innovative technology and development of superior computer-based spring designs. To continue its success it must have sufficient cash resources to plan and fund research and development in both manufacturing technology and engineering design.

When we prepare a cash budget, we add expected receipts to the beginning cash balance and then deduct expected expenditures. If the expected final cash balance is inadequate, any additional cash requirements appear in the budget as planned increases from short-term loans. If the expected final cash balance exceeds the desired balance, the excess is used to repay loans or in acquiring short-term investments. The information for preparing the cash budget is primarily taken from the operating and capital expenditures budgets. But further data and calculations are sometimes necessary to compute the final amounts.

Exhibit 26.16 presents the cash budget for Hockey Den. The beginning cash balance for October is taken from the September 30, 1999, balance sheet in Exhibit 26.5.

Exhibit 26.16

Cash Budget

HOCKEY DEN
Cash Budget
October, November, and December 1999

	October	November	December
Beginning cash balance	$20,000	$ 20,000	$ 22,272
Cash receipts from customers (Exhibit 26.17)	82,000	92,000	104,000
Total cash available	102,000	112,000	126,272
Cash disbursements			
Payments for merchandise (Exhibit 26.18)	58,200	49,200	80,400
Sales commissions (Exhibit 26.14)	10,000	8,000	14,000
Salaries:			
Sales (Exhibit 26.14)	2,000	2,000	2,000
Administrative (Exhibit 26.15)	4,500	4,500	4,500
Accrued income taxes payable (Exhibit 26.5)	20,000		
Dividends ($150,000 x 2%)		3,000	
Interest on bank loan:			
October ($10,000 x 1%)	100		
November ($22,800 x 1%)		228	
Purchase of equipment			25,000
Total cash disbursements	94,800	66,928	125,900
Preliminary balance	7,200	45,072	372
Additional loan from bank	12,800		19,628
Repayment of loan from bank		(22,800)	
Ending cash balance	$20,000	$ 22,272	$ 20,000
Loan balance, end of month	$22,800	$ -0-	$ 19,628

The budgeted sales of Hockey Den are shown in Exhibit 26.6. An analysis of past sales records indicates 40% of Hockey Den's sales are for cash. The remaining 60% are credit sales and these customers can be expected to pay in full during the month following sales. We can compute the budgeted cash receipts from customers as shown in Exhibit 26.17.

	September	October	November	December
Sales	$70,000	$100,000	$80,000	$140,000
Ending accounts receivable (60%)	$42,000	$ 60,000	$48,000	$ 84,000
Cash receipts from:				
Cash sales (40%)		$ 40,000	$32,000	$ 56,000
Collections of prior month's receivables		42,000	60,000	48,000
Total cash receipts		$ 82,000	$92,000	$104,000

Exhibit 26.17

Computing Budgeted Cash Receipts

Exhibit 26.17 shows October's budgeted cash receipts consist of $40,000 from expected cash sales ($100,000 × 40%) plus the anticipated collection of $42,000 of accounts receivable from the end of September. Each month's cash receipts from customers are listed on the second line of Exhibit 26.16.

Hockey Den's purchases of merchandise are entirely on account. Full payments are made during the month following these purchases. This means the cash disbursements for purchases are computed from the September 30, 1999, balance sheet (Exhibit 26.5) and from the merchandise purchases budget (Exhibit 26.9). This computation is shown in Exhibit 26.18.

October payments (September 30 balance)	$58,200
November payments (October purchases)	49,200
December payments (November purchases)	80,400

Exhibit 26.18

Computing Cash Disbursements for Purchases

Because sales commissions and all salaries are paid monthly, the budgeted cash disbursements for these expenses come from the selling expense budget (Exhibit 26.14) and the general and administrative expense budget (Exhibit 26.15). The cash budget is unaffected by amortization expense in the general and administrative expenses budget.

As shown in the September 30, 1999, balance sheet (Exhibit 26.5), accrued income taxes are due and payable in October. The cash budget in Exhibit 26.16 shows this $20,000 expected expenditure in October. Predicted income tax expense for the quarter ending December 31 is 40% of net income and is due in January 2000. It is therefore not reported in the October–December 1999 budget. But it does appear in the budgeted income statement as income tax expense and on the budgeted balance sheet as income tax liability. Hockey Den also pays a cash dividend equal to 2% of the dollar value of common shares in the second month of each quarter. The cash budget in Exhibit 26.16 shows a November payment of $3,000 for this purpose.

Hockey Den has an agreement with its bank that promises additional loans at the end of each month if necessary to keep a minimum cash balance of $20,000. Interest is paid at the end of each month at the rate of 1% of the beginning balance of these loans. Also, if the cash balance exceeds $20,000 at the end of a month, the company uses the excess to repay loans. The interest payments in Exhibit 26.16 equal 1% of the prior month's ending loan balance. For October, this expenditure is 1% of the $10,000 amount reported in the balance sheet of Exhibit 26.5. For November, the company expects to pay interest of $228, computed as 1% of the $22,800 expected loan balance at October 31. No interest is budgeted for December because the company expects to repay the loans in full at the end of November.

Exhibit 26.16 shows the October 31 amount (before any loan-related activity) falls to $7,200. This amount is less than the $20,000 minimum. Hockey Den expects to bring this balance up to the minimum by borrowing $12,800 with a short-term note. At the end of November, the budget shows an expected cash balance of $45,072 before any loan activity. This means the company expects to repay the $22,800 debt. The equipment purchase budgeted for December reduces the expected cash balance to $372, far below the $20,000 minimum. This means the company expects to borrow $19,628 in that month to get back up to the minimum ending balance.

Preparing a Budgeted Income Statement

One of the final steps in preparing the master budget is summarizing the income effects of the plans. The **budgeted income statement** is a managerial accounting report showing predicted amounts revenues and expenses for the budget period. Information needed for preparing a budgeted income statement comes primarily from already prepared budgets.

The volume of information summarized in the budgeted income statement is so large for some companies that spreadsheets are often used to accumulate the budgeted transactions and classify them by their effects on income. We condense the budgeted income statement for Hockey Den and show it in Exhibit 26.19. All information in this exhibit is taken from earlier budgets. It is now possible to predict the amount of income tax expense for the quarter, computed as 40% of the budgeted pre-tax net income. This amount is included in the cash budget and/or the budgeted balance sheet as necessary.

Exhibit 26.19

Budgeted Income Statement

HOCKEY DEN
Budgeted Income Statement
For Three Months Ended December 31, 1999

Sales (Exhibit 26.6, 32,000 units @ $10)		$320,000
Cost of goods sold (32,000 units @ $6)		192,000
Gross profit		128,000
Operating expenses:		
Sales commissions (Exhibit 26.14)	$32,000	
Sales salaries (Exhibit 26.14)	6,000	
Administrative salaries (Exhibit 26.15)	13,500	
Amortization on equipment (Exhibit 26.15)	4,500	
Interest expense (Exhibit 26.16)	328	(56,328)
Net income before income taxes		71,672
Income tax expense ($71,672 x 40%)		(28,669)
Net income		$ 43,003

Did You Know?

With Eyes Open

Most companies allocate dollars based on budgets submitted by department managers. These managers need to be sure the numbers are correct, and they then monitor the budget during the year for discrepancies. But managers must remember that a budget is judged by its success in helping achieve the organization's mission. One analogy is airplane piloting. A pilot must know the destination to properly plan a flight. So too must a department manager know the desired destination to properly plan a budget. [Source: S. M. Rehnberg, "Keep Your Head Out of the Cockpit," *Management Accounting*, July 1995.]

Preparing a Budgeted Balance Sheet

The final step in preparing the master budget is summarizing the company's financial position. The **budgeted balance sheet** shows predicted amounts for the company's assets, liabilities, and shareholders' equity as of the end of the budget period. The budgeted balance sheet of Hockey Den is prepared using information from the other budgets. The sources of amounts shown in its budgeted balance sheet are listed in Exhibit 26.20.

Exhibit 26.20

Sources of Amounts in Budgeted Balance Sheet

Item	Amount	Explanation
Cash	$ 20,000	Ending balance for December from the cash budget in Exhibit 26.16.
Accounts receivable	$ 84,000	60% of $140,000 sales budgeted for December from the sales budget in Exhibit 26.6.
Inventory	$ 48,600	8,100 units in budgeted December ending inventory at the budgeted cost of $6 per unit (from the purchases budget in Exhibit 26.9).
Equipment	$225,000	September 30 balance of $200,000 from the beginning balance sheet in Exhibit 26.5 plus $25,000 cost of new equipment from the cash budget in Exhibit 26.16.
Accumulated amortization	$ 40,500	September 30 balance of $36,000 from the beginning balance sheet in Exhibit 26.5 plus $4,500 expense from the general and administrative expense budget in Exhibit 26.15.
Accounts payable	$ 57,000	Budgeted cost of merchandise purchases for December from the purchases budget in Exhibit 26.9.
Income taxes payable	$ 28,669	Budgeted income tax expense from the budgeted income statement for the fourth quarter in Exhibit 26.19.
Bank loan payable	$ 19,628	Budgeted December 31 balance from the cash budget in Exhibit 26.16.
Common shares	$150,000	Unchanged from the beginning balance sheet in Exhibit 26.5.
Retained earnings	$ 81,803	September 30 balance of $41,800 from the beginning balance sheet in Exhibit 26.5 plus budgeted net income of $43,003 from the budgeted income statement in Exhibit 26.19 minus budgeted cash dividends of $3,000 from the cash budget in Exhibit 26.16.

An eight-column spreadsheet, also called *work sheet*, can be used to prepare the budgeted balance sheet (and income statement). The first two columns would show the post-closing trial balance as of the last day of the period prior to the budget period. The budgeted transactions and adjustments are entered in the third and fourth columns in the same manner as end-of-period adjustments are entered on an ordinary work sheet. For example, if the budget calls for credit sales of $250,000, the Sales account title is entered on the work sheet in the Account Title column. The Sales account is then credited and Accounts Receivable debited for $250,000 in the third and fourth columns. After all budgeted transactions and adjustments are entered, the post-closing trial balance amounts in the first two columns are combined with the budget amounts in the third and fourth columns and sorted to the proper Income Statement and Balance Sheet columns. Balances in these columns are used to prepare the budgeted income statement and balance sheet.

Exhibit 26.21

Budgeted Balance Sheet

HOCKEY DEN Budgeted Balance Sheet December 31, 1999		
Assets		
Cash		$ 20,000
Accounts receivable		84,000
Inventory (8,100 units @ $6)		48,600
Equipment	$225,000	
Less accumulated amortization	(40,500)	184,500
Total assets		$337,100
Liabilities and Shareholders' Equity		
Liabilities:		
Accounts payable	$ 57,000	
Income taxes payable	28,669	
Bank loan payable	19,628	$105,297
Shareholders' equity:		
Common shares	150,000	
Retained earnings	81,803	231,803
Total liabilities and equity		$337,100

Flash back

11. In preparing a budgeted balance sheet:
  a. Plant and equipment is determined by analyzing the capital expenditures budget and the balance sheet from the beginning of the budget period.
  b. Liabilities are determined by analyzing the general and administrative expense budget.
  c. Retained earnings are determined from information contained in the cash budget and the balance sheet from the beginning of the budget period.

12. What sequence is followed in preparing the budgets comprising the master budget?

Answers—p. 1268

Zero-Based Budgeting

USING THE INFORMATION

LO 6 Analyze expense planning using zero-based budgeting.

This chapter focused on the preparation of budgets within an organization. In most cases, annual budgets are based on figures from the previous year, and adjusted for changes in operating conditions. But in some cases companies encounter totally new circumstances. Consider, for example, the marketing department of a company that plans to promote its products for the very first time at a trade show. How does it prepare a budget for the trade show? Zero-based budgeting is one solution to this problem.

Companies using zero-based budgeting start each budgeting period at "ground zero." They assume no previous history for the set of activities being planned. Instead, they prepare a detailed list of activities to be carried out, the resources required to carry out these activities, and the expenses of acquiring these resources. This type of expense planning requires managers to justify the amounts budgeted.

Environmental Manager

You are the new manager responsible for environmental matters of a chemical company. This is a new position within the company. You are asked to develop a budget for your function. How do you proceed?

You Make the Call

Answer—p. 1268

Summary

LO1 **Describe the importance and benefits of budgeting.** Planning is a management responsibility of crucial importance to business success. Budgeting is the process used by management to formalize its plans. Budgeting promotes analysis by management and focuses its attention on the future. Budgeting also provides a basis for evaluating performance, serves as a source of motivation, is a means of coordinating business activities, and communicates management's plans and instructions to employees.

LO2 **Explain the process of budget administration.** Budgeting is a detailed activity that requires administration. Two aspects are important: budget committee and budget period. A budget committee oversees the preparation of the budget. The budget period pertains to the time period for which the budget is prepared such as annual, quarterly, or monthly.

LO3 **Describe a master budget and the process of preparing it.** A master budget is a formal overall plan for a company. It consists of specific plans for business operations, capital expenditures, and the financial results of those activities. The budgeting process begins with preparing a sales budget. Based on expected sales volume, merchandisers can budget merchandise purchases, selling expenses, and administrative expenses. Manufacturers also must budget production quantities, direct materials purchases, direct labour costs, and overhead. Next, the capital expenditures budget is prepared, followed by the cash budget, and budgeted financial statements.

LO4 **Prepare each component of a master budget and link them to the budgeting process.** In the process of preparing a master budget, each component budget is designed to provide guidance for persons responsible for activities covered by that budget. The master budget shows how much revenue is to be received from sales and how much expense is to be incurred. Budgets are designed to reflect the activities of one area (such as manufacturing) impacting the activities of others (such as marketing). The various components of a company are directed to pursue activities consistent with and supportive of its overall objectives.

LO5 **Link both operating and capital expenditure budgets to budgeted financial statements.** The operating budgets, capital expenditures budget, and cash budget contain much of the information to prepare a budgeted income statement for the budget period and a budgeted balance sheet at the end of the budget period. Additional information is available from these budgets' supporting calculations and the balance sheet prior to the budget period. Budgeted financial statements show the expected financial consequences of the planned activities described in the budgets.

LO6 **Analyze expense planning using zero-based budgeting.** Companies often budget for the next year based on the current year's budgets. This may not be possible if there is no historical data available as a base. In such situations, zero-based budgeting can be used for expense planning. Managers following the zero-based budgeting approach must prepare a detailed list of the activities to be carried out, the resources required to carry out these activities, and the expenses of acquiring these resources.

Guidance Answers to **You Make the Call**

Sales Manager

There are two issues you must deal with. First, given that fashions and designs are constantly changing, you cannot rely heavily on previous budgets because they may be irrelevant. As a result, you must carefully analyze the market to understand what designs are in vogue and how long they will last. This information will help you plan the product mix of designs you are willing to offer and estimate demand for your designs. The second issue is one of the budgeting period. Because of continuous change, you may not be able to prepare a budget projecting sales for the year. Your best bet may be to prepare quarterly budgets that you continuously monitor and revise if necessary.

Environmental Manager

Given that yours is a new position, you probably have no historical data to draw on in preparing your budget. In this situation, you must use zero-based budgeting to develop your budget. This requires you to develop a list of activities you plan to conduct, the resources required to carry out these activities, and the expenses associated with these resources. You should challenge yourself to be absolutely certain that the listed activities are necessary and the listed resources are required. This process will strengthen your budget and its likelihood of funding.

Guidance Answers to **Judgment and Ethics**

Budgeting Staffer

The action of this top officer is unethical. This is because the individual is using private information for personal gain. It is also at the expense of the company and its shareholders. As a budgeting staffer, you are low in the company's hierarchical structure and probably unable to directly confront this officer. Yet you should inform an individual with a position of authority within the organization about your discovery. You might also enlist a colleague and explain the situation. The information might be considered more credible if it comes from two people rather than one.

Guidance Answers to Flashbacks

1. Major benefits include: (1) promoting a focus on the future, (2) providing a basis for evaluating performance, (3) providing a source of motivation, (4) coordinating the departments of a business, and (5) communicating plans and instructions.
2. The budget committee's chief responsibility is to provide central guidance to ensure that budget figures are realistic and coordinated.
3. Budget periods usually coincide with accounting periods and therefore cover a month, quarter, or a year. Budgets can also be prepared to cover a long-range period, such as five years.
4. Rolling budgets are budgets that are periodically revised in the process of continuous budgeting.
5. A master budget is a comprehensive or overall plan for a business.
6. *b*
7. The master budget includes operating budgets, the capital expenditures budget, and financial budgets.
8. *c* $(.60 \times 140) + 120 - 50 = 154$
9. Merchandisers prepare merchandise purchases budgets while manufacturers prepare production and manufacturing budgets.
10. With a just-in-time system, the level of inventory is kept to a minimum and orders for merchandise or materials are intended to meet immediate sales demand. A safety stock system maintains an inventory that is large enough to meet sales demands plus an amount to satisfy unexpected sales demands and an amount to cover delayed shipments from suppliers.
11. *a*
12. (1) Sales budget, (2) other operating budgets, (3) capital expenditures budget, (4) cash budget, (5) budgeted income statement, (6) budgeted balance sheet.

Demonstration Problem

The management of Wood Company has asked you to prepare a master budget for the company from the following information. The budget is to cover the months of April, May, and June of 1999.

WOOD COMPANY
Balance Sheet
March 31, 1999

Assets		
Cash	$ 50,000	
Accounts receivable	175,000	
Inventory	126,000	
Total current assets		$351,000
Equipment	480,000	
Accumulated amortization	(90,000)	390,000
Total assets		$741,000

Liabilities and Shareholders' Equity		
Accounts payable	$156,000	
Short-term notes payable	12,000	
Total current liabilities		$168,000
Long-term note payable		200,000
Total liabilities		368,000
Common shares	235,000	
Retained earnings	138,000	
Total shareholders' equity		373,000
Total liabilities and shareholders' equity		$741,000

a. Actual unit sales for March were 10,000 units. Each month's sales are expected to exceed the prior month's results by 5%. The selling price of the product is $25 per unit.

b. The company's policy calls for the ending inventory of a given month to equal 80% of the next month's expected unit sales. The March 31 inventory was 8,400 units, which was in compliance with the policy.

c. Sales representatives' commissions are 12.5% and are paid in the month of the sales. The sales manager's salary will be $3,500 in April and $4,000 thereafter.

d. The general and administrative expenses include administrative salaries of $8,000 per month, amortization of $5,000 per month, and 0.9% monthly interest on the long-term note payable.

e. Thirty percent of the company's sales are expected to be for cash and the remaining 70% will be on credit. Receivables are collected in full in the month following the sale (none is collected in the month of the sale).

f. All purchases of merchandise are on credit, and no payables arise from any other transactions. The purchases of one month are fully paid in the next month. The purchase price is $15 per unit.

g. The minimum ending cash balance for all months is $50,000. If necessary, the company will borrow enough cash to reach the minimum. The resulting short-term note will require an interest payment of 1% at the end of each month. If the ending cash balance exceeds the minimum, the excess will be applied to repaying the short-term notes payable.

h. Dividends of $100,000 are to be declared and paid in May.

i. No cash payments for income taxes are to be made during the second quarter. Income taxes will be assessed at 35% in the quarter.

j. Equipment purchases of $55,000 are scheduled for June.

Required

Prepare the following budgets and other financial information:

1. The sales budget, including sales for July.
2. The purchases budget, the budgeted cost of goods sold for each month and the quarter, and the cost of the June 30 budgeted inventory.
3. The selling expense budget.
4. The general and administrative expense budget.
5. The expected cash receipts from customers and the expected June 30 balance of accounts receivable.
6. The expected cash payments for purchases and the expected June 30 balance of accounts payable.
7. The cash budget.
8. The budgeted income statement.
9. The budgeted statement of retained earnings.
10. The budgeted balance sheet.

Planning the Solution

- The sales budget shows the expected sales for each month in the quarter. Start by multiplying March sales by 105%, and do the same thing for the remaining months. July's sales are needed for the purchases budget. To complete the budget, multiply the expected unit sales by the selling price of $25 per unit.
- Use these results and the 80% inventory policy to budget the size of the ending inventory for April, May, and June. Then, add the budgeted sales to these numbers, and subtract the actual or expected beginning inventory for each month. The result will be the number of units to be purchased in each month. Multiply these numbers by the per unit cost of $15. Find the budgeted cost of goods sold by multiplying the unit sales in each month by the $15 cost per unit. And, find the cost of the June 30 ending inventory by multiplying the units expected to be on hand at that date by the $15 cost per unit.
- The selling expense budget has only two items. Find the amount of the sales representatives' commissions by multiplying the expected dollar sales in each month by the 12.5% commission rate. Then, add the sales manager's salary of $3,500 in April and $4,000 in May and June.
- The general and administrative expense budget should show three items. Administrative salaries are fixed at $8,000 per month and amortization is to be $5,000 per month. Budget the monthly interest expense on the long-term note by multiplying its $200,000 balance by the 0.9% monthly interest rate.
- Determine the amounts of cash sales in each month by multiplying the budgeted sales by 30%. Add to this amount the credit sales of the prior month, which you can compute as 70% of the prior month's sales. April's cash receipts from collecting receivables will equal the March 31 balance of $175,000. The expected June 30 accounts receivable balance equals 70% of June's total budgeted sales.
- Determine expected cash payments on accounts payable for each month by making them equal to the merchandise purchases in the prior month. The payments for April equal the March 31 balance of accounts payable shown on the beginning balance sheet. The June 30 balance of accounts payable equals merchandise purchases for June.
- Prepare the cash budget by combining the given information and the amounts of cash receipts and payments on account that you just computed. Complete the cash budget for each month by either borrowing enough to raise the preliminary balance up to the minimum or paying off the short-term note as much as the balance will allow without falling below the minimum. Also show the ending balance of the short-term note in the budget.
- Prepare the budgeted income statement by combining the budgeted items for all three months. Determine the income before income taxes and multiply it by the 35% rate to find the quarter's income tax expense.
- The budgeted statement of retained earnings should show the March 31 balance plus the quarter's net income minus the quarter's dividends.
- The budgeted balance sheet includes updated balances for all the items that appear in the beginning balance sheet and an additional liability for unpaid income taxes. The amounts for all asset, liability, and equity accounts can be found either in the budgets and schedules or by adding amounts found there to the beginning balances.

Solution to Demonstration Problem

1. The sales budget:

	April	May	June	July
Prior month's sales	10,000	10,500	11,025	11,576
Plus 5% growth	500	525	551	579
Projected unit sales	10,500	11,025	11,576	12,155

	April	May	June	Quarter
Projected unit sales	10,500	11,025	11,576	
Selling price per unit	× $25	× $25	× $25	
Projected sales revenue	$262,500	$275,625	$289,400	$827,525

2. The purchases budget:

	April	May	June	Quarter
Next month's unit sales	11,025	11,576	12,155	
Ending inventory percentage	× 80%	× 80%	× 80%	
Desired ending inventory	8,820	9,261	9,724	
This month's unit sales	10,500	11,025	11,576	
Units to be available	19,320	20,286	21,300	
Beginning inventory	(8,400)	(8,820)	(9,261)	
Units to be purchased	10,920	11,466	12,039	
Budgeted cost per unit	$15	$15	$15	
Projected purchases	$163,800	$171,990	$180,585	$516,375

Budgeted cost of goods sold:

	April	May	June	Quarter
This month's unit sales	10,500	11,025	11,576	
Budgeted cost per unit	× $15	× $15	× $15	
Projected cost of goods sold	$157,500	$165,375	$173,640	$496,515

Budgeted inventory for June 30:

Units	9,724
Cost per unit	× $15
Total	$145,860

3. Selling expense budget:

	April	May	June	Quarter
Budgeted sales	$262,500	$275,625	$289,400	$827,525
Commission percentage . . .	× 12.5%	× 12.5%	× 12.5%	× 12.5%
Sales commissions	32,813	34,453	36,175	103,441
Manager's salary	3,500	4,000	4,000	11,500
Projected selling expenses .	$36,313	$38,453	$40,175	$114,941

4. General and administrative expense budget:

	April	May	June	Quarter
Administrative salaries	$ 8,000	$ 8,000	$ 8,000	$24,000
Amortization	5,000	5,000	5,000	15,000
Interest on long-term note payable (0.9% × $200,000)	1,800	1,800	1,800	5,400
Projected expenses	$14,800	$14,800	$14,800	$44,400

5. Expected cash receipts from customers:

	April	May	June	Quarter
Budgeted sales	$262,500	$275,625	$289,400	
Ending accounts receivable (70%)	$183,750	$192,938	$202,580	
Cash receipts:				
Cash sales (30%)	$78,750	$82,687	$86,820	$248,257
Collections of prior month's receivables	175,000	183,750	192,938	551,688
Total cash to be collected . .	$253,750	$266,437	$279,758	$799,945

6. Expected cash payments to suppliers:

	April	May	June	Quarter
Cash payments (equal to prior month's purchases) .	$156,000	$163,800	$171,990	$491,790
Expected June 30 balance of accounts payable (June purchases)			$180,585	

7. Cash budget:

	April	May	June
Beginning cash balance	$ 50,000	$ 89,517	$ 50,000
Cash received from customers	253,750	266,437	279,758
Total cash available	303,750	355,954	329,758
Cash payments:			
Payments for merchandise	$156,000	$163,800	$171,990
Sales commissions	32,813	34,453	36,175
Salaries:			
Sales	3,500	4,000	4,000
Administrative	8,000	8,000	8,000
Interest on long-term note	1,800	1,800	1,800
Dividends		100,000	
Equipment purchase			55,000
Interest on short-term notes:			
April ($12,000 × 1.0%)	120		
June ($6,099 × 1.0%)			61
Total	202,233	312,053	277,026
Preliminary balance	101,517	43,901	52,732
Additional loan		6,099	
Loan repayment	(12,000)		(2,732)
Ending cash balance	$ 89,517	$ 50,000	$ 50,000
Ending short-term notes	$ -0-	$ 6,099	$ 3,367

8.

WOOD COMPANY
Budgeted Income Statement
Quarter Ended June 30, 1999

Sales		$827,525	(part 1)
Cost of goods sold		(496,515)	(part 2)
Gross profit		$331,010	
Operating expenses:			
Sales commissions	$103,441		(part 3)
Sales salaries	11,500		(part 3)
Administrative salaries	24,000		(part 4)
Amortization	15,000		(part 4)
Interest on long-term note	5,400		(part 4)
Interest on short-term notes	181		(part 7)
Total operating expenses		(159,522)	
Income before income taxes		171,488	
Income taxes (35%)		(60,021)	
Net income		$111,467	

9.

WOOD COMPANY Budgeted Statement of Retained Earnings For the Quarter Ended June 30, 1999		
Beginning retained earnings	$138,000	(given)
Net income	111,467	(income statement)
Total	249,467	
Dividends	(100,000)	(given)
Ending retained earnings	$149,467	

10.

WOOD COMPANY Budgeted Balance Sheet June 30, 1999			
Cash	$ 50,000		(part 7)
Accounts receivable	202,580		(part 5)
Inventory	145,860		(part 2)
Total current assets		$398,440	
Equipment	535,000		(given plus purchase)
Accumulated amortization	(105,000)	430,000	(given plus expense)
Total assets		$828,440	
Accounts payable	$180,585		(part 6)
Short-term notes payable	3,367		(part 7)
Estimated income taxes payable	60,021		(income statement)
Total current liabilities		$243,973	
Long-term note payable		200,000	(given)
Total liabilities		443,973	
Common shares	235,000		(given)
Retained earnings	149,467		(retained earnings
Total shareholders' equity		384,467	statement)
Total liabilities and equity		$828,440	

Glossary

Budget A formal statement of future plans, usually expressed in monetary terms. (p. 1246)

Budgeted balance sheet A managerial accounting report that presents predicted amounts of the company's assets, liabilities, and shareholders' equity as of the end of the budget period. (p. 1265)

Budgeted income statement A managerial accounting report that presents predicted amounts of the company's revenues and expenses for the budget period. (p. 1264)

Budgeting The process of planning future business actions and expressing them as formal plans. (p. 1246)

Capital expenditures budget A plan that lists dollar amounts to be received from disposing of equipment and dollar amounts to be spent on purchasing additional equipment if the proposed production program is carried out. (p. 1261)

Cash budget A plan that shows the expected cash inflows and outflows during the budget period, including receipts from loans needed to maintain a minimum cash balance and repayments of such loans. (p. 1261)

Continuous budgeting The practice of preparing budgets for each of several future periods and revising those budgets as each period is completed; as one period is completed, a new budget is added, with the result that the budget always covers the same number of future periods. (p. 1250)

General and administrative expense budget A plan that shows the predicted operating expenses not included in the selling expenses budget. (p. 1260)

Manufacturing budget A plan that shows the predicted costs for materials, direct labour, and overhead costs to be incurred in manufacturing the units in the production budget. (p. 1256)

Master budget A comprehensive or overall formal plan for a business that includes specific plans for expected sales, the units of product to be produced, the merchandise (or materials) to be purchased, the expense to be incurred, the long-term assets to be purchased, and the amounts of cash to be borrowed or loans to be repaid, as well as a budgeted income statement and balance sheet. (p. 1251)

Merchandise purchases budget A plan that states the units or costs of merchandise to be purchased by a merchandising company during the budget period. (p. 1255)

Production budget A plan showing the number of units to be produced each month. (p. 1256)

Rolling budgets As each monthly or quarterly budget period goes by, a firm adds a new set of monthly or quarterly budgets to replace the ones that have lapsed. (p. 1250)

Safety stock Inventory on hand to reduce the risk of running out; a quantity of merchandise or materials over the minimum needed to satisfy budgeted demand. (p. 1255)

Sales budget A plan showing the units of goods to be sold and the revenue to be derived from the sales; the starting point in the budgeting process because the plans for most departments are related to sales. (p. 1253)

Selling expense budget A plan that lists the types and amounts of selling expenses expected during the budget period. (p. 1259)

Questions

1. Identify the three roles budgeting plays in helping managers control a business.
2. Budgeting promotes good decision making by requiring managers to conduct ______ and by focusing their attention on the _____.
3. What two alternative norms or objectives can be used to evaluate actual performance? Which of the two is generally more useful?
4. What is the benefit of continuous budgeting?
5. Identify the three typical short-term planning time horizons for budgets.
6. Why should each department participate in preparing its own budget?
7. How does budgeting help management coordinate business activities?
8. Why is the sales budget so important to the budgeting process?
9. What is a selling expense budget? What is a capital expenditure(s) budget?
10. What is the difference between a production budget and a manufacturing budget?
11. What is a cash budget? Why do operating budgets and the capital expenditures budget need to be prepared before the cash budget?
12. As the accountant for the athletic apparel division of a major international manufacturer you are charged with the responsibility of preparing the rolling budget. Identify the participants, (for example, the sales manager for the sales budget), you would contact and describe the information each person would provide in preparing the master budget.
13. Because of the nature of the business, do you think management of a local fast food restaurant would participate in long-term budgeting?

Quick Study

QS 26-1
Effective budget guidelines
LO1

What are three guidelines that should be followed if budgeting is to serve effectively as a source of motivation?

QS 26-2
Identify types of budgets
LO3

Which of the following comprise the master budget:

a. Sales budget, operating budgets, historical financial budgets.
b. Operating budgets, historical income statement, budgeted balance sheet.
c. Operating budgets, financial budgets, capital expenditures budget.
d. Priors sales, capital expenditures budget, financial budgets.

QS 26-3
Preparing a purchases budget
LO 4

The July sales budget of the Loop Company calls for sales of $400,000. The store expects to begin July with a $40,000 inventory and to end the month with a $50,000 inventory. The cost of goods sold is typically about 70% of sales. Determine the cost of goods that should be purchased during July.

QS 26-4
Preparing a cash budget
LO 2, 4

Use the following information to prepare a cash budget for the MC Company. The budget should show expected cash receipts and disbursements for the month of March and the balance expected on March 31.

a. Beginning cash balance on March 1, $82,000.
b. Cash receipts from sales, $300,000
c. Budgeted cash payments for purchases, $120,000
d. Budgeted cash disbursements for salaries, $80,000.
e. Other budgeted cash expenses, $55,000.
f. Repayment of bank loan, $30,000.

QS 26-5
Budgeting units manufactured
LO 4

Time Company manufactures watches and has a policy that requires ending inventory to equal 20% of the next month's sales. Time estimates that October's ending inventory will consist of 125,000 watches. Sales for November and December are estimated to be 350,000 and 400,000, respectively. Calculate the number of watches to be produced that would appear on Time's production budget for November.

QS 26-6
Compute ending accounts receivable
LO 5

Light Company anticipates sales for June and July of $420,000 and $398,000, respectively. Cash sales are normally 60% of total sales. Of the credit sales, 10% are collected in the same month as the sale, 70% are collected during the first month after the sale, and the remaining 20% is collected in the second month. Determine the amount of accounts receivable that should be reported on Light's budgeted balance sheet as of July 31.

QS 26-7
Budget committee
LO 2

Explain why the *bottom up* approach to budgeting is viewed as more successful than a top down approach and provide an example.

QS 26-8
Zero-based budgeting
LO 6

Why is zero-based budgeting usually more time-consuming for management and employees.

Exercises

Exercise 26-1
Production budget for two quarters
LO 3, 4

Run Company manufactures an innovative automobile transmission for electric cars. Management predicts that the ending inventory for the first quarter will include 70,000 units. The following unit sales of the transmissions are expected during the rest of the year:

Second quarter	300,000
Third quarter	500,000
Fourth quarter	400,000

Management's policy calls for the ending inventory of a quarter to equal 30% of the next quarter's budgeted sales.

Required

Prepare a production budget showing the transmissions that should be manufactured during the year's second and third quarters.

Exercise 26-2
Merchandise purchases budget for three months
LO 3, 4

Flashlight Company prepared monthly budgets for the current year. The budgets planned for a September ending inventory of 15,000 units. The company follows a policy of ending each month with merchandise inventory on hand equal to a specified percentage of the budgeted sales for the following month. Budgeted sales and merchandise purchases for three months were as follows:

	Sales (Units)	Purchases (Units)
July	120,000	138,000
August	210,000	204,000
September	180,000	159,000

1. Based on this information, compute the following amounts:

a. The percentage relationship between a month's ending inventory and sales budgeted for September.

b. The units budgeted to be sold in October.

c. The units budgeted for July's beginning inventory.

2. Show how the company compiled the merchandise purchases budgets for July, August, and September.

Exercise 26-3
Cash budget for three months
LO 3, 5

Keller Company budgeted the following cash receipts and cash disbursements from operations for the first quarter of the next year:

	Receipts	Disbursements
January	$500,000	$450,000
February	300,000	250,000
March	400,000	500,000

According to a credit agreement with the company's bank, Keller promises to have a minimum cash balance of $30,000 at the end of each month. In return, the bank has agreed that the company can borrow up to $150,000 with interest of 12% per year, paid on the last day of each month. The interest is computed on the beginning balance of the loan for the month. The company is expected to have a cash balance of $30,000 and a loan balance of $60,000 on January 1.

Required

Prepare monthly cash budgets for the first quarter of next year.

Exercise 26-4
Cash budget from transaction data
LO 3, 5

Use the following information to prepare a cash budget for Multimedia, Inc.. The budget should show expected cash receipts and disbursements for the month of July and the balance expected on July 31.

a. Beginning cash balance on July 1: $50,000.

b. Cash receipts from sales: 30% are collected in the month of sale, 50% in the next month, 18% in the second month, and 2% are uncollectible. The following actual and budgeted amounts of sales are known:

May (actual)	$1,720,000
June (actual)	1,200,000
July (budgeted)	1,400,000

c. Payments on purchases: 60% in the month of purchase and 40% in the month following purchase. The following actual and budgeted amounts of merchandise purchases are known:

June (actual)	$430,000
July (budgeted)	600,000

d. Budgeted cash disbursements for salaries in July: $211,000.
e. Budgeted amortization expense for July: $12,000.
f. Other cash expenses budgeted for July: $150,000.
g. Accrued income taxes due in July: $80,000.
h. Bank loan interest due in July: $6,600.

Exercise 26-5
Budgeted income statement and balance sheet
LO 3, 5

Based on the information provided in Exercise 26-4 and the additional information that follows, prepare a budgeted income statement for the month of July and a budgeted balance sheet for July 31:

a. Cost of goods sold is 44% of sales.
b. The inventory at the end of July was $64,000 and Beginning inventory was $80,000.
c. Salaries payable on June 30 were $50,000 and are expected to be $40,000 on July 31.
d. The Equipment account has a balance of $1,600,000 on July 31. On June 30, accumulated amortization was $280,000.
e. The $6,600 cash payment of interest represents the 1% monthly expense on a bank loan of $660,000.
f. Income taxes payable on July 31 were $115,920, and the income tax rate applicable to the company is 30%. Use this information to check the net income value.
g. Ending July 31 Accounts Receivable and Allowance are $1,220,000 and $52,000 respectively. The 2% of sales that prove to be uncollectible are debited to Bad Debts Expense and credited to the Allowance for Doubtful Accounts during the month of sale.
h. The only other balance sheet accounts are Common shares, which has a balance of $600,000, and Retained Earnings, which has a balance of $1,013,600 on June 30.

Exercise 26-6
Calculations of budgeted cash payments
LO 3, 5

Handle Company's cost of goods sold is consistently 60% of sales. The company plans to have a merchandise inventory at the beginning of each month with a cost equal to 40% of that month's budgeted cost of goods sold. All merchandise is purchased on credit, and 50% of the purchases made during a month are paid in that month. Another 35% is paid for during the first month after purchase, and the remaining 15% is paid for during the second month after purchase.

Use the following sales budgets to compute the expected cash payments to be made during October:

August	$150,000
September	350,000
October	200,000
November	300,000

Exercise 26-7
Budgeting monthly cost of goods sold
LO 3, 5

Bear Company purchases all of its camping merchandise on credit. It has recently budgeted the following accounts payable balances and merchandise inventory balances:

	Accounts Payable	Merchandise Inventory
May 31	$120,000	$250,000
June 30	170,000	400,000
July 31	200,000	300,000
August 30	160,000	330,000

Cash payments on accounts payable during each month are expected to be:

May	$1,300,000
June	1,450,000
July	1,350,000
August	1,400,000

a. Calculate the budgeted amounts of purchases for June, July and August.

b. Calculate the budgeted amounts of cost of goods sold for June, July and August.

Exercise 26-8
Budgeting accounts payable balances
LO 2, 4

All-Tec, a merchandising company specializing in home computer speakers, budgets its monthly cost of goods sold to equal 70% of sales. The inventory policy calls for a beginning inventory in each month equal to 25% of the budgeted cost of goods sold for that month. All purchases are on credit, and 20% of the purchases in any month are paid for during the same month. Another 50% is paid during the first month after purchase, and the remaining 30% is paid in the second month after purchase. The following sales budgets have been established:

July	$300,000
August	240,000
September	270,000
October	240,000
November	210,000

a. Calculate the budgeted purchases for July, August, September, and October.

b. Calculate the budgeted payments on accounts payable for September and October.

c. Calculate the budgeted ending balances of accounts payable for September and October.

Exercise 26-9
Zero-based budgeting
LO 2, 6

Jimmy John's foot-long, ball park franks are sold at sporting events around the country. Each year management and employees begin to prepare the master budget in October and present the final budget in late December. The process requires the budget committee to merge several hundred regional budgets into one consolidated budget to begin production planning at the manufacturing plant. This is a challenging process because new regions are added and other regions drop out each year.

Required

As the chair of the budget committee, fill in the following chart and justify the approach taken in preparing the budgets for each region. Regions are defined as new and existing. A new region represents a new customer base, where the market size must be estimated from available data. An existing region is one that has a stable, predictable market.

Region	Budget Process Continuous or Zero-based	Justification
New region		
Existing region		

Problems

Problem 26-1
Production budget and materials purchases budget
LO 3, 4

Sportworld Company produces water skis. Each ski requires two kilograms of carbon fibre. The company's management predicts that there will be 7,000 skis and 12,000 kilograms of the carbon fibre on June 30 of the current year, and that 120,000 skis will be sold during the next quarter. Because the peak selling season will be over, management wants to end the third quarter with only 4,000 finished skis and 5,000 kilograms of carbon fibre in the materials inventory. Carbon fibre can be purchased for approximately $12 per kilogram.

Check Figure Cost of carbon fibre purchases, $2,724,000

Required

Prepare a third-quarter production budget and a third-quarter carbon fibre purchases budget for the company (include the dollar cost of the purchases).

Problem 26-2
Production budget and merchandise purchases budget
LO 3,4

Barton Corporation retails three products that it buys ready for sale. The company's February 28 inventories are:

Product A	15,500 units
Product B	70,000 units
Product C	40,000 units

The company's management has realized that excessive inventories have accumulated for all three products. As a result, the managers have created a new policy that the ending inventory in any month should equal 40% of the expected unit sales for the following month.
Expected sales in units for March, April, May, and June are as follows:

	Budgeted Sales in Units			
	March	April	May	June
Product A	10,000	20,000	30,000	33,000
Product B	66,000	85,000	90,000	80,000
Product C	36,000	30,000	30,000	18,000

Required

Preparation component:

Prepare separate purchases budgets (in units) for each of the three products covering March, April, and May.

Analysis component:

Your answer to the preparation component of this problem should reflect much smaller purchases of all three products in March compared to April and May. What factor caused these smaller purchases to be planned? Suggest some conditions in the business that would cause this factor to affect Barton like it apparently has.

Problem 26-3
Cash budgets with supporting schedules
LO 3,5

Paving Company has a cash balance of $60,000 on June 1. The company's product sells for $125 per unit. Actual and projected sales are:

	Units	Dollars
April (actual)	8,000	$1,000,000
May (actual)	4,000	500,000
June (budgeted)	12,000	1,500,000
July (budgeted)	6,000	750,000
August (budgeted)	7,600	950,000

All sales are on credit. Recent experience shows that 20% of the revenues are collected in the month of the sale, 30% in the next month after the sale, 48% in the second month after the sale, and 2% prove to be uncollectible. The purchase price of the product is $100 per unit. All purchases are payable within 12 days. Thus, 60% of the purchases made in a month are paid in that month and the other 40% are paid in the next month. Paving's management has a policy of maintaining an ending monthly inventory of 25% of the next month's unit sales plus a safety stock of 100 units. The March 31 and May 31 actual inventory levels were consistent with this policy. Cash selling and administrative expenses for the year are $1,200,000, and are paid evenly throughout the year. The company's minimum cash balance for the end of a month is $60,000. This minimum is maintained, if necessary, by borrowing cash from the bank. If the balance goes over $60,000, the company repays as much of the loan as it can without going below the minimum. This loan carries an annual 9% interest rate. On May 31, the balance of the loan was $32,000.

Required

Preparation component

1. Prepare a schedule that shows how much cash will be collected in June and July from the credit customers.
2. Prepare a schedule that shows the budgeted ending inventories for April, May, June, and July.
3. Prepare a schedule showing the purchases budgets for the product for May, June, and July. Present the calculation in units and then show the dollar amount of purchases for each month.
4. Prepare a schedule showing the cash to be paid out during June and July for product purchases.
5. Prepare monthly cash budgets for June and July, including any loan activity and interest expense. Also, show the loan balance at the end of each month.

Check Figure Budgeted ending loan balance for July, $136,782

Analysis component:

6. Refer to your answer to part 5. Note that Paving's cash budget indicates that the company will need to borrow over $40,000 in June and over $60,000 in July. Suggest some reasons why knowing this information in May would be helpful to Paving's management.

Problem 26-4
Monthly cash budgets
LO 3, 5

During the last week of August, the owner of the Disk Company approached the bank for an $80,000 loan to be made on September 1 and repaid on November 30 with annual interest of 12%, plus bank charges for a total of $2,400. The owner planned to increase the store's inventory by $60,000 during September and needed the loan to pay for the merchandise in October and November. The bank's loan officer needed more information about Disk's ability to repay the loan and asked the owner to forecast the store's November 30 cash position.

On September 1, Disk was expected to have a $3,000 cash balance, $120,000 of accounts receivable, and $100,000 of accounts payable. Its budgeted sales, purchases, and cash expenditures for the coming three months are as follows:

	September	October	November
Sales	$220,000	$300,000	$380,000
Merchandise purchases	210,000	180,000	220,000
Payroll	16,000	17,000	18,000
Rent	6,000	6,000	6,000
Other cash expenses	64,000	8,000	7,000
Repayment of bank loan			80,000
Interest on the loan plus bank charges			2,400

The budgeted September purchases include the inventory increase. All sales are on account. The company's regular past experience shows that 25% is collected in the month of the sale, 45% is collected in the month following the sale, 20% in the second month, 9% in the third, and the remainder is not collected. Applying these percentages to the September 1 accounts receivable balance shows that $81,000 of the $120,000 will be collected during September, $36,000 during October, and $16,200 during November. All merchandise is purchased on credit. Eighty percent of the balance is paid in the month following a purchase and the remaining 20% is paid in the second month. The $100,000 of accounts payable at the end of August will be paid as follows: $80,000 in September and $20,000 in October.

Required

Prepare cash budgets for September, October, and November for the Disk Company. Provide additional supplemental schedules as needed.

Check Figure Budgeted total disbursements for November, $299,100

Problem 26-5
Preparation and analysis of budgeted income statements
LO 3, 5

Perkins Company buys one kind of graduation ring at $60 per unit and sells it at $130 per unit. The company's sales representatives receive a 10% commission on each sale. The December income statement shows the following information:

PERKINS COMPANY Income Statement For Month Ended December 31	
Sales	$1,300,000
Cost of goods sold	600,000
Gross profit	700,000
Expenses:	
Sales commissions	130,000
Advertising	200,000
Store rent	24,000
Administrative salaries	40,000
Amortization	50,000
Other	12,000
Total	456,000
Net income	$ 244,000

The company's management believes that the December results would be repeated during January, February, and March without any changes in strategy. However, some changes are being considered. Management believes that unit sales will increase at a rate of 10% each month during the next quarter (including January) if the item's selling price is reduced to $115 per unit and if advertising expenses are increased by 25% and remain at that level for all three months. Even if these changes are made, the purchase price will remain at $60 per ring. Under this plan, the sales representatives would continue to earn a 10% commission and the remaining expenses would remain unchanged.

Required

Using a three-column format, prepare budgeted income statements for January, February, and March, that show the expected results of implementing the proposed changes. Based on the information in the budgeted income statements, recommend whether management should implement the plan.

Check Figure Budgeted net income for February, $150,350

Problem 26-6
Preparing a complete master budget
LO 2, 3, 4

Shortly before the end of 1998, the management of Space Corporation prepared the following budgeted balance sheet for December 31, 1998:

SPACE CORPORATION Budgeted Balance Sheet As of December 31, 1998		
Cash		$ 36,000
Accounts receivable		525,000
Inventory		150,000
Total current assets		711,000
Equipment	$540,000	
Accumulated amortization	67,500	472,500
Total		$1,183,500
Accounts payable	$360,000	
Loan from bank	15,000	
Taxes payable (due March 15, 1999)	90,000	
Total liabilities		$ 465,000
Common shares	472,500	
Retained earnings	246,000	
Total shareholders' equity		718,500
Total		$1,183,500

In anticipation of preparing a master budget for January, February, and March 1999, management has gathered the following information:

a. Space's single product is purchased for $30 per unit and resold for $45 per unit. The expected inventory level on December 31 (5,000 units) is greater than management's desired level for 1999 of 25% of the next month's expected sales (in units). Budgeted sales are:

January	6,000 units
February	8,000
March	10,000
April	9,000

b. Cash sales are 25% of total sales and credit sales are 75% of total sales. Of the credit sales, 60% are collected in the first month after the sale and 40% in the second month after the sale. Sixty percent of the December 31, 1998, balance of accounts receivable will be collected during January and 40% will be collected during February.

c. Merchandise purchased by the company is paid for as follows: 20% in the month after purchase, and 80% in the second month after purchase. Twenty percent of the Accounts Payable balance on December 31, 1998, will be paid during January, and 80% will be paid during February.

d. Sales commissions of 20% of sales are paid each month. Additional sales salaries are $90,000 per year.

e. General and administrative salaries are $144,000 per year. Repair expenses equal $3,000 per month and are paid in cash.

f. The equipment shown in the December 31, 1998, balance sheet was purchased in January 1998. It is being amortized over eight years under the straight-line method with no salvage value. The following new purchases of equipment are planned in the coming quarter:

January	$72,000
February	96,000
March	28,800

This equipment also will be amortized with the straight-line method over eight years, with no salvage value. A full month's amortization is taken for the month in which the equipment is purchased.

g. The company plans to acquire some land at the end of March at a cost of $150,000. The purchase price will be paid with cash on the last day of the month.

h. Space has a working arrangement with the bank to obtain additional loans as needed. The interest rate is 12% per year, and the interest is paid at the end of each month based on the beginning balance. Partial or full payments on these loans can be made on the last day of the month. Space has agreed to maintain a minimum ending cash balance of $36,000 in every month.

i. The income tax rate applicable to the company is 40%. However, income taxes on the first quarter's income will not be paid until April 15.

Required

Prepare a master budget for the first quarter of 1999. It should include the following component budgets:

1. Monthly sales budgets (showing both budgeted unit sales and dollar sales)
2. Monthly merchandise purchases budgets
3. Monthly selling expense budgets
4. Monthly general and administrative expense budgets
5. Monthly capital expenditures budgets
6. Monthly cash budgets
7. Budgeted income statement for the first quarter
8. Budgeted balance sheet as of March 31, 1999

Provide as many supplemental schedules as you need. Round all amounts to the nearest dollar.

Check Figure Budgeted total assets March 31 — $1,346,875

Alternate Problems

Problem 26-1A
Production budget and materials purchases budget
LO 3, 4

Osborne Company produces baseball bats. Each bat requires two kilograms of aluminum alloy. The company's management predicts that there will be 10,000 bats and 14,000 kilograms of aluminum alloy on hand on March 31 of the current year, and that 100,000 bats will be sold during the year's second quarter. Because the peak selling season will have passed, management wants to end the second quarter of the year with only 3,000 finished bats and only 1,000 kilograms of aluminum alloy in the materials inventory. Aluminum alloy can be purchased for approximately $6 per kilogram.

Required

Prepare a second-quarter production budget and a second-quarter aluminum alloy purchases budget for the company (include the dollar cost of the purchases).

Problem 26-2A
Production budget and merchandise purchases budget
LO 3, 4

FMR Corporation retails three products that it buys ready-for-sale. The company's June 30 inventories are:

Product X	40,000 units
Product Y	90,000 units
Product Z	250,000 units

The company's management has realized that excessive inventories have accumulated for all three products. As a result, the managers have created a new policy that the ending inventory in any month should equal 10% of the expected unit sales for the following month.

Expected sales in units for July, August, September, and October are as follows:

	Budgeted Sales in Units			
	July	August	September	October
Product X	70,000	90,000	130,000	140,000
Product Y	100,000	90,000	110,000	100,000
Product Z	300,000	260,000	310,000	260,000

Required

Preparation component

Prepare separate purchases budgets (in units) for each of the three products covering July, August, and September.

Analysis component

Your answer to the preparation component of this problem should reflect much smaller purchases of all three products in July compared to August and September. What factor caused these smaller purchases to be planned? Suggest some conditions in the business that would cause this factor to affect FMR like it apparently has.

Problem 26-3A
Cash budgets with supporting schedules
LO 3, 5

Galaxy Company has a cash balance of $45,000 on March 1. The company's product sells for $20 per unit. Actual and projected sales are:

	Units	Dollars
January (actual)	18,000	$360,000
February (actual)	27,000	540,000
March (budgeted)	15,000	300,000
April (budgeted)	27,000	540,000
May (budgeted)	33,000	660,000

All sales are on credit. Recent experience shows that 40% of the revenues are collected in the month of the sale, 30% in the next month after the sale, 25% in the second month after the sale, and 5% prove to be uncollectible. The purchase price of the product is $12 per unit. All purchases are payable within 21 days. Thus, 30% of the purchases made in a month are paid in that month and the other 70% are paid in the next month. Galaxy Company's management has a policy of maintaining an ending monthly inventory of 30% of the next month's unit sales plus a safety stock of 300 units. The January 31 and February 28 actual inventory levels were consistent with this policy. Cash selling and administrative expenses for the year are $1,440,000, and are paid evenly throughout the year. The company's minimum cash balance for the end of a month is $45,000. This minimum is maintained, if necessary, by borrowing cash from the bank. If the balance goes over $45,000, the company repays as much of the loan as it can without going below the minimum. This loan carries an annual 12% interest rate. At February 28, the balance of the loan was $12,000.

Required

Preparation component

1. Prepare a schedule that shows how much cash will be collected in March and April from the credit customers.
2. Prepare a schedule that shows the budgeted ending inventories for January, February, March, and April.
3. Prepare a schedule showing the purchases budgets for the product for February, March, and April. Present the calculation in terms of units and then show the dollar amount of purchases for each month.
4. Prepare a schedule showing the cash to be paid out during March and April for product purchases.
5. Prepare monthly cash budgets for March and April, including any loan activity and interest expense. Also, show the loan balance at the end of each month.

Analysis component

6. Refer to your answer to part 5. Note that the cash budget indicates that the company will need to borrow nearly $12,000 in March, and that it will be able to repay that new loan plus a prior loan of $12,000 in April. Suggest some reasons why knowing this information in February would be helpful to Galaxy's management.

Problem 26-4A
Monthly cash budgets
LO 3, 5

During the last week of March, the owner of Buy-Right Appliance approached the bank for a $125,000 loan to be made on April 1 and repaid on June 30 with annual interest of 8%, plus bank charges for a total of $3,375. The owner planned to increase the store's inventory by $100,000 during April and needed the loan to pay for the merchandise in May and June. The bank's loan officer needed more information about Buy-Right Appliance's ability to repay the loan and asked the owner to forecast the store's June 30 cash position.

On April 1, Buy-Right Appliance was expected to have a $12,000 cash balance, $135,000 of accounts receivable, and $90,000 of accounts payable. Its budgeted sales, purchases, and cash expenditures for the coming three months are as follows:

	April	May	June
Sales	$350,000	$500,000	$550,000
Merchandise purchases	250,000	200,000	190,000
Payroll	22,500	30,000	37,500
Rent	12,000	12,000	12,000
Other cash expenses	9,000	13,500	16,500
Repayment of bank loan			150,000
Interest on the loan plus bank charges			3,375

The budgeted April purchases include the inventory increase. All sales are on account. The company's regular past experience shows that 10% is collected in the month of the sale, 60% is collected in the month following the sale, 25% in the second month, 3% in the third, and the remainder is not collected. Applying these percentages to the April 1 accounts receivable balance shows that $81,000 of the $135,000 will be collected during April, $33,750 during May, and $4,050 during June. All merchandise is purchased on credit. Eighty percent of the balance is paid in the month following a purchase and the remaining 20% is paid in the second month. The $90,000 of accounts payable at the end of March will be paid as follows: $72,000 in April and $18,000 in May.

Required

Prepare cash budgets for April, May, and June for Buy-Right Appliance. Provide additional supplemental schedules as needed.

Problem 26-5A
Preparation and analysis of budgeted income statements

LO 3, 5

Spencer Company buys one kind of computer graphic chips at $20 and sells it at $50 per chip. The company's sales representatives receive a 10% commission on each sale. The June income statement shows the following information:

SPENCER COMPANY Income Statement For Month Ended June 30	
Sales	$1,000,000
Cost of goods sold	400,000
Gross profit	600,000
Expenses:	
Sales commissions	100,000
Advertising	100,000
Store rent	10,000
Administrative salaries	20,000
Amortization	12,000
Other	24,000
Total	266,000
Net income	$ 334,000

The company's management believes that the June results would be repeated during July, August, and September without any changes in strategy. However, some changes are being considered. Management believes that unit sales will increase at a rate of 10% each month during the next quarter (including July) if the item's selling price is reduced to $45 per unit and if advertising expenses are increased by 20% and remain at that level for all three months. Even if these changes are made, the purchase price will remain at $20 per chip. Under this plan, the sales representatives would continue to earn a 10% commission and the remaining expenses would remain unchanged.

Required

Using a three-column format, prepare budgeted income statements for July, August, and September, that show the expected results of implementing the proposed changes. Based on the information in the budgeted income statements, recommend whether management should implement the plan.

Problem 26-6A
Preparing a complete master budget
LO 2, 4

Shortly before the end of 1998, the management of Chain Corporation prepared the following budgeted balance sheet for December 31, 1998:

CHAIN CORPORATION
Budgeted Balance Sheet
As of December 31, 1998

Cash		$ 160,000
Accounts receivable		400,000
Inventory		180,000
Total current assets		740,000
Equipment	$1,200,000	
Accumulated amortization	120,000	1,080,000
Total		$1,820,000
Accounts payable	$300,000	
Loan from bank	20,000	
Taxes payable (due March 15, 1999)	200,000	
Total liabilities		$ 520,000
Common shares	1,500,000	
Retained earnings (deficit)	(200,000)	
Total shareholders' equity		1,300,000
Total		$1,820,000

In anticipation of preparing a master budget for January, February, and March 1999, management has gathered the following information:

a. Chain Corporation's single product is purchased for $10 per unit and resold for $24 per unit. The expected inventory level on December 31 (18,000 units) is greater than management's desired level for 1999 of 40% of the next month's expected sales (in units). Budgeted sales are:

January	30,000 units
February	24,000
March	40,000
April	50,000

b. Cash sales are 40% of total sales and credit sales are 60% of total sales. Of the credit sales, 70% are collected in the first month after the sale and 30% in the second month after the sale. Seventy percent of the December 31, 1998, balance of accounts receivable will be collected during January and 30% will be collected during February.

c. Merchandise purchased by the company is paid for as follows: 80% in the month after purchase, and 20% in the second month after purchase. Eighty percent of the Accounts Payable balance on December 31, 1998, will be paid during January, and 20% will be paid during February.

d. Sales commissions of 10% of sales are paid each month. Additional sales salaries are $288,000 per year.

e. General and administrative salaries are $336,000 per year. Repair expenses equal $6,000 per month and are paid in cash.

f. The equipment shown in the December 31, 1998, balance sheet was purchased in January 1998. It is being amortized over 10 years under the straight-line method with no salvage value. The following new purchases of equipment are planned in the coming quarter:

January	$240,000
February	120,000
March	96,000

This equipment will also be amortized with the straight-line method over 10 years, with no salvage value. A full month's amortization is taken for the month in which the equipment is purchased.

g. The company plans to acquire some land at the end of March at a cost of $232,000. The purchase price will be paid with cash on the last day of the month.
h. Chain Corporation has a working arrangement with the bank to obtain additional loans as needed. The interest rate is 12% per year, and the interest is paid at the end of each month based on the beginning balance. Partial or full payments on these loans can be made on the last day of the month. Chain Corporation has agreed to maintain a minimum ending cash balance of $160,000 in every month.
i. The income tax rate applicable to the company is 30%. However, income taxes on the first quarter's income will not be paid until April 15.

Required

Prepare a master budget for the first quarter of 1999. It should include the following component budgets:

1. Monthly sales budgets (showing both budgeted unit sales and dollar sales)
2. Monthly merchandise purchases budgets
3. Monthly selling expense budgets
4. Monthly general and administrative expense budgets
5. Monthly capital expenditures budgets
6. Monthly cash budgets
7. Budgeted income statement for the first quarter
8. Budgeted balance sheet as of March 31, 1999

Provide as many supplemental schedules as you need. Round all amounts to the nearest dollar.

Analytical and Review Problem

A & R 26–1

Fei Abella and Cammy Tam were invited by the Racket family for a weekend of tennis during the spring break. During the weekend, Mr. Racket made good on his promise to give Fei another "lesson" on the computer. The lesson was really a demonstration of how the computer is used to plan four or five years ahead under a variety of assumptions. Mr. Racket loaded a spreadsheet program into his microcomputer and loaded the financial statements of Assumed Company. The statements appeared on the screen; Mr. Racket explained the assumptions he was putting into the machine and with the press of a button, projected five-year income statements as well as balance sheets at the end of each year on the screen. He had these printed out and repeated the process with a set of different assumptions. Mr. Racket also demonstrated projections with graphs and bar charts. Amazed and astonished at the speed and the alternatives in presenting financial data, Fei and Cammy thanked Mr. Racket for the demonstration.

On the way back to the university, Fei and Cammy contemplated Mr. Racket's remark at the conclusion of the demonstration which was, "The computer is nothing; the assumptions made are king."

Required

What do you think Mr. Racket meant by the above remark? Explain fully.

BEYOND THE NUMBERS

Reporting in Action

LO 2, 3

Financial statements often serve as a starting point for information in the upcoming budget period. You are assigned the task of determining Canadian Tire's cash paid for dividends in the current year and the budgeted cash needed to pay out next year's dividend. Assume Canadian Tire plans to increase dividends by 10% over the next year and to pay all amounts outstanding by the end of the next fiscal year. Assume that dividends are reported at $108,279,000 on its May 31, 1997, balance sheet in the shareholders' equity section. Dividends payable were $540,000 at the beginning of the fiscal year and $570,000 at the end of the fiscal year.

Required

1. Which financial statement(s) reports information about (a) cash amount paid for dividends, and (b) declared dividend amount to be paid next year? Explain where on the statement(s) this information is listed.
2. Indicate the amount of dividend (a) paid in the year ending May 31, 1997, and (b) to be paid next year, under the assumption in 1.

Comparative Analysis

LO 5

One source of cash savings is improved management of ending inventory. To illustrate, assume **NIKE** and **Reebok** each have $2,000,000 per month in shoe sales in Quebec, and each forecast this level of sales per month for the next 24 months. The competition is intense, with each company showing a 20% contribution margin. Also, assume both NIKE and Reebok have the same fixed costs, and the cost per shoe is the only variable cost for each company. The only difference between NIKE and Reebok is the shoe distribution system. NIKE has a well-established shoe distribution system and requires an ending inventory of only 10% of next month's sales on hand at the end of each month. Reebok is building a new distribution system and requires 40% of next month's sales on hand at the end of each month.

Required

1. Compute how much cash savings are potentially available to Reebok if it can reduce its ending inventory level to match NIKE's 10% level.
2. Explain how information in budgeting ending inventory for both the 40% and 10% required ending inventory conditions can help one justify a "just-in-time" inventory system. You can assume a 15% cost with using money tied up in ending inventory.

Ethics Challenge

LO 1, 2

Both the budget process and the budgets themselves impact management performance. A common practice among not-for-profit businesses and governments is for management to spend any amounts remaining in a budget at the end of a budget period. This practice is often called "use it or lose it." The view is if a manager doesn't spend its allocated budget amount, upper management reduces the next year's budget by the amount not spent. To avoid losing budget dollars, department managers often spend all budgeted amounts regardless of the value added to products or services. We all pay for this government practice.

Required

You are to prepare a short report to your local government offering a solution to this problem.

Communicating in Practice

LO 4

The sequence in preparing budgets is described in the chapter. The sales budget is usually the first and most crucial of the subbudgets in the master budget. Information used to complete the sales budget is crucial because all other budgets use it in planning.

Required

Assume your company's sales staff provides information on expected sales and selling price for items making up the sales budget. Prepare a memorandum to your supervisor outlining concerns with the sales staff's input in the sales budget when its compensation is at least partly tied to budgets. Explain why knowledge of any potential bias in the information provided is important to the budget process.

Taking It to the Net

LO 2, 4

The software industry offers budgeting software templates to meet the needs of many users and industries. This software provides a structured framework to input financial information. Programming is already complete enabling the user to focus on analysis of the information. To see some of the many different spreadsheets available in practice, complete the following requirements.

Required

1. Use the Yahoo search engine and search on the word budgeting. Identify at least five different industries or companies that provide budgeting spreadsheet templates.
2. Select one company listing budgeting spreadsheet templates. List three functions offered in this template that are helpful. You will find many of the competitors offer similar features.

Teamwork in Action

LO 6

In teams of three or four prepare a budget report outlining the cost of attending college (*full time*) for either two semesters (30 hours) or three quarters (45 hours). The focus of this budget is solely on attending college—do not include personal items in the team's budget. Your budget must include tuition, books, supplies, club fees, food plan, and all costs associated with travel to and from college. This is how a team begins under the zero-based budgeting concept. Include a list of any assumptions you use in completing the budget. For example, you might assume some percent increase in tuition or receipt of a scholarship to waive tuition. Be prepared to present your budget report in class.

Hitting the Road

LO 3, 4

To help understand the factors impacting a sales budget, you are to visit three business with the same ownership or franchise membership. Record the selling price of two products at each location, such as regular and premium gas sold at **Shell Canada** stations. You may find a difference in price in at least one of the three locations.

Required

Identify at least three external factors that must be considered when setting the sales budget. What factors possibly explain any differences identified in prices of the businesses you visited? (Note: There is a difference between internal and external factors that impact the sales budget.)

Business Break

LO 2, 6

Commercial credit cards are increasingly a valuable business tool for small business. A commercial credit card is similar to a charge card used by individuals, except with added features. Read "Pick A Card, Not Any Card" in the November 17, 1997, issue of *Business Week*, and answer the following questions.

Required

1. List the advantages of a commercial credit card to a business and its employees.
2. Identify how a commercial credit card helps a business budget expenses (be specific).

27

CHAPTER

Flexible Budgets and Standard Costs

A Look Back

Chapter 26 explained the importance of budgeting. It also described the master budget and its usefulness for planning future company activities.

A Look at This Chapter

This chapter describes flexible budgets, variance analysis, and standard costs. It explains how each is used for purposes of control and monitoring of business activities.

A Look Forward

Chapter 28 focuses on evaluating capital budgeting decisions. It also explains procedures used in evaluating many short-term managerial decisions.

Chapter Outline

A Hole in One

Toronto, ON—In the shadow of high-rise building in downtown Toronto, **G-Max** could be just another trinket shop for wandering tourists. But rolls of twine, manufacturing equipment, and a driving range, make clear that this is a local success story with a difference. This collection is all part of the G-Max manufacturing process.

G-Max makes specialty golf equipment and accessories for individual consumers and organizations. Its specializes in golf balls, with simple colour changes to an entirely redesigned and remanufactured ball. In six years, G-Max has made a name for itself and is quickly becoming the leader in this quirky market. For its most recent fiscal year, earnings are up more than 23%, to $455,000.

Nancy Stricker, 25, is the founder of G-Max. "When I was in high school, I caddied at a golf course and I was amazed at what golfers would do to dazzle friends and clients," says Stricker. "They were always looking for that special item or gag gift." Stricker began by taking golf balls and dressing them up to a buyer's liking. "Names, colours, logos, whatever. I'd fix them up anyway they liked."

Stricker was soon overwhelmed by more than one hundred requests that led her to set up a small manufacturing facility in an old service garage. "People requested all kinds of things. And they were willing to pay for them." Stricker quickly launched into specialty manufacturing of golf balls. "But within a year I was losing control of costs and revenues," says Stricker. "The business was growing so fast that I didn't know what I was doing right and what I was doing wrong. I needed a way to assess how I was doing."

With help from her banker, Stricker implemented an accounting system with budgets and standard costs. "It literally saved my business. It gave me information I needed to make good decisions. Budget reports and cost variances quickly identified problems," says Stricker. "And I quickly moved to solve them."

And the strangest order? "That's easy," says Stricker. "Square, pink golf balls! A consulting firm ordered them for their clients for one of those 'think out of the box' sessions. I guess they wanted to make a point."

Learning Objectives

LO 1 Compare fixed and flexible budgets.

LO 2 Prepare a flexible budget and interpret a flexible budget performance report.

LO 3 Define standard costs and explain their computation and uses.

LO 4 Compute material and labour variances.

LO 5 Describe variances and what they reveal about performance.

LO 6 Compute overhead variances.

LO 7 Explain how standard cost information is useful for management by exception.

LO 8 Record journal entries for standard costs and account for price and quantity variances

LO 9 Analyze changes in sales from expected amounts.

CHAPTER PREVIEW

In Chapter 26, we explained how budgeting organizes and formalizes management's planning activities. We also explained how budgets provide a basis for evaluating actual performance. In this chapter, we extend this discussion and look more closely at how budgets are used to evaluate performance. Evaluations are important for controlling and monitoring business activities. We also describe and illustrate the use of standard costs and variance analyses. This includes explanation of revenue variances. These managerial tools are useful for both evaluation and control of organizations, and in the planning of future activities. Application of these tools can greatly impact the performance of a company as evidenced by G-Max in the opening article.

SECTION 1—FLEXIBLE BUDGETS

Fixed Budget Reports

A master budget reflects management's planned objectives for a future period. We explained in Chapter 26 how a master budget is prepared based on a predicted level of activity such as sales volume for the budget period. This section discusses the effects on the usefulness of budget reports when the actual level of activity is different from the predicted level.

Budgetary Control and Reporting

Budgetary control is the use of budgets by management to monitor and control the operations of a company. This includes use of budgets to see that planned objectives are carried out and met.

Budget reports contain relevant information that compare actual results to planned objectives. This comparison is motivated by a need to both monitor performance and control activities. Budget reports are sometimes viewed as progress reports, or *report cards*, on management's performance in achieving planned objectives. These reports can be prepared at any time and for any period. Three common periods for a budget report are a month, quarter, and year.

The *process of budgetary control* involves at least four steps: (1) develop the budget from planned objectives, (2) compare actual results to budgeted amounts and analyze differences, (3) take corrective and strategic actions, (4) establish new planned objectives and prepare a new budget. Exhibit 27.1 shows this continual process of budgetary control.

Exhibit 27.1

Process of Budgetary Control

Budget reports and related documents are effective tools for managers in getting the greatest benefits from this process.

Fixed Budget Performance Report

In a fixed budgetary control system, the master budget is based on this single prediction for sales volume or other activity level. The budgeted amount for each cost essentially assumes a specific (or *fixed*) amount of sales will occur. A **fixed budget,** also called *static budget*, is one based on a single predicted amount of sales or production volume.

We explained in Chapter 26 that one benefit of a budget is its usefulness in comparing actual results with planned activities. Information useful for analysis is often presented for comparison in a performance report. A **fixed budget performance report** is shown in Exhibit 27.2. This report compares the actual results of **Optel** from November 1999 with the results expected under its fixed budget that predicted 10,000 units of sales (composite)—Optel is a manufacturer of eyeglasses, frames, contact lens, and related supplies. For this report, its production volume equals sales volume. This means the amount of inventory does not change.

This type of performance report designates the differences between budgeted and actual results as *variances*. We see the letters *F* and *U* located beside the numbers in the third column of this report. Their meanings are:

F = **Favourable variance**—when compared to budget, the actual cost or revenue contributes to a *higher* income. This means actual revenue (cost) is greater (lower) than budgeted revenue (cost).

U = **Unfavourable variance**—when compared to budget, the actual cost or revenue contributes to a lower income. This means actual revenue (cost) is *lower* (greater) than budgeted revenue (cost).

This convention is common in practice and is used throughout this chapter.

Exhibit 27.2

Fixed Budget Performance Report

OPTEL
Fixed Budget Performance Report
For Month Ended November 30, 1999

	Fixed Budget	Actual Performance	Variances
Sales: In units	10,000	12,000	
In dollars	$100,000	$125,000	$25,000 F
Cost of goods sold:			
Direct materials	10,000	13,000	3,000 U
Direct labour	15,000	20,000	5,000 U
Overhead:			
Factory supplies	2,000	2,100	100 U
Utilities	3,000	4,000	1,000 U
Amortization of machinery	8,000	8,000	
Supervisory salaries	11,000	11,000	
Selling expenses:			
Sales commissions	9,000	10,800	1,800 U
Shipping expenses	4,000	4,300	300 U
General and administrative expenses:			
Office supplies	5,000	5,200	200 U
Insurance expense	1,000	1,200	200 U
Amortization of office equipment	7,000	7,000	
Administrative salaries	13,000	13,000	
Total expenses	88,000	99,600	11,600 U
Income from operations	$ 12,000	$ 25,400	$13,400 F

F = Favourable variance; and U = Unfavourable variance

Budget Reports for Evaluation

The primary use of budget reports is for management in monitoring and controlling operations. A main part of this activity is the use of budget reports. In the case of Optel's report, management's evaluation is likely to focus on a variety of questions. These questions might include:

- Why is actual income from operations $13,400 higher than budgeted?
- Are amounts paid for each expense item too high?
- Is manufacturing using too much direct material?
- Is manufacturing using too much direct labour?

The performance report in Exhibit 27.2 provides little help in answering these questions. This is because actual sales volume is 2,000 units higher than budgeted. A manager does not know if this higher level of sales activity is the driving force behind variations in total dollar sales and expenses or if other factors have influenced these amounts.

This inability of fixed budget reports to adjust to changes in activity levels is a major limitation of a fixed budget performance report. Its usefulness is reduced because it fails to show whether actual costs are out of line due to a change in actual sales volume or some other factor.

Flexible Budget Reports

This section explains the purposes of both a flexible budget and a flexible budget performance report. We also describe the preparation and reporting of both types of reports.

Purpose of Flexible Budgets

LO1 Compare fixed and flexible budgets.

To help management address questions that arise with the fixed budget performance report, we look to a flexible budget. A **flexible budget,** also called a *variable budget*, is a report based on predicted amounts of revenues and expenses corresponding to the actual level of output. Unlike fixed budgets, a flexible budget is prepared after a period's activities are complete. A flexible budget can be viewed as a fixed budget at an activity level corresponding to the actual level of activity. Many companies prepare and use flexible budgets.

The primary purpose of a flexible budget is to help managers evaluate past performance. A flexible budget is especially useful for evaluations because it reflects the different levels of activities in different amounts of revenues and costs. This means comparisons of actual results with budgeted performance are more likely to identify the reasons for any differences. This also helps managers to focus attention on problem areas and to implement corrective actions. This is in contrast to a fixed budget, whose primary purpose is assisting managers in planning future activities and whose numbers are based on one expected amount of budgeted sales or production.

Preparing Flexible Budgets

LO2 Prepare a flexible budget and interpret a flexible budget performance report.

A flexible budget is designed to reveal the effects of volume on the level of revenues and costs. To prepare a flexible budget, management relies on the distinctions between fixed and variable costs. Fixed and variable costs were described under cost-volume-profit analysis in Chapter 25. Recall that variable costs per unit of activity remain constant as sales change within the relevant range. The total amount of a variable cost changes in direct proportion to a change in level of activity. For fixed costs, the total amount of cost remains unchanged regardless of changes in the level of activity within a relevant (normal) operating range.[1]

[1] In Chapter 25, we explain that some costs are neither strictly variable nor strictly fixed. We assume here that all costs can be reasonably classified as either variable or fixed within a relevant range.

When we create the numbers comprising a flexible budget, we need to express each variable cost as either a constant amount per unit of sales or as a percent of a sales dollar. In the case of a fixed cost, we need to express its budgeted amount as the total amount expected to occur at any sales volume within the relevant range.

Exhibit 27.3 shows a set of flexible budgets of Optel for November 1999. Seven of its expenses are classified as variable costs. Its remaining five expenses are fixed costs. These classifications result from management's investigation of each of the company's expenses following procedures similar to those we explained in Chapter 25. Variable and fixed expense categories are *not* the same for every company, and we must avoid drawing conclusions from specific cases. For example, depending on the nature of a company's operations, office supplies expense can be either fixed or variable with respect to sales.

Exhibit 27.3

Flexible Budgets

OPTEL
Flexible Budgets
For Month Ended November 30, 1999

	Flexible Budget		Flexible Budget for Unit Sales of 10,000	Flexible Budget for Unit Sales of 12,000	Flexible Budget for Unit Sales of 14,000
	Variable Amount per Unit	Total Fixed Cost			
Sales	$10.00		$100,000	$120,000	$140,000
Variable costs:					
Direct materials	1.00		10,000	12,000	14,000
Direct labour	1.50		15,000	18,000	21,000
Factory supplies	0.20		2,000	2,400	2,800
Utilities	0.30		3,000	3,600	4,200
Sales commissions	0.90		9,000	10,800	12,600
Shipping expenses	0.40		4,000	4,800	5,600
Office supplies	0.50		5,000	6,000	7,000
Total variable costs	4.80		48,000	57,600	67,200
Contribution margin	$ 5.20		52,000	62,400	72,800
Fixed costs:					
Amortization, machinery		$ 8,000	8,000	8,000	8,000
Supervisory salaries		11,000	11,000	11,000	11,000
Insurance expense		1,000	1,000	1,000	1,000
Amortization, office equipment		7,000	7,000	7,000	7,000
Administrative salaries		13,000	13,000	13,000	13,000
Total fixed costs		$40,000	40,000	40,000	40,000
Income from operations			$ 12,000	$ 22,400	$ 32,800

The layout for the flexible budgets in Exhibit 27.3 reports sales followed by variable costs and then fixed costs. Both individual and total variable costs are reported and then subtracted from sales. As we explained in Chapter 25, the difference between sales and variable costs equals contribution margin. The expected amounts of fixed costs are listed next, followed by the expected income from operations before taxes.

The first and second columns of Exhibit 27.3 show the flexible budget amounts for variable and fixed costs applied to any volume of sales in the relevant range. The third, fourth, and fifth columns show the flexible budget amounts computed for three different sales volumes. For instance, the third column's flexible budget is based on 10,000 units and shows the same amounts appearing in the fixed budget of Exhibit 27.2. These numbers are the same because the expected volumes are the same for these two budgets.

Recall that Optel's actual sales volume for November is 12,000 units. This level of 2,000 units is more than the 10,000 units originally predicted in the master budget. When differences arise between actual and predicted volume, the usefulness of a flexible budget is apparent. For instance, compare the flexible budget for 10,000 units in the third column (which is the same as the fixed budget in Exhibit 27.2) with the flexible budget for 12,000 units in the fourth column. Note the higher levels for sales and all variable costs reflect nothing more than the increase in sales activity. Any budget analysis comparing actual with planned results that ignored this information would be less useful to management.

To illustrate, when we *evaluate* the performance of Optel, we need to prepare a flexible budget showing actual and budgeted values at 12,000 units. As part of a complete profitability analysis, managers could compare the actual income of $25,400 (from Exhibit 27.2) with the $22,400 income expected at the actual sales volume of 12,000 units. This results in a total variance in income to be explained and understood of $3,000. This variance is markedly different from the $13,400 variance identified in Exhibit 27.2. After receiving the flexible budget based on November's actual volume, management's next step is to determine what caused this $3,000 difference. The next section describes a flexible budget performance report that provides guidance for answering this and similar questions.

Flexible Budget Performance Report

A **flexible budget performance report** lists differences between actual performance and budgeted performance based on actual sales volume or other level of activity. This report helps direct management's attention at those costs or revenues that differ substantially from budgeted amounts.

Exhibit 27.4 shows the flexible budget performance report of Optel for November. We prepare this report after the actual volume is known to be 12,000 units. This report shows a $5,000 favourable variance in total dollar sales. Because actual and budgeted volumes are both 12,000 units, the $5,000 sales variance must have resulted from a selling price that was higher than expected. Further analysis of the facts surrounding this $5,000 sales variance reveals a favourable sales variance of $0.42 as follows:

Actual average price per unit	$125,000/12,000 =	$10.42
Budgeted price per unit	$120,000/12,000 =	10.00
Favourable sales variance per unit	$5,000/12,000 =	$ 0.42

The other variances computed in Exhibit 27.4 should also direct management's attention to areas where corrective actions can help them control Optel's operations. Each variance is analyzed like the previous sales variance. We can think of each expense as the joint result of using a given number of units of an expense item and paying a specific price per unit.

Under this approach, a variance in Exhibit 27.4 is due in part to a difference between *actual price per unit* of input and *budgeted price per unit* of input. This portion is a **price variance.** A variance also is due in part to a difference between *actual quantity* of input used and *budgeted quantity* of input. This portion is a **quantity variance.** We explain more about this technique known as **variance analysis** in the section on standard costs later in the chapter.

Exhibit 27.4

Flexible Budget Performance Report

OPTEL Flexible Budget Performance Report For Month Ended November 30, 1999	Fixed Budget	Actual Performance	Variances
Sales (12,000 units)	$120,000	$125,000	$5,000 F
Variable costs:			
Direct materials	$ 12,000	$ 13,000	$1,000 U
Direct labour	18,000	20,000	2,000 U
Factory supplies	2,400	2,100	300 F
Utilities	3,600	4,000	400 U
Sales commissions	10,800	10,800	
Shipping expenses	4,800	4,300	500 F
Office supplies	6,000	5,200	800 F
Total variable costs	$ 57,600	$ 59,400	$1,800 U
Contribution margin	$ 62,400	$ 65,600	$3,200 F
Fixed costs:			
Amortization of machinery	$ 8,000	$ 8,000	
Supervisory salaries	11,000	11,000	
Insurance expense	1,000	1,200	$ 200 U
Amortization of office equipment	7,000	7,000	
Administrative salaries	13,000	13,000	
Total fixed costs	$ 40,000	$ 40,200	$ 200 U
Income from operations	$ 22,400	$ 25,400	$3,000 F

F = Favourable variance; and U = Unfavourable variance

You Make the Call

Budget Officer

You are the budget officer for a management consulting firm. The heads of both the strategic consulting and tax consulting divisions complain to you about the negative variances on their recent quarterly performance reports. "We worked on more consulting assignments than planned. It's not surprising our costs are higher than expected. But, this report penalizes us for *poor performance*!" How do you react to their complaints?

Answer—p. 1318

Flashback

1. A flexible budget:
   a. Shows fixed costs as constant amounts of cost per unit of activity.
   b. Shows variable costs as constant amounts of cost per unit of activity.
   c. Is prepared based on one expected amount of budgeted sales or production.
2. What is the initial step in preparing a flexible budget?
3. What is the difference between a fixed and a flexible budget?
4. What is contribution margin?

Answers—p. 1319

Mid-Chapter Demonstration Problem

Wei Tian Enterprises presents you with the following incomplete flexible budget for overhead costs:

Overhead Costs	Cost Formula (per hour)	Machine Hours		
		15,000	20,000	25,000
Variable costs:				
Indirect labour			$ 16,000	
Indirect materials			10,000	
Maintenance			24,000	
Utilities			20,000	
Total variable costs			$ 70,000	
Fixed costs:				
Management salaries			$200,000	
Factory rent			40,000	
Insurance			25,000	
Maintenance			10,000	
Total fixed overhead			$275.000	
Total overhead			$345,000	

Required

a. Complete the flexible budget for Wei Enterprises. Assume that cost relationships are valid within the range of machine hours specified by the budget.

b. Estimate the total overhead costs at 28,000 machine hours.

Planning the Solution

- Determine the cost formula for each variable overhead item by dividing each dollar figure under the 20,000 machine hours column by 20,000 machine hours. Note that overhead costs have already been separated into fixed and variable components.
- Using the formula for the portion of the costs, multiply each formula by the number of machine hours given in each column, i.e., 15,000 × \$0.80 = \$12,000 indirect labour costs.
- Total each column to arrive at the total variable cost at each level of activity.
- Fill in the fixed overhead costs for each column.
- Add the total fixed overhead to the total variable overhead costs for each column.
- For part (b) multiply 28,000 machine hours by the variable overhead costs per machine hours and add the total fixed costs to this amount.

Solution to Mid-Chapter Demonstration Problem

a.

Overhead Costs	Cost Formula (per hour)	Machine Hours		
		15,000	20,000	25,000
Variable costs:				
Indirect labour	$0.80	$12,000	$16,000	$20,000
Indirect materials	0.50	7,500	10,000	12,500
Maintenance	1.20	18,000	24,000	30,000
Utilities	1.00	15,000	20,000	25,000
Total variable costs	$3.50	$52,500	$70,000	$87,500

Fixed costs:			
Management salaries . .	$200,000	$200,000	$200,000
Factory rent	40,000	40,000	40,000
Insurance	25,000	25,000	25,000
Maintenance	10,000	10,000	10,000
Total Fixed overhead	$275,000	$275,000	$275,000
Total overhead costs:	$327,500	$345,000	$362,500

b.

Total overhead costs equals $3.50 variable costs per machine hour plus total fixed costs of $275,000.

(28,000 machine hours × $3.50) + $275,000 = $373,000 total estimated overhead costs.

SECTION 2—STANDARD COSTS

We described job order and process cost accounting systems in Chapters 22 and 23. The costs described in these chapters are historical costs. Historical costs are the dollar amounts paid by a company in past transactions. These historical (or actual) costs provide useful information for many analyses.

Management usually needs a standard of comparison to decide whether the historical cost-based amounts are reasonable or excessive. **Standard costs** offer one basis for these comparisons. Standard costs are preset costs that are expected under normal conditions to deliver a product or service. These costs are established through personnel, engineering, and accounting studies using past experiences and other data. They are used by management to assess the reasonableness of actual costs incurred for producing the product or service. When actual costs vary from standard costs, management follows up to identify potential problems and take corrective actions.

LO 3 Define standard costs and explain their computation and uses.

Standard costs are similar to budgeted amounts. They are often used in preparing budgets because these costs represent the anticipated costs that should be incurred under normal conditions. Terms such as *standard material cost, standard labour cost*, and *standard overhead cost* are often used to refer to amounts budgeted for direct materials, direct labour, and overhead.

Materials and Labour Standards

This section explains how we set materials and labour standards. It also shows us how to prepare a standard cost card.

Setting Standard Costs

Managerial accountants, engineers, personnel administrators, and other managers combine their efforts in setting the amounts for standard costs. To identify standards for direct labour costs, we can conduct time and motion studies for each labour operation in the process of providing a product or service. From these studies, management can learn the best way to perform the operation. It then sets the standard labour time required for the operation under normal conditions. In a similar way, standards for materials are set by studying the quantity, grade, and cost of each material used. Standards for overhead costs are explained later in the chapter.

Regardless of the care used in setting standard costs and in revising them as conditions change, actual costs frequently differ from standard costs. These differences often are due to more than one factor. For instance, the actual quantity of material used may differ from standard, and the price paid per unit of material also may differ from standard.

Similar quantity and price differences from standard amounts can occur for labour. For instance, the actual labour time and actual labour rate may vary from what was expected. We also explain later in the chapter how factors can cause actual overhead cost to differ from standard.

Did You Know?

Standard in Vans

Chrysler Canada builds over 1,100 minivans per day in its Windsor, Ontario, plant. Each minivan requires 3,400 parts purchased from 627 suppliers. The plant has 1,400 employees. Imagine the task of setting standard costs for each and every one of the 3,400 parts, the different grades of labour, and the overhead! [Source: A. Vido, "Chrysler and Minivans: Are We There Yet?" *CMA Magazine*, November 1993.]

Illustration of Setting Standard Costs

To illustrate the setting of a standard cost, we consider the case of a baseball bat manufactured by **ProBat**. Engineers of ProBat have determined the manufacture of one bat requires 0.90 kg of high-grade wood. They also recognize there can be loss of material as part of the process, due to inefficiencies and waste. This results in adding an *allowance* of 0.10 kg. This means the standard requirement is 1 kg of wood for each bat.

The 0.90 kg portion is called an *ideal standard*. An ideal standard is the quantity of material that would be required if the process were 100% efficient without any loss or waste. Reality suggests there is usually some loss of material associated with the process. The revised standard of 1 kg is known as the practical standard. A *practical standard* is the quantity of material required under normal application of the process.

High-grade wood can be purchased at a standard price of $25 per kilogram. This is the price the purchasing department determines as the expected price they must likely pay in the budget period. To estimate this price, the purchasing department considers factors such as the quality of materials, future economic conditions, supply factors (shortages and excesses), and any available discounts.

The engineers decide that two hours of labour time (after including allowances) is required to manufacture a bat. The wage rate is $20 per hour (better than average skilled labour is required). ProBat assigns all overhead at the rate of $10 per labour hour. The standard costs of direct materials, direct labour, and overhead for one bat are as shown in Exhibit 27.5 in what's called a *standard cost card*.

Exhibit 27.5

Standard Cost Card

STANDARD COST CARD

Production factor	Cost factor	Total
Direct materials (wood)	*1 kg @ $25 per kg*	$25
Direct labour	*2 hours @ $20 per hour*	40
Overhead	*2 labour hours @ $10 per hour*	20
	Total cost	$85

These amounts can be used to prepare the manufacturing budgets for the budgeted level of production.

Flashback

5. Standard costs:
   a. Change in direct proportion to changes in the level of activity.
   b. Are amounts incurred at the actual level of production for the period.
   c. Equal amounts incurred under normal conditions to provide a product or service.

Answers—p. 1319

Variances

Cost variances, also called *variances*, are differences between actual and standard costs. Cost variances can be favourable or unfavourable. A variance from standard cost is considered favourable if actual cost is less than standard cost. It is considered unfavourable if actual cost is more than standard cost.[2] This section discusses variance analysis and computation.

Variance Analysis

Variances are commonly identified in cost performance reports. When a variance occurs, management examines the circumstances to determine the factors causing it. This often involves analysis, evaluation, and explanation. The results of these efforts should allow management to assign responsibility for the variance. It can then take actions to correct the problem.

To illustrate, Optel's standard material cost for producing 12,000 units of a product is $12,000. But its actual material cost proved to be $13,000. The $1,000 unfavourable variance raises questions. These questions call for answers that, in turn, can lead to changes designed to correct the problem and eliminate this variance in the next period. A performance report can often identify the existence of a problem, but we need to follow up with further investigation to see what can be done to improve future results.

Exhibit 27.6 shows the flow of events in proper management of variance analysis. Four steps are shown: (1) preparation of a standard cost performance report, (2) computation and analysis of variances, (3) identification of questions and their explanations, and (4) corrective and strategic actions.

Exhibit 27.6

Variance Analysis

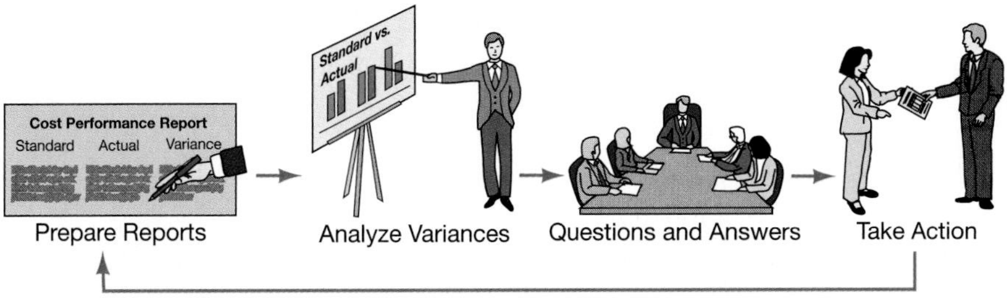

These steps are interrelated and occur frequently in good organizations.

[2] We must recognize that short-term favourable variances can sometimes lead to long-term unfavourable variances. For instance, if management spends less than the budgeted amount on maintenance or insurance, the performance report would identify the difference as a favourable variance. But cutting these expenses can lead to major losses in the long run if machinery wears out prematurely or insurance coverage proves inadequate.

Did You Know?

Strategic Partnership

Strategic partnerships are hot. One manufacturing consultant defines a strategic partnership as a joint effort by the supplier and the manufacturing customer to improve the quality and the delivery of an end product. This partnership requires trust, communication, and sharing in financial rewards. It is based on the idea that there is no sale for either partner until the product is delivered. "In practice, manufacturer-vendor partnerships frequently fall short of the ideal primarily because the compensation system focuses on the purchase price variance. This requires multiple suppliers and a mentality of least cost versus total benefit." [Source: Lawrence, H., "Marriages of Convenience," *CFO Magazine*, July 1991.]

Computing Variances

Management needs information about the factors causing a cost variance. But it must first understand how to compute a variance. In its most simple form, a cost variance (CV) is computed as the difference between actual cost (AC) and standard cost (SC) as shown in Exhibit 27.7.

Exhibit 27.7
Cost Variance Formula

Cost Variance (CV) = **Actual Cost** (AC) − **Standard Cost** (SC)

where:

Actual Cost (AC) = **Actual Quantity** (AQ) × **Actual Price** (AP)

Standard Cost (SC) = **Standard Quantity** (SQ) × **Standard Price** (SP)

A cost variance is further defined by its components. Actual quantity (AQ) is the input (material or labour) consumed in manufacturing the quantity of output. Standard quantity (SQ) is the input allowed for the quantity of output. Actual price (AP) is the amount paid for acquiring the input (material or labour), and standard price (SP) is the price set at the beginning of the budget period.

We explained earlier how two factors cause a cost variance: (1) a difference between actual price and standard price, resulting in a price (or rate) variance, and (2) a difference between actual quantity and standard quantity, resulting in a quantity (or usage or efficiency) variance. To assess the effects of these two factors on a cost variance, we use the formula in Exhibit 27.8.

Exhibit 27.8
Price Variance and Quantity Variance Formulas

Actual Cost AQ × AP — AQ × SP — **Standard Cost** SQ × SP

Price Variance (AQ × AP vs. AQ × SP)

Quantity Variance (AQ × SP vs. SQ × SP)

Cost Variance (Price Variance + Quantity Variance)

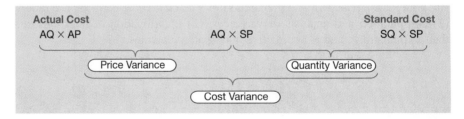

Alternative computations for price and quantity variances are shown in Exhibit 27.9.

Exhibit 27.9
Alternative Price Variance and Quantity Variance Formulas

Price Variance (PV) = [**Actual Price** (AP) − **Standard Price** (SP)] × **Actual Quantity** (AQ)

Quantity Variance (QV) = [**Actual Quantity** (AQ) − **Standard Quantity** (SQ)] × **Standard Price** (SP)

Computing Material and Labour Variances

We illustrate material and labour variances using data from G-Max Company. This company has set the following standard quantities and costs for materials and labour per unit for a golf hat:

Direct materials (.5kg per unit at $2 per kg)	$1.00
Direct labour (1 hr. per unit at $6 per hr.)	6.00
Total standard direct cost per unit	$7.00

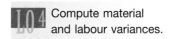

LO 4 Compute material and labour variances.

Material Variances

During May 2000, G-Max Co. budgeted to produce 4,000 units of golf hats. It actually produced only 3,500 units. It also used 1,800 kg of direct material costing $2.10 per kilogram. This means its total material cost was $3,780. This information allows us to compute actual and standard direct material costs for the 3,500 units and its direct material cost variance:

Actual cost	1,800 kg @ $2.10 per kg =	$3,780
Standard cost	1,750 kg @ $2.00 per kg =	3,500
Direct material cost variance (unfavourable) . . .	=	$ 280

The material price and quantity variances for G-Max are computed and shown in Exhibit 27.10.

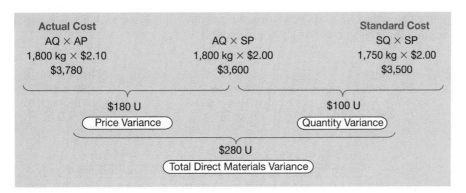

Exhibit 27.10

Material Price and Quantity Variances

Actual Cost		Standard Cost
AQ × AP	AQ × SP	SQ × SP
1,800 kg × $2.10	1,800 kg × $2.00	1,750 kg × $2.00
$3,780	$3,600	$3,500

$180 U (Price Variance) — $100 U (Quantity Variance)

$280 U (Total Direct Materials Variance)

The price variance of $180 is unfavourable because the company paid 10 cents more than the standard price, computed as 1,800 kg × $0.10. The quantity variance of $100 is unfavourable because the company used 50 kg more than the standard quantity, computed as 50 kg × $2. The total direct material variance is $280 and is unfavourable. This information allows management to go to the responsible individuals for explanations and corrective actions.

LO 5 Describe variances and what they reveal about performance.

The purchasing department is usually responsible for the price paid for material. Responsibility for explaining the problem rests with the purchasing manager if the variance is caused by a price higher than standard. The production department is usually responsible for the amount of material used. The production department manager is responsible for explaining the problem if the process used more than the standard amount of materials.

But variance analysis can present challenges. For instance, the production department may have used more than the standard amount of material because the quality of material did not meet specifications and led to excessive waste. In this case the purchasing manager is responsible for explaining why inferior materials were acquired. But the production manager is responsible for explaining what happened if our analysis shows that waste was due to inefficiencies and not poor quality material.

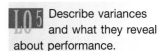

In evaluating price variances, managers must recognize that a favourable price variance may indicate a problem with product quality. **Moosehead Breweries** for example may be able to save 10% to 15% by buying a lower grade barley malt for its better ales. But it is unlikely that the company chief would gamble on quality.

Purchasing should be measured on the quality of the raw materials as well as the purchase price variance.

Labour Variances

Labour cost for a specific product or service depends on the number of hours worked (quantity) and the wage rate paid to employees (price). When actual amounts for a task differ from standard, the labour cost variance can be divided into a rate (price) variance and an efficiency (quantity) variance.

To illustrate, the direct labour standard for 3,500 units of golf hats is one hour per unit, or 3,500 hours at $6 per hour. If 3,400 hours at $6.30 per hour are actually used to complete the units, the actual and standard labour costs for these units are:

Actual cost	3,400 hrs. @ $6.30 per hr. =	$21,420
Standard cost	3,500 hrs. @ $6.00 per hr. =	21,000
Direct labour cost variance (unfavourable)		$ 420

This analysis shows actual cost is only $420 over the standard and suggests no immediate concern. But computing the quantity and price variances reveals a slightly different picture as shown in Exhibit 27.11.

Exhibit 27.11

Labour Rate and Efficiency Standard Cost Variances

Actual Cost		Standard Cost
AH × AR	AH × SR	SH × SR
3,400 hrs. × $6.30	3,400 hrs. × $6.00	3,500 hrs. × $6.00
$21,420	$20,400	$21,000

$1,020 U
Rate Variance

$600 F
Efficiency Variance

$420 U
Total Direct Labour Variance

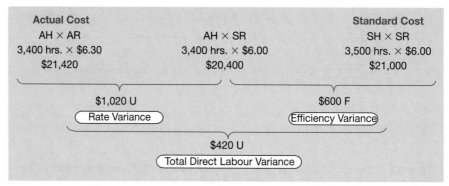

*Where AH is actual direct labour hours; AR is actual wage rate; SH is standard direct labour hours allowed for actual output; SR is standard wage rate.

The analysis in Exhibit 27.11 shows that the favourable efficiency variance of $600 results from using 100 fewer direct labour hours than standard for the units produced. But this favourable variance was more than offset by a wage rate that was $0.30 more than standard. The production manager should explain how the labour hours were reduced. If this experience can be repeated and transferred to other departments, more savings are possible. Also, the personnel administrator, or possibly the production manager, should explain why the wage rate is higher than expected.

One possible explanation of the factors leading to these labour variances might be the use of workers with various skill levels. If so, it is the responsibility of the production manager to assign each task to workers with the skill level appropriate for getting it done. In this case, an investigation might show higher skilled workers were used to produce 3,500 units of golf hats. As a result, fewer labour hours were required for the work. But the wage rate paid to such workers would be higher than standard because of their greater skills. In G-Max's situation, the effect of this strategy would be a higher than standard total cost. This would require actions to remedy this situation.

Human Resource Manager

You are the human resource manager of an electronics assembly plant. You receive the manufacturing variance report for June 2000 and discover a large unfavourable labour efficiency variance. What factors do you investigate to identify the possible causes of this variance?

You Make the Call

Answer—p. 1319

Flashback

6. What is a cost variance?
7. The following information is available for York Co.:

Actual hours worked per unit	2.5
Standard direct labour hours per unit	2.0
Actual production (units)	2,500
Budgeted production (units)	3,000
Actual rate per hour	$3.10
Standard rate per hour	$3.00

   The direct labour efficiency variance is (a) $3,750 U, (b) $3,750 F, (c) $3,875 U, (d) $3,875 F.
8. Refer to Flashback question 27-7. The direct labour rate variance is (a) $500 U, (b) $500 F, (c) $625 F, (d) $625 U.
9. If a material quantity variance is favourable and a material price variance is unfavourable, can the total material cost variance be favourable?

Answers—p. 1319

Standard Overhead Costs

When standard costs are used, a predetermined overhead rate is used to assign standard overhead costs to products or services produced. This predetermined rate is often based on the relation between standard overhead and one of either standard labour cost, standard labour hours, standard machine hours, or another measure of production.

To illustrate, let's return to the case of G-Max. G-Max charges its golf hat with $2 of standard overhead cost per standard direct labour hour. Because the direct labour standard for the golf hat is one hour per unit, the 3,500 units manufactured in May are charged with $7,000 of standard overhead costs, computed as 3,500 hours × $2.

Recall that only 3,400 actual direct labour hours were used by G-Max in producing these units. Yet overhead costs are assigned to units on the basis of standard labour hours, not on the basis of actual labour hours. Standard labour hours are used because the total amount of overhead charged to all units produced should equal the total flexible budget overhead cost for the period. While this is true for variable overhead, the fixed overhead assigned will be equal to the budget only when actual production equals expected production. A difference between actual and expected production will result in what is called fixed overhead volume variance, which we discuss later in the chapter.

Establishing Overhead Standards

Standard overhead costs are the amounts expected to occur at a predicted level of activity. Unlike direct materials and direct labour, overhead includes both variable and fixed costs. This results in the average overhead cost per unit changing as the predicted volume changes.

Because standard costs are also budgeted costs, they must be established before the reporting period begins. This means standard overhead costs are average per unit costs based on the predicted level of activity.

To establish the standard overhead cost rate, management uses the same cost structure that is used to construct a flexible budget when a period is complete. This cost structure identifies the different overhead cost components and classifies them as variable or fixed. To obtain the standard overhead rate, management selects a level of activity (volume) and predicts total overhead cost. It then divides this total by the allocation base to get the standard overhead rate. Standard direct labour hours expected to be used to produce the predicted volume is a common allocation base, and is used in this section.

Exhibit 27.12 shows the overhead cost structure used in developing flexible budgets for G-Max. It also sets the predetermined standard overhead rate for May before the month begins. The first column lists the per unit amounts of variable costs and the monthly amounts of fixed costs. The next four columns show the total costs expected to occur at four different levels of activity. The overhead cost per unit gets smaller as volume of activity increases. This occurs because fixed costs are constant for the month.

Exhibit 27.12

Flexible Overhead Budget

G-MAX
Overhead Costs Scenarios
For Month Ended May 31, 1999

	Flexible Budget Amounts	Different Production Levels (Percent of Monthly Capacity)			
		70%	80%	90%	100%
Production in units	1 unit	3,500	4,000	4,500	5,000
Factory overhead:					
Variable costs (per unit):					
Indirect labour	$ 0.40	$1,400	$1,600	$1,800	$2,000
Indirect materials	0.30	1,050	1,200	1,350	1,500
Power and lights	0.20	700	800	900	1,000
Maintenance	0.10	350	400	450	500
Total	$ 1.00	3,500	4,000	4,500	5,000
Fixed costs (per month):					
Building rent	$1,000	1,000	1,000	1,000	1,000
Amortization, machinery	1,200	1,200	1,200	1,200	1,200
Supervisory salaries	1,800	1,800	1,800	1,800	1,800
Total	$4,000	4,000	4,000	4,000	4,000
Total factory overhead		$7,500	$8,000	$8,500	$9,000
Standard direct labour hours	1 hr./unit	3,500	4,000	4,500	5,000
Predetermined overhead rate per standard direct labour hour		$ 2.14	$ 2.00	$ 1.89	$ 1.80

In setting the standard overhead cost for May, managers of G-Max predicted an 80% capacity level with a predicted production volume of 4,000 golf hats. At this volume the total overhead for May is $8,000. This volume produces a $2 per unit average overhead cost, computed as $8,000 divided by 4,000 units.

Since G-Max has a standard of one direct labour hour for each unit, the predetermined standard overhead application rate for May is $2 per standard direct labour hour. The variable overhead rate remains constant at $1 per direct labour hour regardless of the budgeted production level. The fixed overhead rate changes according to the budgeted production volume. For instance, for the predicted level of 4,000 units of production, the fixed rate is $1 per hour—computed as $4,000 fixed costs divided by 4,000 hours.

When choosing the predicted activity level for a company, management considers many factors. Predicted activity can be set as high as 100% of capacity. But this is rare. Factors causing the activity level to be less than full capacity include difficulties in scheduling work, equipment under repair or maintenance, and insufficient product demand. Good long-run management practices often call for some plant capacity in excess of current operating needs to allow for special opportunities and demand changes.

Measuring Up
In the spirit of continuous improvement, leading companies are setting new standards (benchmarks) for performance. Competitors are comparing their processes and performance standards against these benchmarks established by the leaders. This implies continuous revision of standards in all areas of an organization to improve productivity. Corporations such as **Xerox Canada, Motorola,** and **Magna International** use benchmarking to stay one step ahead of competitors.

Did You Know?

Overhead Variances

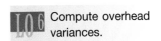

LO 6 Compute overhead variances.

When standard costs are used, the cost accounting system applies overhead to the good units produced using the predetermined standard overhead rate. At the end of the period, the difference between the total overhead cost applied to products and the total overhead cost actually incurred is called **overhead cost variance.** This variance is computed as shown in Exhibit 27.13.

Exhibit 27.13
Overhead Cost Variance Formula

Overhead Cost Variance	=	**Actual Overhead Incurred**	−	**Standard Overhead Applied**
OCV	=	**AOI**	−	**SOA**

Variances are analyzed by cost behaviour to help management identify factors causing the overhead cost variance. This analysis is performed separately for variable and fixed overhead. The results provide information useful to management for taking strategic actions. Similar to our analysis of direct material and direct labour variances, both of these overhead variances can be analyzed into useful components as shown in Exhibit 27.14.

A **spending variance** occurs when management pays an amount different than the budgeted price to acquire overhead items. For instance, the actual wage rate paid to indirect labour might be higher than the budgeted or standard rate. Similarly, actual supervisory salaries might be less than expected. Spending variances can be calculated separately for both fixed and variable costs. Spending variances cause management to investigate the reasons why the amount paid was different than budgeted. Both variable and fixed overhead costs yield their own spending variance.

Analysis of variable overhead includes computation of an **efficiency variance.** An efficiency variance occurs when standard direct labour hours (the allocation base) expected for actual production are different from the actual direct labour hours used. This efficiency variance is unrelated to whether variable overhead was used efficiently. Instead, this variance results from whether or not the overhead allocation base was used efficiently.

Exhibit 27.14

Variable and Fixed Overhead Variances

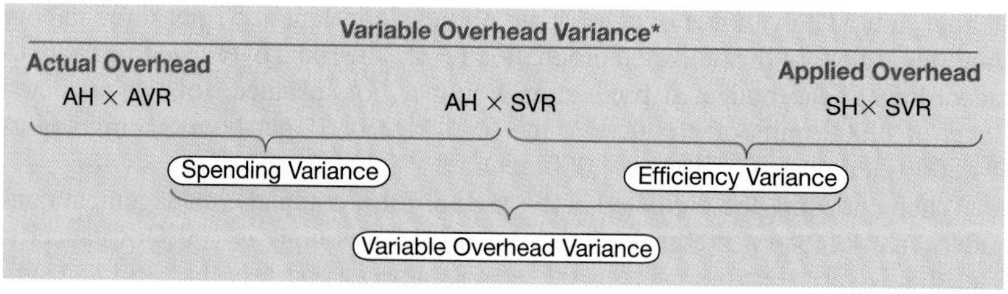

*Where: AH = actual hours; AVR = actual variable overhead rate; SH = standard hours; SVR = standard variable overhead rate.

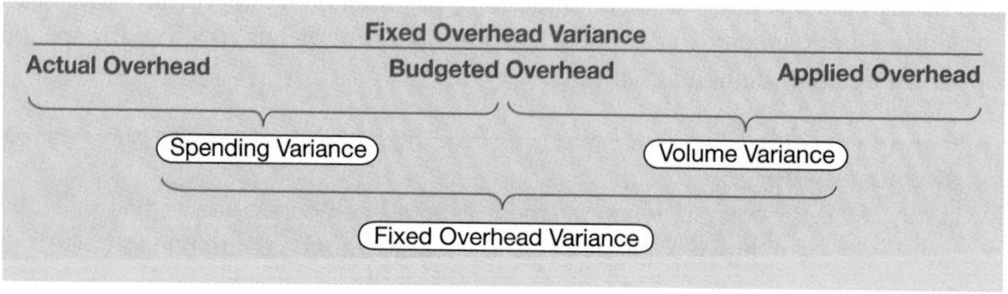

Combining the variable overhead spending variance, the fixed overhead spending variance, and the variable overhead efficiency variance results in controllable variance, see Exhibit 27.15. The **controllable variance** is generally under the control of management.

A **volume variance** occurs when there is a difference between the actual volume of production and the budgeted volume of production. The budgeted fixed overhead amount remains the same regardless of the budgeted volume of production. It is computed based on standard direct labour hours allowed for budgeted production volume. But the applied overhead is based on the standard direct labour hours allowed for the actual volume of production. If there is a difference between budgeted and actual production volumes, there is a difference in the standard direct labour hours allowed for these two production levels. Such a situation yields a volume variance.

A volume variance is not included as part of controllable variance. The actual production level depends upon many factors after a budget is established such as the number of orders received. But management must strive to accurately predict budgeted volume. The practice of continuous budgeting and the use of shorter budgeting periods, as discussed in the previous chapter, are helpful in arriving at accurate budget estimates.

Exhibit 27.15

Framework for Understanding Total Overhead Variance

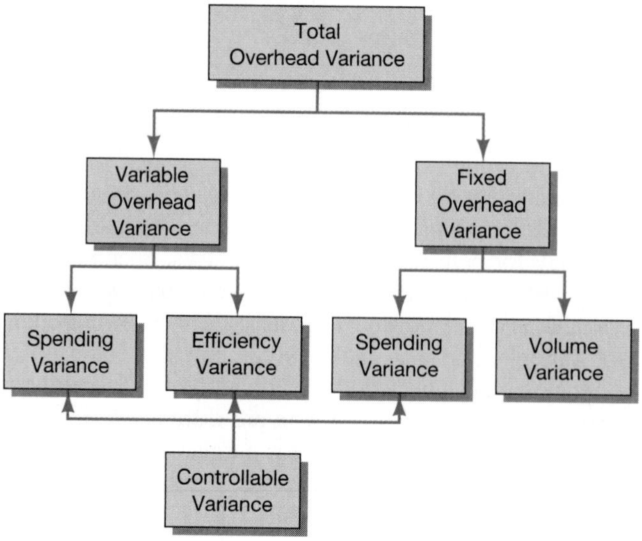

Computing Overhead Variances

To illustrate the computation of overhead variances refer to data from G-Max. We know that 3,500 units are actually produced while 4,000 units were budgeted. Additional data from G-Max shows that actual overhead incurred was $7,650, with the variable portion amounting to $3,650 of the $7,650. Using this information we compute variances for variable and fixed overhead as shown in Exhibits 27.16 and 27.17.

Variable Overhead Variances

Recall that overhead is applied based on direct labour hours as the allocation base. Also recall that 3,400 direct labour hours were used to produce 3,500 units. This compares favourably to the standard requirement of 3,500 direct labour hours at one labour hour per unit. The computation of variable overhead spending and efficiency variances are shown in Exhibit 27.16.

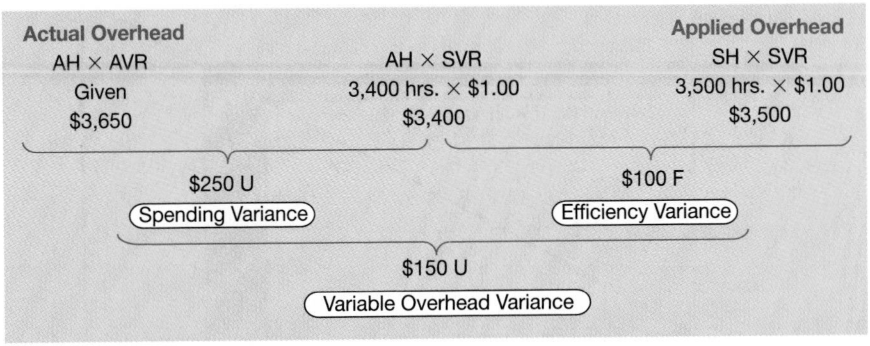

Exhibit 27.16

Computing Variable Overhead Variances

The actual variable overhead amount of $3,650 is reported to us from G-Max. This translates into an actual variable overhead rate of $1.07 per direct labour hour, computed as $3,650 divided by 3,400 units. This reveals that, on average, G-Max incurred $0.07 more per direct labour hour in variable overhead, compared to the standard rate. The middle column of Exhibit 27.16 is computed by multiplying the actual direct labour hours (3,400) by the standard rate of $1 per direct labour hour. The right-hand column is applied overhead. It is computed by multiplying the standard hours allowed for actual production (3,500) by the standard rate of $1 per direct labour hour.

Fixed Overhead Variances

G-Max incurred $4,000 in actual fixed overhead costs, computed as $7,650 total overhead costs minus variable overhead costs of $3,650. This amount is equal to the budgeted overhead for May 1999. G-Max's budgeted fixed overhead application rate is $1 per hour, computed as $4,000 divided by 4,000 direct labour hours (see Exhibit 27.12). The actual production level is 3,500 units. Using this information, we can compute the fixed overhead variances as shown in Exhibit 27.17.

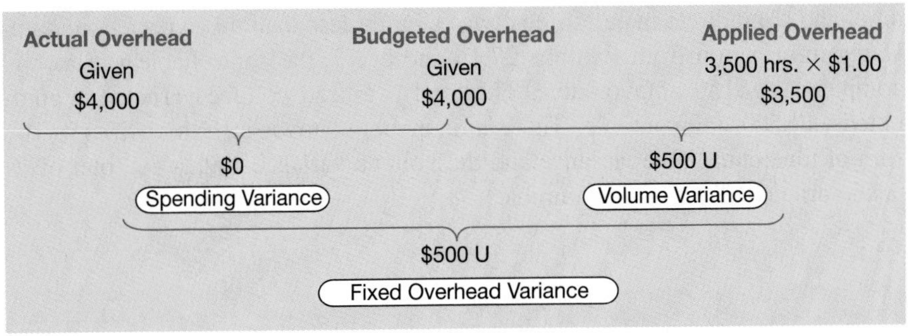

Exhibit 27.17

Computing Fixed Overhead Variances

Applied fixed overhead is computed by multiplying standard hours allowed for actual production (3,500) by the fixed overhead allocation rate ($1). Exhibit 27.17 reveals the fixed overhead spending variance is zero and the volume variance is $500. The volume variance occurs because 500 fewer units were produced than budgeted. This is because 80% of the manufacturing capacity was budgeted but only 70% was used.

The volume variance is shown graphically in Exhibit 27.18. The upward-sloping line reflects the amount of fixed overhead costs expected to be applied to the units produced in May. The horizontal line reflects the $4,000 of total fixed costs expected for May. These two lines cross at the planned operating volume of 4,000 units. At a volume of 3,500 units the overhead costs applied line falls $500 below the budgeted overhead line. This shortfall is the volume variance.

Exhibit 27.18

Volume Variance

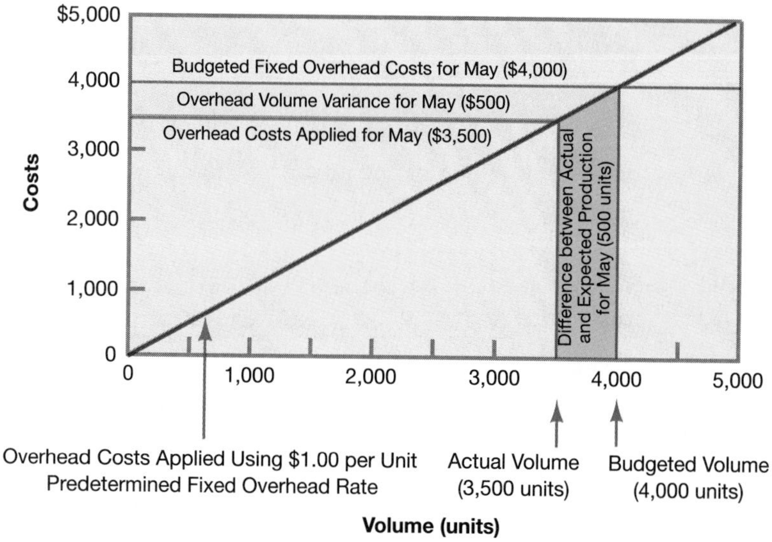

An unfavourable volume variance implies that the company did not reach its predicted operating level. Of course, management would already know this result and the variance does not convey new information. More important, management needs to know why volume is different from the expected level. The main purpose of the volume variance is that it explains the portion of the total variance caused by failing to meet the expected level. This permits management to focus on the controllable variance.

A complete overhead variance report provides managers with information about specific overhead costs and how they differ from budgeted amounts. Exhibit 27.19 shows the May overhead variance report for G-Max. It reveals: (1) all fixed costs and maintenance cost occurred as expected, (2) costs for indirect labour, and power and lights, were higher than expected at the actual volume, and (3) indirect materials cost was slightly less than the expected amount. Using information from Exhibits 27.16 and 27.17, the controllable variance is computed as $150 unfavourable. The total overhead volume variance is computed as $500 unfavourable. These amounts are shown in Exhibit 27.19. The sum of the controllable variance and the volume variance equals the total overhead variance of $650 unfavourable.

Exhibit 27.19

Overhead Variance Report

G-MAX
Factory Overhead Variance Report
For Month Ended May 31, 1999

VOLUME VARIANCE:

Expected production level	80% of capacity
Production level achieved	70% of capacity
Volume variance	$500 (unfavourable)

CONTROLLABLE VARIANCE:

	Flexible Budget	Actual Results	Variances
Variable overhead costs:			
Indirect labour	$1,400	$1,525	$125 U
Indirect materials	1,050	1,025	$ 25 F
Power and lights	700	750	50 U
Maintenance	350	350	—
Total variable costs	$3,500	$3,650	$150 U
Fixed overhead costs:			
Building rent	$1,000	$1,000	
Amortization, machinery	1,200	1,200	
Supervisory salaries	1,800	1,800	
Total fixed costs	$4,000	$4,000	
Total overhead costs	$7,500	$7,650	$150 U

F = Favourable variance; and U = Unfavourable variance

Flash back

10. Under what conditions is overhead volume variance considered favourable?

Answers—p. 1319

Other Standard Cost Uses

This section describes the application of standard costs for control, its use by service and other nonmanufacturing companies, and its impact on the accounting system.

Standard Costs for Control

LO 7 Explain how standard cost information is useful for management by exception.

To control business activities, top management must be able to access the actions of lower-level managers responsible for the company's revenues, costs, and expenses. After a budget is prepared and standard costs are established, management should take actions to gain control when actual costs differ from the standard or budgeted amounts.

Variance reports call management's attention to variations from business plans and other standards. Managers exercise their control function by using these reports to focus on problem areas. This focus on problem areas is known as management by exception.

Management by exception involves managers focusing attention on the most significant variances and giving less attention to areas where performance is reasonably close to the standard. This practice leads management to concentrate on the exceptional or irregular situations. It also means deferring any serious analysis of areas showing actual results that are reasonably close to the plan. Management by exception is especially useful when directed at controllable items.

Judgment and Ethics

Internal Auditor

You are an internal auditor reviewing your company's records. You discover one manager who always spends exactly what is budgeted for supplies and small items of equipment. You also find about 30% of the annual budget for these items is spent just before the end of the year. A talk with this manager reveals he always spends what is budgeted, whether or not supplies and equipment are needed. He offers three reasons for his actions. First, he does not want his budget cut. Second, the company's management by exception calls attention to deviations from the budget. Third, he feels the money was budgeted to be spent. You wonder if the matter should be raised in your report. What do you do?

Answer—p. 1319

Standard Costs for Services and Other Activities

Many managers use standard costs and variance analysis for manufacturing costs. In many cases, the master budget includes selling and general and administrative expenses but subsequent control over these expenses is not based on standard costs and variances.

There are also many managers who recognize that standard costs and variances can help them control their *non*manufacturing expenses. In addition, companies providing services to customers instead of products can use standard costs. Our explanation and application of standard costs and variances can be readily adapted to these nonmanufacturing situations.

Flash back

11. To use management by exception with standard costs:

a. A company must record standard costs in its accounts.

b. Variances from flexible budget amounts should be computed to allow management to focus its attention on significant differences between actual and budgeted performance.

c. Only variances for direct materials and direct labour should be analyzed.

Answers—p. 1319

Standard Cost Accounting System

LO 8 Record journal entries for standard costs and account for price and quantity variances.

We have shown how companies use standard costs in management reports. Most standard cost systems also record these costs and variances in accounts. This practice simplifies recordkeeping and helps in preparation of reports. We do not need knowledge of standard cost accounting practices to understand standard costs and how they are used. But we do need to know how to interpret accounts in which standard costs and variances are recorded. The entries in this section briefly illustrate the important aspects of this process for G-Max's standard costs and variances for May.

The first of these entries is the one to record standard materials cost incurred in May. It is recorded in the Goods in Process Inventory account. This part of the entry is similar to other cost accounting entries. The amount of the debit equals the standard cost ($3,500) instead of the actual cost ($3,780). This entry credits Raw Materials Inventory for actual cost. The difference between standard and actual costs is recorded with debits to two separate materials variance accounts. Both the materials price and quantity variances are recorded as debits because they reflect additional costs greater than the standard cost. This treatment also reflects their unfavourable effect because they represent higher costs and lower net income.

May 31	Goods in Process Inventory	3,500	
	Direct Materials Price Variance	**180**	
	Direct Materials Quantity Variance	**100**	
	Raw Materials Inventory		3,780
	To charge production for standard quantity of materials used (1,750 kg) at the standard price ($2 per kg) and to record direct material price and quantity variances.		

Another important entry is the one to debit Goods in Process Inventory for the standard labour cost of the goods manufactured during May ($21,000) instead of actual cost ($21,420). Actual cost is recorded with a credit to the Factory Payroll account. The difference between standard and actual costs is explained by two variances. The direct labour rate variance is unfavourable and is debited to that account. The direct labour efficiency variance, which is favourable, is credited.

May 31	Goods in Process Inventory	21,000	
	Direct Labour Rate Variance	**1,020**	
	Direct Labour Efficiency Variance		**600**
	Factory Payroll		21,420
	To charge production with 3,500 standard hours of direct labour at the standard $6 per hour rate and to record the direct labour rate and efficiency variances.		

The direct labour efficiency variance is favourable because it represents a lower cost and a higher net income.

The entry to assign standard predetermined overhead to the cost of goods manufactured in the period is also important. It debits the predetermined amount ($7,000) to the Goods in Process Inventory account instead of the actual cost ($7,650). When actual overhead is incurred this amount is debited to the Factory Overhead account. This means when Factory Overhead is applied to Goods in Process Inventory, the amount applied is debited to the Goods in Process Inventory account and credited to the Factory Overhead account. To account for the difference, this entry includes a debit of $250 to the Variable Overhead Spending Variance account, a credit of $100 to the Variable Overhead Efficiency Variance account, and a debit of $500 to the Volume Variance account. An alternative approach, which we show here, is to record the difference with a debit of $150 to the Controllable Variance account and a debit of $500 to the Volume Variance account.

May 31	Goods in Process Inventory	7,000	
	Controllable Variance	**150**	
	Volume Variance	**500**	
	Factory Overhead		7,650
	To apply overhead at the standard rate of $2 per standard direct labour hour (3,500 hours) and to record overhead variances.		

The balances of these six different variance accounts accumulate until the end of the accounting period. Unfavourable variances of some months are often offset by favourable variances of other months.

The variance accounts are temporary owners' equity accounts that are closed at the end of each period. These account balances, which reflect results of events in the period, are closed at the end of the period. Since their balances represent differences between actual and standard costs, they must be added to or subtracted from the manufacturing costs recorded in the period. In this way the recorded manufacturing costs equal the actual costs incurred in the period.

A company must use these actual amounts in external financial statements prepared in accordance with generally accepted accounting principles. If the variances are material, they need to be added to or subtracted from the balances of the Goods in Process Inventory, the Finished Goods Inventory, and the Cost of Goods Sold accounts. If the amounts are immaterial, they are typically added to or subtracted from the balance of the Cost of Goods Sold account.[3]

Flash back

12. A company uses a standard cost system. Prepare the journal entry to record these material variances:

Direct material cost actually incurred	$73,200
Direct material quantity variance (favourable)	3,800
Direct material price variance (unfavourable)	1,300

13. If standard manufacturing costs are recorded in the accounts, how are recorded variances treated at the end of an accounting period?

Answers—p. 1319

Revenue Variances

USING THE INFORMATION

This chapter explained in detail the analysis of cost variances. A similar analysis can be applied to revenue variances. To illustrate, consider the following sales data of G-Max for two different products—fluorescent golf balls and Tiger golf clubs.

	Budgeted	Actual
Sales of golf balls (units)	1,000	1,100
Sales price per golf ball	$ 10	$10.50
Sales of golf clubs (units)	150	140
Sales price per golf club	$ 200	$ 190

LO 9 Analyze changes in sales from expected amounts.

Using this information, we can compute a *sales price variance* and a *sales volume variance* as shown in Exhibit 27.20. Total sales price variance is $850 unfavourable, and the total sales volume variance is $1,000 unfavourable. Neither variance implies anything positive.

[3] This process is similar to that shown in Chapter 22 for eliminating an underapplied or overapplied balance in the Factory Overhead account.

Further analysis of these revenue variances reveals both the sales price and sales volume variances for golf balls are favourable. The unfavourable total sales price and total sales volume variances are due to the golf clubs.

Exhibit 27.20

Computing Revenue Variances

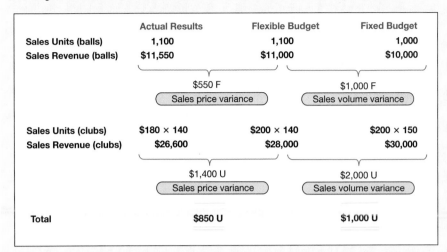

	Actual Results		Flexible Budget		Fixed Budget
Sales Units (balls)	**1,100**		**1,100**		**1,000**
Sales Revenue (balls)	**$11,550**		**$11,000**		**$10,000**
		$550 F Sales price variance		$1,000 F Sales volume variance	
Sales Units (clubs)	**$180 × 140**		**$200 × 140**		**$200 × 150**
Sales Revenue (clubs)	**$26,600**		**$28,000**		**$30,000**
		$1,400 U Sales price variance		$2,000 U Sales volume variance	
Total		**$850 U**		**$1,000 U**	

Sales managers find revenue variance information useful, especially when multiple products are involved. With multiple products, the sales volume variance can be further separated into a *sales mix variance* and a *sales quantity variance*. The sales mix variance is due to a difference between the actual and budgeted sales mix of the products. The sales quantity variance is due to a difference between the *total* actual and budgeted quantity of units sold.

Managers use this information for planning and control purposes. With respect to planning, variance information is used to plan future actions to avoid unfavourable variances. G-Max sold a total of 90 units more than planned but not in the budgeted proportion. It actually sold less than the budgeted quantity of the higher priced golf clubs which contributed to the unfavourable variance. This detail is used by managers to uncover what caused the sales staff to sell more golf balls and fewer golf clubs. With respect to control, managers use this information to evaluate and even reward their salespeople.

Regional Sales Manager
You are the sales manager for a three-product company. A recent performance report from your company's office reveals a large favourable sales volume variance but an unfavourable sales price variance. You are confused because you did not expect to see a large increase in sales volume. What do you do?

You Make the Call

Answer—p. 1319

Summary

LO1 **Compare fixed and flexible budgets.** A fixed budget shows the revenues, costs, and expenses expected to occur at the specified production and sales volume. Therefore, if the actual production and sales volume is at some other level, the amounts in the fixed budget do not provide a reasonable basis for evaluating actual performance. A flexible budget expresses variable costs in per unit terms so that it can be used to develop budgeted amounts for any production and sales volume within the relevant range. As a result, managers compute budgeted amounts after a period for the volume that actually occurred. This budget is more useful in evaluating the actual performance.

LO 2 **Prepare a flexible budget and interpret a flexible budget performance report.** To prepare a flexible budget, management depends on the distinctions between fixed and variable costs. In generating the numbers to be used in preparing a flexible budget, the accountant expresses each variable cost as a constant amount per unit of sales (or as a percentage of a sales dollar). In contrast, the budgeted amount of each fixed cost is expressed as the total amount expected to occur at any sales volume within the relevant range. The flexible budget is then prepared using these amounts for fixed and variable costs for the desired sales volume.

LO 3 **Define standard costs and explain their computation and uses.** Standard costs are the normal costs that should be incurred to produce a product or perform a service. As such, they are the amounts that should be budgeted ahead of time and used in evaluations. Standard costs should be based on a careful examination of the processes used to produce a product or perform a service and the quantities and prices that should be incurred in carrying out those processes. On a performance report, these standard costs (which are really flexible budget amounts) are compared to actual costs and the differences are presented as variances. The variances suggest areas for management attention and possible corrective action.

LO 4 **Compute materials and labour variances.** Materials and labour variances are due to the differences between the actual costs incurred and the budgeted costs. The price (or rate) variance is computed by comparing the actual cost with the flexible budget amount that should have been incurred to acquire the actual quantity of resources. The quantity (or efficiency) variance is computed by comparing the flexible budget amount that should have been incurred to acquire the actual quantity of resources versus the flexible budget amount incurred that should have been incurred to acquire standard quantity of the resource.

LO 5 **Describe variances and what they reveal about performance.** Variances can be used by management to determine that a problem exists. These total cost variances can be broken into price and quantity to direct management's attention to the actions of the lower-level managers responsible for quantities used or prices paid.

LO 6 **Compute overhead variances.** Overhead variances are due to the differences between the actual overhead costs incurred and the overhead applied to production. The spending variance arises because the actual amount incurred was more than the budgeted amount of overhead, whereas the efficiency or volume variance arises due to the difference between the flexible overhead budget and the overhead applied to production. It is important to realize that overhead is not directly traced to a cost object but assigned using an overhead allocation base. Thus, the efficiency variance (in the case of variable overhead) is a result of the overhead application base being used more or less efficiently than planned.

LO 7 **Explain how standard cost information is useful for management by exception.** Standard cost accounting provides management with information about costs that differ from budgeted amounts. Performance reports disclose the costs or areas of operations that have significant variances from normal or budgeted amounts. This disclosure of differences from expected levels allows managers to devote their attention to the exceptions and pay less attention to areas in which operations are proceeding normally.

LO 8 **Record journal entries for standard costs and account for price and quantity variances.** When a company records standard costs in its accounts, the standard costs of materials, labour, and overhead are debited to the Goods in Process Inventory account. Based on an analysis of the material, labour, and overhead costs, each quantity variance, price variance, volume variance, and controllable variance is recorded in a separate account. At the end of the period, if the variances are material, they are allocated among the balances of the Goods in Process Inventory, Finished Goods Inventory, and Cost of Goods Sold accounts. If they are not material, they may be simply debited or credited to the Cost of Goods Sold account.

LO 9 **Analyze changes in sales from expected amounts.** As in the case of costs, actual sales can be different from budgeted sales. Managers can further investigate this difference by computing the sales price and sales volume variances, i.e., the portion of the variance resulting from a difference between the actual and budgeted selling prices and the portion resulting from a difference between the actual and budgeted sales quantities. This information can be useful in that managers can now look further into what caused the price and/or quantity difference.

Guidance Answers to **You Make the Call**

Budget Officer

From the complaints, it appears that the performance report compared the actual results with the fixed budget. While this comparison is useful to determine whether the amount of work actually performed was more or less than what was planned, it is not useful in order to compare whether the divisions were more or less efficient than planned. If the two consulting divisions worked on more assignments than expected, some of their costs will increase. Therefore, the budgeting department should prepare a flexible budget using the actual number of consulting assignments and use this budget to compare the actual performance.

Human Resource Manager

As the HR manager, you may not be directly responsible for any labour efficiency variances. However, you should still investigate the causes for any labour-related variances because labour issues come under Human Resource Management. An unfavourable labour efficiency variance occurs because more labour hours than standard are used during the budget period. There may be at least three reasons for this. First, materials quality may be poor resulting in more labour consumption due to rework. Second, there could have been unplanned interruptions during the period (e.g., strike, breakdowns, accidents). Finally, a different labour mix may have been used by the production manager to expedite orders. This new labour mix may have consisted of a larger proportion of untrained labour, which resulted in more labour hour consumption.

Regional Sales Manager

The fact that the sales price variance is unfavourable suggests that the actual prices were lower than the budgeted prices. As the regional sales manager, you certainly would like to investigate into the matter. Perhaps, your sales persons lowered the price of certain products by offering quantity discounts. You may then want to know what prompted these individuals to offer the discounts (e.g., perhaps the main competitors were offering discounts). Similarly, with respect to the sales volume variance, you may want to break it further into the market share and sales quantity variances. You may find that although the sales quantity variance is favourable, the mix variance may not be. Then you need to investigate further as to why the actual mix is different from the budgeted sales mix.

Guidance Answers to **Judgment and Ethics**

Internal Auditor

This is a situation where the manager of the department is playing safe to cope with the practice of management by exception. It may not be appropriate to classify this manager's action as unethical. However, the action is undesirable and senior management should perhaps be informed about it. The amount involved may not be extremely significant because of the nature of the items purchased and therefore the matter may not be considered very serious. However, it is the internal auditor's role to bring to management's attention such behaviour. Perhaps a good way in which the internal auditor can deal with the situation is to inform about this behaviour in an indirect manner in the report. In addition, the internal auditor can recommend that for the purchase of such discretionary items, the individual department managers must provide a report once every three years and any future budgetary requests must be done using a zero-based budgeting process, and the internal auditor must be given full authority to verify this budget request.

Guidance Answers to Flashbacks

1. *b*
2. The first step is classifying each cost as variable or fixed.
3. A fixed budget is prepared using an expected volume of sales or production, and a flexible budget compares actual costs with the costs that should have been incurred at the actual volume.
4. It is the difference between sales and variable costs.
5. *c*
6. It is the difference between actual cost and standard cost.
7. *a* Total actual hours: $2,500 \times 2.5 = 6,250$
   Total standard hours: $2,500 \times 2.0 = 5,000$
   $QV = (6,250 - 5,000) \times \$3.00 = \$3,750$ U
8. *d* $PV = (\$3.10 - \$3.00) \times 6,250 = \$625$ U
9. Yes, if the materials quantity variance is greater than the materials price variance.
10. The overhead volume variance is favourable when the actual operating level is larger than the expected level.
11. *b*
12.

Goods in Process Inventory	75,700	
Direct Material Price Variance	1,300	
Direct Material Quantity Variance		3,800
Raw Materials Inventory		73,200

13. If the variances are material, they should be prorated among the Goods in Process Inventory, Finished Goods Inventory, and Cost of Goods Sold accounts. If they are not material, they can be closed to Cost of Goods Sold.

Demonstration Problem

The Pacific Company provides the following information about its budgeted and actual results for June 1999. Although the expected volume for June was 25,000 units produced and sold, the company actually produced and sold 27,000 units.

Budget data — 25,000 units (asterisks identify factory overhead items):

Selling price	$ 5.00 per unit	
Variable costs (per unit of output):		
Direct materials	1.24 per unit	
Direct labour	1.50 per unit	
*Factory supplies	0.25 per unit	
*Utilities	0.50 per unit	
Selling costs	0.40 per unit	
Fixed costs (per month):		
*Amortization of machinery	$3,750	
*Amortization of building	2,500	
General liability insurance	1,200	
Property taxes on office equipment	500	
Other administrative expense	750	

Actual results during June — 27,000 units produced:

Selling price (per unit of output)	$ 5.23 per unit
Variable costs (per unit of output):	
Direct materials	1.12 per unit
Direct labour	1.40 per unit
*Factory supplies	0.37 per unit
*Utilities	0.60 per unit
Selling costs	0.34 per unit
Fixed costs (per month):	
*Amortization of machinery	$3,710
*Amortization of building	2,500
General liability insurance	1,250
Property taxes on office equipment	485
Other administrative expense	900

Standard manufacturing costs based on expected output of 25,000 units:

	Per Unit of Output	Quantity Total to Be Used	Total Cost
Direct materials, 4 grams @ $0.31/g	$1.24/unit	100,000 grams	$31,000
Direct labour, 0.25 hrs. @ $6.00/hr.	1.50/unit	6,250 hrs.	37,500
Overhead	1.00/unit		25,000

Actual costs incurred to produce 27,000 units:

	Per Unit of Output	Quantity Total to Be Used	Total Cost
Direct materials, 4 grams @ $0.28/g.	$1.12/unit	108,000 grams	$30,240
Direct labour, 0.20 hrs. @ $7.00/hr.	1.40/unit	5,400 hrs.	37,800
Overhead	1.20/unit		32,400

If standards had been based on an expected output of 27,000 units, standard manufacturing costs would have been:

	Per Unit of Output	Quantity Total to Be Used	Total Cost
Direct materials, 4 grams @ $0.31/g.	$1.24/unit	108,000 grams	$33,480
Direct labour, 0.25 hrs. @ $6.00/hr.	1.50/unit	6,750 hrs.	40,500
Overhead			26,500

Required

1. Develop possible flexible budgets for June showing expected revenues, costs, and income under assumptions of 20,000, 25,000, and 30,000 units of output made and sold.
2. Prepare a performance report that contrasts the actual results with the amounts that would have been budgeted if the actual volume had been expected.
3. Present variance analyses for direct materials, direct labour, and manufacturing overhead.

Planning the Solution

- Prepare a table showing the expected results at the three specified possible levels of output. Compute the variable costs by multiplying the per unit variable costs by the expected volumes. Include fixed costs at the given amounts. Combine the amounts in the table to show the total variable costs, the total contribution margin, total fixed costs, and income from operations.
- Prepare another table that shows the actual results and the amounts that should have been incurred at 27,000 units. Show any differences in the third column, and label them with either an F for favourable if they increase income or a U for unfavourable if they decrease income.
- Using the table format from the chapter, compute these total variances and the individual variances:
  - Total materials variance (including the direct materials quantity variance and the direct materials price variance).
  - Total direct labour variance (including the direct labour efficiency variance and the direct labour rate variance).
  - Total overhead variance (including the overhead volume variance and the overhead controllable variance).

Solution to Demonstration Problem

1. Flexible budgets:

	20,000 Units	25,000 Units	30,000 Units
Sales	$100,000	$125,000	$150,000
Variable costs:			
Direct materials	24,800	31,000	37,200
Direct labour	30,000	37,500	45,000
Factory supplies	5,000	6,250	7,500
Utilities	10,000	12,500	15,000
Selling costs	8,000	10,000	12,000
Total variable costs	77,800	97,250	116,700
Contribution margin	22,200	27,750	33,300
Fixed costs:			
Amortization of machinery	3,750	3,750	3,750
Amortization of building	2,500	2,500	2,500
General liability insurance	1,200	1,200	1,200
Property taxes on office equipment	500	500	500
Other administrative expense	750	750	750
Total fixed costs	8,700	8,700	8,700
Income from operations	$ 13,500	$ 19,050	$ 24,600

2.

THE PACIFIC COMPANY
Flexible Budget Performance Report
For Month of June 1999

	Flexible Budget	Actual Results	Variance
Sales (27,000 units)	$135,000	$141,210	$6,210 F
Variable costs:			
Direct materials	33,480	30,240	3,240 F
Direct labour	40,500	37,800	2,700 F
Factory supplies	6,750	9,990	3,240 U
Utilities	13,500	16,200	2,700 U
Selling costs	10,800	9,180	1,620 F
Total variable costs	105,030	103,410	1,620 F
Contribution margin	29,970	37,800	7,830 F
Fixed costs:			
Amortization of machinery	3,750	3,710	40 F
Amortization of building	2,500	2,500	
General liability insurance	1,200	1,250	50 U
Property taxes on office equipment	500	485	15 F
Other administrative expense	750	900	150 U
Total fixed costs	8,700	8,845	145 U
Income from operations	$ 21,270	$ 28,955	$7,685 F

F = Favourable variance; and U = Unfavourable variance

3. Variance analyses of manufacturing costs:

Material variances:			
Actual cost	108,000 grams @ $0.28	$30,240	
Standard cost	108,000 grams @ $0.31	33,480	
Direct material cost variance (favourable)			$(3,240)
Quantity variance:			
Actual units at standard price	108,000 grams @ $0.31	$33,480	
Standard units at standard price	108,000 grams @ $0.31	33,480	
Variance (none)			-0-
Price variance:			
Actual units at actual price	108,000 grams @ $0.28	30,240	
Actual units at standard price	108,000 grams @ $0.31	33,480	
Variance (favourable)	108,000 grams @ ($0.03)		$(3,240)
Direct material cost variance (favourable)			$(3,240)

Labour variances:			
Actual cost	5,400 hrs. @ $7.00	$37,800	
Standard cost	6,750 hrs. @ $6.00	40,500	
Direct labour cost variance (favourable)			$2,700
Quantity variance:			
Actual hours at standard price	5,400 hrs. @ $6.00	$32,400	
Standard hours at standard price	6,750 hrs. @ $6.00	40,500	
Variance (favourable)	(1,350) hrs. @ $6.00		$(8,100)
Price variance:			
Actual hours at actual price	5,400 hrs. @ $7.00	37,800	
Actual hours at standard price	5,400 hrs. @ $6.00	32,400	
Variance (unfavourable)	5,400 hrs. @ $1.00		5,400
Direct labour cost variance (favourable)			$(2,700)

Overhead variances:			
Total overhead cost incurred	27,000 units @ $1.20	$32,400	
Total overhead applied	27,000 units @ $1.00	27,000	
Overhead cost variance (unfavourable)			$5,400
Volume variance:			
Budgeted overhead at 27,000 units		$26,500	
Standard overhead applied to production (27,000 units @ $1.00 per unit rate)		27,000	
Variance (favourable)			$(500)
Controllable variance:			
Actual overhead incurred		32,400	
Overhead budgeted at operating level achieved		26,500	
Variance (unfavourable)			5,900
Total overhead variance (unfavourable)			$5,400

Glossary

Budgetary control Use of budgets by management to monitor and control the operations of a company. (p. 1294)

Budget report Report comparing actual results to planned objectives; sometimes used as a progress report. (p. 1294)

Controllable variance Two overhead spending variances, and the variable overhead efficiency variance combined together. (p. 1310)

Cost variance The difference between the actual incurred cost and the standard amount. (p. 1303)

Favourable variance Amount calculated when actual value is compared to the budget value, the actual cost or revenue contributes to a higher income. (p. 1295)

Efficiency variance The difference between the actual quantity of an input and the standard quantity of that input. (p. 1309)

Fixed budget A planning budget based on a single predicted amount of sales or production volume; unsuitable for evaluations if the actual volume differs from the predicted volume. (p. 1295)

Fixed budget performance report An internal report that compares actual revenue and cost amounts with fixed budgeted amounts and identifies the differences between them as favourable or unfavourable variances. (p. 1295)

Flexible budget A budget prepared after an operating period is complete in order to help managers evaluate past performance; uses fixed and variable costs in determining total costs. (p. 1296)

Flexible budget performance report An internal report that helps management analyze the difference between actual performance and budgeted performance based on the actual sales volume (or other level of activity); presents the differences between actual and budgeted amounts as variances. (p. 1298)

Management by exception An analytical technique used by management to focus on the most significant variances and give less attention to the areas where performance is close enough to the standard to be satisfactory. (p. 1313)

Overhead cost variance The difference between the total overhead cost applied to products and the total overhead cost actually incurred at the end of a cost period. (p. 1309)

Price variance A difference between actual and budgeted revenue or cost caused by the difference between the actual price per unit and the budgeted price per unit. (p. 1298)

Quantity variance The difference between actual and budgeted revenue or cost caused by the difference between the actual number of units sold or used and the budgeted number of units. (p. 1298)

Spending variance When management pays more or less than the budgeted price or amount to acquire the overhead items. (p. 1309)

Standard costs The costs that should be incurred under normal conditions to produce a specific product or component or to perform a specific service. (p. 1301)

Unfavourable variance Amount calculated when actual value is compared to the budget value, the actual cost or revenue contributes to a lower income. (p. 1295)

Variance analysis A process of examining the differences between actual and budgeted revenues or costs and describing them in terms of the amounts that resulted from price and quantity differences. (p. 1298)

Volume variance The difference between two dollar amounts of fixed overhead cost. The first amount equals the total budgeted overhead cost. The second number is the overhead cost allocated to products using the predetermined fixed overhead rate. (p. 1310)

Questions

1. What limits the usefulness of fixed budget performance reports?
2. Prepare the proper title for a flexible budget performance report for Light Company for the year ending in 1999. Why is the proper title important for this or any report prepared by the accountant?
3. Identify the primary purpose of a flexible budget.
4. In what sense can a variable cost be considered to be constant?
5. What type of analysis does a flexible budget performance report help management make?
6. What is a price variance? What is a quantity variance?
7. What is the purpose of using standard costs?
8. What department is usually responsible for a direct labour cost variance? What department is usually responsible for a direct labour efficiency variance?
9. What is the predetermined standard overhead rate? How is it created?
10. In a two-way analysis of the overhead variance, what is the volume variance?
11. In a two-way analysis of the overhead variance, what is the controllable variance and what creates it?
12. If a company is budgeted to operate at 80% of capacity and actually operates at 75% of capacity, what effect will the 5% reduction have on the controllable variance? The volume variance?
13. Variance analysis, in general, provides, information about _________and _________ variances, nothing more-nothing less.
14. If a company's overhead costs consisted of only variable costs and the actual sales volume was 10% higher than the budgeted sales volume, what kind of *volume variance* would the company experience?
15. What is the relationship among flexible reports, standard costs, variance analysis, and management by exception?
16. Suppose that NIKE has a standard shoe cost for a particular line of women's running shoes sold in Canada. List several factors that might cause the actual cost incurred to vary from the standard.

Quick Study

QS 27-1
Prepare a flexible budget
LO 2

Milestone Company showed the following results for May:

Sales (150,000 units)	$1,275,000
Variable costs	712,500
Fixed costs	300,000

For this level of production, sales were budgeted to be $1,400,000, variable costs, $800,000, and fixed costs, $300,000. Prepare a flexible budget performance report for May.

QS 27-2
Calculate direct material cost
LO 4, 5

Clawson Company's output for the period required a standard direct material cost of $150,000. During the period, the direct material variances included a favourable price variance of $12,000 and a favourable quantity variance of $4,000. What was the actual total direct materials cost for the period?

QS 27-3
Calculate direct labour cost
LO 4, 5

Neely Company's output for the period had an unfavourable direct labour rate variance of $20,000 and an unfavourable direct labour efficiency variance of $10,000. The goods produced during the period required a standard direct labour cost of $400,000. What was the actual total direct labour cost incurred during the period?

QS 27-4
Calculate material used
LO 4, 5

During a recent period, Holloway Company's manufacturing operations experienced a favourable price variance of $4,000 on its direct materials usage. The actual price per kilogram of material was $77.00 while the standard price was $77.50. How many kilograms of material were used during the period?

QS 27-5
Calculate actual overhead
LO 6

School Company's output for the period had a favourable overhead volume variance of $30,000 and an unfavourable overhead controllable variance of $50,400. Standard overhead charged to production during the period amounted to $225,000. What was the actual total overhead cost incurred during the period?

QS 27-6
Interpret management by exception
LO 7

Explain the concept of management by exception and the reason why standard costs assist managers in applying this concept.

QS 27-7
Prepare overhead journal entries
LO 8

Refer to the information presented in QS 27-5. School records standard costs in its accounts. Prepare the journal entry to charge overhead costs to the Goods in Process Inventory account and to record the variances.

QS 27-8
Prepare sales variances
LO 9

Ray's Used Minivans, Inc. specializes in selling used minivans. During the first six months of 1999 the dealership sold 50 minivans at an average price of $9,000 each. The budget for the first six month of 1999 was to sell 45 minivans at an average of $9,500 each. Compute the sales price and sales volume variance for the first six months of 1999 for the dealership.

Exercises

Exercise 27-1
Classifying costs as fixed or variable
LO 2

A company manufactures and sells bicycles. It normally operates eight hours a day, five days per week. On the basis of this general information, classify each of the following costs as fixed or variable. If certain facts would affect your choice, describe at least one reason that would cause you to change your conclusion.

a. Bicycle frames
b. Direct labour.
c. Screws.
d. Repair expense for power tools.
e. Management salaries.
f. Incoming shipping expenses.
g. Office supplies.
h. Amortization on power tools.
i. Taxes on property.
j. Pension cost.
k. Natural gas used for heating.

Exercise 27-2
Preparing a flexible budget
LO 2

Stockton Company prepared the following fixed budget for the first quarter of 1998.

Sales (10,000 units)		$3,000,000
Cost of goods sold:		
Direct materials	$320,000	
Direct labour	680,000	
Production supplies	264,000	
Plant manager's salary	60,000	1,324,000
Gross profit		1,676,000
Selling expenses:		
Sales commissions	120,000	
Packaging	210,000	
Advertising	100,000	430,000
Administrative expenses:		
Administrative salaries	80,000	
Amortization, office equipment	30,000	
Insurance	18,000	
Office rent	24,000	152,000
Income from operations		$1,094,000

Following the format of Exhibit 27.3, prepare a schedule that shows the amounts of the variable costs per unit and the fixed costs per quarter and three possible flexible budgets for sales volumes of 7,500, 10,000, and 12,500 units.

Exercise 27-3
Analysis of fixed budget performance report
LO 1

Land Company's fixed budget performance report for a recent month shows this information:

	Fixed Budget	Actual Results	Variance
Unit sales	6,000	4,800	
Sales	$480,000	$422,400	$57,600 U
Expenses	440,000	394,000	46,000 F
Income from operations	$40,000	$28,400	$11,600 U

The budgeted expenses of $440,000 included $300,000 of variable expenses and $140,000 of fixed expenses. The actual expenses included $130,000 of fixed expenses. Prepare a flexible budget performance report that shows any variances between the budgeted results and the actual results. (List the fixed and variable expenses separately.)

Exercise 27-4
Analysis of fixed budget performance report
LO 1

Shank Company's fixed budget performance report for a recent month shows this information:

	Fixed Budget	Actual Results	Variance
Unit sales	8,400	10,800	
Sales	$840,000	$1,080,000	$240,000 F
Expenses	630,000	756,000	126,000 U
Income from operations	$210,000	$ 324,000	$114,000 F

The budgeted expenses of $630,000 included $588,000 of variable expenses and $42,000 of fixed expenses. The actual expenses included $54,000 of fixed expenses. Prepare a flexible budget performance report that shows any variances between the budgeted results and the actual results. (List the fixed and variable expenses separately.)

Exercise 27-5
Direct material variances
LO 4, 5

Rafferty Company has just finished making 6,000 bookshelves using 8,800 square metres of wood that cost $607,200. The company's direct material standards for one bookshelf are 1.6 square metres of wood at $70 per square metre.

Required

1. Measure the direct material variances incurred in manufacturing these bookshelves.
2. Interpret the variances

Exercise 27-6
Direct labour variances
LO 4, 5

After evaluating Longhorn Company's manufacturing process, management decided to establish standards of 1.5 hours of direct labour per unit of product, and $11 per hour for the labour rate. During October, the company used 3,780 hours of direct labour at a total cost of $45,360 to produce 2,700 units of product. In November, the company used 4,480 hours of direct labour at a total cost of $47,040 to produce 2,800 units of product.

Required

1. Compute the rate variance, the efficiency variance, and the total direct labour cost variance for each of these two months.
2. Interpret the October variances.

Exercise 27-7
Overhead variances
LO 5, 6

Sharp Company established the following standard costs for one unit of its product for 1999:

Direct material (20 kg @ $2.50 per kg)	$ 50.00
Direct labour (15 hrs. @ $8.00 per hr.)	120.00
Factory variable overhead (15 hrs. @ $2.50 per hr.)	37.50
Factory fixed overhead (15 hrs. @ $.50 per hr.)	7.50
Standard cost	$215.00

The $3 ($2.50 + $.50) overhead rate per direct labour hour is based on an expected operating level equal to 75% of the factory's capacity of 50,000 units per month. The following monthly flexible budget information applies to the situation:

	Operating Levels		
	70%	75%	80%
Budgeted output (units)	35,000	37,500	40,000
Budgeted labour (standard hours)	525,000	562,500	600,000
Budgeted overhead:			
Variable overhead	$1,312,500	$1,406,250	$1,500,000
Fixed overhead	281,250	281,250	281,250
Total overhead	$1,593,750	$1,687,500	$1,781,250

During the past month, the company operated at 70% of capacity, employees worked 500,000 hours and incurred the following actual overhead costs:

Variable overhead costs	$1,267,500
Fixed overhead costs	285,000
Total overhead costs	$1,552,500

Required

1. Show how the company computed the predetermined overhead application rate of $3 ($2.50 + $.50) per hour for overhead, variable and fixed.
2. Compute the variable overhead spending and efficiency variances and interpret each.
3. Compute the fixed overhead spending and volume variances and interpret each.

Exercise 27-8
Computing volume and controllable variances
LO 6

Earth Company expected to operate last month at 80% of its productive capacity of 25,000 units per month. At this planned level, the company expected to use 40,000 standard hours of direct labour. The overhead is allocated to products using a predetermined standard rate based on direct labour hours. At the 80% level of operation, the total budgeted cost includes $40,000 of fixed overhead cost and $280,000 of variable overhead cost. During the month, the company actually incurred $340,000 of overhead and 39,000 actual hours while producing 19,500 units of product. Find the overhead volume variance, the overhead controllable variance, and the total overhead variance.

Exercise 27-9
Recording material variances in the accounts
LO 7, 8

Refer to the facts in Exercise 27-5 in working this exercise. Rafferty Company records standard costs in its accounts. Thus, it records its material variances in separate accounts when it assigns raw materials costs to the Goods in Process Inventory account.

Required

1. Show the general journal entry that would be made to charge the direct materials costs to the Goods in Process Inventory account and to record the material variances in their accounts.
2. Assume that the material variances created by the facts in Exercise 27-5 were the only variances accumulated in the accounting period and that they are not considered material. Show the adjusting journal entry that would be made to close the variance accounts at the end of the period.
3. Which variance should be investigated according to the management by exception concept and why?

Exercise 27-10
Recording sales variances
LO 9

Tom's Used Computer Outlet, Inc. specializes in selling used computers. During 1999 the dealership sold 500 computers at an average price of $900 each. The budget for 1999 was to sell 550 computers at an average of $850 each. Compute the sales price and sales volume variance for 1999 and interpret the findings.

Problems

Problem 27-1
Preparing and using a flexible budget
LO 2

Pen Company's master budget for 1999 included the following budgeted income statement. It was based on an expected production and sales volume of 20,000 units.

PEN COMPANY
Fixed Budget
For Year Ended December 31, 1999

Sales		$3,000,000
Cost of goods sold:		
Direct materials	$1,200,00	
Direct labour	260,000	
Machinery repairs (variable cost)	57,000	
Amortization on plant equipment (annual)	250,000	
Utilities (variable cost is 25%)	200,000	
Plant management salaries	140,000	(2,107,000)
Gross profit		893,000
Selling expenses:		
Packaging	80,000	
Shipping	116,000	
Sales salary (a fixed annual amount)	160,000	(356,000)
General and administrative expenses:		
Advertising expense	81,000	
Salaries	241,000	
Entertainment expense	90,000	(412,000)
Income from operations		$ 125,000

Required

1. Classify the items in the fixed budget as variable or fixed and determine their amounts per unit or for the year, as appropriate.
2. Prepare one schedule showing two possible flexible budgets for the company for sales and production volumes of 18,000 and 24,000 units.
3. A consultant has suggested that business conditions are improving. One possible effect could be a sales volume of approximately 28,000 units. The president of the company is confident that this volume is within the relevant range of existing capacity. How much would operating income increase over the 1999 budgeted amount if this level could be reached without having to increase capacity?
4. The consultant's report also describes the possibility of an unfavourable change, in which case production and sales volume for 1999 could fall to 14,000 units. How much income from operations would occur if the volume falls to this level?

Check Figure Budgeted income at 24,000 units, $372,400

Problem 27-2
Flexible budget performance report
LO 1, 2

Refer to the facts in Problem 27-1 in working this problem. Pen Company's actual statement of income for 1999 follows:

PEN COMPANY
Statement of Income from Operations
For Year Ended December 31, 1999

Sales (24,000 units)		$3,648,000
Cost of goods sold:		
Direct materials	$1,400,000	
Direct labour	360,000	
Machinery repairs (variable cost)	60,000	
Amortization on plant equipment (annual)	250,000	
Utilities (fixed cost is $154,000)	218,000	
Plant management salaries	155,000	(2,443,000)
Gross profit		1,205,000
Selling expenses:		
Packaging	90,000	
Shipping	124,000	
Sales salary (annual)	162,000	(376,000)
General and administrative expenses:		
Advertising expense	104,000	
Salaries	232,000	
Entertainment expense	100,000	(436,000)
Income from operations		$ 393,000

Required

Preparation component:

1. Using the flexible budget prepared for Problem 27-1, present a flexible budget performance report for 1999.

Check Figure Total variance in income, $20,600 favourable

Analysis component:

2. Explain the sales variance and the direct materials variance.

Problem 27-3
Computing and reporting material, labour, and overhead variances
LO 3, 4, 5

Peach Company has established the following standard costs per unit for the product it manufactures:

Direct material (10 kg @ $3.00 per kg)	$30.00
Direct labour (4 hrs. @ $6.00 per hr.)	24.00
Overhead (4 hrs. @ $2.50 per hr.)	10.00
Total standard cost	$64.00

The overhead rate was based on an expectation that the operating volume would equal 80% of the productive capacity of 10,000 units per month. The following additional flexible budget information is available:

	Operating Levels		
	70%	80%	90%
Production in units	7,000	8,000	9,000
Standard direct labour hours	28,000	32,000	36,000
Budgeted overhead:			
Variable costs:			
Indirect materials	$8,750	$10,000	$11,250
Indirect labour	14,000	16,000	18,000
Power	3,500	4,000	4,500
Maintenance	1,750	2,000	2,250
Total variable costs	28,000	32,000	36,000
Fixed costs:			
Rent of factory building	12,000	12,000	12,000
Amortization, machinery	20,000	20,000	20,000
Taxes and insurance	2,400	2,400	2,400
Supervisory salaries	13,600	13,600	13,600
Total fixed costs	48,000	48,000	48,000
Total overhead costs	$76,000	$80,000	$84,000

During May, the company operated at 90% of capacity and produced 9,000 units. The following actual costs were incurred:

Direct material (92,000 kg @ $2.95 per kg)		$271,400
Direct labour (37,600 hrs. @ $6.05 per hr.)		227,480
Overhead costs:		
Indirect materials	$10,000	
Indirect labour	16,000	
Power	4,500	
Maintenance	3,000	
Rent of factory building	12,000	
Amortization, machinery	19,200	
Taxes and insurance	3,000	
Supervisory salaries	14,000	81,700
Total costs		$580,580

Required

1. Compute the direct material variances, including the price and quantity variances.
2. Compute the direct labour variances, including the rate and efficiency variances.

3. Prepare a factory overhead variance report that shows the total volume and controllable variances.
4. Prepare a detailed factory overhead variance report (like Exhibit 27.19) that shows the variances for the individual items of overhead.

Check Figure Total overhead controllable variance, $2,300 favourable

---

Problem 27-4
Computing material, labour, and overhead variances
LO 3, 4, 5

Tuna Company established the following standard unit costs for its single product:

Direct material (25 kg @ $4.00 per kg)	$100.00
Direct labour (6 hrs. @ $8.00 per hr.)	48.00
Variable Factory overhead (6 hrs. @ $5.00 per hr.)	30.00
Fixed Factory overhead (6 hrs. @ $7.00 per hr.)	42.00
Total standard cost	$220.00

The overhead rate was based on an expectation that the operating volume would equal 80% of the productive capacity of 60,000 units per quarter. The following additional flexible budget information is available:

	Operating Levels		
	70%	80%	90%
Production in units	42,000	48,000	54,000
Standard direct labour hours	252,000	288,000	324,000
Budgeted overhead:			
Fixed factory overhead	$2,016,000	$2,016,000	$2,016,000
Variable factory overhead	1,260,000	1,440,000	1,620,000

During a recent quarter, the company actually operated at 70% of capacity and produced 42,000 units of product, and actual direct labour totalled 250,000 hours. These units were assigned the following standard costs:

Direct material (1,050,000 kg @ $4.00 per kg)	$4,200,000
Direct labour (252,000 hrs. @ $8.00 per hr.)	2,016,000
Factory overhead (252,000 hrs. @ $12.00 per hr.)	3,024,000
Total standard cost	$9,240,000

Actual costs incurred during the quarter were:

Direct material (1,000,000 kg @ $ 4.25)	$4,250,000
Direct labour (250,000 hrs. @ $7.75)	1,937,500
Fixed factory overhead costs	1,960,000
Variable factory overhead costs	1,200,000
Total actual costs	$9,347,500

Required

1. Compute the total direct material cost variance and the price and quantity variances.
2. Compute the total direct labour variance and the rate and quantity variances.
3. Compute the variable overhead spending and efficiency variances and compute the fixed overhead spending and volume variances.

Check Figure Labour rate variance, $78,500 favourable

Problem 27-5
Flexible budget, variance analysis, and report for overhead costs
LO 2, 3, 5

Hard Drive Company has established the following standard costs for one unit of its product:

Direct material (4.5 kg @ $6.00 per kg)	$27.00
Direct labour (1.5 hrs. @ $12.00 per hr.)	18.00
Overhead (1.5 hrs. @ $16.00 per hr.)	24.00
Total standard cost	$69.00

The predetermined overhead application rate ($16.00 per direct labour hour) is based on an expected volume of 75% of the factory's capacity of 20,000 units per month. Thus, the expected monthly output is 15,000 units. Following are the company's budgeted overhead costs for one month at the 75% level:

HARD DRIVE COMPANY
Monthly Factory Overhead Budget
(at 75% of capacity)

Variable costs:		
Indirect materials	$22,500	
Indirect labour	90,000	
Power	22,500	
Repairs and maintenance	45,000	
Total variable costs		$180,000
Fixed costs:		
Amortization, building	$24,000	
Amortization, machinery	72,000	
Taxes and insurance	18,000	
Supervision	66,000	
Total fixed costs		180,000
Total overhead costs		$360,000

The company incurred the following actual costs when it operated as expected at 75% of capacity during October:

Direct material (69,000 kg @ $6.10) ..		$420,900
Direct labour (22,800 hrs. @ $12.30) ..		280,440
Overhead costs:		
Indirect materials	$21,600	
Indirect labour	82,260	
Power	23,100	
Repairs and maintenance	46,800	
Amortization, building	24,000	
Amortization, machinery	75,000	
Taxes and insurance	16,500	
Supervision	66,000	355,260
Total costs		$1,056,600

Required

1. Classify the items in the overhead budget as variable or fixed and determine their amounts per unit or for the month, as appropriate.
2. Prepare a set of possible flexible overhead budgets for October showing the amounts of each variable and fixed cost at the 65%, 75% and 85% levels.
3. Compute the direct material variances, including the price and quantity variances.

4. Compute the direct labour variances, including the rate and efficiency variances.
5. Prepare a factory overhead variance report that shows the total volume and controllable variances.
6. Prepare a detailed factory overhead variance report (like Exhibit 27.19) that shows the variances for the individual items of overhead.

Problem 27-6
Recording material, labour, and overhead variances

LO 7, 8

Best Company's standard cost accounting system recorded the following information concerning its operations during December:

Standard direct material cost	$130,000
Direct material quantity variance (unfavourable)	5,000
Direct material price variance (favourable)	1,500
Actual direct labour cost	65,000
Direct labour efficiency variance (favourable)	7,000
Direct labour rate variance (unfavourable)	500
Actual overhead cost	250,000
Volume variance (unfavourable)	12,000
Controllable variance (unfavourable)	8,000

Required

Preparation component:

1. Prepare general journal entries dated December 31 to record the company's costs and variances for the month.

Check Figure Goods in Process Inventory (for overhead), $230,000

Analysis component:

2. Identify areas that would attract the attention of a manager who uses management by exception and explain what action the manager should take.

Alternate Problems

Problem 27-1A
Preparing and using a flexible budget

LO 2

Ranch Company's master budget for 1999 included the following budgeted income statement. It was based on an expected production and sales volume of 10,000 units.

RANCH COMPANY Fixed Budget For Year Ended December 31, 1999		
Sales		$250,000
Cost of goods sold:		
Direct materials	$100,000	
Direct labour	20,000	
Patent royalties paid (based on units)	3,000	
Amortization of machinery (annual)	11,920	
Utilities (variable cost is 80%)	8,000	
Supervisory salaries	6,000	(148,920)
Gross profit		101,080
Selling expenses:		
Commissions	9,000	
Shipping	30,000	
Sales salary (annual)	18,000	(57,000)
General and administrative expenses:		
Property taxes	4,000	
Salaries	9,360	
Rent expense	10,000	(23,360)
Income from operations		$ 20,720

Required

1. Classify the items in the fixed budget as variable or fixed and determine their amounts per unit or for the year, as appropriate.
2. Prepare one schedule showing two possible flexible budgets for the company for sales and production volumes of 8,000 and 12,000 units.
3. A consultant has suggested that business conditions are improving. One possible effect could be a sales volume of approximately 14,400 units. The president of the company is confident that this volume is within the relevant range of existing capacity. How much would operating income increase over the 1999 budgeted amount if this level could be reached without having to increase capacity?
4. The consultant's report also describes the possibility of an unfavourable change, in which case production and sales volume for 1999 could fall to 5,000 units. How much income from operations would occur if the volume falls to this level?

Problem 27-2A
Flexible budget performance report
LO 1, 2

Refer to the facts in Problem 27-1A in working this problem. Ranch Company's actual statement of income for 1999 follows:

RANCH COMPANY
Statement of Income from Operations
For Year Ended December 31, 1999

Sales (12,000 units)		$288,000
Cost of goods sold:		
Direct materials	$95,000	
Direct labour	16,000	
Patent royalties paid (based on units)	3,300	
Amortization of machinery (annual)	11,920	
Utilities (variable cost is $7,160)	8,520	
Supervisory salaries	6,720	(141,460)
Gross profit		146,540
Selling expenses:		
Commissions	10,800	
Shipping	37,200	
Sales salary (annual)	19,200	(67,200)
General and administrative expenses:		
Property taxes	4,200	
Salaries	9,360	
Rent expense	10,000	(23,560)
Income from operations		$ 55,780

Required

Preparation component:

1. Using the flexible budget prepared for Problem 27-1A, present a flexible budget performance report for 1999.

Analysis component:

2. Explain the sales variance and the direct materials variance.

Problem 27-3A
Computing and reporting material, labour, and overhead variances
LO 3, 4, 5

Challenger Company has established the following standard costs per unit for the product it manufactures:

Direct material (1,000 grams @ $0.03 per gram)	$ 30.00
Direct labour (2 hr. @ $20.00 per hr.)	40.00
Overhead (2 hr. @ $53.50 per hr.)	107.00
Total standard cost	$177.00

The overhead rate was based on an expectation that the operating volume would equal 60% of the productive capacity of 3,000 units per month. The following additional flexible budget information is also available:

	Operating Levels		
	50%	60%	70%
Production in units	1,500	1,800	2,100
Standard direct labour hours	3,000	3,600	4,200
Budgeted overhead:			
Variable costs:			
Indirect materials	$ 18,000	$ 21,600	$ 25,200
Indirect labour	10,500	12,600	14,700
Power	7,500	9,000	10,500
Maintenance	4,500	5,400	6,300
Total variable costs	40,500	48,600	56,700
Fixed costs:			
Rent of factory building	48,000	48,000	48,000
Amortization, machinery	44,000	44,000	44,000
Taxes and insurance	20,000	20,000	20,000
Supervisory salaries	32,000	32,000	32,000
Total fixed costs	144,000	144,000	144,000
Total overhead costs	$184,500	$192,600	$200,700

During March, the company operated at 70% of capacity and produced 2,100 units. The following actual costs were incurred:

Direct material (2,200,000 grams @ $ 0.028 per gram)		$ 61,600
Direct labour (4,000 hrs. @ $19.50 per hr.)		78,000
Overhead costs:		
Indirect materials	$23,600	
Indirect labour	14,800	
Power	10,000	
Maintenance	3,200	
Rent of factory building	48,000	
Amortization, machinery	44,000	
Taxes and insurance	24,000	
Supervisory salaries	31,600	199,200
Total costs		$338,800

Required

1. Compute the direct material variances, including the price and quantity variances.

2. Compute the direct labour variances, including the rate and efficiency variances.
3. Prepare a factory overhead variance report that shows the total volume and controllable variances.
4. Prepare a detailed factory overhead variance report (like Exhibit 27.19) that shows the variances for the individual items of overhead.

Problem 27-4A
Computing material, labour, and overhead variances
LO 3, 4, 5

Titletown Company established the following standard unit costs for its single product:

Direct material (2.5 kg @ $20.00 per kg)	$ 50.00
Direct labour (3 hrs. @ $15.00 per hr.)	45.00
Variable factory overhead (3 hrs. @ $5.00 per hr.)	15.00
Fixed factory overhead (3 hrs. @ $3.00 per hr.)	9.00
Total standard cost	$119.00

The overhead rate was based on an expectation that the operating volume would equal 90% of the productive capacity of 40,000 units per quarter. The following additional flexible budget information is also available:

	Operating Levels		
	80%	90%	100%
Production in units	32,000	36,000	40,000
Standard direct labour hours	96,000	108,000	120,000
Budgeted overhead:			
Fixed factory overhead	$324,000	$324,000	$324,000
Variable factory overhead	480,000	540,000	600,000

During a recent quarter, the company actually operated at 80% of capacity and produced 32,000 units of product and 100,000 direct labour hours worked. These units were assigned the following standard costs:

Direct material (80,000 kg @ $20.00 per kg)	$1,600,000
Direct labour (96,000 hrs. @ $15.00 per hr.)	1,440,000
Factory overhead (96,000 hrs. @ $8.00 per hr.) . . .	768,000
Total standard cost	$3,808,000

Actual costs incurred during the quarter were:

Direct material (77,500 kg @ $20.40)	$1,581,000
Direct labour (100,000 hrs. @ $14.00)	1,400,000
Fixed factory overhead costs	370,000
Variable factory overhead costs	480,000
Total actual costs	$3,831,000

Required

1. Compute the total direct material cost variance and the price and quantity variances.
2. Compute the total direct labour variance and the rate and efficiency variances.
3. Compute the variable overhead spending and efficiency variances and compute the fixed overhead spending and volume variances.

Problem 27-5A
Flexible budget, variance analysis, and report for overhead costs

LO 2, 3, 5

The Tropical Company has established the following standard costs for one unit of its product:

Direct material (48 kg @ $4.00 per kg)	$192.00
Direct labour (12 hrs. @ $9.00 per hr.)	108.00
Overhead (12 hrs. @ $4.50 per hr.)	54.00
Total standard cost	$354.00

The predetermined overhead application rate ($4.50 per direct labour hour) is based on an expected volume of 50% of the factory's capacity of 10,000 units per month. Thus, the expected monthly output is 5,000 units. Following are the company's budgeted overhead costs for one month at the 50% level:

TROPICAL COMPANY Monthly Factory Overhead Budget (at 50% of capacity)		
Variable costs:		
Indirect materials	$40,000	
Indirect labour	80,000	
Power	20,000	
Repairs and maintenance	30,000	
Total variable costs		$170,000
Fixed costs:		
Amortization, building	20,000	
Amortization, machinery	30,000	
Taxes and insurance	10,000	
Supervision	40,000	
Total fixed costs		100,000
Total overhead costs		$270,000

The company incurred the following actual costs when it unexpectedly operated at 40% of capacity during December:

Direct material (196,000 kg @ $4.00)		$ 784,000
Direct labour (46,000 hrs. @ $9.15)		420,900
Overhead costs:		
Indirect materials	$30,000	
Indirect labour	66,000	
Power	15,600	
Repairs and maintenance	21,000	
Amortization, building	20,000	
Amortization, machinery	30,000	
Taxes and insurance	9,600	
Supervision	39,600	231,800
Total costs		$1,436,700

Required

1. Classify the items in the overhead budget as variable or fixed and determine their amounts per unit or for the month, as appropriate.
2. Prepare a set of possible flexible overhead budgets for December showing the amounts of each variable and fixed cost at the 40%, 50%, and 60% levels.
3. Compute the direct material variances, including the price and quantity variances.
4. Compute the direct labour variances, including the rate and efficiency variances.

Check Figure Overhead volume variance, $20,000 unfavourable

5. Prepare a factory overhead variance report that shows the total volume and controllable variances.
6. Prepare a detailed factory overhead variance report (like Exhibit 27.19) that shows the variances for the individual items of overhead.

Problem 27-6A
Recording material, labour, and overhead variances
LO 7,8

Kraft Company's standard cost accounting system recorded the following information concerning its operations during June:

Standard direct material cost	$220,500
Direct material quantity variance (favourable)	20,250
Direct material price variance (favourable)	14,500
Actual direct labour cost	335,000
Direct labour efficiency variance (favourable)	26,700
Direct labour rate variance (unfavourable)	3,500
Actual overhead cost	359,000
Volume variance (unfavourable)	1,650
Controllable variance (unfavourable)	32,500

Required

Preparation component:

1. Prepare general journal entries dated June 30 to record the company's costs and variances for the month.

Analysis component:

2. Identify areas that would attract the attention of a manager who uses management by exception and describe what action the manager should take.

Analytical and Review Problem

A & R 27-1

While on vacation, Ms. Roberts, president of Roberts Works, took in a seminar on "Reporting to Top Management." One of the seminars was on the use of P/V charts, which Ms. Roberts thought would have applicability to her firm.

Upon returning, Ms. Roberts summoned the controller, Mr. Titus, to her office, told him of the seminar, and asked for a report on how soon such a reporting procedure could be implemented at Roberts Works. The next day a memorandum arrived accomplished by a break-even chart (reproduced below) based on standard budgeted costs and representative of the cost breakdown, and the cost-volume-profit relationship under the current selling price and cost structure.

The president studied the chart and filed it away for reference at month-end. On April 3, on arrival at work, the president found the March Income Statement on her desk (reproduced below). It was not long before Mr. Titus was in the office trying to explain the apparent discrepancy between the income statement and the break-even chart.

ROBERTS WORKS LIMITED
Income Statement
For the Month Ending March 31, 1999

Sales 14,000 units @ $4		$56,000
Cost of sales at standard $2.50		35,000
		$21,000
Selling and administrative costs		11,000
"Normal" net income		$10,000
Variances:		
Material price and usage	$500 cr.	
Labour rate and efficiency	300 dr.	
Budget variance	800 cr.	1,000
		$11,000

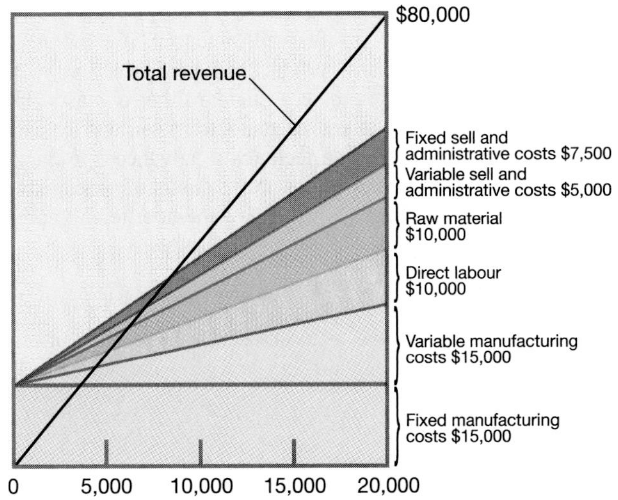

Ms. Roberts was heard saying, "I don't know what kind of accounting you are practising—I can't understand how the break-even chart indicates that at 14,000 unit sales volume net income should be $5,500 and you show in the income statement an amount that is double. If you expect me to have confidence in your reporting, you had better go back to your office and examine the figures and come back with an explanation—and it had better be good, short, and to the point."

Required

As Mr. Titus's assistant, he has asked you to prepare the short (1/2 page) report to reconcile the income statement and break-even chart net incomes.

BEYOND THE NUMBERS

Reporting in Action

LO3

A study of flexible budgets and standard costs gives us several key points about measurement. One is that the unit of measure must be the same to make meaningful comparison and evaluation. When **Alliance** compiles its financial reports in compliance with GAAP, it also follows the same unit of measurement, *Canadian dollars*, for all measurement of business operations. Without this practice, comparisons with other companies and across time are meaningless. This question looks at how Alliance adjusts its accounting values for its subsidiaries that compile financial reports in currencies other than the Canadian dollar.

Required

Read Alliance's note (o) and identify the financial statement where Alliance reports its foreign currency translation.

Comparative Analysis

LO3

As Canadian companies such as **Magna** continue to expand product lines into international markets the foreign currency translation adjustment becomes more important. Yet, at times, users argue that financial reporting is overly complex and financial reports do not provide useful information in support of business decision making because of the many estimates involved. To comply with foreign currency translation adjustment guidelines mandated by GAAP, management must make estimates.

Required

Why is a foreign currency adjustment important to users wanting to compare the performances of Canadian companies to other international companies?

Ethics Challenge

LO 4, 5

Setting standards is challenging. If standards are set too low, suppliers may send inferior products and employees may not work to their full potential. If standards are set too high, suppliers may be unable to offer a quality product at a profitable rate and employees may be overworked. The ethical challenge is to set a standard that is reasonable. As a manager at Computer Chips Inc. you are asked to set the standard material price and quantity for the new 1,000 CKB Mega-Max chip. This is a technically advanced product. To properly set the price and quantity standards, you need to assemble a team of specialists to provide information. Management tells you they will support a five-member team to provide information on the new chip.

Required

Identify the team of five specialists you would assemble to provide information to set the price and quantity standards. Briefly explain why you have chosen each individual.

Communicating in Practice

LO 8

Why use the words *favourable* or *unfavourable* when evaluating variances? The reason is apparent when we look at the closing of accounts. To see this, consider: (1) all variance accounts are closed at the end of each period (temporary accounts), (2) a favourable variance is always a credit balance, and (3) an unfavourable variance is always a debit balance. (Assume all variance accounts are closed to cost of goods sold.)

Required

1. Does cost of goods sold increase or decrease when closing a favourable variance? Does gross margin increase or decrease when a favourable variance is closed to cost of goods sold?
2. Does cost of goods sold increase or decrease when closing an unfavourable variance? Does gross margin increase or decrease when an unfavourable variance is closed to cost of goods sold?
3. Explain the meaning of favourable and unfavourable variance.

Taking It to the Net

LO 3

Compliance to standards is important to the success of a company. A customer will pay a higher price for a product that meets certain standards. This is why the "CSA" label is important to many companies. This voluntary, not-for-profit membership organization tests and certifies products to specified standards. Check out **http://www.cssinfo.com/info/csa.html** and answer the following questions for the basis of a class discussion.

Required

1. Identify one product category that is certified by CSA. Include specific examples of products in this category. Visit a store and locate one product in this category and identify the CSA label.
2. Why would this industry pay for the certification?

Teamwork in Action

LO 5

This chapter links labour rate and time (quantity) standards with specific products. The service industry also uses standard labour rate and time measurements. One example is the standard time to board an aircraft. The reason time plays such an important role in the service industry is because it is viewed as a competitive advantage—best service in the shortest amount of time. Although the labour rate component is difficult to observe, the time component of a service delivery standard is obvious—"lunch to be served in five minutes or less, or it is free."

Required

In teams of three to four students select two industries and identify all the time issues used to create a competitive advantage. Report your findings in a class discussion. You are likely to be surprised by the many different ways time is used to create a competitive advantage.

Hitting the Road

LO 3

Training employees to use specified amounts of materials in production is important. Large companies run by professional management typically invest in this training. Small organizations typically do not. One can observe these different practices in a trip to two different pizza businesses. Visit a local pizza business and a national pizza chain business and then complete the following:

Required

Observe and record the number of raw material items needed to make a typical cheese pizza. Next, observe how the person making the pizza manages the application of each raw material when making the pizza. Record what you observe in a memo format regarding the difference in how quantity applied is managed between the two businesses. Estimate which business is more profitable and why.

Business Break

LO 7

In Germany, labour unions are influential in setting the wage rate and the standard amount of hours worked in a week. This influence, however, can hurt the economy. In particular, a nation's economy can be impacted by labour standards. Read "The German Worker Is Making a Sacrifice" in the July 28, 1997, issue of *Business Week* and answer the following questions.

Required

1. Identify the original problems caused by labour unions regarding the economic health of the German economy.
2. Identify the more recent response by German labour unions in setting wage rate and hours worked in support of bringing economic recovery to Germany. Identify three industries working along with the unions to support the rebirth of the German economy, according to this article.

28

Capital Budgeting and Managerial Decisions

CHAPTER

A Look Back

Chapter 27 discussed flexible budgets, variance analysis, and standard costs. It explained how each is used for controlling and monitoring business activities.

A Look at This Chapter

This chapter focuses on evaluating capital budgeting decisions. It also explains procedures used in evaluating many short-term managerial decisions.

Chapter Outline

Gee-Whiz

Montreal, PQ—At the end of tenth grade, Greg Cass left school to work as an auto mechanic. He found out he hated mechanical work, but he loved electronics. "I found myself tinkering with circuits and other gadgets on cars after work hours," says Cass. He eventually went back to school and earned his high school diploma and then a diploma in computer electronics.

What Cass is now doing is running **Gee-Whiz**, a small computer electronics manufacturer. "It's really tough competing in this industry. Between changing consumer tastes and price fluctuations, it's amazing I have any hair left at all." But Gee-Whiz is bucking the odds and making a name for itself by living on the edge. "We try to be the company with the newest hip thing," says Cass.

While he admits getting burned, such as with his video pager, he is getting it right more times than not. Cass mixes computer savvy with sound techniques to analyze potential investments such as capital budgeting, payback period, and net present value. "I needed some structure in making decisions," says Cass. "There are a lot of techniques out there to help. If the numbers don't add up, I don't do it."

Gee-Whiz Jeans is the new investment for Cass—a jeans manufacturing company. "I'm creating wearable computers woven into jeans," says Cass. "If this works, I'll be merging two industries—electronics and jeans manufacturing. But he admits the development is slow. "I'm over budget and when I'll make a profit is anyone's guess. But I will cut my losses if I have to. I can't hide from the numbers." But don't count Cass out, so far the numbers for Gee-Whiz are pretty rosy.

Learning Objectives

LO 1 Explain the importance of capital budgeting.

LO 2 Compute the payback period and describe its use.

LO 3 Compute accounting rate of return and explain its use.

LO 4 Compute net present value and describe its use.

LO 5 Compute internal rate of return and discuss its use.

LO 6 Describe selection of a hurdle rate for an investment.

LO 7 Describe the importance of relevant costs for short-term decisions.

LO 8 Evaluate short-term managerial decisions using relevant costs.

LO 9 Analyze a capital investment project using break-even time.

CHAPTER PREVIEW

Business decisions involve choosing between alternative courses of action. Although many factors affect business decisions, our analysis typically begins by looking for the alternative that offers the highest return on investment or the greatest reduction in costs. Some decisions are based on little more than an intuitive understanding of the situation because available information is too limited to allow a more systematic analysis. In other cases, intangible factors such as convenience, prestige, and environmental considerations are more important than strictly quantitative factors. But even in these situations, we can reach a more sound decision if we can describe the consequences of alternative choices in financial terms. This chapter explains several methods of analysis that help managers make long-term and short-term decisions such as the one described in the opening article.

SECTION 1—CAPITAL BUDGETING

LO1 Explain the importance of capital budgeting.

We described the *capital expenditures budget* in Chapter 26. It is management's plan for acquiring and selling plant assets. **Capital budgeting** is the process of analyzing alternative long-term investments and deciding which assets to acquire or sell. These plans can also involve developing a new product or process, buying a new machine or a new building, and acquiring an entire company. A fundamental goal for implementing any of these plans is to earn a satisfactory return on investment.

Capital budgeting decisions require careful analysis because they are usually the most difficult and risky decisions that managers make. These decisions are difficult because they require predictions of events that will not occur until well into the future. Many of these predictions are tentative and potentially unreliable. Specifically, a capital budgeting decision is risky because (1) the outcome is uncertain, (2) large amounts of money are usually involved, (3) the investment involves a long-term commitment, and (4) the decision may be difficult or impossible to reverse, no matter how poor it turns out to be.

Capital budgeting covers a wide range of decisions. **Shaw Communications,** for instance, has invested over $800 million in cable and telecommunications distribution systems. Managers use several techniques in evaluating capital budgeting decisions. Nearly all of these techniques involve predicting cash inflows and outflows of proposed investments, assessing the riskiness of those flows, and then choosing the investments to be made.

A capital investment is expected to provide benefits over more than one period. To decide whether to invest or not, management must decide at the present time whether to make such an investment. Given that the cash flows are generated in the future, management restates future cash flows in terms of their present value. This approach applies the time value of money—a dollar today is worth more than a dollar tomorrow. The process of restating future cash flows in terms of their present value is called *discounting*. While it is important to consider the time value of money when evaluating capital investments, managers sometimes apply evaluation methods that do not explicitly consider it.

This chapter describes four methods for comparing alternative investments. These methods call for computing the *payback period*, the *accounting rate of return*, the *net present value*, and the *internal rate of return*. The first two methods do not consider the *time value of money*, whereas the latter two do consider it.

Methods Not Using Time Value of Money

All investments, whether they involve the purchase of a machine or another long-term asset, are expected to produce cash inflows and cash outflows. *Net cash flow* is the cash inflows minus cash outflows for the period. There are methods available for management to perform simple analyses of the financial feasibility of an investment without using the time value of money. This section explains two of the most common methods in this category: (1) payback period and (2) accounting rate of return.

Payback Period

LO 2 Compute the payback period and describe its use.

The **payback period (PBP)** of an investment is the time expected to recover the initial investment amount. Managers prefer investing in assets with shorter payback periods to reduce the risk of an unprofitable investment over the long run. Acquiring assets with short payback periods reduces a company's risk due to potentially inaccurate long-term predictions of future cash flows.

Computing Payback Period

This section explains how we compute the payback period with either equal or unequal cash flows.

Equal Cash Flows

To illustrate use of the payback period with equal cash flows,[1] we look at data from **FasTrac,** a manufacturer of exercise equipment and supplies. FasTrac is considering several different capital investments. One of the investments that FasTrac is considering is purchasing a machine used in manufacturing a new product. This machine costs $16,000 and is expected to have an eight-year life with no salvage value. Management predicts this machine will produce 1,000 units of product each year and that the product will be sold for $30 per unit.

Exhibit 28.1 shows the annual cash flows the asset is expected to generate over its life. It also shows the expected annual revenues and expenses (including amortization and income taxes) from this machine.

Exhibit 28.1
Cash Flow Analysis

FASTRAC
Cash Flow Analysis – New Machinery
January 15, 1999

	Expected Accrual Net Income	Expected Cash Flows
Annual sales of new product	$30,000	$30,000
Deduct annual expenses:		
Cost of materials, labour, and overhead (except amort.)	(15,500)	(15,500)
Amortization of machinery	(2,000)	
Additional selling and administrative expenses	(9,500)	(9,500)
Annual pre-tax income	$ 3,000	
Income taxes (30%)	(900)	(900)
Annual net income	$ 2,100	
Annual net cash flow		$ 4,100

[1] Equal cash flows means cash flows are the same each and every year. Unequal cash flows means not all cash flows are equal in amount.

Net cash flows from the machinery is computed by subtracting expected cash outflows from expected cash inflows. The cash flow column excludes all non-cash revenues and expenses. For FasTrac, amortization is the only noncash item. Alternatively, some managers adjust the projected net income for revenue and expense items that do not affect cash flows. For FasTrac this means taking the net income of $2,100 and adding back the $2,000 amortization.

The formula for computing the payback period of an investment is shown in Exhibit 28.2.

Exhibit 28.2

Payback Period Formula with Equal Cash Flows

$$\textbf{Payback period} = \frac{\textbf{Cost of investment}}{\textbf{Annual net cash flow}}$$

The resulting payback period is the time it will take the investment to generate enough net cash flow to return (or pay back) the cash initially invested to buy it.

In the case of FasTrac the payback period is just under four years as shown here:

$$\text{Payback period} = \frac{\$16{,}000}{\$4{,}100} = 3.9 \text{ years}$$

This means the initial investment is fully recovered just before we reach the halfway point of this machinery's useful life of eight years.

Unequal Cash Flows

Computation of the payback period ratio in the prior section assumes equal net cash flows. But what if the net cash flows are unequal? In this case the payback period is computed using the *cumulative total of net cash flows*. Cumulative refers to the addition of each additional period's net cash flows as we progress through time.

To illustrate, let's look at data for another potential investment that FasTrac is considering. This machine is predicted to produce unequal, or uneven, net cash flows over the next eight years. The relevant data along with computation of the payback period are shown in Exhibit 28.3.

Exhibit 28.3

Payback Period with Unequal Cash Flows

Period*	Expected Net Cash Flows	Cumulative Net Cash Flows
Year 0	$(16,000)	$(16,000)
Year 1	3,000	(13,000)
Year 2	4,000	(9,000)
Year 3	4,000	(5,000)
Year 4	4,000	(1,000)
Year 5	5,000	4,000
Year 6	3,000	7,000
Year 7	2,000	9,000
Year 8	2,000	11,000
		Payback period = 4.2 years

*All cash flows occur at the end of the year indicated.

Year 0 refers to the time of initial investment, and is reflected in the $16,000 cash outflow to acquire the machinery. By the end of Year 1, the cumulative net cash flow is reduced to $(13,000)—computed as the $(16,000) initial cash outflow plus Year 1's $3,000 cash inflow. This process continues throughout the asset's life.

The cumulative net cash flow amount changes from negative to positive in Year 5. Specifically, at the end of Year 4, the cumulative net cash flow is $(1,000). This means that as soon as FasTrac receives a net cash flow of $1,000 in the fifth year, the investment is fully recovered. If we assume cash flows are received uniformly *within* each year, then receipt of the $1,000 occurs about one-fifth of the way through the year. This is computed as $1,000 divided by Year 5's total net cash flow of $5,000, or 0.20. This gives us our payback period of 4.2 years, computed as 4 years plus 0.20 of Year 5.

Recall the opening article and the decision by Gee-Whiz to acquire a jeans fabric processing plant. Gee-Whiz's group put together a five-year forecast of cash flows from this acquisition. While a major reason to acquire it was for the processing technology, Gee-Whiz continued its current operations. Revenue was projected to grow annually based on an assumed increasing market share and stable prices for the current mix of products. Projected cash outflows reflected an increasing advertising budget believed necessary to increase market share and sales revenue. Projected outflows assumed stable raw material costs with modest increases in plant, administrative, and sales costs. Gee-Whiz assumed the fabric could be sold and administered by existing sales and administrative staff. It then compared these cash flows with estimated net cash flows from investing in a start-up fabric processing plant. Cash flows of the start-up alternative were used to set a ceiling on the amount paid for the plant.

Using the Payback Period

Companies desire a short payback period to increase return and reduce risk. The more quickly cash is received, the more quickly it is available for other uses, and the less time its cash investment is at risk of loss. A shorter payback period also improves the company's ability to respond to unanticipated changes and its risk of having to keep an unprofitable investment.

Payback period should never be the only consideration in evaluating investments. This is because it ignores at least two important factors. First, it fails to reflect differences in the timing of net cash flows within the payback period. In the previous case, FasTrac's net cash flows in the first five years were $3,000, $4,000, $4,000, $4,000 and $5,000. If another asset had predicted cash flows of $9,000, $3,000, $2,000, $1,800 and $1,000 in these five years, its payback period would also be 4.2 years. But this second alternative is more desirable because it provides more cash more quickly.

Second, the payback period ignores *all* cash flows after the point where its costs are fully recovered. For example, one investment may pay back its cost in 3 years but stop producing cash after 4 years. But a second investment might require 5 years to pay back its cost yet continue to produce net cash flows for another 15 years. A focus on only the payback period would mistakenly lead one to choose the first investment over the second.

Flash back

1. Capital budgeting is:
   a. Concerned with analyzing alternative sources of capital, including debt and equity.
   b. An essential activity for all companies as they consider what assets to acquire.
   c. Best done by intuitive assessments of the value of assets and their potential usefulness.
2. Why are capital budgeting decisions often difficult?
3. A company is considering the purchase of new equipment costing $75,000. Annual net cash flows from this equipment are $30,000, $25,000, $15,000, $10,000, and $5,000. The payback period is (a) 4 years, (b) 3.5 years, or (c) 3 years.
4. If amortization is an expense, why is it added back to net income from an investment to compute the net cash flow from this investment?
5. If two investments have the same payback period, are they equally desirable? Explain.

Answers—p. 1372

Accounting Rate of Return

LO3 Compute accounting rate of return and explain its use.

Another method used by managers in capital budgeting decisions is to compute and apply the accounting rate of return. This section explains the method.

Computing Accounting Rate of Return

The **accounting rate of return,** also called *return on average investment*, is computed by dividing the after-tax net income from a project by the average amount invested in the project. To illustrate, let's return to the potential $16,000 machinery investment by FasTrac described in Exhibit 28.1. Our first step is to compute the (1) after-tax net income and (2) average amount invested. The after-tax net income of $2,100 is already available from Exhibit 28.1. We are then left with computing average amount invested.

We begin by assuming net cash flows are received evenly throughout each year. This means the average investment for each year is computed as the average of its beginning and ending book values. If FasTrac's $16,000 machine is amortized $2,000 each year, then the average amount invested in the machine for each year is computed as shown in Exhibit 28.4. The average for any year is the average of the beginning and ending book values.

Exhibit 28.4

Computing Average Amount Invested

	Beginning Book Value	Annual Amortization	Ending Book Value	Average Book Value
Year 1	$16,000	$ 2,000	$14,000	$15,000
Year 2	14,000	2,000	12,000	13,000
Year 3	12,000	2,000	10,000	11,000
Year 4	10,000	2,000	8,000	9,000
Year 5	8,000	2,000	6,000	7,000
Year 6	6,000	2,000	4,000	5,000
Year 7	4,000	2,000	2,000	3,000
Year 8	2,000	2,000	-0-	1,000
Total		$16,000		$64,000/8 years

Next, we need the average book value for the asset's entire life. This amount is computed by taking the average of the individual yearly averages. This average equals $8,000, computed as $64,000 divided by 8 years (see right most column of Exhibit 28.4). Because FasTrac uses straight-line amortization, we can find the average book value for the eight years as the sum of the beginning and ending book values divided by 2 as shown in Exhibit 28.5.

Exhibit 28.5

Average Amount Invested Under Straight-Line Amortization

$$\textbf{Annual Average investment} = \frac{\textbf{Beginning book value + Ending book value}}{\textbf{2}}$$

$$= \frac{\$16{,}000 + \$\,0}{2} = \$8{,}000$$

If an investment carries a salvage value, then the average amount invested when using straight-line amortization is computed as (Original cost + Salvage value) / 2.

Once we determine the after-tax net income and the average amount invested, the accounting rate of return on the investment can be computed. This final step divides the estimated annual after-tax net income by the average amount invested as shown in Exhibit 28.6.

$$\text{Accounting rate of return} = \frac{\text{Annual after-tax net income}}{\text{Annual average investment}}$$

Exhibit 28.6

Accounting Rate of Return Formula

This yields an accounting rate of return for FasTrac of:

$$\text{Accounting rate of return} = \frac{\$2{,}100}{\$8{,}000} = 26.25\%$$

Using Accounting Rate of Return

It is managements's responsibility to decide whether or not 26% is a satisfactory rate of return. To make this decision we must factor in the riskiness of an investment. For instance, we cannot say an investment with a 26% return is preferred over one with a lower return unless we recognize differences in risk. This means an investment's return is satisfactory or unsatisfactory only when it is related to returns from other investments with similar lives and risk.

When accounting rate of return is used to select between capital investments, the one with the least risk, the shortest payback period, and the highest return for the longest time is often identified as the best. But this analysis is sometimes challenging because different investments often yield different rankings depending on the measure used.

Perhaps because accounting rate of return is readily computed, it is often used in evaluating investment opportunities. But its usefulness is limited because its use of the amount invested is based on book values for future periods. Amortization methods are used to allocate costs among years, not to predict market values of assets. The accounting rate of return is also limited when an asset's net incomes are expected to vary from year to year. This requires that the rate be computed using *average* annual net incomes. Yet this accounting rate of return fails to distinguish between two investments with the same average annual net income but where one yields higher amounts in early years and the other in later years.

Flash back

6. The following data relate to a machinery purchase that a company is considering:

Cost	$180,000
Salvage value	15,000
Annual income	40,000

The machine's accounting rate of return, assuming net cash flows from the investment are received evenly throughout the year (ignore income taxes), is (a) 22%, (b) 41%, or (c) 21%.

7. Is a 15% accounting rate of return for a machine a good rate?

Answers—p. 1372

Methods Using Time Value of Money

This section describes methods that help managers with capital budgeting decisions and that use the time value of money. The two methods described are (1) net present value and (2) internal rate of return.

To apply the methods in this section, we need a basic understanding of the concept of present value. An expanded explanation of present value concepts is in Appendix II. We can use the present value tables in Appendix II to solve several of the problems at the end of this chapter.

Did You Know?

The Winner Is?
How do we choose among the methods for evaluating capital investments? Management surveys consistently show the internal rate of return (IRR) as the most popular method. This is followed by the payback period and net present value (NPV). The internal rate of return measures the return of a project and is easily understood; while payback period is a quick measure of when an investment is fully recovered. Few companies use the accounting rate of return (ARR). Yet nearly all companies use more than one of these methods.

Net Present Value

LO4 Compute net present value and describe its use.

An investment in a new plant asset is expected to produce a stream of future net cash flows. A business should not acquire an asset unless its expected net cash flows are sufficient to provide a satisfactory return on investment and recover the amount initially invested. One way to make this decision is to compare the cost of the asset to the projected cash flows at a single point in time. Net present value (NPV) is one method to compare cost to projected cash flows.

Computing Net Present Value

A NPV analysis uses the time value of money applied to future cash inflows and cash outflows so that management can evaluate the benefit and cost of a project at one point in time. To illustrate, let's return to the proposed machinery purchase by FasTrac described in Exhibit 28.1. Does this machine provide a satisfactory return while recovering the amount invested? Recall this machine requires a $16,000 investment. Its annual net cash flows are expected to be $4,100 for the next eight years. If we know the annual return that FasTrac requires on its investments, we can compute the net present value of this investment.

Net present value is computed by discounting the future net cash flows from the investment at the required rate of return and then subtracting the initial amount invested as shown in Exhibit 28.7. We assume net cash flows from this machine are received at the end of each year and that FasTrac requires a 12% rate of return.[2]

Exhibit 28.7

Net Present Value with Equal Cash Flows

	Net Cash Flows	Present Value of $1 at 12%*	Present Value of Net Cash Flows
Year 1	$ 4,100	0.8929	$ 3,661
Year 2	4,100	0.7972	3,269
Year 3	4,100	0.7118	2,918
Year 4	4,100	0.6355	2,606
Year 5	4,100	0.5674	2,326
Year 6	4,100	0.5066	2,077
Year 7	4,100	0.4523	1,854
Year 8	4,100	0.4039	1,656
Total	$32,800		$20,367
Amount invested			(16,000)
Net present value			$ 4,367

* Present Value of $1 factors are taken from Table II.1 in Appendix II.

The first column of Exhibit 28.7 shows the annual net cash flows. Present value of 1 factors, also called *discount factors*, are shown in the second column. They are taken from Table II.1 in Appendix II and assume net cash flows are received at the end of each year. *To simplify present value computations and for*

[2] This assumption simplifies computations and is commonly made in practice.

assignment material at the end of this chapter, we assume net cash flows are received at the end of each year.

Annual net cash flows from the first column of Exhibit 28.7 are multiplied by the discount factors in the second column to give present values shown in the third column. The final three lines of this exhibit show the final net present value computations. The asset's $16,000 initial cost is deducted from the $20,367 total present value of all future net cash flows to give us this asset's net present value of $4,367. This means the machine is expected to (1) recover its cost, (2) provide a 12% compounded return, and (3) generate another $4,367. We can summarize the analysis by saying the value of this machine's future net cash flows to FasTrac exceeds the $16,000 investment by $4,367.

Net Present Value Decision Rule

The decision rule in applying the net present value method is: When the expected cash flows from an asset are discounted at the required rate and yield a *positive* net present value, the asset should be acquired. This decision rule is reflected in the following chart:

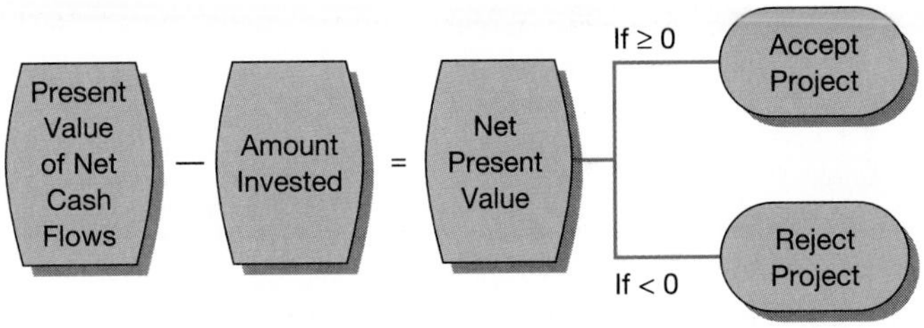

When comparing several investment opportunities of about the same cost and the same risk, the one with the highest positive net present value is preferred.

Systems Manager

You are a systems manager. Top management recently adopted new policies to control equipment purchases. The new policy says all proposals for purchases in excess of $5,000 must be submitted with cash flow predictions to the financial analysis group for capital budget analysis. This group has authority to approve or disapprove a proposal. Another systems manager, who is a friend, wants to upgrade his department's computers at a $25,000 cost. Your friend is considering submitting several purchase orders all under $5,000 to avoid the proposal process. He says the computers will increase profits, and wants to avoid a delay. How do you advise your friend?

Answer—p. 1372

Simplifying Computations

The computation in Exhibit 28.7 uses separate present value of $1 factors for each of the eight years. Then, each year's net cash flow is multiplied by its present value of $1 factor to determine its present value. The individual present values for each of the eight net cash flows are added to give us the total present value of the asset.

This computation can be simplified in two ways when annual net cash flows are equal in amount. One simplification is to add the eight annual present values of $1 factors for a total of 4.9676. This amount is multiplied by the annual net cash flow of $4,100 to get the $20,367 total present value of the net cash flows.[3]

[3] We can simplify this computation even further using Table II.3 which gives the present value of 1 to be received periodically for a number of periods. To determine the present value of these eight annual receipts discounted at 12%, go down the 12% column of Table II.3 to the factor on the eighth line. This factor is 4.9676. We then compute the $20,367 present value for these eight annual $4,100 receipts, computed as 4.9676 × $4,100.

A second simplification is to use a calculator with compound interest functions or a spreadsheet program. Whatever procedure is chosen it is important to understand the concepts behind these computations. The actual technique we use does not matter as long as we apply it properly.

Unequal Cash Flows

Net present value analysis can also be applied when net cash flows are unequal. To illustrate, let's assume FasTrac can choose only one capital investment from among *Projects A, B, or C.* Each project requires a $12,000 investment. Future net cash flows for each project are shown in the first column of Exhibit 28.8.

Exhibit 28.8

Net Present Value with Unequal Cash Flows

	Net Cash Flows			Present Value of	Present Value of Net Cash Flows		
	A	B	C	$1 at 10%	A	B	C
Year 1	$ 5,000	$ 8,000	$ 1,000	0.9091	$ 4,546	$ 7,273	$ 909
Year 2	5,000	5,000	5,000	0.8264	4,132	4,132	4,132
Year 3	5,000	2,000	9,000	0.7513	3,757	1,503	6,762
Total	$15,000	$15,000	$15,000		$12,435	$12,908	$11,803
Amount invested					(12,000)	(12,000)	(12,000)
Net present value					$ 435	$ 908	$ (197)

All three projects in Exhibit 28.8 have the same expected total cash flows of $15,000. Project A is expected to produce equal amounts of $5,000 each year. Project B is expected to produce a larger amount in the first year. Project C is expected to produce a larger amount in the third year. The middle (fourth) column shows the present value of 1 factors from Table II.1. Since the patterns of net cash flows are different, we know these projects will give different net present values.

Computations in the right-most columns of Exhibit 28.8 show that Project A has a $435 positive net present value. Project B has the largest net present value of $908 because it brings in cash more quickly. Project C has a $197 *negative* net present value because it brings in cash less quickly. If FasTrac requires a 10% return, then Project C should be rejected because its net present value implies a return *under* 10%. If only one project can be accepted, then Project B appears best because it yields the highest net present value.

Salvage Value and Accelerated Amortization

FasTrac estimated the $16,000 machine would have no salvage value at the end of its useful life. But in many cases an asset is expected to have a salvage value. If so, this amount is an additional net cash flow received at the end of the final year of the asset's life. All other computations remain the same.

Recall the opening article discussion of Gee-Whiz's acquisition of a jeans processing plant. This company's acquisition analysis used the series of predicted cash flows and assumed the ability to sell the processing plant at about 10 times earnings at the end of five years. In its analysis, the plant's expected selling price was treated like salvage value.

Amortization also affects NPV analysis. FasTrac computes amortization using the straight-line method. But accelerated amortization is also commonly used, especially for income tax computations. Amortization for tax purposes is called capital cost allowance (CCA). Revenue Canada specifies maximum rates that companies may use for tax purposes. For example, automobiles may be amortized at 30% declining balance and office furniture may be amortized at 20%. It is common for Canadian companies that use accelerated amortization to use the rates that are specified by Revenue Canada. Accelerated amortization produces larger amortization deductions in the early years of an asset's life and smaller deductions in later years. This pattern results in smaller income tax payments in early years and larger payments in later years.

Accelerated amortization does not change the basics of a present value analysis, but it can change the result. Using accelerated amortization for tax reporting affects the net present value of an asset's cash flows because it produces larger net cash inflows in the early years of the asset's life and smaller ones in later years. Because early cash flows are more valuable than later ones, being able to use accelerated amortization for tax reporting always makes an investment more desirable.

Using Net Present Value

In deciding whether to proceed with a capital investment project, we go ahead if the NPV is positive and reject the proposal if the NPV is negative. If there are several projects of similar investment amounts and risk levels, we can compare the net present values of the different projects and rank them on the basis of their NPVs. But if the amount invested differs substantially across projects, then NPV is of limited value for comparison purposes.

To illustrate, suppose Project X requires an investment of $1 million and provides a NPV of $100,000. But Project Y requires an investment of only $100,000 and returns a NPV of $75,000. Ranking on the basis of NPV puts Project X ahead of Y. Yet X's NPV is only 10% of the investment whereas Y's NPV is 75% of its investment. It is important to note that when reviewing projects with different risks, the NPVs of the individual projects are computed using different discount rates. The greater the risk, the higher the discount rate.

Internal Rate of Return

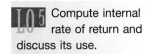

LO 5 Compute internal rate of return and discuss its use.

Another means to evaluate capital investments is to use the internal rate of return (IRR). The *internal rate of return* refers to the discount rate that results in a zero NPV from investment. This means if we compute the total present value of a project's net cash flows using the IRR as the discount rate and then subtract the initial investment from this total present value, we get a zero NPV.

Computing Internal Rate of Return

To illustrate, we use the data for Project A of FasTrac from Exhibit 28.8 to compute its IRR. Exhibit 28.9 shows the two-step process in computing IRR.

Exhibit 28.9

Computing Internal Rate of Return

Step 1: Compute present value factor for FasTrac's three-year project.

$$\text{Present value factor} = \frac{\text{Amount invested}}{\text{Net cash flows}} = \frac{\$12{,}000}{\$5{,}000} = 2.4000$$

Step 2: Identify present value factor of 2.4000 in Table II.3 for the three-year row. The factor is approximately equal to the 12% discount rate factor of 2.4018. This implies the IRR is 12%.*

* Since the present value factor of 2.4000 is not exactly equal to the 12% factor of 2.4018, we can more precisely estimate the IRR as follows:

Discount rate	Present value factor
12%	2.4018
15%	2.2832
	0.1186=difference

$$\text{IRR} = 12\% + \left[3\% \times \frac{2.4018 - 2.4000}{0.1186}\right] = \underline{\underline{12.05\%}}$$

When cash flows are equal such as with Project A, we can compute the present value factor by dividing the initial investment by its net cash flows. We then look up in an annuity table to determine the discount rate equal to this present value factor. For Project A of FasTrac, we look across the three-period row of Table II.3 and find that the discount rate corresponding to the present value factor of 2.4000 is roughly equal to the 2.4018 value for the 12% rate. This row is reproduced here:

	Rate				
Periods	1%	5%	10%	12%	15%
3	2.9410	2.7232	2.4869	2.4018	2.2832

The 12% rate is the Project's IRR. A more precise estimate of the IRR can be computed following the procedure shown in the note to Exhibit 28.9. Spreadsheet software and calculators can also compute this IRR.

Unequal Cash Flows

If net cash flows are unequal, we must use trial and error to compute the IRR. We do this by selecting any reasonable discount rate and computing the NPV. If the amount is positive (negative), we recompute the NPV using a higher (lower) discount rate. We continue these steps until we reach a point where two consecutive computations result in a NPV having different signs (positive and negative). Since the NPV is zero using IRR, we know that the IRR lies between these two discount rates. We can then estimate its value. Spreadsheet programs and calculators can do these computations for us.

Did You Know?

Deciding What's New

Cyto Technologies is a rapidly growing bio-tech company using both financial and nonfinancial criteria to evaluate its investments in new products. In addition to using the IRR, it assesses the potential for spin-off products, long-term positioning, technical success, strategic fit, manufacturing capabilities, and using marketing and distribution channels. [Source: S. Kalagnanam, and S. Schmidt, "Analyzing Capital Investments in New Products," *Management Accounting,* January 1996, pp. 31–36.]

Using Internal Rate of Return

When we use the IRR to evaluate a project, we compare the IRR with a predetermined hurdle rate. A **hurdle rate** is a minimum acceptable rate of return and is applied as shown here:

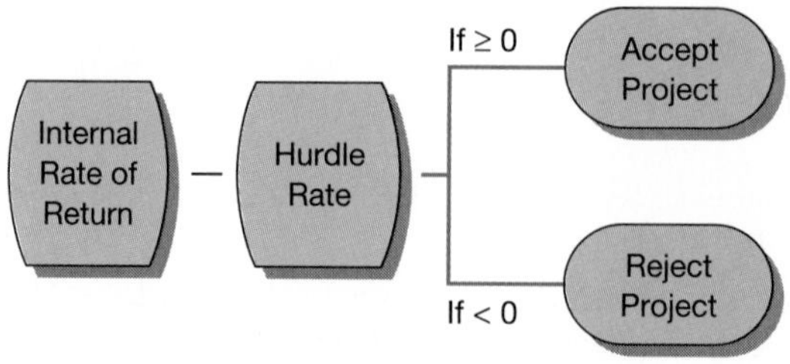

LO 6 Describe selection of a hurdle rate for an investment.

Top management selects the discount rate used as the hurdle in evaluating capital investments. While financial formulas aid in this selection, the choice of a minimum rate is subjective and left to management discretion.

In the case of projects financed from borrowed funds, the hurdle rate must exceed the interest rate paid on these funds. This is because the return on an investment must cover interest and provide an additional profit to reward the company for its risk. For instance, if money is borrowed at 10%, a required after-tax return of 15% is often acceptable in industrial companies with average risk. We must remember that lower risk investments require a lower rate of return compared with higher risk investments.

If the project is internally financed, the hurdle rate is often based on actual returns from comparable projects. If the IRR is higher than the hurdle rate, the project is accepted. In the case of multiple projects, they are often ranked by the extent to which IRR exceeds the hurdle rate. The hurdle rate for individual projects is often different depending on the risk involved. Also IRR is not subject to the limitations of NPV when comparing projects with different amounts invested. This is because the IRR is expressed as a percent rather than an absolute dollar value.

In analyzing its jeans processing plant acquisition, Gee-Whiz used an 18% required return on investment. Based on this rate, the bid price was accepted by its competitor and the processing plant became Gee-Whiz Jeans.

Capital budgeting decisions involve estimates not certainties. This became apparent to Gee-Whiz Jeans less than two years after acquisition when it admitted that it failed to fully take into account changes in customer and distribution channels. This led to higher administrative, delivery, and sales costs than anticipated. The expected increase in market share also had not occurred. Its share actually had declined, as it had under previous ownership. Poor results were experienced despite increased funds spent on advertising and marketing.

R&D Manager
You are the R&D manager of a hi-tech company. For a new product currently being developed under your management, you decide to use a 12% discount rate to compute its NPV. The controller expresses concern that your discount rate is too low. How do you respond?

You Make the Call

Answer—p. 1371

Comparing Capital Budgeting Methods

We explained four methods managers use to evaluate capital investment projects. But how do they compare with each other? This section addresses that question.

Both payback period and the accounting rate of return do not consider the time value of money, whereas both net present value and the internal rate of return do; see Exhibit 28.10. The payback period is a simple method giving managers an estimate of how soon they will recover the initial investment. Managers often consider this method when they have limited cash to invest and a number of projects to choose from. The accounting rate of return is a percent that is computed using accrual income instead of cash flows. It is an average rate for the entire investment period and does not reflect annual returns.

Net present value considers all estimated net cash flows for the expected life of the project. It can be applied to equal and unequal cash flows, and can reflect changes in the level of risk over the life of a project. But because it is a dollar measure, a comparison of projects of unequal sizes is difficult. The internal rate of return also considers all cash flows from a project. It is readily computed when the cash flows are equal, but requires some trial and error estimation when cash flows are unequal. Since the IRR is a percent measure, it is readily used to compare projects with different investment amounts. But changes in risks over the life of a project are not reflected in the IRR. Exhibit 28.10 highlights differences between these four methods.

Exhibit 28.10

Comparing Methods of Analyzing Capital Investments

	Payback Period	Accounting Rate of Return	Net Present Value	Internal Rate of Return
Measurement basis	Cash flows	Accrual income	Cash flows Profitability	Cash flows Profitability
Measurement unit	Years	Percent	Dollars	Percent
Strengths	Easy to understand Allows comparisons of projects	Easy to understand Allows comparison of projects	Reflects time value of money Reflects varying risk over a project's life	Reflects time value of money Allows comparisons of dissimilar projects
Limitations	Ignores time value of money Ignores cash flows after payback period	Ignores time value of money Ignores annual rates over life of project	Difficult to compare dissimilar projects	Ignores varying risk over life of project

Flash back

8. A company can invest in only one of two projects. Each project requires a $20,000 investment and is expected to generate end-of-period cash flows as follows:

	Annual Cash Flows	
	Project A	Project B
Year 1	$12,000	$4,500
Year 2	8,500	8,500
Year 3	4,000	13,000
	$24,500	$26,000

Assuming a discount rate of 10%, which project has the greater net present value?

9. Two investment alternatives are expected to generate annual cash flows with the same net present value (assuming the same discount rate applied to each). Using this information, can you conclude the two alternatives are equally desirable?

10. When two investment alternatives have the same total expected cash flows but differ in the timing of those flows, which method of evaluating those investments is superior? (a) accounting rate of return, or (b) net present value.

Answers—p. 1372

Mid-Chapter Demonstration Problem

Davenport Company is considering three investment opportunities that would involve purchasing asset X, asset Y, or asset Z. Straight-line amortization would be used in each case, and the salvage value would be received at the end of the life of the investment. In estimating the periodic net income from each asset, the only noncash expense is amortization. The following predictions are available about these investments.

	Asset		
	X	Y	Z
Purchase price	$40,000	$40,000	$40,000
Salvage	$1,000	-0-	$10,000
Useful life	6 years	8 years	8 years
Expected net incomes (losses)			
Year 1	$3,500	$11,000	$(3,750)
Year 2	3,500	9,000	4,250
Year 3	3,500	7,000	8,250
Year 4	3,500	5,000	16,250
Year 5	3,500	3,000	(1,750)
Year 6	3,500	1,000	(1,750)
Year 7	-0-	(1,000)	(1,750)
Year 8	-0-	(3,000)	21,250
Total income	$21,000	$32,000	$41,000

Required

Rank the three investments first to third, based on each of the following analytical techniques:

a. Payback period, assuming that the cash flows from each investments are received evenly throughout each year.

b. Return on average investment, assuming that the net income from each investment is received evenly throughout each year.

c. Net present value, using 8% per year as the discount rate. For this analysis, assume that the cash flows are received at the end of each year.

Planning the Solution

- Begin by calculating the annual amortization cost for each of the three assets. Then, predict the annual net cash flows for the three alternatives for each of the eight years by adding the predicted net income, the amortization expense, and the salvage value (only in the asset's final year).
- Find the payback for each of the three assets. The calculations for asset X can be found as a ratio. The payback periods for assets X and Y must be found by calculating their cumulative cash flows. Then rank the three opportunities, with the shortest payback period receiving the highest rank.
- Find the return on average investment for each of the three assets. To begin, find each asset's average annual net income by dividing the total income by the number of years in its life. Next, find the average investment over that life by finding the average annual income by the annual investment to get a percentage. Finally, rank the three alternatives, with the highest rate of return getting the highest ranking.
- Find the net present value of the future net cash flows from the three investments. Set up a three-column table for each asset. The first column should show the net cash inflow for each year in the asset's life. The second column should show table values for the present value of $1 discounted at 8%. The third column should be the product of the future cash flow and the table value. Then take the sum of the yearly present values and subtract the initial cost. The result is the net present value of each project. Finally, rank the three projects, with the largest net present value getting the highest ranking.

Annual amortization and cash flows from each of the three investments:

	X	Y	Z
Annual amortization expense:			
Cost	$40,000	$40,000	$40,000
Salvage value	(1,000)	-0-	(10,000)
Amortization base	$39,000	$40,000	$30,000
Life	6 years	8 years	8 years
Annual amortization	$6,500	$5,000	$3,750
Annual cash flows (net income plus amortization plus salvage in final year):			
	X	Y	Z
Year 1	$10,000	$16,000	$ -0-
Year 2	10,000	14,000	8,000
Year 3	10,000	12,000	12,000
Year 4	10,000	10,000	20,000
Year 5	10,000	8,000	2,000
Year 6	11,000	6,000	2,000
Year 7	-0-	4,000	2,000
Year 8	-0-	2,000	35,000
Total	$61,000	$72,000	$81,000

Solution to Mid-Chapter Demonstration Problem

a. Payback method:

Investment X:

$$\text{Payback period} = \frac{\text{Cost of asset}}{\text{Annual net cash flows}}$$

$$= \frac{\$40,000}{\$10,000} = 4 \text{ years}$$

Investment Y:

	Annual Net Cash Flows	Cumulative Net Cash Flows
Year 1	$16,000	$16,000
Year 2	14,000	30,000
Year 3	12,000	42,000

Thus, the $40,000 cost is paid back in slightly less than three years.

Investment Z:

	Annual Net Cash Flows	Cumulative Net Cash Flows
Year 1	$ -0-	$ -0-
Year 2	8,000	8,000
Year 3	12,000	20,000
Year 4	20,000	40,000

Thus, the $40,000 cost is paid back in four years.

Ranking: Investment Y is ranked first because it will pay back the cost in less than three years. Investments X and Z are tied for second with payback periods of four years.

b. Return on average investment: Because the cash flows are spread evenly throughout each period, the average investment is calculated as the average of the original cost and the salvage value.

Average net income per year:			
Total income over life	$21,000	$32,000	$41,000
Estimated useful life	6 years	8 years	8 years
Average annual net income	$3,500	$4,000	$5,125
Average investment:			
Purchase price (initial book value)	$40,000	$40,000	$40,000
Salvage value (final book value)	1,000	-0-	10,000
Sum	$41,000	$40,000	$50,000
Average (sum/2)	$20,500	$20,000	$25,000
Average return on investment	17.1%	20.0%	20.5%
Rank	Third	Second	First

c. Net present value (using 8% per year as the discount rate):

Investment X:

	Net Cash Flows	Present Value at 8%	Present Value of Cash Flows
Year 1	$10,000	0.9259	$ 9,259
Year 2	10,000	0.8573	8,573
Year 3	10,000	0.7938	7,938
Year 4	10,000	0.7350	7,350
Year 5	10,000	0.6806	6,806
Year 6	11,000	0.6302	6,932
Total	$61,000		$46,858
Original cost of asset			(40,000)
Net present value			$ 6,858

Investment Y:

	Net Cash Flows	Present Value at 8%	Present Value of Cash Flows
Year 1	$16,000	0.9259	$14,814
Year 2	14,000	0.8573	12,002
Year 3	12,000	0.7938	9,526
Year 4	10,000	0.7350	7,350
Year 5	8,000	0.6806	5,445
Year 6	6,000	0.6302	3,781
Year 7	4,000	0.5835	2,334
Year 8	2,000	0.5403	1,081
Total	$72,000		$56,333
Original cost of asset			(40,000)
Net present value			$16,333

Investment Z:

	Net Cash Flows	Present Value at 8%	Present Value of Cash Flows
Year 1	$ -0-	0.9259	$ -0-
Year 2	8,000	0.8573	6,858
Year 3	12,000	0.7938	9,526
Year 4	20,000	0.7350	14,700
Year 5	2,000	0.6806	1,361
Year 6	2,000	0.6302	1,260
Year 7	2,000	0.5835	1,167
Year 8	35,000	0.5403	18,911
Total	$81,000		$53,783
Original cost of asset			(40,000)
Net present value			$13,783

On the basis of the net present value, the investments are ranked as follows:

Y	$ 16,333	First
Z	13,783	Second
X	6,858	Third

SECTION 2—MANAGERIAL DECISIONS

This section focuses on the use of management and cost accounting information for several important managerial decisions. The emphasis is on the use of quantitative measures to help managers make decisions. Most of these involve short-term decision making. Methods for long-term managerial decisions are described in the first section of this chapter and in several other chapters of this book. A primary goal of this section is to explain what costs and other financial factors are most relevant to these decisions. We also provide a framework to help structure an analysis of the situation.

Decisions and Information

This section explains how managers make decisions and the information relevant to these decisions.

Decision Making

Managerial decision making involves five steps: (1) define the decision problem, (2) identify alternative courses of action, (3) collect relevant information to evaluate each alternative, (4) select the preferred course of action, and (5) analyze and assess decisions made. These five steps are illustrated in Exhibit 28.11.

Exhibit 28.11

Managerial Decision Making

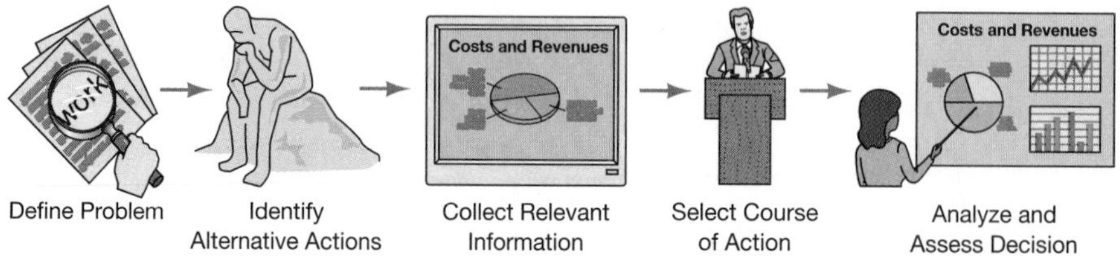

Managerial and financial accounting information play an important role in most management decisions. The accounting system is expected to mainly provide *financial* information such as performance reports and budget analyses for decision making. But *nonfinancial* information that bears on factors such as environmental effects, political sensitivities, and social responsibility is also important.

Relevant Costs

LO7 Describe the importance of relevant costs for short-term decisions.

Most financial measures of revenues and costs provided by cost accounting systems are based on historical costs. While historical costs are important and useful for many tasks such as product pricing and the control and monitoring of business activities, we sometimes find that *relevant costs*, or *avoidable costs*, are more valuable for certain managerial decisions. Three types of costs were identified and explained in Chapter 21: sunk costs, out-of-pocket costs and opportunity costs.

A **sunk cost** arises from a past decision and cannot be avoided or changed. These costs are irrelevant to future decisions. An example is the cost of production equipment previously purchased by a company. Most of a company's *allocated* costs, especially fixed overhead such as amortization and administrative expenses, are sunk costs.

An **out-of-pocket cost** requires a future outlay of cash and is relevant for current and future decision making. These costs are usually the result of management's decisions. Future purchases of production equipment involve out-of-pocket costs.

Analysis of relevant costs must consider opportunity costs. An **opportunity cost** is the potential benefit lost by taking a specific action when two or more alternative choices are available. An example is a student giving up wages from a job to attend summer school. Companies are continually faced with several alternative courses of action from which they must choose. For instance, a company making standardized products might be approached by a customer with a request to supply a special (nonstandard) product. A decision to accept or not accept the special order must consider not only the profit to be made from the special order but also the profit given up by devoting time and resources to this order instead of pursuing an alternative project. The profit given up is an opportunity cost.

Consideration of opportunity costs is important. Its implications extend to internal resource allocation decisions. For instance, a computer manufacturer must decide between internally manufacturing a chip versus buying it externally. In another case, management of a multidivision company must decide whether to continue operating or discontinue a particular division.

Management must also consider the relevant benefits associated with a decision. **Relevant benefits** refer to the additional or *incremental* revenue that is generated by selecting a particular course of action over another. For instance, a student must decide the relevant benefits of taking one course over another course. In sum, both relevant costs and relevant benefits are crucial to managerial decision making.

Managerial Decision Tasks

Managers confront many different types of tasks that require analysis of alternative actions and making a decision. We describe several different types of decision tasks in this section. We set these tasks in the context of FasTrac, the exercise supplies and equipment manufacturer introduced earlier. *We treat each of these decision tasks as separate from each other.*

LO 8 Evaluate short-term managerial decisions using relevant costs.

Accepting Additional Business

FasTrac is operating at its normal level of 80% of full capacity. It produces and sells approximately 100,000 units of product annually. FasTrac's annual average and total costs are shown in Exhibit 28.12.

Exhibit 28.12

Average and Total Historical Costs

	Per Unit	Total
Sales (100,000 units)	$10.00	$1,000,000
Direct materials	$ 3.50	$ 350,000
Direct labour	2.20	220,000
Factory overhead	1.10	110,000
Selling expenses	1.40	140,000
Administrative expenses	0.80	80,000
Total expenses	$ 9.00	$ 900,000
Operating income	$ 1.00	$ 100,000

FasTrac's marketing department identifies a customer who wants to buy and export the company's product to another country. This customer offers to buy 10,000 units of product at $8.50 per unit. While the price offer is low, FasTrac is considering the proposal because this sale would be several times larger than any previous sale made by the company. Also, the units will be exported, and this new business will not affect domestic sales.

To determine whether this order should be accepted or rejected, management needs to know whether net income will increase if the offer is accepted. The analysis in Exhibit 28.13 shows that if management relied on per unit average historical costs, the sale would be rejected because it yields a loss.

Exhibit 28.13

Additional Business Analysis Using Historical Costs

	Per Unit	Total
Sales (10,000 units)	$ 8.50	$85,000
Direct materials	$ 3.50	$35,000
Direct labour	2.20	22,000
Factory overhead	1.10	11,000
Selling expenses	1.40	14,000
Administrative expenses	0.80	8,000
Total expenses	$ 9.00	$90,000
Operating loss	$(0.50)	$ (5,000)

But historical costs are *not* relevant to this decision. Instead, the relevant costs are the additional costs called incremental costs. **Incremental costs,** also called *differential costs*, are the additional costs incurred if a company pursues a certain course of action. FasTrac's incremental costs are those related to the added volume that this new order would bring.

To make its decision, FasTrac must analyze the costs of this new business in a different manner. The following additional information is available:

- Manufacturing 10,000 additional units requires direct materials of $3.50 per unit and direct labour of $2.20 per unit (same as other units).
- 10,000 additional units can be manufactured with $5,000 of incremental factory overhead costs for power, packaging, and indirect labour (all variable costs).
- Incremental commissions and selling expenses from this sale would be $2,000 (all variable costs).

- Incremental administrative expenses of $1,000 for clerical efforts are needed (all fixed expenses).

Using this information, we show in Exhibit 28.14 how accepting this new business affects FasTrac's net income.

Exhibit 28.14

Additional Business Analysis Using Relevant Costs

	Current Business	Additional Business	Combined
Sales	$1,000,000	$85,000	$1,085,000
Direct materials	$ 350,000	$35,000	$ 385,000
Direct labour	220,000	22,000	242,000
Factory overhead	110,000	5,000	115,000
Selling expenses	140,000	2,000	142,000
Administrative expense	80,000	1,000	81,000
Total expenses	$ 900,000	$65,000	$ 965,000
Operating income	$ 100,000	$20,000	$ 120,000

The relevant costs analysis in Exhibit 28.14 suggests the additional business should be accepted. The additional business would provide $85,000 of added revenue while incurring only $65,000 of added costs. This would yield $20,000 of additional pre-tax income. Moreover, FasTrac would have more income at any price exceeding $6.50 per unit. A $6.50 price would be identical to the $65,000 incremental cost divided by the 10,000 added units.

An analysis of incremental costs of additional volume is always relevant for this type of decision. But we must proceed cautiously when the additional volume approaches or exceeds the existing available capacity of the factory. If the additional volume requires the company to expand its capacity by obtaining more equipment, more space, or more personnel, the incremental costs could quickly exceed the incremental revenue.

Another cautionary note is the effect on existing sales. For FasTrac, all new units are sold outside its normal domestic sales channels. But if accepting additional business causes existing sales to decline, then this information must be included in our analysis. The contribution margin lost from a decline in sales is an opportunity cost. Also, if future cash flows over several time periods are affected, then their net present value is computed and used in making this analysis.

The key point is that management must not blindly use average historical costs, especially allocated overhead costs. Instead, the managerial accounting system needs to provide information about the incremental costs to be incurred if the additional business is accepted.

Production Supervisor

You are the production supervisor for a custom manufacturer. A new customer inquires about a special order product that is currently not manufactured by your company. The controller asks you to provide information relevant to this decision. What information do you provide?

You Make the Call

Answer—p. 1372

Make or Buy

Incremental costs are used in deciding whether to make or buy a component of a product. To illustrate, FasTrac has excess productive capacity that can be used to manufacture Part #417. This part is a component of its major product. The component is currently purchased and delivered to the plant at a cost of $1.20 per unit. FasTrac estimates that to make Part #417 would cost $0.45 for direct materials, $0.50 for direct labour, and an undetermined amount for factory overhead.

Our task is to figure out how much overhead should be added to these costs so we can decide to make or buy Part #417. If FasTrac's normal predetermined overhead application rate is 100% of direct labour cost, we might be tempted to conclude that overhead cost is $0.50 per unit, computed as 100% of the $0.50 direct labour cost. We would then mistakenly conclude that total cost is $1.45, computed as $0.45 of materials plus $0.50 of labour plus $0.50 of overhead. Our decision in this case would be that the company is better off buying the part at $1.20 each than making it for $1.45 each.

But as we explained earlier, only incremental overhead costs are relevant. This means we must ignore the normal predetermined overhead rate. Instead we need to compute an *incremental overhead rate*. Incremental overhead costs might include, for example, power for operating machines, extra supplies, cleanup costs, materials handling, and quality control. We can prepare a per unit analysis such as that shown in Exhibit 28.15.:

Exhibit 28.15

Make versus Buy Analysis

	Make	Buy
Direct materials	$ 0.45	—
Direct labour	0.50	—
Overhead costs	[?]	—
Purchase price	—	$1.20
Total incremental costs ..	$0.95 + [?]	$1.20

If incremental overhead costs are less than $0.25 per unit, then the total cost of making the component is less than the purchase price of $1.20. This implies FasTrac should make the part.

FasTrac's decision rule in this case is any amount of overhead less than $0.25 per unit yields a total cost for Part #417 that is less than the $1.20 purchase price. But FasTrac must consider several factors in deciding whether to make or buy the part, including product quality, timeliness of delivery (especially in a just-in-time setting), reactions of customers and suppliers, and other intangibles such as employee morale and workload. It must also consider whether making the part requires incremental fixed costs to expand plant capacity. When these added factors are considered, small cost differences may not matter.

A key point is that average historical cost provided by a cost accounting system is not the most relevant to a make or buy decision. Instead, incremental costs are most relevant.

Did You Know?

Outsourcing

Make or buy decisions can apply to services as well as to manufacturing activities. Firms engage in outsourcing of services such as accounting, billing, customer service, human resource management and logistics to cut costs, obtain access to world-class capabilities, and allow the company to focus on its core competencies. Outsourcing also makes sense when risks need to be shared or when resources are not available internally. Canada's outsourcing market is estimated to be in the $15–$20 billion range and is engaged in by firms of all sizes. To work well, outsourcing should be part of a firm's strategic planning and the firm should have a clear picture of what it wants to accomplish.

Scrap or Rework Defects

Costs incurred in manufacturing units of product not meeting quality standards are sunk costs. This means they have been incurred and cannot be changed. These costs are irrelevant in any decision on whether to sell the units as scrap or rework them so they meet quality standards.

To illustrate, let's assume FasTrac has 10,000 defective units of a product that costs $1 per unit to manufacture. These units can be sold as is for $0.40 each. Alternatively, they can be reworked for $0.80 per unit, and then sold for their full price of $1.50 each. Should FasTrac sell the units as scrap or rework them?

To make this decision, management must recognize the original manufacturing costs of $1 per unit are sunk, or unavoidable. This means these costs are *entirely irrelevant* to the decision. In addition, we must be certain that all costs of reworking defects including interfering with normal operations are accounted for in our analysis. For instance, suppose reworking the defects means FasTrac is unable to manufacture 10,000 *new* units with an incremental cost of $1 per unit and a selling price of $1.50 per unit. Our analysis of this situation is shown in Exhibit 28.16.

Exhibit 28.16

Scrap versus Rework Analysis

	Scrap	Rework
Sale of scrapped/ reworked units	$4,000	$15,000
Less rework of defects		(8,000)
Less opportunity cost of not making new units		**(5,000)**
Net return	$4,000	$ 2,000

If reworking defects requires FasTrac to give up making 10,000 new units, it incurs an opportunity cost equal to the lost $5,000 net return from making and selling new units. This opportunity cost is the difference between the $15,000 revenue (10,000 units × $1.50) from selling these new units and their $10,000 manufacturing costs (10,000 units × $1). This analysis yields a $2,000 difference in favour of scrapping the defects. If we had *failed* to include the opportunity costs of $5,000, the rework option would show a return of $7,000 instead of $2,000. This would mistakenly make reworking appear more favourable than scrapping.

Inadequate Information

The Government of Canada had its first government-wide audit of material management in 1980. In 1996, it was learned that many of the problems discovered in 1980 still existed. The Auditor General found that inadequate information for decision making was a reoccurring problem. For example, in the area of ship repair and overhaul, all relevant costs were not taken into account when a contract was awarded to the lowest bidder (lower by $71). Meanwhile, the ships in need of repair had to be shipped to an out-of-town shipyard at an additional cost of $30,000 while one of the unsuccessful bidders had facilities in town. [Source: Gary Barber, "Material Must Be Better Managed," *CMA Management Accounting Magazine*, March 1997, p. 35.]

Did You Know?

Flash back

11. A company receives a special order for 200 units of its product. To stamp the buyer's name on each unit, the company must incur an additional fixed cost of $400 above its normal manufacturing costs. Without the order, the company is operating at 75% of capacity and produces 7,500 units of product at the following costs:

Direct materials	$ 37,500
Direct labour	60,000
Factory overhead (30% variable)	20,000
Selling expenses (60% variable)	25,000

The special order will not affect normal unit sales and will not increase fixed overhead and selling costs. Variable selling expenses on the special order are reduced to one-half the normal amount. The price per unit necessary to earn $1,000 on this order is (a) $14.80, (b) $15.80, (c) $19.80, (d) $20.80, or (e) $21.80.

12. What are the incremental costs of accepting this additional volume of business?

Answers—p. 1372

Sell or Process Further

Relevant costs are an important part of the decision to sell partially completed products as is or to process them further and then sell. To illustrate, let's suppose FasTrac has 40,000 units of a partially finished Product Q. FasTrac has already spent $0.75 per unit to manufacture these 40,000 units of Product Q at a total cost of $30,000. The 40,000 units can be sold to another manufacturer as raw material for $50,000. Alternatively, FasTrac can process them further and produce finished products X, Y, and Z at an incremental cost of $2 per unit. The added processing yields the products and revenues shown in Exhibit 28.17.

Exhibit 28.17

Revenues from Processing Further

Product	Price	Units	Revenue
X	$4.00	10,000	$ 40,000
Y	6.00	22,000	132,000
Z	8.00	6,000	48,000
Spoilage	—	2,000	-0-
Total		40,000	$220,000

FasTrac must decide whether this added revenue from selling finished products exceeds the cost of finishing them. Exhibit 28.18 shows the two-step analysis for this decision. First, FasTrac needs to compute its incremental revenue from further processing Q into products X, Y and Z. This amount is the difference between the $220,000 revenue from further processing and selling products X, Y and Z, and the $50,000 FasTrac will lose from not selling Q as is (the $50,000 is an opportunity cost). Second, FasTrac needs to compute its incremental cost from further processing Q into X, Y, and Z. This amount is the $80,000 further processing costs, computed as 40,000 units × $2 incremental cost. This analysis shows FasTrac can earn incremental income of $90,000 from a decision to further process Q.

The earlier $30,000 manufacturing cost for the 40,000 units of Product Q does not appear in Exhibit 28.18. This cost is a sunk cost and is irrelevant to the decision in that it has already been incurred.

Exhibit 28.18

Sell or Process Analysis

Revenue if processed	$220,000
Revenue if sold as is	(50,000)
Incremental revenue	$170,000
Cost if processed	(80,000)
Incremental income	**$ 90,000**

Flash back

13. A company has already incurred a cost of $1,000 in partially producing its four products. Selling prices for these products are listed below when partially and fully processed. Also shown are additional costs necessary to finish these partially processed units:

Product	Unfinished Selling Price	Finished Selling Price	Further Processing Costs
Alpha	$300	$600	$150
Beta	450	900	300
Gamma	275	425	125
Delta	150	210	75

Which of these products should not be processed further? (a) Alpha (b) Beta (c) Gamma (d) Delta

14. Under what conditions is a sunk cost relevant to decision making?

Answers—p. 1372

Selecting Sales Mix

When a company sells a mix of products, some are likely more profitable than others. Management is often wise to concentrate sales efforts on more profitable products. But if production facilities or other factors are limited, an increase in the production and sale of one product usually requires a company to reduce the production and sale of others. In this case management must identify the most profitable combination, or *sales mix*, of products. It then focuses on selling this sales mix of products.

To identify the best sales mix, management must know the contribution margin of each product. It must also know what facilities are required to produce these products and any constraints on these facilities and markets for the products.

To illustrate, let's assume FasTrac makes and sells two products, A and B. The same machines are used to produce both products. The products have the following selling prices and variable costs per units:

	Product A	Product B
Selling price	$5.00	$7.50
Variable costs	3.50	5.50
Contribution margin	$1.50	$2.00

The variable costs are included in the analysis because they are the incremental costs of producing these products within the existing capacity of 100,000 machine hours per month. Three cases are reviewed.

Case 1: Assume (a) each product requires 1 machine hour per unit for production and (b) the market for these products is unlimited. Under these conditions, FasTrac should produce as much of Product B as it can because of its larger contribution margin per unit. At full capacity, FasTrac would produce $200,000 of contribution margin (computed as $2 per unit × 100,000 machine hours).

Case 2: Assume (a) Product A requires 1 machine hour per unit, (b) Product B requires 2 machine hours per unit, and (c) the market for these products is unlimited. Under these conditions, FasTrac should produce as much of Product A as it can because it produces $1.50 of contribution margin per machine hour while Product B produces only $1 per machine hour. Exhibit 28.19 shows the relevant analysis.

Exhibit 28.19

Sales Mix Analysis Using Relevant Costs

	Product A	Product B
Selling price	$5.00	$7.50
Variable costs	3.50	5.50
Contribution margin	$1.50	$2.00
Machine hours per unit	1.0	2.0
Contribution margin per machine hour	$1.50	$1.00

At its full capacity of 100,000 machine hours, FasTrac produces 100,000 units of Product A. This would yield $150,000 of contribution margin. In contrast, if all 100,000 hours are used to produce Product B, only 50,000 units would be produced with a contribution margin of $100,000. These results suggest that when a company has no excess capacity, only the most profitable product should be manufactured.

Case 3: A need for a mix of different products arises when market demand is not sufficient to allow a company to sell all that it produces. For instance, assume (a) Product A requires 1 machine hour per unit, (b) Product B requires 2 machine hours per unit, and (c) the market for Product A is limited to 80,000 units. Under these condition, FasTrac should produce no more than 80,000 units of Product A. This would leave another 20,000 machine hours of capacity for making Product B. FasTrac should use this spare capacity to produce 10,000 units of Product B. This sales mix maximizes FasTrac's contribution margin at $140,000 under these conditions.[4]

Eliminating a Segment

When a segment such as a department or division is performing poorly we must consider eliminating it. But segment information on net income (loss) or contribution to overhead is not sufficient for this decision. Instead, we must look at the segment's avoidable expenses and unavoidable expenses. **Avoidable expenses,** also called *escapable*, are deductions that would not be incurred if the segment is eliminated. **Unavoidable expense,** also called *inescapable*, are deductions that would continue even if the segment is eliminated.

To illustrate, FasTrac is considering eliminating its treadmill division because total expenses of $48,300 are greater than its sales of $47,800. Analysis of this division's operating expenses is shown in Exhibit 28.20.

FasTrac's analysis shows it can avoid expenses of $41,800 if it eliminates the treadmill division. Since this division's sales are $47,800, it also means FasTrac will lose $6,000 of income if it eliminates the segment. *Our decision rule is that a segment is a candidate for elimination if its revenues are less than its avoidable expenses.* Avoidable expenses can be viewed as the costs of generating this segment's revenues. When avoidable expenses are greater than revenues, the segment should be eliminated.

[4] A mathematical technique called *linear programming* is useful for finding the optimal sales mix for several products subject to many market and production constraints.

Exhibit 28.20

Analysis of Divisional Operating Expenses

	Total	Avoidable Expenses	Unavoidable Expenses
Cost of goods sold	$30,200	$30,200	—
Direct expenses:			
Salaries expense	7,900	7,900	—
Amortization expense, Equipment	200	—	$ 200
Indirect expenses:			
Rent and utilities expense	3,150	—	3,150
Advertising expense	200	200	—
Insurance expense	400	300	100
Service department costs:			
Share of office department expenses	3,060	2,200	860
Share of purchasing expenses	3,190	1,000	2,190
Total	$48,300	$41,800	$6,500

When considering elimination of a segment we must assess its impact on other segments. While a segment may be unprofitable on its own, it might still contribute to the sales and profits of other segments. This means it is possible to continue a segment even when its revenues are less than its avoidable expenses. Similarly, a profitable segment might be discontinued if its space, assets, or staff can be more profitably used by expanding existing segments or by creating new ones. Our decision to keep or eliminate a segment requires a more complex analysis than simply looking at a segment's performance report. While such reports provide useful information, they do not provide all the information necessary for this decision.

Flash back

15. What is the difference between avoidable and unavoidable expenses?

16. A segment is a candidate for elimination if (a) its revenues are less than its avoidable expenses, (b) it has a net loss, or (c) its unavoidable expenses are greater than its revenues.

Answers—p. 1372

Qualitative Factors in Decisions

Managers must consider qualitative factors in making managerial decisions. To illustrate, let's consider a make versus buy decision where a manager is considering buying from an outside supplier instead of continuing to make a component. Several qualitative factors must be considered. First, the quality, delivery, and reputation of the proposed supplier are important. Second, the effects from discontinuing the making of the component can include potential layoffs and worker morale.

Consider another situation where a company is examining a one-time additional sale to a new customer at a special low price. Qualitative factors to consider include the effects of a low price on the image of the company and the threat of regular customers demanding a similar price. They must also consider whether this customer is really a one-time customer. If not, can it continue to offer this low price in the long-term? In sum, management cannot rely solely on financial numbers to make managerial decisions.

Break-Even Time

USING THE INFORMATION

LO 9 Analyze a capital investment project using break-even time.

The first section of this chapter explained several methods to evaluate capital investments. One of these methods was payback period. Our computation of payback period did not require us to use the time value of money. We explained how this is a limitation of the method. **Break-even time (BET)** of an investment project is a variation on the payback period that overcomes the limitation of not using the time value of money.

Break-even time is computed by first restating future cash flows in terms of their present values. This requires us to discount the cash flows. Second, we then compute the payback period using these restated (discounted) cash flows.

To illustrate, let's return to the case of FasTrac described in Exhibit 28.1. This involved a $16,000 investment in machinery. The annual net cash flows from this investment are projected at $4,100 for eight years. Exhibit 28.21 shows the computation of break-even time for this investment decision.

Exhibit 28.21

Break-Even Time Analysis

Year	Cash flows	Present Value of 1 at 10%	Cash Flows	Cumulative Present Value of Cash Flows
0	$(16,000)	1.0000	$(16,000)	$(16,000)
1	4,100	0.9091	3,727	(12,273)
2	4,100	0.8264	3,388	(8,885)
3	4,100	0.7513	3,080	(5,805)
4	4,100	0.6830	2,800	(3,005)
5	4,100	0.6209	2,546	(459)
6	4,100	0.5645	2,314	1,855
7	4,100	0.5132	2,104	3,959
8	4,100	0.4665	1,913	5,869

The right-hand column of this exhibit shows break-even time is between 5 and 6 years, or about 5.2 years. This is the time it takes for the project to break even after considering the time value of money. Cash flows earned after 5.2 years contribute to generating a net present value that, in this case, is $5,872.

Break-even time is a useful measure for managers because it informs them as to when they can start expecting the cash flows to yield net positive returns. It also tells us that if BET is less than the estimated life of the investment, management can expect a positive net present value from the investment. This method allows managers to compare and rank alternative investments on the basis of BET, where lowest BET gets the highest rank.

You Make the Call

Investment Manager

You are an investment manager for a company. Management asks you to evaluate three alternative investments. Investment recovery time is crucial because cash is scarce. Also, the time value of money is important in your decision. Which methods do you use to evaluate these investments?

Answer—p. 1372

Summary

LO1 Explain the importance of capital budgeting. Capital budgeting is the process of analyzing alternative investments and deciding which assets to acquire or sell. Generally, capital budgeting involves predicting the cash flows to be received from alternative possibilities, evaluating their merits, and then choosing which ones should be pursued.

LO2 Compute the payback period and describe its use. One method of comparing possible investments computes and compares their payback periods. This period is an estimate of the time that can be expected to pass before the cumulative net cash inflow from the investment equals its initial cost. The payback period analysis is limited because it fails to reflect the riskiness of the cash flows, differences in the timing of cash flows within the payback period, and all cash flows that occur after the payback period.

LO3 Compute accounting rate of return and explain its use. A project's expected accounting rate of return is computed by dividing the periodic after-tax net income by the average investment in the project. When the net cash flows are received evenly throughout each period, the average investment is computed as the average of the investment's initial book value and its salvage value. One major limitation of the accounting rate of return is its dependence on predictions of future value derived from amortization methods. It also fails to reflect year-to-year variations in expected net incomes.

LO4 Compute net present value and describe its use. The net present value of an investment is determined by predicting the future cash flows that it is expected to generate, discounting them at a rate that represents an acceptable return, and then subtracting the initial cost of the investment from the sum of the present values. This technique can deal with any pattern of expected cash flows and applies a superior concept of return on investment. However, it is limited by the subjectivity inherent in predicting future cash flows and in selecting the discount rate.

LO5 Compute internal rate of return and discuss its use. The internal rate of return (IRR) is the discount rate which results in a zero net present value. When the cash flows are equal, we can compute the present value factor corresponding to the IRR by dividing the initial investment by the annual cash flows. We then look up the annuity tables to determine the discount rate corresponding to our present value factor. If the cash flows are uneven, we must use trial and error to compute the IRR.

LO6 Describe selection of a hurdle rate for an investment. Top management should select the hurdle (discount) rate to be used for evaluating capital investments. Although financial formulas can aid this selection, the choice of a satisfactory minimum rate is largely subjective. However, the required earnings rate should be higher than the rate at which money can be borrowed because the return on an investment must cover the interest and provide an additional profit to reward the company for its risk.

LO7 Describe the importance of relevant costs for short-term decisions. In the case of short-term decision making, a company must rely on the relevant costs pertaining to an alternative course of action rather than historical costs. Out-of-pocket expenses and opportunity costs are relevant because these are avoidable, whereas sunk costs are irrelevant because they result from past decisions and are therefore unavoidable. In addition to the relevant costs, managers must also consider the relevant benefits associated with an alternative course of action.

LO8 Evaluate short-term managerial decisions using relevant costs. Examples of such decisions include accepting additional business, make or buy, sell as is or process further, etc. Relevant costs are useful in evaluating such decisions. For example, in deciding whether to produce and sell additional units of product, the relevant factors are the incremental costs and revenues from the additional volume, i.e., incremental income.

LO9 Analyze a capital investment project using break-even time. The break-even time (BET) is another measure for evaluating capital investment projects. It is computed by first restating the future cash flows in terms of their present values (i.e., discounting the cash flows) and then calculating the payback period using these restated cash flows. This method is superior to payback because it considers the time value of money.

Guidance Answers to **You Make the Call**

R&D Manager

The controller may be concerned that the new product is risky and should therefore be evaluated using a higher rate of return. As the R&D manager, you should conduct a thorough technical analysis, obtain detailed market data and information about similar products available in the market. These factors might provide sufficient information to support the use of a lower return. Essentially, you must be able to convince the controller that the risk level does not necessarily increase solely because the company is dealing with a new product, and that the company has the capability and the resources to handle the new product.

Production Supervisor

As the person who will most likely be responsible for the production of the new product (if the order is accepted), you should identify as much detail as possible regarding the production implications of the order. You must provide details pertaining to the estimated direct costs of the product, requirements of any special equipment or processing (handling, packaging, etc.) and the costs associated with them. You must also identify if there might be manufacturing capacity constraints which may affect the production of other regular products if this order is accepted. All these details will allow the controller to identify and list all the relevant costs that must be considered in determining a price to be quoted.

Investment Manager

Given that the time factor is important, you must determine the payback period or the break-even time. The latter is superior because it also accounts for the time value of money which is an important consideration in your company.

Guidance Answers to **Judgment and Ethics**

Systems Manager

The dilemma faced by your friend is whether to abide by rules that are designed to prevent abuse or to "bend" those rules to acquire an investment that he believes will actually benefit the firm. This situation is very realistic, and representative of the real world. Because breaking up the total order into small components is fundamentally dishonest, you should advise your friend against such an action. You should point out the consequences of being caught at a later stage, particularly the embarrassment in front of his peers and subordinates. Your friend should be encouraged to develop a proposal for the entire package and then do all that he can to expedite its processing, particularly by pointing out the significant benefits associated with the investment. When faced by an internal control system that is not working, there is virtually never a legitimate reason to overcome its shortcomings by dishonesty. Rather, a direct assault on those limitations will make more sense, and will certainly be the ethical thing to do.

Guidance Answers to Flash backs

1. *b*
2. They are usually based on predictions of events that might occur well into the future.
3. *b*
4. Amortization expense is subtracted from revenues in computing net income. However, it does not use cash and should be added back to net income to compute net cash flows.
5. Not necessarily. One investment may continue to generate cash flows beyond the payback period for a longer time than the other. Also, the timing of their cash flows within the payback period may differ.
6. *b* Average investment = ($180,000 + $15,000)/2 = $97,500
   Return on average investment = $40,000/$97,500 = 41%
7. It cannot be determined without comparing it to the returns expected from alternative investments with similar risk.
8. Project A

Year	Present Value of $1 at 10%	Project A Net Cash Flows	Project A Present Value of Net Cash Flows	Project B Net Cash Flows	Project B Present Value of Net Cash Flows
1	.9091	$12,000	$10,909	$4,500	$4,091
2	.8264	8,500	7,024	8,500	7,024
3	.7513	4,000	3,005	13,000	9,767
Total		$24,500	$20,938	$26,000	$20,882
Amount to be invested			(20,000)		(20,000)
Net present value of investment			$938		$882

9. No, the information is too limited to draw that conclusion. One investment may have more risk than the other.
10. Net present value.
11. Variable costs per unit for special order:

Direct materials ($37,500/7,500)	$5.00
Direct labour ($60,000/7,500)	8.00
Variable factory overhead [(.30 × $20,000)/7,500]	.80
Variable selling expenses [(.60 × $25,000 × .5)/7,500]	1.00
Total	$14.80

Cost to produce special order:
(200 × $14.80) + $400 = $3,360
Required price per unit:
($3,360 + $1,000)/200 = $21.80

12. They are the additional costs that will result from accepting the additional business.
13. *d*
14. It is never relevant because it results from a past decision.
15. Avoidable expenses are those that the company will not incur if a department is eliminated, whereas unavoidable expenses are those that will continue even after the department is eliminated.
16. *a*

Demonstration Problem

Determine the appropriate action in each of the following decision situations:

a. Packer Company has been operating at 80% of its 100,000 units per year capacity for manufacturing its product. A chain store has offered to buy an additional 10,000 units at $22 each and sell them in an area where Packer currently has no outlet. Consider the following facts:

	Per Unit	Total
Costs at 80% of capacity:		
Direct materials	$ 8.00	$ 640,000
Direct labour	7.00	560,000
Total (fixed and variable) overhead	12.50	1,000,000
Totals	$27.50	$2,200,000

In producing the 10,000 additional units, fixed overhead costs would remain at their present level but incremental variable overhead costs of $3.00 per unit would be incurred. Should the company accept or reject this order?

b. Green Company uses Part JR345 in manufacturing its products. In the past, it has always purchased this part from a supplier for $40 each. It recently upgraded its own manufacturing capabilities and has enough excess capacity (including trained workers) to begin manufacturing Part JR345 instead of buying it. The bookkeeper has prepared the following projection of the cost of making the part, assuming that overhead should be allocated to the part with the normal predetermined application rate of 200% of the direct labour cost.

Direct materials	$11.00
Direct labour	15.00
Total fixed and variable overhead (200% of direct labour cost)	30.00
Total	$56.00

The required volume of output of the part will not require any incremental fixed overhead cost. Incremental variable overhead cost will be $17 per unit. Should the company make or buy this part?

c. Gold Company's manufacturing process causes a relatively large number of defective parts to be produced. The defective parts can be (1) sold for scrap, (2) melted down to recover the metal for reuse, or (3) reworked and otherwise repaired. If defective parts are reworked, the output of other good units is reduced because there is no excess capacity. In fact, each unit reworked means that one new unit cannot be produced. The following information is available about 500 defective parts currently on hand:

Proceeds of selling as scrap	$2,500
Additional cost of melting down all defective parts	$400
Cost of metal purchases that can be avoided by using recycled metal	$4,800
Cost to rework 500 defective parts:	
Direct materials	$ -0-
Direct labour	1,500
Incremental overhead	1,750
Cost to produce 500 new parts:	
Direct materials	$6,000
Direct labour	5,000
Incremental overhead	3,200
Selling price of each good unit	$ 40

Should the company melt down the parts, sell them as scrap, or rework them?

d. White Company can invest in one of two projects, TD14 or TD21. Each project would require an initial investment of $100,000 and would produce the following annual cash flows:

	TD14	TD21
Year 1	$ 20,000	$ 40,000
Year 2	30,000	40,000
Year 3	70,000	40,000
Total	$120,000	$120,000

Under the assumption that the company requires a 10% compounded return from its investments, use present values to determine which project, if any, should be accepted.

Planning the Solution

- Determine whether the Packer Company should accept the additional business by finding the incremental costs of materials, labour, and overhead that will be incurred if the order is accepted. Leave out those fixed costs that will not be increased by the order. If the incremental revenue will exceed the incremental cost, accept the order.
- Determine whether the Green Company should make or buy the component by finding the incremental cost of making each unit. If the incremental cost exceeds the purchase price, the component should be purchased.
- Determine whether the Gold Company should sell the defective parts, melt them down and recycle the metal, or rework them. To compare the three choices, examine all costs incurred and disposal proceeds received in going from the current condition of having 500 defective units to the condition of having 500 new units. For the scrapping tactic, include the costs of producing 500 brand new units and subtract the $2,500 proceeds from selling the old ones. For the melting tactic, include the costs of melting the defective units, add the net cost of new materials in excess over those obtained from recycling, and add the direct labour and overhead costs. For the reworking tactic, merely add the costs of direct labour and incremental overhead. Then, select the alternative that has the lowest cost. Notice that the cost assigned to the 500 defective units is sunk and not considered in choosing among the three alternatives.
- Prepare the net present value of each investment using a 10% discount rate for each year. Assume all cash flow in at the end of the period unless stated otherwise by the author.

Solution to Demonstration Problem

a. This decision concerns accepting additional business. Because the unit costs seem to be $27.50, it appears as if the offer to sell for $22.00 should be rejected. However, the $27.50 cost includes some fixed costs. When the analysis includes only the incremental costs, the per unit cost is reduced as follows:

Direct materials	$ 8.00
Direct labour	7.00
Variable overhead	3.00
Total incremental cost	$18.00

The offer should be accepted because it will produce $4.00 of additional profit per unit (computed as $22 price less $18 incremental cost), which is a total profit of $40,000 for the 10,000 units.

b. This is a make or buy decision. The bookkeeper's analysis is faulty because it includes the nonincremental overhead of $13 per unit. When only the incremental overhead of $17 is included, the unit cost of manufacturing the part is:

Direct materials	$11.00
Direct labour	15.00
Variable overhead	17.00
Total incremental cost	$43.00

It would be better to continue buying the part for $40 instead of making it for $43.

c. This is a scrap or rework decision. The goal is to identify the alternative that produces the greater benefit to the company. To compare the alternatives on an equal basis, determine the net cost of obtaining 500 marketable units. The comparison is as follows:

	Sell As Is	Melt and Recycle	Rework Units
Incremental cost to produce 500 marketable units:			
Direct material:			
Cost of new materials	$ 6,000	$6,000	
Value of recycled metal		(4,800)	
Net materials cost		1,200	
Melting costs		400	
Total direct material cost.	6,000	1,600	
Direct labour	5,000	5,000	$1,500
Incremental overhead	3,200	3,200	1,750
Total cost to produce 500 marketable units	14,200	9,800	3,250
Less proceeds of selling defective units as scrap			
Opportunity cost*	(2,500)		5,800
Net cost	$11,700	$9,800	$9,050

*The opportunity cost of $5,800 is the lost contribution margin from not being able to produce and sell 500 units because of reworking, computed as ($40.00 − 28.40) × 500 units.

The incremental cost of obtaining 500 marketable parts is smallest if the defective parts are reworked.

d.

TD14

	Net Cash Flows	Present Value of $1 at 10%	Present Value of Net Cash Flows
Year 1	$ 20,000	0.9091	$ 18,182
Year 2	30,000	0.8264	24,792
Year 3	70,000	0.7513	52,591
Total	$120,000		95,565
Amount invested			(100,000)
Net present value			**$ (4,435)**

TD21

	Net Cash Flows	Present Value of $1 at 10%	Present Value of Net Cash Flows
Year 1	$ 40,000	0.9091	$ 36,364
Year 2	40,000	0.8264	33,056
Year 3	40,000	0.7513	30,052
Total	$120,000		99,472
Amount invested			(100,000)
Net present value			**$ (528)**

Glossary

Accounting rate of return A rate used to evaluate the acceptability of an investment; equals the after-tax periodic income from the project divided by the average investment in the asset; also called *return on average investment.* (p. 1348)

Avoidable costs/expenses An out-of-pocket cost/expense that requires a future outlay of cash and is relevant for future decision making; costs/expenses that would not be incurred if the department/product/service were eliminated. (p. 1368)

Break-even time A time-based measurement used to evaluate the acceptability of an investment; equals the time expected to pass before the *present value* of the net cash flows from an investment equals its initial cost. (p. 1370)

Capital budgeting The process of analyzing alternative investments and deciding which assets to acquire or sell. (p. 1344)

Hurdle rate A mininum acceptable rate of return (set by management) for an investment. (p. 1354)

Incremental cost An additional cost incurred only if the company accepts the additional volume. (p. 1362)

Net present value A dollar amount used to evaluate the acceptability of an investment; an estimate of an asset's value to the company; computed by discounting the future cash flows from the investment at a satisfactory rate and then subtracting the initial cost of the investment. (p. 1350)

Opportunity cost The costs that represent the potential benefits lost by choosing an alternative course of action. (p. 1361)

Out-of-pocket cost A cost incurred or avoided as a result of management's decisions. (p. 1361)

Payback period A time-based measurement used to evaluate the acceptability of an investment; the time expected to pass before the net cash flows from an investment return its initial cost. (p. 1345)

Relevant benefits Additional or incremental revenue generated by selecting a particular course of action over another. (p. 1361)

Sunk cost A cost that cannot be avoided or changed in any way because it arises from a past decision; irrelevant to future decisions. (p. 1361)

Unavoidable costs/expenses No further out-of-pocket cost/expense required regardless of future decision making; costs/expenses that would continue even if the department/product/service were eliminated. (p. 1368)

Questions

1. What is capital budgeting?
2. Capital budgeting decisions require careful analysis because they are generally the ______ ______ and ______ decisions that management faces.
3. Identify four reasons why capital budgeting decisions are risky.
4. Why is an investment more attractive if it has a short payback period?
5. Identify two disadvantages of the payback period method of comparing investments.
6. What is the average amount invested in a machine during its life if it costs $200,000 and has a predicted five-year life with a $20,000 salvage value? Assume that the net income is received evenly throughout each year.
7. Why is the present value of $100 that you expect to receive one year from now less than $100 received today? What is the present value of $100 that you expect to receive one year from now, discounted at 12%?
8. If the present value of the expected net cash flows from a machine, discounted at 10%, exceeds the amount to be invested, what can you say about the expected rate of return on the investment? What can you say about the expected rate of return if the present value of the net cash flows, discounted at 10%, is less than the amount of the investment?
9. Why is the value of an investment increased by using accelerated amortization (instead of straight-line) for income tax reporting?
10. Why should the required earnings rate always be higher than the rate at which money can be borrowed when making a typical capital budgeting decision.?
11. A company manufactures and sells 500,000 units of product at $30 per unit in domestic markets. The product costs $20 per unit to manufacture ($13 variable cost per unit, $7 fixed cost per unit). Can you describe a situation under which the company may be willing to sell an additional 25,000 units of the product in an international market at $15 per unit?
12. What is an out-of-pocket cost? What is an opportunity cost? Are opportunity costs recorded in the accounting records?
13. Any costs that have been incurred in manufacturing a product are sunk costs. Why are sunk costs irrelevant in deciding whether to sell the product in its present condition or to make it into a new product through additional processing?
14. Identify the incremental costs incurred by BETA Shoes for shipping one additional pair of dress shoes to an **Eaton's** retail outlet, along with the normal order of 1,000 pairs of dress shoes.

Quick Study

QS 28-1
Compute payback period
LO 2

Brooks Company is considering investment TD that requires an immediate payment of $18,000 and provides an expected cash return of $6,000 annually for four years. What is the payback period?

QS 28-2
Evaluate payback alternatives
LO 2

Freeman Company is considering two alternative investments. Investment 20TD has a payback period of 3.5 years and Investment 25TD has a payback period of 4.00 years. Why might Freeman analyze the two alternatives and choose 25TD over 20TD?

QS 28-3
Compute return on investment
LO 3

Pad Company is considering an investment expected to generate an average net income after taxes of $1,300 for three years. The investment cost $30,000 and has an estimated $4,000 salvage value. Compute the rate of return on this investment.

QS 28-4
Compute net present value
LO 4

If Fox Company invests $50,000 now, it can expect to receive $10,000 at the end of each year for seven years plus $6,000 at the end of the seventh year. What is the net present value of the investment, assuming Fox demands a 10% return on the investment?

QS 28-5
Evaluate incremental costs
LO 7

Marker Company incurs $6 per unit cost related to one of its products that it currently manufactures and sells for $9 per unit. Instead of manufacturing and selling this product, Marker can purchase a similar product for $5 and sell it for $8. If this is done, unit sales would remain unchanged and $5 of the costs assigned to the product would be eliminated. Should Marker continue to manufacture the product or purchase the alternative product?

QS 28-6
Analyze scarce resources
LO 7

Byte Company can sell all the units of computer memory 233BTY and 300BTY, but has limited production capacity. It can produce two units of 233BTY per hour or three units of 300BTY per hour and has 4,000 production hours available. Product 233BTY has a contribution margin of $5 and Product 300BTY has a contribution margin of $4. What is the most profitable sales mix for Byte Company?

QS 28-7
Compute BET
LO 9

Cut-To-Fit, Inc., a work shoe manufacturer, is evaluating the cost/benefits of new equipment that would custom build each pair of work shoes. The customer would have his/her foot scanned by digital computer equipment and this information would be fed into the new equipment, which would then specify exactly how the raw materials should be cut to provide a perfect fit to the customer. The new equipment costs $100,000 and is expected to generate an additional $35,000 in cash flow for 5 years. A bank will make a loan to Cut-To-Fit, Inc. for the entire $100,000 at a 10% interest rate. Use the table below to determine the break-even in time for this equipment.

Year	Cash Flows	Discount Factor (10%)	Discounted Cash Flows	Cumulative Discounted Cash Flows
0	$(100,000)	1.0000		
1	35,000	0.9091		
2	35,000	0.8264		
3	35,000	0.7513		
4	35,000	0.6830		
5	35,000	0.6209		

Exercises

Exercise 28-1
Payback period, equal cash flows
LO 2

Compute the payback periods for these two unrelated investments:

a. A new automatic control system for an existing machine is expected to cost $260,000 and have a useful life of five years. The system should save $75,000 (after 30% taxes) each year, after deducting straight-line amortization on the system. The predicted salvage value of the system is $10,000.

b. A machine costs $190,000, has a $10,000 salvage value, is expected to last nine years, and will generate an after-tax net income of $30,000 per year after straight-line amortization.

Exercise 28-2
Payback period, unequal annual net cash inflows
LO 2

Champ Company is considering the purchase of an asset for $90,000. The asset is expected to produce the following net cash flows:

	Net Cash Inflows
Year 1	$ 30,000
Year 2	20,000
Year 3	30,000
Year 4	60,000
Year 5	19,000
Total	$159,000

The cash flows would occur evenly throughout each year. Compute the payback period for this investment.

Exercise 28-3
Payback period from income statement data
LO 2

A machine can be purchased for $300,000 and used for five years to generate these net incomes:

Year 1	$ 20,000
Year 2	50,000
Year 3	100,000
Year 4	75,000
Year 5	200,000

In projecting the expected net incomes, double-declining balance amortization was deducted, based on a five-year life and a salvage value of $50,000. Present computations to show the payback period for the machine. Ignore income taxes.

Exercise 28-4
Computing average return on investment
LO 3

Asset X is expected to cost $500,000 and generate an after-tax net income of $15,000 each year. Management also predicts that asset X will have an eight-year service life and a $100,000 salvage value. Compute the average return on investment for asset X.

Exercise 28-5
Payback and return on average investment
LO 2

Link Company is considering the purchase of equipment that would allow the company to add a new product to its line. The equipment is expected to cost $240,000 with a 12-year life and no salvage value. It will be amortized on a straight-line basis. The company expects to sell 96,000 units of the equipment's product each year. The expected net income for the year related to the equipment is as follows:

Sales	$150,000
Costs:	
Materials, labour, and overhead (except for amortization on the new equipment)	80,000
Amortization on the new equipment	20,000
Selling and administrative expenses	15,000
Total expenses	115,000
Operating income	35,000
Income taxes (30%)	10,500
Net income	$ 24,500

Required

Compute (a) the payback period and (b) the return on average investment for this equipment.

Exercise 28-6
Net present value of an investment
LO 4

After evaluating the risk of the investment described in Exercise 28-5, the Link Company concludes that it must earn at least an 8% compounded return on the investment in the equipment. Use this rate to determine the net present value of the investment in the equipment.

Exercise 28-7
Net present values of investments
LO 4

The Mouse Company can invest in each of three cheese-making projects, 1, 6, and 7. Each project would require an initial investment of $190,000 and would produce the following annual cash flows:

	1	6	7
Year 1	$ 10,000	$ 80,000	$150,000
Year 2	90,000	80,000	50,000
Year 3	140,000	80,000	40,000
Total	$240,000	$240,000	$240,000

Required

1. Assuming that the company requires a 12% compounded return from its investments, use net present values to determine which project or projects should be acquired.
2. Using the answer obtained from part 1, is the internal rate of return greater than or less than 12% for project 6?

Exercise 28-8
Analysis of additional volume
LO 7

Camp Company expects to sell 200,000 units of its product during the next period with the following results:

Sales	$3,000,000
Costs and expenses:	
Direct materials	400,000
Direct labour	800,000
Factory overhead	200,000
Selling expenses	300,000
Administrative expenses	514,000
Total costs and expenses	2,214,000
Net income	$ 786,000

The company has an opportunity to sell 20,000 additional units at a price of $12 per unit. The additional sales would not affect the regular sales. Direct material and direct labour unit costs would be the same for the additional units as they are for the regular units. However, the additional volume would create these incremental effects on costs:

- Total factory overhead would increase by 15%.
- Total administrative expenses would increase by $86,000.

Required

Prepare an appropriate analysis to determine whether the company should accept or reject the offer to sell the additional units at the reduced price.

Exercise 28-9
Make or buy decision
LO 7, 8

Green Company currently manufactures a part at a cost of $3.40 per unit. This cost is based on a normal production rate of 50,000 units per year. The variable costs are $1.50 per unit, fixed costs related only to the part are $50,000 per year, and allocated fixed costs are $45,000 per year. These allocated costs would continue whether the company makes or buys the part. Green is considering buying the part from a supplier that has quoted a price of $2.70 per unit. This price would be guaranteed for a three-year period.

Required

Should the company continue to manufacture the part or should it purchase the part from the outside supplier? Support your answer with an analysis.

Exercise 28-10
Analysis of additional processing of a product
LO 7, 8

The Newton Company has 20,000 units of Product A that were manufactured for a total cost of $20 per unit. The 20,000 units can be sold at this stage for $500,000. Alternatively, they can receive further processing at a total additional cost of $300,000 and be converted into 4,000 units of Product B and 8,000 units of Product C. Product B can be sold for $75 per unit and Product C can be sold for $50 per unit.

Required

Prepare an analysis that shows whether the units of Product A should be processed further.

Exercise 28-11
Analysis of sales mix
LO 7

Dial Company owns a machine that can produce two different products. Product TLX can be produced at the rate of two units per hour and Product MTV can be produced at the rate of five units per hour. The capacity of the machine is 2,200 hours per year. The highly specialized products are sold to a single customer who has agreed to buy all of the company's output up to a maximum of 3,750 units of Product TLX and 2,000 units of Product MTV. Selling prices and variable costs per unit to produce the products are:

	Product TLX	Product MTV
Selling price	$12.50	$7.50
Variable costs	3.75	4.50

Required

Determine the most profitable sales mix for the company and compute the contribution margin that results from that sales mix.

Exercise 28-12
Income effects of eliminating departments
LO 7, 8

All Cheese Company's management expects the next year to produce the following net incomes for its five departments:

	Dept. M	Dept. N	Dept. O	Dept. P	Dept. T
Sales	$63,000	$ 35,000	$56,000	$42,000	$28,000
Expenses:					
Avoidable	9,800	36,400	22,400	14,000	37,800
Unavoidable	51,800	12,600	4,200	29,400	9,800
Total	$61,600	$ 49,000	$26,600	$43,400	$ 47,600
Net income (loss)	$ 1,400	$(14,000)	$29,400	$ (1,400)	$(19,600)

Required

Prepare a combined income statement for the company under each of the following conditions:

a. Management does not eliminate any departments.

b. Management eliminates those departments expected to show net losses. Explain findings.

c. Management eliminates only those departments that generate less sales dollars than avoidable expenses.

Exercise 28-13
Comparing payback and BET
LO 2, 9

This chapter presented two ways to evaluate investment proposals using time in years as a measure, payback and BET. Refer to QS 28-7 and complete the BET computation and next, complete the payback period for this investment.

Required

1. Report the time measures for each measurement technique.
2. Discuss the value of a BET measure over the payback method.
3. List two conditions where payback and BET measures would be very similar.

Problems

Problem 28-1
Payback, return on investment, and net present value
LO 2, 3

The Print Company is planning to add a new product to its line. To assemble this product, the company would have to buy a new machine at a cost of $300,000. The asset is expected to have a four-year life and a $20,000 salvage value. This additional information is available:

Expected annual sales of new product	$1,150,000
Expected costs:	
Direct materials	300,000
Direct labour	420,000
Factory overhead excluding amortization on new machine	210,000
Selling and administrative expenses	100,000
Income taxes	30%

All sales are for cash and all costs are out-of-pocket, except the amortization on the new machine.

Required

1. Compute the amount of straight-line amortization that would be taken in each year of the asset's life.
2. Determine the amounts of net income and cash flow expected in each year of the asset's life.
3. Compute the payback period on the investment in the new machine, assuming that the cash flows occur evenly throughout each year.
4. Compute the rate of return on the average investment in the new machine, assuming that the net income occurs evenly throughout each year.
5. Compute the net present value of the investment with a discount rate of 7%, assuming that all cash flows occur at the end of each year. (Be sure to include the salvage value as a cash flow in the last year of the asset's life.)

Check Figure Net present value of investment, $70,915

Problem 28-2
Payback, return on investment, and net present value
LO 2, 3

The Mold Company has the opportunity to invest in one of two new molding projects. Project Y requires an investment of $240,000 for new machinery having a four-year life and no salvage value. Project Z requires an investment of $240,000 for new machinery having a three-year life and no salvage value. The two projects would produce the following predicted annual results:

	Project Y	Project Z
Sales	$250,000	$200,000
Expenses:		
Direct materials	35,000	25,000
Direct labour	50,000	30,000
Factory overhead including amortization	90,000	90,000
Selling and administrative expenses	18,000	18,000
Total expenses	193,000	163,000
Operating income	57,000	37,000
Income taxes (30%)	17,100	11,100
Net income	$ 39,900	$ 25,900

The company uses straight-line amortization and the cash flows occur evenly throughout the year; for requirement 4, assume cash flows occur at the end of each period.

Required

Preparation component:

Check Figure Return on average investment in Project Y, 33.25%

1. Find the annual cash flows expected for the two projects.
2. Find the payback period expected for the two projects.
3. Find the rate of return on average investment expected for the two projects.
4. Find the net present value of the investment for the two projects, using 8% as the discount rate.

Analysis component:

5. Select the project that you would recommend to management, and explain your choice.

Problem 28-3
Computing cash flows and net present values with alternative tax amortization methods

LO 4

The Flight Corporation is considering a new wing development project that would require a $30,000 investment in special test equipment with no salvage value. The project would produce $12,000 of income before amortization at the end of each year for six years. The company's income tax rate is 40%. In compiling its tax return and computing its income tax payments, assume the company can choose between these two alternative amortization schedules:

	Straight-Line Amortization Schedule	Accelerated Amortization Schedule
Year 1	$ 3,000	$ 6,000
Year 2	6,000	9,600
Year 3	6,000	5,760
Year 4	6,000	3,456
Year 5	6,000	3,456
Year 6	3,000	1,728
Total	$30,000	$30,000

Required

Preparation component:

1. Produce a five-column table that shows these items for each of the six years: (a) income before amortization, (b) straight-line amortization expense, (c) taxable income, (d) income taxes, and (e) net cash flow. The net cash flow equals the amount of income before amortization minus the income taxes.
2. Produce a five-column table that shows these items for each of the six years: (a) income before amortization, (b) accelerated amortization expense, (c) taxable income, (d) income

taxes, and (e) net cash flow. The net cash flow equals the amount of income before amortization minus the income taxes.

3. Compute the net present value of the investment if straight-line amortization is used. Use 10% as the discount rate.
4. Compute the net present value of the investment if accelerated amortization is used. Use 10% as the discount rate.

Check Figure Net present value of investment (accelerated), $10,635

Analysis component:

5. Explain why the accelerated amortization method increases the net present value of this project.

Problem 28-4
Income results of added sales
LO 7,8

Design Products, Inc. manufactures underwater markers that it sells to wholesalers at $4 per package. The company manufactures and sells approximately 300,000 packages of markers each year to shipwreck treasure hunting teams, and normal costs for the production and sale of this quantity are as follows:

Direct materials	$384,000
Direct labour	96,000
Factory overhead	288,000
Selling expenses	120,000
Administrative expenses	80,000
Total	$968,000

A wholesaler has offered to buy 50,000 packages of markers for $3.44 each. These markers would be marketed under the wholesaler's name and would not affect Design Products' sales through its normal channels. A study of the costs of the new business reveals the following information:

- Direct material costs are 100% variable.
- The per unit direct labour costs for the additional units would be 50% greater than normal because their production would require overtime pay at one-and-one-half times the usual labour rate.
- One-fourth of the normal annual overhead costs are fixed at any production level from 250,000 to 400,000 units. The remaining three-fourths of the annual overhead cost is variable with volume.
- There will be no additional selling costs if the new business is accepted.
- Accepting the new business would increase administrative expenses by a fixed amount of $4,000.

Required:

Prepare a three-column comparative income statement that shows:

1. Operating income for one year without the special order.
2. Operating income that would be received from the new business.
3. Combined results for one year from normal business and the new business.

Check Figure Combined operating income, $276,000

Problem 28-5
Results of alternative sales mixes
LO 7,8

The Packer Company is capable of producing two products, G and B, with the same machine in its factory. These facts are known:

	Product G	Product B
Selling price	$60.00	$80.00
Variable costs	20.00	45.00
Contribution	$40.00	$35.00
Machine-hours to produce 1 unit	0.4	1.0
Maximum unit sales per month	550	175

The company presently operates the machine for a single eight-hour shift for 22 working days each month. The management is thinking about operating the machine for two shifts, which will increase the machine's availability by another eight hours per day for 22 days per month. This change would require additional fixed costs of $3,250 per month.

Required

1. Determine the contribution margin per machine hour that each product generates.
2. How many units of G and B should the company produce if it continues to operate with only one shift? How much total contribution margin is produced each month with this mix?
3. If the company adds another shift, how many units of G and B should the company produce? How much total contribution margin would be produced each month with this mix? Should the company add the new shift?
4. Suppose that the company determines it can also increase the maximum sales of Product G to 725 units per month by spending $4,500 per month in marketing efforts. Should the company pursue this tactic together with the double shift?

Check Figure Units of B to be produced, 132 units

Problem 28-6
Analysis of avoidable and unavoidable expenses

LO 7, 8

The management of Home Appliance Company is trying to decide whether to eliminate Department 200, which has produced losses or low profits for several years. The company's 1998 departmental income statement shows the following results:

HOME APPLIANCE COMPANY
Income Statement
For Year Ended December 31, 1998

	Dept. 100	Dept. 200	Combined
Sales	$436,000	$290,000	$726,000
Cost of goods sold	262,000	207,000	469,000
Gross profit from sales	174,000	83,000	257,000
Operating expenses:			
Direct expenses:			
Advertising	17,000	12,000	29,000
Store supplies used	4,000	3,800	7,800
Amortization of store equipment	5,000	3,300	8,300
Total direct expenses	26,000	19,100	45,100
Allocated expenses:			
Sales salaries	65,000	39,000	104,000
Rent expense	9,440	4,720	14,160
Bad debts expense	9,900	8,100	18,000
Office salary	18,720	12,480	31,200
Insurance expense	2,000	1,100	3,100
Miscellaneous office expenses	2,400	1,600	4,000
Total allocated expenses	107,460	67,000	174,460
Total expenses	133,460	86,100	219,560
Net income (loss)	$ 40,540	$ (3,100)	$ 37,440

In analyzing the decision to eliminate Department 200, the management has looked at the following items of information:

a. The company has one office worker who earns $600 per week or $31,200 per year and four salesclerks who each earn $500 per week or $26,000 per year.
b. Currently, the full salaries of two salesclerks are charged to Department 100. The full salary of one salesclerk is charged to Department 200. Because the fourth clerk works half-time in both departments, her salary is divided evenly between the two departments.
c. The sales salaries and the office salary currently assigned to Department 200 would be avoided if the department were eliminated. However, management prefers another plan.

Two salesclerks have indicated that they will be quitting soon. Management thinks that their work can be done by the other two clerks if the one office worker works in sales half-time. The office worker's schedule will allow this shift of duties if Department 200 is eliminated. If this change is implemented, half the office worker's salary would be reported as sales salaries and half would be reported as office salary.

d. The store building is rented under a long-term lease that cannot be changed. Therefore, the space presently occupied by Department 200 will have to be used by the current Department 100. The equipment used by Department 200 will be used by the current Department 100.

e. Closing Department 200 will eliminate its expenses for advertising, bad debts, and store supplies. It will also eliminate 70% of the insurance expense allocated to the department for coverage on its merchandise inventory. In addition, 25% of the miscellaneous office expenses presently allocated to Department 200 will be eliminated.

Required

Preparation component:

1. Prepare a three-column schedule that lists (a) the company's total expenses (including cost of goods sold), (b) the expenses that would be eliminated by closing Department 200, and (c) the expenses that will continue.
2. Prepare a forecasted income statement for the company reflecting the elimination under the assumption that sales and the gross profit will not be affected. The statement should also reflect the reassignment of the office worker to one-half time as a salesclerk.

Check Figure 2. Forecasted net income without Department 200, $31,510

Analysis component:

3. Prepare a reconciliation of the company's combined net income with the forecasted net income assuming Department 200 is eliminated. Also compare Department 200's revenues and its avoidable expenses and explain why you think the department should or should not be eliminated.

Alternate Problems

Problem 28-1A

Payback, return on investment and net present value

LO 2, 3

The Continental Company is planning to add a new product to its line. To assemble this product, the company would have to buy a new machine at a cost of $100,000. The asset is expected to have a five-year life and a $25,000 salvage value. This additional information is available:

Expected annual sales of new product	$350,000
Expected costs:	
Direct materials	150,000
Direct labour	50,000
Factory overhead excluding amortization on new machine	100,000
Selling and administrative expenses	23,000
Income taxes	20%

All sales are for cash and all costs are out-of-pocket, except the amortization on the new machine.

Required

1. Compute the amount of straight-line amortization that would be taken in each year of the asset's life.
2. Determine the amounts of net income and cash flow expected in each year of the asset's life.
3. Compute the payback period on the investment in the new machine, assuming that the cash flows occur evenly throughout each year.
4. Compute the rate of return on the average investment in the new machine, assuming that the net income occurs evenly throughout each year.
5. Compute the net present value of the investment with a discount rate of 12%, assuming that all cash flows occur at the end of each year. (Be sure to include the salvage value as a cash flow in the last year of the asset's life.)

Problem 28-2A
Payback, return on investment, and net present value

LO 2, 3

The Green Company has the opportunity to invest in one of two projects. Project A requires an investment of $480,000 for new machinery having a three-year life and no salvage value. Project B also requires an investment of $480,000 for new machinery having a four-year life and no salvage value. The two projects would produce the following predicted annual results:

	Project A	Project B
Sales	$750,000	$800,000
Expenses:		
Direct materials	125,000	250,000
Direct labour	130,000	80,000
Factory overhead including amortization	330,000	276,000
Selling and administrative expenses	120,000	120,000
Total expenses	705,000	726,000
Operating income	45,000	74,000
Income taxes (30%)	13,500	22,200
Net income	$ 31,500	$ 51,800

Assume that the company uses straight-line amortization and that the cash flows occur evenly throughout the year, except that for requirement 4 assume cash flows occur at the end of each period.

Required

Preparation component:

1. Find the annual cash flows expected for the two projects.
2. Find the payback period expected for the two projects.
3. Find the rate of return on average investment expected for the two projects.
4. Find the net present value of the investment for the two projects, using 10% as the discount rate.

Analysis component:

5. Select the project that you would recommend to management, and explain your choice.

Problem 28-3A
Computing cash flows and net present values with alternative tax amortization methods

LO 4

The Grill Corporation is considering a project that would require a $25,000 investment in an asset having no salvage value. The project would produce $15,000 of income before amortization at the end of each year for six years. The company's income tax rate is 30%. In compiling its tax return and computing its income tax payments, the company can choose between these two alternative amortization schedules:

	Straight-Line Amortization Schedule	Accelerated Amortization Schedule
Year 1	$ 2,500	$ 5,000
Year 2	5,000	8,000
Year 3	5,000	4,800
Year 4	5,000	2,880
Year 5	5,000	2,880
Year 6	2,500	1,440
Total	$25,000	$25,000

Required

Preparation component:

1. Produce a five-column table that shows these items for each of the six years: (a) income before amortization, (b) straight-line amortization expense, (c) taxable income, (d) income taxes, and (e) net cash flow. The net cash flow equals the amount of income before amortization minus the income taxes.
2. Produce a five-column table that shows these items for each of the six years: (a) income before amortization, (b) accelerated amortization expense, (c) taxable income, (d) income taxes, and (e) net cash flow. The net cash flow equals the amount of income before amortization minus the income taxes.
3. Compute the net present value of the investment if straight-line amortization is used. Use 15% as the discount rate.
4. Compute the net present value of the investment if accelerated amortization is used. Use 15% as the discount rate.

Analysis component:

5. Explain why the accelerated amortization method increases the net present value of this project.

Problem 28-4A
Income results of added sales
LO 7, 8

Wire Company manufactures bottled water that it sells to wholesalers in the local area at $1.00 per bottle. The company manufactures and sells approximately 200,000 bottles each month, and normal costs for the production and sale of this quantity are as follows:

Direct materials	$30,000
Direct labour	12,000
Factory overhead	50,000
Selling expenses	7,500
Administrative expenses	31,500
Total	$131,000

An out-of-province distributor has offered to buy 20,000 bottles next month for $0.80 each. These bottles would be marketed in other provinces and would not affect Wire's sales through its normal channels.

A study of the costs of the new business reveals the following information:

- Direct material costs are 100% variable.
- The per unit direct labour costs for the additional units would be 100% greater than normal because their production would require special double overtime pay to meet the distributor's deadline.
- Eighty percent of the normal annual overhead costs are fixed at any production level from 120,000 to 300,000 units. The remaining 20% of the annual overhead cost is variable with volume.
- There will be no additional selling costs if the new business is accepted.
- Accepting the new business would increase administrative expenses by a fixed amount of $750.

Required

Prepare a three-column comparative income statement that shows:

1. Operating income for one year without the special order.
2. Operating income that would be received from the new business.
3. Combined results for one year from the usual business and the new business.

Problem 28-5A
Results of alternative sales mixes

LO 7, 8

The Branck Company is capable of producing two products, Product 22 and Product 47, with the same machine in its factory. These facts are known:

	Product 22	Product 47
Selling price	$175	$200
Variable costs	100	150
Contribution	$ 75	$ 50
Machine hours to produce 1 unit	0.8	0.5
Maximum unit sales per month	525	450

The company presently operates the machine for a single eight-hour shift for 23 working days each month. The management is thinking about operating the machine for two shifts, which will increase the machine's availability by another eight hours per day for 23 days per month. This change would require additional fixed costs of $5,000 per month.

Required

1. Determine the contribution margin per machine hour that each product generates.
2. How many units of Product 22 and Product 47 should the company produce if it continues to operate with only one shift? How much total contribution margin is produced each month with this mix?
3. If the company adds another shift, how many units of Product 22 and Product 47 should the company produce? How much total contribution margin would be produced each month with this mix? Should the company add the new shift?
4. Suppose that the company determines it can also increase the maximum sales of Product 47 to 500 units per month by spending $500 per month in marketing efforts. Should the company pursue this tactic together with the double shift?

Problem 28-6A
Analysis of avoidable and unavoidable expenses

LO 7, 8

The management of The TeeTime Company is trying to decide whether to eliminate Department G, which has produced low profits or losses for several years. The company's 1997 departmental income statement shows the following results:

THE TEETIME COMPANY
Income Statement
For Year Ended December 31, 1997

	Dept. A	Dept. G	Combined
Sales	$700,000	$175,000	$875,000
Cost of goods sold	461,300	125,100	586,400
Gross profit from sales	238,700	49,900	288,600
Operating expenses:			
Direct expenses:			
Advertising	27,000	3,000	30,000
Store supplies used	5,600	1,400	7,000
Amortization of store equipment	14,000	7,000	21,000
Total direct expenses	46,600	11,400	58,000
Allocated expenses:			
Sales salaries	70,200	23,400	93,600
Rent expense	22,080	5,520	27,600
Bad debts expense	21,000	4,000	25,000
Office salary	20,800	5,200	26,000
Insurance expense	4,200	1,400	5,600
Miscellaneous office expenses	1,700	2,500	4,200
Total allocated expenses	139,980	42,020	182,000
Total expenses	186,580	53,420	240,000
Net income (loss)	$ 52,120	$ (3,520)	$ 48,600

In analyzing the decision to eliminate Department G, the management has looked at the following items of information:

a. The company has one office worker who earns $500 per week or $26,000 per year and four salesclerks who each earn $450 per week or $23,400 per year.

b. Currently, the full salaries of three salesclerks are charged to Department A. The full salary of one salesclerk is charged to Department G.

c. The sales salaries and the office salary currently assigned to Department G would be avoided if the department were to be eliminated. However, management prefers another plan. Two salesclerks have indicated that they will be quitting soon. Management thinks that their work can be done by the two remaining clerks if the one office worker works in sales half-time. The office worker's schedule will allow this shift of duties if Department G is eliminated. If this change is implemented, half the office worker's salary would be reported as sales salaries and half would be reported as office salary.

d. The store building is rented under a long-term lease that cannot be changed. Therefore, the space presently occupied by Department G will have to be used by the current Department A. The equipment used by Department G will be used by the current Department A.

e. Closing Department G will eliminate its expenses for advertising, bad debts, and store supplies. It will also eliminate 65% of the insurance expense allocated to the department for coverage on its merchandise inventory. In addition, 30% of the miscellaneous office expenses presently allocated to Department G will be eliminated.

Required

Preparation component:

1. Prepare a three-column schedule that lists (a) the company's total expenses (including cost of goods sold), (b) the expenses that would be eliminated by closing Department G, and (c) the expenses that will continue.
2. Prepare a forecasted income statement for the company reflecting the elimination under the assumption that sales and the gross profit will not be affected. The statement should also reflect the reassignment of the office worker to one-half time as a salesclerk.

Analysis component:

3. Prepare a reconciliation of the company's combined net income with the forecasted net income assuming Department G is eliminated. Also compare Department G's revenues and its avoidable expenses and explain why you think the department should or should not be eliminated.

Analytical and Review Problems

A & R Problem 28-1

Five investment opportunities of equal cost offer the following cash flow patterns:

Year	A	B	C	D	E
1	$ 4,000	$ 2,000	$ 2,500	$ 3,000	$ 1,000
2	4,000	2,000	2,500	3,000	1,000
3	4,000	2,000	2,500	3,000	1,000
4	4,000	2,000	2,500	3,000	1,000
5	4,000	2,000	2,500	3,000	1,000
6	1,000	3,000	2,500	2,000	4,000
7	1,000	3,000	2,500	2,000	4,000
8	1,000	3,000	2,500	2,000	4,000
9	1,000	3,000	2,500	2,000	4,000
10	1,000	3,000	2,500	2,000	4,000
Total	$25,000	$25,000	$25,000	$25,000	$25,000

Required

Rank the five alternatives in terms of desirability and justify your ranking.

A & R Problem 28-2

George Disposal has been offered an opportunity to submit a bid for the right to provide a garbage disposal service for the local municipality. The contract would run for five years. Mr. Disposal estimates that his net cash receipts from the disposal business would amount to $120,000 annually. If this bid is accepted, Mr. Disposal would have to make an initial investment of $24,000 in specialized equipment.

Required

What is the maximum amount that Mr. Disposal can afford to bid for the disposal service business, assuming that he requires a 15% return on his investment? (Do not consider income taxes.)

BEYOND THE NUMBERS

Reporting in Action

LO 4

Read notes 1 and 3 in **Atlantis's** annual report in Appendix I, and answer the following questions.

Required

1. In note 1, identify the two types of amortization methods used by Atlantis.
2. The maximum capital cost allowance rate specified by Revenue Canada for vehicles is 30%. How does this rate compare with the amortization rate used by Atlantis?
3. Using your answers from 1 and 2, why do you think Atlantis would use an accelerated amortization method when it reduces reported earnings in the early years of the investment period?
4. If the tax laws do not change for amortization, do you expect Atlantis to follow the same amortization method in later years? Check your response with Atlantis's current statements.

Comparative Analysis

LO 7

Reebok and **NIKE** sell several different products. Some are profitable and others are not. Teams of employees in each company make advertising, investment, and product mix decisions. For both companies, a certain portion of advertising is done on a local basis to a target audience.

Required

1. Find one major ad of a product or group of products for each company in your local newspaper. Contact the newspaper and ask them the approximate cost of this ad space (for example, cost of one page or one-half page of advertising).
2. Estimate how many products must be sold from this ad for it to justify the cost of the advertisement. Begin by taking the selling price of the product advertised for each company and assume a 20% contribution margin.
3. What is the importance of effective advertising when making a product mix decision? Be prepared to present your ideas in class.

Ethics Challenge

LO 4

A consultant commented that "Too often the numbers look good, but feel bad." This comment stems from estimation errors commonly found in capital budgeting proposals relating to the number of years that a project is assumed to generate cash flows. First, it is very difficult to reliably predict cash flow several years into the future. Second, the present value of cash flows many years into the future (say beyond 10 years) is often very small.

Required

1. Record the value today of $100 to be received in 10 years, at a 12% discount rate. What do you conclude?
2. Why is having an understanding of this concept important when evaluating several investment projects?

Communicating in Practice

LO 2,3

Payback, ROI and NPV are common techniques used in evaluating long-run investment opportunities. Identify the type of measurement perspective each offers and list the advantages and disadvantages of each. Be prepared to present your ideas to the class.

Taking It to the Net

We often must compete for good jobs. Today, more companies are using the Net to search for good employees. Our knowledge of this new job search tool can potentially help us obtain that "special opportunity." Check out the following Web sites and read how to prepare a résumé to be competitive in our information age:

http://www.cacee.com/
www.resumix.com/resume/resume_tips.html
www.occ.com/occ/JLK/HowToEResume.html

Required

Be prepared to turn in a rough draft of your résumé following the advice provided.

Teamwork in Action

LO 2,3

In teams of three or four, identify four conditions why an international airline company such as **Air Canada** or **Canadian Airlines** would make an investment in a project when all analyses such as payback and net present value indicate it would be a bad investment. (Hint: Think about qualitative issues and remember numbers do not always tell the whole story.) Provide an example of an investment project supporting your answer.

Hitting the Road

LO 1,4

"What does a new car really cost?" Visit or call your local auto dealership and inquire about leasing a car. Ask about the down payment and the required monthly payments. You are likely to find the salesperson does not discuss the cost of the car. The sales focus will be on the affordability of the monthly payments. This chapter gives you the tools to compute the cost of the car, in current dollars, and to estimate the profit from leasing for an auto dealership.

Required

1. Compare the cost-to-lease to the buy decision for the car in current dollars. Use the information given to you by the dealership you contact. (Assume you will make a final payment at the end of the lease and own the car upon completion of the lease.)
2. Is it more costly to buy or lease the car? By how much?

Business Break

LO 1,2

The business of office equipment continues to change. While the 1980s office equipment included products like ink blotters, adding machines, and thermal faxes, today's products are quick to change and often expensive. It is now not uncommon for a manager to require a three-year payback on all office equipment investments. But quantifying the benefits of office equipment is often difficult. Read "The Digital Copier Comes of Age" in *Business Week*, December 8, 1997.

Required

1. List three advantages of the new digital copier.
2. How would you try to measure these advantages to justify the price paid?

I

Financial Statement Information

APPENDIX

This appendix includes financial statement information from (a) **Alliance Communications Corporation** and (b) **Atlantis Communications Inc.** All of this information is taken from their annual reports. An **annual report** is a summary of the financial results of a company's operations for the year and its future plans. It is directed at external users of financial information, but also affects actions of internal users.

An annual report is also used by a company to showcase itself and its products. Many include attractive pictures, diagrams and illustrations related to the company. But the *financial section* is its primary objective. This section communicates much information about a company, with most data drawn from the accounting information system.

The layout of the financial section of an annual report is fairly standard and usually includes:

- Financial History and Highlights
- Message to Shareholders
- Management Discussion and Analysis
- Management Report
- Auditor's Report
- Financial Statements
- Notes to Financial Statements
- List of Directors and Managers

This appendix provides most of this information for Alliance Communications Corporation and Atlantis Communications Inc. This appendix is organized as follows:

- Alliance: I-1 to I-33
- Atlantis: I-34 to I-60

Many assignments at the end of each chapter refer to information in this appendix. We encourage readers to spend extra time with these assignments as they are especially useful in reinforcing and showing the relevance and diversity of financial reporting.

CORPORATE PROFILE

Alliance Communications Corporation is a global producer, distributor and broadcaster of filmed entertainment. Headquartered in Toronto with offices in Montreal, Vancouver, Los Angeles, Paris and Shannon, Alliance shares trade in Toronto and Montreal under AAC, and on NASDAQ under the symbol ALLIF.

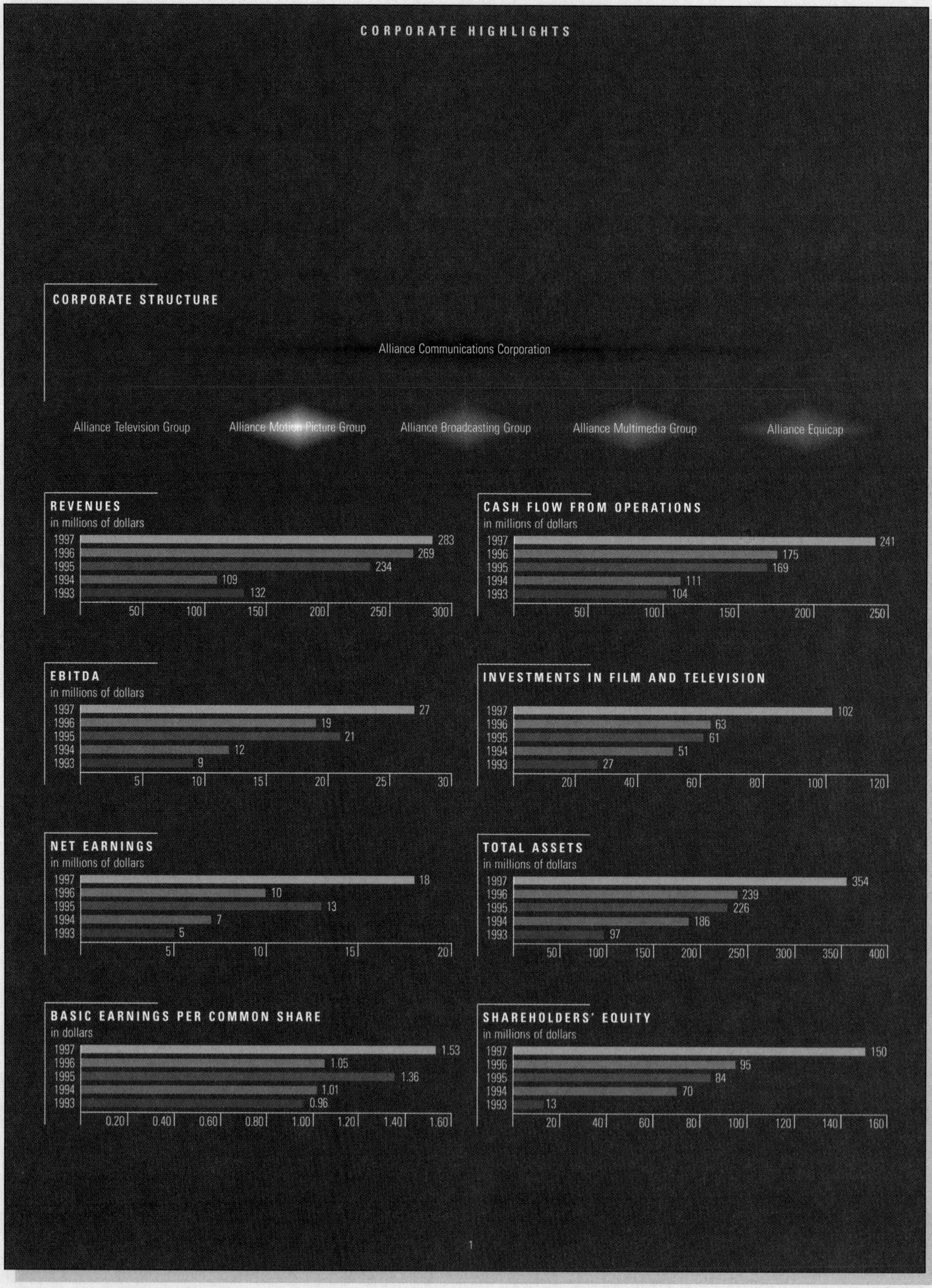
CORPORATE HIGHLIGHTS
CORPORATE STRUCTURE
Alliance Communications Corporation
Alliance Television Group
Alliance Motion Picture Group
Alliance Broadcasting Group
Alliance Multimedia Group
Alliance Equicap
REVENUES
in millions of dollars
1997 283
1996 269
1995 234
1994 109
1993 132
50 100 150 200 250 300
CASH FLOW FROM OPERATIONS
in millions of dollars
1997 241
1996 175
1995 169
1994 111
1993 104
50 100 150 200 250
EBITDA
in millions of dollars
1997 27
1996 19
1995 21
1994 12
1993 9
5 10 15 20 25 30
INVESTMENTS IN FILM AND TELEVISION
1997 102
1996 63
1995 61
1994 51
1993 27
20 40 60 80 100 120
NET EARNINGS
in millions of dollars
1997 18
1996 10
1995 13
1994 7
1993 5
5 10 15 20
TOTAL ASSETS
in millions of dollars
1997 354
1996 239
1995 226
1994 186
1993 97
50 100 150 200 250 300 350 400
BASIC EARNINGS PER COMMON SHARE
in dollars
1997 1.53
1996 1.05
1995 1.36
1994 1.01
1993 0.96
0.20 0.40 0.60 0.80 1.00 1.20 1.40 1.60
SHAREHOLDERS' EQUITY
in millions of dollars
1997 150
1996 95
1995 84
1994 70
1993 13
20 40 60 80 100 120 140 160
1

CORPORATE HIGHLIGHTS

AWARDS AND HONOURS

MOTION PICTURE AWARDS

Berlin Film Festival	C.I.C.A.E. Award	Welcome to the Dollhouse
Cannes International Film Festival	Special Jury Prize	Crash
Fantasporto, Portugal	Critics Award	Denise Calls Up
Fantasporto, Portugal	Audience Award	Denise Calls Up
Genie Awards	Best Achievement in Sound Editing	Crash
Genie Awards	Best Achievement in Film Editing	Crash
Genie Awards	Best Achievement in Art Direction	Lilies
Genie Awards	Best Achievement in Costume Design	Lilies
Genie Awards	Golden Reel Award	Crash
Genie Awards	Best Motion Picture	Lilies
Genie Awards	Best Overall Sound	Lilies
Genie Awards	Best Adapted Screenplay	Crash
Genie Awards	Best Achievement in Cinematography	Crash
Genie Awards	Best Achievement in Direction	Crash
Deauville Festival of American Cinema	Grand Prize	The Daytrippers
Sundance Film Festival	Filmmaker's Trophy Award	In the Company of Men

CANNES INTERNATIONAL FILM FESTIVAL AWARDS (MAY 1997)

Cannes International Film Festival	Grand Prix	The Sweet Hereafter
Cannes International Film Festival	International Critics Prize	The Sweet Hereafter
Cannes International Film Festival	Ecumenical Prize	The Sweet Hereafter

TELEVISION AWARDS

Banff International Television Festival	Best Continuing Series	Due South
Banff International Television Festiva	Best Animated Program	ReBoot
Golden Gates, San Francisco	Golden Gate Award	Due South
Worldfest Houston	Gold Award	Mirror Mirror
Worldfest Houston	Silver Award	Reboot
Gemini Awards	Chrysler Canada Award	Due South
Gemini Awards	Best Dramatic Series	Due South
Gemini Awards	Best Performance by an Actress	North of 60
Gemini Awards	Best Animated Program or Series	Reboot
Gemini Awards	Best Performance by a Supporting Actor	North of 60
Gemini Awards	Best Direction	Straight Up
Gemini Awards	Best Performance by an Actress	Mother Trucker: The Diana Kilmury Story
Worldfest Houston	Gold Special Jury Award	The Hunchback

PRIMETIME EMMY AWARDS NOMINATIONS (JULY 1997)

Outstanding Art Direction for a Miniseries or a Special	The Hunchback
Outstanding Costume Design for a Miniseries or a Special	The Hunchback
Outstanding Hairstyling for a Miniseries or a Special	The Hunchback
Outstanding Makeup for a Miniseries or a Special	The Hunchback
Outstanding Costume Design for a Miniseries or a Special	The Inheritance

SELECTED HIGHLIGHTS

May 20/96 Crash wins Special Jury Prize at Cannes Film Festival.

June 1/96 Diane Keaton signs first look deal with Alliance.

June 25/96 Alliance signs exclusive television deal with Director John Woo.

July 23/96 Crash becomes first Canadian motion picture to capture, in its opening week, first place at the French box office.

Aug. 22/96 Alliance completes cross border offering, realizing net proceeds of $32.9 million.

Sept. 4/96 Alliance wins coveted analog license to launch History Television.

Sept. 18/96 Alliance realizes profit in Mainframe investment and retains international distribution deal.

Sept. 19/96 Alliance forms Equicap Financial Corporation. Robert Beattie named division head.

Oct. 30/96 Principal photography begins on Atom Egoyan's The Sweet Hereafter.

Nov. 15/96 The English Patient opens in Canada culminating in $13 million at the box office.

Nov. 27/96 Crash wins 6 Genie awards including the Golden Reel Award for top grossing film. Lilies wins Genie award for Best Motion Picture.

Jan. 13/97 Alliance/Shaw Partnership files application for a national Video on Demand programming service.

Jan. 13/97 Alliance begins production with international partners on Captain Star, the Company's first conventional animation series.

Jan. 23/97 Alliance increases ownership in Showcase Television to 99%.

Jan. 23/97 Alliance acquires 20% interest in La Fete Group.

Feb. 27/97 Alliance forms joint venture with UK theatrical distributor, Electric Pictures.

Mar. 2/97 Alliance wins 7 Gemini Awards including Best Dramatic Series for Due South.

Mar. 4/97 Alliance begins principal photography on John Woo's Once a Thief, the series, for delivery on fiscal 1998.

Mar. 24/97 Films distributed in Canada by Alliance Releasing win 12 Academy Awards led by The English Patient.

MESSAGE TO SHAREHOLDERS

Fiscal 1997 was a year of success for Alliance. On the one hand, the company experienced earnings growth momentum, particularly in the core production, distribution and broadcasting businesses. On the other hand, Alliance's long term strategies began to bear fruit as the company achieved a number of its targeted objectives.

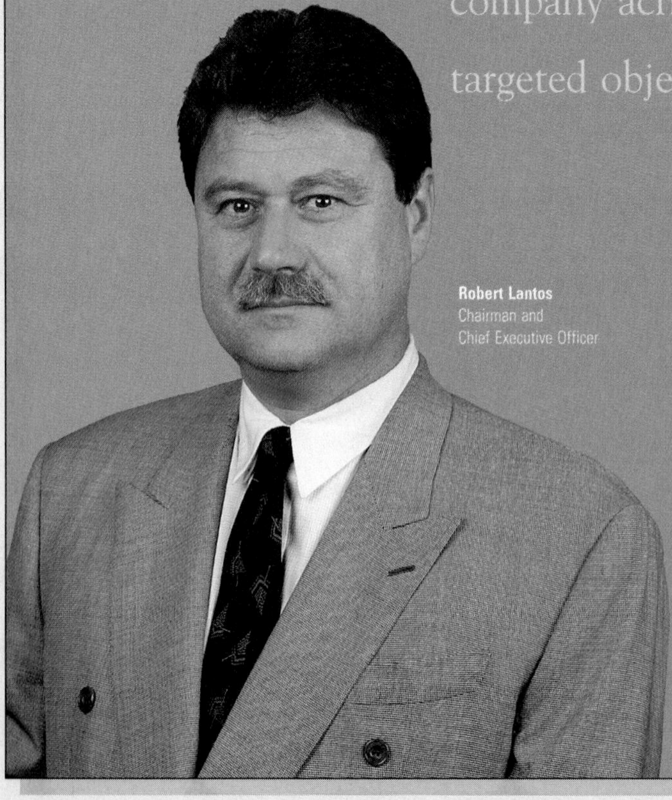

Robert Lantos
Chairman and
Chief Executive Officer

MESSAGE TO SHAREHOLDERS

We pursued our two-pronged strategy with determination and confidence:

1. TO MAXIMIZE OUR ACCESS TO THE MARKET BY BUILDING OUR DIRECT DISTRIBUTION REACH.

- We renewed long term Canadian distribution agreements with the two top US independent motion picture producers, Miramax and New Line.

- We successfully applied to the CRTC for a license to launch a new specialty network - History Television - a highly-prized and fiercely contested service which was awarded one of the last analog licenses and which will be launched on a new specialty tier by all major Canadian Cable Systems in September 1997.

- We consolidated our ownership of Showcase Television through the acquisition of most of the minority interest thereby increasing our equity from 55% to 99%.

- We ensured long term revenue growth for Showcase Television, obtaining the CRTC's approval to increase the service's permitted advertising time to 12 minutes per hour from its original 8 minute maximum.

- We expanded the reach of the now profitable Showcase Television to 3.5 million homes which will grow to 4 million in September 1997 through a new carriage agreement with Videotron and CF Cable in Montreal.

- Through a 50-50 joint venture with Shaw Communications, we applied for and received a license to launch a national Video-On-Demand service in English and French, a new distribution medium which we believe will have a significant long term impact on revenues.

- We entered the UK theatrical distribution market, teaming with distributor Electric Pictures.

- We expanded into the US first-run syndication market through distribution agreements with Polygram Filmed Entertainment.

- We acquired a 20% interest in Canada's leading childrens' film producer, Quebec's Les Productions La Fete, with an option to double our equity.

- We launched an in-house ad sales division in our Broadcasting Group, replacing the previous agency arrangements and resulting in immediate revenue growth.

- We acquired Canadian distribution rights to approximately 100 hours of drama from producer Telescene.

- We expanded our Canadian video operations into the distribution of non-theatrical product, including titles from Nelvana's animation catalogue.

Victor Loewy
President - Alliance Motion Picture Distribution
Vice Chairman - Alliance Communications Corporation

2. TO BUILD AND IMPROVE OUR CONTENT LIBRARY.

- We retain long term distribution rights by producing proprietary projects. We ensure continued production growth through increased investment in in-house development, exclusive deals with carefully targeted high profile talent, and by recruiting skilled creative executives.
This philosophy has already begun to yield dividends as highlighted in television by John Woo's *Once A Thief*, Diane Keaton's *Northern Lights* and Larry Gelbart's *Fast Track*, and in motion pictures by Atom Egoyan's *The Sweet Hereafter* and by the upcoming David Cronenberg's *eXistenZ*, Istvan Szabo's *Sunshine*, and Costa-Gavras' *No Other Life*.

Throughout the year, we continued our relentless pursuit of excellence. The quality of our product determines our stature in the industry and the prices we command in the international marketplace.

In turn, our peers rewarded us with some of the industry's highest laurels:

- Once again we won the top Canadian television and film honours. At the Gemini Awards, *Due South* was named Best Dramatic Series for the third consecutive year – the tenth time an Alliance produced series won this award. Also for the third time, *Due South* won the Chrysler Canada Award for Most Popular Television Program and *ReBoot* won the Gemini for Best Animated Program.

- *Crash* won a Special Jury Prize at the 1996 Cannes Film Festival.

- In May 1997, *The Sweet Hereafter*, the fourth Alliance collaboration with director Atom Egoyan, was the most decorated film at this year's Cannes Film Festival, winning three major awards including the Grand Prix. It is now three years in a row that an Alliance film has won an award in Cannes.

- Motion pictures acquired for Canada by Alliance such as *The English Patient*, *Shine*, *Secrets & Lies* and *Sling Blade* won 12 Academy Awards this year.

- In July 1997, Alliance received five prime time Emmy nominations, four for *The Hunchback* and one for *The Inheritance*.

Ultimately, our strategy is – to put it bluntly – to make money – which is exactly what we accomplished in fiscal 1997 with a 27% growth in earnings from $10.4 million to $13.2 million, a 42% growth in EBITDA from $18.8 million to $26.7 million, and a 66% growth in pre-tax earnings from $12.3 million to $20.4 million. (These results are exclusive of the Mainframe related gain). Our distribution-driven, diversified production strategy ensures that this growth will continue in fiscal 1998 and in the years to follow.

From left to right: **Atom Egoyan**, director and producer of *The Sweet Hereafter*. **John Woo**, director and executive producer of *Once a Thief*, the movie. **David Cronenberg**, writer, director and producer of *Crash*. **Dianne Keaton**, executive producer and star of *Northern Lights*

MESSAGE TO SHAREHOLDERS

A report to our shareholders must be more than just corporate cheerleading. A critical analysis of the company must also take into account its vulnerabilities and unfulfilled expectations. This year at Alliance:

1. We targeted the UK market because, after the US, it is the world's strongest source of independent movies. To support the initiative we competed for a lottery franchise in order to better access British film subsidies.

We assembled a strong and diverse group of partners. Under the name Studio Pictures, we competed for a franchise award which, had it succeeded, would have triggered some $60 million of off-balance sheet production financing over five years. Although we were not successful, we achieved our goal of expanding Alliance's production reach into the UK, forging an important tie with one of the UK's leading film production executives, George Faber, the former head of BBC Films. Mr. Faber's Company Pictures, in which Alliance is a shareholder, now has an overall production deal with Alliance. The British distributor Electric Pictures formed the platform for our move into the UK distribution market.

2. Our television production slate suffered from an imbalance between series and movies. With only two series in production, television movies dominated the slate. Movies are more costly per hour than series. This negatively impacted our gross margins. The imbalance has been addressed. Fiscal 1998 features our largest television production slate ever with 120 hours confirmed for delivery this year. The slate is now dominated by series, with six in production and several pilots underway. Because we own extensive rights in perpetuity to all our productions, even the less profitable television movies are valuable additions to our library and will continue to generate revenues well beyond their amortization cycle.

3. In 1994, we invested in a start-up television station in Hungary, Budapest TV3. Our strategy was to create a new market for our library and, parallel with our investment, we entered into a long term product supply agreement with TV3.

The Company's diverse day to day business activities are managed by a Management Executive Committee comprised of Robert Lantos, Victor Loewy and shown here from left to right: **Roman Doroniuk** Chief Financial Officer, **George Burger** Executive Vice-President, **Jeff Rayman** Chairman, Alliance Multimedia President, Alliance Equicap

While the station has been modestly successful, we are experiencing collection difficulties on our supply agreement which has now been suspended. Our investment in TV3 is not material (approximately $1.3 million) and we believe that its value is not at present impaired. With TV3 not proving to be of strategic value to our library sales, the Company may sell its interest in the station.

THE EQUICAP FACTOR

Our focus on expansion and the strengthening of our core businesses over the past three years has significantly reduced Equicap's share of the overall earnings picture of Alliance. The potential negative impact of ending Equicap's tax shelter activities on the Company's earnings has been minimized.

In fiscal 1997, Equicap's tax shelter business contributed approximately $4.5 million to our net earnings, or 34% excluding the Mainframe gain, down from 38% in fiscal 1996. Net earnings in our core businesses increased from 1996 to 1997 by 34%, excluding the Mainframe gain.

Our growing production slate, renewed distribution output deals, growth in our broadcasting business and revenues generated by our library will ensure that our overall earnings growth is not compromised by a reduced contribution from Equicap in fiscal 1998 and beyond. We are confident that we have successfully replaced Equicap's tax shelter earnings with valuable and predictable profits from our growing core activities.

While we anticipate no earnings from tax shelters in fiscal 1999, we do expect growing revenue and earning streams from Equicap's new ventures led by Equicap Financial Corporation.

HIDDEN ASSETS

A brief inventory of some extraordinary assets whose value is not fully reflected on the balance sheet:

1. We have amassed a world class library of movies, television drama and animation — the largest and most valuable library ever assembled by a Canadian company. It consists of over 1,000 hours of international rights and more than 8,000 hours of Canadian rights (including nearly 3,000 motion pictures). The growth of our international rights library is propelled by our philosophy to produce proprietary projects. Our Canadian rights library is the beneficiary of our strong theatrical distribution operation which consistently feeds our Canadian library with new titles.

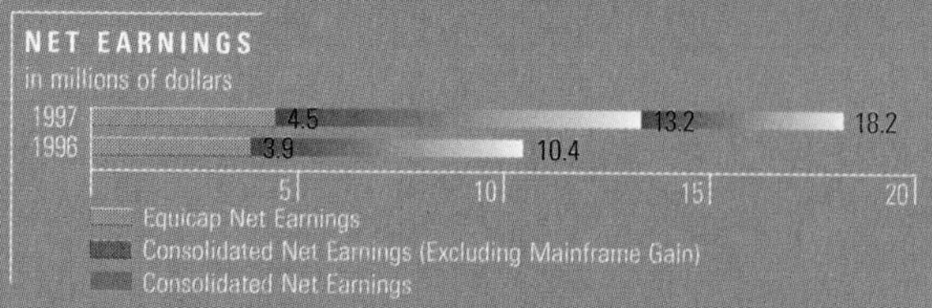

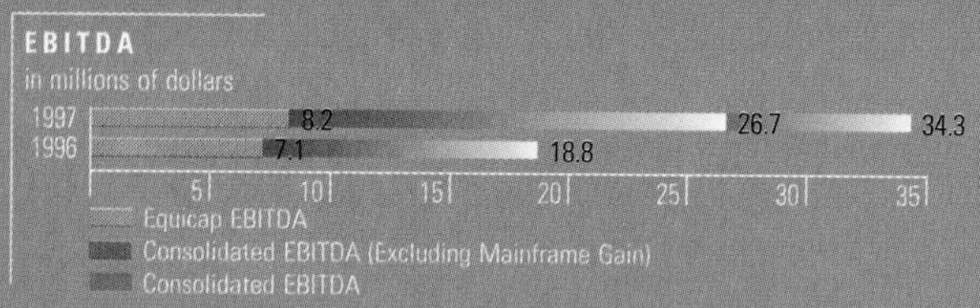

MESSAGE TO SHAREHOLDERS

In the business of filmed entertainment, library revenues are an essential pillar of strength. They represent a steadily increasing high margin income stream from off-balance sheet assets. For a library to generate meaningful revenues it has to achieve a certain critical mass and it must contain some highly desirable lead titles. Alliance's library has both. Since fiscal 1994, library revenues have grown at a compound annual rate of 42% from $4.5 million to $13.0 million and all of the titles in our library have been principally fully amortized. We define library revenues as sales of programs after their first cycle, typically three years after completion. There are more aggressive definitions practised in the industry which, in our opinion, mix library revenues with current revenues.

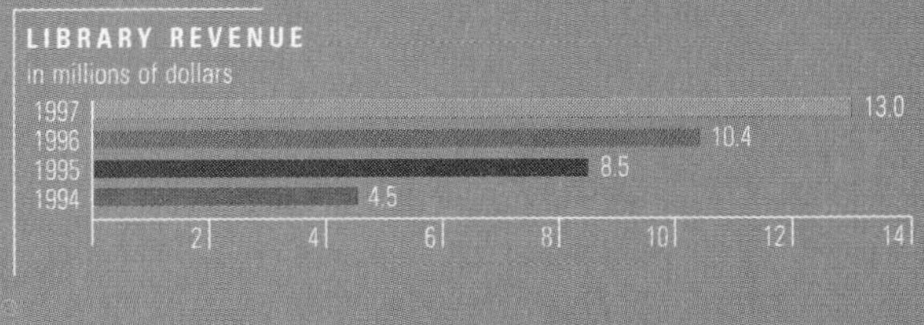

A major portion of Alliance's product is still in its first cycle of exploitation thus ensuring future growth in library revenue as these rights revert to the Company.

2. When we took Alliance public four years ago, we had no broadcast assets. Today, we have three specialty services:

I) Showcase Television, which is now generating operating revenue of $20 million with a subscriber growth rate of 20,000 households per month.

II) History Television, which even prior to its September 1997 launch, has begun to generate advertising sales.

The launching of History Television will bring economies of scale to Showcase Television as the two services share origination facilities, advertising sales force, administration and management.

One of the reasons we acquired the minority interests in Showcase Television was to be free to fully realize upon these efficiencies.

We consider Showcase Television and History Television to be "beachfront properties" as they are among the last specialty services to receive wide national cable carriage. With all analog slots now occupied, future specialty licences in English Canada will likely be issued on the basis of digital carriage only and will require a long period before achieving the level of consumer penetration necessary for profitability.

Our specialty networks have value beyond their earnings multiple. They are irreplaceable. Together with our strength in Canadian theatrical and home video distribution, our broadcast assets provide us with a uniquely diversified reach into the Canadian market.

III) Video-On-Demand (in partnership with Shaw Communications) which will bring the video store to the consumer's living room.

All three services are important new opportunities for Alliance's library.

3. In the years since our IPO, we have built a growing animation business from a start-up position. The two computer generated series which we co-produce with Mainframe and distribute world-wide, *ReBoot* and *Beast Wars*, are at the leading edge of CGI. They are widely sold internationally and are in the US market in first-run syndication. Both are ratings hits in Canada where they are among the top-rated shows on YTV.

Our first 2-D conventional animated series, *Captain Star*, is an international co-production with various European partners such as the UK's HTV. It debuts in Canada in September on the new cartoon network, Teletoon.

An Alliance animation library is now beginning to take shape, containing 91 episodes of high-end animation to which we control international distribution rights.

Our 1994 investment in Mainframe Entertainment has strengthened our balance sheet with a ten-fold after tax cash return on our capital plus a 7% carried interest in the now publicly traded company. While we have reduced our equity position, we have maintained our principal strategic objective through a distribution agreement which provides us with international rights to Mainframe product.

Thanks to our strategic focus, we have carefully laid the groundwork for future growth. We have identified our weak spots and have replaced them with new building blocks, positioning the Company to focus on its strengths.

In closing, we record with great regret the passing of our friend and distinguished colleague, Andrew Sarlos, O.C., LL.D.(Hon), F.C.A., who served Alliance with distinction as a Director of the Company from 1992. He is greatly missed. At the same time, we record with pleasure the election to the Board in 1996 of Donald Sobey, Chairman of the Empire Group. We warmly welcome Mr. Sobey.

Robert Lantos

MANAGEMENTS DISCUSSION AND ANALYSIS

ALLANCE COMMUNICATIONS CORPORATION

RESULTS OF OPERATIONS

Fiscal 1997 marked renewed earnings growth with record net earnings, revenues and cash flow from operations.

Net earnings for the year ended March 31, 1997 increased 75.0% to $18.2 million compared to $10.4 million for the year ended March 31, 1996. Excluding the gain on sale of investment, net earnings in fiscal 1997 increased 26.9% to $13.2 million. EBITDA increased 42.0% to $26.7 million for the year ended March 31, 1997 from $18.8 million for the year ended March 31, 1996.

Revenues in fiscal 1997 increased 5.1% to $282.6 million compared to fiscal 1996 revenues of $268.9 million. Revenues increased in all businesses with the exception of Motion Pictures, where revenues declined due to the timing of the delivery of Alliance-produced motion pictures. Gross profit increased 16.2% to $68.8 million in fiscal 1997 from $59.2 million in fiscal 1996 while the gross margin increased to 24.3% in fiscal 1997 from 22.0% in fiscal 1996.

Cash flow from operations in fiscal 1997 increased 37.9% to $240.7 million from $174.5 million in fiscal 1996.

The following table presents a consolidated financial summary of the Company's businesses.

For the years ended March 31, 1997, March 31, 1996 and March 31, 1995
(In thousands of Canadian dollars)

							% Increase (Decrease)	
	1997	%	1996	%	1995	%	1997 over 1996	1996 over 1995
REVENUES BY BUSINESS:								
Alliance Television	$ 110,463	39.1	$ 104,676	38.9	$ 106,540	45.5	5.5	(1.7)
Alliance Motion Pictures	113,331	40.1	121,416	45.1	100,709	43.1	(6.7)	20.6
Alliance Equicap	24,967	8.8	23,204	8.6	23,582	10.1	7.6	(1.6)
Alliance Broadcasting	19,884	7.0	16,836	6.3	2,586	1.1	18.1	551.0
Alliance Multimedia	13,954	5.0	2,813	1.1	394	0.2	396.1	614.0
Total Revenues	$ 282,599	100.0	$ 268,945	100.0	$ 233,811	100.0	5.1	15.0
DIRECT OPERATING EXPENSES BY BUSINESS:								
Alliance Television	$ 88,699	80.3	$ 80,486	76.9	$ 83,282	78.2	10.2	(3.4)
Alliance Motion Pictures	90,762	80.1	109,331	90.0	87,743	87.1	(17.0)	24.6
Alliance Equicap	12,372	49.6	11,920	51.4	11,573	49.1	3.8	3.0
Alliance Broadcasting	11,218	56.4	7,299	43.4	827	32.0	53.7	782.6
Alliance Multimedia	10,765	77.1	753	26.8	260	66.0	1329.6	189.6
Total Direct Operating Expenses	$ 213,816	75.7	$ 209,789	78.0	$ 183,685	78.6	1.9	14.2
GROSS PROFIT BY BUSINESS:								
Alliance Television	$ 21,764	19.7	$ 24,190	23.1	$ 23,258	21.8	(10.0)	4.0
Alliance Motion Pictures	22,569	19.9	12,085	10.0	12,966	12.9	86.8	6.8
Alliance Equicap	12,595	50.4	11,284	48.6	12,009	50.9	11.6	(6.0)
Alliance Broadcasting	8,666	43.6	9,537	56.6	1,759	68.0	(9.1)	442.2
Alliance Multimedia	3,189	22.9	2,060	73.2	134	34.0	54.8	1,437.3
Total Gross Profit	$ 68,783	24.3	$ 59,156	22.0	$ 50,126	21.4	16.3	18.0

MANAGEMENTS DISCUSSION AND ANALYSIS

ALLANCE COMMUNICATIONS CORPORATION

FISCAL 1997 COMPARED TO FISCAL 1996

Revenues in fiscal 1997 were $282.6 million, an increase of $13.7 million or 5.1%, compared to $268.9 million in fiscal 1996. This increase was due to revenue growth in all businesses, with the exception of a slight decline in Alliance Motion Pictures.

Alliance Television revenues in fiscal 1997 were $110.5 million, an increase of $5.8 million or 5.5%, compared to $104.7 million in fiscal 1996. This increase was due to an $8.1 million increase in production revenues, partially offset by a $2.3 million decrease in distribution revenues. In the current year, 56 hours of television production were delivered compared to 57 hours in the prior year. These hours were comprised of 35 hours of series delivered in fiscal 1997 compared to 46 hours in fiscal 1996, 18 hours of television movies delivered in fiscal 1997 compared to 10 hours in fiscal 1996 and three hours of television pilots delivered in fiscal 1997 compared to one hour in fiscal 1996. On average, therefore, the size of the average hourly production budget increased substantially over the prior year as television movie budgets per hour are generally much higher than television series' budgets per hour. The decreased distribution revenues were due to exceptional revenues being earned in the prior year on certain titles which was not repeated in the same magnitude in the current year.

Alliance Motion Pictures revenues in fiscal 1997 were $113.3 million, a decrease of $8.1 million or 6.7%, compared to $121.4 million in fiscal 1996. This decrease was due primarily to the production division where revenues decreased by $15.2 million over the prior year from $32.2 million in fiscal 1996 to $17.0 million in the current year. In the current year, the production division delivered one motion picture, Crash, whereas in the prior year three motion pictures were delivered. In Alliance Releasing, the Company's Canadian distribution business, revenues in fiscal 1997 were $82.0 million, an increase of $2.2 million or 2.8%, compared to $79.8 million in fiscal 1996. Within Alliance Releasing, theatrical revenues increased $1.4 million compared to the prior year, video revenues decreased $2.4 million compared to the prior year and television revenues increased $3.0 million compared to the prior year, due primarily to the timing of the releases in the various media formats. Theatrical successes in the current year included: The English Patient; Shine; Michael; and Trainspotting. Le Monde revenues were $11.7 million, an increase of $7.2 million or 160.0%, compared to $4.5 million in fiscal 1996 due to the growing library of titles. Top revenue performers in the current year included: Lethal Tender; Dead Silence; Hostile Intent; and Ravager. Alliance Independent Films' revenues of $2.7 million decreased $2.2 million or 44.9%, compared to $4.9 million in the prior year due to the decline in the amount of new product acquired and delivered in the current year. Deliveries in the current year included: Denise Calls Up; Welcome to the Dollhouse; and When Night is Falling.

Alliance Equicap revenues in fiscal 1997 were $25.0 million an increase of $1.8 million or 7.8%, compared to fiscal 1996 revenues of $23.2 million due primarily to the success of production services deals in the current year. In addition, the current year's revenues include Equicap Financial Corporation, which started up operations in the fall of 1996. Equicap Financial Corporation closed six deals in the period October 1996 to March 1997 for arrangement fee revenues and interest income of $0.6 million.

Alliance Broadcasting revenues in fiscal 1997 were $19.9 million, an increase of $3.1 million or 18.5%, compared to $16.8 million in fiscal 1996 due primarily to increased advertising sales. Cable revenues were slightly higher due to an increase in the subscriber base net of the impact of a lower average subscriber rate.

MANAGEMENTS DISCUSSION AND ANALYSIS

ALLANCE COMMUNICATIONS CORPORATION

Alliance Multimedia revenues in fiscal 1997 were $14.0 million, an increase of $11.2 million or 400.0%, compared to $2.8 million in fiscal 1996. Distribution revenues of $12.0 million were recognized in fiscal 1997 as 26 episodes of Beastwars were delivered. TMP-The Music Publisher ("TMP") revenues increased to $2.0 million, an increase of $0.9 million or 81.8%, compared to $1.1 million in fiscal 1996 due to the timing of collections of foreign royalties and also from the successes of Amanda Marshall's debut album which contained five TMP songs and the TMP song "Heaven Help My Heart", recorded by both Wynonna Judd and Tina Arena.

Gross profit in fiscal 1997 was $68.8 million, an increase of $9.6 million or 16.2%, compared to $59.2 million in fiscal 1996. This increase was due primarily to Alliance Motion Pictures where the gross profit increased $10.5 million year-over-year. As a percentage of revenues, gross profit in fiscal 1997 was 24.3%, compared to 22.0% in fiscal 1996, due to increased margins in Alliance Motion Pictures and the change in the revenue mix, partially offset by decreased margins in Alliance Television. The increased margins in Alliance Motion Pictures were due primarily to an increased margin in the production division where the margin improved from - 11.8% on the motion pictures delivered in the prior year to 15.9% on Crash, which was delivered in the current year. The decreased margins in Alliance Television were due to the increased production costs per hour of delivering higher quality television movies in the current year such as: The Hunchback; The Inheritance and Toe Tags (pilot) as well as an increased proportion of television movies versus television series. Television series generally have better margins but accounted for a lower percentage of production in fiscal 1997.

Other operating expenses in fiscal 1997 were $42.0 million, an increase of $1.6 million or 4.0%, compared to $40.4 million in fiscal 1996. Other operating expenses as a percentage of revenues decreased slightly to 14.9% compared to 15.0% in fiscal 1996. Other operating expenses are comprised of corporate overhead and operating expenses other than direct operating expenses. These expenses include such items as general and administrative expenses, salaries and benefits, office rental, communications costs and professional fees. In fiscal 1997, $13.9 million of operating expenses related to corporate overhead, compared to $12.3 million in fiscal 1996. Corporate overhead included non-recurring charges of $2.1 million in fiscal 1997: $1 million relating to Equicap bonus costs; $600,000 relating to the Company's unsuccessful UK franchise bid; and $500,000 relating to head office moving costs, compared to $1.3 million in fiscal 1996: $800,000 relating to severance costs; and $500,000 relating to the Company's unsuccessful efforts to acquire the broadcast assets of John Labatt Limited. Before non-recurring charges, corporate overhead increased to $11.8 million in fiscal 1997 from $11.0 million in fiscal 1996. The increase in other operating expenses was primarily due to head count increases in new and expanding businesses such as Alliance Pictures International and Equicap Financial Corporation.

Net interest expense in fiscal 1997 was $1.3 million, an increase of $0.4 million or 44.4%, compared to $0.9 million in fiscal 1996, reflecting increased cash requirements in the current year, partially offset by the equity offering proceeds and lower interest rates.

The Company's effective tax rate for fiscal 1997 increased to 35.0% from 15.7% in fiscal 1996 due to a shift in the mix of earnings before income taxes to income tax jurisdictions with less favourable income tax rates. In addition, in the current year, the gain on sale of investment was taxed at approximately 34%.

Net earnings in fiscal 1997 were $18.2 million, an increase of $7.8 million or 75.0%, compared to $10.4 million in fiscal 1996.

MANAGEMENTS DISCUSSION AND ANALYSIS

ALLANCE COMMUNICATIONS CORPORATION

FISCAL 1996 COMPARED TO FISCAL 1995

Revenues in fiscal 1996 were $268.9 million, an increase of $35.1 million or 15.0%, compared to $233.8 million in fiscal 1995. This increase was due primarily to significant revenue growth in Alliance Motion Pictures, as well as the inclusion of revenues for a full year in Alliance Broadcasting, which started commercial operations in January 1995.

Alliance Television revenues in fiscal 1996 were $104.7 million, a decrease of $1.8 million or 1.7%, compared to $106.5 million in fiscal 1995. This decrease was due primarily to lower international revenues partially offset by higher North American revenues.

Alliance Motion Pictures revenues in fiscal 1996 were $121.4 million, an increase of $20.7 million or 20.6%, compared to $100.7 million in fiscal 1995. This increase was due primarily to increased revenues in Alliance Releasing, where revenues in fiscal 1996 were $79.8 million, an increase of $21.3 million or 36.4%, compared to $58.5 million in fiscal 1995. Within Alliance Releasing, this increase was due primarily to increased Canadian home video revenues as a result of a number of successful home video releases, including Pulp Fiction, Mortal Kombat, Don Juan DeMarco and Johnny Mnemonic, as well as the continued exploitation of Dumb and Dumber, The Swan Princess and The Mask, which were released theatrically in fiscal 1995. These increases were slightly offset by a $3.0 million decrease in Canadian theatrical revenues in fiscal 1996.

Alliance Equicap revenues in fiscal 1996 were $23.2 million which was approximately the same as fiscal 1995. In fiscal 1996, Equicap focused on structured production financings, which provided private investors with access to tax incentives provided by the Canadian government.

Alliance Broadcasting revenues in fiscal 1996 were $16.8 million, an increase of $14.2 million or 546.2%, compared to $2.6 million in fiscal 1995. This increase was due primarily to fiscal 1996 revenues reflecting the first full year of operations of Showcase, while the previous year reflected only one quarter of operations. Revenues were recognized in the first quarter of operations.

Alliance Multimedia revenues in fiscal 1996 were $2.8 million, an increase of $2.4 million or 600.0%, compared to $0.4 million in fiscal 1995. Distribution revenues of $1.7 million were recognized in fiscal 1996 as episodes of ReBoot were delivered to YTV. Fiscal 1996 also reflected the first full year of operations of TMP where revenues were $1.1 million, an increase of $0.7 million or 175.0%, compared to $0.4 million in fiscal 1995.

Gross profit in fiscal 1996 was $59.2 million, an increase of $9.1 million or 18.2%, compared to $50.1 million in fiscal 1995. This increase was due primarily to the inclusion of gross profit realized from Showcase Television's first full year of operations and distribution revenues realized upon the delivery of ReBoot. Gross profit in fiscal 1996 was 22.0%, compared to 21.4% in fiscal 1995, due to the change in the revenue mix and increased margins in Alliance Television, partially offset by decreased margins in Alliance Motion Pictures. Decreased margins in Alliance Motion Pictures were due primarily to an increase in the provision for investment in film and television programs in fiscal 1996. In addition, margins on films delivered in fiscal 1996 were not as favourable as the margins on films delivered in fiscal 1995.

Other operating expenses in fiscal 1996 were $40.4 million, an increase of $11.8 million or 41.3%, compared to $28.6 million in fiscal 1995. In fiscal 1996, $12.3 million of other operating expenses related to corporate overhead, compared to $11.7 million in fiscal 1995. Corporate overhead included non-recurring charges of $1.3 million in fiscal 1996 compared to $0.6 million in fiscal 1995. Before non-recurring charges, corporate overhead decreased to $11.0 million in fiscal 1996 from $11.1 million in fiscal 1995. The overall increase in other operating expenses was due to expansion of the Los Angeles office and international operations, increased expenses in Alliance Broadcasting associated with Showcase Television's first full year of operations, overall head count and wage increases and certain one-time expenditures, such as severance costs and costs associated with the company's unsuccessful efforts to acquire the broadcast assets of John Labatt Limited.

Net interest expense in fiscal 1996 was \$0.9 million, an increase of \$0.6 million or 200.0%, compared to \$0.3 million in fiscal 1995, reflecting increased interest costs as the opening cash balance was drawn down early in the fiscal year to finance production costs, acquisitions of distribution product and development costs.

The Company's effective tax rate for fiscal 1996 decreased to 15.7% from 22.0% in fiscal 1995 due to a shift in the mix of earnings before income taxes to non-Canadian operations with favourable income tax rates.

Net earnings in fiscal 1996 were \$10.4 million, a decrease of \$2.6 million or 20.0%, compared to \$13.0 million in fiscal 1995.

LIQUIDITY AND CAPITAL RESOURCES

Cash flow from operations increased significantly during fiscal 1997 to \$240.7 million from \$174.5 million for fiscal 1996 and \$169.1 million for fiscal 1995. Earnings before interest, provision for income taxes, depreciation, amortization and minority interest ("EBITDA") increased to \$26.7 million during fiscal 1997 after dropping to \$18.8 million in fiscal 1996 from \$21.5 million in fiscal 1995.

Alliance has traditionally financed its working capital requirements principally through cash generated by operations, revolving bank credit facilities and sales of equity. The greatest demand for working capital exists in the start-up phase of production, which traditionally occurs in August and September, although it is progressively becoming less and less seasonal in nature as the company diversifies its business.

The nature of the Company's business is such that significant initial expenditures are required to produce and acquire television programs and films, while revenues from these television programs and films are earned over an extended period of time after their completion and acquisition. As Alliance's activities grow, its financing requirements are expected to grow. The Company believes it has sufficient resources to fund its operations through fiscal 1998 from cash generated by operations, existing bank facilities and the net proceeds of the U.S. equity offering in August 1996.

Alliance typically borrows from banks to provide interim production financing. All revenues associated with these productions are pledged as security for these loans. The majority of these borrowings relate specifically to television program and film production.

On October 28, 1994, prior to the reorganization of the share capital of the Company, the Company issued an unsecured, subordinated 6.5% convertible debenture maturing April 5, 2002 to Onex Corporation for \$16.5 million cash. The debenture is convertible into common shares of the Company at any time at \$19 per share. Interest is payable in cash or additional convertible debentures at the Company's option. Commencing October 28, 1999, the debenture or any portion thereof will be redeemable at the option of the Company, provided certain conditions are met, at the issue price, together with accrued and unpaid interest to the date of redemption. The debenture provides the Company with the option to pay for the redemption of the debenture by issuing common shares to the debenture holder at a price equal to 90% of the weighted average trading price of the common shares for the last 20 consecutive trading days prior to redemption or the maturity date.

In fiscal 1995, the Company obtained a $75 million credit facility from a Canadian chartered bank. The bank facility provided for a $20 million demand operating line, a $50 million term production financing facility and a $5 million facility to hedge foreign exchange exposure.

In August 1996, the Company completed a cross-border offering of 3,020,000 class B non-voting shares for net proceeds of $32.9 million.

In December 1996, the Company's bank facility was increased to $122 million to provide for a $65 million demand operating line, a $50 million term production financing facility, a $5 million facility to hedge foreign exchange exposure and a $2 million lease facility. As at March 31, 1997, the Company had loans outstanding under its term production facility on productions in progress in the amount of $15.9 million. The Company applied $12.5 million of its cash against the $15.9 million loans for net operating loan and bank indebtedness of $3.4 million as at March 31, 1997. See note 5 to the Consolidated Financial Statements.

In March 1997, Equicap Financial Corporation obtained a $25 million non-recourse revolving line of credit with a Canadian Chartered bank. The line of credit forms part of the funds made available for film projects financed by Equicap Financial Corporation.

RISKS AND UNCERTAINTIES

The Company capitalizes production and distribution costs as incurred to investment in film and television programs and such costs are amortized to direct operating expenses in accordance with SFAS 53. Under SFAS 53, all costs incurred in connection with an individual film or television program, including production costs, release prints and advertising costs, are capitalized as investment in film and television programs. These costs are stated at the lower of unamortized cost and estimated net realizable value. Estimated total production costs for an individual film or television program are amortized in the proportion that revenues realized relates to management's estimate of the total revenues expected to be received from such film or television program. As a result, if revenue estimates change with respect to a film or television program, the Company may be required to write down all or a portion of the unamortized costs of such film or television program. No assurance can be given that a write down will not have a significant impact on the Company's results of operations and financial condition.

Results of operations for any period are significantly dependent on the number and timing of television programs and films delivered or made available to various media. Consequently, the Company's results of operations may fluctuate materially from period to period and the results for any one period are not necessarily indicative of results for future periods. Ultimately, profitability depends not only on revenues but on the amount paid to acquire or produce the film or television program and the amount spent on the prints and advertising campaign used to promote it.

The Company currently finances a portion of its production budgets from Canadian governmental agencies and incentive programs, such as Telefilm Canada and federal and provincial tax credits, as well as international sources in the case of the Company's co-productions. There can be no assurance that local cultural incentive programs which the Company may access in Canada and internationally, will not be reduced, amended or eliminated. Any change in these incentive programs may have an adverse impact on the Company.

MANAGEMENTS DISCUSSION AND ANALYSIS

ALLANCE COMMUNICATIONS CORPORATION

A significant portion of the Company's revenues and expenses is in U.S. dollars, and therefore subject to fluctuation in exchange rates. There is risk that a significant fluctuation in exchange rates may have an adverse impact on the Company's results of operations.

Commissions earned by Alliance Equicap have been principally related to sales of limited partnership units to private investors in connection with structured production financings. Recent changes to Canadian income tax legislation have eliminated tax incentives available to investors in connection with certain financings. Consequently, it is expected that Alliance Equicap's revenues in fiscal 1998 will be substantially less than in fiscal 1997.

OUTLOOK

The Company achieved record results in fiscal 1997 and plans to continue to build on this success. The Company will continue to pursue its long term strategy of expanding its libraries and increasing its direct distribution reach. The Company's proven ability to deliver and distribute high quality product combined with its strong financial position, makes it well positioned to achieve its aggressive growth strategy.

QUARTERLY REVIEW

The business of the Company fluctuates during the year as indicated by the table below, which summarizes quarterly results for the fiscal year ended March 31, 1997:

(In thousands of Canadian dollars except share information)

	1st Qtr.	2nd Qtr.	3rd. Qtr.	4th Qtr.	Total
Revenues	$ 63,516	$ 54,617	$ 64,956	$ 99,510	$ 282,599
Gross Profit	12,402	15,688	16,066	24,627	68,783
EBITDA	3,026	3,529	6,850	13,341	26,746
Net Earnings	955	6,260	4,081	6,892	18,188
Basic Earnings Per Share	$ 0.10	$ 0.53	$ 0.32	$ 0.53	$ 1.53

AUDITORS' REPORT

ALLIANCE COMMUNICATIONS CORPORATION

To the shareholders of Alliance Communications Corporation:

We have audited the consolidated balance sheets of Alliance Communications Corporation as at March 31, 1997 and 1996 and the consolidated statements of earnings and retained earnings and changes in financial position for each of the years in the three year period ended March 31, 1997. These financial statements are the responsibility of the company's management. Our responsibility is to express an opinion on these financial statements based on our audits.

We conducted our audits in accordance with Canadian generally accepted auditing standards. Those standards require that we plan and perform an audit to obtain reasonable assurance whether the financial statements are free of material misstatement. An audit includes examining, on a test basis, evidence supporting the amounts and disclosures in the financial statements. An audit also includes assessing the accounting principles used and significant estimates made by management, as well as evaluating the overall financial statement presentation.

In our opinion, these consolidated financial statements present fairly, in all material respects, the financial position of the company as at March 31, 1997 and 1996 and the results of its operations and the changes in its financial position for each of the years in the three year period ended March 31, 1997 in accordance with Canadian generally accepted accounting principles.

Coopers & Lybrand

Chartered Accountants

North York, Ontario, Canada
May 30, 1997
(except as to note 21 which is as of June 17, 1997)

CONSOLIDATED BALANCE SHEETS

ALLIANCE COMMUNICATIONS CORPORATION

As at March 31, 1997 and March 31, 1996
(In thousands of Canadian dollars)

	1997	1996
ASSETS		
Cash and short-term investments	$ 10,777	$ 5,090
Accounts receivable	82,184	53,081
Distribution contracts receivable	76,272	64,948
Loans receivable	9,283	-
Investment in film and television programs (note 2)	101,531	63,274
Film and television programs in progress	22,955	22,398
Program exhibition rights	11,821	9,151
Development costs and investment in scripts	13,103	7,762
Property and equipment (note 3)	10,314	6,848
Broadcasting licences, net of accumulated amortization of $30 (1996 - $nil)	7,236	-
Other assets (note 4)	8,246	6,346
	$ 353,722	$ 238,898
LIABILITIES		
Operating loan and bank indebtedness (note 5)	$3,361	$ 5,617
Accounts payable and accrued liabilities	86,268	47,440
Distribution revenues payable	23,223	26,238
Loans payable (note 6)	-	2,083
Income taxes (note 12)	10,927	10,818
Deferred revenue	62,980	32,706
Convertible debenture (note 7)	16,500	16,500
Minority interest	39	2,116
	203,298	143,518
SHAREHOLDERS' EQUITY		
Capital stock (note 8)	88,836	52,295
Retained earnings	60,893	42,705
Cumulative translation adjustments	695	380
	150,424	95,380
	$ 353,722	$ 238,898

Signed on behalf of the Board,

David J Kassie
Director

Ellis Jacob
Director

The accompanying notes form an integral part of these financial statements.

CONSOLIDATED STATEMENTS OF EARNINGS AND RETAINED EARNINGS

ALLIANCE COMMUNICATIONS CORPORATION

For the years ended March 31, 1997, March 31, 1996 and March 31, 1995
(In thousands of Canadian dollars, except per share data)

	1997	1996	1995
REVENUES	$ 282,599	$ 268,945	$ 233,811
DIRECT OPERATING EXPENSES	213,816	209,789	183,685
GROSS PROFIT	68,783	59,156	50,126
OTHER EXPENSES			
Other operating expenses	42,037	40,363	28,643
Amortization	5,160	5,038	5,164
Interest (note 10)	1,296	893	282
Minority interest	(142)	562	(596)
	48,351	46,856	33,493
EARNINGS BEFORE UNDERNOTED	20,432	12,300	16,633
GAIN ON SALE OF INVESTMENT (NOTE 11)	7,544	-	-
EARNINGS BEFORE INCOME TAXES	27,976	12,300	16,633
PROVISION FOR INCOME TAXES (NOTE 12)	9,788	1,935	3,658
NET EARNINGS FOR THE YEAR	18,188	10,365	12,975
RETAINED EARNINGS, BEGINNING OF YEAR	42,705	32,340	19,365
RETAINED EARNINGS, END OF YEAR	$ 60,893	$ 42,705	$ 32,340
BASIC EARNINGS PER COMMON SHARE (NOTE 13)	$ 1.53	$ 1.05	$ 1.36

The accompanying notes form an integral part of these financial statements

CONSOLIDATED STATEMENTS OF CHANGES IN FINANCIAL POSITION

ALLIANCE COMMUNICATIONS CORPORATION

For the years ended March 31, 1997, March 31, 1996 and March 31, 1995
(In thousands of Canadian dollars)

	1997	1996	1995
CASH AND SHORT-TERM INVESTMENTS PROVIDED BY (USED IN):			
OPERATING ACTIVITIES			
Net earnings for the year	$ 18,188	$ 10,365	$ 12,975
Items not affecting cash:			
Amortization of investment in film and television programs	190,226	185,534	169,460
Amortization of program exhibition rights	9,363	6,807	-
Amortization of development costs and investment in scripts	2,351	1,800	1,342
Amortization of property and equipment and pre-operating costs	2,401	2,934	3,518
Amortization of broadcasting licences and goodwill	408	304	304
Gain on sale of investment (note 11)	(7,544)	-	-
Minority interest	(142)	562	(596)
Deferred income taxes	3,529	1,594	3,284
Net changes in other non-cash balances related to operations (note 14)	21,950	(35,373)	(21,173)
	240,730	174,527	169,114
INVESTING ACTIVITIES			
Investment in films and television programs	(228,483)	(188,156)	(177,414)
Film and television programs in progress	(557)	7,516	(5,328)
Program exhibition rights	(12,033)	(6,333)	(10,236)
Development costs and investment in scripts	(7,692)	(5,226)	(2,278)
Net additions to property and equipment	(5,237)	(2,973)	(6,280)
Net proceeds from sale of investment (note 11)	7,684	-	-
Business acquisitions	(9,425)	135	(2,765)
Cash balances of acquired businesses	-	-	4,308
Long-term investments	(2,219)	(992)	(617)
	(257,962)	(196,029)	(200,610)
FINANCING ACTIVITIES			
Operating loan and bank indebtedness	(2,256)	5,617	-
Increase in loans receivable	(9,283)	-	-
Increase (decrease) in loans payable	(2,083)	712	1,086
Issue of convertible debenture	-	-	16,500
Issue of common shares	36,541	1,403	21,818
Exercise of warrants	-	-	(20,984)
	22,919	7,732	18,420
INCREASE (DECREASE) IN CASH AND SHORT-TERM INVESTMENTS	5,687	(13,770)	(13,076)
CASH AND SHORT-TERM INVESTMENTS, BEGINNING OF YEAR	5,090	18,860	31,936
CASH AND SHORT-TERM INVESTMENTS, END OF YEAR	$ 10,777	$ 5,090	$ 18,860

The accompanying notes form an integral part of these financial statements

NOTES TO THE FINANCIAL STATEMENTS

ALLIANCE COMMUNICATIONS CORPORATION

Alliance Communications Corporation ("the Company") is a fully integrated global supplier of entertainment products whose origins are in television and motion picture production and distribution. The Company also has interests in broadcasting, computer generated animation facilities, music publishing and financing services.

1. SIGNIFICANT ACCOUNTING POLICIES

(a) Generally Accepted Accounting Principles

These consolidated financial statements have been prepared in accordance with Canadian generally accepted accounting principles ("Canadian GAAP"). These principles conform in all material respects with the accounting principles generally accepted in the United States ("U.S. GAAP") except as described in note 20.

(b) Principle of Consolidation

The consolidated financial statements include the accounts of Alliance Communications Corporation and all of its subsidiaries.

(c) Revenue Recognition

Revenue is derived from sale of distribution rights and equity in productions and theatrical or television exhibition. Revenue is recognized as earned when the film or television program is completed and delivered, when amounts are due from the exhibitor or when a contract is executed that irrevocably transfers distribution rights to a licensee or equity to an investor, and there is reasonable assurance of collectability of proceeds.

The Company recognizes as revenue only the net benefits from sales to limited partnerships when the investor has irrevocably committed to acquire the related equity.

Fees related to loan origination, including loan restructuring or renegotiating, are recognized as revenue over the expected term of the loan.

Cable service subscriber fee revenue is accrued as earned. Advertising revenue is recognized when advertisements are aired.

Revenue for music publishing is derived from the collection of royalties on the rights owned and is recognized when received.

Amounts received and receivable and not recognized as revenue are included in deferred revenue.

(d) Short-term Investments

Short-term investments are carried at the lower of cost and market value.

(e) Loans Receivable

Loans receivable are stated net of unearned income and an allowance for credit losses. An allowance for credit losses is maintained in an amount considered adequate to absorb estimated credit-related losses. The allowance is increased by provisions for credit losses which are charged to income, and reduced by write-offs net of expected recoveries. The Company conducts ongoing credit assessments of its loan portfolio on an account-by-account basis and establishes specific allowances when doubtful accounts are identified.

(f) Investment in Film and Television Programs

Investment in film and television programs represents the unamortized costs of motion picture and television programs which have been produced by the Company or for which the Company has acquired distribution rights. Such costs include all production, print and advertising costs which are expected to be recovered from future revenues, net of estimated future liabilities related to the product.

Amortization is determined based on the ratio that current revenues earned from the film and television programs bear to expected gross future revenues. Based on management's estimates of gross future revenues as at March 31, 1997, it is expected that the investment in film and television programs will be absorbed principally over the next three years.

Investment in film and television programs is written down to the net recoverable amount if the investment is greater than the net recoverable amount. Net recoverable amount is defined as the total future revenues expected to be earned from film and television programs, net of future costs.

(g) Film and Television Programs in Progress
Film and television programs in progress represents the accumulated costs of uncompleted motion picture and television programs which are being produced by the Company.

(h) Program Exhibition Rights
Program exhibition rights represents the rights to various long-term contracts acquired from third parties to broadcast television programs and motion pictures. Program exhibition rights and corresponding liabilities are recorded at the time the Company becomes committed under a license agreement and the product is available for telecast. The carrying value of the program exhibition rights is amortized over the lesser of two years and the contracted exhibition period beginning in the month the film or television program is premiered.

(i) Development Costs and Investment in Scripts
Development costs and investment in scripts represents expenditures made on projects prior to production. Advances or contributions received from third parties to assist in development are deducted from these expenditures. Upon commencement of production, development costs and investment in scripts are charged to the production. Development costs and investment in scripts are amortized on the straight-line basis over three years commencing in the year following the year such costs are incurred when production has not commenced. Development costs and investment in scripts are written off when determined not to be recoverable.

(j) Government Financing and Assistance
The Company has access to several government programs that are designed to assist film and television production and distribution in Canada. Amounts received in respect of production assistance are recorded as revenue in accordance with the Company's revenue recognition policy for completed film and television programs. Government assistance with respect to distribution rights is recorded as a reduction of investment in film and television programs. Government assistance towards current expenses is included in net earnings for the year.

(k) Property and Equipment
Property and equipment are carried at cost less accumulated amortization. Amortization is provided, commencing in the year after acquisition, using the following rates and methods:

Computer hardware
- 30% principally by declining balance
Computer software
- 100% principally by declining balance
Furniture and fixtures
- 20% principally by declining balance
Equipment
- 30% principally by declining balance
Leasehold improvements
- straight-line over the lease term
Broadcast and transmission equipment
- straight-line over 5 years

(l) Broadcasting Licences
In acquisitions involving broadcasting undertakings, fair value is assigned to the broadcasting licences acquired. Broadcasting licences are amortized on a straight-line basis over a period of forty years. When there is an expectation that the net carrying amount of the licence will not be recovered, the licence is written down to its net recoverable amount.

(m) Other Assets
Other assets include pre-operating costs related to the period before commencement of commercial operations of Showcase Television Inc. and other businesses. The amount is being amortized on a straight-line basis over a period of five years.

Other assets also include long-term investments which are accounted for at cost when the conditions for equity accounting are not present and goodwill which is amortized on a straight-line basis over a period of five years.

(n) Distribution Revenues Payable
Distribution revenues payable represents the excess of receipts from the distribution of film and television programs over commissions earned and distribution costs incurred and are payable to the licensor of the film or television program.

(o) Foreign Currency
Assets and liabilities denominated in currencies other than Canadian dollars are translated at exchange rates in effect at the balance sheet date. Revenue and expense items are translated at average rates of exchange for the year. Translation gains or losses are included in the determination of earnings except for gains or losses arising on the translation of the accounts of the foreign subsidiaries considered to be self-sustaining, which are deferred as a separate component of shareholders' equity.

(p) Non-Cash Balances Related to Operations
Non-cash balances related to operations are comprised of the aggregate of the following assets and liabilities: accounts receivable; distribution contracts receivable; other assets excluding long-term-investments and goodwill; accounts payable and accrued liabilities; distribution revenues payable; income taxes; deferred revenue; and cumulative translation adjustments.

(q) Use of Estimates
The preparation of financial statements in conformity with generally accepted accounting principles requires management to make estimates and assumptions that affect the reported amounts of assets and liabilities and disclosure of contingent assets and liabilities at the dates of the financial statements and the reported amounts of revenues and expenses during the reporting periods. Actual results could differ from those estimates.

(r) Comparative Amounts
Certain amounts presented in the prior period have been reclassified to conform with the presentation adopted in the current year.

2. INVESTMENT IN FILM AND TELEVISION PROGRAMS
(In thousands of Canadian dollars)

	1997	1996
Completed film and television programs produced, net of amortization	$ 37,218	$ 22,837
Film and television programs acquired, net of amortization	64,313	40,437
	$ 101,531	$ 63,274

NOTES TO THE FINANCIAL STATEMENTS
ALLIANCE COMMUNICATIONS CORPORATION

The Company expects that 92% of completed film and television programs produced, net of amortization, and 72% of acquisition costs related to film and television programs acquired, net of amortization, will be amortized during the three year period ending March 31, 2000.

The Company earns revenues from films and television programs which are fully amortized and are not valued in the accounts.

3. PROPERTY AND EQUIPMENT

(In thousands of Canadian dollars)

	1997		1996	
	Cost	Accumulated Amortization	Cost	Accumulated Amortization
Computer hardware and software	$ 5,243	$ 2,142	$ 4,040	$ 1,387
Furniture and fixtures	3,206	985	2,061	742
Equipment	1,438	975	1,316	704
Leasehold improvements	4,340	881	1,876	771
Broadcast and transmission equipment	1,570	500	1,482	323
	15,797	5,483	10,775	3,927
Net property and equipment		$ 10,314		$ 6,848

4. OTHER ASSETS

(In thousands of Canadian dollars)

	1997	1996
Pre-operating costs, net of accumulated amortization of $1,338 (1996 - $708)	$ 2,507	$ 2,231
Prepaid expenses	1,344	1,622
Long-term investments	3,688	1,609
Goodwill, net of accumulated amortization of $1,162 (1996 - $784)	707	884
	$ 8,246	$ 6,346

5. OPERATING LOAN AND BANK INDEBTEDNESS

(In thousands of Canadian dollars)

	1997	1996
Bank indebtedness - gross	$ 15,871	$ 18,760
Interest expense on bank indebtedness	$ 1,010	$ 961
Weighted average interest rate	6.09%	9.04%

Operating loan and bank indebtedness is netted on the balance sheet with cash and short-term investments to the extent a right of offset exists.

The Company's assets and the assets of its subsidiaries have been pledged as collateral for the bank indebtedness.

At March 31, 1997, the Company had unused credit facilities aggregating $131,729,000 (1996 - $61,240,000) subject to margin calculations. These facilities are primarily used for bridge financing of productions.

6. LOANS PAYABLE

(In thousands of Canadian dollars)

	1997	1996
Interest bearing loans at prime plus 1%, unsecured with no specific repayment date	$ nil	$ 2,083

NOTES TO THE FINANCIAL STATEMENTS

ALLIANCE COMMUNICATIONS CORPORATION

7. CONVERTIBLE DEBENTURE

On October 28, 1994, the Company issued a convertible, unsecured, subordinated debenture for $16,500,000 cash, bearing interest at 6.5% per year and maturing on April 5, 2002. The debenture is convertible at the option of the holder into common shares of the Company at any time after October 28, 1995 at a conversion price of $19 per share. Interest is payable in cash or additional convertible debentures at the Company's option.

Commencing October 28, 1999, the debenture will be redeemable at the option of the Company, provided certain conditions are met, at the issue price, together with accrued and unpaid interest to the date of redemption. The Company has the option to pay for the redemption of the debenture by issuing its own common shares to the debenture holder at a price equal to 90% of the weighted average trading price of the common shares for the last 20 consecutive trading days prior to redemption or the maturity date.

8. CAPITAL STOCK

a) The authorized capital stock of the Company consists of an unlimited number of common shares. The common shares are comprised of Class A Voting Shares (the "Voting Shares") and Class B Non-Voting Shares (the "Non-Voting Shares") which have identical attributes except that the Non-Voting Shares are non-voting and each of the Voting Shares is convertible at any time at the holder's option into one fully paid and non-assessable Non-Voting Share. The Non-Voting Shares may be converted into Voting Shares only in certain circumstances.

b) During fiscal 1997, the following transactions occurred:
In August 1996, 3,020,000 Non-Voting Shares were issued pursuant to a public offering at a gross price of US$8.50 per share for proceeds of CDN$32,920,000, net of issue expenses and income tax benefits;

In September 1996, 10,000 Non-Voting Shares were issued in connection with the acquisition of film and television programs at $13.62 per share for proceeds of $136,000;

In January 1997, 95,421 Non-Voting Shares were issued in connection with a long-term investment in another company at $11.79 per share for proceeds of $1,125,000;

In January and February 1997, 162,807 Non-Voting Shares were issued in connection with the acquisition of an additional 44% ownership interest in Showcase Television Inc. at $11.84 per share for proceeds of $1,927,000 (note 9); and

During fiscal 1997, 62,100 Voting Shares were converted into Non-Voting Shares. In addition, 37,020 employee stock options for 18,509 Voting Shares and 18,511 Non-Voting Shares were exercised pursuant to the Company stock option plan for proceeds of $433,000.

c) During fiscal 1996, the following transactions occurred:
On April 26, 1995, the Company reorganized its share capital and created the Voting Shares and Non-Voting Shares, converted each existing common share into one-half of a Voting Share and one-half of a Non-Voting Share, and cancelled all of the existing authorized and issued common shares; and

During fiscal 1996, 117,478 employee stock options were exercised pursuant to the Company stock option plan for proceeds of $1,403,000.

d) During fiscal 1995, the following transactions occurred:
In May 1994, 1,530,000 shares were issued pursuant to the exercise of 1,530,000 warrants to acquire common shares and the receipt of proceeds of $20,984,000 released from escrow net of issue expenses and income tax benefits;

In October 1994, 13,900 shares were issued in connection with the purchase of a 75% interest in Partisan Music Productions Inc., carrying on business as TMP - The Music Publisher, at $16.33 per share for aggregate proceeds of $227,000; and

During fiscal 1995, 51,936 employee stock options were exercised pursuant to the Company stock option plan for proceeds of $607,700.

e) As a result, the issued capital stock is as follows:
(In thousands of Canadian dollars)

	1997	1996
Common shares:		
Voting Shares, 4,905,134 (1996 - 4,948,725)	$ 26,057	$ 26,169
Non-Voting Shares, 8,313,882 (1996 - 4,945,043)	62,779	26,126
	$ 88,836	$ 52,295

f) The Company has an Amended and Restated 1993 Employee Stock Option Plan which provides for the issuance of up to 1,750,000 common shares. These options generally vest in equal annual amounts over three to five years. No options are exercisable for periods of more than ten years after date of grant. Options granted under the plan may not have an option price less than the fair market value of the Non-Voting Shares on the date the option is granted.

Options outstanding were split 50% Voting Shares and 50% Non-Voting Shares on May 15, 1995. All new options granted after May 15, 1995 are options to purchase Non-Voting Shares.

Stock option activity for 1995, 1996 and 1997 is as follows:

(In thousands of Canadian dollars)

	Number of Shares			Weighted Average
	Voting	Non-Voting	Total	Exercise Price
Outstanding at March 31, 1994	360,633	360,633	721,266	$ 11.80
Granted	276,203	276,203	552,406	14.24
Exercised	(25,968)	(25,968)	(51,936)	13.29
Cancelled	(14,850)	(14,850)	(29,700)	11.34
Outstanding at March 31, 1995	596,018	596,018	1,192,036	12.88
Granted	-	537,520	537,520	14.75
Exercised	(58,739)	(58,739)	(117,478)	11.70
Cancelled	(99,409)	(99,416)	(198,825)	12.85
Outstanding at March 31, 1996	437,870	975,383	1,413,253	13.69
Granted	5,000	121,120	126,120	14.25
Exercised	(18,509)	(18,511)	(37,020)	11.71
Cancelled	(17,934)	(17,925)	(35,859)	12.85
Outstanding at March 31, 1997	406,427	1,060,067	1,466,494	$ 13.81
Exercisable at March 31, 1997	291,628	503,604	795,232	$ 13.20
Exercisable at March 31, 1996	216,962	216,962	433,924	12.47
Exercisable at March 31, 1995	172,943	172,944	345,887	11.78

At March 31, 1997, 1,466,494 options were outstanding with exercise prices ranging from $11.70 to $16.375 and with a weighted average remaining contractual life of 4.9 years.

NOTES TO THE FINANCIAL STATEMENTS

ALLIANCE COMMUNICATIONS CORPORATION

9. BUSINESS ACQUISITIONS

During fiscal 1997, the Company acquired an additional 44% ownership interest in Showcase Television Inc. for total consideration of $9,207,000. The consideration was in the form of $7,280,000 cash and 162,807 common shares of the Company. The fair value assigned to the broadcasting licence in this acquisition was $7,266,000. After completion of this acquisition, the Company had a 99% ownership interest in Showcase Television Inc.

10. INTEREST

(In thousands of Canadian dollars)

	1997	1996	1995
Interest expense on long-term debt	$ 1,073	$ 1,195	$ 476
Interest income	(1,282)	(1,550)	(359)
Other	1,505	1,248	165
	$ 1,296	$ 893	$ 282

Interest paid for the year ended March 31, 1997 amounted to $1,925,000 (1996 - $2,040,000, 1995 - $1,332,000).

11. GAIN ON SALE OF INVESTMENT

In September 1996, Mainframe Entertainment Inc. repurchased a portion of the Company's investment in Mainframe for net proceeds of $7,684,000 resulting in a pre-tax gain on sale of $7,544,000. The Company retained a 15% ownership interest in Mainframe (note 21).

12. INCOME TAXES

The differences between the effective tax rate reflected in the provision for income taxes and the Canadian statutory income tax rate are as follows:

	1997	1996	1995
Corporate statutory income tax rate	44.6%	44.6%	44.0%
Add (deduct) the income tax rate effect of:			
Foreign operations subject to different income tax rates	(11.9)	(31.9)	(24.6)
Expenses not deductible for income tax purposes	2.8	2.3	3.4
Other	(0.5)	0.7	(0.8)
	35.0%	15.7%	22.0%

The subsidiaries' non-capital tax losses are approximately $1,180,000, which are available for offset against those subsidiaries' future taxable income. The benefits of these losses, which have not been reflected in these accounts, expire in various years to fiscal 2002.

Details of income taxes are as follows:

(In thousands of Canadian dollars)

	1997	1996
Depreciation	$ 388	$ 185
Financing fees	(1,803)	(995)
Prepaid royalties	5,217	20,067
Development costs	-	3,450
Investment in film and television programs	-	7,622
Other	1,719	1,927
Net operating loss carry-forwards	(2,822)	(21,438)
Deferred income taxes	2,699	10,818
Taxes payable	8,228	-
	$ 10,927	$ 10,818

13. EARNINGS PER SHARE

Earnings per common share is calculated on the basis of 11,919,000 (1996 - 9,840,000, 1995 - 9,543,000) weighted average common shares outstanding.

Fully diluted earnings per common share for 1997 is $1.44 (1996 - $0.99, 1995 - $1.31). This reflects the effects of employee stock options and convertible debenture outstanding as at March 31, 1997 and 1996 and 1995.

14. STATEMENT OF CHANGES IN FINANCIAL POSITION

(In thousands of Canadian dollars)

	1997	1996	1995
Cash provided by (used in):			
Accounts receivable and distribution contracts receivable	$ (40,427)	$ (26,569)	$ (22,388)
Accounts payable and accrued liabilities	38,828	(248)	5,551
Distribution revenue payable	(3,015)	(6,532)	13,223
Deferred revenue	30,274	(498)	(14,607)
Other	(3,710)	(1,526)	(2,952)
Net changes in non-cash working capital balances related to operations	$ 21,950	$ (35,373)	$ (21,173)

15. GOVERNMENT FINANCING AND ASSISTANCE

Revenues include $14,101,000 of production financing obtained from the government for the year ended March 31, 1997 (1996 - $13,824,000, 1995 - $8,881,000). This financing is repayable from distribution revenues in respect of which the financing was made. As revenues from these productions are not currently known, the amounts ultimately repayable to government agencies are not determinable. In addition, revenues include $2,290,000 of government grants (1995 - $693,000, 1994 - $2,406,000).

Investment in film and television programs includes a reduction of $10,291,000 (1996 - $10,810,000, 1995 - $10,209,000) with respect to government assistance for distribution of certain programs. In addition, revenues include $859,000 (1996 - $1,023,000, 1995 - $1,492,000) of government grants. Government assistance may be repayable in whole or in part depending upon future revenues generated by certain individual film and television programs. The potential amounts repayable are not determinable.

16. RELATED PARTY TRANSACTIONS

Included in accounts receivable is $218,000 (1996 - $nil) due from officers of the Company.

17. COMMITMENTS AND CONTINGENCIES

a) The Company is committed with respect to operating leases for office premises and equipment expiring at various dates to May 2007. The future minimum payments under the terms of such leases are as follows:

(In thousands of Canadian dollars)	
1998	$ 2,982
1999	1,679
2000	1,366
2001	1,423
2002	959
Thereafter	3,007
	$ 11,416

Rent expense for 1997 is $2,053,000 (1996 - $1,525,000, 1995 - $1,418,000).

b) The Company is involved in various legal actions. In the opinion of management, any resulting liability is not expected to have a material adverse effect on the Company's financial position.

c) The Company has a letter of credit of US$2,500,000 outstanding at March 31, 1997 (1996 - US$2,500,000, 1995 - US$2,500,000).

18. SEGMENTED INFORMATION

The Company is vertically integrated and operates exclusively in the production, distribution and structured production financing of television programs and motion pictures, broadcasting and music publishing industries, which are considered the dominant industry segments.

Revenues include $113,216,000 (1996 - $100,902,000, 1995 - $105,588,000) derived from foreign sources.

19. FINANCIAL INSTRUMENTS

Fair Value of Financial Instruments

The estimated fair values of financial instruments as at March 31, 1997 and March 31, 1996 are based on relevant market prices and information available at the time. The carrying value of cash and short-term investments, accounts receivable, loans receivable, long-term investments, operating loan and bank indebtedness, accounts payable and accrued liabilities, distribution revenues payable, loans payable, and convertible debenture approximates the fair value of these financial instruments. Financial instruments with a carrying value different from their fair value include:

(In thousands of Canadian dollars)

	1997		1996	
	Carrying Value	Fair Value	Carrying Value	Fair Value
Financial Assets:				
Assets for which fair value approximates carrying value	$ 105,932	$ 105,932	$ 59,780	$ 59,780
Distribution contracts receivable	76,272	74,066	64,948	63,283
Financial Liabilities:				
Liabilities for which fair value approximates carrying value	$ 129,352	$ 129,352	$ 97,878	$ 97,878

The fair value of distribution contracts receivable is based on discounting future cash flows using rates currently available for similar instruments. The Company has not written these receivables down as it expects to recover their carrying amounts fully by holding them to maturity.

Concentration of Credit Risk
Accounts receivable from the federal government and a government agency in connection with production financing represents 41% of total accounts receivable at March 31, 1997. The Company believes that there is minimal risk associated with the collection of these amounts. The balance of accounts receivable and distribution contracts receivable is widely distributed amongst customers. Loans receivable include amounts due from a relatively small number of customers. The Company maintains an allowance for credit losses in an amount considered adequate to absorb estimated credit-related losses.

20. RECONCILIATION TO UNITED STATES GAAP

The consolidated financial statements of the Company have been prepared in accordance with Canadian GAAP. The following adjustments and/or additional disclosures, would be required in order to present the financial statements in accordance with U.S. GAAP, as required by the United States Securities and Exchange Commission.

Under U.S. GAAP, the net earnings and earnings per common share figures and shareholders' equity for the years ended March 31, 1997, 1996 and 1995 would be adjusted as follows:

(In thousands of Canadian dollars)

	Net Earnings			Shareholders' Equity	
	1997	1996	1995	1997	1996
Canadian GAAP	$ 18,188	$ 10,365	$ 12,975	$ 150,424	$ 95,380
Adjustment to development costs and investment in scripts net of income taxes of $92 (1996 - $648, 1995 - $447)(a)	115	808	(562)	(401)	(516)
Adjustment to operating expenses with respect to stock options (b)	(77)	90	(457)	(799)	(722)
Adjustment to revenue with respect to television license agreements net of income taxes of $662 (1996 - $90, 1995 - $243)(c)	(2,062)	(2,501)	(125)	(5,718)	(3,656)
Adjustment to income tax provision excluding cumulative effect adjustment noted below (d)	-	-	166	193	193
Adjustment to retained earnings with respect to stock options.	-	-	-	799	722
U.S. GAAP excluding cumulative effect adjustment	16,164	8,762	11,997	144,498	91,401
Cumulative effect of income tax adjustment for years prior to April 1, 1993 (d)	-	-	-	(285)	(285)
U.S. GAAP	$ 16,164	$ 8,762	$ 11,997	$ 144,213	$ 91,116
Earnings Per Common Share Based on U.S. GAAP(e)					
Primary	$ 1.35	$ 0.88	$ 1.23		
Fully Diluted	$ 1.30	$ 0.86	$ 1.17		

NOTES TO THE FINANCIAL STATEMENTS

ALLIANCE COMMUNICATIONS CORPORATION

a) Accounting for Development Costs and Investment in Scripts
Under Statement of Financial Accounting Standards No. 53 "Financial Reporting by Producers and Distributors of Motion Picture Films" (SFAS 53), expenditures associated with the development of stories and scenarios are expensed as incurred while expenditures for properties such as film rights to books, stage plays, original screenplays, etc. are expensed if the property has been held for three years and has not been set for production. Under Canadian GAAP, development costs and investment in scripts is amortized over three years commencing in the year following the year such costs are incurred. The net difference of the two adjustments is disclosed as a U.S. GAAP reconciling item.

b) Accounting for Stock Options and Share Issuances
During fiscal 1997, the Company adopted the disclosure-only provisions of Statement of Financial Accounting Standards No. 123 "Accounting for Stock-Based Compensation" (SFAS 123) but, as permitted, continues to apply Accounting Principles Board Opinion No. 25 "Accounting for Stock Issued to Employees" (APB 25) in accounting for its employee stock option plan for U.S. GAAP reconciliation purposes.

For the year ended March 31, 1996, compensatory employee stock options were issued and vested in the year. In accordance with APB 25, the difference between the quoted market price and the option price is recorded as compensation expense over the vesting period.

For the years ended March 31, 1997 and 1995, no compensatory employee stock options were issued which resulted in a compensation expense, however, a compensatory expense was recognized for options issued in prior years as they vested in the year.

Under SFAS 123, the Company's pro forma net earnings for U.S. GAAP would be $15,123,000 (1996 - $8,459,000) and primary earnings per common share would be $1.26 (1996 - $0.85).

As the provisions of SFAS 123 have not been applied to options granted prior to January 1, 1995, the resulting pro forma compensation cost may not be representative of that to be expected in future years.

For disclosure purposes the fair value of each stock option grant is estimated on the date of grant using the Black-Scholes option pricing model with the following weighted average assumptions used for stock options granted in 1997 and 1996, respectively: expected dividend yields of 0.0% for both years, expected volatility of 41.4% and 39.9%, risk-free interest rate of 5.9% and 6.5% and expected life of 3 years for all grants. The weighted average fair value of the stock options granted in 1997 and 1996 was $4.77 and $5.30, respectively.

c) Revenue Recognition From Television License Agreements
Under Canadian GAAP, revenues from license agreements for television programs are recognized as earned when the television program is completed and delivered, when amounts are due from exhibitor or when a contract is executed that irrevocably transfers distribution rights to a licensee, and there is reasonable assurance of collectability of proceeds. Under SFAS 53, revenues from license agreements for television programs are recognized at the time the license periods commence instead of at the time the license agreements are executed.

NOTES TO THE FINANCIAL STATEMENTS

ALLIANCE COMMUNICATIONS CORPORATION

d) Accounting for Income Taxes
Effective April 1, 1993, the Company adopted Statement of Financial Accounting Standards No. 109 "Accounting for Income Taxes" (SFAS 109) for U.S. GAAP reconciliation purposes. The adoption of SFAS 109 changes the Company's method of accounting for income taxes from the deferral method to the asset and liability method. SFAS 109 requires recognition of deferred tax liabilities and assets for the expected future tax consequences of assets and liabilities that have been recognized in the financial statements.

As a result of the adoption of SFAS 109, the Company recognized an additional expense of $285,000, representing the cumulative effect of the change on results for year prior to April 1, 1993.

Under U.S. GAAP, the provision for income taxes for the year ended March 31, 1997 would be $9,218,000 (1996 - $2,493,000, 1995 - $2,802,000).

The application of SFAS 109 would increase broadcasting licences and income taxes by approximately $5,850,000 at March 31, 1997 (1996 - $nil).

e) Earnings per Common Share
Under Accounting Principles Board Opinion No. 15 "Earnings per Share" (APB 15), earnings per share is based on the weighted average number of common shares issued and outstanding and common stock equivalents, including stock options and warrants.

Certain stock options and shares are considered to have been outstanding from the beginning of the year for the earnings per common share calculations at March 31, 1997, 1996 and 1995. The treasury stock method was applied in the earnings per common share calculations.

Primary earnings per common share is calculated on the basis of 11,985,000 (1996 - 9,922,000, 1995 - 9,719,000) weighted average shares outstanding.

For U.S. GAAP disclosure purposes, the Company will adopt the new U.S. GAAP standard for computing earnings per share, Statement of Financial Accounting Standards No. 128 "Earnings Per Share" (SFAS 128) for the year ended March 31, 1998. The effect of applying SFAS 128 to years prior to March 31, 1998 does not produce a materially different earnings per share as computed under APB 15.

f) Consolidated Statements of Cash Flows
The Company's cash flows determined in accordance with U.S. GAAP would be as follows:

(In thousands of Canadian dollars)

	1997	1996	1995
Operating activities	$ 238,383	$ 174,282	$ 166,992
Investing activities	(252,676)	(195,037)	(198,479)
Financing activities	19,867	7,732	18,193
Effect of exchange rates on cash	113	(747)	218
Increase (decrease) in cash and cash equivalents	$ 5,687	($13,770)	$ (13,076)

21. SUBSEQUENT EVENT
On June 17, 1997, the Company sold a portion of its investment in Mainframe Entertainment Inc. in connection with Mainframe's initial public offering for net proceeds of $4,594,000 and realized a pre-tax gain on sale of $4,535,000. The Company retained a 7% ownership interest in Mainframe.

ATLANTIS®
20TH ANNIVERSARY
1978–1998

Contents

Financial Highlights

For the years ended December 31 (in millions of dollars, except per share information)	1997	1996	Change
Operating Results			
Revenue	$ 178	$ 138	29 %
Net earnings before unusual items	$ 5.6	$ 3.4	65 %
Net earnings	$ 5.6	$ 6.9(1)	(19)%
Financial Position			
Completed programs	$ 46.9	$ 44.7	5 %
Cash, net of loans payable	$ 19.8	$ 3.1	539 %
Interim financing	$ 67.1	$ 27.2	147 %
Shareholders' equity	$ 97.1	$ 68.8	41 %
Per Share Information			
Net earnings before unusual items	$ 0.55	$ 0.35	57 %
Net earnings	$ 0.55	$ 0.72(1)	(24)%
Book value	$ 7.82	$ 7.16	9 %
Shares Outstanding *(millions)*			
Average for the year	10.1	9.6	5 %
At year end	12.4(2)	9.6	29 %

Note (1): 1996 Net earnings include the gain on sale of the Company's interest in YTV of $3.5 million or $0.37 per share.
(2): Includes the conversion into common shares of 2.3 million Special Warrants issued in December 1997.

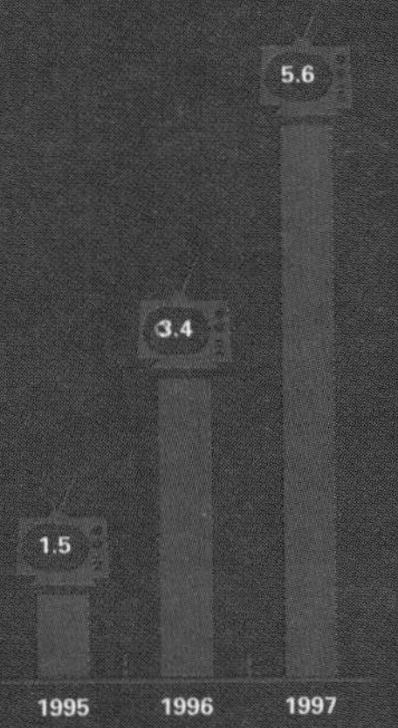

Net earnings before unusual items ($ millions)

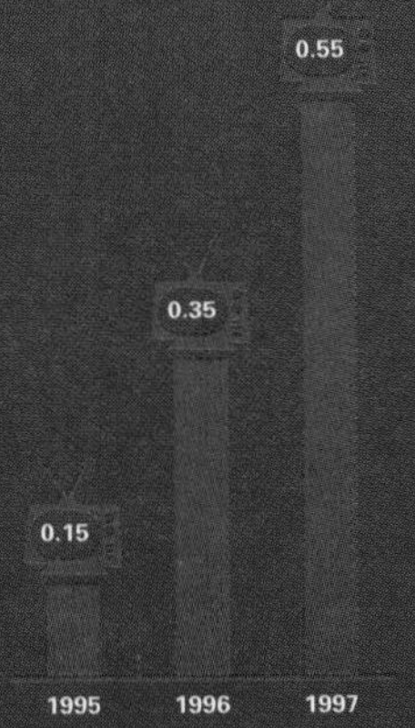

Net earnings per share before unusual items ($)

1997 Highlights

- ★ ATLANTIS delivered 104 hours of original television drama, up 18 per cent from 1996, representing the renewal of four existing series, two new series and two television movies.
- ★ ATLANTIS' series *Gene Roddenberry's Earth: Final Conflict*® was the highest-rated original one-hour series to have entered U.S. syndication in the past two years.
- ★ ATLANTIS' television movie *Borrowed Hearts: A Holiday Romance* was the highest-rated program on all of American television for the last week of November 1997, garnering 30 million viewers in the U.S. and Canada.
- ★ ATLANTIS acquired 50 per cent of Calibre Digital Pictures, a leading animation and digital effects company, and reached an agreement to acquire Ironstar Communications, a Canadian distributor with a library of 300 hours.
- ★ ATLANTIS successfully launched Home & Garden Television (HGTV) Canada and imported the Food Network into over four million homes on October 17, 1997.
- ★ ATLANTIS applied to the CRTC (Canadian Radio-television and Telecommunications Commission) for five new Canadian cable channels: Food Network Canada, National Geographic Channel Canada, FIT TV Canada, Canada's Health Network and People Channel and is a minority partner in the CHAOS TV application.
- ★ ATLANTIS completed a successful $20 million equity offering in December 1997.
- ★ ATLANTIS' stock price closed the year at $10.50, a 50 per cent increase over the prior year.

Message to Shareholders

Nineteen ninety-seven was a year of operational, financial and strategic success for Atlantis Communications Inc. We achieved significant growth in revenues and net income and we did so in a manner that achieved our primary goal – to increase the ongoing sustainability and reliability of the growth in our operating results. The strategies we employed to achieve this primary goal in 1997 will be continued going forward.

Michael MacMillan, Chairman and Chief Executive Officer *(right),* **Lewis Rose,** President *(left),* on the set of *Traders*

Our first key strategy, given that the largest segment of our business is the production and distribution of original prime time television drama, was to increase the production of series that were renewable from year to year (as opposed to stand alone television movies). We wanted series that provide ongoing opportunities for future exploitation once a critical mass of episodes has been produced. We wanted series where Atlantis controlled major distribution rights.

All four of our one-hour series were renewed in 1997 – *Traders, PSI FACTOR®: Chronicles of the Paranormal, The Outer Limits* and *The Adventures of Sinbad;* as well, we launched two new series – *Cold Squad* and *Gene Roddenberry's Earth: Final Conflict®*. Importantly, the newer series – *Cold Squad, Gene Roddenberry's Earth: Final Conflict®* and *PSI FACTOR®: Chronicles of the Paranormal* – are all series where the Canadian and major international distribution rights are controlled by Atlantis.

Already, five of our series from 1997 have been renewed for 1998 and our two new series announced to date – *The World of Peter Cottontail* and *Sixth Grade Alien* – are also series to which Atlantis controls Canadian and all international distribution rights.

Reliable and sustainable earnings are also created through "output" or "package" deals, whereby customers commit to acquire a certain volume of programming prior to the programs being produced or even identified. Atlantis recently entered into a major "package" deal with the leading European entertainment company, Endemol Entertainment of The Netherlands. Endemol agreed to license European, African and Middle Eastern rights to a number of television series and movies produced by Atlantis in 1998 and each of the next two years, as well as a selection of Atlantis' library catalogue. This arrangement will continue to increase the predictability of our growth and provide revenue to Atlantis of $115 million over the three years.

The second key strategy we employed last year was to leverage the strength of our distribution infrastructure to take advantage of Atlantis' knowledge of and relationships within the Canadian and international television marketplace. We sought to add additional product lines to be exploited by our distribution company, Atlantis Releasing, so that we could grow our sales with only modest incremental costs.

This is why we were pleased to be named the exclusive Canadian distributor of CBS television programming. The CBS appointment began in 1997 and has an initial three-year term. This means that Atlantis is the distributor in Canada of such shows as *Touched By An Angel, 60 Minutes* and *Brooklyn South,* among others.

Likewise, our recent purchase of Canadian distributor Ironstar Communications gives Atlantis access to Ironstar's program library for both Canadian and international exploitation.

It was for similar distribution leverage purposes that we decided to increase the children's program component of our catalogue. By adding animation and more live action children's series to our production activity we feed our established distribution strength while complementing our core prime time drama catalogue. Thus, in 1997, we acquired 50 per cent of Calibre Digital Pictures, a successful Canadian animation company which creates all types of animation including leading edge computer generated animation. Calibre continues to grow under the leadership of its founder, Neil Williamson, and we intend to purchase the remainder of Calibre within two years.

In 1998 we are growing our animation and live action children's initiatives with success. We recently licensed two new series to YTV Canada, which we are currently placing with other buyers internationally. These are the live action series *Sixth Grade Alien,* based on new books by best selling children's author Bruce Coville and the animated series *The World of Peter Cottontail,* based on the celebrated books by author Thornton W. Burgess. We are fortunate to mark our entry into animation with a property as well known and popular as *The World of Peter Cottontail.*

The final key strategy for 1997 was to continue aggressively to develop our broadcasting activities. Last year we secured national analogue carriage of our new specialty channel Home & Garden Television (HGTV) Canada, which launched on October 17, 1997. Already, HGTV Canada is attracting a positive viewer and advertiser response and we are optimistic for its continued growth and financial success.

On September 30, 1997 Atlantis applied to the CRTC for permission to launch five new specialty channels, controlled by Atlantis – People Channel, National Geographic Channel Canada, Food Network Canada, FIT TV Canada and Canada's Health Network. We believe that each of these concepts will, if approved by the CRTC, be an excellent complement to our two existing channels, Life Network and HGTV Canada.

As an interim measure, Atlantis is the exclusive agent for Food Network (U.S.), which we are currently importing into four million Canadian cable homes. Our agreement with the owners of Food Network (U.S.), E.W. Scripps Co. (the owner of HGTV in the U.S. and our partner in HGTV Canada), is that when the CRTC approves our Food Network Canada application, Food Network (U.S.) will voluntarily withdraw from Canada. Then, Food Network Canada, which Atlantis will control and manage, will replace it.

E.W. Scripps Co. will become a 29 per cent shareholder in the Canadian channel, and Shaw Communications will own 20 per cent.

In recognition of the importance of our broadcasting activities, in 1997 we created a new business unit called Atlantis Broadcasting, incorporating Life Network, HGTV Canada, Food Network and the pending applications. Juris Silkans, who has played a key role in the development of Life Network and HGTV Canada, now has an expanded leadership role as President of Atlantis Broadcasting.

The North American television marketplace continues to change substantially and quickly; viewers clearly enjoy having an increased choice of channels to watch. As well, they obviously enjoy watching "themed" channels where they reliably know the type of programming to be presented.

In Canada and the U.S., viewing of specialty and pay channels has now risen to approximately 30 per cent of total television viewing. This is astounding growth, particularly in the last few years. Television advertising revenue in North America has not yet caught up to reflect this fundamental shift in how viewers are using television. We believe that advertising spending will shift to reflect the trends in actual viewing; as such, specialty channels like ours have an exciting and substantial growth opportunity.

In 1998 our broadcasting focus will be to grow HGTV Canada through its first full year, while we prepare for the CRTC hearings on the new channel applications, anticipated to be in the first quarter of 1999. Meanwhile, we are pursuing other possibilities of expanding the "brand" value of our existing channels both within Canada and through international opportunities.

I am particularly pleased that the strategies and initiatives described here have also been reflected in increased shareholder value. The Atlantis stock price began 1997 at $7.00 and finished the year at $10.50 – an increase of exactly 50 per cent. In the first months of 1998 the price has continued to strengthen. We completed a successful equity issue in December 1997, raising approximately $20 million of equity at $9.00/share. That equity issue combined with the increase in share price has materially increased the size of our market capitalization.

This year marks the 20th anniversary of Atlantis and the theme of this year's annual report celebrates these two decades. We are very proud of what we have accomplished and created. The growth and success of Atlantis over these 20 years reflects the growth of our industry worldwide. When we started Atlantis there was no meaningful use of VCRs in homes; there was no significant pay television or specialty television; there was limited private ownership of television networks outside of North America. Atlantis' growth was possible, in part, because of the new methods of delivering filmed entertainment to viewers. Looking ahead, the methods of delivering entertainment and information will continue to diversify and evolve with the advent of the Internet, digital signals and other, still unknown, opportunities. As these new technologies become real, we will again be reminded that, as in the past, it is the content, not the hardware, which ultimately matters the most. That is where we come in.

To ensure that we participate fully in this exciting future we will need to continue to attract and retain the best and the brightest to our management team and attract the best creative talent to all of our productions. That, I believe, is how we arrived at our position today. Over the past few years we have significantly strengthened our management, both corporately and within each of our operating companies. Included in those positive moves was the 1997 appointment of Lewis Rose as President of Atlantis Communications Inc.

Looking forward to the next two decades I am particularly thankful for the continuing friendship and business partnership with Seaton McLean. Seaton co-founded Atlantis with Janice Platt and me, amongst others, in 1978. Seaton has provided Atlantis its inspiration and leadership every step of the way for each of those 20 years.

Similarly, I look forward to the ongoing and vital contributions and friendships with Ted Riley and Peter Sussman who have shared most of the past 20 years with us and who initiated and led our expansion internationally and into the U.S.

Atlantis has extremely talented and dedicated employees. The achievements of 20 years and the prospect for future growth would, clearly, never have been possible without our terrific team, both past and present.

I also offer a heartfelt thank you to our casts, crews, writers, directors and all those who participate in the production of our programs, including producers, suppliers, broadcast customers and financiers, as well as to our shareholders and our Board of Directors whose advice is always appreciated.

Atlantis begins its third decade with a clear sense of opportunity, excitement and growth. The best is yet to come.

Michael I.M. MacMillan
Chairman and
Chief Executive Officer

Management's Discussion and Analysis

The following discussion and analysis for the years ended December 31, 1997 and 1996 should be read in conjunction with the consolidated financial statements and the notes to the consolidated financial statements included in this annual report.

Atlantis Communications Inc. is a leading international producer, distributor and broadcaster of popular high-quality television programming for audiences worldwide. Television Production includes the production of television programs, as well as ownership and management of studios and post-production facilities. Television Distribution includes the licensing of both proprietary Atlantis-produced and third-party acquired television programming. Atlantis' Broadcasting interests include 100% of the specialty channel Life Network, and a controlling 67% interest in the specialty channel Home & Garden Television (HGTV) Canada. Atlantis Broadcasting also is the exclusive agent in Canada for Food Network, FiT TV and America's Health Network.

The impact of the two broad business areas, Television Production/Distribution and Broadcasting, on the Company's results and financial position is discussed below.

Operating Results

Revenue

The Company's total revenue of $178.0 million increased by $40.0 million (29%) in 1997. Revenue from the Production/Distribution business increased by $35.8 million (32%) to $149.4 million, while revenue from the Broadcasting business increased by $4.1 million (19%) to $26.0 million, and Other Revenue, primarily from investments, increased by $0.1 million to $2.6 million.

Production/Distribution Revenue

Production/Distribution revenue consists of program licence revenue, other program revenue, and post-production revenue. The results of the Production/Distribution operations may vary significantly in any period depending on the number of hours of television programs delivered in that period. As a result, the Company's earnings for any one period are not necessarily indicative of results for future periods.

Program Licence Revenue

Program licence revenue is comprised of pre-sale licencing revenue (licensing of Atlantis-produced programs prior to the delivery of the program) as well as after-sale licencing revenue (licensing of completed Atlantis-produced programs or completed programs acquired from third parties). Program licence revenue is recognized when a program is delivered, the licence period begins and the collectability of proceeds is reasonably assured. In the case of a television series, revenue is recognized on a pro-rata episodic basis.

Program licence revenue increased $45.8 million (50%) to $137.4 million, largely as a result of increased revenue from pre-sale licencing and after-sales of *Gene Rodden-*

Revenue Analysis

(millions)	1997		1996	
Production/Distribution Revenue				
Program Licence	**$ 137.4**	**77%**	$ 91.6	66%
Other Program	**$ 10.9**	**6%**	$ 20.8	15%
Post-Production	**$ 1.1**	**1%**	$ 1.2	1%
	$ 149.4	**84%**	$ 113.6	82%
Broadcast Revenue	**$ 26.0**	**15%**	$ 21.9	16%
Other Revenue	**$ 2.6**	**1%**	$ 2.5	2%
Total Revenue	**$ 178.0**	**100%**	$ 138.0	100%

berry's Earth: Final Conflict® and *Cold Squad*, two new series added to the Atlantis slate during 1997. An increase in the number of episodes delivered of both *PSI FACTOR®: Chronicles of the Paranormal* and *The Adventures of Sinbad* also contributed to the significant year over year increase in program licence revenue. The 1997 library revenues increased by $5.6 million (52%) to $16.3 million and included the sale of all 65 episodes of the family drama *Neon Rider* to Pax Net, the new Paxson Communications Network in the U.S.

Atlantis continues to generate the majority (89%) of its program licence revenues from outside Canada, with 47% (46% – 1996) from the United States and 42% (43% – 1996) from other markets around the world (see chart). This reflects the global appeal of Atlantis' programming.

Other Program Revenue
Other program revenue is comprised of revenue raised by the Company from third-party sources to fund production costs. This revenue includes non-recourse investments in programs by government agencies and broadcasters and financing from the Canada Television and Cable Production Fund in both years. During 1996, other program revenue also included interest income from limited partnership syndications and proceeds from the sale of copyright to limited partnership syndications. Other program revenue is recognized when a program is delivered and the collectability of proceeds is reasonably assured. In the case of a television series, revenue is recognized on a pro-rata episodic basis.

Other program revenue declined by $9.9 million (48%) to $10.9 million. The decrease was due to the fact that 1996 was the final year in which the Company recognized revenue related to interest income and proceeds from sales of copyright to limited partnership syndications. The revenue recognized on these limited partnership syndications in 1996 was $11.9 million and related to purchase agreements entered into prior to December 31, 1995. During 1995, amendments to the Income Tax Act arising from the February 1995 Federal Budget were implemented to eliminate new limited partnership syndications of Canadian certified film and television productions effective December 31, 1995.

Other program revenue of $10.9 million in 1997, primarily represents financing from government incentive and regulatory programs, up from $8.9 million in 1996. In early 1998, the Federal government announced a three-year commitment for the CTCPF (Canada Television Cable Production Fund), but there is no assurance as to the eligibility criteria for programs, the funding caps, or the availability of funds for Atlantis programs given the first come first served nature of the Licence Fee Program.

Program Licence Revenue – Geographic Analysis

(millions)	1997		1996	
Canada	**$ 15.5**	**11%**	$ 10.1	11%
United States	**$ 64.1**	**47%**	$ 42.3	46%
Other Markets	**$ 57.8**	**42%**	$ 39.2	43%
Total Program Licence Revenue	**$ 137.4**	**100%**	$ 91.6	100%

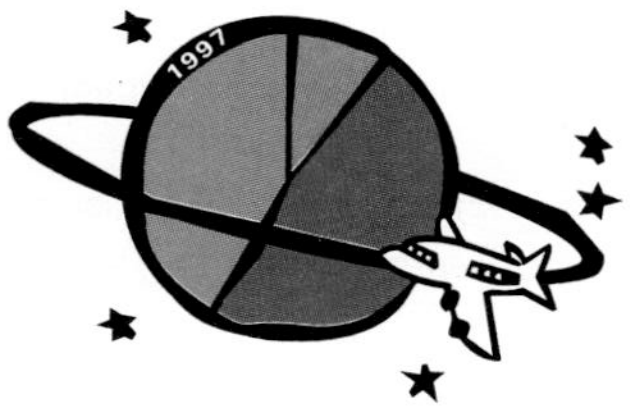

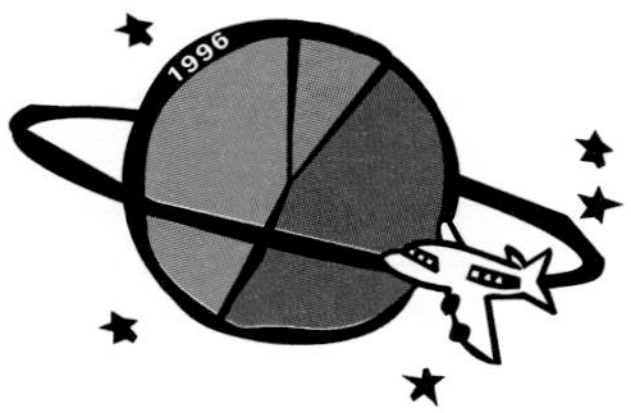

The Company continues to emphasize the creation of more commercial, market-driven programming which can be increasingly financed by pre-sale licences from the international market, with reduced reliance on the domestic market and related government incentives.

Post-Production Revenue
Post-production revenue is comprised of revenue from sound mixing, picture editing, and sound editing services for both television and theatrical films provided by a wholly-owned subsidiary, Casablanca Sound & Picture Inc., and is recognized as services are performed. In 1997, post-production revenue was $1.1 million ($1.2 million – 1996) after elimination of $4.0 million ($2.8 million – 1996) in respect of services performed for production companies in the associated Atlantis group of companies.

Broadcast Revenue
Broadcast revenue in 1997 is derived from the operation of the Company's specialty television channels: Life Network and HGTV Canada. Broadcasting revenue is comprised of two principal sources: cable subscriber revenue and advertising revenue. Cable subscriber revenue increased by $0.4 million (3%) to $13.8 million as the number of households that receive Life Network increased by 300,000 to 5.7 million at December 31, 1997. The HGTV Canada signal

was received by over 4.0 million households at December 31, 1997 and was still in the free preview period at that date.

Advertising, ancillary and other revenue increased by $3.7 million (44%) to $12.2 million in 1997. This increase was due to continued advertiser confidence in Life Network's ability to deliver significant ratings from a desirable audience demographic, together with the launch of HGTV Canada on October 17, 1997 which provided synergies for the sales effort. The results have been a continued increase in sales of commercial time at more favourable rates during 1997.

Amortization

Amortization of $150.1 million in 1997 ($116.1 million – 1996) was comprised of amortization of completed programs, costs of distributing programs, amortization of broadcast rights and development costs.

Amortization of Atlantis-produced programs as a percentage of Production/Distribution revenue was 88% in 1997, which compares to 87% in 1996.

The Company's completed program asset represents the original cost of completed programs, net of accumulated amortization. The completed program inventory contains 745 hours of Atlantis-produced programming, including 104 hours delivered in 1997.

1997 Production Activity

Production Initiated in 1997	Episode Length (hours)	Total Series/ Movie Budget ($ millions)	Number of Hours Delivered Q1	Q2	Q3	Q4	1997	1998	Key Broadcasters
T.V. Series									
Gene Roddenberry's Earth: Final Conflict® I	1.0	37	—	—	3.0	10.0	**13.0**	9.0	Tribune Entertainment – U.S. Syndication, CTV/ Baton Broadcasting System
Cold Squad I	1.0	11	—	—	—	6.0	**6.0**	5.0	CTV/Baton Broadcasting System
Outer Limits IIIB	1.0	41	—	—	—	2.0	**2.0**	20.0	Showtime, MGM – U.S. Syndication, Global
PSI FACTOR®: Chronicles of the Paranormal II	1.0	23	—	1.0	6.0	9.0	**16.0**	6.0	EYEMARK Entertainment (CBS) – U.S. Syndication, Global
The Adventures of Sinbad II	1.0	31	—	—	5.0	8.0	**13.0**	9.0	All American – U.S. Syndication, Global
Traders III	1.0	18	—	—	4.0	10.0	**14.0**	8.0	Global, CBC
T.V. Movies									
Borrowed Hearts: A Holiday Romance	2.0	6	—	—	2.0	—	**2.0**	—	CBS, CTV/Baton Broadcasting System
The Return of Alex Kelly	2.0	7	—	—	—	2.0	**2.0**	—	CBS, CTV/Baton Broadcasting System
			—	1.0	20.0	47.0	**68.0**	57.0	

Production Initiated in 1996 and delivered in 1997	Episode Length (hours)	Total Series/ Movie Budget ($ millions)	1996	Number of Hours Delivered Q1	Q2	Q3	Q4	1997	1998	Key Broadcasters
T.V. Series										
Flash Forward II	0.5	8	8.0	3.0	—	—	—	**3.0**	—	ABC, Disney Channel, Family Channel (Canada), Global
Outer Limits IIIA	1.0	41	5.0	7.0	8.0	2.0	—	**17.0**	—	Showtime, MGM – U.S. Syndication, Global, TMN, Superchannel
PSI FACTOR®: Chronicles of the Paranormal I	1.0	22	16.0	5.0	1.0	—	—	**6.0**	—	EYEMARK Entertainment (CBS) – U.S. Syndication, Global
The Adventures of Sinbad	1.0	32	12.0	7.0	3.0	—	—	**10.0**	—	All American – U.S. Syndication, Global
			41.0	22.0	12.0	2.0	—	**36.0**	—	
Total number of hours delivered				22.0	13.0	22.0	47.0	**104.0**	57.0	

In addition, the Atlantis library contains 362 hours of acquired programs (including 300 hours obtained in the Ironstar acquisition which closed in early 1998). Atlantis also represents other third-party programs such as the CBS catalogue.

The Company utilizes the individual film forecast computation method in amortizing its completed programs. Capitalized production and/or acquisition costs, together with the estimated total cost of any residual payments, or other participations related to a particular program, are amortized in the ratio that revenue generated by the program in a particular period bears to management's estimate of total gross revenue, to be realized from that program over the next four years. Although the value of the completed programs at December 31, 1997, is expected to be fully amortized by December 31, 2001, management is confident that the library will continue to generate revenue well beyond the amortization period.

At December 31, 1997, the Company had amortized 92% of the original cost of its completed programs. The Company anticipates that these programs will be fully amortized after four years.

Amortization is based on management's estimates of future revenues, and as such, any significant negative variation between the estimated revenue and the actual revenue realized over time in respect of a program may require a write-down of that program. Management controls this risk by periodically reviewing and updating the estimates and assumptions involved in the calculations used to amortize the program inventory in the context of a continually changing marketplace.

The Company has applied for tax credits under federal and provincial tax credit programs. This funding, along with government grants, has been reflected as a reduction to the cost of completed programs in the amount of $16.5 million ($9.9 million – 1996), and a reduction of $2.6 million ($2.5 million – 1996) to the cost of programs in process.

Amortization of Broadcast rights in 1997 was 60% of total Broadcast revenue, compared with 75% in 1996. The Company's Broadcast rights asset represents the original cost of broadcast programming net of accumulated amortization. The Broadcast rights are amortized over the exclusivity period of the contract, if applicable, or otherwise over one-half of the duration of the contract.

The decrease in the ratio of Broadcast rights amortization to total Broadcast revenue can be attributed to the change in the required level of spending on Canadian content as required by condition of licence between Life Network's first and second year of operation. In 1997, Life Network's conditions of licence required it to maintain Canadian program expenditures at a level equal to 65% of the previous year's revenue from regulated broadcast activities less a 5% allowable variance. In its first full year of operation, ended August 31, 1996, Life Network expended $15.2 million on Canadian program expenditures, which was within the 5% allowable variance of the initial year requirement of $16.0 million in Canadian program expenditures.

HGTV Canada's conditions of licence will require it to maintain Canadian program expenditures at a level equal to 50% of the previous year's revenue from regulated broadcast activities within a 5% allowable variance. For its first year of operation, an expenditure level was not established as part of the licence conditions. Management expects that both Life Network and HGTV Canada will continue to meet this condition of licence at future fiscal year ends.

Operating Expense

Operating expense, net of capitalized operating expenses which relate directly to programs and development projects, increased by $0.3 million (2%) to $14.1 million in 1997. Gross operating expenses increased by $3.3 million (17%) to $22.9 million.

The entire increase in gross operating expenses is attributable to the Broadcasting group where additional costs were incurred for the start-up of the HGTV Canada channel and to accommodate growth at Life Network. The Company capitalized $2.1 million of pre-operating expenses for HGTV Canada, which represented $3.0 million of operating expenses net of advertising and ancillary revenue of $0.9 million. These capitalized operating costs will be amortized over five years from the commencement of commercial operations.

While gross operating expenses of $13.0 million did not increase in the Television Production/Distribution area, additional operating costs were capitalized to reflect the increased level of production activity for television programming during 1997.

Depreciation

Depreciation includes depreciation expense for fixed assets and the amortization expense related to goodwill, deferred start-up costs and other assets.

Depreciation expense increased by $1.3 million to $3.0 million in 1997. The increase relates to the goodwill associated with the Life Network acquisition, amortization of deferred start-up costs associated with Life Network and additional depreciation on capital expenditures made during 1997. The majority of the capital expenditures of $5.7 million were for broadcasting equipment associated with the start-up of HGTV Canada ($3.6 million) and information technology and financial systems investment throughout the Company ($0.8 million).

Gain on Sale of Investment
On August 30, 1996, the Company sold its 28% interest in YTV for net proceeds of approximately $25 million. The Company accounted for its share of equity earnings from YTV, as well as for amortization of related goodwill incurred in connection with the acquisition of its interest in YTV, up until the date of disposition. The gain on the sale of this investment was $5.3 million before taxes ($3.5 million or $0.37 cents per share, on an after-tax basis). The proceeds of disposition were retained by the Company in general cash reserves and contributed to the increase in the Company's cash and marketable securities at December 31, 1996 and the reduction in the Company's interest expense in 1996.

Interest Expense
Interest expense decreased by approximately $0.4 million (29%) in 1997. This decrease was primarily due to an increase in the average cash position of the Company throughout 1997. Interest expense attributable to interim financing is included in the production costs of the particular program to which it relates, and therefore does not appear as interest expense on the Company's Consolidated Statement of Earnings.

Income Taxes
The Company's effective income tax rate for 1997 was 43.7% of earnings before taxes (1996 – 34.7%). This effective tax rate reflects a 15.8% reduction in the effective income tax rate due to the utilization of loss carry-forwards, an increase in the income tax rate due to non-deductible expenses (5.8%), an accrual for income tax contingencies (8.4%) and other adjustments (0.7%).

The Company is currently undergoing audits of the taxation years ended 1992 to 1994 by Revenue Canada and the taxation years ended 1993 to 1995 by the Ontario Ministry of Revenue. The Company has not been reassessed by either body, and as such, any reassessment may result in additional tax liability not currently reflected in the Company's financial statements.

EBITDA (Earnings before interest, taxes, depreciation and amortization)
EBITDA for 1997 increased by $5.7 million (71%) to $13.7 million. The improvement in EBITDA results from increased margin from the production, distribution and broadcast of television programs, partially offset by a slight increase in net operating expenses.

Net Earnings
Net earnings for 1997 were $5.6 million, compared with net earnings before unusual items of $3.4 million for 1996. The total 1996 net earnings of $6.9 million included an after-tax gain of $3.5 million, or $0.37 per share, on the sale of the Company's interest in YTV (see Gain on Sale of Investment).

Net earnings per share in 1997, before unusual items, increased by $0.20 or 57% to $0.55 from $0.35 in 1996. Total net earnings per share in 1997 were $0.55 compared with $0.72 in 1996, which included the $0.37 per share after-tax gain described above.

The 1997 per share calculation is based on a weighted average of 10,067,074 shares outstanding (1996 – 9,603,294 shares). There were 10,119,244 shares outstanding at December 31, 1997.

Earnings before income taxes, before unusual items, were $9.8 million in 1997 compared with $4.9 million in 1996. The increase in earnings before income taxes, before unusual items, is a result of the increased margin from the production, distribution and broadcast of television programs ($6.0 million), plus a reduction in interest expense ($0.4 million). The increase in earnings was partially offset by increases in operating expenses ($0.2 million) and depreciation ($1.3 million).

Liquidity and Capital Resources

Cash and Cash Equivalents
During 1997, the Company's cash and cash equivalents increased by $15.6 million to $29.7 million at December 31, 1997. Net cash (cash and cash equivalents less loans payable) increased by $16.7 million to $19.8 million at December 31, 1997. In addition to these cash reserves, the Company has unused operating lines of credit of $22.4 million with Canadian chartered banks, and separate interim financing arrangements for productions.

The Company also has financing commitments, from a Canadian chartered bank for $29.4 million, which support the applications for five new specialty channels. The financing will be available to fund the Company's investment and operating debts in the specialty channels, should licence(s) be awarded.

The Company is generally required to make significant initial expenditures either to produce its own television programs or to acquire programs from third parties. As the revenues from these programs are received by the Company over an extended period of time, the Company has traditionally financed its working capital requirements in this initial period through cash generated by operations and its lines of credit. In the case of television series, where cash flow requirements are more substantial, the Company uses self-liquidating interim financing loans, primarily from Canadian chartered banks.

Cash used in Operating Activities

During 1997, the Company had a net cash inflow of $133 million compared with $137 million in 1996. The net use of cash was to primarily finance accounts receivable associated with the increased production activity and interim funding of applications for federal and provincial tax credit programs for both the 1996 and 1997 programs. This use of cash was partially offset by an increase in gross margin from television production, distribution and broadcasting activity.

Cash used in Investing Activities

During 1997, the Company had a cash outflow from investing activity of $181 million compared with $128 million in 1996. The 1997 cash outflow included increased investments in programs in process and completed programs due to the increased production activity ($30 million), increased expenditures for capital and other assets mainly associated with the start-up of HGTV Canada ($4 million) and the investment in Calibre Digital Pictures ($2 million).

The remaining variance results from activities in 1996, where the Company received proceeds of $25 million on the sale of its interest in YTV, partially offset by the purchase of the remaining 43% interest in the Life Network for $9 million.

Cash provided from Financing Activities

During 1997, the Company funded its operating and investment activities mainly through the use of interim financing and a private placement of Special Warrants that took place in December 1997. The cash provided from financing activities was $64 million for 1997 ($1 million – 1996).

Interim Financing

During 1997, the Company received $40 million of interim financing ($5 million – 1996) to support the increased production activity and the applications for tax credits under federal and provincial tax credit programs.

Interim financing on programs is debt which the Company raises in respect of a specific program in order to bridge the cash flow requirements of that program during its production. Interim financing is generally 100% secured by assigned accounts receivable of the program to which it relates. As such, the debt is self-liquidating. Interest expense attributable to interim financing is included in the production costs of the particular program to which it relates, and therefore does not appear as interest expense on the Company's Consolidated Statement of Earnings.

During 1997, the Company actively financed its programs through the use of an interim $45 million Production Revolver Facility with the Royal Bank of Canada. During 1997, the Company re-negotiated the terms of this facility, in conjunction with its lines of credit to obtain a more favourable overall credit package which provides lower borrowing costs and more efficient administration. The overall average interest rate for interim financing during 1997 was 4.7%, compared with 7.3% during 1996. The lower rate for 1997 is a result of the improved borrowing terms of the Production Revolver Facility and a lower average Canadian prime borrowing rate during 1997.

Private Placement of Special Warrants

On December 23, 1997, the Company issued 2,292,400 Special Warrants for cash consideration of $20.6 million ($9 per share). The Company's share issue costs including the underwriters' fees and expenses totaled $1.9 million ($1.0 million after taxes). On February 9, 1998, all of the Special Warrants were converted into subordinate voting shares on a one-for-one basis. As at April 2, 1998, there were 8,180,645 subordinated voting shares outstanding (12,418,144 total shares).

Year 2000

The year 2000 poses a challenge to businesses that are reliant on computer systems or other equipment that use the last two digits to represent a year. The Company has performed an analysis of the risks and uncertainties arising from the year 2000 issue and developed a plan to address the risks and uncertainties. The plan is reviewed on an ongoing basis by executive management and the Board of Directors. The scope of the analysis includes all computer hardware products, computer software products, broadcasting, production, post-production, animation equipment, and general office equipment. This analysis will be expanded to include the systems of the Company's key suppliers, customers and bankers during 1998.

The Company's inventory of software includes mainly third-party products and some custom-developed applications. The custom-developed applications, which have been implemented recently, were designed with four digit date processing and are fully year 2000 compliant.

An inventory of substantially all third-party hardware and software products has been taken and the state of year 2000 readiness evaluated. A significant number of products are already year 2000 compliant and supplier certifications from other third-party vendors have been obtained or are being pursued as part of the implementation plan. The Year 2000 plan includes some limited testing of major systems to ensure year 2000 compliance, in addition to relying on supplier certifications and the experience of their clients who conduct tests on these products. Contingency plans will be developed for any product where supplier certification has not been provided during fiscal 1998.

The costs associated with the Year 2000 plan are mainly administrative costs and will be incurred by existing in-house staff from 1997 through the year 1999. These costs will be expensed as incurred and are not expected to be material. The Company's existing budget for information technology includes the replacement of desktop technology and key financial operating systems during fiscal 1998. The replacement products that have been selected for implementation during 1998 are year 2000 compliant.

The Company presently believes that through testing and upgrading its systems and working with third-party vendors, it will ensure a smooth transition for the Company and its customers.

Outlook

The Company is committed to growth through excellence in television programming.

For 1998, five of the Company's six 1997 television series have been re-ordered for a further season of production, along with orders for two new children's television series, two series' pilots and one network movie. This totals over 125 hours of television production that is already committed and is expected to be delivered during 1998.

In an increasing global market for television programs, a significant amount of pre-sale revenue is required to create programs that are of a high quality and meet the necessary commercial appeal in the marketplace. In order to secure substantial pre-sale revenue for many projects, the Company has entered into program package/output arrangements with key customers including Endemol Entertainment for Europe, Africa and the Middle East and TV3 for New Zealand. The Endemol arrangement, signed in April 1998, also included a significant sale of the available rights for Endemol's territories of a variety of Atlantis' drama programs from its library.

The television production and distribution industry is experiencing consolidation both within Canada and North America and on a global basis, which may limit the number of customers and suppliers in the marketplace. In order to ensure that the Company remains competitive, it may from time to time pursue investment opportunities in the industry which expand its scale and scope in order to maximize its future growth and profit potential. During 1997, the Company acquired an interest in Calibre Digital Pictures to expand its capability in the area of animation and special effects. The investment opportunities will be carefully evaluated in terms of their overall strategic and financial value to the Company.

In 1997, the Company's broadcasting operation filed applications with the Canadian Radio-television and Telecommunications Commission ("CRTC") for five new specialty broadcasting services which Atlantis controls. They are: Food Network Canada, Canada's Health Network, People Channel, National Geographic Channel Canada and FIT TV Canada.
In addition, the Company participated as a 20% shareholder in Shaw Communications Inc.'s application for CHAOS TV. Over the next fiscal year, no decisions from the CRTC are expected with regard to the specialty broadcasting applications. The Company expects that the CRTC will hold hearings regarding the applications during the first quarter of 1999 and is optimistic that it will be successful in expanding its broadcasting operation beyond its current two channels, Life Network and HGTV Canada. Management believes that the addition of new broadcasting services to its existing operation will create synergies and improve overall operating results.

Management believes that the key events of 1997: continued development of a growing television program slate with international appeal; the significant growth in Life Network and the launch of HGTV Canada; the Company's entry into the animation and special effects business through the acquisition of Calibre Digital Pictures; coupled with the addition of new product lines such as the CBS representation agreement; and the application for five new specialty broadcast services, which Atlantis controls, are consistent with the Company's growth strategy to enhance shareholder value.

Management's Report

The accompanying financial statements and all information contained in this annual report of Atlantis Communications Inc. are the responsibility of Management and have been approved by the Board of Directors. Financial and operating data elsewhere in the annual report is consistent with the information contained in the financial statements. The financial statements and all other information have been prepared by Management in accordance with generally accepted accounting principles. The financial statements include some figures and assumptions based on Management's best estimates which have been derived with careful judgement.

In fulfilling its responsibilities, Management of the Company has developed and maintains a system of internal accounting controls. These controls ensure that the financial records are reliable for preparing the financial statements. The Board of Directors of the Company carries out its responsibility for the financial statements through its Audit Committee. The Audit Committee reviews the Company's annual consolidated financial statements and recommends their approval by the Board of Directors. The auditors have full access to the Audit Committee with and without Management present.

The financial statements have been audited by Deloitte & Touche Chartered Accountants, whose findings are contained in this annual report.

Michael I.M. MacMillan
Chairman and Chief Executive Officer

Lewis N. Rose
President

Kerri Golden
Chief Financial Officer

Auditors' Report

To the Shareholders of Atlantis Communications Inc.

We have audited the consolidated balance sheets of Atlantis Communications Inc. as at December 31, 1997 and 1996 and the consolidated statements of earnings and retained earnings and changes in financial position for the years then ended. These financial statements are the responsibility of the Company's management. Our responsibility is to express an opinion on these financial statements based on our audits.

We conducted our audits in accordance with generally accepted auditing standards. Those standards require that we plan and perform an audit to obtain reasonable assurance whether the financial statements are free of material misstatement. An audit includes examining, on a test basis, evidence supporting the amounts and disclosures in the financial statements. An audit also includes assessing the accounting principles used and significant estimates made by management, as well as evaluating the overall financial statement presentation.

In our opinion, these consolidated financial statements present fairly, in all material respects, the financial position of the Company as at December 31, 1997 and 1996 and the results of its operations and the changes in its financial position for the years then ended in accordance with generally accepted accounting principles.

Toronto, Ontario
April 02, 1998

Deloitte & Touche
Chartered Accountants

Consolidated Balance Sheets

As at December 31 (in thousands of Canadian dollars, except for per share information)	**1997**	1996
Assets		
Cash and cash equivalents *(Note 2)*	**$ 29,669**	$ 14,099
Accounts receivable *(Note 3)*	**145,611**	75,645
Development costs	**4,147**	4,561
Programs in process	**40,308**	22,829
Completed programs *(Note 4)*	**46,932**	44,698
Broadcast rights *(Note 5)*	**13,517**	11,260
Notes receivable *(Note 6)*	**20,526**	140,673
Investments *(Note 7)*	**3,513**	1,500
Fixed assets *(Note 8)*	**12,537**	8,937
Deferred income taxes	**4,284**	—
Other assets *(Note 9)*	**12,503**	10,624
	$ 333,547	$ 334,826
Liabilities		
Accounts payable and accrued liabilities	**$ 42,592**	$ 24,591
Broadcast rights payable	**4,457**	5,043
Distribution revenue payable	**10,996**	9,419
Interim financing on programs *(Note 10)*	**67,055**	27,230
Loans payable *(Note 11)*	**9,847**	10,952
Deferred revenue	**78,842**	45,904
Notes payable *(Note 6)*	**20,526**	140,673
Deferred income taxes	**—**	2,186
Non-controlling interest	**2,145**	—
	236,460	265,998
Shareholders' Equity		
Capital stock *(Note 12)*	**76,705**	52,961
Retained earnings	**20,382**	15,867
	97,087	68,828
	$ 333,547	$ 334,826
Book value per share *(Note 13)*	**$ 7.82**	$ 7.16

See accompanying notes

On behalf of the Board:

Michael I.M. MacMillan
Director

Donald W. Paterson
Director

ATLANTIS

Consolidated Statements of Earnings and Retained Earnings

For the years ended December 31 (in thousands of Canadian dollars, except for per share information)	**1997**	1996
Revenue	**$ 177,960**	$ 137,984
Expenses		
Amortization	**150,101**	116,134
Operating	**14,129**	13,856
Depreciation	**3,029**	1,694
	167,259	131,684
Earnings before undernoted	**10,701**	6,300
Gain on sale of investment *(Note 9)*	**—**	5,272
Earnings before interest and income taxes	**10,701**	11,572
Interest	**947**	1,339
Earnings before income taxes	**9,754**	10,233
Provision for (recovery of) income taxes *(Note 14)*		
Current	**9,887**	2,954
Deferred	**(5,625)**	593
	4,262	3,547
Earnings before equity earnings and non-controlling interest	**5,492**	6,686
Equity earnings from investment	**73**	318
Non-controlling interest	**—**	(138)
Net earnings for the year	**5,565**	6,866
Retained earnings, beginning of year	**15,867**	9,001
Share issue costs *(Note 12)*	**(1,050)**	—
Retained earnings, end of year	**$ 20,382**	$ 15,867
Earnings per share *(Note 15)*	**$ 0.55**	$ 0.72

See accompanying notes

Consolidated Statements of Changes in Financial Position

For the years ended December 31 (in thousands of Canadian dollars)	**1997**	1996
Cash provided by (used in):		
Operating activities		
Net earnings for the year	**$ 5,565**	$ 6,866
Items not affecting cash		
Amortization and depreciation	**153,130**	117,828
Gain on disposition of an investment	**—**	(5,272)
Deferred income taxes	**(5,625)**	593
Non-controlling interest and equity earnings	**(73)**	(180)
	152,997	119,835
Changes in other non-cash balances	**(19,842)**	17,067
	133,155	136,902
Investing activities		
Development costs	**(2,565)**	(2,219)
Programs in process	**(19,749)**	(5,478)
Completed programs	**(129,945)**	(112,166)
Broadcast rights	**(18,436)**	(19,038)
Investments	**(1,940)**	(400)
Proceeds on sale of investment	**—**	25,145
Net additions to fixed assets	**(5,755)**	(1,831)
Acquisition of Life Network	**—**	(9,473)
Other assets	**(2,754)**	(2,899)
	(181,144)	(128,359)
Financing activities		
Notes receivable	**120,148**	(256)
Interim financing	**39,825**	5,097
Loans payable	**(1,105)**	(4,331)
Notes payable	**(120,148)**	256
Non-controlling interest	**2,145**	—
Capital stock issued	**23,744**	50
Share issue costs	**(1,050)**	—
	63,559	816
Increase in cash and cash equivalents	**15,570**	9,359
Cash and cash equivalents, beginning of year	**14,099**	4,740
Cash and cash equivalents, end of year	**$ 29,669**	$ 14,099

See accompanying notes

Notes to Consolidated Financial Statements

December 31, 1997 and 1996 (in thousands of Canadian dollars, except for per share information)

ATLANTIS COMMUNICATIONS INC., together with its subsidiaries (the "Company") is an international producer, distributor and broadcaster of television programs.

1. Summary of Significant Accounting Policies

Generally accepted accounting principles

These consolidated financial statements have been prepared in accordance with generally accepted accounting principles.

The Company has adopted United States Financial Accounting Standards Board Statement No. 53 for revenue recognition and amortization of program costs, as there are no Canadian accounting standards specific to the television industry.

Principles of consolidation

These consolidated financial statements include the financial statements of the Company, its subsidiaries, an equity ownership in Calibre Digital Design Inc. ("Calibre"), and a 50% joint venture interest in Cinevillage Inc. ("Cinevillage"). Calibre is accounted for using the equity method. Cinevillage is accounted for using the proportionate consolidation method to reflect the Company's share of assets, liabilities, revenues and expenses in the joint venture.

Revenue recognition

The Company's primary sources of revenue are derived from the production and distribution of television programs, and revenue derived from broadcast activities. Production and distribution revenue is comprised of program licence revenue, other program revenue, and post-production revenue.

Program licence revenue is derived from licensing distribution rights to broadcasters and syndicators. The Company recognizes program licence revenue when the program is delivered, the licence period begins, and the collectability of the revenue is reasonably assured. In the case of a television series, revenue is recognized on a pro-rata episodic basis.

Other program revenue is comprised of non-recourse investments in programs by government agencies and broadcasters and financing from the Canada Television and Cable Production Fund. The Company recognizes other program revenue when a program is delivered and the collectability of the revenue is reasonably assured. In the case of a television series, revenue is recognized on a pro-rata episodic basis.

Broadcast revenue is derived from the operations of the Company's specialty cable television channel, Life Network Inc. ("Life Network"), and is comprised of two principal sources: cable subscriber revenue, and advertising revenue. Cable subscriber revenue is recognized as the services are provided. Advertising revenue is recognized when the commercials are aired. Revenue of Home & Garden Television Canada Inc. ("HGTV") has been deferred as the channel is in the pre-operating stage.

Development costs

The Company capitalizes costs, including related overhead, incurred with respect to literary works and other underlying rights it intends to adapt for production. Non-recourse development financing received by the Company has been offset against the related development costs. Development costs are assessed periodically on a project by project basis, and are written off when determined not to be recoverable.

Programs in process

Programs in process represent the costs incurred by the Company in the production of television programs where principal photography has commenced, but where the programs were not delivered at year end. These costs include production expenditures, interest and overhead, net of federal and provincial tax credits and grants. Programs in process are not amortized as no revenue has been recognized.

Completed programs

Completed programs represent the costs incurred by the Company in the production of television programs which have been produced and delivered, or for which the Company has acquired distribution rights from third parties. These costs include production expenditures, acquisition costs, interest, overhead, third-party participation and print and advertising costs, net of federal and provincial tax credits and grants.

Completed programs are stated at the lower of cost, net of amortization, and net realizable value. The net realizable value of a completed program is the Company's share of the estimated future revenue to be earned from the program, net of the estimated future costs.

The individual film forecast method is used to amortize the cost of completed programs. Amortization for each completed program is based on the ratio that current revenue earned from that program bears to estimated future revenue, including subsequent licensing periods.

Broadcast rights

Broadcast subsidiaries are committed, under various contracts, to pay for the rights to broadcast programming. Broadcast rights and corresponding liabilities are recorded when the licence period begins and the program becomes available for use. Broadcast rights are stated at the lower of cost, net of amortization, and net realizable value. The cost of each contract is amortized over the exclusivity period, if applicable, and otherwise over one-half of the duration of the contract.

Investments

Investments in shares of associated companies over which the Company has significant influence, are accounted for by the equity method. Other investments are carried at cost.

Fixed assets

Fixed assets are carried at cost less accumulated depreciation. Depreciation is provided using the following rates and methods:

Building	5% declining balance
Broadcast and production equipment	20 – 30% declining balance
Furniture and other equipment	20 – 30% declining balance
Leasehold improvements	20% straight-line
Vehicles	30% declining balance

Other assets

Other assets include pre-operating costs and goodwill. Pre-operating costs primarily relate to HGTV and Life Network. HGTV is currently in the pre-operating stage. All start-up costs incurred during the pre-operating stage are being capitalized and will be amortized over five years from commencement of commercial operations.

Life Network was in the pre-operating stage to December 31, 1994. All start-up costs related to the pre-operating stage are being amortized from the commencement of operations on January 1, 1995 over 56 months.

Goodwill represents the excess of the cost of investments over the assigned values of assets and liabilities acquired, and is amortized using the straight-line method over periods not exceeding 40 years. The balance is reviewed on an annual basis and, in the event of a permanent impairment to goodwill, such as material change in the business practices or significant operating losses, the Company will record a reduction in the unamortized portion of goodwill.

Distribution revenue payable

Distribution revenue payable represents amounts owing to investors, co-producers and other third-party participants.

Deferred revenue

Completed program revenue is deferred until the program is delivered. Program licence revenue is also deferred until the licence meets the revenue recognition criteria as described in this note.

Government financing, tax credits and grants

The Company has access to government financing that is designed to assist television production and distribution in Canada. Financing from government agencies is considered revenue, and is recognized in accordance with the Company's revenue recognition policy. Federal and provincial tax credits and grants related to programs in process and completed programs are recorded as a reduction in the cost of the respective program.

Use of estimates

The preparation of financial statements in conformity with generally accepted accounting principles requires management to make estimates and assumptions that affect the amounts reported in the financial statements. Actual results could differ from these estimates.

Amortization of completed programs is based on management's estimates of future revenue. Accordingly, any significant negative variation between the estimated revenue and the actual revenue realized over time in respect of a program, may require a write-down of that program. Due to a continually changing marketplace, management controls this risk by periodically reviewing and updating these estimates and assumptions.

The Company is currently undergoing audits by Revenue Canada and the Ontario Ministry of Revenue. As the result of these audits is unknown and as no reassessments have been made to date, a reassessment may result in additional tax liability not currently reflected in the Company's financial statements.

Income taxes

The Company accounts for income taxes using the deferral method.

2. Cash and Cash Equivalents

Bank demand loans have been netted against cash and marketable securities. The Company has unused operating lines of credit of $22,400 with Canadian chartered banks, secured by general security agreements over the Company and a first floating charge over the assets of certain subsidiaries. Outstanding borrowings of $1,350 ($Nil – 1996), are due upon demand and bear interest at prime.

3. Accounts Receivable

Accounts receivable includes $39,818 ($8,934 – 1996) of receivables which are non interest bearing and are due subsequent to December 31, 1998.

4. Completed Programs

	1997		1996	
	value	**%**	value	%
Original cost of completed programs	**$ 596,786**	**100 %**	$ 477,056	100 %
Less: accumulated amortization	**(549,854)**	**(92)**	(432,358)	(91)
Completed programs, net of accumulated amortization	**$ 46,932**	**8 %**	$ 44,698	9 %

As at December 31, 1997, the Company anticipates that approximately 99% of these original program costs will be amortized after three years and 100% after four years.

5. Broadcast Rights

	1997		1996	
	value	**%**	value	%
Original cost of broadcast rights	**$ 28,789**	**100 %**	$ 21,462	100 %
Less: accumulated amortization	**(15,272)**	**(53)**	(10,202)	(48)
Broadcast rights, net of accumulated amortization	**$ 13,517**	**47 %**	$ 11,260	52 %

6. Notes Receivable and Notes Payable

Notes receivable from limited partnerships become due on various dates up to January 15, 1999 and are exactly matched by dates and amounts of the Notes payable. These Notes receivable are secured by assignments of promissory notes from a financial corporation which are in turn secured by financial instruments and the promissory notes of the private investors in the limited partnerships.

7. Investments

	1997	1996
Calibre Digital Design Inc. – equity basis	**$ 2,435**	$ —
Other investments – at cost	**1,078**	1,500
	$ 3,513	$ 1,500

The Company's share of the difference between the replacement cost and the net book value of Calibre's assets at the date of purchase was $1,304. This difference is being amortized over a period of 60 months, beginning on June 1, 1997.

8. Fixed Assets

	1997		1996	
	Cost	**Accumulated Depreciation**	Cost	Accumulated Depreciation
Building (including land of $363)	**$ 3,592**	**$ 1,266**	$ 3,582	$ 1,171
Broadcast and production equipment	**10,671**	**4,213**	5,691	1,654
Furniture and other equipment	**4,863**	**2,307**	3,305	1,743
Leasehold improvements	**2,193**	**1,062**	1,738	835
Vehicles	**82**	**16**	29	5
	$ 21,401	**$ 8,864**	$ 14,345	$ 5,408
Net Book Value		**$ 12,537**		$ 8,937

As at December 31, 1997, $3,219 ($3,620 – 1996) of the equipment described above, less accumulated depreciation of $1,275 ($1,202 – 1996), was subject to capital leases.

9. Acquisitions and Divestiture

Investment in Calibre Digital Design Inc.

On May 31, 1997, the Company acquired 50% of the voting shares (60% equity) of Calibre for $2,545, including $1,045 relating to restructuring and integration costs. This acquisition has been accounted for using the equity method.

Acquisition of 43% of Life Network

In 1996, the Company increased its ownership in Life Network from 57% to 100%. The Company acquired the remaining interest for aggregate consideration of $9,473 comprised of cash, rights and 474,981 treasury shares of the Company. Also included in this amount is approximately $2,000 relating to restructuring and integration costs. Part of the consideration, including the treasury shares, was paid subsequent to December 31, 1996 (see Note 12). The 43% interest in Life Network was acquired from related parties, including management and a significant shareholder of the Company.

The increase in ownership of Life Network was accounted for as a purchase. As a result of the acquisition, goodwill, included in other assets, increased by $6,466, and non-controlling interest decreased by $3,007.

Divestiture of 28% of YTV Canada, Inc.

In 1996, the Company sold its 28% interest in YTV Canada, Inc. for net proceeds of $25,145. The pre-tax gain on the sale of YTV amounted to $5,272, or $3,532 ($0.37 per share) on an after-tax basis.

10. Interim Financing on Programs

Interim financing on programs at December 31, 1997 bears interest at various rates up to U.S. prime rate plus 1.0% (U.S. prime rate plus 1.0% – 1996). Of the outstanding balance, $2,537 represents U.S. dollar borrowings. The loans are fully secured by direct assignments of accounts receivable.

The Company has available $45,000 under an interim production credit facility, secured by direct assignments of accounts receivable. Outstanding borrowings of $35,018 at December 31,1997 ($Nil – 1996) bear interest at prime plus 5/8%.

11. Loans Payable

	1997	1996
Mortgages payable		
Bear interest from a fixed rate of 9.99% to 3.0% above average cost of funds to the mortgagee, secured by land and building, maturing at the latest October 2005	**$ 3,421**	$ 3,576
Bank term loans		
Bear interest at rates up to prime rate plus 1.5%, secured by various assets and distribution licencing agreements or territories, maturing at the latest November 2001	**3,244**	2,790
Other debt	**1,581**	2,580
Obligation under capital leases	**1,601**	2,006
	$ 9,847	$ 10,952

Principal payments are due as follows:

1998	$ 4,438
1999	1,548
2000	1,107
2001	244
2002	255
Thereafter	2,255
	$ 9,847

12. Capital Stock

	1997		1996	
	# of Shares	**Value**	# of Shares	Value
Authorized				
Multiple Voting Shares (MVS)	**4,237,499**		4,237,499	
Subordinate Voting Shares (SVS)	**Unlimited**		Unlimited	
Preference Shares	**Unlimited**		Unlimited	
Share Purchase Warrants (SPW)	**2,292,400**		—	
Issued and Outstanding				
Share Purchase Warrants	**2,292,400**	**$ 20,631**	—	$ —
Multiple Voting Shares (ten dollars book value)	**4,237,499**	**—**	4,237,499	—
Subordinate Voting Shares	**5,881,745**	**56,074**	5,371,550	52,961
Total Voting Shares	**10,119,244**	**56,074**	9,609,049	52,961
Total Capital Stock		**$ 76,705**		$ 52,961

The MVS carry 10 votes per share and SVS carry one vote per share. MVS are convertible into SVS on a one-for-one basis. The MVS and SVS rank equally with respect to dividends and capital distributions, however, there are restrictions on ownership and transfer of the MVS. The MVS and SVS are currently constrained to limit non-Canadian ownership to levels which will not adversely affect the Company in carrying on any regulated business. Currently the CRTC limits non-Canadian ownership to 33 1/3% of the Company's voting shares. The SVS are entitled to specific rights, including coattail provisions, in the event of a take-over bid.

On December 23, 1997, the Company issued 2,292,400 Special Warrants for cash consideration of $20,631 ($9 per share). The Company's share of issue costs including underwriters' fees and expenses totalled $1,895 ($1,050 net of related taxes). On February 9, 1998, all of the Special Warrants were converted into subordinate voting shares on a one-for-one basis. During 1997, the Company issued 13,414 SVS to the Directors as consideration for services in the amount of $99, and 15,600 SVS, with an ascribed value of $94, were issued in connection with 1996 bonuses payable. In addition, 6,200 options with a total value of $37 were exercised by option holders.

In 1997, the Company paid the consideration which was accrued at December 31, 1996 in conjunction with the acquisition of the remaining interest in Life Network (Note 9). In conjunction with this acquisition, the Company issued 474,981 SVS on January 20, 1997, with a total value of $2,850.

During 1996, the Company issued 7,405 SVS to the Directors as consideration for services in the amount of $50.

Options

As at December 31, 1997, there were 1,453,964 options (960,164 – 1996) authorized to purchase SVS, and 1,014,323 options (884,469 – 1996) to purchase SVS were outstanding at prices ranging from $5.95 to $14.50 per share with a weighted average price of $8.72 ($10.08 – 1996). These options vest over time and will expire, at the latest, by May 2002.

Subsequent to December 31, 1997, 76,500 options were issued at $10.25. These options vest over time and will expire, at the latest, by February 2003. Subsequent to December 31, 1997, 20,934 options were cancelled or expired, and 6,500 options were exercised.

13. Book Value Per Share

Book value per share represents the total of shareholders' equity divided by the number of shares and Special Warrants outstanding at year end.

14. Income Taxes

(a) The effective rates of income taxes provided in the statements of earnings vary from the rates specified in the tax statutes as follows:

	1997	1996
Combined basic federal and provincial income tax rate	**44.6 %**	44.6 %
Non-deductible expenses	**5.8**	—
Reduction due to income taxed in other jurisdictions	**—**	(4.6)
Gain on sale of investment taxed at capital gains rate	**—**	(5.7)
Use of loss carry-forwards	**(15.8)**	(3.5)
Increase in income tax accrual	**8.4**	—
Other	**0.7**	3.9
	43.7 %	34.7 %

During the year the Company accrued an additional amount for income tax contingencies.

(b) Loss carry-forwards of certain of the Company's subsidiaries, for which no benefit has been recognized, amount to $133 as at December 31, 1997 ($4,083 – 1996) and are available for utilization against future taxable income. As at December 31, 1997, the loss carry-forwards expire as follows:

2002	$ 35
2003	98
	$ 133

15. Earnings Per Share

	1997		1996	
	Basic	**Fully Diluted**	Basic	Fully Diluted
Operating earnings per share	**$ 0.55**	**$ 0.52**	$ 0.35	$ 0.34
Earnings per share from unusual items	—	—	0.37	0.33
Total earnings per share	**$ 0.55**	**$ 0.52**	$ 0.72	$ 0.67
Weighted average number of shares	**10,067,074**	**11,195,706**	9,603,294	10,844,792
Number of shares outstanding at December 31	**10,119,244**	**13,425,967**	9,609,049	10,493,518

Earnings per share from unusual items in 1996 represents the after-tax earnings per share from the gain on sale of YTV (see Note 9).

16. Government Financing, Tax Credits and Grants

Revenue includes $10,589 of government program financing for the year ended December 31, 1997 ($8,947 – 1996). A portion of this amount is repayable depending on the future revenue of the individual program, and therefore has been reflected in the determination of the net realizable value of the program as a future cost. Completed program costs for the year ended December 31, 1997 are net of $16,471 of federal and provincial tax credits and grants ($9,877 – 1996). Programs in process costs for the year ended December 31, 1997 are net of $2,591 of federal and provincial tax credits and grants ($2,493 – 1996).

17. Financial Instruments

Fair values

The estimated fair values of financial instruments as at December 31, 1997 and December 31, 1996 are based on the relevant market prices and information available at that time. The fair value estimates are not indicative of the amounts that the Company might receive or incur in actual market transactions.

	1997		1996	
	Book Value	**Fair Value**	Book Value	Fair Value
Financial assets				
Assets for which fair value approximates book value	**$ 29,669**	**$ 29,669**	$ 14,099	$ 14,099
Accounts receivable	**145,611**	**142,843**	78,448	78,061
Notes receivable	**20,526**	**19,650**	140,673	139,813
Financial liabilities				
Liabilities for which fair value approximates book value	**$ 133,846**	**$ 133,846**	$ 77,128	$ 77,128
Obligations under capital lease	**1,601**	**1,549**	—	—
Notes payable	**20,526**	**19,650**	140,673	139,813

Cash and marketable securities, accounts payable and accrued liabilities, broadcast rights payable, distribution revenue payable, loans payable and interim financing on programs are all short-term in nature and as such, their carrying value approximates fair value.

The fair value of accounts receivable on balances due subsequent to December 31, 1998, was estimated using discount rates based on an average of market interest rates.

The fair value of notes receivable and notes payable was estimated based on quoted market prices or discounted cash flows, using discount rates based on market interest rates. Amounts recorded as fair value relating to notes receivable and payable are based on amounts due and receivable subsequent to December 31, 1998. The terms of these instruments require the notes receivable to be matched with the notes payable.

Forward contracts

The Company has committed to the sale of 800 million Italian Lira on February 27,1998, at an exchange rate of U.S. $0.00647.

The Company has committed to the sale of U.S. $31,786 under forward exchange contracts. The contracts are at rates of exchange ranging from Cdn. $1.3592 to $1.4205, and maturing at various dates to August 15, 2000.

The unrealized loss on forward exchange contracts at December 31, 1997 is $821. This loss has not been recorded as the contracts are considered to be hedges.

Concentration of credit risk

Accounts receivable from one customer, excluding receivables from government programs, represents 14% (24% – 1996) of total accounts receivable at December 31, 1997. The Company believes that there is no risk associated with the collection of this amount. The balance of accounts receivable are widely disbursed amongst customers.

18. Contingent Liabilities and Commitments

(a) In addition to the mortgage payable obligation (Note 11), the Company has jointly and severally guaranteed an additional $3,500 to a mortgagee of Cinevillage.

(b) The Company has entered into agreements with program investors on a number of projects under which the Company has guaranteed payments to such investors in aggregate of $297 as at December 31, 1997 ($2,357 – 1996). The Company anticipates that revenues from each of the programs in connection with which guarantees were given will meet or exceed obligations to respective program investors.

(c) The Company is committed to further payments totaling $1,500 related to marketing the launch of HGTV. These payments will be made during the current year.

(d) As at December 31, 1997 the Company is committed to future minimum operating lease payments as follows:

1998	$ 2,442
1999	2,215
2000	1,515
2001	492
2002	492
Thereafter	—
	$ 7,156

19. Segmented Information

(a) The Company's only significant activity is the production, distribution and broadcasting of television programs and ancillary rights.

(b) Revenue for the year ended December 31, 1997 includes $121,925 ($81,405 – 1996) derived from non-Canadian sources.

20. Supplementary Information

The Company has a 50% investment in Cinevillage. The Company's proportionate share in the assets, liabilities and net earnings from operations of Cinevillage is as follows:

	1997	1996
Assets, including fixed assets, at cost less accumulated depreciation of $1,398 ($1,275 – 1996)	**$ 2,423**	$ 2,548
Liabilities	**3,532**	3,708
Net income (loss)	**$ 52**	$ (258)

21. Comparative Figures

Certain comparative figures have been reclassified to conform with the current year's presentation.

Present and Future Values

II

APPENDIX

Learning Objectives

LO1 Describe the earning of interest and the concepts of present and future values.

LO2 Apply present value concepts to a single amount by using interest tables.

LO3 Apply future value concepts to a single amount by using interest tables.

LO4 Apply present value concepts to an annuity by using interest tables.

LO5 Apply future value concepts to an annuity by using interest tables.

Appendix Outline

- **Present and Future Value Concepts**
- **Present Value of a Single Amount**
- **Future Value of a Single Amount**
- **Present Value of an Annuity**
- **Future Value of an Annuity**

APPENDIX PREVIEW

The concepts of present value are described and applied in Chapter 17. This appendix helps to supplement that discussion with added explanations, illustrations, computations, present value tables, and additional assignments. We also give attention to illustrations, definitions, and computations of future values.

Present and Future Value Concepts

LO1 Describe the earning of interest and the concepts of present and future values.

There's an old saying, *time is money.* This saying reflects the notion that as time passes, the assets and liabilities we hold are changing. This change is due to interest. *Interest* is the payment to the owner of an asset for its use by a borrower. The most common example of this type of asset is a savings account. As we keep a balance of cash in our accounts, it earns interest that is paid to us by the financial institution. An example of a liability is a car loan. As we carry the balance of the loan, we accumulate interest costs on this debt. We must ultimately repay this loan with interest.

Present and future value computations are a way for us to estimate the interest component of holding assets or liabilities over time. The present value of an amount applies when we either lend or borrow an asset that must be repaid in full at some future date, and we want to know its worth today. The future value of an amount applies when we either lend or borrow an asset that must be repaid in full at some future date, and we want to know its worth at a future date.

The first section focuses on the present value of a single amount. Later sections focus on the future value of a single amount, and then both present and future values of a series of amounts (or annuity).

Present Value of a Single Amount

We graphically express the present value (p) of a single future amount (f) received or paid at a future date in Exhibit II.1.

Exhibit II.1

Present Value of a Single Amount

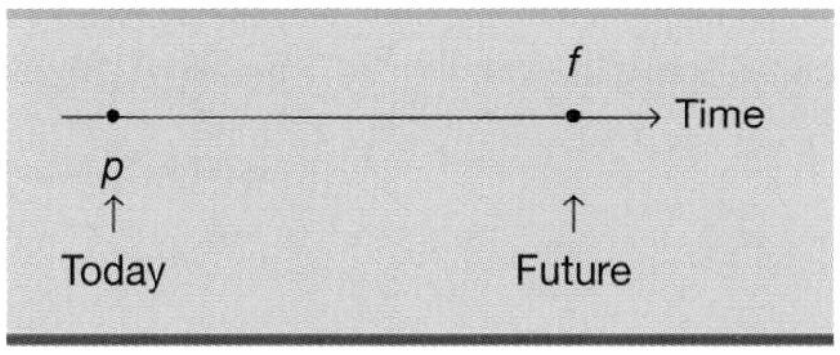

LO2 Apply present value concepts to a single amount by using interest tables.

The formula to compute the present value of this single amount is shown in Exhibit II.2 where: p = present value; f = future value; i = rate of interest per period; and n = number of periods.

Exhibit II.2

Present Value of a Single Amount Formula

$$p = \frac{f}{(1 + i)^n}$$

To illustrate the application of this formula, let's assume we need $220 one period from today. We want to know how much must be invested now, for one period, at an interest rate of 10% to provide for this $220.[1] For this illustration the p, or present value, is the unknown amount. In particular, the present and future values, along with the interest rate, are shown graphically as:

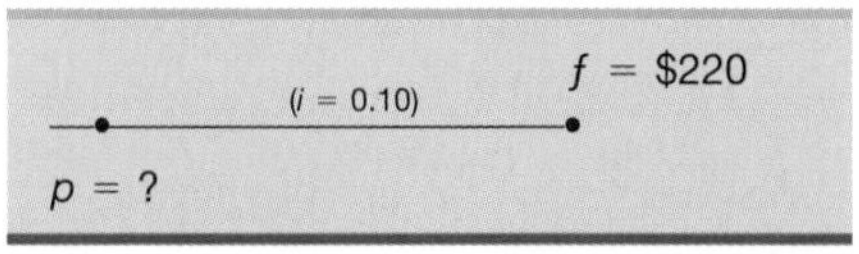

Conceptually, we know p must be less than $220. This is obvious from the answer to the question: Would we rather have $220 today or $220 at some future date? If we had $220 today, we could invest it and see it grow to something more than $220 in the future. Therefore, if we were promised $220 in the future, we would take less than $220 today. But how much less?

[1] Interest is also called a *discount*, and an interest rate is also called a *discount rate.*

To answer that question we can compute an estimate of the present value of the \$220 to be received one period from now using the formula in Exhibit II.2 as:

$$p = \frac{f}{(1 + i)^n} = \frac{\$242}{(1 + .10)^1} = \$200$$

This means we are indifferent between \$200 today or \$220 at the end of one period.

We can also use this formula to compute the present value for *any number of periods.* To illustrate this computation, we consider a payment of \$242 at the end of two periods at 10% interest. The present value of this \$242 to be received two periods from now is computed as:

$$p = \frac{f}{(1 + i)^n} = \frac{\$242}{(1 + .10)^2} = \$200$$

These results tells us we are indifferent between \$200 today, or \$220 one period from today, or \$242 two periods from today.

The number of periods (n) in the present value formula does not have to be expressed in years. Any period of time such as a day, a month, a quarter, or a year can be used. But, whatever period is used, the interest rate (i) must be compounded for the same period. This means if a situation expresses n in months, and i equals 12% per year, then we can assume 1% of an amount invested at the beginning of each month is earned in interest per month and added to the investment. In this case, interest is said to be compounded monthly.

A present value table helps us with present value computations. It gives us present values for a variety of interest rates (i) and a variety of periods (n). Each present value in a present value table assumes the future value (f) is 1. When the future value (f) is different than 1, we can simply multiply present value (p) by that future amount to give us our estimate.

The formula used to construct a table of present values of a single future amount of 1 is shown in Exhibit II.3.

Exhibit II.3

Present Value of 1 Formula

$$p = \frac{1}{(1 + i)^n}$$

This formula is identical to that in Exhibit II.2 except that f equals 1. Table II.1 at the end of this appendix is a present value table for a single future amount. It is often called a **present value of 1 table.** A present value table involves three factors: p, i, and n.[2] Knowing two of these three factors allows us to compute the third. To illustrate, consider the three possible cases.

Case 1 (solve for p when knowing i and n). Our example above is a case in which we need to solve for p when knowing i and n. To illustrate how we use a present value table, let's again look at how we estimate the present value of \$220 (f) at the end of one period (n) where the interest rate (i) is 10%. To answer this we go to the present value table (Table II.1) and look in the row for 1 period and in the column for 10% interest. Here we find a present value (p) of 0.9091 based on a future value of 1. This means, for instance, that \$1 to be received 1 period from today at 10% interest is worth \$0.9091 today. Since the future value is not \$1, but is \$220, we multiply the 0.9091 by \$220 to get an answer of \$200.

[2] A fourth is f, but as we already explained, we need only multiple the "1" used in the formula by f.

Case 2 (solve for n when knowing p and i). This is a case in which we have, say, a \$100,000 future value (f) valued at \$13,000 today (p) with an interest rate of 12% (i). In this case we want to know how many periods (n) there are between the present value and the future value. A case example is when we want to retire with \$100,000, but have only \$13,000 earning a 12% return. How long will it be before we can retire? To answer this we go to Table II.1 and look in the 12% interest column. Here we find a column of present values (p) based on a future value of 1. To use the present value table for this solution, we must divide \$13,000 (p) by \$100,000 (f), which equals 0.1300. This is necessary because a present value table defines f equal to 1, and p as a fraction of 1. We look for a value nearest to 0.1300 (p), which we find in the row for 18 periods (n). This means the present value of \$100,000 at the end of 18 periods at 12% interest is \$13,000 or, alternatively stated, we must work 18 more years.

Case 3 (solve for i when knowing p and n). This is a case where we have, say, a \$120,000 future value (f) valued at \$60,000 (p) today when there are nine periods (n) between the present and future values. Here we want to know what rate of interest is being used. As an example, suppose we want to retire with \$120,000, but we only have \$60,000 and hope to retire in nine years. What interest rate must we earn to retire with \$120,000 in nine years? To answer this we go to the present value table (Table II.1) and look in the row for nine periods. To again use the present value table we must divide \$60,000 (p) by \$120,000 (f), which equals 0.5000. Recall this is necessary because a present value table defines f equal to 1, and p as a fraction of 1. We look for a value in the row for nine periods that is nearest to 0.5000 (p), which we find in the column for 8% interest (i). This means the present value of \$120,000 at the end of nine periods at 8% interest is \$60,000 or, in our example, we must earn 8% annual interest to retire in nine years.

Flash back

1. A company is considering an investment expected to yield \$70,000 after six years. If this company demands an 8% return, how much is it willing to pay for this investment?

Answer—p. II-9

Future Value of a Single Amount

We use the formula for the present value of a single amount and modify it to obtain the formula for the future value of a single amount. To illustrate, we multiply both sides of the equation in Exhibit II.2 by $(1 + i)^n$. The result is shown in Exhibit II.4.

Exhibit II.4

Future Value of a Single Amount Formula

$$f = p \times (1 + i)^n$$

Future value (f) is defined in terms of p, i, and n. We can use this formula to determine that \$200 invested for 1 period at an interest rate of 10% increases to a future value of \$220 as follows:

LO3 Apply future value concepts to a single amount by using interest tables.

$$\begin{aligned} f &= p \times (1 + i)^n \\ &= \$200 \times (1 + .10)^1 \\ &= \$220 \end{aligned}$$

This formula can also be used to compute the future value of an amount for *any number of periods* into the future. As an example, assume $200 is invested for three periods at 10%. The future value of this $200 is $266.20 and is computed as:

$$f = p \times (1 + i)^n$$
$$= \$200 \times (1 + .10)^3$$
$$= \$266.20$$

It is also possible to use a future value table to compute future values (f) for many combinations of interest rates (i) and time periods (n). Each future value in a future value table assumes the present value (p) is 1. As with a present value table, if the future amount is something other than 1, we simply multiply our answer by that amount. The formula used to construct a table of future values of a single amount of 1 is shown in Exhibit II.5.

Exhibit II.5

Future Value of 1 Formula

$$f = (1 + i)^n$$

Table II.2 at the end of this appendix shows a table of future values of a single amount of 1. This type of table is called a **future value of 1 table.**

It is interesting to point out some items in Tables II.1 and II.2. Note in Table II.2 for the row where $n = 0$, that the future value is 1 for every interest rate. This is because no interest is earned when time does not pass. Also notice that Tables II.1 and II.2 report the same information in a different manner. In particular, one table is simply the inverse of the other.

To illustrate this inverse relation let's say we invest $100 annually for a period of five years at 12% per year. How much do we expect to have after five years? We can answer this question using Table II.2 by finding the future value (f) of 1, for five periods from now, compounded at 12%. From the table we find $f = 1.7623$. If we start with $100, the amount it accumulates to after five years is $176.23 ($100 × 1.7623).

We can alternatively use Table II.1. Here we find the present value (p) of 1, discounted five periods at 12%, is 0.5674. Recall the inverse relation between present value and future value. This means $p = 1/f$ (or equivalently $f = 1/p$).[3] Knowing this we can compute the future value of $100 invested for five periods at 12% as:

$$f = \$100 \times (1 / 0.5674) = \$176.24$$

A future value table involves three factors: f, i, and n. Knowing two of these three factors allows us to compute the third. To illustrate, consider the three possible cases.

Case 1 (solve for f when knowing i and n). Our example above is a case in which we need to solve for f when knowing i and n. We found that $100 invested for five periods at 12% interest accumulates to $176.24.

Case 2 (solve for n when knowing f and i). This is a case where we have, say, $2,000 ($p$) and we want to know how many periods (n) it will take to accumulate to $3,000 ($f$) at 7% ($i$) interest. To answer this, we go to the future value table (Table II.2) and look in the 7% interest column. Here we find a column of future values (f) based on a present value of 1. To use a future value table, we must divide $3,000 ($f$) by $2,000 ($p$), which equals 1.500. This is necessary because a future value table defines p equal to 1, and f as a multiple of 1. We

[3] Proof of this relation is left for advanced courses.

look for a value nearest to 1.50 (f), which we find in the row for six periods (n). This means \$2,000 invested for six periods at 7% interest accumulates to \$3,000.

Case 3 (solve for i when knowing f and n). This is a case where we have, say, \$2,001 (p) and in nine years (n) we want to have \$4,000 (f). What rate of interest must we earn to accomplish this? To answer this, we go to Table II.2 and search in the row for nine periods. To use a future value table, we must divide \$4,000 (f) by \$2,001 (p), which equals 1.9990. Recall this is necessary because a future value table defines p equal to 1, and f as a multiple of 1. We look for a value nearest to 1.9990 (f), which we find in the column for 8% interest (i). This means \$2,001 invested for nine periods at 8% interest accumulates to \$4,000.

Flash back

2. Assume you are a winner in a \$150,000 cash sweepstakes. You decide to deposit this cash in an account earning 8% annual interest and you plan to quit your job when the account equals \$555,000. How many years will it be before you can quit working?

Answers—p. II-9

Present Value of an Annuity

An annuity is a series of equal payments occurring at equal intervals. One example is a series of three annual payments of \$100 each. The present value of an ordinary annuity is defined as the present value of equal payments at equal intervals as of one period before the first payment. An ordinary annuity of \$100 and its present value (p) is illustrated in Exhibit II.6.

Exhibit II.6

Present Value of an Ordinary Annuity

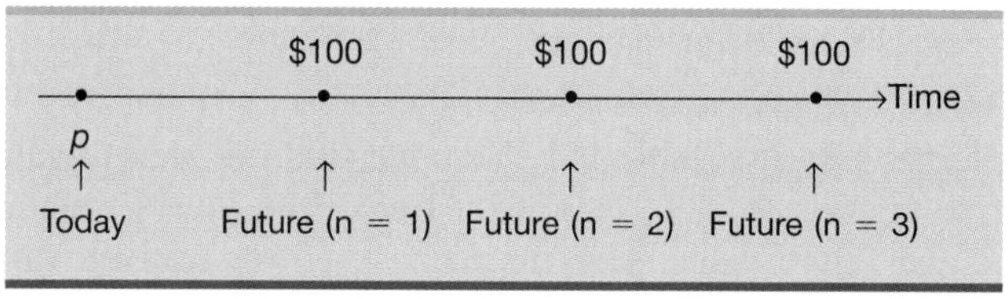

LO4 Apply present value concepts to an annuity by using interest tables.

One way for us to compute the present value of an ordinary annuity is to find the present value of each payment using our present value formula from Exhibit II.3. We then would add up each of the three present values. To illustrate, let's look at three, \$100 payments at the end of each of the next three periods with an interest rate of 15%. Our present value computations are:

$$p = \frac{\$100}{(1 + .15)^1} + \frac{\$100}{(1 + .15)^2} + \frac{\$100}{(1 + .15)^3} = \$228.32$$

This computation also is identical to computing the present value of each payment (from Table II.1) and taking their sum or, alternatively, adding the values from Table II.1 for each of the three payments and multiplying their sum by the \$100 annuity payment.

A more direct way is to use a present value of annuity table. Table II.3 at the end of this appendix is one such table. This table is called a **present value of an annuity of 1 table.** If we look at Table II.3 where $n = 3$ and $i = 15\%$, we see the present value is 2.2832. This means the present value of an annuity of 1 for 3 periods, with a 15% interest rate, is 2.2832.

A present value of annuity formula is used to construct Table II.3. It can also be constructed by adding the amounts in a present value of 1 table.[4] To illustrate, we use Tables II.1 and II.3 to confirm this relation for the prior example: We can also use business calculators or spreadsheet computer programs to find the present value of an annuity.

From Table II.1		From Table II.3	
$i = 15\%, n = 1$	0.8696		
$i = 15\%, n = 2$	0.7561		
$i = 15\%, n = 3$	0.6575		
Total	2.2832	$i = 15\%, n = 3$	2.2832

Flashback

3. A company is considering an investment paying $10,000 every six months for three years. The first payment would be received in six months. If this company requires an annual return of 8%, what is the maximum amount they are willing to invest?

Answer—p. II-9

Future Value of an Annuity

We can also compute the future value of an annuity. The future value of an *ordinary annuity* is the accumulated value of each annuity payment with interest as of the date of the final payment. To illustrate, let's consider the earlier annuity of three annual payments of $100. Exhibit II.7 shows the point in time for the future value (f). The first payment is made two periods prior to the point where future value is determined, and the final payment occurs on the future value date.

Exhibit II.7

Future Value of an Ordinary Annuity

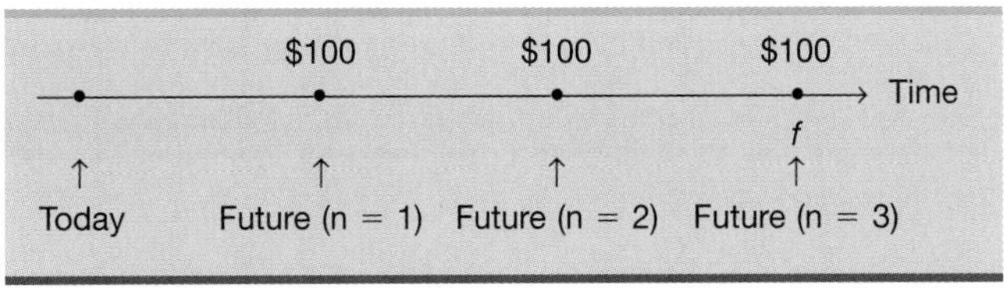

LO5 Apply future value concepts to an annuity by using interest tables.

One way to compute the future value of an annuity is to use the formula to find the future value of *each* payment and add them together. If we assume an interest rate of 15%, our calculation is:

$$f = \$100 \times (1 + .15)^2 + \$100 \times (1 + .15)^1 + \$100 \times (1 + .15)^0 = \$347.25$$

[4] The formula for the present value of an annuity of 1 is: $p = \dfrac{1 - \dfrac{1}{(1 + i)^n}}{i}$

This is identical to using Table II.2 and finding the sum of the future values of each payment, or adding the future values of the three payments of 1 and multiplying the sum by $100.

A more direct way is to use a table showing future values of annuities. Such a table is called a future value of an annuity of 1 table. Table II.4 at the end of this appendix is one such table. We should note in Table II.4 that when $n = 1$, the future values are equal to 1 ($f = 1$) for all rates of interest. That is because the annuity consists of only one payment and the future value is determined on the date of that payment — no time passes between the payment and its future value.

A formula is used to construct Table II.4.[5] We can also construct it by adding the amounts from a future value of 1 table. To illustrate, we use Tables II.2 and II.4 to confirm this relation for the prior example:

From Table II.2		From Table II.4	
$i = 15\%, n = 0$	1.0000		
$i = 15\%, n = 1$	1.1500		
$i = 15\%, n = 2$	1.3225		
Total	3.4725	$i = 15\%, n = 3$	3.4725

Note the future value in Table II.2 is 1.0000 when $n = 0$, but the future value in Table II.4 is 1.0000 when $n = 1$. Is this a contradiction? No. When $n = 0$ in Table II.2, the future value is determined on the date where a single payment occurs. This means no interest is earned, since no time has passed, and the future value equals the payment. Table II.4 describes annuities with equal payments occurring at the end of each period. When $n = 1$, the annuity has one payment, and its future value equals 1 on the date of its final and only payment. Again, no time passes from the payment and its future value date.

Flashback

4. A company invests $45,000 per year for five years at 12% annual interest. Compute the value of this annuity investment at the end of five years.

Answers—p. II-9

[5] The formula for the future value of an annuity of 1 is: $f = \frac{(1 + i)^n - 1}{i}$

Summary

LO1 Describe the earning of interest and the concepts of present and future values. Interest is payment to the owner of an asset for its use by a borrower. Present and future value computations are a way for us to estimate the interest component of holding assets or liabilities over a period of time.

LO2 Apply present value concepts to a single amount by using interest tables. The present value of a single amount to be received at a future date is the amount that can be invested now at the specified interest rate to yield that future value.

LO3 Apply future value concepts to a single amount by using interest tables. The future value of a single amount invested at a specified rate of interest is the amount that would accumulate at a future date.

LO4 Apply present value concepts to an annuity by using interest tables. The present value of an annuity is the amount that can be invested now at the specified interest rate to yield that series of equal periodic payments.

LO5 Apply future value concepts to an annuity by using interest tables. The future value of an annuity to be invested at a specific rate of interest is the amount that would accumulate at the date of the final equal periodic payment.

Guidance Answers to Flashbacks

1. $70,000 × 0.6302 = $44,114 (using Table II.1, $i = 8\%$, $n = 6$).
2. $555,000/$150,000 = 3.7000; Table II.2 shows this value is not achieved until after 17 years at 8% interest.
3. $10,000 × 5.2421 = $52,421 (using Table II.3, $i = 4\%$, $n = 6$).
4. $45,000 × 6.3528 = $285,876 (using Table II.4, $i = 12\%$, $n = 5$).

Quick Study

QS II-1 Identifying interest rates in tables LO1

You are asked to make future value estimates using the future value of 1 table (Table II.2). Which interest rate column do you use when working with the following rates?

a. 8% compounded quarterly
b. 12% compounded annually
c. 6% compounded semiannually
d. 12% compounded monthly

QS II-2 Present value of an amount LO2

Flaherty is considering an investment which, if paid for immediately, is expected to return $140,000 five years hence. If Flaherty demands a 9% return, how much is she willing to pay for this investment?

QS II-3 Future value of an amount LO3

CII, Inc., invested $630,000 in a project expected to earn a 12% annual rate of return. The earnings will be reinvested in the project each year until the entire investment is liquidated 10 years hence. What will the cash proceeds be when the project is liquidated?

QS II-4 Present value of an annuity LO4

Beene Distributing is considering a contract that will return $150,000 annually at the end of each year for six years. If Beene demands an annual return of 7% and pays for the investment immediately, how much should it be willing to pay?

QS II-5
Future value of an annuity
L05

Claire Fitch is planning to begin an individual retirement program in which she will invest $1,500 annually at the end of each year. Fitch plans to retire after making 30 annual investments in a program that earns a return of 10%. What will be the value of the program on the date of the last investment?

QS II-6
Interest rate on an investment
L02

Ken Francis has been offered the possibility of investing $2,745 for 15 years, after which he will be paid $10,000. What annual rate of interest will Francis earn? (Use Table II.1.)

QS II-7
Number of periods of an investment
L02

Megan Brink has been offered the possibility of investing $6,651. The investment will earn 6% per year and will return Brink $10,000 at the end of the investment. How many years must Brink wait to receive the $10,000? (Use Table II.1.)

Exercises

Exercise II-1
Using present and future value tables
L01

For each of the following situations identify (1) it as either (a) present or future value and (b) single amount or annuity case, (2) the table you would use in your computations (but do not solve the problem), and (3) the interest rate and time periods you would use.

a. You need to accumulate $10,000 for a trip you wish to take in four years. You are able to earn 8% compounded semiannually on your savings. You only plan on making one deposit and letting the money accumulate for four years. How would you determine the amount of the one-time deposit?

b. Assume the same facts as in (a), except you will make semiannual deposits to your savings account.

c. You hope to retire after working 40 years with savings in excess of $1,000,000. You expect to save $4,000 a year for 40 years and earn an annual rate of interest of 8%. Will you be able to retire with more than $1,000,000 in 40 years?

d. A sweepstakes agency names you a grand prize winner. You can take $225,000 immediately or elect to receive annual installments of $30,000 for 20 years. You can earn 10% annually on investments you make. Which prize do you choose to receive?

Exercise II-2
Number of periods of an investment
L02

Bill Thompson expects to invest $10,000 at 12% and, at the end of the investment, receive $96,463. How many years will elapse before Thompson receives the payment? (Use Table II.2.)

Exercise II-3
Interest rate on an investment
L02

Ed Summers expects to invest $10,000 for 25 years, after which he will receive $108,347. What rate of interest will Summers earn? (Use Table II.2.)

Exercise II-4
Interest rate on an investment
L04

Betsey Jones expects an immediate investment of $57,466 to return $10,000 annually for eight years, with the first payment to be received in one year. What rate of interest will Jones earn? (Use Table II.3.)

Exercise II-5
Number of periods of an investment
LO4

Keith Riggins expects an investment of $82,014 to return $10,000 annually for several years. If Riggins is to earn a return of 10%, how many annual payments must he receive? (Use Table II.3.)

Exercise II-6
Interest rate on an investment
LO5

Steve Algoe expects to invest $1,000 annually for 40 years and have an accumulated value of $154,762 on the date of the last investment. If this occurs, what rate of interest will Algoe earn? (Use Table II.4.)

Exercise II-7
Number of periods of an investment
LO5

Katherine Beckwith expects to invest $10,000 annually that will earn 8%. How many annual investments must Beckwith make to accumulate $303,243 on the date of the last investment? (Use Table II.4.)

Exercise II-8
Present value of an annuity
LO4

Sam Weber financed a new automobile by paying $6,500 cash and agreeing to make 40 monthly payments of $500 each, the first payment to be made one month after the purchase. The loan bears interest at an annual rate of 12%. What was the cost of the automobile?

Exercise II-9
Future value of an amount
LO3

Mark Welsch deposited $7,200 in a savings account that earns interest at an annual rate of 8%, compounded quarterly. The $7,200 plus earned interest must remain in the account 10 years before it can be withdrawn. How much money will be in the account at the end of the 10 years?

Exercise II-10
Future value of an annuity
LO4

Kelly Malone plans to have $50 withheld from her monthly paycheque and deposited in a savings account that earns 12% annually, compounded monthly. If Malone continues with her plan for 2 1/2 years, how much will be accumulated in the account on the date of the last deposit?

Exercise II-11
Present value of bonds
LO2, 3

Spiller Corp. plans to issue 10%, 15-year, $500,000 par value bonds payable that pay interest semiannually on June 30 and December 31. The bonds are dated December 31, 1999, and are to be issued on that date. If the market rate of interest for the bonds is 8% on the date of issue, what will be the cash proceeds from the bond issue?

Exercise II-12
Future value of an amount plus an annuity
LO3,5

Starr Company has decided to establish a fund that will be used 10 years hence to replace an aging productive facility. The company will make an initial contribution of $100,000 to the fund and plans to make quarterly contributions of $50,000 beginning in three months. The fund is expected to earn 12%, compounded quarterly. What will be the value of the fund 10 years hence?

Exercise II-13
Present value of an amount
LO3

McAdams Company expects to earn 10% per year on an investment that will pay $606,773 six years hence. Use Table II.1 to compute the present value of the investment.

Exercise II-14
Future value of an amount
LO3

Catten, Inc., invests $163,170 at 7% per year for nine years. Use Table II.2 to compute the future value of the investment nine years hence.

Exercise II-15
Present value of an amount and annuity
LO2, 4

Compute the amount that can be borrowed under each of the following circumstances:

a. A promise to pay $90,000 in seven years at an interest rate of 6%.

b. An agreement made on February 1, 2000, to make three payments of $20,000 on February 1 of 2001, 2002, and 2003. The annual interest rate is 10%.

Exercise II-16
Present value of an amount
LO2

On January 1, 2000, a company agrees to pay $20,000 in three years. If the annual interest rate is 10%, determine how much cash the company can borrow with this promise.

Exercise II-17
Present value of an amount
LO2

Find the amount of money that can be borrowed with each of the following promises:

Case	Single Future Payment	Number of Years	Interest Rate
a.	$ 40,000	3	4%
b.	75,000	7	8%
c.	52,000	9	10%
d.	18,000	2	4%
e.	63,000	8	6%
f.	89,000	5	2%

Exercise II-18
Present values of annuities
LO4

C&H Ski Club recently borrowed money and agreed to pay it back with a series of six annual payments of $5,000 each. C&H subsequently borrowed more money and agreed to pay it back with a series of four annual payments of $7,500 each. The annual interest rate for both loans is 6%.

a. Use Table II.1 to find the present value of these two annuities. (Round amounts to the nearest dollar.)

b. Use Table II.3 to find the present value of these two annuities.

Exercise II-19
Present value with semiannual compounding
LO1, 4

Otto Co. borrowed cash on April 30, 2000, by promising to make four payments of $13,000 each on November 1, 2000, May 1, 2001, November 1, 2001, and May 1, 2002.

a. How much cash is Otto able to borrow if the interest rate is 8%, compounded semiannually?

b. How much cash is Otto able to borrow if the interest rate is 12%, compounded semiannually?

c. How much cash is Otto able to borrow if the interest rate is 16%, compounded semiannually?

Table II.1

Present Value of 1 Due in *n* Periods

	Rate											
Periods	1%	2%	3%	4%	5%	6%	7%	8%	9%	10%	12%	15%
1	0.9901	0.9804	0.9709	0.9615	0.9524	0.9434	0.9346	0.9259	0.9174	0.9091	0.8929	0.8696
2	0.9803	0.9612	0.9426	0.9246	0.9070	0.8900	0.8734	0.8573	0.8417	0.8264	0.7972	0.7561
3	0.9706	0.9423	0.9151	0.8890	0.8638	0.8396	0.8163	0.7938	0.7722	0.7513	0.7118	0.6575
4	0.9610	0.9238	0.8885	0.8548	0.8227	0.7921	0.7629	0.7350	0.7084	0.6830	0.6355	0.5718
5	0.9515	0.9057	0.8626	0.8219	0.7835	0.7473	0.7130	0.6806	0.6499	0.6209	0.5674	0.4972
6	0.9420	0.8880	0.8375	0.7903	0.7462	0.7050	0.6663	0.6302	0.5963	0.5645	0.5066	0.4323
7	0.9327	0.8706	0.8131	0.7599	0.7107	0.6651	0.6227	0.5835	0.5470	0.5132	0.4523	0.3759
8	0.9235	0.8535	0.7894	0.7307	0.6768	0.6274	0.5820	0.5403	0.5019	0.4665	0.4039	0.3269
9	0.9143	0.8368	0.7664	0.7026	0.6446	0.5919	0.5439	0.5002	0.4604	0.4241	0.3606	0.2843
10	0.9053	0.8203	0.7441	0.6756	0.6139	0.5584	0.5083	0.4632	0.4224	0.3855	0.3220	0.2472
11	0.8963	0.8043	0.7224	0.6496	0.5847	0.5268	0.4751	0.4289	0.3875	0.3505	0.2875	0.2149
12	0.8874	0.7885	0.7014	0.6246	0.5568	0.4970	0.4440	0.3971	0.3555	0.3186	0.2567	0.1869
13	0.8787	0.7730	0.6810	0.6006	0.5303	0.4688	0.4150	0.3677	0.3262	0.2897	0.2292	0.1625
14	0.8700	0.7579	0.6611	0.5775	0.5051	0.4423	0.3878	0.3405	0.2992	0.2633	0.2046	0.1413
15	0.8613	0.7430	0.6419	0.5553	0.4810	0.4173	0.3624	0.3152	0.2745	0.2394	0.1827	0.1229
16	0.8528	0.7284	0.6232	0.5339	0.4581	0.3936	0.3387	0.2919	0.2519	0.2176	0.1631	0.1069
17	0.8444	0.7142	0.6050	0.5134	0.4363	0.3714	0.3166	0.2703	0.2311	0.1978	0.1456	0.0929
18	0.8360	0.7002	0.5874	0.4936	0.4155	0.3503	0.2959	0.2502	0.2120	0.1799	0.1300	0.0808
19	0.8277	0.6864	0.5703	0.4746	0.3957	0.3305	0.2765	0.2317	0.1945	0.1635	0.1161	0.0703
20	0.8195	0.6730	0.5537	0.4564	0.3769	0.3118	0.2584	0.2145	0.1784	0.1486	0.1037	0.0611
25	0.7798	0.6095	0.4776	0.3751	0.2953	0.2330	0.1842	0.1460	0.1160	0.0923	0.0588	0.0304
30	0.7419	0.5521	0.4120	0.3083	0.2314	0.1741	0.1314	0.0994	0.0754	0.0573	0.0334	0.0151
35	0.7059	0.5000	0.3554	0.2534	0.1813	0.1301	0.0937	0.0676	0.0490	0.0356	0.0189	0.0075
40	0.6717	0.4529	0.3066	0.2083	0.1420	0.0972	0.0668	0.0460	0.0318	0.0221	0.0107	0.0037

Table II.2

Future Value of 1 Due in *n* Periods

	Rate											
Periods	1%	2%	3%	4%	5%	6%	7%	8%	9%	10%	12%	15%
0	1.0000	1.0000	1.0000	1.0000	1.0000	1.0000	1.0000	1.0000	1.0000	1.0000	1.0000	1.0000
1	1.0100	1.0200	1.0300	1.0400	1.0500	1.0600	1.0700	1.0800	1.0900	1.1000	1.1200	1.1500
2	1.0201	1.0404	1.0609	1.0816	1.1025	1.1236	1.1449	1.1664	1.1811	1.2100	1.2544	1.3225
3	1.0303	1.0612	1.0927	1.1249	1.1576	1.1910	1.2250	1.2597	1.2950	1.3310	1.4049	1.5209
4	1.0406	1.0824	1.1255	1.1699	1.2155	1.2625	1.3108	1.3605	1.4116	1.4641	1.5735	1.7490
5	1.0510	1.1041	1.1593	1.2167	1.2763	1.3382	1.4026	1.4693	1.5386	1.6105	1.7623	2.0114
6	1.0615	1.1262	1.1941	1.2653	1.3401	1.4185	1.5007	1.5869	1.6771	1.7116	1.9738	2.3131
7	1.0721	1.1487	1.2299	1.3159	1.4071	1.5036	1.6058	1.7138	1.8280	1.9487	2.2107	2.6600
8	1.0829	1.1717	1.2668	1.3686	1.4775	1.5938	1.7182	1.8509	1.9926	2.1436	2.4760	3.0590
9	1.0937	1.1951	1.3048	1.4233	1.5513	1.6895	1.8385	1.9990	2.1719	2.3579	2.7731	3.5179
10	1.1046	1.2190	1.3439	1.4802	1.6289	1.7908	1.9672	2.1589	2.3674	2.5937	3.1058	4.0456
11	1.1157	1.2434	1.3842	1.5395	1.7103	1.8983	2.1049	2.3316	2.5804	2.8531	3.4785	4.6524
12	1.1268	1.2682	1.4258	1.6010	1.7959	2.0122	2.2522	2.5182	2.8127	3.1384	3.8960	5.3503
13	1.1381	1.2936	1.4685	1.6651	1.8856	2.1329	2.4098	2.7196	3.0658	3.4523	4.3635	6.1528
14	1.1495	1.3195	1.5126	1.7317	1.9799	2.2609	2.5785	2.9372	3.3417	3.7975	4.8871	7.0757
15	1.1610	1.3459	1.5580	1.8009	2.0789	2.3966	2.7590	3.1722	3.6425	4.1772	5.4736	8.1371
16	1.1726	1.3728	1.6047	1.8730	2.1829	2.5404	2.9522	3.4259	3.9703	4.5950	6.1304	9.3576
17	1.1843	1.4002	1.6528	1.9479	2.2920	2.6928	3.1588	3.7000	4.3276	5.0545	6.8660	10.7613
18	1.1961	1.4282	1.7024	2.0258	2.4066	2.8543	3.3799	3.9960	4.7171	5.5599	7.6900	12.3755
19	1.2081	1.4568	1.7535	2.1068	2.5270	3.0256	3.6165	4.3157	5.1417	6.1159	8.6128	14.2318
20	1.2202	1.4859	1.8061	2.1911	2.6533	3.2071	3.8697	4.6610	5.6044	6.7275	9.6463	16.3665
25	1.2824	1.6406	2.0938	2.6658	3.3864	4.2919	5.4274	6.8485	8.6231	10.8347	17.0001	32.9190
30	1.3478	1.8114	2.4273	3.2434	4.3219	5.7435	7.6123	10.0627	13.2677	17.4494	29.9599	66.2118
35	1.4166	1.9999	2.8139	3.9461	5.5160	7.6861	10.6766	14.7853	20.4140	28.1024	52.7996	133.176
40	1.4889	2.2080	3.2620	4.8010	7.0400	10.2857	14.9745	21.7245	31.4094	45.2593	93.0510	267.864

Table II.3

Present Value of an Annuity of 1 per Period

Periods	Rate 1%	2%	3%	4%	5%	6%	7%	8%	9%	10%	12%	15%
1	0.9901	0.9804	0.9709	0.9615	0.9524	0.9434	0.9346	0.9259	0.9174	0.9091	0.8929	0.8696
2	1.9704	1.9416	1.9135	1.8861	1.8594	1.8334	1.8080	1.7833	1.7591	1.7355	1.6901	1.6257
3	2.9410	2.8839	2.8286	2.7751	2.7232	2.6730	2.6243	2.5771	2.5313	2.4869	2.4018	2.2832
4	3.9020	3.8077	3.7171	3.6299	3.5460	3.4651	3.3872	3.3121	3.2397	3.1699	3.0373	2.8550
5	4.8534	4.7135	4.5797	4.4518	4.3295	4.2124	4.1002	3.9927	3.8897	3.7908	3.6048	3.3522
6	5.7955	5.6014	5.4172	5.2421	5.0757	4.9173	4.7665	4.6229	4.4859	4.3553	4.1114	3.7845
7	6.7282	6.4720	6.2303	6.0021	5.7864	5.5824	5.3893	5.2064	5.0330	4.8684	4.5638	4.1604
8	7.6517	7.3255	7.0197	6.7327	6.4632	6.2098	5.9713	5.7466	5.5348	5.3349	4.9676	4.4873
9	8.5660	8.1622	7.7861	7.4353	7.1078	6.8017	6.5152	6.2469	5.9952	5.7950	5.3282	4.7716
10	9.4713	8.9826	8.5302	8.1109	7.7217	7.3601	7.0236	6.7101	6.4177	6.1446	5.6502	5.0188
11	10.3676	9.7868	9.2526	8.7605	8.3064	7.8869	7.4987	7.1390	6.8052	6.4951	5.9377	5.2337
12	11.2551	10.5753	9.9540	9.3851	8.8633	8.3838	7.9427	7.5361	7.1607	6.8137	6.1944	5.4206
13	12.1337	11.3484	10.6350	9.9856	9.3936	8.8527	8.3577	7.9038	7.4869	7.1034	6.4235	5.5831
14	13.0037	12.1062	11.2961	10.5631	9.8986	9.2950	8.7455	8.2442	7.7862	7.3667	6.6282	5.7245
15	13.8651	12.8493	11.9379	11.1184	10.3797	9.7122	9.1079	8.5595	8.0607	7.6061	6.8109	5.8474
16	14.7179	13.5777	12.5611	11.6523	10.8378	10.1059	9.4466	8.8514	8.3126	7.8237	6.9740	5.9542
17	15.5623	14.2919	13.1661	12.1657	11.2741	10.4773	9.7632	9.1216	8.5436	8.0216	7.1196	6.0472
18	16.3983	14.9920	13.7535	12.6593	11.6896	10.8276	10.0591	9.3719	8.7556	8.2014	7.2497	6.1280
19	17.2260	15.6785	14.3238	13.1339	12.0853	11.1581	10.3356	9.6036	8.9501	8.3649	7.3658	6.1982
20	18.0456	16.3514	14.8775	13.5903	12.4622	11.4699	10.5940	9.8181	9.1285	8.5136	7.4694	6.2593
25	22.0232	19.5235	17.4131	15.6221	14.0939	12.7834	11.6536	10.6748	9.8226	9.0770	7.8431	6.4641
30	25.8077	22.3965	19.6004	17.2920	15.3725	13.7648	12.4090	11.2578	10.2737	9.4269	8.0552	6.5660
35	29.4086	24.9986	21.4872	18.6646	16.3742	14.4982	12.9477	11.6546	10.5668	9.6442	8.1755	6.6166
40	32.8347	27.3555	23.1148	19.7928	17.1591	15.0463	13.3317	11.9246	10.7574	9.7791	8.2438	6.6418

Table II.4

Future Value of an Annuity of 1 per Period

Periods	Rate 1%	2%	3%	4%	5%	6%	7%	8%	9%	10%	12%	15%
1	1.0000	1.0000	1.0000	1.0000	1.0000	1.0000	1.0000	1.0000	1.0000	1.0000	1.0000	1.0000
2	2.0100	2.0200	2.0300	2.0400	2.0500	2.0600	2.0700	2.0800	2.0900	2.1000	2.1200	2.1500
3	3.0301	3.0604	3.0909	3.1216	3.1525	3.1836	3.2149	3.2464	3.2781	3.3100	3.3744	3.4725
4	4.0604	4.1216	4.1836	4.2465	4.3101	4.3746	4.4399	4.5061	4.5731	4.6410	4.7793	4.9934
5	5.1010	5.2040	5.3091	5.4163	5.5256	5.6371	5.7507	5.8666	5.9847	6.1051	6.3528	6.7424
6	6.1520	6.3081	6.4684	6.6330	6.8019	6.9753	7.1533	7.3359	7.5233	7.7156	8.1152	8.7537
7	7.2135	7.4343	7.6625	7.8983	8.1420	8.3938	8.6540	8.9228	9.2004	9.4872	10.0890	11.0668
8	8.2857	8.5830	8.8923	9.2142	9.5491	9.8975	10.2598	10.6366	11.0285	11.4359	12.2997	13.7268
9	9.3685	9.7546	10.1591	10.5828	11.0266	11.4913	11.9780	12.4876	13.0210	13.5795	14.7757	16.7858
10	10.4622	10.9497	11.4639	12.0061	12.5779	13.1808	13.8164	14.4866	15.1929	15.9374	17.5487	20.3037
11	11.5668	12.1687	12.8078	13.4864	14.2068	14.9716	15.7835	16.6455	17.5603	18.5312	20.6546	24.3493
12	12.6825	13.4121	14.1920	15.0258	15.9171	16.8699	17.8885	18.9771	20.1407	21.3843	24.1331	29.0017
13	13.8093	14.6803	15.6178	16.6268	17.7130	18.8821	20.1406	21.4953	22.9534	24.5227	28.0291	34.3519
14	14.9474	15.9739	17.0863	18.2919	19.5986	21.0151	22.5505	24.2149	26.0192	27.9750	32.3926	40.5047
15	16.0969	17.2934	18.5989	20.0236	21.5786	23.2760	25.1290	27.1521	29.3609	31.7725	37.2797	47.5804
16	17.2579	18.6393	20.1569	21.8245	23.6575	25.6725	27.8881	30.3243	33.0034	35.9497	42.7533	55.7175
17	18.4304	20.012	21.7616	23.6975	25.8404	28.2129	30.8402	33.7502	36.9737	40.5447	48.8837	65.0751
18	19.6147	21.4123	23.4144	25.6454	28.1324	30.9057	33.9990	37.4502	41.3013	45.5992	55.7497	75.8364
19	20.8109	22.8406	25.1169	27.6712	30.5390	33.7600	37.3790	41.4463	46.0185	41.1591	63.4397	88.2118
20	22.0190	24.2974	26.8704	29.7781	33.0660	36.7856	40.9955	45.7620	51.1601	57.2750	72.0524	102.444
25	28.2432	32.0303	36.4593	41.6459	47.7271	54.8645	63.2490	73.1059	84.7009	98.3471	133.334	212.793
30	34.7849	40.5681	47.5754	56.0849	66.4388	79.0582	94.4608	113.283	136.308	164.494	241.333	434.745
35	41.6603	49.9945	60.4621	73.6522	90.3203	111.435	138.237	172.317	215.711	271.024	431.663	881.170
40	48.8864	60.4020	75.4013	95.0255	120.800	154.762	199.635	259.057	337.882	442.593	767.091	1,779.09

Accounting Concepts and Alternative Valuations

III

APPENDIX

Chapter Outine

Section 1— Accounting Concepts

- **Accounting Concepts and Principles**
- **Descriptive and Prescriptive Concepts**
- **Financial Statement Concepts**
  - Objectives of Financial Reporting
  - Qualities of Useful Information
  - Elements of Financial Statements
  - Recognition and Measurement

Section 2—Alternative Accounting Valuations

- **Historical Cost Accounting and Price Changes**
  - Impact of Price Changes on the Balance Sheet
  - Impact of Price Changes on the Income Statement
- **Valuation Alternatives to Historical Cost**
  - Constant Dollar Accounting
  - Current Cost Accounting
  - Mark to Market Accounting

APPENDIX PREVIEW

Accounting concepts are not laws of nature. They are broad ideas developed as a way of *describing* current accounting practices and *prescribing* new and improved practices. In this Appendix we explain the accounting concepts the CICA developed in an effort to guide future changes and improvements in accounting. We also discuss alternatives to the historical cost measurements reported in financial statements. Understanding these alternatives helps us with interpreting information in these statements.

A Look At This Appendix

This appendix describes accounting concepts, how they are developed, and the conceptual framework in accounting. It also discusses alternative valuations to historical cost accounting.

Learning Objectives

LO 1 Explain both descriptive and prescriptive concepts and their development.

LO 2 Describe the financial statement concepts for accounting.

LO 3 Explain how price changes impact conventional financial statements.

LO 4 Discuss valuation alternatives to historical cost.

SECTION 1 ACCOUNTING CONCEPTS

Accounting Concepts and Principles

LO1 Explain both descriptive and prescriptive concepts and their development.

Accounting *concepts* serve two main purposes. First, they provide descriptions of existing accounting practices. They act as guidelines that help us understand and use accounting information. Knowing how concepts are applied enables us to effectively use accounting information in different situations, and understanding accounting concepts is easier and more useful than memorizing a long list of procedures. Second, accounting concepts are important for the Accounting Standards Board (AcSB), which is charged with developing acceptable practices for financial reporting in Canada and with improving the quality of such reporting.

We defined and illustrated several important accounting *principles* in this book. Several of these major principles are listed in Exhibit III.1. Accounting principles describe in general terms the practices as currently applied.

We first explained these principles in Chapter 2, but we referred to them frequently in the book. The term *concepts* include both these principles as well as other general rules. The AcSB also uses the word *concepts* in this same way.

Exhibit III.1

Partial List of Accounting Principles

- **Business entity principle**
- **Conservatism principle**
- **Consistency principle**
- **Cost principle**
- **Full-disclosure principle**
- **Going-concern principle**
- **Matching principle**
- **Materiality principle**
- **Objectivity principle**
- **Revenue recognition principle**
- **Time period principle**

As business practices evolved in recent years, accounting concepts were sometimes difficult to apply in dealing with new and different types of transactions. This occurs because they are intended as general descriptions of current accounting practices. They do not necessarily describe what should be done. Since concepts do not identify weaknesses in accounting practices, they do not lead to major changes or improvements in accounting practices.

The AcSB, however, is charged with improving financial reporting. It was generally agreed that a new set of concepts needed to be developed for this purpose. They also decided this new set of concepts should not merely *describe* what is being done in current practice. Instead, the new concepts should *prescribe* (or guide) what ought to be done to improve things. Before we describe the concepts developed by the AcSB, we look more closely at the differences between descriptive and prescriptive uses of accounting concepts.

Descriptive and Prescriptive Concepts

Concepts differ in how they are developed and used. Generally, when concepts are intended to describe current practice, they are developed by looking at accepted practices and then making rules to encompass them. This bottom-up, or *descriptive*, approach is shown in Exhibit III.2.

Exhibit III.2

"Bottom-Up" Development of Descriptive Concepts

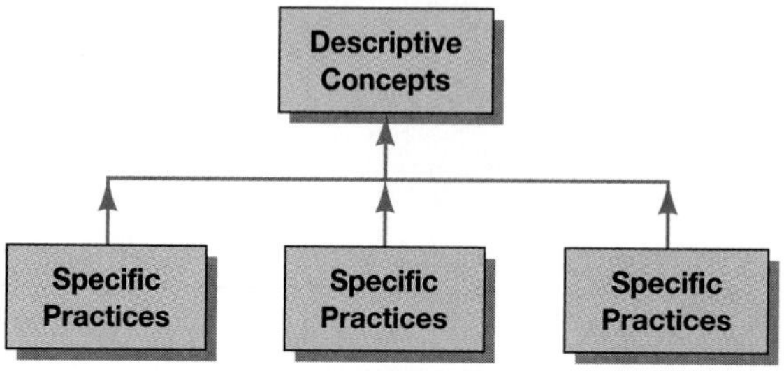

It shows arrows going from specific practices to concepts. The outcome of this process is a set of concepts that summarize practice. This process, for instance, leads us to the concept that asset purchases are recorded at cost.

But these concepts often fail to show how new problems might be solved. For example, the concept that assets are recorded at cost doesn't provide direct guidance for situations where assets have no cost because they are donated to a company by a local government. The bottom-up approach is based on the presumption that current practices are adequate. They don't lead to development of new and improved accounting methods. The concept that assets are initially recorded at cost doesn't encourage asking the question of whether they should always be carried at that amount.

Alternatively, when concepts are intended to *prescribe* (or guide) improvements in accounting practice, they are likely to be designed by a top-down approach as shown in Exhibit III.3.

Exhibit III.3

"Top-Down" Development of Prescriptive Concepts

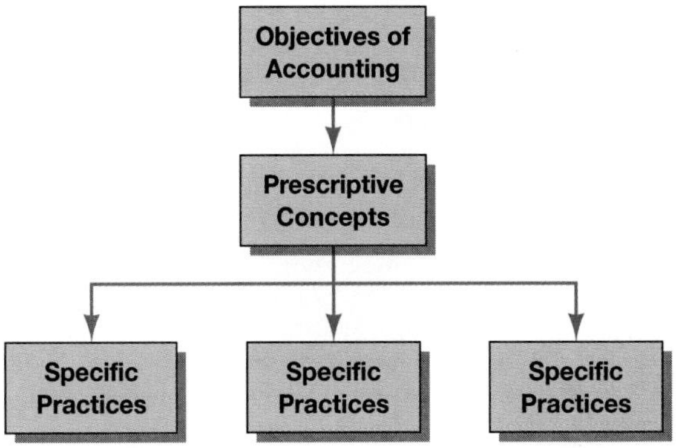

The top-down approach starts with broad accounting objectives. The process then generates broad concepts about the types of information that should be reported. These concepts lead to specific practices that ought to be used. The advantage of this approach is that these concepts are good for solving new problems and evaluating old answers. Its disadvantage is the concepts may not be very descriptive of current practice. The suggested practices may not even be in current use.

Since the AcSB uses accounting concepts to prescribe accounting practices, the Board used a top-down approach. The Board's concepts are not necessarily more correct than others. But new concepts are intended to provide better guidelines for developing new and improved accounting practices. The AcSB continues to use them as a basis for future actions and already has used them to justify many important changes in financial reporting.

It is crucial in setting accounting standards that the issues be properly identified and described. Section 1000, "Financial Statement Concepts" of the *CICA Handbook* helps the AcSB do this by providing common objectives and terms. Section 1000 also helps the Board focus on the important factors in accounting standard setting and, hopefully, reduces some of the political aspects of policy making.

Flash back

III-1. What is the starting point in a top-down approach to developing accounting concepts?

III-2. What is the starting point in a bottom-up approach to developing accounting concepts?

Answers—p. III-9

Financial Statement Concepts

LO 2 Describe the financial statement concepts for accounting.

During the 1970s the accounting profession in both Canada and the United States turned its attention to the apparent need for improvement in financial reporting. In 1980 *Corporate Reporting: Its Future Evolution,* a research study, was published by the Canadian Institute of Chartered Accountants, and in 1989 "Financial Statement Concepts," section 1000 of the *CICA Handbook,* was approved. In the United States the Financial Accounting Standards Board (FASB) published, in the 1978–85 period, six statements regarded as the most comprehensive pronouncement of the conceptual framework of accounting. FASB (SFAC 1) and Accounting Standards Board (*CICA Handbook,* section 1000) identified the broad objectives of financial reporting.

The Financial Accounting Standard Board's approach to developing a conceptual framework is diagrammed in Exhibit III.4. The Board has issued six

Statements of Financial Accounting Concepts (SFAC). These concepts statements are not the same as the FASB's *Statements of Financial Accounting Standards (SFAS)*. The *SFASs* are authoritative statements of generally accepted accounting principles, whereas the *SFACs* are guidelines the Board uses in developing new standards. Accounting professionals are not required to follow the *SFACs* in practice.

Exhibit III.4

Conceptual Framework

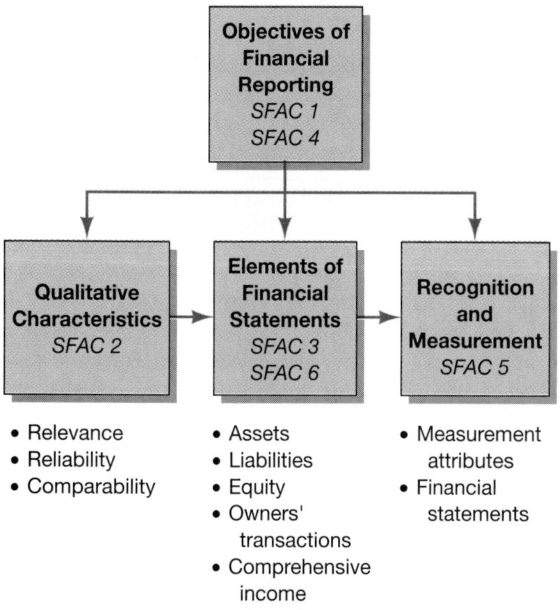

Objectives of Financial Reporting

"Financial Statement Concepts" identified the broad objectives of financial reporting. The most general objective stated in the *CICA Handbook,* par. 1000.12, is to "communicate information that is useful to investors, creditors, and other users in making resource allocation decisions and/or assessing management stewardship." From this beginning point the Accounting Standards Board (AcSB) expressed other, more specific objectives. These objectives recognize that (1) financial reporting should help users predict future cash flow and (2) in making such predictions, information about a company's resources and obligations is useful if it possesses certain qualities. All of the concepts in the "Financial Statement Concepts" are intended to be consistent with these general objectives. Of course, present accounting practice already provides information about a company's resources and obligations. Thus, although the conceptual framework is intended to be prescriptive of new and improved practices, the concepts in the framework are also descriptive of many current practices.

Did You Know?

On-Line Concepts
The CICA has a Web site [www.cica.ca] where we can access exposure drafts and the latest news from the Accounting Standards Board. This site also provides access to many current standards and happenings in accounting.

Qualities of Useful Information

Exhibit III.4 shows the next step in the conceptual framework was to identify the qualities (or qualitative characteristics) that financial information should have if it is to be useful in decision making. The Board discussed the fact that information is useful only if it is understandable to users. But the Board assumed users have the training, experience, and motivation to analyze financial reports. With this decision, the Board indicated financial reporting should not try to meet the needs of unsophisticated or casual users.

In *Section 1000*, the Board stated information is useful if it is (1) relevant, (2) reliable, and (3) comparable. Information is *relevant* if it can make a difference in a decision. Information has this quality when it helps users predict the future or evaluate the past and is received in time to affect their decisions.

Information is *reliable* if users can depend on it to be free from bias and error. Reliable information is verifiable and faithfully represents what is intended to be described. Users can depend on information only if it is neutral. This means the rules used to produce information are not designed to lead users to accept or reject any specific decision.

Information is *comparable* if users can use it to identify differences and similarities between companies. Complete comparability is possible only if companies follow uniform practices. But even if all companies uniformly follow the same practices, comparable reports do not result if the practices are inappropriate. For example, comparable information is not provided if all companies ignored the useful lives of their assets and depreciate them over two years.

Comparability also requires consistency (see Chapter 7). This means a company should not change its accounting practices unless the change is justified as a reporting improvement. Another important concept discussed in *Section 1000* is materiality (see Chapter 10). An item is material if it affects decisions of users. Items not material are often accounted for in the easiest way possible using cost-benefit criteria.

Elements of Financial Statements

Exhibit III.4 shows an important part of the conceptual framework is the elements of financial statements. This includes defining the categories of information that are contained in financial statements. The Board's discussion of financial statement elements included defining important items such as assets, liabilities, equity, revenues, expenses, gains and losses. In earlier chapters, we drew on many of these definitions. Recently, the Board has issued recommendations for not-for-profit accounting entities.[1]

Recognition and Measurement

The Board has established concepts for deciding (1) when items should be presented (or recognized) in financial statements and (2) how to assign numbers to (or measure) those items. The Board generally concluded that items should be recognized in financial statements if they meet the following criteria:

Defined.	Item meets the definition of an element of financial statements.
Measurable.	Has a relevant attribute measurable with sufficient reliability.
Relevant.	Information about it is capable of making a difference in user decisions.
Reliable.	Information is representationally faithful, verifiable, and neutral.

The question of how an item is measured raises a fundamental question of whether financial statements should be based on cost or on current value. The Board's discussion of this issue is more descriptive of current practice than it is prescriptive of new measurement methods.

Paragraph 1000.04 of the *CICA Handbook* states that a full set of financial statements should show:

1. Balance Sheet (financial position at the end of the period.)
2. Income Statement (earnings for the period.)
3. Statement of Retained Earnings
4. Statement of Cash Flows (cash flows during the period.)
5. Notes to financial statements and supporting schedules to which the financial statements are cross-referenced are an integral part of such statements.

---

[1] *CICA Handbook,* sections 4400ff, "Not-for-Profit Organizations."

Flashback

III-3. The AcSB's financial statement concepts are intended to:

a. Provide a historical analysis of accounting practice.

b. Describe current accounting practice.

c. Provide concepts that are prescriptive of what should be done in accounting practice.

III-4. The notion that accounting practices should be consistent from year to year most directly relates to the AcSB's concept that information reported in financial statements should be (a) relevant, (b) material, (c) reliable, or (d) comparable.

III-5. What characteristics of accounting information make it reliable?

III-6. What do the elements of financial statements refer to?

Answers—p. III-9

SECTION 2 ALTERNATIVE ACCOUNTING VALUATIONS

Historical Cost Accounting and Price Changes

Most agree that conventional (historical cost based) financial statements provide useful information to users. But many also believe conventional financial statements inadequately account for the impact of changing prices. When prices changes, users often look for alternative valuations along with the conventional statements when making decisions.

LO3 Explain how price changes impact conventional financial statements.

Impact of Price Changes on the Balance Sheet

Conventional financial statements reflect transactions recorded using historical costs. Amounts in statements are usually not adjusted even though subsequent price changes alter their values.[2] As an example, consider Company X who purchases 10 acres of land for $25,000. At the end of each accounting period, Company X reports a balance sheet showing "Land ... $25,000." Several years later, after sharp price increases, Company Y purchases 10 acres of land next to and nearly identical to Company X's land. But Company Y paid $60,000 for its land. Exhibit III.5 shows the conventional balance sheet disclosures for these two companies for the land account.

Exhibit III.5
Conventional Balance Sheet Comparison

	Company X	Company Y
Land	$25,000	$60,000

Absent the details, a user is likely to conclude that either Company Y has more land than Company X or that Company Y's land is more valuable. In reality, both companies own 10 acres that are identical. The difference is due to price changes.

[2] One exception to this is with the reporting of certain investments in debt and equity securities at their market values. We explained this exception in Chapters 10 and 17.

Impact of Price Changes on the Income Statement

The inability of a conventional balance sheet to reflect price changes also shows up in the income statement. As an example, consider two companies that purchase identical machines but at different times. Company A purchases the machine for $10,000 in 1998, while Company Z purchases the machine in 2000 when its price is $18,000. Both machines are depreciated on a straight-line basis over a 10-year period with no salvage value. Exhibit III.6 shows amortization expense in the conventional annual income statements for these two companies.

	Company A	Company Z
Amortization expense, machinery	$1,000	$1,800

Exhibit III.6

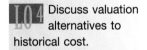

Conventional Income Statement Comparison

Although identical assets are being amortized, the income statements show a sharply higher amortization expense for Company Z.

Valuation Alternatives to Historical Cost

LO 4 Discuss valuation alternatives to historical cost.

This section discusses three alternatives to historical cost valuation for financial statements.

Constant Dollar Accounting

One alternative to conventional financial statements is to restate dollar amounts of cost incurred in earlier years for changes in the general price level. This means a specific dollar amount of cost in a previous year is restated as the number of dollars spent if the cost is paid with dollars having the current amount of purchasing power. Restating accounting numbers into dollars of equal purchasing power yields *constant dollar* financial statements. Constant dollar accounting changes the unit of measurement, but it is still based on historical cost.

Current Cost Accounting

All prices do not change at the same rate. When the general price level is rising, some specific prices may be falling. *Current cost* accounting measures financial statement elements at current values. It is not based on historical cost. The result of measuring expenses in current costs is that revenue is matched with current (at the time of the sale) costs of the resources used to earn the revenue. This means operating profit is not positive unless revenues are large enough to replace all of the resources consumed in the process of producing those revenues. Those who argue for current costs believe that operating profit measured in this fashion provides an improved basis for evaluating the effectiveness of operating activities. On the balance sheet, current cost accounting reports assets at amounts needed to purchase them as of the balance sheet date. Liabilities are reported at amounts needed to satisfy the liabilities as of the balance sheet date.

Mark-to-Market Accounting

We can also report assets (and liabilities) at current selling prices. On the balance sheet, this means assets are reported at amounts received if the assets were sold. Liabilities are reported at amounts needed to settle the liabilities. This method of valuation is called the current selling price method or, more commonly, *mark-to-market* accounting.

One argument supporting current selling prices of assets is that the alternative to owning an asset is to sell it. This means the sacrifice a business makes to hold an asset is the amount it would receive if the asset were sold. Also, the benefit derived from holding a liability is the amount the business avoids paying by not settling it. Shareholders' equity in this case represents the net amount of cash from liquidating the company. This net liquidation value is the amount that can be invested in other projects if the company were liquidated. It is a relevant basis for evaluating whether the income the company earns is enough to justify remaining in business.

Some proponents of current selling price believe it should be applied to assets but not liabilities. Others argue it applies equally well to both. Still others believe it should be applied only to assets held for sale. As Chapters 10 and 16 explain, companies use the current selling price approach to value some investments. Investments in trading securities are reported at their fair (market) values, with the related changes in fair values reported on the income statement. Investments in securities available for sale are also reported at their fair values, but the related changes in fair values are not reported on the conventional income statement. Instead, they are reported as part of shareholders' equity.

Summary

LO 1 **Explain both descriptive and prescriptive concepts and their development.** Descriptive accounting concepts provide general descriptions of current accounting practices and are most useful in learning about accounting. Prescriptive accounting concepts guide us in the practices that should be followed. These prescriptive concepts are most useful in developing accounting procedures for new types of transactions and making improvements in accounting practice. A bottom-up approach to developing concepts begins by examining the practices currently in use. Then, concepts are developed that provide general descriptions of those practices. A top-down approach begins by stating the objectives of accounting. From these objectives, concepts are developed that guide us in identifying the types of accounting practices one should follow.

LO 2 **Describe the financial statement concepts for accounting.** The CICA's Financial Statement Concepts begins by stating the broad objectives of financial reporting. Next, it identifies the qualitative characteristics accounting information should possess. The elements contained in financial reports are then defined, followed by recognition and measurement criteria.

LO 3 **Explain how price changes impact conventional financial statements.** Conventional financial statements report transactions in terms of historical dollars received or paid. The statements usually are not adjusted to reflect general price level changes or changes in the specific prices of the items reported. This can impact the statements with items not reflecting current values, which can lead to errors in judgment by users.

LO 4 **Discuss valuation alternatives to historical cost.** Constant dollar accounting involves multiplying cost by a factor reflecting the change in the general price level since the cost was incurred. Current cost accounting involves reporting on the balance sheet the dollar amounts needed to purchase the assets at the balance sheet date, and on the income statement the amounts needed to acquire operating assets on the date they are used. Mark-to-market accounting involves reporting current selling prices of assets and liabilities.

Guidance Answers to Flashbacks

III-1. A top-down approach to developing accounting concepts begins by identifying appropriate objectives of accounting reports.

III-2. A bottom-up approach to developing accounting concepts starts by examining existing accounting practices and determining the general features that characterize those procedures.

III-3. *c*

III-4. *d*

III-5. To have the qualitative characteristic of being reliable, accounting information should be free from bias and error, should be verifiable, should faithfully represent what is supposed to be described, and should be neutral.

III-6. The elements of financial statements are the objects and events that financial statements should describe; for example, assets, liabilities, revenues, and expenses.

Questions

1. Can a concept be used descriptively and prescriptively?
2. Which three qualitative characteristics of accounting information did the CICA identify as being necessary if the information is to be useful?
3. What is implied by saying that financial information should have the qualitative characteristic of relevance?
4. What are the four criteria an item should satisfy to be recognized in the financial statements?
5. Some people argue that conventional financial statements fail to adequately account for inflation. What general problem with conventional financial statements generates this argument?
6. What is the fundamental difference in the adjustments made under current cost accounting and under historical cost/constant dollar accounting?
7. What are three alternatives to historical cost valuation for financial statements?

Quick Study

QS III-1
Accounting concepts
LO 1, 2

Identify the following statements as true or false:

_____ 1. Accounting concepts are good examples of laws of nature.
_____ 2. There are really no viable alternatives to historical cost measurements for financial statement reporting.
_____ 3. Practices suggested by applying CICA's Financial Statement Concepts must be in current use in practice.
_____ 4. Accounting professionals are not required to follow the Financial Statement Concepts in practice.
_____ 5. Only the Financial Statement Concepts describe authoritative generally accepted accounting principles.
_____ 6. Relevance, as an important quality of financial information, is placed above reliability in the conceptual framework hierarchy.
_____ 7. When concepts are intended to prescribe improvements in accounting practice, they are likely to be designed by a top-down approach.

QS III-2
Qualities of accounting information
LO 2

Match the desired qualities of financial information to the proper descriptions of the qualities. Use the following codes:

A. Relevant
B. Reliable
C. Comparable

_____ 1. Timely
_____ 2. Neutral
_____ 3. Verifiable
_____ 4. Requires consistency
_____ 5. Makes a difference in decision making
_____ 6. Useful in identifying differences between companies
_____ 7. Faithful representation
_____ 8. Free from bias and error
_____ 9. Predictive

QS III-3
Impact of price changes on the balance sheet
LO 3

Identify *four* accounts from the following list that you feel are most susceptible to changing prices.

a. Accounts receivable
b. Inventories
c. Land
d. Equipment
e. Accounts payable

f. Cash
g. Long-term equity investments
h. Prepaid expenses
i. Income taxes payable

Exercises

Exercise III-1
Review of accounting principles

LO 1

Match the principle to its proper description

Principle

_____ **1.** Business Entity principle
_____ **2.** Going-concern principle
_____ **3.** Objectivity principle
_____ **4.** Revenue recognition principle
_____ **5.** Matching priñciple
_____ **6.** Time period principle

Decription

A. Requires that financial statement information be supported by something other than someone's opinion or imagination.
B. Requires that revenue be recognized at the same time that it is earned.
C. Assumes that the business will continue operating instead of being closed or sold.
D. Requires expenses to be reported in the same period as the revenues that were earned as the result of the expenses.
E. Requires every business to be accounted for separately and distinctly from its owners.
F. Requires identifying the activities of a business with specific time periods such as quarters or years.

Exercise III-2

LO 1, 2

Write a brief report explaining the difference between descriptive and prescriptive concepts. Indicate why the CICA's Financial Statement Concepts is designed to be prescriptive, and discuss the issue of whether specific concepts can be both descriptive and prescriptive.

Exercise III-3
Mark-to-market valuation

LO 4

Review Alliance's balance sheet in Appendix I. Identify three account balances that would likely change if its balance sheet were prepared on a mark-to-market basis rather than using generally accepted accounting principles.

Exercise III-4
Mark-to-market valuation

LO 4

Assume that your employer has asked you to prepare the company's balance sheet using mark-to-market accounting. You realize that some accounts have valuations that don't differ from the historical cost basis, such as cash, accounts receivable, accounts payable, and prepaid expenses. However, there are four accounts that you need to locate market values for. These accounts are inventory, land, equipment, and temporary investments. Identify possible sources you may need to consult for these market values.

Codes of Professional Conduct

Selections from the ICAO Rules of Professional Conduct[1]

Principles

- A member or student shall conduct himself or herself at all times in a manner which will maintain the good reputation of the profession and its ability to serve the public interest.
- A member or student shall perform his or her professional services with integrity and care and accept an obligation to sustain his or her professional competence by keeping himself or herself informed of, and complying with, developments in professional standards.
- A member who is engaged in an attest function such as an audit or review of financial statements shall hold himself or herself free of any influence, interest or relationship, in respect of his or her client's affairs, which impairs his or her professional judgement or objectivity or which, in the view of a reasonable observer, would impair the member's professional judgement or objectivity.
- A member or student has a duty of confidence in respect of the affairs of any client and shall not disclose, without proper cause, any information obtained in the course of his or her duties, nor shall he or she in any way exploit such information to his or her advantage.
- The development of a member's practice shall be founded upon a reputation for professional excellence. The use of methods of advertising which do not uphold professional good taste, which could be characterized as self-promotion, and which solicit, rather than inform, is not in keeping with this principle.
- A member shall act in relation to any member with the courtesy and consideration due between professional colleagues and which, in turn, he or she would wish to be accorded by the other member.

Standards of Conduct Affecting the Public Interest

201 Maintenance of reputation of profession
202 Integrity and due care
203 Professional competence

---

[1] ICAO, *Rules of Professional Conduct* (Toronto: Institute of Chartered Accountants of Ontario). Other provincial institutes have similar provisions.

204 Objectivity
205 False or misleading documents and oral representations
206 Compliance with professional standards
207 Informing clients and associates of possible conflicts of interest
208 Unauthorized benefits
209 Improper use of confidential information
210 Confidentiality of information
211 Duty to report breach of rules of professional conduct
212 Handling of trust funds and other property
213 Unlawful activity
214 Fee quotations
215 Contingency fees and services without fees
216 Payment or receipt of commissions
217 General advertising
218 Retention of documentation and working papers

Compliance with the ICAO Rules of Professional Conduct depends primarily on a member's understanding and voluntary actions. However, there are provisions for reinforcement by peers and the public through public opinion, and ultimately by disciplinary proceedings, where necessary. Adherence to the Rules helps ensure individual and collective ethical behaviour by CAs.

Selections from the Code of Professional Ethics for Management Accountants[2]

Introduction

- Professional Ethics is the behaviour of a professional toward peers, other professionals and members of the public. They concern the performance of professional duties in accordance with recognized standards of accounting and professional integrity.
- The codes of professional ethics vary from province to province in certain details in order to comply with provincial legislation and the by-laws of the provincial societies. The following discussion covers the elements common to these codes. Reference should be made to the relevant code of ethics for specific information.
- Every member of the Society is duty bound to uphold and increase the competence and prestige of the accounting profession. In keeping with high standards of ethical conduct, members will conduct their professional work with honesty, impartially, courtesy, and personal honour. Any breach of the principles of professional ethics will constitute discreditable conduct. The offending member will be liable to disciplinary measures the by-laws of the Society consider appropriate.
- A professional approach to resolving a problem of ethics requires that the rules of behaviour establish minimum, not maximum standards. Where the rules are silent, an even greater burden of responsibility falls upon the member to ensure that the course of action followed is consistent with general standards established by the Society.

General

- Members shall, in exercising their professional responsibilities, subordinate personal interest to those of the public, the employer, the Society and the profession.

[2] The Society of Management Accountants of Ontario, *Management Accountants Handbook.* (Toronto: SMAC).

- Any member convicted of any criminal offence or who has been a party to any fraud or improper business practice may be charged with professional misconduct and be required to appear before a Society disciplinary tribunal. If found quilty of such charges by the tribunal, the member may be subject to dismissal from membership in the Society and to forfeiture of the right to use the CMA designation, or to other penalties provided in the by-laws.
- A certificate of conviction in any court in Canada shall be sufficient evidence of a criminal conviction.
- No member shall report any false or misleading fact in a financial statement, or knowingly misrepresent any statement.

Relations with the Public

- Subject to provincial legislation, a Certified Management Accountant may offer services to the public as a management or cost accountant or consultant with the status of proprietor, partner, director, officer, or shareholder of an incorporated company and may associate with non-members for this purpose. A member associated with any company must abide by the rules of professional conduct of the Society. Certified members may use the initials CMA on the letterhead, professional cards or announcement in any public forum of the businesses with which they are associated.
- The right of Certified Management Accountants to sign an audit certificate or perform a review engagement varies from jurisdiction to jurisdiction across Canada. Members of the Society must comply with local legislation.
- No person except a Certified member, shall on letterhead, nameplates, professional cards or announcements claim membership in the Society.
- When practising as a management accountant in preparing or expressing an opinion on financial statements intended to inform the public or management, a member shall disclose all material facts, require all and sufficient information to warrant expression of opinion, and will report all material misstatements or departures from generally accepted accounting principles.
- Improper use by a member of a client's or employer's confidential information or affairs is discreditable conduct.
- The member will treat as confident any information obtained concerning a client's affairs. The member also has a duty to inform the client of any member interest, affiliation or other matter of which the client ought reasonably to be informed, or which might influence the member's judgement.

Relations with Employers

- No member shall use an employer's confidential information or business affairs to acquire any personal interest, property or benefit.
- A member shall treat as confidential any information, or documents concerning the employer's business affairs and shall not disclose or release such information or documents without the consent of the employer, or the order of lawful authority.
- A member shall inform the employer of any business connections, affiliations or interests of which the employer might reasonably expect to be informed.
- No member shall knowingly be a party to any unlawful act of the employer.

Relations with Professional Accountants

- No member shall criticize the professional work of another professional accountant except with the knowledge of that accountant unless the member reviews the work of others as a normal responsibility.
- Members will uphold the principle of appropriate and adequate compensation for work and will endeavour to provide opportunities for professional development and advancement for accountants employed by them or under their supervision.

Chart of Accounts

Assets

Current Assets

101 Cash
102 Petty Cash
103 Cash equivalents
104 Temporary investments
105 Allowance to reduce temporary investments to market
106 Accounts receivable
107 Allowance for doubtful accounts
108 Legal fees receivable
109 Interest receivable
110 Rent receivable
111 Notes receivable
115 Subscription receivable, common shares
116 Subscription receivable, preferred shares
119 Merchandise inventory
120 _________ inventory
121 _________ inventory
124 Office supplies
125 Store supplies
126 ______ supplies
128 Prepaid insurance
129 Prepaid interest
131 Prepaid rent
132 Raw materials inventory
133 Goods in process inventory, ______
134 Goods in process inventory, ______
135 Finished goods inventory

Long-Term Investments

141 Investment in ______ shares
142 Investment in ______ bonds
144 Investment in ______
145 Bond sinking fund

Capital Assets

151 Automobiles
152 Accumulated amortization, automobiles
153 Trucks
154 Accumulated amortization, trucks
155 Boats
156 Accumulated amortization, boats
157 Professional library
158 Accumulated amortization, professional library
159 Law library
160 Accumulated amortization, law library
161 Furniture
162 Accumulated amortization, Furniture
163 Office equipment
164 Accumulated amortization, office equipment
165 Store equipment
166 Accumulated amortization, store equipment
167 ______ equipment
168 Accumulated amortization, ______ equipment
169 Machinery
170 Accumulated amortization, machinery
173 Building ______
174 Accumulated amortization, building ______
175 Building ______
176 Accumulated amortization, building ______
179 Land improvements, ______
180 Accumulated amortization, land improvements ______
181 Land improvements ______
182 Accumulated amortization, land improvements ______
183 Land

Natural Resources

185 Mineral deposit
186 Accumulated depletion, mineral deposit

Intangible Assets

191 Patents
192 Leasehold
193 Franchise
194 Copyright
195 Leasehold improvements
196 Organization costs
197 Deferred income tax debits

Liabilities

Current Liabilities

201 Accounts payable
202 Insurance payable
203 Interest payable
204 Legal fees payable
205 Short-term notes payable
206 Discount on short notes payable
207 Office salaries payable
208 Rent payable
209 Salaries payable
210 Wages payable
211 Accrued payroll payable
214 Estimated warranty liability

215 Income taxes payable
216 Common dividends payable
217 Preferred dividends payable
218 UI payable
219 CPP payable
221 Employees' medical insurance payable
222 Employees' retirement program payable
223 Employees' union dues payable
224 PST payable
225 GST payable
226 Estimated vacation pay liability

Unearned Revenues

230 Unearned consulting fees
231 Unearned legal fees
232 Unearned property management fees
233 Unearned _______ fees
234 Unearned _______
235 Unearned janitorial revenue
236 Unearned _______ revenue
238 Unearned rent _______

Long-Term Liabilities

251 Long-term notes payable
252 Discount on notes payable
253 Long-term lease liability
254 Discount on lease liability
255 Bonds payable
256 Discount on bonds payable
257 Premium on bonds payable
258 Deferred income tax credit

Equity

Owners' Equity

301 _______, capital
302 _______, withdrawals
303 _______, capital
304 _______, withdrawals
305 _______, capital
305 _______, withdrawals

Corporate Contributed Capital

307 Common shares
309 Common shares subscribed
310 Common stock dividends distributable
313 Contributed capital from the retirement of common shares
315 Preferred shares
317 Preferred shares subscribed

Retained Earnings

318 Retained earnings
319 Cash dividends declared
320 Stock dividends declared

Revenues

401 _______ fees earned
402 _______ fees earned
403 _______ services revenue
404 _______ services revenue
405 Commission earned
406 Rent earned
407 Dividends earned
408 Earnings from investment in _______
409 Interest earned
410 Sinking fund earnings
413 Sales
414 Sales returns and allowances
415 Sales discounts

Cost of Sales

501 Amortization of patents
502 Cost of goods sold
503 Depletion of mine deposit
505 Purchases
506 Purchases returns and allowances
507 Purchases discounts
508 Transportation-in

Manufacturing Accounts

520 Raw materials purchases
521 Freight-in on raw materials
530 Factory payroll
531 Direct labour
540 Factory overhead
541 Indirect materials
542 Indirect labour
543 Factory insurance expired
544 Factory supervision
545 Factory supplies used
546 Factory utilities
547 Miscellaneous production costs
548 Property taxes on factory building
550 Rent on factory building
551 Repairs, factory equipment
552 Small tools written off
560 Amortization of factory equipment
561 Amortization of factory building

Standard Cost Variance Accounts

580 Direct material quantity variance
581 Direct material price variance
582 Direct labour quantity variance
583 Direct labour price variance
584 Factory overhead volume variance
585 Factory overhead controllable variance

Expenses

Amortization (Depreciation and Depletion Expenses)

601 Amortization expense, _______
602 Amortization expense, copyrights
603 Depletion expense, _______
604 Amortization expense, boats
605 Amortization expense, automobiles
606 Amortization expense, building _______
607 Amortization expense, building _______
608 Amortization expense, land improvements _______
609 Amortization expense, land improvements _______
610 Amortization expense, law library
611 Amortization expense, trucks
612 Amortization expense, _______ equipment
613 Amortization expense, _______ equipment
614 Amortization expense, _______
615 Amortization expense, _______

Employee Related Expense

620 Office salaries expense
621 Sales salaries expense
622 Salaries expense
623 _______ wages expense
624 Employees' benefits expense
625 Payroll taxes expense

Financial Expenses

630 Cash over and short
631 Discounts lost
633 Interest expense

Insurance Expenses

635 Insurance expense, delivery equipment
636 Insurance expense, office equipment
637 Insurance expense, _______

Rental Expenses

640 Rent expense
641 Rent expense, office space
642 Rent expense, selling space

643 Press rental expense
644 Truck rental expense
645 ______ rental expense

Supplies Expense

650 Office supplies expense
651 Store supplies expense
652 _________ supplies expense
653 _________ supplies expense

Miscellaneous Expenses

655 Advertising expense
656 Bad debts expense
657 Blueprinting expense
658 Boat expense
659 Collection expense
661 Concessions expense
662 Credit card expense
663 Delivery expense
664 Dumping expense
667 Equipment expense
668 Food and drinks expense
669 Gas, oil, and repairs expense
671 Gas and oil expense
672 General and administrative expense
673 Janitorial expense
674 Legal fees expense
676 Mileage expense
677 Miscellaneous expenses
678 Mower and tools expense
679 Operating expenses
681 Permits expense
682 Postage expense
683 Property taxes expense
684 Repairs expense, ______
685 Repairs expense, ______
687 Selling expenses
688 Telephone expense
689 Travel and entertaining expense
690 Utilities expense
691 Warranty expense
695 Income taxes expense

Gains and Losses

701 Gain on retirement of bonds
702 Gain on sale of machinery
703 Gain on sale of temporary investments
704 Gain on sale of trucks
705 Gain on ______
801 Loss on disposal of machinery
802 Loss on exchange of equipment
803 Loss on exchange of ________
804 Loss on market decline of temporary investments
805 Loss on retirement of bonds
806 Loss on sale of investments
807 Loss on sale of Machinery
808 Loss on sale of ________
809 Loss on _________
810 Loss or gain from liquidation

Clearing Accounts

901 Income summary
902 Manufacturing summary

Credits

Chapter 21, page 991, photo © T. Anderson, The Image Bank

Chapter 22, page 1035, photo © Canapress Photo Service (Jacques Boissinot)

Chapter 23, page 1105, photo © Sylvain Grandadam/Tony Stone Images

Chapter 24, page 1155, photo © Dick Hemingway: Photography

Chapter 25, page 1205, photo © Comstock Photofile Limited

Chapter 26, page 1245, photo © Canapress Photo Service (Allan Boyko)

Chapter 27, page 1293, photo © Canapress Photo Service (Frank Gunn)

Chapter 28, page 1343, photo © Ron Sangha/Tony Stone Images

Index